LAW IN THE MAKING

BY

SIR CARLETON KEMP ALLEN

SEVENTH EDITION

OXFORD UNIVERSITY PRESS
LONDON OXFORD NEW YORK

Oxford University Press

OXFORD LONDON NEW YORK
GLASGOW TORONTO MELBOURNE WELLINGTON
CAPE TOWN SALISBURY IBADAN NAIROBI LUSAKA ADDIS ABABA
BOMBAY CALCUTTA MADRAS KARACHI LAHORE DACCA
KUALA LUMPUR SINGAPORE HONG KONG TOKYO

First edition published by the Clarendon Press 1927
Second Edition 1930
Third Edition 1939
Fourth Edition 1946
Fifth Edition 1951
Sixth Edition 1958
Seventh Edition 1964
First published as an Oxford University Press paperback 1961
Reprinted 1966, 1969

PREFACE TO THE SEVENTH EDITION

THE last edition of this book, which has since been reproduced in paperback form, appeared in 1958. I am surprised that there is a call for another edition, and still more surprised to find myself preparing it. Let it be regarded, as indeed it must be, with the indulgence due to 'last words'.

A good many changes and amendments have been made in detail, and case-law has been brought up to the end of 1962 and, where possible, a little beyond. Revision and rearrangement have been particularly necessary in the chapters on precedent and legislation. The most substantial change has been in the concluding chapters on subordinate legislation, which have been largely rewritten and amplified, to take account of the Franks Report and the Tribunals and Inquiries Act, 1958. To make room for this new matter, the account of the German *Adelrecht* and the discussion of Léon Duguit's theories, neither of which subjects seems now to be of very lively interest, have been omitted.

For the rest, I would only repeat what I have said in previous editions, namely, that ageing books, like ageing mortals, are susceptible only of a certain amount of rejuvenation. It is nearly half a century since this book first appeared, and, without affectation, it is a constant, though naturally an agreeable, surprise to its writer that it can have kept some measure of vitality for so long. With the years it has—again like mortal man—undergone many changes of mind and body and has 'put on weight' of physique if not of wisdom. It could not have kept its health at all but for the help and counsel of friends, some of whom, alas, have departed, while others have changed their estate since I first had the benefit of their learning and advice. Two of my most kindly mentors in earlier days were the late Sir Paul Vinogradoff and the late Sir William Holdsworth. Let me also recall my indebtedness to my former tutor, the late Professor F. de Zulueta; the late Sir John Miles, sometime Warden of Merton College; Sir David Keir, Master of Balliol College; the late Professor J. L. Brierly; the late Professor Paul Collinet; Professor P. E. Corbett, of Yale University; Mr. C. H. S. Fifoot, Hon. Fellow of Hertford College; Professor S. E. Thorne, of Harvard University; Professor A. L. Goodhart, until recently Master of University College, Oxford; the late Professor H. F. Jolowicz; Professor W. Friedmann, of Columbia University. In this edition I owe, and gratefully acknowledge, a special debt to Professor H. W. R. Wade for help and criticism in the concluding chapters.

Finally, I should like to pay tribute to the skill and vigilance of the staff of the Clarendon Press, who throughout the lifetime of this book have saved me from many errors and negligences and have often made suggestions which were so pertinent that the author has been mortified at not having thought of them himself.

C. K. A.

Oxford
27 November 1963

LAW IN TH[illegible]
MAKING

TABLE OF CONTENTS

TABLE OF STATUTES

TABLE OF CASES

Figures printed in heavy type refer to cases which are discussed or quoted in the text. Ordinary type indicates cases cited in footnotes.

LIST OF ABBREVIATIONS

Arch. für civ. Pr.	*Archiv für civilistische Praxis*
DPR.	*Deutsches Privatrecht*
E.H.R.	*English Historical Review*
H.L.R.	*Harvard Law Review*
Halsbury, *L. of E.*	Halsbury's *Laws of England* (2nd or 3rd ed., as indicated)
Holdsworth, *H.E.L.*	Sir W. S. Holdsworth, *History of English Law*
J.S.C.L.	*Journal of the Society of Comparative Legislation* (now *Journal of Comparative Legislation and International Law*)
L.Q.R.	*Law Quarterly Review*
M.L.R.	*Modern Law Review*
Pand.	*Pandekten*
P. & M.	Pollock & Maitland, *History of English Law*
S.S.*	Selden Society
S.R. & O. or *S.I.*	*Statutory Rules and Orders* (till 1948), *Statutory Instruments* (after 1948)
Statt. R.	*Statutes of the Realm*
Vin. Abr.	*Viner's Abridgement*
Z.S.S.	*Zeitschrift der Savigny Stiftung*

* When Selden Society publications are referred to with the prefix 'vol.', this indicates the number of the volume in the whole series; when in brackets without the prefix 'vol.', the reference is to the number in the special Year Book series.

INTRODUCTION

LAW AND ITS SOURCES

In these pages we shall be concerned with the sources of law, but not those sources which are commonly called 'literary'. The 'documentation' of law is a study for the legal historian. The term 'sources' is here used to connote those agencies by which rules of conduct acquire the character of law by becoming objectively definite, uniform, and, above all, compulsory.

Two views of the genesis of law

Many artificial classifications of the sources of law have been attempted—e.g. into 'formal' and 'material';[1] but for our present discussion we need consider only two antithetic conceptions of the growth of law, and it is still necessary for every student of jurisprudence to define his attitude towards these two conflicting views. In the one, the essence of law is that it is imposed upon society by a sovereign will. In the other, the essence of law is that it develops within society of its own vitality. In the one case, law is artificial: the picture is that of an omnipotent authority standing high above society, and issuing *downwards* its behests. In the other case, law is spontaneous, growing *upwards*, independently of any dominant will. The second view does not exclude the notion of sanction or enforcement by a supreme established authority. This, in most societies, becomes necessary at some stage in the ordinary course of social growth. But authority so set up and obeyed by agreement is not the sole and indispensable source of all law. It is itself a creation of law. In the other view, it is and must be the creator of law. It enforces law, so to say, because it has the right to do what it likes with its own. According to this doctrine, the existence of a dominating

[1] This distinction, which appeared in earlier editions of Salmond's *Jurisprudence*, has been discarded by the present editor, Dr. Glanville Williams.

sovereign will is an absolute pre-requisite to all law. There may be social observances existing before it or without it, but they are *not law* in any proper significance of that term. Before any rules deserving the name of law can be said to exist, there must be a sovereign from which they can derive authority.

The Austinian sovereign—sole source of law

In the doctrine of Austin, this position is consistently maintained. There may be 'immediate and mediate', 'direct and indirect or oblique' sources, but again and again he insists that the full dignity of the term 'source' can be properly applied only to the sovereign. Legislation, then, is the most appropriate, because the most direct, expression of the sovereign's will. But nobody ever supposed that law consisted solely of legislation. The most extreme Austinian dogma could not abolish the immemorial distinction between *ius* and *lex*. Common Law, custom, precedent, equity were, to say the least, distinct and operative elements in English law in Austin's day as much as in our own. Austin classifies them as 'subordinate sources' of law, and the explanation which he gives of that term really amounts to denying that they are sources at all.

'In one of its senses, the source of a law is its direct or immediate author. For either directly or remotely, the sovereign, or supreme legislator, is the author of all law; and all laws are derived from the same source; but immediately and directly laws have different authors. As proceeding from *immediate* authors of different characters or descriptions, laws are talked of (in the language of metaphor) as if they arose and flowed from different fountains or sources: in other words, the *immediate* author of a given rule (whether that author be the sovereign or any individual or body legislating in subordination to the sovereign) is styled the fountain, or the source, from which the rule in question springs and streams. But this talk is rather fanciful than just; for applying the metaphor with the consistency which even poetry requires, rules established immediately by the supreme legislature are the only rules springing from a *fons* or *source*. Individuals or bodies legislating in subordination to the sovereign are more properly *reservoirs* fed from the source of all law, the supreme legislature, and again emitting the borrowed waters which they receive from that Fountain of Law.'[1]

The analytical standpoint

This view may gain some plausibility when it is urged that Austin's task was solely to analyse the existing elements of a modern legal system. The severely 'analytical' jurist, while admitting that various historical elements have gone to make up the material of law, may claim that he deliberately excludes those elements from consideration, being concerned only to dissect the legal arrangement as he finds it; and he finds it, in the modern world, invariably subordinated to the control of a sovereign power.[2] But this is to beg the whole question. The different materials found to exist in the law cannot be understood independently of their historical evolution. Their origin—whatever their present scope and effect—is essentially a matter of social history; and to predicate that this origin is and must be a single sovereign, of modern type, is to stultify the inquiry *in limine*. This weakness is very noticeable throughout Austin's

[1] *Jurisprudence*, Lect. XXVIII. It is curious that Austin, consciously or unconsciously, exactly reverses a metaphor used by Blackstone: 'Justice is not derived from the King, as from his free gift; but he is the steward of the public, to dispense it to whom it is *due*. He is not the spring, but the reservoir; from whence right and equity are conducted by a thousand channels, to every individual': 1 *Comm.* 266.

[2] This, unless I have misunderstood him, appears to be the general position of Professor C. A. W. Manning in 'Austin Today; or "The Province of Jurisprudence" Re-examined' (*Modern Theories of Law*). Interesting and ingenious though Professor Manning's interpretations are, they cannot, except by a powerful exercise of the imagination, be extracted from anything which Austin actually wrote or seems to have meant. To say that Austin was 'responsible only for a particular account of the relation between law and communal psychology', that 'his sovereign is after all an abstraction, and his sovereignty and command just a brace of ideas', and that he was engaged primarily in a study of 'social statics', is really to transfer ideas and arguments from one plane to another, both in time and in conception, at the will of the interpreter; nor does it strengthen the interpretation to say that Austin did not 'vividly realize what it was he was attempting', and that it is doubtful whether he 'saw what he was after'. Austin's objective may have been limited, but he would have been surprised to learn that he was in any doubt about it. There is always a danger in taking the dogmatic and explicit doctrines of a former age (for if Austin was anything he was dogmatic and explicit) and paraphrasing them into the terminology and philosophical fashions of a later era.

treatment of the sources of law. He could not be content with pure analysis, but, in spite of himself, felt the necessity of supporting his main thesis by historical illustrations. Unfortunately, his examples, drawn almost entirely from Roman Law, are sometimes surprisingly inapposite, and nowhere more than in this part of his discussion does he show himself the victim of fixed ideas. Observe, for example, the domination of the preconceived English Parliamentary sovereign in the following remarkable statement:

> 'If our House of Lords and House of Commons sometimes sat and voted in one assembly, and sometimes separately as at present, they would afford an exact parallel to the manner in which the sovereign was divided in the Roman Republic. Acts passed by the two bodies assembled in one House would correspond to *leges curiatae* and *centuriatae;* acts originating in the one House and adopted by the other would be *plebiscita* or *senatusconsulta*.'

Though Austin could not anticipate nineteenth-century research into Roman legislative organs, it is difficult to understand how, even in his own day, he arrived at this extraordinary analogy. Or again, take this account of the praetorian law:

> 'It was not made in the way of decisions in particular cases, but consisted of general laws, made and promulged in the way of direct legislation; by virtue of a power assumed at first by the Praetors, with the acquiescence of the supreme legislature, and subsequently confirmed to them by its express recognition and authority.'

The 'express recognition and authority' was presumably Hadrian's codification of the *ius honorarium*; but this was essentially declaratory of a body of law which had grown to maturity, and to say that until the reign of Hadrian the praetorian law was applied 'with the acquiescence of the supreme legislature' is mere fiction. No such thing ever happened in fact. What Austin really means, consistently with his doctrine of 'imposed' law, is that 'acquiescence' *ought* to have happened in fact. As it did not, the whole remarkable structure of Roman equitable law becomes, in Austin's eyes, to that extent discredited. It is 'merely an incondite mass of occasional and insulated rules, that had grown, by a slow and nearly insensible aggregation, through a long succession of ages'. This 'incondite mass' became the *viva vox iuris civilis*. This bastard offspring of 'subordinate' legislation radically affected, and in some capital respects wholly changed, every important department of Roman Law. To regard it as anything but a source of law in itself is to distort manifest facts.

Modern criticisms of it

The conception of subordinate sources of law existing, as it were, on sufferance, is a corollary to the doctrine of unlimited sovereignty, 'as great as possibly men can be imagined to make it', which Austin adopted enthusiastically from Hobbes; sovereignty, in the celebrated phrase of the French constitution of 1791, 'indivisible, inalienable, and imprescriptible'. We need not recapitulate familiar criticisms of the main Austinian, or more properly Hobbesian, position. Whatever room may still be left for controversy, it may be said without temerity that at least two qualifications of Leviathan sovereignty are now generally conceded: and to concede them is to deny the doctrine two of its most vital postulates. (1) Whatever be the constitutional instrument which secures the observance and enforcement of law—and some sanction of this kind is certainly indispensable—there is no historical justification for the view that this power must always and necessarily be a determinate 'human superior' which at the same time *creates* all law. It is impossible in every form of society governed by law to disengage and personify a 'sovereign', as thus understood, with the artificial precision which Hobbes and Austin assume. (2) The sovereign power, whatever its nature, is not to be conceived merely as a means of saving society from itself. To Hobbes (again followed specifically by Austin) the alternatives are unmistakable. 'And though of so unlimited a power men may fancy many evil consequences, yet the consequences of the want of it, which is perpetual war of every man against his neighbour, are much worse.' Modern studies of the natural history of law have cast much doubt upon this supposed state of natural social warfare. The group-instinct, out of which society has grown, is based on co-operation, not on strife, and no human group ever have survived without combining to resist or to adapt, for the common advantage, adverse conditions of physical environment. Indeed, the principle need not be confined to human societies; it is not the habit of any group of creatures to exist only for internecine strife. Hobbes's famous *homo homini lupus* was an inapt metaphor, for the wolf is not the natural enemy of the wolf, and the pack is based on combination, not on warfare. This admitted, the determinate sovereign's title to absolute authority is gravely challenged. A group existing by combination and unity of aim is bound to provide itself with rules; it is not, in mere desperation, necessarily compelled to surrender its will to a supreme lawgiver in order to save itself from disruption. Law, in short, begins to grow as soon as society begins to grow; it is not invented and imposed *ab extra* at any specific stage of development.

Influence of Austinian jurisprudence

But again it may be urged that these criticisms, even if conceded, have a purely academic or antiquarian interest. Whatever may have been the history of primitive societies, the law of the modern civilized world is, as a fact, invariably enforced by some kind of ultimate sanction; is it not, then, substantially true to say, with Austin, that this sanctioning power is the source of the authority of law? The argument has undoubtedly carried weight with many practical minds. The attraction of the Austinian theory of law has lain in its simplicity and consistency. In social no less than in spiritual life, doubts and questionings beget a natural desire for infallible authority; and since law is inevitably bound up with the crucial question of justice, such problems will certainly never be absent from it. The comfort of certainty lies in a sovereign which is a definite, constant, and tangible basis for the operation of all law. Without it, we are told, nothing remains but unreal speculation. One of the most remarkable features of the political philosophy of Hobbes, and of the jurisprudence of Austin, is that despite the unsparing attacks to which they have been continuously subjected, their vitality is still far from exhausted. For a systematic exposition of the methods of English jurisprudence, we still have to turn to Austin. Nobody has replaced him. Many a student must feel that he reads Austin only in order to controvert him; yet Austinian jurisprudence, despite all the broadsides and notwithstanding the further disadvantage of an unattractive manner of presentation, so far maintains its influence that it may still be described as the characteristic jurisprudence of England, and it has of late years received increasing attention and respect from Continental jurists.[1]

Its acknowledged weaknesses

But consistency and authority may be bought too dear. Apart from its historical, or rather non-historical aspect, the analytical doctrine has not proved itself to be the only practical and consistent scheme of modern law. In one sense, it might be said that the emergence of totalitarian states in the modern world has raised Austinian doctrine to its apotheosis; but the political principles of these states are so frankly opportunistic that it is exceedingly difficult to determine the juridical basis of their systems of legislation and justice. In communities which still call themselves 'democratic', and especially in those of federal pattern, it has become increasingly evident that Austin's indivisible sovereignty is quite inappropriate. Even in England, where, as we

[1] See, e.g., Somló, *Juristische Grundlehre*, *passim*; Lévy-Ullmann, *Éléments d'introduction générale à l'étude des sciences juridiques*, Parts I and II; Radbruch, 'Anglo-American Jurisprudence through Continental Eyes', 52 *L.Q.R.* 530; Schwarz, 'Austin and the German Jurisprudence of his Time', *Politica*, Aug. 1934. On the connexion between Austin and the doctrines of Kelsen and Roguin, see Pound, 'Fifty Years of Jurisprudence', *Journal of the Society of Public Teachers of Law*, 1937, 17.

have said, Austin has not been definitely replaced and his doctrines are still perpetuated, there has been for many years a growing realization that a new conception of law is made necessary by the changed conditions of a community which has become, in large measure, 'socialized'. It is true that Austin's critics are by no means agreed among themselves, and it is largely owing to their disagreements that the unitary sovereign still sits, though insecurely, upon his throne. It is not our task here to attempt to reconcile the critics, or to enter upon any general examination of the theory of sovereignty. But it is relevant to our purpose to glance rapidly at the principal movements in the theory of jurisprudence which have brought us to the now prevailing point of view—one which must radically affect our method of approaching the study of the sources of law.

The Byzantine tradition

Maine's well-known criticisms have probably been the most influential among English lawyers in calling in question the theory of a *determinate* sovereign as the postulate of all efficient social organization. His conclusions were based upon well-attested features of Eastern societies; and we may regard it as the converse of his thesis that Hobbes and Austin, far from establishing a permanent and universal type of society, depict no more than a single phase in the development of Western civilization. That phase is governed by a conception of sovereignty which, if it is not solely derived from, is powerfully influenced by the Roman, or more strictly the Byzantine, theory of monarchy. If Caesar and Tacitus are to be believed, an absolute principate was not native to the Germanic peoples; but the pomp of Byzantine imperialism was enthusiastically adopted, and even exaggerated, by the barbarians who conquered the Romans, and who were faced with the problem of ruling, over an enormous area, provincials accustomed to absolutist forms of government. Some writers, like Allen in his description of *The Royal Prerogative in England*, have exaggerated the *direct* adoption of Roman institutions;

but the influence, direct and indirect, was certainly widespread and sustained, and was destined to permeate European institutions for many centuries. It need hardly be observed that it was not the only doctrine of government which philosophy had offered the world. It would have caused surprise, and no little pain, to Plato or Aristotle. But its influence has been continuous and is not yet exhausted. With Dante, Byzantine sovereignty becomes not only an epic but a gospel. It is Justinian himself who appears in glory to Dante and Beatrice, sings the splendour of the Roman Empire, and admonishes those who would seek to derogate from its unified pre-eminence. In the *De Monarchia* it is the special mission of Rome to govern the world in one divinely ordained hegemony. As there must be one God of the universe, one Christ of the Church, one head of the family, so there must be one sovereign ruler, and one only, of every human society. More—there must be one leader of the whole world; and for that task the Roman people is destined not only by the will of God, manifested in many ways, but by the human right of conquest. When all allowance has been made for nationalistic bias and poetic fervour, Dante's exaltation of the unitary sovereign was no mere figment. In its spiritual or ecclesiastical manifestation, it still holds sway; in its temporal aspect, it embodied what was to be, for Europe, a long contest between absolutism and individual liberty. Three hundred years later it finds an apostle less imaginative, but even more convinced, in Bodin. The exercise of power—the basis of this conception of sovereignty—is the centre of Hobbes's political doctrine, which had so great an influence both in England and abroad. And there was no lack of practical demonstration of personified power. In the German States of the seventeenth century, some three hundred imperators held sway. Small wonder that jurists like Pufendorf, Thomasius, and Christian Wolff were deeply concerned with the theory of political power, of which they often had intimate and sharp personal experience. It is a comparatively short time since France emerged from more than a thousand years of monarchy not inaccurately epitomized, at its height, in Louis XIV's famous aphorism.

The feudal and the monarchical principles in England

But the Middle Ages also gave birth to the principle of feudalism, founded upon the notion of contract, not of command. The coexistence of these two fundamentally different theories of government leads to a curious dualism, nowhere better illustrated than in the development of monarchical doctrine in England. The Anglo-Saxon kings were no imperators, and their Norman and Angevin successors were essentially feudal overlords. In Bracton's day, as has been observed by Pollock and Maitland, 'the theory that in every State there must be some man or definite body of men, some sovereign without duties and without rights, would have been rejected'. Bracton is in two minds between the Romanistic and the feudal conception. He reproduces familiar Roman generalities about the sovereign's dignity and preeminence; but, faithful to the Common Law and feudal principles in which he is steeped, he makes cautious reservations concerning the limits of royal power. Thus in procedure by assize he leaves the subject remediless against his sovereign, with no hope of redress save in 'the Lord, the avenger, who says, "To me vengeance, I will repay" ': but he hastens to add a qualification which goes near to contradicting all that has gone before: 'unless there be some one who says that the body corporate of the realm and the body of barons ought to do this and may do it in the court of the King himself'. He insists in rhetorical terms on the King's attributes of superiority and power; but adds, in words which have become famous as an early declaration of a vital constitutional principle: 'But the King himself ought not to be subject to man, but subject to God and to the law, for the law makes the King. Let the King, then, attribute to the law what the law attributes to him, namely, dominion and power, for *there is no king where the will and not the law has dominion.*' So, again, the King is subject to his own Court, that is, to the barons and nobles who compose it; they are associates of the King, 'and he who has an associate, has a master, and therefore if the King be without a bridle . . . they ought to put a bridle upon him'. If the associates themselves are without a bridle, then indeed the King's subjects are in desperate case, and can only 'exclaim and say, O Lord Jesus Christ, bind their jaws with a rein and with a bridle'. This is pure feudalism.

It is not until the decline of feudalism that Romanistic sovereignty begins to take definite shape in England. Under the Tudors, Bracton's generalizations about the superiority of the monarch would have been a commonplace; but it would have been dangerous indeed to maintain the right to 'bridle' the sovereign. In legal theory, the kingship begins to emerge as what Maitland has called 'a juristic abortion'—the corporation sole. The king serves as a framework for an elaborate structure of 'metaphysical—or we might say metaphysiological—nonsense'. He becomes two persons with two bodies and two capacities, yet with only *one* person! Our law reports begin to shadow forth mystical abstractions excelled in obscurity only by St. Athanasius. More and more superhuman attributes adhere to the King's Majesty, until they approach dangerously near to blasphemy, and James Stuart frankly 'adorns his person with some sparkles of divinity'. The inevitable reaction took the form of one royal 'martyrdom' and two revolutions, and the crisis of 1688 may be said to have expelled Caesarism from this realm. It dwindled in practice till in another hundred years it had become the shadow of a shade. That it persisted in theory, however, may be sufficiently gathered from Blackstone's account of the royal prerogative. That rhapsodical recital of all the perfections has not even yet wholly disappeared from our constitutional theory, although everybody knows its reality to be none and even its symbolism to be little.

The doctrine, of which it is the last echo in our law—a doctrine, perhaps, not truly held by Blackstone, yet reproduced in an imitative manner—is the conception of law as *will* as against the conception of law as *reason*. 'There is no King'—let us recall Bracton's words—'where the will and not the law has dominion.' This law to which dominion is due is the law founded not upon arbitrary command but upon that fundamental Reason which must govern corporate as well as individual conduct.

The revolt of rationalism

Reason is the sovereign, almost the god, of eighteenth-century individualism. That movement was not independent of germinal processes which may be traced back to the Renaissance; for no great movement appears suddenly and unaccountably, like a meteor in the sky; but, as so often happens, the influence of a single mind gave it an impulse which made its future momentum irresistible. Because he turned men's interest away from the formal problems of academic philosophy towards the infinitely more absorbing problems of living personality, Descartes became, no less than Hobbes, 'the father of modern philosophy'. Though he was not specially concerned with questions of law and government, his exaltation of inalienable, indestructible Reason was difficult to reconcile with the will of a Dantesque *princeps*. John Locke was still in his teens when Descartes died. 'The first books', he said, 'which gave him a relish of philosophical things were those of Descartes.' By the time—nearly the end of his life, and the end of the seventeenth century—that he published the *Essay* which was to be 'the philosophical Bible' of the eighteenth century, Locke had rejected much of Descartes's teaching; but he carried on one torch lit by his predecessor. 'Reason must be our last guide and judge in everything; the subject part of mankind might . . . with Egyptian bondage, expect Egyptian darkness, were not the candle of the Lord set up by Himself in men's minds, which it is impossible for the breath or power of man wholly to extinguish.' Law itself becomes an emanation from a natural order of things, a natural rule of reason, and breach of the law is merely 'varying from the right rule of reason'. The 'state of nature' becomes a state of liberty, not of strife; and the liberty of each member of society can be curtailed only by his own consent in his own interest. Duties as well as rights are of the essence of the sovereign: sovereignty unlimited and irresponsible is not to be admitted under any guise, human, as with Hobbes, or divine, as with Filmer. Even the legislature is restricted by the governing principle that 'these laws ought to be designed for no other end ultimately, but the good of the people'. The royal prerogative itself is merely a form of discretion confided to the executive—a bold precept in 1690, and a striking anticipation of the doctrine which a modern teacher, Dicey, has made familiar to all lawyers.

The eighteenth century, then, had ample stimulus towards its gospel of individual will, individual reason, and individual liberty. Finding its evangelist in Rousseau, that gospel forces a trial of strength between the established Caesarism and the new 'general will'. Sovereignty there is in plenty, but it is claimed for the many, not for the one or the few. The *power* of Byzantine supremacy, undirected towards any social or moral end, becomes not only an anomaly but a menace. The State must exercise power not for itself but for its members. This was a direct challenge to the settled tradition of government. It was accompanied by an idealistic optimism, an impetuous faith in human perfectibility and in the irresistible march of progress. Reason, the essence of being, and Liberty, the essence of law, found an incomparable advocate in Kant; the State's duty to the individual took philosophic shape in Fichte. The 'natural progress' of Adam Smith imports a new and complacent optimism into economic theory. Bentham, like Rousseau, 'compels men to be free'. And dry doctrines of politics are soon to be accompanied by a high harmony of lyricism: Wordsworth is moved to great utterance, Shelley hurls defiance at princes, Byron performs spectacular exploits in the cause of Hellenic liberty.

One of the most remarkable features of Austin's writings is that all these accumulated forces seem to have left him entirely unaffected. He does not revolt against eighteenth-century individualism: he seems to be quite impervious to it. His doctrine was reactionary even in his own day. He carries the reader back to Hobbes and Bodin as if the eighteenth century were a blank page.

The revolt against rationalism

A conscious revolt was certain to come from other quarters. Nowhere is it more explicit or more eloquent than in Burke. In the dignified personal references which close the *Thoughts on the French Revolution*, he justly claims for himself a true love of liberty and a true hatred of oppression throughout his public career; but his sane conservatism inspired in him an equal hatred of unbridled individualism and the vain imaginings of a fictitious 'equality'. In his protest against the exaggerated claims of Ego to take precedence over all other facts of social existence, he stands with the political and theocratical movement of reaction against eighteenth-century individualism. In his insistence on the solemnity and the continuity of tradition, he anticipates the historical school of the nineteenth century. The champion of the American colonists was assuredly no disciple of Caesarism; but his sympathies are closer to the Leviathan than to the General Will.

Bentham's condemnation of the French Revolution was no less severe than Burke's; but the lessons he drew from it were very different. His *Étatisme*, however solicitous for the general and the individual good, is in direct opposition to that of Rousseau; the individual becomes not so much an active contributor to the sum of social good as a passive recipient of benefits; and Bentham hardly stopped to inquire whether material benefits necessarily constitute happiness, or indeed, whether they are benefits at all unless they satisfy conscious desires. In another respect Bentham breaks with the spirit of the eighteenth century. For him no metaphysics, no Cartesian abstractions: the real or supposed origins of society and of the social instinct have no interest for him: he is concerned only to remedy existing disabilities. His idealism relates to the future, in no sense to the past. Yet, as an idealism of perfectibility, it is unlimited. He is perhaps the most remarkable example in literature of an essentially practical mind unconscious of any bounds to the practicable. From this paradoxical temper results the paradox of fact, so well elaborated by Dicey, that the apostle of individualism was destined to become the founder of State-socialism.

The theological reaction

The exaggeration of *homo omnium mensura* invited a theological as well as a political reaction. Even to Burke there is something actually impious in the excessive exaltation of Reason. The French 'theocrats' of the early nineteenth century—Saint-Martin, de Maistre, de Bonald, Ballanche, Lamennais—found it necessary to remind overweening man that the only omnipotent Reason in the universe was the Supreme Reason of God, and that the rationalist was in danger of arrogating to himself superhuman attributes. God's law in society was not natural equality, but natural inequality, and it behoved man to think upon his frailties rather than upon his excellences, looking to a Higher Power alike for the genesis and the governance of social life.

The historical reaction

But this was a partial reversion to mechanical explanations of society. The greater counterblast to eighteenth-century 'a-priorism' came not from Faith but from another manifestation of Reason, very different from its predecessor. Even the eighteenth-century doctors themselves were not quite unaware that their theories were built upon prodigious assumptions. Locke, for example, is uncomfortably conscious that an answer is required to the question, 'Where, *as a matter of historical fact*, is your social contract to be found?' His own answer, however, is mere evasion. The historical movement in jurisprudence may be called the revolt of fact against fancy. Burke adumbrated it in his warnings not to construct schemes for the future without having first assimilated the lessons of the past. In its more scientific aspect it directed attention not to the abstract ideal, but to the physical environment of law—a theme by no means new, since it formed the core of Montesquieu's teaching, but one which had been forgotten amid the intense speculation of the eighteenth century. A pamphlet evoked by an academic controversy recalled men's attention to it with singular force. The opening passage of Savigny's *On the Vocation of our Age for Legislation and Jurisprudence* summarized a doctrine first suggested by Hugo and now destined to become the starting-point of a new school of thought:

> 'In the earliest times to which authentic history extends, the law will be found to have already attained a fixed character, peculiar to the people, like their manners, language, and constitution. Nay, these phenomena have no separate existence, they are but the particular faculties and tendencies of an individual people, inseparably united in nature, and only wearing the semblance of distinct attributes to our view. That which binds them into one whole is the common conviction of the people, the kindred consciousness of an inward necessity, excluding all notion of an accidental and arbitrary origin.'

Ihering said that with the appearance of Savigny's earliest work, *Das Recht des Besitzes*, in 1803, modern jurisprudence was born. A new scientific method opposed a sane scepticism both to the assumptions of the preceding age and to factitious theories of the growth or the reformation of societies. It is difficult for us today to realize how novel this attitude seemed to a generation which had not learnt, or had forgotten, to regard law and history as vitally interdependent.

Savigny's 'pessimism'

Savigny's conception of law is directly opposed to the glorification of individual Reason. The picture which, to many minds, he seemed to paint was that environmental conditions impelled societies along predestined paths to a foreordained end. Whereas the eighteenth century has been more and more chidden for its optimism, the Historical School has been accused of a juristic pessimism. If the rationalists erred in idolizing the future, the historical jurists erred in idolizing the past. They tended, it is said, to hang traditions like fetters upon the hands of reformative enterprise. Their distrust of legislation, especially when codified, showed a discouraging scepticism of Will and a disbelief in the efficacy of human effort to master material surroundings. It is easy to exaggerate this criticism, and exaggeration has not been lacking. Savigny's spirit was not that of supine resignation. In 1839, when he published the first volumes of his great 'System', he expressly defended himself against the charge of fatalism, and disclaimed any desire to 'subject the present to the government of the past'. It is the jurist's business to exercise a 'vivid creative energy' upon inherited conditions.

'The altering of single, nay of many legal doctrines, is doing nothing towards the object [i.e. changing existing legal principles]; for . . . the mode of thought, with the speculation of questions that may arise, will still be influenced by the pre-existing system, and the subserviency of the present to the past will manifest itself even when the present is purposely opposed to the past. There is consequently no mode of avoiding this overruling influence of the existing matter; it will be injurious to us so long as we ignorantly submit to it; but beneficial, if we oppose to it a vivid creative energy—obtain the mastery over it by a thorough grounding in history, and thus appropriate to ourselves the whole intellectual wealth of preceding generations. We have therefore no choice but either, as Bacon says, *sermocinari tanquam e vinculis*, or to learn by the profound study of jurisprudence how to use the historical matter freely as our instrument: there is no other alternative.'

Nevertheless, it is not easy to see how creative energy is to succeed in its aims if there is 'no mode of avoiding this overruling influence of the existing matter': for situations frequently occur when the existing matter must be deliberately and decisively overruled. There is, therefore, some justice in the criticism that Savigny and his school undervalued the function of creative will. As Savigny taught his generation that jurisprudence cannot be divorced from history, so he might himself have been reminded that it cannot be wholly divorced from philosophy. It is impossible to regard human law as a purely material phenomenon. It is not original protoplasm, but a derivative product, and ultimately its source must be conscious Will and Reason, though these are vastly influenced by the circumstances of environment.

However, 'teleology' was not the task which Savigny set himself. That was reserved for another, and perhaps even greater, jurist of the nineteenth century—Rudolf von Ihering. Savigny's main thesis was how law becomes, not whither it tends, or whither enlightened effort may make it tend. The exclusion of this aspect of law led him and his followers into difficulties, just as the exclusion of history had led the 'a-priorists' into even greater difficulties. But it is the lot of the pioneer of thought, either by overstatement or understatement, to do injustice to his own case. If his main thesis find acceptance and permanence, he has not wholly failed, whatever modifications subsequent criticism may impose. Savigny's main thesis remains substantially unimpaired; and it was a final negation of the unitary sovereign conceived as the sole and inevitable source of law. The true import of the historical and comparative approach to law—expounded in singularly illuminating fashion and purged of many of the early exaggerations—was first conveyed to English readers by Sir Henry Maine, with profound effect on the jurisprudence of this country.

Jurisprudence and biology

Burke and Savigny have been described as 'Darwinians before Darwin'; but Savigny was not very long 'before Darwin'. His last published work appeared only six years before *The Origin of Species*, and he was still alive when that book detonated upon the world. As at the beginning of his life-work a new era opened up in legal history, so at its end a new era, of similar tendency, began in natural history. Evolution, whether philosophically or scientifically considered, was no new doctrine; but the principle of natural selection, formulated as a law and not merely as an hypothesis, influenced every department of thought as few scientific doctrines had done before. The 'species question', so wittily described by Huxley, and still within living memory, was no mere learned controversy; 'overflowing the narrow bounds of purely scientific circles', wrote Huxley, 'it divides with Italy and the Volunteers the attention of general society'. Twenty-one years later, the same writer was able to state with confidence that the essentials of the doctrine had established themselves in intelligent opinion as beyond controversy. This is not the place to discuss, even if we were competent to do so, later views and queries; whatever questions may still remain open, it is at least certain that Darwinian biology has enormously influenced every branch of study since it was first propounded. Jurisprudence, already set upon the path of a new historical method, could not escape that influence. Even the mind uninstructed in principles of natural science could not fail to be impressed, almost awed, by one fact which emerged more and more clearly from the new biology—the extraordinary interdependence of all known forms of life. Daily and with growing astonishment men have learnt by what intricate processes organisms, to all appearance unrelated, vitally influence each other in generation, subsistence, and dissolution. When Huxley wrote, he estimated that not less than half a million forms of life were known to science; today only a very rash biologist, we conceive, would so much as venture a guess. Among these myriad creatures there is not one which, in the infinite complexities of their mutual action and reaction, *may* not be the cause of far-reaching transformations in natural or human history. Thus the powerful stimulus to biological investigation gave, potentially at least, to every organism, however obscure, an unprecedented importance. Nothing could escape the insatiable microscope.

Sociology and the 'organic school': and comparative jurisprudence

Society became an organism like everything else—the most important organism of all in the view of a new school of students who called themselves 'sociologists'. Even before the Darwinian doctrine had been formulated, Comte had pleaded for the study of social institutions as a science with its own technique. However ill he may have succeeded in constructing a system of philosophy, the method he advocated was destined to prove fruitful in other hands. Whether or not 'sociology' has justified the large claims which have been made for it, if we place ourselves in the year 1860 it is not difficult to imagine the stimulus which was given to it by the newly awakened interest in biology. It was the biological aspect of society, suggested by Darwin, rather than its mathematico-political aspect, suggested by Comte, which inspired the teaching of Herbert Spencer. Doubtless, in the enthusiasm of real or supposed discovery, he carried the method to indefensible extremes. The comparison between the anatomy of an animal organism and a body politic is instructive and suggestive, and this Spencer successfully demonstrated; but to push the comparison beyond the limits of analogy is to mistake the metaphorical for the actual. It is, indeed, to return to a form of barren anthropomorphism which was popular in the Middle Ages, but which has been long since discredited. Much of Spencer's 'organic' dissection of society reads nowadays like complicated allegory, the more misleading for its very ingenuity. Somewhat cruelly, but not altogether unjustly, M. Bergson has compared his method to that of a man whose sole idea of construction is the fitting together of the pieces of a puzzle. Yet, as we shall see, the 'organic' and sociological view has not been without its effect on jurisprudence. The interdependence of organisms, in its sociological aspect, means the mutual relations of all members of civilized society, and the distribution of a sense of responsibility far wider than can be comprised within the formula sovereign-and-subject. The Spencerian analysis, it is true, by over-insistence on 'organic' analogies, laid itself open to the charge of being as mechanical as any of the earlier *a priori* doctrines, which did not profess to be 'scientific'. But at least it directed attention to the necessity of considering law in relation to other social phenomena. It remained for Gierke to contrast with the mechanical operation of real or supposed laws in society the no less dynamic operation of will, and especially group-will. The later generations of sociologists have found it necessary to approach their inquiry with far more regard to psychology than to biology. If there be anything corresponding to biology in jurisprudence today, it is to be found in that study of racial origins and early social institutions which for the last century has steadily grown under the style of 'comparative' jurisprudence. The study of law has been obliged to extend its scope far beyond the particular form of Occidental society which was the basis of the old analytical jurisprudence. The gaps which still yawn in this young and growing branch of study, and which have drawn upon it some impatient criticism, are attributable to deficiency of data rather than to faults of method. Whatever the doubts and imperfections of modern sociological jurisprudence, whatever problems it may yet have to solve, it appears to be the natural outcome of a continuous movement in legal thought which makes it impossible to regard law, a primary function of society, as the product solely of sovereign power.

Recent tendencies

The problems of the nature and sources of law, and of state-sovereignty, have become increasingly complex in our own age, and the extremely varied, and often antagonistic, methods of approach which have been apparent in recent years reflect the profound transformations of the social, political, and legal institutions of the modern world. As might be expected in the existing conditions, two main tendencies of juristic speculation, the one idealistic and the other materialistic, have developed and seem, at the first view, to stand in opposition to each other. Yet, while we may discern in them, as in the whole story of juristic thought, the eternal process of thesis and antithesis, action and reaction, at many points they have more community of aim than their adherents always seem to realize.

'Revived Natural Law'

The idealistic tendency has been given the somewhat misleading title of 'the revived Law of Nature'—misleading, because in all but a few of its various forms, this doctrine is essentially different from the Law of Nature as it was understood in former ages; it has taken on, in accordance with the prevailing fashion of thought, a *relativistic* complexion quite incompatible with the bygone conception of a supreme law of which all positive law was merely declaratory. Its only point of contact with the old Natural Law is that a moral idealism is its resonant keynote. It represents a revolt against the determinism of the Historical School on the one hand and the artificial finality of the Analytical School on the other hand; though, as we shall see, it has itself provoked, in the school of 'Pure Law', a reaction towards a form of analytical system more rigid than any which prevailed in the nineteenth century. I have already suggested that the charge of 'pessimism', so often levelled at the Historical School, has been exaggerated; but it is true that the principal lesson of that movement was certainly to concentrate the gaze upon the facts, events, and actual tendencies—in short, the objective phenomena—of legal development. From Ihering came the reinstatement of the power of subjective will and purpose over these objective phenomena; and from the modern apostles of 'the revived Law of Nature' comes the reaffirmation of the ethical content of law in its ideal of justice, which is a greater and more enduring element, in the view of this school, than either the accidents of circumstance or the material aims and wants of man.

The very diversity of forms which this conception has assumed in recent years is a testimony to its vitality and to the attraction which it possesses for different types of mind. Its extreme form, as found in the works of such writers as V. Cathrein and G. Renard, is a return to, or reassertion of, the theological conception of a Law of God which is the ultimate governor of all the laws of men. Based on the Thomist system, this teaching is confined almost entirely to adherents of the Roman Catholic faith and philosophy. A wider influence has been exercised by the revival, with certain differences of interpretation, of the Kantian philosophy of law, particularly in the voluminous writings, dating from 1888, of Rudolf Stammler. Founding himself on the 'critical' system of Kant, Stammler set before himself two principal objects in the study of law and justice: first, by distinguishing merely technical or adventitious elements of legal systems from their basic principles, to ascertain the true nature of law as distinct from other social rules; and second, to determine the Hypothetical and Categorical Imperatives of law considered as a form of human reason. 'All positive law', he says, 'is an attempt at just law.' By the abstraction of his imperatives, Stammler hoped—though his formulations have been much controverted—to establish certain constants of thought by which man might judge how nearly law succeeded in its attempt at justice—justice being, in this conception, a 'harmony' of wills or purposes within the framework of social life. Stammler did not (as did the old theories of Natural Law) deny authority to law which failed to conform to the overruling requirements of justice; he attempted to shape a rational method or form—an epistemological instrument—by which the relative rightness of law could be determined in any given circumstances, and which would serve as a guide, when the law failed before this test, to bring it nearer to its essential aim. The core of his teaching has been well described as follows:

R. Stammler

'Law is a certain structural formation of those purposes which move men to action. To discover the general principles of this formation we must abstract the purposes from the living social world of their origin and ask ourselves what is essential for the understanding of them as an harmonious and orderly system of ends. We shall then discover by the help of logical analysis certain absolutely valid principles of juridical organization, which will guide us safely in judging what purposes are deserving of legal recognition and how these purposes are jurally related.'[1]

Stammler's chief departure from Kant was in his distinction between the absolute and the social ideal. He emphasized the 'specific legal content' of law in its relation to the necessarily changing circumstances of particular times, places, and societies. The law which, in its 'specific legal content', subserved the social will-harmony in the particular circumstances to which it applied might thus be 'objectively just' while it still fell short of the ideal of the absolutely just. Thus Stammler offered a technique for the determination of what may be called the relatively just (this being the highest at which most law can aim), and arrived at a standpoint which is frequently termed a 'natural law with variable content'.

J. Kohler

It is open to question whether this conception does not contain a philosophical contradiction, but it has had a powerful appeal for jurists who, while fully conscious of the lessons of the historical movement, still believe that it is not solely material considerations which govern the conception and development of law. Thus some jurists, of whom the most eminent is Josef Kohler, far from finding a merely mechanical determinism in all the fluctuations and contrasts of comparative legal history, have been the more convinced by them of an evolutionary tendency, an ever-swelling current of moral progress, in social history. This was a recurrent theme with Sir Henry Maine; and Kohler, a disciple of Hegel, vehemently protests against such materialistic legal interpretations

[1] F. Hallis, *Corporate Personality*, 35. See further on Stammler, Friedmann, *Legal Theory*, 3rd ed., 100 ff., and C. K. Allen, 'Justice and Expediency', in *Interpretations of Modern Legal Philosophies*.

as that of Ihering, which was vitiated, he avers, by 'a deplorable dilettantism; only an unphilosophical mind could find satisfaction in it'. Kohler concludes the preface to one of his best-known works[1] with the vigorous affirmation: 'A unity of spirit rules mankind and evolution forces its way out of universal substance. . . . Materialism is dead; the philosophy of Spirit still lives.' And again: 'Mankind constantly progresses in culture in the sense that permanent cultural values are produced, and that man becomes more and more god-like in knowledge and mastery of the earth. Only when based on this foundation can the requirements of the law be recognized as the requirements of the advancing culture which the law is to serve; and only in this way can the true aim of the law be known for what it is.' This, assuredly, is not Natural Law in its earlier incarnation, and Kohler is as much convinced as Stammler of 'variable content'. 'There is no eternal law. The law that is suitable for one period is not so for another; we can only strive to provide every culture with its corresponding system of law.' But in this Hegelian conception there certainly resides a supreme law in the principle of evolution, progress, or culture; though jesting Pilate may well ask, 'What is culture?' and may well question whether man's knowledge and mastery of the earth have necessarily made him 'god-like'. The history of societies and of morals since 1914 hardly encourage that comfortable belief.

The French Natural Law School

The teaching of Stammler has had its most marked influence in France, where writers like Saleilles, Gény, Charmont, Le Fur, and Demogue have devoted themselves with enthusiasm to the 'revived' Natural Law. All these writers—and certain other Continental jurists, notably del Vecchio, with them—are unanimous, on the one hand, in disclaiming any desire to resurrect the absolute Natural Law of the philosophers and the theologians, and, on the other hand, in proclaiming

[1] *Rechtsphilosophie*, translated (A. Albrecht) as *The Philosophy of Law* (*Modern Legal Philosophy Series*).

their dissatisfaction with the empiricism of the purely historical or anthropological approach. They are all convinced that law, whether in the form of legislation or of judicial decision, cannot perform its true function, and cannot, indeed, operate even with the maximum of practical efficiency, unless it adds a certain transcendental element to the purely utilitarian aim. Neither the material needs of man (they hold) nor the forces of habit and tradition are enough in themselves; some measure of creative idealism is ever necessary to give law its highest efficacy as a social cement. But the ideal which must be sought is essentially relative; it is not, like the old Law of Nature, immutable, or apprehended only by revelation as an eternal verity; it is essentially 'the ideal of an epoch', and herein lies its 'variable content'. When the writers of this school attempt to tell us how it is to be discovered, it must be confessed that they fall into extreme vagueness which, by contrast with the formidable categories of Stammler, leave more to the imagination but offer less to the perception. We hear much of the 'social conscience', of the *Rechtsgefühl* of the community, which seems only to be Savigny's *Volksgeist* or *Rechtsüberzeugung* with a moralistic colouring, just as the 'ideal of an epoch' seems only to be Savigny's *Zeitgeist* in livelier hue. One Dutch writer, H. Krabbe, believes so strongly in the 'social conscience', or the 'recognition' of law by those to whom it applies, that he admits no other authority as a true source of law; which seems to mean—subject to the same logical objections—that law is to the individual, or to groups of individuals, what the theory of 'auto-limitation' is to the State; again a notion which was roughly symbolized in the old Social Contract. The collective conscience here becomes the corporate aspect of the Natural Law (if it can be so termed); as for the individual judge or legislator who has to explore and expound the collective conscience, much emphasis is laid (e.g. by F. Gény) on his instinct or 'intuition'—in short, on his own moral sense and his own intelligence;[1] so that we seem to be moving in a somewhat baffling circle of subjectivity. Reduced to its simplest terms, the 'revived natural law' seems to mean little more than that the magistrate must judge as justly as he can, and the legislator must make laws as wisely as he can, in accordance with the prevailing ideas of justice and utility, with which, it is to be hoped (and, after all, it cannot be more than a hope), the law-makers and law-dispensers of a particular community are imbued by training and experience. Thus stated, the New Natural Law does not seem to contain any very novel truth, or to be very felicitously named; and it probably would not have been so much canvassed on the Continent had it not been associated with a movement for a more liberal and elastic judicial technique (*la libre recherche scientifique*) than has been orthodox in most European countries, and also with controversies concerning the nature and limits of the powers of the State. Apart from these special problems, its chief value, as I have indicated, has been to counteract the tendency to exaggerate the purely historical and fortuitous circumstances of legal growth, at the expense of the moral principles from which law may sometimes be judicially separated, but can never be divorced *a vinculo matrimonii*.

The later Socio-logical School

In sharp contrast to these liberal aspirations is a modern school of thought which carries on the tradition of the early sociologists, devoting its attention not so much to the ethical content and aim of law as to the actual social circumstances which give rise to legal institutions and which condition their scope and operation. This is the 'functional' view of law, regarded as one, and only one, of many factors in the morphology of society. It is essentially concerned not with man as an individual but with man-in-association. In this cast of thought it stands in the direct line of descent from doctrines which we have seen growing throughout the nineteenth century,

[1] In Gény's theory, however, it is an instinct always developed and disciplined by the influences of judicial *technique*.

and which have regarded man less as the Rational Being of the eighteenth century than as a component part of a totality inspired by a common purpose, whether it be the entire *Volk* of Savigny and Beseler or the fractional but autarchical *Gemeinschaft* of Gierke. The whole theory of the Sociological School is a protest against the orthodox conception of law as an emanation from a single authority in the State, or as a complete body of explicit and comprehensive propositions applicable, by accurate interpretation, to all claims, relationships, and conflicts of interest. In a foreword to his most influential work[1] Eugen Ehrlich boldly observes:

E. Ehrlich

'It is often said that a book must be written in a manner that permits of summing up its content in a single sentence. If the present volume were to be subjected to this test, the sentence might be the following: At the present as well as at any other time, the centre of gravity of legal development lies not in legislation, nor in juristic science, nor in judicial decision, but in society itself. This sentence, perhaps, contains the substance of every attempt to state the fundamental principles of the sociology of law.'

Ehrlich's is still an authoritative voice in the current phase of sociological jurisprudence, though much of his theory, and even more of his technique, have been tempered and clarified by later jurists, especially in the United States, like Pound, Timasheff, Huntington Cairns, and Julius Stone. Ehrlich, and indeed all the modern Sociological School, stand at the opposite pole from the conception of the sovereign as a unitary source of law; there is no theme more insistent in his work than the heterogeneity of the sources from which law is derived. On every page he demands scrutiny not of the 'propositions' of law, as lawyers know them, but of what he calls the 'facts' (*Tatsache*) of law, as students of social institutions find them. He distinguishes between three

[1] *Grundlegung der Soziologie des Rechts*, translated (W. L. Moll) as *Fundamental Principles of the Sociology of Law*. Ehrlich's views on custom as a source of law are discussed *post*, pp. 122 ff.

different kinds of norms. Legal rules, formulated either by statutes or codes or Common Law acceptation, are 'norms for decision'. But Ehrlich does not conceive them as formulations which embody the whole or even the greater part of 'law', properly understood. A law, he holds, is essentially a rule of conduct, and 'norms for decision' are merely rules of conduct for those whose business it is to settle legal disputes. (This, I would interject, is a very disputable connotation of 'conduct'.) There are many other rules of conduct in society which are self-generating and which depend upon no superior sanctioning authority. Society is a congeries of sub-societies, and man is found everywhere to be not merely a 'member of society', but a unit in innumerable different associations. He is, as it were, an electron in an atom forming part of the whole matter of society. Each of these constituent atoms has a spontaneous 'inner order' of its own, which is as truly 'law' as 'state-law'. It may not have the whole authority of State compulsion behind it, but Ehrlich denies that the complete sanction of force is a necessary attribute of law; innumerable social rules, he observes, which are in fact operative and efficacious, lack any sanction but the *opinio necessitatis*. The principles of 'inner order' which govern corporate groupings and relationships Ehrlich describes as 'legal norms', and they are no less legal because they are 'fact-norms'. It is important, in order to grasp Ehrlich's thesis, to bear constantly in mind his distinction between 'norms for decision' and 'legal norms'.

What, then, is the nexus between 'norms for decision', which are commonly regarded as 'law', and all the multifarious 'fact-norms'? Ehrlich is bound to accord to the 'norms for decision' a kind of validity which is so different, at least in degree, from that of his other norms that it raises doubts about the whole of his terminology. For he cannot deny to the 'norms for decision' a special kind of authority; the last word rests with them, whatever the force of the 'fact-norms'. He tells us that 'the norms prescribed by the legal proposition can either secure absolute enforcement for the norms that flow from the facts of the law, or they can hinder them or invalidate them; and, lastly, they can attach legal consequences to them that bear no relation whatsoever to the legal consequences that flow from the facts'. In other words, the 'norms for decision' have the power of confirming the 'fact-norms' and clothing them with new authority, or of giving them quite different effect from that which had been previously attributed to them, or indeed of denying them altogether the value of norms, and, in effect, suppressing them.

It is clear, therefore, that on the threshold of this doctrine stands a problem of postulation. We have to decide at the outset—and the matter is really one of terminology—whether we propose to regard all accepted rules of conduct as 'laws', or whether we will apply that term only to those rules of conduct which are supported by a special and pre-eminent kind of authority. We seem to be moving in a circle, and involving ourselves in a patent terminological contradiction, if we say that the 'norms for decision' can *legally* deprive the 'fact-norms' of *legal* effect, or 'can attach *legal* consequences to them that bear no relation whatsoever to the *legal* consequences that flow from the facts'. We cannot, as the phrase is, have it both ways; if the consequences which flow from the 'norms for decision' are legal, then the different consequences which flow from the 'fact-norms' cannot also be legal.

Ehrlich's attempts to define the nature and scope of the 'facts of law', or to frame any clear conception of the 'inner order' of associational functions, cannot be regarded as successful; and this is not surprising, when we remember that the 'facts of law' are really the facts of the whole of life itself. It is for that reason that Ehrlich found the greatest difficulty in setting any boundaries to his subject, and ended by setting none whatever. While he believed that it was possible to frame a 'general legal science' upon sociological principles, it became evident, especially in his later writings, that this science could not be 'general' without taking all knowledge as its province; and there seems to be no reason why it should stop short at research into material 'sociological' phenomena, since the biological, the metaphysical, the psychological, the spiritual, and the aesthetic are no less relevant to the study of man-in-association than the more concrete and ascertainable social phenomena. One example may serve to show the scope of Ehrlich's 'facts of law'.

'The factory, the bank, the railroad, the great landed estate, the labour union, the association of employers, and a thousand other forms of life—each of these likewise has an order, and this order has a legal side as well as that of the mercantile establishment, which is regulated only in detail by the Commercial Code. In addition, there are countless forms in which the activity of these associations manifests itself outwardly, above all in contracts. In studying the manufacturing establishment, the legal investigator must pursue the countless, highly intricate paths that lead from the acceptance of the order to the delivery of the finished products to the customer, to wit, the position of the representative and of the commercial traveller, the three departments that are to be found in every manufacturing establishment (the sales department, the technical department, and the manufacturing department), the arrival of the orders, the preparation and the preservation of drawings, the computation of the cost of the undertaking, the calculation for the purpose of checking up, the execution of the order on the basis of the drawings, the functions of the manufacturing department, of the master workman, the management of the warehouse, the computation of wages by the piece and by time, the distribution of wages among the individual workmen, the importance of the certificate showing that the material has been handed over, the price list, the supervision at the gates by porters. Of equal importance for the legal side of the order of the undertaking is the keeping of books, the taking of inventories, the supervision over the warehouse, the preservation of drawings and models, the employment of workmen and of apprentices, the working regulations, and the committees of the workmen.'

It is difficult to see why we should not add to this inventory the technical details of the production of the raw materials, and of the manufacture, of every kind of commodity known to civilization. It goes without saying that history, economics, and ethnography must be included within the scope of jurisprudence. And this is only a beginning. 'This exposition would altogether fail of its purpose if it were understood to convey the idea that . . . the methods which I have indicated in any way exhaust the methodology of the sociology of law. New scientific aims will always make new scientific methods necessary.' For example, Ehrlich saw an important connexion between law and political geography. Towards the end of his life he established a 'Seminar of Living Law' in which his disciples were employed on the 'cartography' of every conceivable phase of social activity. I mean no disrespect to the labours of a very learned, sincere, and original jurist if I call this kind of project Megalomaniac Jurisprudence. The boundaries between the different branches of knowledge are indeed difficult to define, but experience has shown again and again that knowledge of everything usually ends in wisdom in nothing. Limitations of time, space, and human capacity are 'facts of law' and facts of life; and if, say, every dispute in contract were to pass through the processes which Ehrlich pictures, complete justice might perhaps be achieved, but it would be of little satisfaction to the parties, for they would certainly be dead before the forensic process was complete. These considerations warn us to place some practicable limits upon our conceptions and definitions of 'law'.

Roscoe Pound

The sociological jurisprudence of Professor Roscoe Pound, which has had great influence in the United States, has scrupulously avoided exaggerations of this kind; indeed, a dominant note of Pound's whole doctrine is its distrust of all juristic dogmatism. He is a moderate of the moderates—a relativist with a strong conviction of the provisional nature of all legal creeds and expedients. It would not be accurate to describe his attitude as purely pragmatic or utilitarian; he is no enemy of the abstract philosophy of law, nor does he underestimate the part which speculative idealism has played in the development of legal institutions. But he is impressed by certain limitations of legal philosophy which history has constantly illustrated—in particular, the influence upon philosophical theory of contemporary exigencies which convert what purports to be absolute truth into a thesis conditioned by circumstances of time and place. When we consider the various prevailing philosophies which have succeeded each other in men's thoughts and aims, it is evident that they have been affected by particular conjunctions of circumstances almost as much as the concrete arrangements and expedients of society itself. Again and again whole trends of thought have been coloured by the desire to justify a theory of government, to solve a pressing governmental problem of the day, to resolve doubts created by a phase of social change, or to bridge transition from one order of society to another. Nowadays these prevailing philosophies go by the name of 'ideologies'. They all, says Professor Pound, tend to be 'modes of rationalizing the juristic desires of the time', and though each in its turn has considered itself a decisive revelation of truth, none of them is or can be final. The first lesson, then, is that all juristic truth is relative truth.

Pound is equally undisposed to accept the dogma of the Analytical School that what Ehrlich calls the 'propositions of law' are all-comprehensive, self-sufficient, and self-explanatory. Nor does he regard with any greater favour the 'laws' of social growth and coexistence which the earlier sociologists thought they had discovered, and which writers like Ehrlich are apt to assume without formulating: nor yet such an all-powerful social 'law' as Duguit posits. The whole trend of Professor Pound's legal teleology is cautiously experimental—to the point, indeed, where some may think it hesitating and unsatisfying; but there is much warrant in experience for believing that modesty of objective in social experiment is more fruitful in the long run than a vaulting ambition which o'erleaps itself. This view, of course, will not satisfy the *exalté*, who will miss in the work of Professor Pound and other sociological jurists the stimulus of an ideal which, to the mood of faith, may be all the more worth pursuing because it is unattainable. It is, perhaps, a matter of temperament in each individual whether or not he is resigned to the acceptance of serviceable substitutes in place of absolute standards. Certainly it is true, as we have seen, that while soaring conceptions of eternal law have left men ill provided with working-tools, narrowly materialistic interpretations of law and history have left them hungering for something which they seem to feel is of more enduring substance.

However this may be, Professor Pound's legal philosophy is essentially one of practical compromise. He believes, with Ihering, that 'interests' are the chief subject-matter of law, and that the task of law in society is the 'satisfaction of human wants and desires'. These are ever changing with the flux of circumstance, and, in the pursuit of its purpose of 'social control', law is faced with two perpetual problems: first, the maintenance of a balance between stability and change; and second, the ascertainment of those 'social desiderata' which it is both possible and desirable for the law to satisfy. Thus arises the problem of the 'valuation of interests'—the selection of the most socially valuable objectives of state-regulation. For this difficult task, what criterion is available? Here again Professor Pound declines to commit himself to any rigid canon. His general answer seems to be—and it cannot altogether escape the criticism that it is rather the acknowledgement than the acceptance of a challenge—that the most important thing is that the jurist should first of all be aware of the real nature of his responsibility, and then, in furtherance of social aims, should do the best he can, in the most sensible way he can, on the best information he can get. If it is objected that this is, after all, what the jurist has always striven to do, the answer presumably is that he has not always been sufficiently conscious of the true direction which his effort should take. 'I do not believe the jurist has to do more than recognize the problem and perceive that it is presented to him as one of securing all social interests so far as he may, of maintaining a balance or harmony among them that is compatible with the securing of all of them.' This, it is true, leaves the jurist with an indefinite commission, but it requires of him something more attainable than the gigantic task which Ehrlich imposes upon him. 'For the purpose of understanding the law of to-day,' writes Professor Pound,

> 'I am content with a picture of satisfying as much of the whole body of human wants as we may with the least sacrifice. I am content to think of law as a social institution to satisfy social wants—the claims and demands involved in the existence of civilized society—by giving effect to as much as we may with the least sacrifice, so far as such wants may be satisfied or such claims given effect by an ordering of human conduct through politically organized society. For present purposes I am content to see in legal history the record of a continually wider recognizing and satisfying of human wants or claims or desires through social control; a more embracing and more effective securing of social interests; a continually more complete and effective elimination of waste and precluding of friction in human enjoyment of the goods of existence—in short, a continually more efficacious social engineering.'

This is the picture of Sociological Jurisprudence which might, perhaps, be better described as Experimental Jurisprudence. The immediate practical means which Professor Pound advocates for the technique of his engineering are: 'study of the actual social effects of legal institutions and legal doctrines, study of the means of making legal rules effective, sociological study in preparation for law-making, study of juridical method, a sociological legal history, and the importance of reasonable and just solutions of individual cases' (the 'individualization' of legal decisions) 'where the last generation was content with the abstract justice of abstract rules'. For the particular sphere of American law, Professor Pound has suggested a more detailed programme.

Pound's metaphor of 'engineering' has been criticized[1] as suggesting a system of merely mechanical expedients mechanically administered to social exigencies. But a metaphor must not be pressed too far, and this hardly seems to be Professor Pound's meaning. Engineering, after all, is a matter of nice calculation and ingenious resource, as well as of cogs and wheels and levers. A more substantial criticism, I believe, is that if we overemphasize the experimental aspect of law we shall be in danger of falsifying the manner in which it does in fact operate within a large part of its territory. Experiment implies initiative, and a ceaselessly 'engineering' law suggests the picture of a science which is always seeking new instruments, new expedients, for new needs—new 'goods', in short, for the good life. The picture is accurate enough for a great deal of what is called 'social legislation' in the modern state, and this is nowadays a preponderant part of law. It is true that in the world of today no enlightened system of law is content with being merely static: it must also be dynamic, and a great deal of thought and knowledge is necessary in order to make it usefully dynamic. But all law is not legislation, and with regard to a large area of the legal field the experiments of the law, if they can be so called—the engineering appliances, if you will—are brought to bear *ex post facto*. If a right is to be regarded, in Ihering's formula, as a 'legally protected interest', it seems that what frequently happens is that society discovers or creates its own interests, as circumstances demand, and when they have taken definite shape the law steps in at the appropriate moment and protects

[1] Vinogradoff, *Collected Papers*, ii. 324.

them, generally adding something, as the Sociologists themselves say, by the 'creative role of interpretation'. We have only to glance at rapidly developing branches of the law such as torts or commercial law to see this process constantly at work. This is why, in the early stages of law, 'the remedy comes before the right'—which, if literally accepted, is a logical absurdity; what it really means is that primitive law is chiefly concerned with devising means to recognize and protect rights which men have found for themselves. This is also why it is so often said that 'law lags behind social needs', the fact being that law frequently does not lend its assistance, and indeed cannot do so, until the social needs have become manifest and articulate. As Ehrlich insisted, men-in-society are constantly finding and regulating their own 'wants and desires', and the assistance of the law is often supplementary and declaratory. It is possible, without great strain of language, to consider this work of reinforcement, adjustment, and reconciliation as a kind of experimentation, for it certainly needs ingenuity and a shrewd appreciation of social circumstances; but we should be careful to distinguish between that part of modern law which is deliberately exploratory or inventive, and that part which is confirmatory. Nor should we forget that while, as I have said, much of modern law is dynamic, much is, and must be, static, in the sense that it aims at regulation of behaviour and the maintenance of order. As Professor Pound himself has said, whole theories of law, in the past, have been content with the dominating purpose of keeping the peace; and any student of English Common Law knows how much of it grew up round the central notion of the King's Peace. That is not the whole of the law today, but it is still a large and essential part of it. If we are to regard the law as an engine, let us think of it as a dynamo. Sometimes the dynamo drives a crane, a drill, a riveter, or even a mechanical shovel: but frequently it also actuates a gyroscope to maintain stability.

It is necessary, again, if we are to think of 'wants and desires' as the essential subject-matter of law, that we should give that term the widest interpretation—so wide, indeed, that it becomes difficult to draw a dividing line between the scope of sociological jurisprudence and that of any other kind of jurisprudence, even the most abstract. The sociological point of view suffers from the same besetting sin as the utilitarian: it is apt to thrust on society what, in accordance with theoretical principles, society *ought* to want and desire, just as Bentham offered, as actual goodness and happiness, what *ought* to make men good and happy—and what, doubtless, *would* make men good and happy if they were not sometimes strangely obstinate about their likes and dislikes. Since, to sociological investigation, the ponderables are obviously much more tractable material than the equally important imponderables, there is a danger—though I do not suggest that all sociological jurists have been unaware of it—that too much attention may be concentrated on the purely physical aspects of social and individual life. We have seen in the modern world communities where all the most carefully calculated boons of social 'planning' were in large measure sterilized by the denial of the elementary boon of personal freedom. Material advantages may be conferred by the contrivance of law, but one of the 'wants and desires' to which men are still attached is to be as free from legal contrivance as is reasonably possible. The good life is not capable of being reduced to a blue-print. Ihering's famous definition of law[1] was: 'The form of the guarantee of the conditions of the life of society, assured by the State's power of constraint.' But what are the 'conditions of the life of society'? Ihering answers that they are

'the subjective conditions which govern it. They are not merely the conditions upon which physical existence depends, but also all the goods, all the enjoyments, which, in the view of the

[1] *Zweck im Recht*, para. 181.

individual, alone give savour to his life. Honour is not a condition of physical existence, and yet, for a man of honour, what is life worth if honour is lost? To preserve it, he will readily risk his life. Liberty and nationality are not conditions of physical existence; but there was never a liberty-loving people which would not prefer death to helotage. The man who destroys himself out of disgust with life may yet unite in his own person all the objective conditions which are necessary for existence. In a word, the goods and the enjoyment which man feels to be essential to his life are not of a merely material nature, but have also an intangible, idealistic value; they comprise everything for which humanity may strive: honour, love, education, religion, the arts, the sciences. The question of the conditions of life, both of the individual and of society, is a question of national and individual education.'

It is the 'subjective conditions' of coexistence which present the greatest problem, as yet insufficiently envisaged, to sociological jurisprudence.

'Realistic' Jurisprudence

A type of relativistic legal philosophy which has developed strongly and has had a marked influence on juristic thinking in recent years, is described as 'realist' —not, perhaps, altogether happily; for, as Professor Pound pointed out in the early days of this movement, all the successive 'schools' of jurisprudence in history have claimed to find the path to the only 'real' law.

L. Duguit

Though his successors of later schools do not seem to acknowledge any special debt to him, one of the first true realists was a jurist of French constitutional law, Professor Léon Duguit of Bordeaux, who wrote prolifically in the early years of the present century. His work attracted much attention for some years, but its influence has waned. An enthusiastic disciple of Comte, he insisted that law is simply a phenomenon of *fact*, an *objective situation* as between State and individual on the one hand and between individual and individual on the other hand. The first essential, he held, was to banish from law all 'metaphysic', and particularly the notion of *right*. (We shall meet these doctrines again.) In Comte's words, 'the only right which any man can possess is the right always to do his duty'. Duty to what? Not to the State, for the State, though elaborately personified in so much juristic theory, is a mere fiction. *L'État est mort!* It, too, is merely a phenomenon of political *fact*, and its function in modern society is not the exercise of authority or power, but that of acting as a central, directing agency for the performance of *public service*. In other words, the notion of public service replaces the conception of sovereignty as the foundation of public law. All derives from one basic, predominant principle, which necessarily involves the interplay of reciprocal duties—the principle of *social interdependence* leading to *social solidarity*. 'Solidarity is nothing more or less than the fact of interdependence uniting the members of human society, and particularly the members of a social group, by reason of the community of needs and the division of labour.' The development of this theme led Duguit into his theory of *group decentralization* or *federal syndicalism*—a form of disseminated autonomy in which the part played by the State was little more than that of a regulator or overseer. Its effect, according to Duguit, would be to establish a general 'balance of power' in the community. The theory had some distant affinities with the doctrines of Fascism which were later to develop in Italy and which passed under a cloud in the Second World War.

Duguit's attempt to evaporate all ethical essence out of law, to banish *right* from jurisprudence and substitute for it only *service*, cannot be said to have been either consistent or convincing. He laid himself open to the criticism, which was not wanting, that his ultra-materialism was in reality only a disguised form of idealism, and that in postulating an irrefragable social law of solidarity, which he conceived as a mere existing fact, he was really seeking to establish a constant of law which other jurists called 'natural' or 'natural with variable content'. In the end, he could not escape the 'metaphysic' which he so much distrusted, and which, as we shall see, has been the bogy of other realists.[1]

In the sense in which it is now used by its principal exponents, the term 'real' is intended to point to the contrast which frequently exists between law as it *seems* in its dogmatic formulation and as it *is* in its actual working and effects. There is no doubt that this contrast is often striking and usually unfortunate, because it confuses the public mind and tends to bring the law into disrepute. Most practising lawyers accept it with a shrug and adapt their technique to it, but the legal and social reformer cannot and should not be so easily reconciled to it. To take an example from our own society, it is the law of England that divorce can be granted only on proof of a matrimonial offence, that the parties are therefore at arm's length, and that collusion between them is fatal to a petition. Everybody, including the judges, knows that in thousands of cases that is not how the law actually works. It is clearly of importance to the community that this difference between theory and practice should be realized and confronted.

American realism

The main trend of the American realist movement has been to call in question legal *certainty*, to attack what is called *conceptualism*, and to emphasize those many influences which produce 'accidents of litigation' through the variable elements of forensic method and especially of *judicial technique*.

Mr. Justice Oliver Wendell Holmes is universally recognized as one of the greatest legal minds of modern times and any words of his deserve the utmost respect. As long ago as 1897, in a brilliant address ('The Path of the Law') he used a famous phrase: 'The prophecies of what the courts will do in fact, and nothing more pretentious, are what I mean by the law.' This arresting dictum became at one time a kind of sacred text for much realist doctrine. There is nothing new or startling

[1] A fuller discussion of Duguit's theories will be found in the present writer's *Legal Duties*, 158 ff.

in it to any legal practitioner. No honest lawyer advising a prospective litigant can do more than opine what he believes, or hopes, a court will decide. If it were otherwise, there would be no legal disputes at all, since an infallible prophecy could be made simply by reference to the authorities. But the Holmes 'predictions' do not mean, and never have meant, that law consists merely of a series of fortuitous events, or, as it has been put, that law is not what it *is* but what it *does*. It is strange that Holmes should ever have been interpreted in such manner, for the remainder of his celebrated address, while it calls for a constant and vigilant re-examination of established rules and pretends no respect for those which are empty or outworn, is an eloquent plea for the study of law as a rational system based on history, tradition, and logic. 'Theory', this master tells us, 'is the most important part of the dogma of the law.' The lawyer's 'predictions' are valueless unless based on principles diligently sought and intelligently understood. To master the law means 'to look straight through all the dramatic incidents and to discern the true basis for prophecy'. The weakness of realism has been to concentrate too much attention on the 'dramatic incidents' and to regard them as the whole substance of law.

The question of 'certainty' will be considered later (*post*, pp. 346 ff.) in connexion with the operation of legal precedent. Meanwhile, it may be asked whether insistence on the 'basic myth' of certainty is not itself something of a myth? In a vast number of legal relationships there is a reasonable measure of certainty—as much as is vouchsafed in most human affairs—but in the innumerable combinations of circumstances and personalities which may give rise to legal disputes, only a very naïve mind imagines that laws can operate with the same precision as, let us say, what are called the 'laws' of natural forces and substances. Even these latter are far less 'certain' than they were once supposed to be, and scientists today are extremely cautious in all their generalizations. If by the 'myth of certainty' is meant a belief that human laws can be applied by a sort of mathematical or mechanical method, then it is a delusion which the realists are right to expose. But who really believes anything of the kind? No experienced practitioner; still less any Bumble of the great public which regards the uncertainty of law as one of its most asinine characteristics. The charge, however, may lie with some measure of justice against certain academic jurists, especially of the analytical school, who tend to show an excessive faith in mere concepts as the milk of the legal word.

'Conceptualism' is an awkward word, but it is perhaps as good as any other to denote what is undoubtedly a besetting sin of juristic method. It is a kind of abuse or misdirection of logic in the construction of artificial rules or categories which are plausible in the abstract but have little correspondence with the concrete. It was this kind of *Begriffsjurisprudenz*—a barren and not very difficult intellectual exercise, by no means confined to the law—which Ihering repudiated and satirized. It is, of course, convenient to be able to appeal to real or supposed canons under which any given legal problem can be subsumed, and law cannot be applied without some such master principles; but there is a tendency in legal dialectic to invent these rules of thumb when they apply only very imperfectly to the many human situations which are the territory of law. This has been aptly expressed by Professor J. L. Montrose[1] as 'the way in which the analytical lawyer, who condemns "well-meaning vagueness" and produces definite rules which are often evaluated as "logically" determined, may sometimes be shown to have employed a pseudo-logic and to have sacrificed the greater utility of comprehensiveness and justice for the lesser utility of mechanical precision'. In the pages of this book the reader will

[1] 'Distinguishing Cases and the Limits of Ratio Decidendi', 19 *M.L.R.* 525, 529.

meet with various examples of these legal freaks and of factitious distinctions which work injustice in their application because they subordinate substance to form. Thus the categories or degrees of duties which have crept into the commonest of all torts, negligence, have proved to be far too rigid and artificial and are now being gradually abandoned. The great danger here is that once these fallacies have established themselves the conservatism of lawyers is apt to regard them as self-justified and sacrosanct. Most Common Law rules are based on accumulated experience which it is rash to despise; but there are many exceptions, and legal development is paralysed if we allow ourselves to believe that in law whatever is, is right; and there is abundant evidence that this has been a common infirmity of legal minds.

Realists, therefore, approach all settled and traditional doctrines of the law in a spirit of scepticism. Provided that it does not run to mere showy eccentricity posing as 'originality', or degenerate into dissent merely for bravado—and these are the temptations—scepticism is no unhealthy frame of mind for the jurist, for without it law will stagnate and fall behind its social mission. The arch-sceptic of English jurisprudence was Jeremy Bentham, who was not prepared to accept any legal rule or institution at its face value. His critical energy, compounded in an exceptional degree of the destructive and the constructive, led him into some excesses and even absurdities; but without his indomitable nonconformity English law would be far other today than it is. The scepticism of the realists is therefore a wholesome antidote to the complacency to which lawyers are prone. It is, however, always necessary to remember that there is a difference between refusing to approve a legal rule without first evaluating it and rejecting a rule simply because it *is* a rule. Some realists have shown a tendency in that direction.

As for judicial technique, the problems with which

American realists have been concerned must be viewed in their own local setting. The influence of judicial decision in shaping the law is bound to be particularly powerful in a country where, at the very centre, there is a Supreme Court which has the reponsibility of interpreting the federal constitution and adapting it to changing conditions; a country, too, which is the birthplace of the pragmatic philosophy. Again, the conglomerate of the United States exhibits such a multiplicity both of laws and of jurisdictions as has seldom existed within a single community; and the maintenance of what is, despite many disparities, a real cohesion and a vigorous jurisprudence throughout so vast a system has been one of the great legal achievements not only of the New World but of legal history. Diversity, however, inevitably gives rise to special problems of its own. One of them is that uniformity of principle and of judicial method, difficult enough to preserve even within a circumscribed legal system, becomes almost impossible of achievement, and the task of the lawyer in reconciling and threading his way through the maze of decisions is perplexing indeed. This situation is complicated by unevenness of judicial attainment, which ranges from a standard as high as any in the world to the manifest shortcomings of popularly elected judges. Furthermore, the scope of judicial discretion, and of what is called on the Continent 'free law-finding', has for long past been wider than in England, which is far more tenacious of the doctrine of *stare decisis*—largely, it may be, because the ascertainment and application of authority does not present the same practical difficulties as in America, though, as we shall see, those difficulties are growing.

The 'human factor' in judicial decision is not, of course, peculiar to the United States. It will never be excluded anywhere so long as judges are men and not automata. But can it be eliminated from any process, simple or complicated, scientific or intellectual, which involves human agency? It is difficult to see how, even by the extensive use of psychology (which the realists favour), it is possible to reduce the illimitable range of these personal variables to any kind of helpful generalizations. No judge in the world can rid himself entirely of prepossessions and idiosyncrasies. The bad judge allows himself to be governed by them, to the detriment of justice, though in any well-ordered legal system there will generally be a higher authority to correct him. The good judge tries, as far as he can, to banish bias from his adjudication. This is difficult but not wholly impossible. It is, in fact, done every day with no small measure of success. Conscientious judges are constantly giving decisions against their own inclinations. The 'human factor' is certainly important in a legal operation, just as it is in a surgical operation; but its inevitable intrusions do not mean that judicial determinations are completely at the mercy of personal vagaries or are to be measured only by 'the length of the Chancellor's foot'.

The realist movement has suffered, like most evangelisms, from its own exaggerations. In its earliest polemics it evinced such a distrust of orthodox 'paper rules' that it seemed to deny the value of all legal principles and to regard law merely as a jumble of uncoordinated happenings. This was plainly an untenable position and it has now been greatly modified. Psychology has been similarly exaggerated. Thus in his well-known *Law and the Modern Mind*, which has attracted much attention, Judge Jerome Frank traced the 'child-like' quest for legal certainty to a 'father-complex'. It is surely unnecessary to seek a Freudian explanation for the very simple fact that in a precarious existence men naturally crave for more certainty than is possible to obtain, whether it be in fluctuating temporal affairs or (as is evident in all theology) in spiritual speculations. It does not need Freud to tell us that when a man is uncertain about his legal rights he would very much like to be freed from his doubts. Again, the variability of judicial *science et technique*, as Gény called it, was at one time so disproportionately emphasized that all judgements seemed to become mere spasms, so to speak, of an incalculable intuitionism, or 'hunch', as it was called. (There is indeed such a thing as judicial intuition, but it is not just the lucky guess of the moment, but the product of intimacy with what Professor Pound has called 'the taught tradition of the law'.) These extravagances have diminished as the different aspects of realism have been canvassed in much learned controversy. The realist movement as it is today links up closely with the sociological. It places perhaps more stress on factual investigation of the law's actual working and results than on the aims of 'social engineering' which law *ought* to set before itself; but the trend is the same, for it is by practical ascertainment and collation of the facts of law-in-action that weaknesses of orthodox rubrics are disclosed and the way is opened for revision. In this approach, however, there is some danger (as in sociological programmes) that methodology may become an end in itself—that the accumulation of facts, figures, and data may come to be regarded as in itself a contribution to legal and legislative science, whereas it can never be more than an amorphous mass until it is interpreted and illuminated by creative intelligence. There has, no doubt, been some waste of humdrum labour in this respect, but the effort is in the right direction, and American lawyers have shown far more enterprise and a livelier spirit of inquiry than their British brethren. Not that England is without its censors of the law; there is little complacency in the works of many recent writers on our law. There is a standing Law Reform Committee which has achieved valuable results, and the phenomena of law-in-action are not infrequently examined and reported upon by Royal Commissions, Committees, and the like, which may have considerable effect on reformative or consolidating legislation. There is much 'sociological jurisprudence', and even 'realism', to be found in British Blue Books, but it must be added in sorrow that too often they take the form of rather unsatisfactory compromises and also that their bolder recommendations, even if accepted, take, on the average, about twenty years to mature.

The realist movement (it prefers not to be called a 'school') has been summed up by one of its leading and most vigorous exponents, Professor K. Llewellyn, as a 'ferment'. Fermentation is necessary in legal chemistry, for without it the liquor of the law becomes sour and stale. Grown out of its youthful exuberances and disabused of its hasty conclusion that law is to be found only in facts and deeds, this movement brings to modern jurisprudence a spirit of vigilance and exploration which is capable in the right hands of contributing substantially to the understanding of law not as a bloodless abstraction but as a living force in society.[1]

Scandinavian realism

A somewhat different doctrine, which carries 'realism' to an uncompromising extreme, has been expounded in recent years by what has come to be known as the 'Scandinavian school' of jurists.[2] It is based principally on the teaching of the philosopher Axel Hägerström, to whom all the writers of this persuasion acknowledge their indebtedness.

If American realism is 'rule-sceptical', Scandinavian realism may be described as 'metaphysics-sceptical'. It insists vehemently on dissociating all legal phenomena from 'metaphysics', which Ross, following Hägerström, considers to be largely derived from primitive 'magic',[3]

[1] The voluminous literature of realism cannot be mentioned in detail here, but there is no better concise exposition of its main standpoint than the late Professor Max Radin's 'Legal Realism', 31 *Columbia Law Review*, 824. For a fuller survey see Friedmann's *Legal Theory*.

[2] The main sources, for English readers, are: (the late) Axel Hägerström, *Inquiries into the Nature of Law and Morals* (translated); (the late) A. C. Lundstedt, *Superstition or Rationality in Action for Peace?* (1925) (translated), and *Legal Thinking Revised* (1956) (written in very imperfect English); K. Olivecrona, *Law as Fact* (1939) (translated); Alf Ross, *Towards a Realistic Jurisprudence* (1946), and *On Law and Justice* (1958) (written in English).

[3] Hägerström was a Professor of Philosophy, but one of his major works (written in German) was on the Roman law of obligations. This I have not read, but, according to his followers, it laid much stress on the elements of

and on regarding them simply as *social facts*, ascertained by *empirical science*. Again and again this principle is asserted. 'Legal notions', writes Ross, 'must be interpreted as conceptions of social reality, the behaviour of man in society, and as nothing else.' All positive law is thus a social technique. Every method of reasoning which is not purely empirical is valueless and illusory, being based on *a priori* preconceptions for which there is no 'scientific' basis. 'Law', writes Olivecrona, 'is nothing but a set of social facts.' The rules of law are in no sense the will of the State, or indeed the will of anything or anybody, in the sense of commands, but are 'independent imperatives' (or, as Ross prefers to call them, 'directives') issued from time to time by various constitutional agencies; and their sole effect is that they 'operate on the mind of the judge' and lead to certain *applications* of the law which are the *facts* of the legal system. The business of 'doctrinal jurisprudence', which is the only true kind of jurisprudence, is simply to discover and expound, without value-judgements, these rules 'for the establishment and functioning of the State machinery of force'. All *a priori* notions, and especially those of such ideologies as natural law and abstract justice, must be banished from any estimate of the 'validity' or the 'binding force' of law. Its validity is to be estimated solely by its existence as a social fact, which attracts the force-machinery of the State. It is not clear in Olivecrona's theory whether it is legitimate to seek any social purpose in the facts of law, but the whole notion of 'social welfare' is dismissed by Ross as being again 'metaphysical' and therefore empty.

The rejection of 'jurisprudential idealism' is accompanied by a ruthless slaughter of many traditional legal notions. Most theories of law are simply 'a persistent infantilism'. Rights become 'imaginary' or 'fictitious',

'magic' in the development of Roman Law. This suggestion of superstition and magic constantly reappears in his disciples' discussion of 'metaphysical' conceptions of law.

apparently because they are, of course, abstractions until tested and adjudged by legal process. *Stare decisis* is an illusion, customary law is only a form of ideology. Pound's 'social engineering' is a chimera. A legal norm is, as we have seen, a 'directive' not to the community, but to judges and administrators. Law is not the creation of the State, for the mere existence of the State or of the community presupposes law. Legislation does not operate with any 'binding force'; it makes enacted law *psychologically* effective, by the use of a certain form 'which has a grip on the minds of the people'. There is no ethical content in law; on the contrary, morals are created by law itself. And so on. All theories which differ from this empirical science are dismissed summarily as 'meaningless' or 'illusory' or plain 'nonsense'. It would seem that most jurists and philosophers have been living in a kind of trance of illusion. This intolerance is most marked in the writings of the late Professor Lundstedt, whose arrogance of statement is not improved by the obscurity and incoherence of his argumentation.

This school of thought has affinities with American realism, which, however, it regards as placing too much emphasis on the behaviourism of judges and not enough on the exorcism of metaphysics. It has great respect for Kelsen's doctrines, but differs from them on the fundamental issue that Kelsen's *Grundnorm* is an utter surrender to speculative metaphysics. Kelsen's system, as we shall see, lives in the world of the *Sollen* (metaphysics again!) and not of the *Sein*, and therefore is not realistic.

Again, this doctrine has much in common with the sociological school of jurisprudence, and indeed Ross concedes that 'the basis of jurisprudence must be a sociological outlook'; but it differentiates itself on the ground that sociology divagates into many inquiries (presumably unreal?) merely *surrounding* legal norms, and is too apt to become 'natural-law philosophy in disguise'.

The essence of the theory is summed up in Ross's dictum that 'all metaphysics are a chimera and there is no cognition other than the empirical'. That is a proposition of epistemology too large for present discussion, but it must be accepted as the basis of the jurisprudence of this whole school. One may sympathize with some of its renunciations of metaphysics and speculation—for example, with Ross's assault on the *a priori* assumptions of natural law. But if there is no 'scientific' basis for such doctrines, what is the 'scientific' basis for the interpretation of *fact*? Is this 'reality' really 'objective'? Is it definitely and certainly ascertainable by empirical science—indeed, can the term 'science' be properly applied to it? Even in America we have had 'fact-sceptics' as well as 'rule-sceptics'. Mere fact is a lifeless and meaningless thing until its significance has been estimated; and it can only be estimated by subjective interpretation. Law in all its forms is a phenomenon of the relationship between men in society; it is susceptible of many different meanings, according to the interpreter, and can never be said to be an objective, indisputable 'reality', proven beyond cavil or dispute. We are not here dealing with concrete substances and forces, as natural science does (though, as we have seen, cautiously and tentatively), but with human phenomena in all their varieties and complexities. It is questionable whether they can ever be the material of an exact science. Even sociology holds a precarious title as a science; still more dubious is a science of laws as mere social facts. The attempt to reduce one of the most important of human activities to bare fact, stripped of all content and purport, unrelated to human design and social development, must in the end make of 'doctrinal jurisprudence' an extremely barren exercise of the intelligence. It cannot escape value-judgements which will be equally 'metaphysical' with all the other approaches to law which it so scornfully rejects.

Despite certain affinities, which have been mentioned,

The Theory of Pure Law

of inquiry and method, the so-called Theory of Pure Law stands in opposition to all this realism. In its origin it chiefly represented a revolt against those 'ideological' types of jurisprudence which have been evolved as mere instruments of government in totalitarian states. It is associated with the 'Viennese school', which has had a powerful intellectual influence, and of which the leader is Professor Hans Kelsen. In his prolific writings there is nothing which Kelsen has more relentlessly attacked than 'ideology' in legal theory; indeed, this may be described as the core of his doctrine; and his equally unsparing assaults on 'natural law', in both its ancient and modern forms, is only another aspect of the same teaching. Kelsen's reasoning is austere, taut, forcible; though it constantly deals in abstractions which seem somewhat rarefied to the English reader, its severe and almost Euclidean economy of demonstration is a refreshing contrast to the discursiveness of some of the exponents of the New Natural Law. This characteristic of it has appealed strongly to many minds which have become both wearied and bewildered by the excesses of 'metajuristic' speculation (as Kelsen would call it) in the field of law.

H. Kelsen

Kelsen describes his science of law as 'pure' (*rein*), and again and again insists that law 'properly so called' (in Austin's phrase) must be kept unspotted from elements which, not rightfully belonging to it, merely confuse and contaminate it. But how delimit it? For this difficult task Kelsen finds his starting-point in Kant's system of Pure Reason. 'Clear frontiers' in the realm of thought was a cardinal doctrine with Kant, and one of the most important of these frontiers was that which he drew between the domain of the *Sein* (the Is) and of the *Sollen* (the Shall Be). Kelsen's first postulate is that law exists solely in the world of *Sollen*, and that every legal principle is therefore that kind of rule which Continental jurisprudence has long known as a *norm*. Law, says Kelsen again and again, is essentially a 'normative science'. Now the essential characteristic of a 'norm' is that it is something hypothetical or 'relative'; in the broadest sense, it might even be called 'conventional'. It depends upon a certain initial assumption which does not arise out of the necessities of nature but is laid down by an operation of human will and reason. Assuming such-and-such a general proposition (the product of man's own will and reason), then such-and-such *must* follow as a consequence (to be *enforced* by man's own will). Assuming that it is unlawful to forge another's signature (a principle entirely of man's own creation), then the forger *must* be punished. This is the world of the *Sollen*, and in that world norms are the elaborated rules of what human will and reason say *shall be*. In the world of the *Sein*, of the actual observed phenomena of physical existence, it is quite otherwise. The scientist who observes and records phenomena makes no initial assumption; and, so far as he is preoccupied with laws or rules at all, they are laws of induction, concerned not with what *must* or *shall* be, but only with what *will* be. An apple parts from a tree; it *will* fall to the ground by the forces of nature, and not because any process of human will or reason had decreed, antecedently, that it *shall* or *must* fall. Thus the 'laws' of natural science are (to resort to Austin again) laws merely 'by analogy', and are 'improperly so called'. The norms in the realm of the *Sollen* are wholly different in origin and nature, resembling 'improper' laws solely in the attribute of *uniformity*.

This philosophical distinction, though it may seem to the lawyer to be of little practical relevance, is essential to the understanding of Kelsen's doctrine. A cardinal problem, however, is to find the true dividing line between law and other moral or social 'sciences'.[1] Kelsen points out that a great many other 'sciences' besides law

[1] I am aware that the use of the word 'science' in this sense may be accused of question-begging. Kelsen, however, adopts Kant's conception of a science as being a *system* of knowledge, or 'totality of cognitions', arranged according to principles. All law is, to Kelsen, a *Deutungsschema*, and he frequently so describes it.

are 'normative'—all philosophy, logic, economics, for example, and indeed any system of knowledge which is not concerned solely with the behaviour of material phenomena. Kelsen finds the distinguishing mark of law in the element of *compulsion*.[1] All law must possess an 'apparatus of compulsion'. Thus Kelsen and his followers stand with Austin in regarding law as essentially imperative. It follows that, looking at law from the standpoint of the individual, Kelsen, like Duguit,[2] finds the whole essence of law in duty, and not in right; he denies to this duty any inherent moral content whatever;[3] legal duty is simply what the law commands, and what the law commands has no necessary relation whatever to the norms of ethics. But who or what is the commander? In whom does the authority for the enforcement of the norm reside? Austin, concentrating his attention on the English legal system, found a comparatively simple answer to this troublesome question. Kelsen's answer is much more complex. He cannot but be aware that in many modern States it is far from easy to disengage any single, supreme authority, and say, 'Here rests the last word.' But he holds that in all civilized states it is possible to trace one's way back to a basic norm, the *Grundnorm*—a grand, indispensable postulate—to which all the roads of the law lead, by however devious routes.

This, like every other legal norm, has no necessary connexion with order, or justice, or expediency, or any other of the principles which have been commonly associated with the theory of the State and society. It is to be regarded solely as matter of fact—the will of that (whatever it is) or of those (whoever they may be) who have the power to express their will and to impose it on the community. Just as the State, to Duguit, exists not *de*

[1] *Contra*, see Ehrlich, *op. cit.*, ch. iv. Ehrlich maintained that many other 'norms', besides law, possess a compulsive sanction. And see *post*, Chapter I.

[2] See the present writer's 'Legal Duties', in the volume of that name.

[3] I believe this to be a fallacy, since *moral* obligation is inseparable from the notion of duty. But it does not follow that every legal duty necessarily implies a legal right. See 'Legal Duties', *op. cit.*

jure but *de facto* only, in the will of those who happen for the time being to control it, so the sanctioning authority of any system of laws is, to Kelsen, merely an historical fact, and, to that extent, an accidental fact. (Cf. the doctrine of the Scandinavian realists.) In many modern States this *Grundnorm* is to be found in a written constitution. Where no such explicit formulation exists, Kelsen is by no means clear in guiding our search. This is the least convincing part of his doctrine, and, as we shall see, in one sphere at least it involves him in grave inconsistencies.

In a single sentence[1] Kelsen summarizes his theory of law as 'a structural analysis, as exact as possible, of the positive law, an analysis free of all ethical or political judgements of value'. Because it is concerned only with the actual and not with the ideal law, it is described as *positivistic*. Because it claims to strip the law of all illusions and distractions, it styles itself *realistic*—but in a very different sense from that which we have already considered. And because it strives to purge juristic theory of many elements which it believes to be mere adulterants, it claims to be *pure*.

Now, to many English readers, this doctrine, despite its elaborate philosophical apparatus, will seem only like beating at an open door. English lawyers have not found much difficulty in keeping their theory free of the 'ideological', and they are not accustomed to confuse law with morals. Our legal literature abounds in majestic generalities about the Law of God, the Law of Nature, and the Law of Reason—nor have those conceptions been without their influence upon our legal development; but, at least in modern times, our judges have seldom hesitated between the relative claims of explicit, though imperfect, law on the one hand and of ideal justice, psychology, or sociology on the other. Not only is Natural Law of merely antiquarian interest to the ordinary student of our legal system, but he is frankly puzzled—and scarcely inter-

[1] 50 *L.Q.R.* 498.

ested—by modern manifestations of 'revived' Natural Law, whether with 'variable content' or not. Since his language does not suffer from the philological accident that the same word (*Recht*) means both 'right' and 'law', the English lawyer will be but faintly interested in Kelsen's assaults upon the traditional distinction between *objektives Recht* and *subjektives Recht*. Again, no reader of Austin is likely to confuse the positive law with the 'deontological', not even if he has read (which is improbable) Austin's curious and uneasy lectures on the Law of Nature. Nor is the English lawyer prone to confuse the legal and the political. Our law has had its political vicissitudes, and at certain periods of its history it has been threatened with degradation into an instrument of government; it might, indeed, have suffered that dismal fate but for the resistance of men like Sir Edward Coke. But today there is nothing more repellent to Anglo-Saxon legal instinct than the corruption of law by political 'ideology', and in their hostility to that most insidious virus in the body politic the Viennese School have the cordial sympathy of nearly all Anglo-American jurists.

But while it is desirable, and, indeed, imperative, to restrain the scope of positive law within its proper limits, and to protect it from extraneous elements which can only obscure its true function, it is doubtful whether the task of the jurist is complete when he has reduced all law merely to a 'structural analysis', or to a scheme of purely intellectual conceptions. We have already noted the dangers of abstract conceptions as the be-all and end-all of jurisprudence. Law touches actual life at so many points that it is extremely difficult, without an arbitrary scholasticism, to segregate its purely intellectual content from its human significance. It is perfectly true that law, considered only as a body of rules or a scheme of logic, is, and must be, a *system of concepts*, and can only be apprehended as such. But if, having disengaged our concepts and having arranged them in a *Deutungsschema* of flawless logical pattern, we stop at that point, what a barren task have we engaged upon! It is surely necessary, when we have by intellectual analysis determined our subject-matter, to examine, and to examine anxiously, its relevance to other manifestations of individual and social life. In doing this we are, let it be granted, not engaged upon the same process of pure ratiocination which must be employed in the subsumption of a particular case under an ascertained legal rule; we are engaged upon a process of synthesis rather than analysis, and this is complementary, not merely supplementary, to the meaning-scheme of 'pure' law. Without the examination not only of law, but of the *implications of law* as a function of society, the 'pure' essence distilled by the jurist is a colourless, tasteless, and unnutritious fluid which soon evaporates. But because we apply a critical as well as an analytical method to the juridical order, we do not on that account forget that the existing positive law still remains positive law, and must be administered as such. It is in this respect that Kelsen, in his just anxiety to repudiate the muddled jurisprudence which has often confounded law with ethics, does less than justice to some of the theories which he attacks. When Ehrlich, for example, discusses the 'sociology' of law, he does not forget that the substantive law is a scheme of concepts—indeed, he writes of law as 'a purely intellectual thing, existing solely in the minds of men'. When Ihering wrote of the teleology of law, he did not mean that 'pure' law should be used as an instrument for what the judge thought to be a desirable social end; and when Professor Pound writes of the 'social engineering' of law, he does not for a moment mean that every judge is a licensed social engineer, free to practise any and all experiments on the community. If it gives Professor Kelsen any satisfaction to call these studies of law 'metajuristic', we need not quarrel with him; the important consideration is that unless the 'pure' juristic is supplemented by the 'metajuristic', it is of little value to human life or even to human thought. But it surely does not follow that metajuristics are to be introduced into the actual *sphere of operation* of juristics, to the confusion of the administration of justice.

It was because certain followers of Kelsen realized that the 'pure' theory of law was in danger of degenerating into an arid *Begriffsjurisprudenz* that they developed the notion of the *creativeness* of 'pure' law. We have seen that the *Grundnorm*, which Kelsen seems usually to conceive as the constitution of a State, is the foundation of all other legal norms. But how are these other legal norms, many and diverse as they are, to be related to the *Grundnorm*? Clearly they can be arrived at only by countless individual acts of deduction and application on the part of legislators and judges, and (Kelsen adds) even administrators. Thus the entire body of the law becomes a 'pyramid' (*Stufenbau des Rechts*), ever mounting up from the basic norm; or, to reverse the metaphor, Kelsen speaks of the law as a 'hierarchic structure' descending from the supreme positive norm to the smallest manifestation of it. Each one of these acts of deduction and application is a *creative* act, and the whole juridical order is thus a coherent system of progressive delegation (*Erzeugungszusammenhang*); and by this process of 'concretization' (as it is termed) the law is rendered perpetually 'self-creative'. This doctrine, first propounded by A. Merkl, has been approved and adopted by Kelsen, and now forms an integral part of his theory. To the 'creative function' of the judge we shall have occasion to refer more than once in the ensuing pages. Here we would only say that it seems to be too lightly assumed, in this picture of the *Stufenbau*, that the pyramid is necessarily a perfect and consistent piece of architecture. If all legal norms could be deduced, one from another, with the same mechanical certainty as stone can be placed on stone in an accurately designed building, half our legal problems would be solved, and the judge, far from being 'creative', would be a mere slot-machine. If, on the other hand, the judge introduces into his task (as some hold) so great an individual element that he becomes truly 'creative', this seems to be a very large concession to the 'meta-juristic' and would mean that a great deal of the 'purity' of law would be diluted by individual vagaries in the complex process of hierarchic delegation. A patchwork, rather than a pyramid, would have been a more appropriate metaphor to describe this body of law; and it will be the object of these pages to show that law is indeed a patchwork; and, since patchwork is often of strong and serviceable texture, the law need not be ashamed of that homely designation.

Perhaps the most debatable part of Kelsen's doctrine is his conception of the *Grundnorm*. This, for all its impressive title, seems to be little more than Austin's sovereign in a new guise, and is open to all the same objections. Just as Austin simplified his problem by fixing his gaze on the Parliament of the English system, so Kelsen simplifies his problem by basing much of his theory on the written constitutions with which he is most familiar. The truth is that in many states it is impossible to detach any *Grundnorm* which has anything like the definiteness of a written constitution; and even in countries of *droit écrit* there seems to be no reason why we should stop short at the constitution; we have to look for the *Grundnorm* of the constitution itself. The *Grundnorm*, for example, in the United States remains as elusive as it was when critics first pointed out the difficulty of applying to it Austin's diagrammatic doctrine of sovereignty. When judges, whose authority is delegated by the constitution, have the power of interpreting their own mandate and even of limiting the action of the legislature, where is the *Grundnorm* of their jurisdiction? If the ensuing chapters of this book achieve their object in the smallest degree, they will suggest that the *Grundnorm* of all law is made up of many elements, no one of which can be set up, without an extreme degree of arbitrariness, as the Norm of Norms.

The artificiality of the Viennese doctrine is nowhere

more apparent than in its picture of International Law. Kelsen insists that International Law is to be considered as essentially a 'juridical order', and that all other interpretations of it are not only valueless but mischievous. But it is obvious that there must be great difficulty, at the outset, in fitting so incomplete a system as International Law to Kelsen's rectilinear design of a 'normative science'. He himself shows—as, indeed, he could not deny—that International Law lacks most of the characteristics of 'law properly so called'—in particular, constituted organs for legislation, adjudication, and legal execution. Most of all it lacks that 'apparatus of compulsion' which he teaches us is indispensable to all law in the true sense. How, then, can this inchoate 'juridical order' be described as law? The Viennese School answers that it is a type of, or at least an analogy to, *primitive law*; it is at the same stage of evolution as the legal systems of early uncivilized communities, which also lacked the constitutional organs and the explicit rules of modern States, and which were governed solely by customary law. This is an unconvincing similitude. Analogies of this kind are good servants but bad masters, and when they are made the basis of a juristic theory they exhibit the limitation of all analogies—namely, that they are apt to confuse similarity with identity. Even admitting (which we should not be prepared to do) that modern International Law is *like* the law of primitive societies, it is highly misleading to base any juristic conclusions on the comparison between modern States, with all their complex, planned organization, and the social systems of communities which were governed not only by custom but by superstition, sacerdotal religion, tribal law, and a hundred other influences, or what the Scandinavian realists call 'magic', now extinct in the civilized world. The analogy becomes all the more strained when we remember that it is only dimly and uncertainly that we can descry these 'natural' societies at all, and that even when we can, or think we can, unveil them from the mists of antiquity, we find the most bewildering diversity among them.

Even if we admit the analogy with primitive law, we must still ask for the sanction. Kelsen lays down repeatedly that the sanctions of International Law are two kinds of force—war and reprisals. This is a remarkable conclusion. War, as known to International Law, is in no sense a sanction in the true legal sense. Although much has been written about the 'just war', this is essentially a moral, political, or 'metajuristic' conception. International Law is not concerned, except incidentally, with the causes of war, and its 'laws of war' are rules which are intended only to regulate a conflict existing *de facto*, but which have nothing to say to war *de jure*. Indeed, we may go farther: in the present state of the world, war, an instrument of national or political will, has only a *de facto* existence and is not a juristic phenomenon at all. It cannot be a sanction, for a legal sanction (at all events, the sanction of force) must always be imposed by a superior and acknowledged authority—which does not at present exist in the international community. It was hoped by many that the League of Nations and the United Nations might develop into such an authority, but recent history has not fortified the hope. Kelsen, however, evades the difficulty by assimilating war and reprisals to the self-help of primitive communities. This, we would urge again, is to reduce legal doctrine to a mere figure of speech; and, even as a metaphor, it is far from exact. History does not tell us of any society in which self-help has been a legal sanction in and of itself—that is, without reference to some higher authority which ultimately will reinforce the individual's own means of redress. Indeed, a society in which self-help was the sole 'legal' sanction would not be a society in any recognizable sense of the term, but merely an animal condition of anarchy. Hobbes and other writers on natural law have supposed this condition of humanity to have once existed, and indeed it may have existed in some incalculably remote age when the life of anthropoid men was 'nasty, brutish, and short'; but we know nothing of it, and in the most primitive societies of which we have any evidence, either in history or among existing uncivilized peoples, self-help is always subject to some superior regulating authority, however rudimentary.

If it is difficult to find the 'apparatus of compulsion' in International Law, its *Grundnorm* is even more elusive. Searching for the basic norm to which all International Law can be referred, the Viennese School has fallen back, after some perilous flirtations with Natural Law, upon the maxim *pacta sunt servanda*. This appears to be a contradiction of the whole positivist conception of the *Grundnorm*. For how can a doctrine of good faith be a 'hypothetical' norm? It is essentially and manifestly a 'positive' norm; it lies in the ethical sphere, or, to adopt the philosophy of the Viennese School, it is valid not because it *is*—because it happens to have been laid down and accepted as the source of authority—but 'because of its content', like all the norms of ethics. Further, it lacks, as we have seen, that element of effective compulsion which is indispensable to the *Grundnorm*. And finally, even if the doctrine *pacta sunt servanda* is to be taken as the basic norm of international treaty-law, what relevance has it to the innumerable rules of International Law which have grown up by practice and have nothing to do with treaties? The answer, though it is at present somewhat half-hearted, which seems to be suggested by Kelsen and some of his followers is that the basis of *all* primitive customary law (a term which apparently is made to include modern International Law) is the principle *pacta sunt servanda*. To say that the foundation of primitive customary law is the same as that of the law of consensus and contract in a developed society seems to be carrying jurisprudence into the realm of poetic fantasy. And finally—though it must be said in sorrow—many recent examples cause us to wonder whether, as a principle of international morality, *pacta sunt servanda* is now as firmly established as it was even in the days of Grotius.

It would be a grave misrepresentation to suggest that Professor Kelsen, in his voluminous and deeply learned writings, has been concerned only with an abstract conception of law as an intellectual exercise. His 'normative' view has led him to re-examine, with a most stimulating originality, many of the traditional doctrines of jurisprudence. In this respect his contribution has been of great value and has had a notable effect on current jurisprudence. In particular, his theories of the nature of the State and of legal personality—which lie beyond the scope of this book—deserve the closest attention. Kelsen's is undoubtedly one of the most vivid and courageous minds in recent legal thought, and his doctrines have had a considerable vogue on the Continent, though, for reasons which have been suggested, they are not so influential in England. The Viennese School has done good service in bringing back law from the strange paths in which it has tended to wander in troublous years; but in the anxiety to keep law 'pure' it has raised it to such a remote and inaccessible altitude that it has difficulty in drawing the breath of life. Long before the rise of the Viennese School, Professor François Gény had anticipated the weaknesses of its method.

'If we consider', he wrote,[1] 'the various attempts which have been made to erect a pure juridical science on the postulate of an inevitable and imperious logic, permeating the whole legal order, what results do they give us which really accord with reason? We undoubtedly find in them the analysis, often very acute, of the conditions necessary to constitute a given juridical situation—either one which exists in fact, or one which is theoretically possible. We are also shown, as the result of deductions which are often unexceptionable, the consequences of this situation, derived

[1] *Méthode d'interprétation*, i. 133.

either from its essential nature or from qualifying circumstances which may affect it. But, having determined these factors, in ideal scheme, and in such a way as to present the problem, if we then expect, by the force of pure logic, to arrive at a solution which we can apply to the facts of real life, we are the victims of a palpable illusion. All we have done, in reality, is to manufacture a logic of pure affirmations, of concepts without any objective foundation, of sentiments (to put it plainly) rather than reasons, and prejudices based on tradition or on the unconscious bent of the mind. Fascinated by his own ingenuity, the jurist does not always perceive the unreality of his own constructions and the practical barrenness of their results. . . . The whole scaffolding of conceptions and constructions, erected *a priori*, possesses no absolute or permanent value from the point of view of the actual operation of law, which is the sole aim of the proper business of a "positive" jurist. This is a principle which our traditional learning has too often forgotten.'

Method of regarding sources of law

The preceding observations have been directed towards showing—since it seems to us essential to the inquiry—that the study of the sources of law cannot be approached with the preconception that they are derived from a single origin, either the sovereign or any other. It is a very different matter to say that there is no legal sovereign at all. As everybody knows, a great deal of current theory is directed to demolishing the whole conception of sovereignty. Here, as in so many controversies, the issue seems to be largely one of terminology. If by sovereignty is meant the absolutist conception of command from superior to inferior, we may agree that it is entirely inappropriate to modern society, except that form of society, lately established over half the Western world and much of the Eastern, which exalts a dictatorial State to a degree of material, spiritual, and emotional domination probably unprecedented in history. But if by sovereignty is meant a constitutional power set up in a civilized society as part of its social machinery for the enforcement of law, recognized by common consent, and obeyed as a necessary instrument of government, entirely different considerations arise. A view sometimes expressed, but not noticeably gaining in popularity, is that no such constituted sanction is necessary for law, the true and sole sanction residing in popular recognition.[1] This is a question outside our present purpose. We need only say that there seems to us to be a world of difference between, on the one hand, conceiving a pre-existing unitary sovereign as the source of law and, on the other hand, recognizing that in every modern State there must be some ultimate means of enforcing the law which society has developed in the natural process of its growth. Or, to put it in other words, there is a difference between considering law as the creation of the sanctioning power and considering the sanctioning power as the creation of law. We shall, indeed, assume in what follows that a definite sanction of this kind exists in all mature legal systems. But, without entering upon an examination of its elements in different forms of modern States, we regard it as part, not as the cause, of law: as posterior, not as anterior, to the growth of legal rules.

Accordingly, we shall be concerned with those sources of law which have been the most frequent subjects of jurisprudential study, though it is not pretended that they are exhaustive. They will be considered here in the order in which they normally appear in social development. Custom, as the raw material of law, is our natural starting-point, although, as we shall see, there are those who hold that judicial interpretation is anterior even to custom and is, indeed, the true genesis of it. Whether this be so or not, it is certain that the influences of popular usage and of magisterial interpretation are never far separated in social history, and perhaps it is neither possible nor profitable to insist on any uniform chronology. The subject of judicial interpretation leads us to that form of it which is of special interest in our own legal system—the doctrine and operation of precedent.

[1] e.g. Krabbe, *The Modern Idea of the State*, whereon see Vinogradoff, 'The Juridical Nature of the State' (*Collected Papers*, ii. 350), and MacIver, *The Modern State*, 478.

Whether equity, which is next considered, is properly to be regarded as a source of law, has been much disputed, but the view here advanced is that so constant and apparently indispensable a factor in legal development deserves consideration as a 'source' rather than as a mere adventitious element. Finally, we pass to the constitutional organs of law-making in developed societies—legislation original and subordinate.

I

CUSTOM: NATURE AND ORIGIN

1. NATURE OF CUSTOM

Habit and social custom

ALL creatures are creatures of habit. In the lower forms of life, habitual behaviour, mysterious in origin and operation, is called instinct. Scientists have been concerned with the relation between instinct and inherited characteristics, glandular secretions and nervous reflexes. These speculations lie beyond our inquiry; suffice it that there seems to be only a fine line between the instinctive behaviour of certain higher organisms and that of primitive man. But at a certain stage of his development, man, while retaining some instinctive reactions, comes to possess an increasing degree of choice in his habit and customs. It is, however, difficult for him, whatever degree of 'free' will he may seem to attain, to become entirely emancipated from customary influences. The mere existence of a society, the mere plurality of individuals, give rise to customs from which no single member of the totality can completely divorce himself. 'Men's thoughts', wrote Bacon, 'are much according to their inclinations; their discourse and speeches according to their learning and infused opinions; but their *deeds* are after as they have been accustomed.' Our 'highly developed', 'civilized' societies of the modern world are just as replete with social customs as the 'primitive' societies of the past or the 'backward' societies of today. These customs are doubtless more rationalized and for the most part less superstitious than once they were;[1] but they are quite as numerous and quite as powerful. In varying degrees they all possess a

[1] People who automatically, and without in the least knowing why, exclaim 'Bless you!' when somebody sneezes would be astonished to learn how far back they are going into ancient superstitions. This, and many other examples

sanction: to disregard them involves some kind of penalty. It may be slight and in some cases almost ineffectual; but it always exists. Society invariably takes a revenge for the breach of any of its conventions. No man can be compelled to be moral, as the not infrequent attempts at this kind of compulsion have shown; but the open defiance of current morality involves social reprobation, a severe and often a cruel punishment, except to the few who are content to forfeit social esteem. The real punishment of our criminals lies not in the deprivation of their liberty but in the stigma which society itself, not the judge or the jailer, brands upon them. Many would prefer, as a matter of personal comfort, to defy the dictates of fashion, but few are prepared to face the ridicule which defiance involves. A large section of the population of England would consider themselves social outcasts if they did not provide a certain kind of funeral, far beyond their means, for their deceased relatives. The average Englishman could no more be induced to wear his hair long than the average Chinese mandarin of the old régime could have been induced to wear his finger-nails short.

Legal custom and its sanction

Yet none of these customs is completely obligatory. Their sanction, though in many cases powerful, is imperfect. No man is under an absolute compulsion to visit the barber, or to wear garments of usual design, or to be moral or polite or cleanly or amiable. Legal custom occupies a place by itself in that its sanction is more certain in its operation than that of any other. The effect of the sanction is usually negative rather than positive: if the custom is not followed, certain desired legal consequences will not be brought about. Law, backed by the opinion and at later stages by the tribunals of the community, will forbid those relationships to be effected; sometimes it will go further, and actually punish the

of superstitious survivals, are to be found in Sir Thomas Browne's *Pseudodoxia,* and a more modern treatment of the subject would probably be no less rich in instances.

citizen who persists in ignoring a custom. No option, however small, is left to the individual, as in other social customs. A man may, if he chooses, argue that it is a waste of time and money to cut his hair; in consequence, he may, if he is sensitive, be made uncomfortable, but he will not lose a single right of citizenship or property. He may argue with as much, or as little, reason that the custom of signing, sealing, and delivering a deed is an absurd anachronism; but if he ignores this quaint survival in a transfer of stock, then *nihil agit*.

The Austinian view

Most of the customs in modern societies are non-legal and therefore not obligatory, in the fullest sense of that word. The majority of the rules which govern legal relationships have by this time been formulated in statutes or decisions; only to a very limited extent do they consist of tacit usages. But it is not difficult either to imagine or to find definite records of societies in which there is no such explicit formulation of rules. How far in these societies legal custom is a spontaneous growth, and how far it is the creation of individual dominating minds, is a question which we shall have to examine in its place.[1] It is at least certain that in many societies of which we have evidence, before any clearly articulated system of law-making and law-dispensing has developed, the conduct of men in society is governed by customary rules. To call these *legal* rules is something of an anachronism, for in very many cases they are equally rules of religion and morality, which, at this early stage, have not become distinguished from law;[2] but they are 'legal' in the sense which is nowadays attached to that term, inasmuch as they are binding and obligatory rules of conduct (not merely of faith and conviction), and that the breach of them is a breach of positive *duty*. Austin denies them the force of law until they have been expressly recognized

[1] *Post*, pp. 112 ff.

[2] *Contra*, however, see A. S. Diamond, *Primitive Law*, Part II. For a most discerning account of the relationship between custom, ethics, law, and interpretation in a modern 'primitive' society, see Max Gluckman, *The Judicial Process among the Barotse of Northern Rhodesia*.

by the sovereign. This is consistent with his general doctrine of sovereignty, for, without the *cachet* of supreme authority, custom cannot be conceived as a command. The operation of custom in society was, indeed, one of the most formidable obstacles to the whole conception of Austinian sovereignty. There was no escaping the fact that custom was constantly followed and obeyed before ever judicial authority had pronounced upon it.[1] Austin conceded that there are certain so-called laws of conduct 'set by men not political superiors', but held that these cannot properly be called laws because they are not the commands of a determinate political superior. This conclusion certainly follows when it has once been assumed that all law must be an explicit command: but it is precisely the binding force of custom which challenges the initial assumption itself. Austin had to invent the term 'positive morality' for custom; but, in spite of ingenious distinctions,[2] he failed to explain satisfactorily why the body of rules which he classified as 'positive morality' (unconvincingly distinguished from the morality which 'may signify the law set by God') lacked the true character of law.

Custom and 'positive morality'

Non-litigious custom

Custom, as has been said, grows up by conduct, and it is therefore a mistake to measure its validity solely by the element of express sanction accorded by courts of law or by any other determinate authority. The characteristic feature of the great majority of customs is that they are essentially non-litigious in origin. They arise not from any conflict of rights adjusted by a supreme arbiter, nor from any claim of *meum* against *tuum*, but from practices prompted by the convenience of society and of the individual, so far as they are prompted by any

[1] The standard definitions of custom in English law attribute to it the highest degree of inherent validity. 'A custom, in the intendment of law, is such a usage as hath obtained the force of a law, and is in truth a binding law to such particular places, persons and things which it concerns. . . . But it is *ius non scriptum*, and made by the people only of such place where the custom is': Viner, *Abr.* vii. 164, citing *Tanistry Case*, Dav. 31b.

[2] See especially Lects. I and V, Campbell's ed., 89 and 175.

conscious purpose at all. 'It is not conflicts', it has been said,[1]

> 'that initiate rules of legal observance, but the practices of every day directed by the give-and-take considerations of reasonable intercourse and social co-operation. Neither succession, nor property, nor possession, nor contract started from direct legislation or from direct conflict. Succession has its roots in the necessary arrangements of the household on the death of its manager, property began with occupation, possession is reducible to *de facto* detention, the origins of contract go back to the customs of barter. Disputes as to rights in primitive society are pre-eminently disputes as to the application of non-litigious custom.'

The starting-point of all custom is convention rather than conflict, just as the starting-point of all society is co-operation rather than dissension.

1. The Common Law as custom

But it may be said that these considerations are applicable only to primitive societies. It is, however, impossible to understand the true nature of modern law without some knowledge of its origins in social custom. A foreign lawyer, wedded to his code, might challenge this proposition; but the English lawyer who has to deal constantly with the Common Law will not find it startling. For what is the Common Law? Assuredly it is not merely an agglomeration of spontaneous customary rules, unless we are to ignore the vital influence of judicial interpretation upon our law. But neither is it primarily the artificial creation of expert minds, as are codes and statutes. Its roots strike deep into the soil of national ideas and institutions. 'Habent enim Anglici', says Bracton,[2] 'plurima ex consuetudine quae non habent ex lege': and it is not without significance that he did not adopt Azo's term *ius* for the whole English system, but was careful to call it 'lex et consuetudo'.[3] 'The Common Law', writes

Bracton

[1] Vinogradoff, *Historical Jurisprudence*, i. 368.

[2] F. 1.

[3] *Lex* is to Bracton *lex scripta*, emanating from sovereign authority; and we may see again his hesitation between Bolognese and feudal tradition, already noticed (*ante*, p. 10), in his doubts as to how far the *consuetudines* which the Common Law was absorbing deserved the full title of 'law'. He

Sir Frederick Pollock[1] (who points out that *ius commune* 'means originally the rule acknowledged by all parties as applicable'), 'is a customary law if, in the course of about six centuries, the undoubting belief and uniform language of everybody who had occasion to consider the matter were able to make it so. To this day "coutume" is the nearest equivalent that learned Frenchmen can find for its English name.'

Black-stone: particular and general customs

Coke[2] describes custom as 'one of the main triangles of the laws of England'. Blackstone, in a well-known passage,[3] has attempted to define the Common Law of England:

> 'This unwritten or common law is properly distinguishable into three kinds: 1. General customs; which are the universal rule of the whole kingdom, and form the common law, in its stricter and more usual signification. 2. Particular customs; which for the most part affect only the inhabitants of particular districts. 3. Certain particular laws; which by custom are adapted and used by some particular courts, of pretty general and extensive jurisdiction.'

He gives a number of examples and then describes them as 'all these doctrines which are not set down in any written statute or ordinance, but depend merely upon immemorial usage, that is, upon common law, for their support'.

The 'particular customs' to which Blackstone refers have had a greater importance in the past than at the present time, especially in the feudal land law; but they

solves the problem by insisting that the *consuetudines* should be the sanctioned product of royal authority *or its representatives* (Council or Court), not of casual uninstructed opinion: 'cum legis vigorem habeat quicquid de consilio et consensu magnatum et reipublicae communi sponsione, auctoritate regis sive principis praecedente, iuste fuerit definitum et approbatum' (i. 1). This compromise, even allowing for the centralizing influence which the Royal Courts were steadily exercising over local custom, does not completely account for the operative force of the innumerable *consuetudines* (which Bracton goes on to recognize specifically) 'in diversis comitatibus, civitatibus, burgis et villis'.

[1] *First Book of Jurisprudence* (6th ed.), 254. And see Salmond, *Jurisprudence* (11th ed.), 232 ff. [2] Co. Litt. 110b. [3] 1 *Comm.* 67.

are by no means unimportant even today, and in one sphere at least, commercial law, 'particular' usages are constantly before the Courts. Something will be said later of their nature and application.[1]

Blackstone's 'general customs' or 'customs of the realm' are those fundamental principles in legal relationships which for the most part are not to be found in any express formulation, but are assumed to be inherent in our social arrangements. They are, in short, the Common Law itself.[2] Their origin, discoverable only in social practices of which we have, at most, fragmentary evidence, is necessarily obscure. There has sometimes been too great a tendency to frame *a priori* generalities about them, and to attribute them to unseen, mystical agencies when very often they can be traced to quite definite human invention. St. Germain says of them in *Doctor and Student*:[3]

> 'And because the said customs be neither against the law of God, nor the law of reason, and have alway been taken to be good and necessary for the commonwealth of all the realm; therefore they have obtained the strength of a law, insomuch that he that doth against them doth against justice: and these be the customs that properly be called the *common law*.'

But, as we shall see,[4] a good many of the examples he gives are attributable not to any primordial law of God

[1] *Post*, pp. 135 ff. The very important part played by borough customs (see *post*, pp. 104 ff.) in the development of our general law has received less than its due share of attention from English students, but has been greatly illuminated by Miss Mary Bateson's invaluable collection of *Borough Customs* (S.S., vols. 18 and 21).

[2] *Beaulieu* v. *Finglas* (1401), Y.B. 2 H. IV. 18 (Pasch. pl. 5). In some of the old cases, a distinction is drawn between common custom and Common Law. Thus in Hobart's report of *Rich* v. *Kneeland* (1613), 1 Hob. 17, a note to the judgement observes: 'And it was resolved that, though it was laid as a custom of the realm, yet indeed it is common law.' The distinction is not clear, but seems to mean that the rule in question was not merely one of popular observance but had been sanctioned by the Courts. The 'custom of the realm' in regard to common carriers and innkeepers is indistinguishable from Common Law, and is almost entirely the product of judicial decisions. See Littleton J., Appendix, *post*, p. 615.

[3] Ch. vii.

[4] *Post*, p. 124f.

or reason or necessity, but, in a very great measure at least, to the inventive intelligence of Bench and Bar. Nevertheless, whatever the actual origin of a custom, once it has established itself by general and long-continued practice it is difficult to distinguish from the Common Law itself. 'What is the effect in England', asked Swinfen Eady L.J. in *Bebb* v. *Law Society*, [1914] 1 Ch. 286, 296, 'of long-continued usage, usage through the centuries without departure in any single instance? Bovill C.J. in *Chorlton* v. *Lings* (1868), L.R. 4 C.P. 374, 383, . . . puts it in this way. After referring to certain exceptional instances, he says: "But these instances are of comparatively little weight, as opposed to uninterrupted usage to the contrary for several centuries; and what has been commonly received and acquiesced in as the law raises a strong presumption of what the law is, and at least throws upon those who question it the burthen of proving that it is not what it has been so understood to be." '[1]

Family Law

The operation of pure social custom is apparent in many branches of our law, and nowhere more clearly than in our family law. Monogamy itself is tribal custom, influenced, but not created, by Christianity.[2] It is true that we have prescribed ceremonials for marriage, that bigamy is a crime in England, and that for persons whose status is determined by English law none but monogamous marriage is recognized as valid.[3] But the

[1] See also Tindal C.J. in *Veley* v. *Burder* (1841), 12 A. & E. 265, 302, and Best J. in *Blundell* v. *Catterall* (1821), 5 B. & Ald. 268, 279; and cf. F. A. Greer (afterwards Greer L.J. and Lord Fairfield), 'Custom in the Common Law', 9 *L.Q.R.* 153, 158.

[2] And probably of slow development: see Vinogradoff, *Historical Jurisprudence*, i. 238.

[3] The rule goes no farther than this, that parties to polygamous marriages cannot obtain matrimonial relief in English courts (*Hyde* v. *H.* (1866), L.R. 1 P. & D. 130). Polygamous marriage, however, is recognized by English law as creating matrimonial status in countries where it is legal. This view, previously doubtful but advanced by the present writer in 1931 (see *Legal Duties*, 68 ff.), was confirmed by *Baindail* v. *B.*, [1946] P. 122 (approving *Srini Vasan* v. *S.V.*, [1946] P. 67). See further *Risk* v. *R.*, [1951] P. 50, *Bamgbose* v. *Daniel*, [1955] A.C. 107, and *Coleman* v. *Shang*, [1961] A.C. 481.

custom of monogamy goes back to the earliest known social origins of our race. It is, again, purely by custom that a wife takes her husband's name. In France this rule was enacted by a law of 6th February 1893. Nobody has ever thought it worth while to give it statutory form in England, but it would be fantastic to doubt that it is the settled law of the land.[1] And so throughout the greater part of our familial law. Parental authority, the rights of guardianship, control, and education, are not only customary but belong so peculiarly to the father as 'master of his own house, king and ruler in his own family' (the words are those of the Court of Appeal), that the courts will interfere with them as little as possible.[2] Until 1926,[3] the father could not, except on an actual separation of the spouses, voluntarily surrender these fundamental rights over and duties to his offspring;[4] nor could a mother do so in respect of her illegitimate child.[5]

The assumptions of the Common Law

It is a constant source of wonder to foreigners that our law is built up to so great an extent on *assumptions*: that in the most fundamental matters (Austin notwithstanding) there are so few direct commands and prohibitions.[6] Where shall we find any 'sovereign' rule which expressly defines and forbids libel, or false imprisonment, or negligence? Not only the judges but Parliament

On the whole subject see W. E. Beckett, 'The Recognition of Polygamous Marriages under English Law', 48 *L.Q.R.* 341, and 'J. H. C. M.', 62 *L.Q.R.* 116.

[1] There is but scanty direct judicial authority on the point; but see *Fendall orse. Goldsmid* v. *G.* (1877), L.R. 2 P.D. 263, and *Cowley* v. *C.*, [1901] A.C. 450.

[2] *Agar-Ellis* v. *Lascelles* (1878), 10 Ch.D. 49, 75. Cf. *Lough* v. *Ward*, [1945] 2 All E.R. 338. But see *Ward* v. *Laverty*, [1925] A.C. 101. Modern legislation has, of course, interfered increasingly in the interests of children who are neglected, ill treated, 'in need of care and protection', or incorrigibly delinquent.

[3] Adoption of Children Act, 1926 (now repealed and substantially re-enacted by the Adoption Act, 1950).

[4] *Agar-Ellis* v. *Lascelles, ubi sup.*

[5] *Humphrys* v. *Polak*, [1901] 2 K.B. 385.

[6] 'Nine-tenths, at least, of the law of contract, and the whole, or nearly the whole, of the law of torts, are not to be discovered in any volume of the statutes': Dicey, *Law and Opinion in England*, 360.

itself, in regulating such matters of civil liability, constantly assume an hypothesis of existing law: for example, an inquirer will search in vain the important statutes relating to libel for a definition of that very common tort. It would never occur to the House of Commons to lay down what constitutes actionable negligence in law; the conception of duty which underlies it is rooted far deeper than any English statute seeks to go. In criminal law, it is true, a wider field has been covered by legislation. Indeed, so much of our criminal law has now been embodied in statute that there seems to be no very cogent argument against the codification of the whole of it. Statute has filled up gaps in the Common Law by 'new' crimes, like embezzlement, false pretences, publication of false balance-sheets, and the like. But the foundations of criminal liability are still firmly embedded in the Common Law, and to this day our statute-book contains no definition of the highest crime but one known to the law, and the most heinous known to humanity—wilful murder. The definition of this crime which is to be found in Coke, and in any treatise on criminal law, is a mosaic of principles put together through ages of practice and interpretation. In all branches, the assumptions on which our law is built up are so many and so vital that it is tempting to regard them all as spontaneous outcrops of the national genius. This, as we shall see, is not entirely true; but it is more nearly true than the conception of them purely as commands, direct or indirect.[1]

Constitutional Law

Again, custom and convention are operative throughout the very machinery of English government itself. 'Constitutional Law' is correctly, indeed inevitably, described by our writers as 'The Law *and Custom* of the Constitution'. To say truth, this branch of our law—if

[1] On this passage see Gluckman, *The Judicial Process among the Barotse*, 332, who objects to confining the principle to English law, and holds that similar assumptions exist in 'all systems of law'. Reference to England, of course, does not exclude the possibility of similar assumptions in other systems (with which I am not here concerned), though I am not prepared to generalize as widely as Professor Gluckman about 'all systems of law'.

it can properly be considered a separate branch—contains a great more custom than law, in the ordinary sense of those terms. It is unnecessary to insist that the very hinge of the Parliamentary system—Cabinet government—has grown up in the main by usage, and by usage has, in recent times, visibly changed its character. It and its head, the most responsible individual in the kingdom, elude definition in our written law. We cannot advance a step in constitutional law without inquiring into 'Parliamentary practice', which frequently has no explicit sovereign sanction whatever, and yet is of the utmost moment to the system of government. Too often we forget that these tacit *de facto* usages limit materially the so-called absolute sovereignty of the legislature.

2. Foreign custom

English lawyers are constantly reminded of the force of custom in legal systems other than their own. This does not apply in the same degree to lawyers of other European countries. French jurists, for example, may have to deal with the native law of African and other colonies; but local usages are overshadowed by the Code, and custom is hardly considered a source of law at all. Its study has, indeed, been strangely neglected by French jurists, and it is comparatively recently that their interest in it has been awakened, chiefly by Professor François Gény. The Civil Code prescribes no method of proof and no period of antiquity for custom, though it recognizes, as it was bound to do, the numerous commercial customs which exist in French society as in all others; and the rules of interpretation which have grown up round these mercantile usages have gradually been extended to customs of all kinds.[1]

But the Englishman who had to administer law in India, or to practise before the Privy Council, could not be unconscious of the part which custom has played and still plays in the legal development of civilizations even more complex than his own. It is well known that

[1] *Code Civ.*, Arts. 1135, 1159, 1160; Gény, *Méthode d'interprétation*, i. 317 ff.; and, on the whole place of custom in law, *ibid.* i, Part III, Section ii.

acquaintance with Indian customary law first inspired Sir Henry Maine to embark upon his researches into the growth of law, and consequently to put a new complexion on the accepted English dogmas on this subject. But a lawyer in India hardly needed the writings of historical jurists to remind him that custom was a vital legal element in the society with which he had to deal. It was a fact self-evident in innumerable relations of everyday life. The authority of legislation, as we understand it (the term, of course, not including sacred declaratory codes), is a very modern phenomenon in Indian society and has been largely due to importation from outside. It was a method of government virtually unknown to the Hindu rulers. 'The great body of existing law', said J. D. Mayne,[1] 'consists of ancient usages, more or less modified by Aryan or Brahmanical influence.' The Code of Manu accords the utmost authority to custom, even as against revealed and sacred law, for it is the duty of pundits and rulers alike to found their ordinances upon immemorial usage, 'the root of all piety'. They must have regard not merely to the sanctioned practices of virtuous men, though these possess a special validity, but to 'the usages of castes, of districts, of guilds, and of families'.[2] If we dilute the pietistic terminology of sacred, 'inspired' literature, the sanctity of custom means that immemorial usage is deemed to be based on a fundamental reasonableness,[3] though not in every instance on what Western ideas would regard as a fundamental morality.[4] The

[1] *Hindu Law and Usage* (8th ed.), 47. On the whole subject, see Maine, *Village Communities*, Lect. II, and Roy, *Customs and Customary Law in British India* (Tagore Lectures, 1908).

[2] i. 108, 110; viii. 41; and cf. ii. 6, 12, 18, 20; iv. 115, 156, 179; viii. 46; *Sacred Books of the East*, ed. Max Müller, vol. xxv; Roy, *op. cit.* 15.

[3] The 'custom of virtuous men' is indeed nothing else than the 'custom handed down in regular succession since time immemorial among the four chief castes': ii. 18, and cf. iv. 178.

[4] Thus prostitution was recognized by Hindu law among some classes (dancing-girls in pagodas) and gave rise to certain questions, of which English courts took cognizance, of adoption and inheritance. On the other hand, it is sternly discountenanced by Mohammedan law.

general principles laid down by the Code of Manu have been consistently followed and extended by all the authoritative commentators.[1] From the outset, British rule recognized the scope and validity of native custom, and as early as 1781[2] the legislature expressly 'saved' local custom where it differed from the general law; and in 1868, in a leading case,[3] the Judicial Committee of the Privy Council affirmed the principle in the most explicit terms. Though during the course of the nineteenth century the bulk of British law in India was codified, the inviolability of custom was repeatedly maintained both by the general law and by the legislation of different provinces—always provided, it need hardly be said, that the necessary judicial tests were satisfied. These tests were in the main the same as those applied to English customs;[4] but they were applied more frequently, because they occupied a larger place in the life of the people and because of a complexity of races, castes, and religions unknown in English civilization. Especially in regard to inheritance their intricacies were many and difficult. Similarly today English judges constantly have to deal with native customs (of which many examples might be cited) in those colonies and dependencies which still have the right to appeal to the Privy Council.

II. ORIGIN OF CUSTOM

No problem of jurisprudence, except perhaps that of corporate personality, has given rise to more lively controversy than the origin of custom. The difficulties of the inquiry are, first, that it necessarily deals with early social phenomena which are not ascertainable by positive evidence, and second, that the motive forces which it has

[1] Roy, *op. cit.* 15. Narada, i. 40, goes to the farthest limit: 'Custom is powerful and overrules the sacred law.'

[2] 21 Geo. III, c. 70, s. 17; and cf. Indian Reg. IV of 1793, s. 15.

[3] *Collector of Madura* v. *Mootoo Ramalinga*, 12 Moo. I.A. 397.

[4] See Excursus B, p. 157.

to consider, both in the individual and in society, are in large measure psychological and impalpable.

1. Theory of custom in Roman Law

We turn naturally to the world's greatest legal system for guidance concerning the rise and scope of custom; but here Roman jurisprudence is singularly indistinct.[1] Throughout the Corpus Iuris custom appears in connexion with institutions of widely different kinds, and it is extremely difficult to construct any consistent theory, so obscure and often contradictory are the references. Two main titles, D. 1. 3 and C. 8. 52, deal specifically with the topic: the latter is laconic, and as for the former, there is probably no title in the Digest which shows so little homogeneity and which has been the centre of so much discussion. Not inaptly the gloss upon C. 8. 52 observes: 'Sed quae est longa consuetudo? Licet enim rubrica quaerat, non tamen solvit lex huius tituli.'

The genius of Roman Law unsympathetic to custom

Custom inevitably raises questions of historical origins, and from its very nature the Corpus Iuris could deal with historical origins only in the barest outline, as in the well-known sketch of Pomponius in D. 1. 2 (*De Origine Iuris*), which is a masterpiece of concision rather than of illumination. Besides, the habit of mind, as well as the professional practice, of the jurists did not incline them to the discussion either of abstract questions of

[1] The actual customary origins of many institutions of Roman Law form an attractive question of historical jurisprudence, on which much valuable work has been done and continues to be done by modern civilians: see, for example, Pernice's criticisms of Brie, *Die Lehre vom Gewohnheitsrecht*, in *Z.S.S.* (*Röm. Abth.*), xx. 127, and Ehrlich's views, mentioned *post*, pp. 122 ff. This problem is, however, beyond the scope of our present inquiry, and the observations here made are concerned with the juristic theory (so far as formulated) of custom in Roman Law, rather than with the historical growth of tribal and customary institutions among the Romans and their subject peoples. Our material is drawn principally from the Corpus Iuris, which, of course, refers in the main to Roman Law at a late stage of its development. There is force in the contention of A. A. Schiller ('Custom in Classical Roman Law', 24 *Virginia Law Review*, No. 3, Jan. 1938) that the conception and scope of custom were much less clearly apprehended in the classical than in the post-classical period, though the extreme indefiniteness which he ascribes to the former period may be due chiefly to our lack of evidence about it. Cf. Cuq, *Institutions Juridiques*, pp. 15 f., and the views of E. Ehrlich, discussed *post*, *loc. cit.*

jurisprudence or of legal antiquities. They themselves were habitually concerned with technical interpretation, and their primary business was with formulated law, not with the *de facto* law of customary observance.[1] It was accepted as a fact of general recognition, though of somewhat academic interest, that the original law of Rome had been customary; but this historical postulate is of more moment to the orators and historians than to the jurists.[2] The tradition of codification early enters into the legal field, first with the semi-legendary[3] Leges Regiae, and next with the Twelve Tables. The Twelve Tables inaugurate an enormously long period—some thousand years—of juristic and praetorian interpretation, not to mention republican and imperial legislation, and all circumstances strongly combine against the growth of a general customary law throughout the Empire. Nor would it have been at all compatible with the absolute sovereignty of the later Empire, especially with the codification of Justinian. That local and peregrine custom must have played an important part in the heterogeneous Byzantine Empire was long believed but never sufficiently understood until L. Mitteis explored the subject.[4] There are numerous references in the Corpus Iuris to a *consuetudo loci*,[5] *consuetudo provinciae*,[6] *mos provinciae*,[7] *consuetudo regionis*,[8] and *mos regionis*,[9] but their exact meaning is still matter of great doubt.[10]

[1] Brie, *op. cit.* And see Schulz, *Principles of Roman Law*, 19 ff.

[2] The *locus classicus* is Cicero, *De Inv.* ii. 65 ff.: 'initium ergo eius (i.e. iuris) ab natura ductum videtur; quaedam autem ex utilitatis ratione aut perspicua nobis aut obscura in consuetudinem venisse; post autem approbata quaedam a consuetudine aut . . . legibus esse firmata', &c. Cf. D. 1. 2. 2. 1: 'populus sine lege certa, sine iure certo', &c.

[3] Though beyond doubt an actual code, of origin probably traditional and sacerdotal rather than regal or comitial: Girard, *Textes de Droit romain*, 1 ff. It is characteristic of imperial jurisprudence that Pomponius dogmatically impresses these laws with the seal of sovereign authority: D. 1. 2; Girard, *loc. cit.*

[4] *Reichsrecht u. Volksrecht in den östlichen Provinzen des römischen Kaiserreichs*, 1891.

[5] D. 2. 12. 4; 3. 4. 6. 11.

[6] D. 22. 5. 3. 6.

[7] D. 26. 7. 7. 10.

[8] D. 18. 1. 17; 21. 2. 6.

[9] D. 22. 1. 1. pr.; C. 4. 65. 8.

[10] See Brie, *op. cit.* 21–22.

Mos, consuetudo, and consensus utentium

Nevertheless, while an explicit theory of custom is absent from the surviving sources of Roman Law, its recognition in a great variety of circumstances leaves no doubt of its practical importance. *Usus*, though omitted by Gaius, is inserted by Justinian in his enumeration of the sources of law.[1] *Mos*, *mores*, and *consuetudo* are terms of considerable frequency throughout the Corpus Iuris, and at first sight appear to be used interchangeably. On closer examination, however, it seems clear that *mos* refers to something more primordial and less tangible than *consuetudo* and *usus*, which resolve themselves into the *actual practice* and observance of custom. *Mores* are those general habits of life, that disposition towards certain institutions (patriarchy is the most conspicuous example),[2] which reside in the genius of the Roman people.[3] In the Savignian theory they would be closely identified, it may be presumed, with the *Überzeugung;* and this 'conviction' is expressed in the language of the jurists in the oft-repeated doctrine of the *consensus utentium*. That doctrine finds perhaps its most explicit, certainly its most succinct, formulation in the definition of Ulpian: 'Mores sunt tacitus consensus populi, longa consuetudine inveteratus.'[4] Similarly Cicero expresses the conventional view: 'consuetudine autem ius esse putatur id, quod voluntate omnium sine lege vetustas comprobarit.'[5] The

[1] Inst. i. 2. 9. Of the various institutions referred to in the Corpus Iuris as founded purely on custom, the following may suffice as illustrations: D. 49. 15. 19. pr. (*postliminium*: here *mores* are equated to *naturalis aequitas*); D. 50. 13. 5. 1 (*existimatio*); D. 27. 10. 1 (interdiction of prodigal); D. 28. 6. 2 (pupillary substitution—cf. Inst. ii. 16. pr. and D. 29. 8. pr.); D. 24. 1. 31 (gifts between husband and wife). It is noteworthy that all these passages except the first two are from Ulpian, who seems to have attached greater importance to custom than any other jurist. Gaius mentions succession by adoption as having been introduced 'eo iure quod consensu receptum est', iii. 82; and similarly *pignoris capio*, iv. 26–27.

[2] Gai. i. 55; Inst. i. 9. 2.

[3] The peculiarly Roman colouring sometimes appears in the expression 'mos (mores) civitatis' or 'nostrae civitatis': D. 29. 2. 8. pr.; 18. 1. 34. 1; 50. 16. 42. Doubtless a great many of these practices and forms of procedure were so generally, and almost automatically, accepted that they were never recorded in our surviving sources of law: see Schulz, *op. cit.* 20 ff.

[4] *Reg.* pr. 4.

[5] *De Inv.* ii. 67.

conception of custom as based on consent, a corporate act of will on the part of the people, automatic rather than express,[1] becomes an almost tedious formula of the jurists; its exact nature and process they do not seem to have examined, any more than the apostles of the Social Contract examined the actual mechanics of consensus in their supposed contract. The doctrine becomes the less convincing in view of the fact that the same foundation of popular consent was assumed, constitutionally and legally, to lie at the base of all legislation:[2] a theory which throughout the Empire steadily diminished in verisimilitude, and certainly under the absolute monarchy was no better than a fiction.

Reasonableness

Yet if it is dangerous to base customary practices on any elements of deliberate will and consent, it is easy to see that the consensus which the Roman writers really had in mind was that uniformity or unanimity of practice which is necessarily characteristic of custom. Nowadays we say that this uniformity is founded on an *opinio necessitatis*, a recognition of the custom as being *obligatory* in order to achieve a certain end. No such doctrine is explicit in Roman theory;[3] but just as there is a supposed consensus in the adoption of custom, so that consensus itself is based upon a reasonable social necessity, which is expressed as the 'ratio quae suasit consuetudinem'.[4] This inherent reasonableness, associated, it would seem, with an objective utility rather than a subjective logic, is a necessary element in all custom which is entitled to judicial consideration; and although there is no clear doctrine that *error* and *irrationality* in its inception are

[1] 'Velut tacita civium conventio'; D. 1. 3. 35 (Hermogenian).

[2] Most notably in D. 1. 3. 32. 1 (Julian): 'ipsae leges nulla alia ex causa nos teneant, quam quod iudicio populi receptae sunt.' It may be, however, that the *leges* here referred to are republican, not imperial.

[3] Brie, *op. cit.* 23.

[4] C. 8. 52. 1: 'nam et consuetudo praecedens et ratio quae consuetudinem suasit custodienda est.' The same doctrine appears in non-juristic writings: e.g. Quintilian, *Inst. Or.* v. 10. 13: 'quae persuasione etiam si non omnium hominum, eius tamen civitatis aut gentis, in qua res agitur, in mores recepta sunt'. Cf. Cicero, *De Inv.* ii. 65 (*utilitatis ratio*).

sufficient to invalidate a custom actually observed in practice, such a usage must not be admitted as a valid precedent for other similar usages.[1]

Antiquity

If *mos* and *ratio* are the *inner content* of custom, *consuetudo* is its actual practice, and emphasis is constantly laid on the antiquity and frequency of that practice. Custom is almost invariably conceived by the jurists as *perpetua* or *inveterata*, and it is doubtful whether any custom of recent origin came within their purview at all. However supreme the imperial formulation of law, there is a natural, prudential desire not to remove the ancient landmark. This temper is well illustrated in the correspondence of the younger Pliny. Pliny inquires of the Emperor whether senators appointed in Bithynia contrary to a technical provision of the Lex Pompeia are to be deprived of their offices; though the statute is clear, he hesitates to act according to the rigour of the law when a custom, though by no means *inveterata*, has established itself to the contrary. Trajan sympathizes with his doubt, and gives the diplomatic reply that existing appointments shall not be annulled but that for the future the statute shall be strictly observed.[2] In the case of inveterate custom not opposed to statute, the conservative tendency would be even stronger; indeed, the judge is expressly forbidden to ignore it.[3] What exactly

[1] This appears to be the meaning of Celsus in D. 1. 3. 39, taken in conjunction with Paulus, D. h.t. 14: 'Quod non ratione introductum, sed errore primum, deinde consuetudine optentum est, in aliis similibus non optinet'; and Paulus: 'Quod vero contra rationem iuris receptum est, non est producendum ad consequentias.' Further, Julian, D. h.t. 15: 'In his, quae contra rationem iuris constituta sunt, non possumus sequi regulam iuris.' These are dark sayings, but I follow Brie, *op. cit.*, in interpreting them to mean that a custom contrary to the ordinary *ratio iuris* may not be bad in itself (Julian certainly seems to imply this) but, in modern phrase, 'is not to be extended' *ad similia* or *ad consequentia*. It exists, in short, only on sufferance and somewhat under displeasure. On the other hand, C. 8. 52. 2 is emphatic that custom cannot be valid *ut rationem vincat*. See Jolowicz, *Roman Foundations of Modern Law*, 27. On the general theory of the reasonableness of custom see *post*, pp. 140 ff., and Appendix, *post*, p. 614.

[2] *Epist. ad Traianum*, cxiv and cxv.

[3] D. 1. 3. 38; Inst. iv. 17. pr.; D. 22. 5. 3. 6; and (strongest) C. 8. 52 ('ne quid contra longam consuetudinem fiat').

constituted antiquity in law was never definitely laid down. It is probable that, in the absence of any positive rule, judges, especially in the provinces, must have found themselves sometimes embarrassed, and this doubtless was the reason for the constitution of Leo and Zeno in A.D. 474, which provided that in case of doubt as to the antiquity of any particular custom, the magistrate should have recourse to the decision of the emperor.[1]

Scope of operation

With regard to the actual operation of custom in the scheme of Roman Law, modern students are left in great doubt owing to their inevitable ignorance of the practice of the courts.[2] But it is evident throughout the leading titles of the Digest and Codex, as well as in many other references, that the place assigned to custom as an operative source of law was by no means unimportant: and it is therefore difficult to understand why the subject did not receive a more systematic exposition. Like the *ius honorarium*, it *supplements* the written law, and is a self-contained authority where statute is silent.[3] Besides thus filling the interstices in the enacted law, it may serve to *interpret* statutory provisions, especially when they are conflicting or ambiguous; thus Paulus's famous maxim, 'Optima est legum interpres consuetudo'.[4] And though it is to be gathered from express references and from the general tenor of imperial legislation that custom could

[1] C. 1. 14. 11.

[2] Only one passage of Ulpian (D. 1. 3. 34), and that highly obscure through its unusual and probably corrupt expression 'contradicto iudicio', seems to suggest that judicial recognition was a prerequisite to the validity of custom. But the practice of the Courts in taking cognizance of and testing alleged customs must have been extremely important. Unfortunately we have only indirect and vague references to the *mos iudiciorum* in this connexion, and these are to be found in the orators rather than the jurists: Brie, *op. cit.* 52 ff., citing Savigny, *System*, i. 148, n. (h) hereon.

[3] D. 1. 3. 32 (Julian): 'De quibus causis scriptis legibus non utimur . . .'; D. h.t. 33 (Ulpian): '. . . in his quae non ex scripto descendunt'. Cf. Tertullian, *De Corona*, 4: 'Even in civil matters custom is received instead of law, when positive legal enactment is wanting (*cum deficit lex*)' (Ante-Nicene Library, *Writings of Tertullian*, i. 337).

[4] D. 1. 3. 37; cf. D. h.t. 38, '. . . in ambiguitatibus quae ex legibus proficiscuntur'.

not be allowed to prevail against definite statutory provision or (more doubtfully) against the *ratio iuris*,[1] yet in one respect we find a larger function ascribed to it than our own law has ever admitted.[2] In spite of conflicting evidence in the sources, there is reason to suppose that the *negative* aspect of *consuetudo*—i.e. *desuetudo*—was recognized as definitely and properly abrogative of statute. Julian is explicit on the point in D. 1. 3. 32. 1, and still more conclusive is the general rule stated in Inst. i. 2. 11: 'Ea vero, quae ipsa sibi quaeque civitas constituit, saepe mutari solent vel tacito consensu populi vel postea lege lata.' This seems to be confirmed by the frequent mention in the Corpus Iuris of statutes which have fallen into disuse.[3] The subject, however, is much controverted, and the genuineness of the passage attributed to Julian has been vigorously attacked.[4] The divestitive legal period of desuetude seems to have been as much at large as the vestitive period of consuetude; at all events, the available sources do not attempt to establish any standard. We may suppose without rashness that it required even stricter proof than the *vetustas* of custom, for it is improbable that the imperial will would have brooked so formidable a check except within well-defined limits, and only when the inefficacy of the abrogated enactment had been unmistakably proved in practice.[5]

[1] C. 8. 52. 2. Nov. 134. 1 is an example of the express prohibition of custom: '. . . neque vero consuetudines nominare aut quaerere, quas forsitan aliqui praedecessorum in proprium lucrum iniuste adinvenerunt'. On the whole subject, see Jolowicz, *op. cit.* 29 ff.

[2] See *post*, pp. 478 ff.

[3] D. 9. 2. 27. 4 (second chapter of Lex Aquilia) (cf. Inst. iv. 3. 12); D. 11. 1. 1. 1 (interrogatories to heir-claimant); Inst. i. 5. 3 (*dediticii*); Inst. iv. 4. 7 (XII T. penalties for *iniuria*); C. 6. 51. 1. 1 (Lex Papia); Nov. 89. 15 (a constitution of Constantine: '[de naturalibus suis] non utendo perempta est'). The desuetude of the XII Tables, and of statutes in general, is discussed with spirit in Gellius, *Noct. Att.* xx. 1. 9 ff. The same principle seems to have been recognized in Greek law: see Vinogradoff, *Historical Jurisprudence*, ii. 80. On desuetude in English law, see *post*, pp. 478 ff.

[4] See Steinwenter, 'Zur Lehre vom Gewohnheitsrechte', in *Studi Bonfante*, ii. 419 ff.

[5] Brie, *op. cit.* 37 ff.

2. *The Historical School*

It will be seen that, in Roman theory, custom, as a source of law, occupied a considerable place. It may well be doubted whether any Roman jurist would have gone as far as the Analytical School in denying it any legal validity unless it was derived from or sanctioned by a determinate sovereign. On the other hand, so far as there is any consistent theory of custom at all in Roman Law, it is clearly relegated to a subordinate position among the sources of law, and, with the single surprising exception of its abrogative effect upon statutory law, it was not conceived as competing on equal terms with the authority of constitutional law-making organs. It is not, indeed, until comparatively recent times that custom has been erected to a primary place among the materials of law. To the German Historical School[1] all law is essentially the product of natural forces associated with the *Geist* of each particular people, and nothing is more representative of these evolutionary processes than the autochthonous customs which are found to exist in each community, and which are as indigenous as its flora and fauna. Custom carries its own justification in itself, because it would not exist at all unless some deep-seated need of the people or some native quality of temperament gave rise to it. Savigny might well have said of custom, 'Whatever is, is right.' This is his own account of it:[2]

'The true basis of positive law . . . has its existence, its reality, in the common consciousness of the people. This existence is an invisible thing; by what means can we recognize it? We do so when it reveals itself in external act, when it steps forth in usage, manners, custom; in the uniformity of a continuing and therefore lasting manner of action we recognize the belief of the people as its common root and one diametrically opposite to bare chance. Custom therefore is the badge (*Kennzeichen*) and not a ground of origin (*Entstehungsgrund*) of positive law.'

[1] On the Historical School generally, see Vinogradoff, *Historical Jurisprudence*, i, ch. vi; Stone, *The Province and Function of Law*, 421 ff.; Paton, *Jurisprudence* (2nd ed.), 14 ff.; Friedmann, *Legal Theory* (4th ed.), 158 ff.; Lloyd, *Introduction to Jurisprudence*, ch. 10; Kantorowicz, 'Savigny and the Historical School of Law', 53 *L.Q.R.* 326.

[2] *System*, § 12, Holloway's trans.

Puchta carried the principle even farther. To him custom was not only self-sufficient and independent of legislative authority, but was a condition precedent of all sound legislation. He found the basis of customary law in the collective purpose of the nation, and express legislation could be useful only in so far as it embodied this purpose as already manifested in custom. From this view arose the distrust with which the Historical School regarded all legislation, especially when in the form of a code.

The Volksgeist

The starting-point is a *Volksgeist* which exists *de facto* and must be accepted, without any attempt to explain it, as a natural phenomenon. It is primarily a sociological, not a legal, fact; law is but one among many of its manifestations. But custom comes early among those manifestations, and it is essentially a reflex of the *Geist*. In itself it creates nothing. It is not the hammer, it is the spark struck from the anvil. Its effect is to *make known* the existing *Geist*. 'Die Gewohnheit macht das Recht nicht, sie läßt es nur erkennen.' In reality, it is *instinct* coming to the surface in practical relationships. That particular instinct in the general *Geist* which applies to legal arrangements is the *Rechtsüberzeugung* or *Rechtsbewußtsein*. It would seem to include not only an instinct for a particular kind of legal institution, but also a general consciousness of right and wrong as expressed in legal arrangements. All law, whether applied by judges or ordained by the sovereign, must accord with this native *Rechtsüberzeugung;* otherwise it is misconceived, pernicious, and doomed to failure. The effort of every enlightened legal system should be to dispense the law which was and which is and which is to be; artificial expedients are justified only when pressing new needs arise in society. It is true that in the application of the indigenous law human agents must intervene; but their business is to utilize what they find, not to use it as material for their own inventive ingenuity. Custom is above all else a *rule of conduct*; but judges and interpreters are concerned with logical decisions, not with rules of conduct. The origin, the self-contained validity, of custom is an entirely different question from its application, and the two things should never be allowed to merge. And even when the interpreter has to exercise his individual judgement in the disputes which are certain to arise about the meaning of law, he does so as 'the representative of the people'. He, too, must come within the ambit of the *Volksgeist*, and he is a just and efficient judge only in so far as he adheres to its dictates in forming his conclusions.

The merest glance at these summarized principles, which I hope accurately represent the main purport of Savigny's teaching, is sufficient to show their deeply sociological colouring. If Savigny was an evolutionist before the evolutionists, so he was a sociologist before the sociologists. Without disrespect to their scholarly genius, it is difficult not to feel that unconsciously (for they could hardly guess what would be built upon the foundations which they laid) Savigny and his followers were National Socialists before the National Socialists. Be that as it may, the logical and historical difficulties which reside in Savigny's doctrine, if it be accepted unqualified, are many and serious; and, especially when he came to consider the *Juristenrecht*,[1] he had much ado to remain consistent with his own principles.

Customs of ruling classes

Many customs which have taken deep root in society do not appear to be based on any general conviction of their rightness or necessity, or upon any real and voluntary *consensus utentium*. Slavery was the almost universal practice of the ancient world. It was not, however, accepted without stern criticism from those who concerned themselves with its moral, as opposed to its merely utilitarian, aspects. It is true that Plato shows towards it a complacency which is somewhat surprising according to modern notions; he treats it as an institution universally admitted to be useful,[2] and contents himself with good

[1] See *post*, pp. 112 ff.

[2] *Legg*. vi. 776 D.

counsels for the humane treatment of slaves.[1] Before Aristotle, and contemporaneously with him, the ethics of slavery appear to have been debated with some liveliness;[2] and Aristotle specifically examines the arguments in a well-known passage of the *Politics*.[3] He defends 'natural' slavery, in accordance with a theory of what may be called natural inequalitarianism, but is by no means unimpressed by the considerations on the other side,[4] from which, indeed, he can escape only by somewhat specious reasoning.[5] The slavery which he defends is so greatly attenuated by reformatory doctrine that it really ceases to be the slavery of actual practice; as his learned expositor, W. L. Newman, observes,[6] Aristotle

'deserves to be remembered rather as the author of a suggestion for the reformation of slavery than as the defender of the institution. The slavery he defends is an ideal slavery which can exist only where the master is intellectually and morally as high as the slave is low. . . . His theory of slavery implies, if followed out to its results, the illegitimacy of the relation of master and slave in a large proportion of the cases in which it existed.'

In the theory of at least one group of Roman jurists, who were probably influenced by philosophical and especially Stoic speculations concerning the Law of Nature, Aristotle's theory of natural inequality is exactly reversed, and slavery is frankly admitted to be 'contra naturam',[7] whereas liberty is a 'naturalis facultas eius

[1] Indeed, counsels of perfection; *ibid.* 777 D: ἡ δὲ τροφὴ τῶν τοιούτων μήτε τινὰ ὕβριν ὑβρίζειν εἰς τοὺς οἰκέτας, ἧττον δέ, εἰ δυνατόν, ἀδικεῖν ἢ τοὺς ἐξ ἴσου. But he had no false sentiment about 'keeping the servant in his proper place', or meting out due punishment: *ibid.* E, *ad fin.* The only repellent feature he seems to have found in slavery was the enslavement of *Greeks*, which deeply offended his nationalism: *Legg.*, *loc. cit.*, and cf. *Rep.* v. 469 B and C, and Arist. *Pol.* i. 6, 1255ᵃ 6 ff.

[2] Newman, *The Politics of Aristotle*, i. 139 ff.

[3] i. 3, 1253ᵇ ff.

[4] i. 6, 1255ᵃ 1.

[5] e.g. i. 6, 1255ᵇ 10: The abuse of authority over the slave is wrong because, the slave being part of his master, injury of the part is injury of the whole! No general principles of humanitarianism emerge from the discussion.

[6] *Op. cit.* 151.

[7] Inst. i. 3. 2, quoting Florentinus *apud* D. 1. 5. 4. 1; cf. Tryphoninus, D. 12. 6. 64.

quod cuique facere libet'.[1] As is well known, slavery was the chief example cited in support of Ulpian's (dubious) distinction between the *ius naturale* and the *ius gentium*.[2] Though Christianity tolerated slavery,[3] enlightened opinion, if it did not actually condemn it, had always cast the gravest doubts upon its justification,[4] and the whole tendency of the later Roman Law was strongly *in favorem libertatis*.[5] Why, then, was it so long tolerated, whether in its unmitigated form or in the modified form of serfdom? Why were the final and decisive attacks upon it delayed until the eighteenth century A.D.? The mere fact that barbarous customs of war made it part of the *ius gentium* was hardly enough to endue it with such obstinate vitality; and to suppose that it was based upon a conviction resident in the mass of humanity—many of whom were, according to Aristotelian principles, 'natural slaves'—would be fanciful.

The truth is that slavery was a custom based upon the needs not of a popular majority but of a ruling minority. Ideally, that minority might consist of the mental and moral aristocrats of Plato and Aristotle; actually, it consisted of the 'property-owning classes', and it was they who kept it so long in existence, for economic reasons, which were characteristic of the ancient world but by no means peculiar to it. In our time we have seen, most unhappily, a reversion to chattel slavery, far more inhuman than that which existed in Rome and Athens. There are countries in the modern world where slavery, under

[1] Inst. i. 3. 1, again quoting Florentinus, D. 1. 5. 4. pr.; cf. Ulpian, D. 1. 1. 4 and 50. 17. 32.

[2] D. 1. 1. 4. According to A. J. Carlyle (*Mediaeval Political Theory in the West*, i. 39 ff.), Ulpian, Florentinus, and Tryphoninus are the only jurists who support the distinction, and they seem to have developed no very clear doctrine. Possibly the name of Pomponius should be added, on the strength of D. 1. 1. 2; but it is not clear whether he is there cited as in agreement with Ulpian's general doctrine, or merely as giving an example of the *ius* which is *solis hominibus inter se commune*.

[3] St. Paul, 1 Cor. vii. 20–23; Col. iii. 22–25.

[4] Newman, *op. cit.* 155 ff.

[5] Buckland, *The Roman Law of Slavery*. On the whole subject see Carlyle, *op. cit.*, vol. i, *passim*.

the guise of penal forced labour, is practised on a very large scale as an essential part of the planned national economy. The same process will be found repeatedly in history—customs establish themselves not because they correspond with any conscious, widespread necessity, but because they fit the economic convenience of the most powerful caste. 'Wherever there is an ascendant class,' wrote Mill,[1] 'a large portion of the morality of the country emanates from its class interests, and its feelings of class superiority.' The weaker members, who form the majority of society, accept these customs either because they are imposed by irresistible force, or because they suit on the whole the general arrangements of society, which those in subordinate positions accept through *vis inertiae* or at least are powerless to repulse. This is very apparent in perhaps the most important body of custom which has ever existed in Europe—feudal custom. It is impossible to think of feudal custom as merely 'broad-based upon a people's will'. The bulk of it was founded upon the notion of *service*, not simply convenience or conviction. Service, or *rent*, was not, it is true, an obligation confined to any one class; the powerful baron, as a customer of the king, had his duties of service like anybody else. But the great bulk of services and rents were of a rural and agricultural kind, and they were undoubtedly imposed on the hewers of wood and drawers of water for the benefit of their superiors.[2] We must not on this account conclude that the feudal system was one of bare tyranny of the strong over the weak; but neither is it to be supposed that this elaborate customary system, which has so deeply affected all our institutions, took its origin solely from a popular *Bewußtsein*.

Customs local and international

Many customs, again, are so essentially local in origin that they cannot be said to arise from any widespread conviction. The vigour and rapidity with which these local usages reproduce themselves is one of the most

[1] *On Liberty*, Intro.

[2] Vinogradoff, *English Society in the Eleventh Century*, 383.

remarkable features of custom, and will call for separate consideration.[1] Neither England nor any other European country can claim that the merchant customs which have established themselves in its law are the product of any particular national genius. It was overlooked by the Historical School that what we now understand by nationalism is a comparatively modern conception. In the Middle Ages—indeed, probably as late as the seventeenth century—the boundaries which divided European peoples were those of religion rather than of race. The *ius gentium* has been a real and powerful influence in civilization, and not a mere abstract aspiration. In the cosmopolitanism of commercial and many other customs the *Volksgeist* loses much of its meaning. And the pretended purity of its lineage is often highly suspect. What allowance is made for the importation of custom by conquest, invasion, and 'peaceful penetration'? Law is seldom of pure-blooded stock, and 'national' is a dangerous word to use, without qualification, of almost any legal institution.[2]

3. *Development of custom*
Inner and outer manifestations

When we speak of 'conviction' or 'spirit'—the nearest, though inadequate, approach we can make to the German terminology—we think of something intangible, psychological, non-material. But are we not making a large assumption in positing any conscious 'conviction' in those societies and at those times when custom most naturally comes into being? Custom is

[1] *Post*, pp. 128 ff.

[2] Self-flattery in this respect is not unknown in our Common Law. Doubtless it gave Fortescue a patriotic glow, after describing the early conquests and invasions of Britain, to declare roundly that 'in all the times of these several nations and their kings, this realm was still ruled with the self-same customs, that it is now governed withal': *De Laud.*, ch. 17. With no less unction did Popham C.J. state gravely in Court 'that the laws of England had continued as a rock without alteration in all the varieties of people that had possessed this land, namely, the Romans, Britons, Danes, Saxons, Norman, and English'; and Coke applauds this gratifying sentiment (cited Spence, *Equitable Jurisdiction*, i. 125). But a very slight acquaintance with legal history informs us that this is rhetoric addressed to the heart rather than to the reason. Even the patriotism of Blackstone could not go so far: see 1 *Comm.* 64.

conduct. No conduct of any intelligent human being, or group of intelligent human beings, can be wholly willless or reasonless. It has its internal and external aspects: the internal in mind and emotions, the external in conduct or, if we wish to avoid qualitative terms, in mere contractions of the muscles, 'irritability' or 'response to stimulus'. When we are dealing with a state of society in which reflection about social institutions is *ex hypothesi* embryonic, it is not easy to distinguish between the *inner* manifestations of social tendencies—feelings, desires, will, consciousness—and their *outer* manifestations in mere conduct. To probe only the psychological genesis of social custom must lead to much inconclusive speculation; to see in custom nothing but *de facto* conduct will be to ignore the basis of will and desire which, in some degree, must underlie the conduct of all rational creatures. The German historical jurists tended to concentrate attention on the inner or metaphysical aspect. Puchta, for example, is concerned with it almost exclusively: to him the *practice* of custom—custom as actual conduct in society, and therefore operative law—is merely the inseparable companion of customary law, a kind of necessary sub-product; but the real substance of the law itself is to be found in the immanent *Rechtsüberzeugung*. This attitude leads to abstractions which become the more elusive the more we seek to analyse them; for when we are dealing with law, a concrete institution of human society, we cannot be content with mere abstractions. We hear, for example, much of a *Volkswille;* but what meaning are we to attach to this supposed corporate will of societies in which the notion of corporate existence is rudimentary and inarticulate? It means even less than the *volonté générale* of the much more highly organized society of Rousseau. It means, indeed, nothing, except perhaps in the single instance of tribal self-defence or aggression; and it has long since been abandoned even by the modern disciples of Puchta and Savigny. They insist, and with reason, that the early popular 'conviction' about law, if it is anything, is a state of consciousness, not an act of will.[1]

Corporate life of society

The conviction or consciousness of the people has, in more recent jurisprudence, been associated with the conception of the people as a corporation. Behind all Teutonic theory of the nineteenth century lies the idea of the corporate life and thought of the people, and above all of the German people. But to Savigny and Puchta this corporate *Geist* remains in the shadowy world of the spirit. It was reserved for a later German jurist, scarcely less distinguished, to clothe the corporate spirit with flesh and blood. To Gierke[2] every true human association becomes a real and living entity animated by its own individual soul; of all such leagues, State-organized nations are the greatest, and the corporate spirit, the People-spirit, is the very core of the separate personality which each possesses.

> 'The development of law lies in human action. But the subject of this action is not individuals, but communities (*Gemeinschaften*). The individual man who co-operates in the process always acts as a component *member* and in furtherance of a human *community*.'[3]

This is not intended to mean the stunting or suppression of individuality; the relationship is one of mutual benefit; in proportion as the individual labours in the interest of the community, so he adds to his own strength and stature. But always the community, at least in this jurist's view of history, is the highest achievement of human endeavour. Gierke approached his subject in the same historical spirit as Savigny, and, like Savigny, made

[1] Gierke, *DPR*. i. 163 ff.

[2] On his significance generally see Vinogradoff, *Historical Jurisprudence*, i. 131 ff.

[3] Gierke, *DPR*. i. 125. A later interpretation of the Group principle, which places the emphasis on the 'idea' rather than the *will* of the collectivity, and which presents the State as a congeries of 'institutions', is to be found in the works of Professor M. Hauriou (the Elder) and Professor G. Renard: see 'The Institutional Theory', in *Modern Theories of Law*, by Sir Ivor Jennings, who links this theory with Roman Catholic Thomistic doctrines. See also Stone, *The Province and Function of Law*, 695 ff.

it a lifework; like Savigny, again, he exalted and cherished the spirit of his nation; but with him that spirit is no longer a mystic attribute irreducible to exact cognizance, but the essence and distinguishing mark of a real *person*.

'Conviction' or 'practice' as generating custom? Rational and irrational customs

Whether this personality be 'real' or 'fictitious', whether the doctrine does not merely attach attributes of the phenomenal to what really belongs to the world of the noumenal, is still a controversy on which we need not enter. But let us note that in Gierke's conception of the 'corporate life of the people' the development of law is to be found in the 'outer manifestation' of conduct rather than in the 'inner manifestation' of conviction. 'The development of law', to repeat his words, 'lies in human *action*.' In the infancy of a people it is the thing *done* or *made*, the thing grasped by the senses rather than by the intellect, which prevails. The aspirations of the people will express themselves in the concrete forms of plastic arts, not in abstractions, for the popular mind is as yet incapable of abstractions. Ingenuity and imagination are expended on creating *emblems* which embody a meaning not explicitly understood. Law, according to this view of it, streams from the soul of a people like national poetry, it is as holy as the national religion, it grows and spreads like language; religious, ethical, and poetical elements all contribute to its vital force. But the shapes in which it presents itself are physical, tangible, and immediate, full of fantasy and force, but weak and unavailing when any abstraction enters in or any general idea becomes disengaged from discrete phenomena. It is an error (Gierke maintains) to apply sophisticated ideas of consciousness to this naïve state of mind. In this stage of social development, what we should call general ideas presented themselves to men's minds not as mental pictures but as states of fact. When men spoke of peace, they thought of the *fact* of peace and the material circumstances which it involved: breach of the peace meant to them the *act* of lawless violence; vindication of the peace meant the actual prosecution of revenge, either by self and kindred, or by appointed judges; loss of peace—outlawry—meant the miserable condition of exclusion from the guarantees of life and limb; punishment meant the actual infliction of a foreordained retribution. Power over persons was the power of the strong hand; property was the investment of individuals with material goods, to have and to hold. Procedure was not a rationalized system, but was shaped into immutable forms and sacramental words; rights and duties were not debated in the abstract, but the very persons and things themselves in dispute must be 'actually and bodily present'—the rod or spear of ownership, the clod of earth from the debatable land, the debtor in default, the slave claimed free: these were not mere empty symbols, but convenient devices to make the invisible visible and the intangible tangible. Institutions were always expressed in terms of the concrete and the formalistic; the idea of any immanent general principle in law was wholly lacking. It is only when a nation is well advanced in its development that the force of the abstract begins to assert itself and symbols cease to satisfy the mind. The world of thought prevails over the world of facts. The physical and the sensuous become ancillary to the intellectual: everything urges from 'separateness' to 'togetherness', and general principles of rule, harmony, and co-ordination establish themselves. The corporate life of a young society is full of vital creative force; from it grow religion and poetry, law and custom, as the branches from a tree, but the forms it creates are not *conscious* social institutions. These come only with the full maturity of the people; if they are lost and there is retrogression to 'separateness' in ideas and habits, this is the stage of decay and disintegration, and ruin is not far distant.[1]

[1] *Genossenschaftsrecht*, ii. 7 ff. It must be confessed that Gierke's eloquent, sometimes almost rhapsodical, description of early society seems to contain no small element of imagination, and is somewhat reminiscent of those bright-hued pictures of a Golden Age which were once so popular. It is not, I hope, an excess of scepticism to regard with some distrust all generalizations about

We must not, then, in searching for the *conviction* in the corporate life of a people, underestimate the effect of the actual *practice* of custom. These two elements are not mutually exclusive but interdependent and complementary. In the earliest stages of society, practice plays the greater part and custom grows by the force of concrete example; but as general notions begin to be apprehended in the abstract, conviction and practice become complementary to each other and settle into a perpetual process of action and reaction. To this extent a 'conviction' of some kind, in some degree, must lie behind all customs—they would never arise at all unless some motive for them existed in reason or convenience. Often, it is true, the rational basis is extremely obscure. A custom may seem entirely arbitary, a mere freak or throwback, but this is usually because we have insufficient evidence of its origin; further investigation, or a chance discovery, may show that there is an excellent practical reason for what seemed at first sight entirely fortuitous. It is puzzling, for example, to find a single locality like Kent or Nottingham adopting rules of inheritance directly at variance with a well-established 'custom of the realm' like primogeniture; but research has shown very sufficient reasons for the apparent arbitrariness of gavelkind and Borough English custom.[1] It is true, *pace* Savigny, that the reason and utility on which such customs rest often arise from purely local conditions, not from any widespread *Geist*; still, they are based on discernible motives, and the farther we trace the custom back, the clearer the motives become. We must be chary of characterizing any custom, however seemingly abnormal, as irrational unless we have all the evidence before us.

the state of mind of primitive man. The evidence is scantier than the imaginative opportunities. It is impossible not to detect in the whole of Gierke's philosophy, as in so much German thinking of his age, the seeds of a nationalism which was later to run mad.

[1] Vinogradoff, *Villeinage in England*, 185, 205 ff.; P. & M. i. 165; Spence, *Equitable Jurisdiction*, i. 4.

But we cannot ignore the converse process, that of practice generating conviction. There are many customs which cannot be attributed to any conscious conviction without metaphysical ingenuity which savours of pure invention. In the experience both of communities and of individuals, circumstances often arise in which it is necessary to choose between several equally desirable or undesirable alternatives. A traveller comes to a parting of the ways, and knows not which of several roads leads to his destination; on what principle does he select one or the other? When it is a question of taking one from among a number of articles equal in appearance and value—fruit, pens, pins, pound notes, cards, pieces of paper, what you will—on what principle of conviction or motive is the selection made? It is extremely difficult, if it be possible at all, to find the rational basis of such acts of choice. It is not denied that logically and psychologically *any* act of choice necessarily involves a preference, a contrast and selection, between a definite better and a definite worse; but the determining elements in the process of preference are too recondite for analysis. The small acts of daily life are full of such apparently arbitrary choices, which are not made the more explicable by the general description 'habit'. So it is also in the growth of many customs. What is there of 'conviction' in adopting the left or the right as the rule of the road? The custom varies erratically in different countries, and even, on the Continent, in different parts of the same country. And this is legal, not merely social, custom; for to choose the wrong side of the road may involve the most painful consequences in law.[1] Why do Westerns write from left to right, and many Easterns from right to left? Innumerable local customs are associated with particular days of the year: why one date more than another? 'A custom', says Blackstone,[2] 'in a parish that no man shall put his beasts into the common

[1] See Christian's interesting note to 1 Bl. *Comm.* 74.

[2] 1 *Comm.* 77.

till the 3rd of October, would be good; and yet it would be hard to show the reason why that day in particular is fixed upon, rather than the day before or after.' A great many commercial customs appear to be quite arbitrary; publishers and bakers defy the laws of mathematics by making 12 equal 13, and rabbit-merchants, it would seem, have considered 1,000 to be synonymous with 1,200.[1] A little industry could collect a large number of these apparently erratic anomalies among the customs of localities and merchants.[2] Does any fundamental *Bewußtsein* underlie them? We must remind ourselves again that they are not always as irrational as they seem. Thus, to take Blackstone's example, there is a reason why the common pasture should not be available until October, for it is not till that month that the crops will have been removed. Similarly, '12 copies (or loaves) to be reckoned as 13' is merely a child-like device for allowing discount or reducing the price of a dozen. The rabbit-merchants' 1,200 is ten long hundreds of six score each, the old 'Anglicus numerus' of Anglo-Norman Surveys.[3] But, as Blackstone asks, why the 3rd of October rather than the 2nd or the 4th? Customs may, in a greater or less degree, all be rational in their inception, but it often happens that, *once they have been inaugurated*, elements of the non-rational enter in, and, having once entered, abide. A point has to be fixed, a line to be drawn, somewhere. Often, as has been said, it is possible to find unsuspected explanations; but one cannot always resist a suspicion that the explanations suffer from the dubious plausibility of the 'aetiological'. Thus it is sometimes suggested—though I do not know that it has ever been pressed as a serious theory—that in England the left is chosen as the rule of the road in order to leave the right side clear and the right hand free for self-defence. A Frenchman, then, prefers to defend himself with his

[1] *Smith* v. *Wilson* (1832), 3 B. & A. 728.

[2] See note to *Wigglesworth* v. *Dallison*, 1 Sm. L.C. (13th ed.), 597.

[3] Pollock, *Contracts* (13th ed.), 202.

strong left arm?[1] Such explanations, which are also not unknown to philologists, invite scepticism. More truly says the Digest,[2] in its blunt fashion: 'Non omnium quae a maioribus constituta sunt ratio reddi potest.'[3] 'Customs are apt to develop into traditions which are stronger than law and remain unchallenged long after the reason for them has disappeared.'[4] It is a very characteristic quality of custom—perhaps, indeed, its strongest—that the mere fact of its practice and repetition invest it with a sanctity which is often more compelling than reason, logic, or utility. Maine has observed:[5]

> 'A process commences which may be shortly described by saying that *usage which is reasonable generates usage which is unreasonable*. Analogy, the most valuable of instruments in the maturity of jurisprudence, is the most dangerous of snares in its infancy. Prohibitions and ordinances, originally confined, for good reasons, to a single description of acts, are made to apply to all acts of the same class, because a man menaced with the anger of the gods for doing one thing, feels a natural terror in doing any other thing which is remotely like it.'

Imitation

Why does the thing done become the thing which *must* be done? In the answer to this question, the part played by sheer imitation in social custom has, as I venture to think, been greatly neglected.[6] It is practically ignored by the German historical jurists, and until recently

[1] Tarde (*Les Lois de l'Imitation*, 349) offers an interesting explanation of the custom of writing from left to right. The copy of this work which has been available to me once belonged to the late Professor A. V. Dicey. In the margin of this page I observe an emphatic query, which emboldens me to venture the opinion that Tarde's reasoning is more ingenious than convincing.

[2] 1. 3. 20.

[3] 'It cannot be said that a custom is founded on reason, though an unreasonable custom is void; for no reason, even the highest whatsoever, would make a custom or law; so it is no particular reason that makes any custom law, but the usage and practice itself, without regard had to any reason of such usage': per Trevor C.J., *Arthur* v. *Bokenham* (1708), 11 Mod. 160. Cf. Coke C.J. in *Hix* v. *Gardiner* (1614), 2 Bulstr. 196.

[4] *Edwards* v. *Att.-Gen. for Canada*, [1930] A.C. 124, 134.

[5] *Ancient Law*, 16 (italics mine).

[6] See, however, Maine, *Early Law and Custom*, on the effect of imitation on clan-organization (following Lyall); and Vinogradoff, *Historical Jurisprudence*, i. 169 ff.

little attempt has been made to investigate it. Yet imitation is one of the commonest and most influential elements in the life of every individual and every society. To say that we are all creatures of habit is to blush for a platitude; yet platitudes are often truths which are accepted more unquestioningly than they are apprehended clearly. If we dispassionately examine our ordinary conduct, we shall find that far more of our daily actions are purely imitative, and far fewer purely rational, than it flatters us to admit. To make each separate act a thing of deliberate reason requires more time, more independence of judgement, and more hardihood than ordinary human life allows or ordinary human nature achieves. 'The most intellectual of men', writes Walter Bagehot,[1]

> 'are moved quite as much by circumstances which they are used to as by their own will. The active voluntary part of a man is very small, and if it were not economized by a sleepy kind of habit, its results would be null. We could not do every day out of our own heads all we have to do. We should accomplish nothing, for all our energies would be frittered away in minor attempts at petty improvements. One man, too, would go off from the known track in one direction, and one in another; so that when a crisis came requiring massed combination, no two men would be near enough to act together. It is the dull traditional habit of mankind that guides most men's actions, and is the steady frame in which each new artist must set the picture that he paints. And all this traditional part of human nature is, *ex vi termini*, most easily impressed and acted on by that which is handed down.'

It is not mere weakness or indolence that constrains us to submit in a reasonable degree to the dictates of fashion. It is easy to sneer at the conventionally minded, and it is true, as Mill observed in his essay *On Liberty*, that the 'despotism of custom' may be 'the standing hindrance to human advancement'. But where no great principle is involved, adherence to the usual is the merest prudence.

[1] *The English Constitution*, ch. i. Bagehot, in *Physics and Politics* (No. 3), also had many shrewd observations on the effect of 'mimicry' in 'nation-making'.

To be singular in the ordinary matters of use and wont is worth neither the effort nor the discomfort. Not to be singular—to follow the prescribed mode—is at least a guarantee of security. It is based upon the reasonable expectation without which social relationships become anarchical. What has been done once and has produced a certain result will, if done again in the same way, produce the same result. The trite way is not only the safe way, but generally it is also the short way. And so, from following the trite way ourselves, we easily come to believe that for others to deviate from it is not only foolish but anti-social. This belief is for the most part founded not on any conviction of ultimate rightness or wrongness but simply on our tenacity to habit.

Tarde's thesis

The most systematic attempt which has been made, so far as the present writer is aware, to examine the workings of the imitative faculty in man and society is G. Tarde's profound and fascinating study, *Les Lois de l'Imitation*.[1] To Tarde imitation is no mere curiosity of psychology, it is one of the primary laws of nature. Nature perpetuates itself by repetition: and the three fundamental forms of repetition are rhythm or *undulation*, *generation*, and *imitation*. With the biological aspects of these principles we cannot deal here, nor are they Tarde's main concern; suffice it that there is ample evidence to support them in post-Darwinian natural science. Applying them to the evolution of human societies, Tarde sees imitation as one of the necessary inherent principles by which society perpetuates itself. It is no mere casual phenomenon, recurring with unaccountable frequency: it is a wholly indispensable quality in the continuity of a society—if society is to have any continuity, or, in other words, life. 'La société, c'est l'imitation.' Nowhere is the force of imitation more

[1] A suggestive, but ill-developed, view of will and imitation, based on Bain's theory of the will, is to be found in Korkunov, *General Theory of Law*, § 20. See also William James, *Psychology*, ii. 408, and on Tarde generally see Stone, *The Province and Function of Law*, 662 ff.

marked than in the deep-seated conservatism of custom and law. 'Le droit . . . n'est ici qu'une suite et une forme du penchant de l'homme à l'imitation. . . . La solidarité juridique a un caractère exclusivement social, mais pourquoi? Parce qu'elle suppose la similitude par imitation.' A social group is defined as 'une collection d'êtres en tant qu'ils sont en train de s'imiter entre eux ou en tant que, sans s'imiter actuellement, ils se ressemblent et que leurs traits communs sont des copies anciennes d'un même modèle.' Custom is the great stabilizing factor in society exactly because, by its imitative influence, it is for ever striving to maintain the 'copies of the same model'. It is to the life of society what physical reproduction is to the order of nature. But the nineteenth century has acquainted us with another constant principle in the order of nature—that of 'variation'. The variations of custom may be said to be prevailing *fashions*. Custom is the thing of immemorial antiquity, fashion is the thing of the moment. We have only to look round us to see how imperious it is in its demands and its effects, and how indefinitely it varies and fluctuates, comes and goes. If in the mysterious realm of mass-psychology we are searching for an unmistakable, ever-present, and inexhaustible *Geist* or 'corporate spirit', surely there is none which more frequently forces itself on the attention than this instinct of imitation permeating every department of social life like the very atmosphere which it breathes. The sceptic may reject, for want of proof—or perhaps for lack of faith—the nebulous abstractions of the *Volksgeist* or of the corporate personality of the people. But while he may well shrink from attempting to analyse the psychological qualities of the imitative faculty, he can scarcely deny its vigorous existence and its manifold results.

Suggestive influence of imitation

Tarde insists that many of the influences which contribute to the force of imitation are 'extra-logical'. Partaking of the nature of the fundamental impulse to repetition and reproduction, they are concerned not so much with reason as with feeling and instinct. Indeed, he insists almost too strongly upon this aspect of the matter, for he seems to leave insufficient scope for that kind of imitation which is deliberate and logically reasoned—a form of mimicry which has undoubtedly played its part in the propagation of custom. Yet in a great variety of instances which fall within common experience the impulse to imitation does not appear to be rational at all. It seems to exercise some kind of hypnotic influence, or shall we say a force of attraction, which is no more demonstrably the product of reason and choice than polar attraction is the product of the needle and the magnet. Whether or not it is purely instinctive, and possibly congenital, is disputed by biologists. Tarde calls it 'magnetization' or 'somnambulism'. It is for the psychologist to explain, if he can, this curious effect of imitation on the minds not only of men but of large groups of men; that is hardly the task of a lawyer. We certainly do not explain the matter by using such terms as 'automatic' or 'subconscious'. But however baffling this phenomenon may be, few will deny that it exists. Everybody is familiar with popular 'crazes'. These are quite different from mere passing fashions. As we have said, there is generally a very simple reason for 'following the fashion': it is less trouble to do so than not to do so. But there seems to be no reason why 'crazes' should suddenly appear and disappear. A whole community will sometimes, for no apparent reason, throw itself passionately into the pursuit of a particular game or pastime or competition. The extraordinary infection of these trivialities is something quite outside logic and reason; and it is, needless to say, a trifle by comparison with the infection of inventions,[1] ideas, creeds, language, morals, art, and institutions. In his essay 'Shakespeare and the Drama',[2] Tolstoy calls attention to 'those epidemic

[1] 'Is it not trite that the invention of gunpowder has profoundly modified our social and political organization?': Maitland, *Collected Papers*, iii. 298.

[2] *Works of Tolstoy*, ed. Aylmer Maude, xxi. 307.

"suggestions" to which men ever have been and are subject'. Such suggestion, he continues, 'always has existed and does exist in the most varied spheres of life. As glaring instances, considerable in scope and in deceitful influence, one may cite the medieval Crusades, which afflicted not only adults but even children, and other "suggestions" startling in their senselessness, such as faith in witches,[1] in the utility of torture for the discovery of truth, the search for the elixir of life, the philosopher's stone, or the passion for tulips, valued at several thousands of guldens a bulb, which took hold of Holland. Such irrational "suggestions" always have existed and do exist in all spheres of human life—religious, philosophical, political, economic, scientific, artistic, and, in general, literary—and people clearly see their insanity only when they free themselves from them. But so long

[1] The extraordinary influence on medieval Europe of the belief in witchcraft has been described by Lecky, *Rise of Rationalism*, vol. i, ch. i. It was less powerful in England than on the Continent; but even in England there was something approaching a 'witch-scare' in the late sixteenth and early seventeenth centuries. In 1580 Jean Bodin published a *Démonomanie des Sorciers* in which he strongly urged the burning of sorcerers and witches. Bishop Jewel's jeremiads on the subject inspired Elizabeth with such genuine alarm that she appointed a special commission which conducted a savage campaign against witches. In 1582 seventeen women of the village of St. Osyth, in Essex, were barbarously executed. The superstition was greatly stimulated by James I's peculiar interest in it, as shown by his 'Daemonologie', and trials were frequent throughout the seventeenth century. The trial of the witches at Bury St. Edmunds in 1664, before Sir Matthew Hale, is recorded in 6 St. T. 647. The 'scare' died down towards the end of the seventeenth century. Holt C.J. did much to discourage it (see Holdsworth, *H.E.L.* vi. 518), especially by the trial of Hathaway in 1702 as a cheat and impostor for falsely pretending to be bewitched (14 St. T. 643). The last conviction for witchcraft in England seems to have been that of Jane Wenham at Hertford in 1712. The numerous statutes relating to witchcraft, dating from before the Conquest, were not repealed till 1736 (9 Geo. II, c. 5). Much curious learning on the subject is to be found in Reginald Scott's *Discoverie of Witchcraft* (1548) and in the evidence at the trial of the Bury St. Edmunds witches, above-mentioned. See also Stephen, *Hist. Cr. L.* ii. 430 ff. Belief in witchcraft is by no means extinct even now in some rural districts, for example in certain remote parts of Wales. Within living memory a woman was tried at the Cardiff Assizes for having obtained some hundreds of pounds from a farmer by professing to supply him with charms: see A. G. Bradley's *Exmoor Memories*, 148.

as they are under their influence, the suggestions appear to them so certain, so true, that to argue about them is regarded as neither necessary nor possible.' Tolstoy's main theme is startling—it is that Shakespeare is a writer totally devoid of merit, artistic or moral, and that the high esteem in which he is held is merely another example of popular hypnotic suggestion, intensified by the modern power of the press! We can hardly share Tolstoy's astonishment that he could find none to agree with him in this highly original view; but his other examples are striking and notorious. Tarde takes as a modern example of an imitative 'craze' the strange and unpleasant habit of chewing gum, which has spread so widely in some countries. The habit of snuff-taking, so prevalent in the eighteenth century, also suggests itself; and the almost complete disappearance of that habit gives rise to melancholy doubts whether the practice of smoking may not some day disappear from male, and even female, society. The 'cross-word puzzle' is a curious example of the imitative 'craze' in our own day. So, perhaps, was the singular habit, once taken with great solemnity, of identifying arbitrary symbols, like the swastika, or clothing of a particular colour, with political creeds.

Examples of imitative customs: borough customs

We must certainly reckon with this force of attraction —I will avoid the term 'hypnotism'—in the propagation of custom.

'The transmission and "reception"', it has been said,[1] 'of devices and institutions of all kinds is constantly modifying the course of social evolution in all its stages. It is not only Roman law, the printing press, and firearms that have wandered through the world and been accepted by representatives of the most varied cultures: systems of script, funeral by cremation, the erection of megalithic monuments, may also be cited as cases in point. Archaeologists and ethnologists have been very active lately in showing the remarkable currents of cultural influence running

[1] Vinogradoff, *Historical Jurisprudence*, i. 169. Cf. Maine, *Ancient Law*, ch. vii, on the spread of the custom of primogeniture.

across the continents of the Old World or across the Pacific Ocean.'

Not infrequently institutions spread like a 'craze': and this is true not only of isolated usages but of whole codes of laws. In France and Germany, in the twelfth and thirteenth centuries, there was a continual process of legal imitation between many towns previously governed by quite distinct customs. The customs of Lorris, for instance, spread with great rapidity in France. In Germany nearly all the municipal laws of the Rhine towns were derived from Cologne; while Lübeck served in the same way as a model for the Baltic towns. The famous Law of Magdeburg was not only extensively copied in Germany but spread into Siberia, Bohemia, Poland, and Moravia—indeed, its influence can be traced throughout practically the whole of Eastern Europe. Penal law is full of similar examples of imitation. Until the eighteenth century, torture as a means of legal proof bespatters all Europe with blood.[1] Some are inclined to think that the popularity of the jury since the eighteenth century—a popularity maintained despite glaring defects and anomalies—is only another example of an epidemic superstition.[2] It is beyond doubt that, at least for purposes of criminal procedure, the English jury was deliberately copied by country after country in Europe throughout the nineteenth century.[3]

In our own medieval law we have a remarkable example of the force of imitation in the development of local and national civic institutions. The borough, with its court, its peculiar privileges and duties, and usually its gild merchant, possessed from the earliest times a notable individuality and a high significance in national

[1] It was never legal in England by the Common Law, but was frequently admitted by exercise of the royal prerogative: see Holdsworth, *H.E.L.* v. 170 ff. and 185 ff.

[2] Tarde, *op. cit.*

[3] See Maitland, 'The Body Politic', in *Collected Papers*, iii. 285, 298—an instructive paper generally on the part played by imitation in social development.

life.[1] Its importance was augmented by the sanction of the numerous royal charters which were granted throughout the twelfth and thirteenth centuries, and which became one of the chief distinguishing marks of the borough. The process of imitation and adoption which we have just observed at work in France and Germany is also to be found in the 'affiliation' of medieval boroughs in England.

> 'When a prosperous village or a newly-founded town wished to secure the franchises of a free borough, or when a borough sought an extension of its liberties, it was natural for the community to look for a model among its more privileged and flourishing neighbours.'[2]

In this way a number of 'parent' boroughs are widely imitated, and customs originally peculiar to one locality—often customs which deeply affect the citizen's rights of person and property[3]—become widespread throughout the land. Thus, to take one or two of the examples collected by the industry of Dr. Gross,[4] the code of London is imitated in forty-nine English towns, that of Winchester in twenty-four; Oxford, York, Hastings, Dublin, Kilkenny, Rhuddlan, and Newcastle serve as 'parent' boroughs to many more.

But the process does not end here. If we look at Dr. Gross's tables, we find that Bristol and Hereford are imitated by a great number of towns in England, Ireland, and Wales. Later researches have shown that in this instance a strong foreign influence has entered in, and that a great many of the customs which were attributed to Bristol are in fact derived from the Norman town of Breteuil.[5] The laws of Breteuil themselves seem to have been derived from Verneuil, King John having granted it the liberties of that town in 1189. With great

[1] *Ante*, p. 73, n. 1.

[2] Gross, *The Gild Merchant*, i. 242.

[3] They are fully described in P. & M. i. 634 ff.

[4] *Op. cit.* i. 254 ff.

[5] Miss Mary Bateson, 'The Laws of Breteuil', 15 and 16 *E.H.R.*; Petit-Dutaillis, *Studies Supplementary to Stubbs's Constitutional History* (2nd ed.), 88 ff.

rapidity during the twelfth and thirteenth centuries Breteuil, a strong but by no means pre-eminent community of France, played the same part in England as Lorris in France, or Freiburg and Magdeburg in Germany.[1]

This example of imitation is characteristic. The process was not purely mechanical. The laws of Breteuil were in some respects peculiarly favourable to the burgess,[2] and for that reason were naturally popular. There is a more personal reason. In 1060 William of Normandy had given the charge of the new Castle of Breteuil to William Fitzosbern,[3] who after the Conquest became Earl of Hereford and of the Isle of Wight. William Fitzosbern doubtless introduced the customs he knew best into Hereford; and their extension would in some measure be due to the fact that he was commissioned by the king to build castles and was given practically *carte blanche* in the creation of boroughs.[4] In the case of other 'parent' boroughs, 'the need', as Dr. Gross observes,[5] 'of a reliable precedent . . . was especially felt in an age when even the magistrates of most towns were unskilled in law, and when the king and baron were ever ready to nullify chartered rights, the one by a quibbling "quo warranto", the other by evasions and encroachments'. But these considerations do not entirely account for the extent of borough-affiliation. As in most cases of imitation which is not merely simian, there is, in the first instance, a rational ground for the impulse to imitate; but *once the process is begun*, it goes far beyond the stimuli of expediency and utility alone, and gathers momentum of its own motion. And thus it comes about repeatedly in history that the greatest results may ensue from the most unsuspected causes. The influence of the mimetic faculty has not been confined to casual or trivial social phenomena: it has also affected fundamental institutions. 'Nothing', wrote Sir Henry Maine,[6]

[1] Petit-Dutaillis, *loc. cit.* [2] *Ibid.* 89; Miss Bateson, 16 *E.H.R.* 342.
[3] Stubbs, i. 389; P. & M. ii. 267. [4] Miss Bateson, *ibid.* 335.
[5] *Op. cit.* i. [6] *Early Law and Custom*, 284.

'seems to me to have more affected primitive society, and yet to have been more neglected by those who have theorized upon it, than the imitative faculty which man has always possessed. . . . On superficial consideration, we are apt to think that man's mimetic faculty confines itself to matters of taste and personal habit. But, in truth, there is no successful, or conspicuous, or simply fashionable model which men, in the various stages of their progress, will not endeavour to imitate. The habit of political imitation, which has always been strong, still survives. "Make us a king to judge us, *like all the nations*," said the Israelites to Samuel (1 Sam. viii. 5). "Give us a constitution to regulate our liberty, like that of one particular nation," is the corresponding modern and Western command.'

So far we have considered custom as a legal and social phenomenon growing up by forces inherent in society—forces partly of reason and necessity, and partly of suggestion and imitation. But there is another view which would regard custom as of a far more artificial origin than this. The consideration of that view must be reserved for another chapter.

II

CUSTOM: INTERPRETATION AND APPLICATION

I. INTERPRETATION OF CUSTOM

Juristic control of custom

WHEN a society possesses accredited lawgivers or tribunals, it is part of their function to supervise the operation of custom; for, since custom contemplates legal relationships, it must be subject to review by the constituted judicial authorities which control all legal relationships. In the ordinary terminology of jurisprudence, the interpreters of custom are generically described as *jurists*, their science, to adopt a convenient German term, as *Juristenrecht*. It need hardly be observed that this expression is not confined to 'jurists' in the sense of learned writers upon legal topics; it includes all those whose special function is to expound and apply customary law. Thus in ancient societies it will comprise the semi-fabulous code-makers and lawgivers; and in England, though not to the same extent as on the Continent, it must also include the judges themselves.

Two principal views have been advanced concerning the relation between customary law and expert interpretation.

1. *View of the Historical School:* Juristenrecht *subordinate to* Volksrecht

The first is represented by Savigny and the Historical School. Now here the apostles of popular evolutionary law were in a difficulty. They could not, as good historians, be unaware that the interpretation of specialists has always played an important part in the development of legal systems; and this influence had all the appearance of being highly creative. But to concede to individuals, as distinct from the *Volk*, a creative function of this kind was to drive a stake into the heart of the *Rechtsüberzeugung*. How, then, account for the undeniably persistent phenomenon of the interpreter and his influence in moulding custom? The answer must be given in Savigny's own words:[1]

> 'The law, originally the common property of the collective people, in consequence of the ramifying relations of actual life, is so developed in its details that it can no longer be comprehended by the people at large. A separate class of legal experts thereupon comes into existence, which, itself an element of the people, represents the community in this domain of thought. In the peculiar consciousness of this class, the law is only an extension of the characteristic development of the *Volksrecht*. This latter henceforth leads a double life. In its fundamentals it continues to exist in the common consciousness of the people; but the precise determination and application of details is the special task of the class of jurisconsults.'

A more recent statement of the same view describes the magistrate or judge as 'the recognized and permanent organ through which the mind of the people expresses itself in shaping that part of the law which the State power does not formally enact'.[2]

In this view, the legal interpreter is entitled to the name of jurist only in so far as he remains the *representative of the people*. It is inevitable that as law expands in scope and complexity, there must grow up a class of persons 'learned in the law' (*Rechtskundige*). To them recourse may be had in case of dispute, and they, not only in the arena of litigation, but in the study as well, will lucubrate the amassed wisdom of the law. These two functions—the elaboration of the pure theory of law, and its application to concrete cases—Savigny recognizes as distinct. But both are within the periphery of the same essential task—the exposition of the existing law derived from the characteristic customs of the community. It is not the interpreter's business to add anything of his own. He is a conduit-pipe, not a source. True, an efficient conduit-pipe is not made by any casual

[1] *System*, i, § 14.

[2] Bryce, *Studies in History and Jurisprudence*, 690.

method out of any chance material; and it is only by assiduous training that the jurist can become a straight, sound, efficient conduit-pipe. But to attempt to be more than this is to attempt what is both impossible and mischievous; it is to usurp the office of the community, nay, of nature itself.

This theme is not a mere generalization in Savigny and Puchta. It is elaborated with the highest patience, and in particular it is applied to the case which lay nearest to Savigny's heart—the influence of jurists on the development of medieval German law. The abundant apparent exceptions to the general rule, and the considerable difficulties in its way, are not shirked, though they are sometimes treated with a somewhat hesitating logic. But the cardinal doctrine remains constant. The entire legitimate function of the interpreter must be restrained within the central fact of the *Rechtsentwicklung*, or evolution of law.

Practical objections to this view

Without delving into obscure factors in primitive societies, a plain man, regarding the matter as one of simple fact, will immediately feel grave objections to this theory. When a judge grants a writ of Habeas Corpus, and takes occasion to say that the freedom of the individual from unlawful restraint is one of the most fundamental and ancient rules of English law, he may be said, in a sense, to be echoing a principle resident in the conviction of most of the British community. But when a judge decided a disputed question of property according, let us say, to the Rule in Shelley's Case, in what real sense could he be said to be a representative of the people? Could it be pretended that a pious faith in the sanctity of seisin burned in the bosom of the Commonwealth, suffusing all its members with a healthy glow? Was the community plunged in gloom when an Act of Parliament incontinently swept the rule out of existence? The truth is that the judge who played a new variation on the Rule in Shelley's Case was operating in a sphere as remote from 'popular consciousness' as a mathematician who had discovered a new law of Elliptical Functions. The present writer cannot go the whole distance with those who say that the Rule in Shelley's Case was merely 'made' out-and-out by judges; but its origin is certainly not to be found in mass-psychology. Yet it was no less the law of the land than Habeas Corpus, and might affect a citizen's rights no less. It is impossible to believe, in view of plain facts, that the *vox iurisconsulti* is necessarily the *vox populi*.

For here, as always, the judge is performing a function not merely subsidiary to the operation of law but inherent in its very nature. Law exists in order to be applied; and it must be applied through some human agency. If all men apprehended rules in precisely the same manner, if they were all at one about their rights and duties, there would be no need for legal exposition, and indeed little need at all for 'law', as that term is usually understood. But since unanimity is impossible, there arises very early in the development of law the necessity for analysis and application through the medium of the skilled, impartial interpreter. The veriest tiro in legal study is soon made aware how omnipresent the influence of the interpreter has been. It has not always been an influence for good; 'professionalism', both in ancient and in modern societies, has too often impeded progress and brought justice into disrepute. But in another and more characteristic aspect—in the devoted search after exactitude and the quest of justice for its own sake—the expert interpretation of the law has rendered incalculable service to mankind. The force and discipline of legal reasoning have not only been a constant attraction to commanding minds but have made the lawyer a model of that dispassionate thinking, clear vision, and nice appreciation of evidence, without which it is impossible to progress far in the orderly conduct of mundane affairs.

It is hardly necessary to dwell on the many examples in legal history of the potent effect which individual

Influence of jurists on development of law: examples

geniuses, or groups of geniuses, have had upon the development of law.[1] The very word 'jurist' at once suggests that remarkable group of men who, during the first two centuries of the Roman Empire, built an imperishable legal monument. It would be a grave exaggeration to say that the classical jurists made Roman Law, either ancient or modern. It cannot even be said, Savigny notwithstanding, that Roman Law itself was entirely indigenous. Nevertheless, the work achieved by the classical jurists, and the vitality of their influence, are among the most remarkable proofs in history that the indestructibility of matter is as nothing compared with the indestructibility of mind. Let us remember that they were a class of hard-working practitioners or officials—not rulers or prophets or demi-gods, not legislators except in a derivative sense, and not aided by any of the glamour of myth or fable. Yet for two thousand years they have never lifted their hands from European legal institutions. More than once it seemed that their influence had been destroyed by adverse circumstances. In the third century A.D., when Ulpian's work was done and there began for Rome a long period of disruption and decadence, it might well have seemed that the labours of the great jurists had been thrown away. In the fourth and fifth centuries Roman Law seemed to have fallen into a state of desperate confusion, only slightly remedied by successive attempts at codification on the part of both Romans and barbarians. He would have been a very bold prophet who could have predicted for the dead giants of the past the resurrection which they were to receive at the command of Justinian. The world's greatest codification is compiled, in by far its greatest part, from the learning of jurists dead two, three, four, and five hundred years. But even this resurrection seemed to have been of no avail. Darkness fell on the learning of the jurists, as on all learning, for

[1] The subject is brilliantly discussed in Pound's *Interpretation of Legal History*, ch. vi.

five hundred years. The flame of the classical tradition sank to a wan flicker with little promise of heat or light. Humble clerks just kept it alive with their encyclopaedias and glosses. And then, in Provence, in Lombardy, at Ravenna, and at Bologna, comes the second resurrection. Learning returns to the 'milk of the word', sterilized of the barbaric germs which have been infecting it for five centuries. Now, and for all time, the jurists' title to immortality is established. Not a single country in Europe has been unaffected by them, not even England, which was the least receptive of their influence. Our medieval law has a direct connexion with Bologna. Not only was Bracton largely indebted to Azo, but our 'English Justinian' visited the School of Bologna in 1273 on his return from the Holy Land, and took from it a legal adviser whom he entrusted with high offices of State. For seven years this Franciscus, son of Accursius, was to Edward I *familiaris noster*, *Juris Civilis professor*, and until shortly before the time of his death he was in receipt of a pension from his royal employer.[1] Who can estimate his influence on the opinions and decisions of our most famous lawyer king?

Our own law is impregnated with the influence of great expositors. Bracton's debt to Bologna is now generally admitted; our own debt to Bracton is owed not only for a treatise of capital importance on medieval law but in a large measure for the foundation of a system of precedents which, rightly or wrongly, has become an indispensable part of our system.[2] Littleton's task was no less than to make cosmos out of the chaos into which our land law had been gradually slipping for some 150 years. One trembles to conjecture what our law of real property might have become if this profound student had not grasped the principle that *lex plus laudatur quando ratione probatur*, and had not penetrated through a maze of technicalities to the 'arguments and reason of the law'.[3]

[1] Spence, *Equitable Jurisdiction*, i. 131.

[2] *Post*, pp. 187 ff.

[3] Holdsworth, *H.E.L.* ii. 573.

Justly Coke said of him that 'by this excellent work which he had studiously learned of others, he faithfully taught all the professors of law in succeeding ages'. Coke himself is a landmark, rugged but deep-set, on the high road of our law. To his strong personality we owe not only a harvest of untiring industry but an ideal of the Common Law and of the judicial office which is the bedrock of our administration of justice.[1] In the eighteenth century Blackstone, though lacking the originality of his great predecessors, rendered a remarkable service to the prestige of English law at a period when legal education was at its nadir. The success of his Commentaries is unparalleled in legal literature, and to this day we have not been able to replace them.

How far are jurists 'representatives of the people'?

These are but a few among many modern examples of the *pouvoir prétorien* of eminent jurists—a power which not even express legislation has been able to destroy.[2] To what extent can these craftsmen of the law be called 'representatives of the people'? Every man, be he genius or simpleton, is a product of his age. It is only by way of paradox that we speak of this or that great man being 'born before his time' or 'in advance of his age'. The greatest conceivable intellect can work only with the material which its environment vouchsafes to it, and can express itself only in language, and only

[1] Even Austin, who spared no great name his strictures, could not withhold a tribute from 'this most illustrious of our prudentes'; though, characteristically, he commends him for the very quality in which he is most lacking, 'the *coherence* of his mastery of rules': Lect. xxx. 563; *Codification and Law Reform*, Works, ii. 1130.

[2] The most famous example is Justinian's stern prohibition of all commentaries, glosses, and interpretations of the Digest: Introd. to Digest, *Const. Deo Auctore* (especially § 12) and *Const. Tanta* (especially §§ 19 ff.). C. 7. 45. 13 is sometimes interpreted as an attempt to put an end to all juristic interpretations; but see *post*, pp. 172 ff. In 1794 recourse to learned opinion and precedent was forbidden by the Prussian *Allgemeines Landrecht*, Einl., § 6: 'Auf Meinungen der Rechtslehrer, oder ältere Aussprüche der Richter, soll, bei künftigen Entscheidungen, keine Rücksicht genommen werden': a provision concerning which Gény (*Méthode d'interprétation*, ii. 60) justly observes that 'its very brutality prevented it from being taken literally'. On the unpopularity of jurists in the sixteenth century, see Vinogradoff, *Roman Law in Mediaeval Europe* (2nd ed.), 141 ff.

about things, which are intelligible to contemporary minds. It would have been as impossible for Ulpian to reform Roman Law by excluding slavery and admitting the modern principle of equality before the law as it would have been impossible for Littleton to introduce a system of land registry. Among judges and jurists, some are conservative and reactionary, some are innovating and long-sighted, some narrow, others liberal; but none can escape the actual circumstances in which he lives, or attempt to apply the laws of Utopia to existing society. In the material at their disposal, all produced by contemporary causes, the *Volksgeist* occupies an important place. Though it is always dangerous to dogmatize about national character, we shall not greatly venture if we say that the classical jurists of Rome could not have been so great had they not been born of, or assimilated by, a race with a peculiar genius for law, at a time when the fruits of that genius were ripe for harvest. But that is to say no more than is applicable to all the great spirits of history. We cannot on this account ignore the influence of individual minds. Julius Caesar and Napoleon assuredly were men of their age; but it would be affectation to pretend that by their individual genius they did not change the current of the world's history. This is equally true of the great jurists who have influenced the course of legal development at many times in many nations. Roman Law was, as to the great bulk of it, the creature of the Roman people, a system which no single individual or group of individuals could have invented of his own initiative; yet the great jurists of the Empire, by the force of their remarkable talents, gave to it a character which has had the profoundest consequences for European society. Only by a strain of language and of reason can we say that this was the handiwork of circumstances and not of men.

It goes, however, to the opposite extreme to say that custom is entirely the product of individual invention and not of social forces. It is true that many systems of

2. *Views of certain comparative jurists: Custom the product of* Juristenrecht

law have their tradition of the great lawgiver favoured by divine inspiration, or, at the least, endowed with preternatural wisdom, and thus possessed of a 'sanction' which leaves no room for doubt or disobedience. No reader of Maine needs to be reminded that ancient law is full of codes fabulously attributed to inspired legislators, but in reality consisting of collections of customary law known to and administered by a judicial or religious aristocracy. It is in the stage preceding these collections of written laws that Maine offers a more questionable theory. Maine, it need hardly be said, stood in line with the general doctrine of the German Historical School (though there is no evidence that he was directly influenced by it), but in his view of the origin of custom he diverges from it. Early in *Ancient Law* occurs the well-known passage:

Maine

> 'Custom is a conception posterior to that of Themistes or judgements. However strongly we, with our modern associations, may be inclined to lay down *a priori* that the notion of a custom must precede that of a judicial sentence, and that a judgement must affirm a custom or punish its breach, it seems quite certain that the historical order of the ideas is that in which I have placed them. The Homeric word for a custom in the embryo is sometimes "Themis" in the singular—more often "Dike", the meaning of which visibly fluctuates between a "judgement" and a "custom" or "usage".'

As Maine himself implies, a lawyer or historian trained in 'received' notions will find it difficult to swallow this piece of strong meat without at least a gulp. It has, on the face of it, the air of paradox in as great a degree as the *Rechtsbewußtsein* has the air of metaphor. The conservative student must be pardoned if he rubs his eyes a little at a statement like the following, made by a jurist later than Maine: 'It is doubtful whether, at all stages of legal history, rules laid down by judges have not generated custom, rather than custom generated the rules'.[1]

[1] J. C. Gray, *The Nature and Sources of the Law*, 297. For a vigorous

E. Lambert

The same view has been urged with much force by later students of comparative jurisprudence, and by nobody more thoroughly than Professor E. Lambert of Lyons.[1] French jurists, as has been mentioned, are on the whole not greatly preoccupied with the subject of custom, and, not unnaturally in view of the traditional legal methods of their country, they find it hard to reconcile themselves to any creative or formative function in the judge or jurisconsult. Lambert's thesis is a concentrated attack on this settled view. 'Jurisprudence', he writes,[2]

> 'is an indispensable propelling factor (*un propulseur*) in customary law, and it *propels to inevitable results*. It is enough to say that extra-judicial practice . . . ultimately conforms, with varying degrees of rapidity, to the directions which are imposed upon it by judicial practice, once that practice has become settled. When those who use the custom (*les interéssés*) are clearly convinced, through information supplied by men who are in touch with practical affairs, that there is no reason to suppose that the Courts will depart from the line of conduct they have laid down, they then adapt their own conduct to this jurisprudence, in the same manner and for the same reasons that they adapt themselves to rules laid down by the legislator. This is in no sense spontaneous consent, or essentially voluntary conformity, but obligatory resignation.'

The opposite view, which is based on the theory of the *consensus utentium*, is traced to Romano-Canonical doctrine, as exhibited chiefly by the Glossators and Post-glossators. Lambert holds it to be disproved by all the comparative evidence of known legal systems, and proceeds to examine that evidence with abundant patience and erudition. As an example of a contemporary society living under customary law, he takes England with her Common Law, and emphasizes the influence of judicial

statement of this doctrine as against Blackstone's 'immemorial user', see Bentham, *A Comment on the Commentaries*, 222 f.

[1] *La Fonction du Droit civil comparé.*

[2] *Op. cit.* i. 172. *La jurisprudence* has its usual sense of *judicial* learning, as opposed to enacted law.

precedent in 'general' custom and of judicial tests in 'particular' custom. He examines in turn Greek, Irish, and Indian law (following Maine), Hebraic, Mussulman, French, and Germanic, and gives special attention to custom in Roman Law, particularly the Twelve Tables and the *Juristenrecht* of the classical jurists. We must not follow him into all these researches, but we may state in his own words the general significance which he attaches to these many manifestations of the same influence. It will be seen that he ranges himself with Josef Kohler, whose copious work in comparative jurisprudence has been the foundation of much subsequent study.

'It is only by the protracted influence of arbitral or judicial decisions . . . that law becomes differentiated from ethics and morals; that it is crystallized in juridical rules (*normes*); that, slowly indeed, . . . it prevails over the notion of State guarantee, the sanction of social constraint . . . Jurisprudence remains not only the natural instrument for the development of customary law, but also one of the chief instruments which effect a necessary harmony between the variations of the social and economic setting and those legal systems which have been the subject of codes. Kohler . . . constantly returns to the principle that in every legal system, whether contemporary or in the historic past, a faithful examination of the theory of legal sources always reveals the presence, among the most productive agencies in law, of this essential element, *the creative force of jurisprudence*.'[1]

E. Ehrlich

Approaching the question with a sociological interest, Eugen Ehrlich[2] also laid great stress on the influence of the *Juristenrecht*. He devoted particular attention to the customary law of Rome. He maintained that, at least until imperial times, what the Romans understood by customary law was entirely *Juristenrecht*. The *ius privatum*

[1] *Op. cit.* i. 216 ff.

[2] *Beiträge zur Theorie der Rechtsquellen; Grundlegung der Soziologie des Rechts*. For a criticism of Ehrlich's views, especially concerning custom in Roman Law, see Vinogradoff, 'The Problem of Customary Law', *Collected Papers*, ii. 410, and *ante*, pp. 28 ff. See further Stone, *The Province and Function of Law*, 381 ff., and Friedmann, *Legal Theory* (4th ed.), 199 ff.

—'naturalia praecepta aut gentium aut civilibus'—was really, from the earliest times, only a part of the *ius civile*: and the *ius civile* means nothing more or less than *Juristenrecht*.[1] Until, therefore, the emperors take all law unto themselves, the jurists are the most important factor in developing the substantive law. And this is characteristic of all systems. *Mores et consuetudo*, Ehrlich maintained, cannot become law without the intervention of jurisprudence. But this jurisprudence is not to be considered either as the sole original source of customary law, nor yet as a mere inanimate intermediary. The cardinal error of the historical jurists, in Ehrlich's view, was that they did not distinguish between *legal rules applied by the Courts* (*Rechtssätze*) and *legal arrangements existing in society* (*Rechtsverhältnisse*, *Rechtseinrichtungen*). These are quite distinct, the one artificial, a product of human reason and logic, the other spontaneous and innate—e.g. family and property law, associations spontaneously formed in society, and the elements of contractual obligation. The function of the jurist is twofold: he must discover by his own investigation what are the existing streams of legal conviction in the community, and must then frame uniform generalizations for the arrangements actually existing in society. But the latter of these two functions has a technique of its own, a technique of reasoning quite other than 'conviction' and 'consciousness', which are in truth not technique at all; and it was because he did not realize this that Savigny frequently mistook for *Rechtsentwicklung* what was peculiar to the 'art' of the *Juristenrecht*. On the other hand, Ehrlich could not go as far as Beseler in entirely dissociating the *Juristenrecht* from the *Volksrecht*. There should be a fundamental accord between them; but it is certain that when the processes of juristic reasoning are brought into play, they will affect the character and very often the actual form of the usage arising out of the *Volksrecht*.

[1] Where a distinct branch of peculiar customary law is recognized, it generally means local law in the provinces: *Soziologie des Rechts*, 357.

English Common Law

This dualism in the development of legal institutions may be well illustrated from our own Common Law. More and more we have been compelled by historical research to modify those large claims which have been made from time to time—for example, by Blackstone—for the primordial popular indwelling of our basic legal principles. We have seen that every student of the Common Law constantly has to reckon with the large customary element which it contains; but it is equally well known to legal historians nowadays that the 'custom of the realm' was in a very large measure the custom of the courts, not of the people—*Gerichtsrecht* rather than *Volksrecht*. Blackstone, it is true, half-heartedly reproduces what Lambert calls the Romano-Canonical theory of the *consensus utentium*. Having explained that Ulpian's famous principle, *Quod principi placuit legis habet vigorem*, was always alien to English institutions, he continues:

> 'And indeed it is one of the characteristic marks of English liberty, that our common law depends upon custom; which carries this internal evidence of freedom along with it, that it probably was introduced by the voluntary consent of the people.'[1]

Serjeant Stephen[2] was careful to omit this hesitating passage: and Blackstone's best-known editor, Christian, enters a caveat against it, quoting Lord Hale to the effect 'that many of those things that we now take for common law, were undoubtedly acts of parliament, though not now to be found of record'. This is unquestionable; but what is even more certain is that 'many of those things that we now take for common law' were developed by the sovereign's judges. The cardinal fact in the settlement of our medieval law is the gradual domination of a permanent central tribunal over the jurisdiction of local courts. This process, beginning under Henry I, may be said to have become irresistible under Henry III; royal justice establishes approximate uniformity in essentials

[1] 1 *Comm.* 74. [2] *Comm.* (11th ed.), 59 f.

as against the bewildering diversity of local custom, and the supreme custom becomes the custom of the King's Court. There is still great variety of usages in manors, boroughs, and localities; but in what may be called the working basis of a general system of justice, the royal courts carry on, and have ever since continued, a perpetual process of reconciliation and harmonization, so that local divergences, though always respected and often jealously safeguarded, do not impair the symmetry of the main fabric. Beyond doubt, the greater part of this process of consolidation was the conscious task of the King's expert advisers.[1] Its effect has not been fully realized until modern times. Our old books, in the desire to generalize about the principles of the Common Law, are often naïvely unconscious of its artificial ingredients. For example, in the passage already cited[2] from *Doctor and Student*, St. Germain gives the following as examples of customs 'that properly be called the common law'—the system of courts and judicature; freedom from arbitrary imprisonment (as confirmed by Magna Carta); freedom and equality of justice; primogeniture and other customs of inheritance; certain feudal customs, such as wardship and marriage; feoffment with livery of seisin; the principle that a term of years is a chattel-real; distress for rent; trial by jury. Excepting perhaps the general principles of 'freedom', there is scarcely an item in this catalogue which cannot be traced to the direct influence of judicial practice, or—e.g. trial by jury—to a direct borrowing or importation. To take one example only, it might be thought that primogeniture is pure native custom. On the contrary, it seems to have been established as a general custom of the realm by the deliberate encouragement of the judges. It certainly did not occupy the position of a general custom at the end of the twelfth century, but seems to have been regarded as peculiarly appropriate to military tenures. Yet after the lapse of another century,

[1] P. & M. i. 86, 132, 161 ff., *et passim*.

[2] *Ante*, p. 73.

it had become the general rule of descent. The persuasive learning of the judge is not difficult to detect behind this development.[1]

3. Action and reaction of customary law and expert interpretation

Wherever we turn, then, we find this constant action and reaction between native customary law and the 'art' of the interpreter. It is exceedingly difficult to say where the one ends and the other begins; but it is certainly impossible, in the face of overwhelming evidence to the contrary, to regard the judge merely as a mechanical impersonal instrument for the application of self-sufficient customary law.

Are we, then, to accept Maine's view in its entirety, and see in the jurist and the doomsman the true fountain and origin of all customary law? The truth seems to lie between these two opposing views.

Custom of sociological origin: the jurist 'finds the law' but influences it

Many of Maine's examples in *Ancient Law* are taken from the highly instructive, but by no means conclusive, evidence of epic poetry. The broad general principle he states needs larger corroboration than this. Lambert covers a wider field; and in his insistence upon the creative power, in so many different circumstances, of *la jurisprudence*, he tends to undervalue a fact which he himself states in express terms. Customary law, he says, becomes crystallized in rules elaborated by interpreters;

> 'but the law itself already existed in the form of juridical sentiment, before the first instruments of arbitration were ever established; and it is this juridical sentiment, much more than the labours of arbitrators and judges, which settles the earliest series of precedents, from which springs juristic custom properly so called—a thing quite distinct from conventional usages or the usages of daily life.'

It seems quite impossible, however powerful the effect of interpretation may be, to picture any creative period in the growth of custom without presupposing this initial 'juridical sentiment' in the community at large. It may be vague and uncertain, capricious in its effects until skilled understanding has disciplined it into wieldy

[1] P. & M. ii. 262 ff.; cf. Pollock, *First Book of Jurisprudence* (6th ed.), 255.

forms; but it exists as the starting-point of all efficacious customary law. Maine made a notable contribution to jurisprudence when he emphasized the part played in primitive societies by the codification of customary law; but he certainly exaggerated the creative function of the codifier and the lawgiver. The very word 'lawgiver' is somewhat misleading. Again and again we find the hierophant of justice conceived not as the 'giver' but as the 'finder' of law. Even the semi-divine legislator, in whom we now see the codifier of existing law, is to primitive faith a receptacle of inspiration rather than an inventor of social rules. As for the doomsman, it is true, as Maine insisted, that his influence is to be found everywhere. We Anglo-Saxons have had our *witan;* the Frisians their *asegas*; Scandinavian peoples their *laghmen* and *lögsögumathr;* the French their *échevins*, the Germans their *Schöffen;* and it is the same among the Hindus and Brahmins, and all the priestly castes of Roman, Greek, and Celtic peoples. These are the 'learned in the law' to whom the community looks for enlightenment; but they are called upon not to make new rules for new circumstances but to apply, with special wisdom and skill, those principles which have been developed in social intercourse—crudely, perhaps, but substantially—by necessity, convenience, an elementary sense of justice, or pure imitation.

'Social customs themselves obviously did not take their origin from an assembly or tribunal. They grew up by gradual process in the households and daily relations of the clans, and the magistrate only came in at a later stage, when the custom was already in operation, and added to the sanction of general recognition the express formulation of judicial and expert authority.'[1]

Even in our medieval Common Law, though, as we have seen, the Royal Courts exercised a constant harmonizing and formative influence, the customs with which they had to deal were not mere inventions but rested on a

[1] Vinogradoff, *Historical Jurisprudence*, i. 363.

basis of pre-existing popular observance. Many of them were not peculiar to England but were characteristic of the feudal civilization of North-Western Europe; and a considerable part of the function of the judges was to ascertain by the best available evidence—particularly by the jury of recognition—whether an alleged custom did in fact exist in popular practice, and, if so, what was its precise nature and extent.[1]

Much, then, of Savigny's doctrine still contains an important lesson for modern students of law: there *is* a native law of the community, and its origins are to be found in sociological, not in artificial, elements. But in the development of this fundamental law, interpretation by constituted authority plays an indispensable part, and this in an increasing degree as the system of law develops into more complex but more settled forms. We must distinguish between the spontaneous social *Rechtsverhältnisse* which establish themselves by inscrutable processes in communities, and the learned and logical science of the *Juristenrecht*. The perpetual process of interpretation must inevitably produce an equally active metabolism in the subject-matter of usage. Customs become modified, sometimes to such an extent that they cease to exist. But always the jurist or the magistrate has to deal with practices derived in the first instance from actual social relationships. He never creates or invents custom, in the true sense of those words. The Austinian doctrine that custom is in no sense 'law' until a court or statute has ratified it, is too rigid and presents only part of the truth: though, upon Austin's premisses, it is a strictly logical, and indeed inevitable, conclusion. The exact relationship between custom and law we shall consider presently; meanwhile, let us note two distinct tributaries which ceaselessly flow into the main stream.

[1] See Vinogradoff, 'Some Considerations on the Methods of Ascertaining Legal Customs', *Collected Papers*, ii. 403. Cf. *ibid.* (ii. 410), 'The Problem of Customary Law'. Both these essays, though brief, are of capital value to the student of the nature and history of customary law.

For the most part, custom arises spontaneously from actual social practice, which soon acquires an imperative character through the forces of convenience, imitation, and instinctive traditionalism; but as judicial logic is brought to bear upon it—and this is very likely to happen as disputes arise in the course of time—new elements are necessarily added to it by the process of scrutiny and interpretation. Sometimes it remains substantially intact, sometimes it is so essentially transmuted that it seems to be the invention of the interpreter, and sometimes, though rarely, it ceases altogether to possess, or even to claim, an obligatory character.

II. APPLICATION OF CUSTOM

Custom contains its own legal validity

The scope of custom diminishes as the formulation of legal rules becomes more explicit and as a more elaborate machinery is set up for the making and administering of law. Though minor customs and usages spring up even nowadays, especially in commercial relationships, the great formative period of the more important customs belongs to the past. Ancient customs, however, are still an integral part of modern law, and the courts frequently have to deal with them. How do the courts regard them?

The primary function of modern judicial analysis is to examine the nature and reality of *existing* custom, not to invent new customs or arbitrarily to abolish those which are proved to exist in immemorial practice. In this respect English law is peculiarly instructive, because our courts have built up a system of well-defined principles for this task of judicial analysis. We shall find that the chief purport of these rules or tests is to determine whether the general and particular customs of our law are, *as a matter of established fact*, proved to be recognized social practice. Beyond this English courts seldom go, if ever; and it is, I submit, a mistake to represent modern judges as exercising any extensive critical faculty with regard to established usages. To this extent custom is still self-contained, self-sufficient, and self-justified law in England—that, in the main, with exceptions which will presently be noted, and which do not seriously affect the guiding principle, *if a custom is proved in an English court by satisfactory evidence to exist and to be observed, the function of the court is merely to declare the custom operative law*. In other words, the custom does not derive its inherent validity from the authority of the court, and the 'sanction' of the court is declaratory rather than constitutive. But in order to merit recognition, the custom has to satisfy certain tests, all of which tend in one direction—proof of the actual existence and operation of the custom.

It is *recognized* as law if it satisfies certain tests

Custom *exceptional* and *limited*

In approaching this subject we must first note two elementary and unvarying characteristics of custom in modern society.

First, every custom is in some fundamental respect an *exception* from the ordinary law of the land.[1]

Second, every custom is *limited* in its application. It does not apply to the generality of citizens, but only to a particular *class* of persons or to a particular *place*. Although it must always govern a plurality of persons—for there is no such thing as a custom inherent only in one person—the plurality must be restricted.

Legality

These two rules really amount to stating the same proposition in two different ways. A custom applying to all the Queen's subjects is not truly a custom at all in the legal sense, for, as Coke says,[2] 'that is the common law'.[3]

[1] Co. Litt. 113a; Com. Dig. *Copyhold* (S), 4; *Horton* v. *Beckman* (1796), 6 T.R. 760, 764.

[2] Co. Litt. 110b.

[3] *Fitch* v. *Rawling* (1795), 2 H.Bl. 393 (see *post*, p. 628), *Gifford* v. *Yarborough* (1828), 5 Bing. 163, per Best C.J. at p. 164; *Coventry* v. *Wills* (1863), 12 W.R. 127 (a case in which it was attempted to establish a right by custom 'in all the Queen's subjects' to witness horse-races on Newmarket Heath). In *Fitch* v. *Rawling*, *ubi sup.*, at p. 398, Buller J. observed: 'How that which may be claimed by all the inhabitants of England, can be the subject of a custom, I cannot conceive. Customs must in their nature be confined to individuals of a particular description, and what is common to all mankind

Customs, then, are *local variations* of the general law. But they must not be more than variations. They can never be set up against a positive rule of statutory law. If an Act of Parliament lays down that every pound avoirdupois throughout the kingdom shall be 16 oz.,[1] a local custom that every pound of butter sold in a certain market shall be 18 oz. is bad and unenforceable.[2] The London Stock Exchange, despite the express provisions of Leeman's Act,[3] has persistently refused to specify the serial numbers of the shares in a contract for the sale of banking shares;[4] underwriters have constantly disregarded s. 4 of the Marine Insurance Act, 1906, which provides that every insurer of a cargo or bottom must have an 'insurable interest' in the same:[5] but the courts could not, without bringing statute law into contempt, countenance such customs. If a statute plainly conflicts with a pre-existing custom, the latter is automatically abrogated.

Neither can a custom conflict with any fundamental principle of the Common Law.[6] It is one thing for a

can never be claimed as a custom.' On 'custom of the realm', see *ante*, p. 73, n. 2, and cf. *post*, p. 615.

[1] 13 & 14 Car. II, c. 26.

[2] *Noble* v. *Durell* (1789), 3 T.R. 271.

[3] 30 & 31 Vict., c. 29.

[4] *Perry* v. *Barnett* (1885), 15 Q.B.D. 388.

[5] *Cheshire* v. *Vaughan*, [1920] 3 K.B. 240. Similarly underwriters consistently ignored the construction which had been placed on the Life Assurance Act, 1774, by *Godsall* v. *Boldero* (1805), 9 East 72 (viz. that an insurable interest in a life policy must persist until the death of the assured), and this was one of the reasons, as Parke B. plainly stated, why *Godsall* v. *Boldero* was overruled in 1854 by *Dalby* v. *India and London Life Assurance Co.*, 15 C.B. 365.

[6] *Smith* v. *Lane* (1585), And. 191; *Peplow* v. *Rowley* (1615), Croc. Jac. 357. See Salmond, *Jurisprudence* (11th ed.), 246 n., where the term 'fundamental' is criticized as being too vague. It seems to me as expressive a word as any to indicate a rule of the Common Law which, in the opinion of the court, is definite and settled beyond any reasonable doubt or argument. There may, of course, be differences of judicial opinion, and differences of degree, on this point, but there are many rules or underlying principles of the Common Law which are so indisputable that they may be regarded as fundamental; see the observations of Parker J. in *Johnson* v. *Clark*, [1908] 1 Ch. 303, cited *post*, pp. 145 ff. and see *post*, pp. 293 ff.

custom to be a local variation of the general law, another for it to negate the very spirit of law. It is, as we shall see, sometimes a nice problem to decide which of these two effects a custom produces.

Proof of existence

As for the other recognized tests, they can be distinguished and classified by many different methods.[1] For convenience, and because they are the most commonly accepted, I adopt here those given by Blackstone, who follows in the main Coke on Littleton. It will be found that they all serve one main purpose, as has already been suggested—viz. proof of the existence of the custom. It is an ancient principle of our law that a custom, since it claims a privilege out of the ordinary course of law, is *stricti iuris*,[2] especially if it 'goes to the destruction of an estate'—i.e. derogates from vested rights of property.[3] Customs go back into distant ages; they are set up with various motives for the furtherance of various interests, and the initial problem is always to decide whether the custom prayed in aid has a good foundation *in fact*. This finding of fact is for the jury;[4] but the 'judicial tests' are applied as matter of law to determine in the first place whether there is any evidence on which the jury can find the custom proved. The question of fact, though the principal, is not the sole consideration. In a modern State, the court has power to say at once that the custom, even if proved to demonstration, is contrary to a subsequent positive rule of law, and must be discontinued. Further, it has always been laid down that the court has

[1] See Jethro Brown, *Austinian Theory of Law*, 315 ff.

[2] *Zinzan* v. *Talmage* (1680), Pollex. 561. The expression, as meaning simply 'requiring strict proof', is of course an inaccurate rendering of the Roman term *stricti iuris*. 'All customs which are against the common law of England ought to be taken strictly, nay very strictly, even stricter than any act of Parliament that alters the common law': per Trevor C.J., *Arthur* v. *Bokenham* (1708), 11 Mod. 148, 160.

[3] *King* v. *Dilliston* (1689), 3 Mod. 221, 224.

[4] 1 Bl. *Comm.* 75. See *ibid.* for the special and curious mode of proof for customs of London. It was at one time the practice that, in case of doubt, these customs should be certified by the Recorder, on behalf of the Lord Mayor and Aldermen. In *Day* v. *Savadge* (1615), Hob. 85 (*post*, p. 622), the issue was whether the custom alleged was to be tried by certificate or by the jury.

power to declare a custom, though proved in fact, unreasonable in its origin and no longer to be observed. As I shall attempt to show, this latter rule belongs to theory rather than to practice and has little effect upon the operation of custom in English law.

For the rest, the 'judicial tests' are only various modes of weighing the evidence for and against the existence of alleged customs. Let us consider them seriatim.

Antiquity

The first is that the custom must have existed from time immemorial, 'time whereof the memory of man runneth not to the contrary'. This, by its very statement, is purely a question of continuous, and therefore certain, existence. A mere habit, practice, or fashion which has existed for a number of years nobody supposes to be *ipso facto* an obligatory custom: antiquity is the only reliable proof of resistance to the changing conditions of different ages.[1] But antiquity is a relative term, and if it were applied as a test without qualification, every custom would necessitate indefinite archaeological research. Our law, therefore, has set an arbitrary limit to 'legal memory', fixing it at A.D. 1189, the first year of the reign of Richard I. This was established by analogy with the

[1] The learned editor (Dr. Glanville Williams) of the 11th ed. of Salmond's *Jurisprudence* (246 n.) objects that this statement is unconvincing, because in the nineteenth century alone conditions of life in England have changed more than at any other period, and it might fairly be supposed that a custom which had survived them for a long period had given sufficient proof of its acceptance and observance. I do not think that this affects my point that there must be, in the eye of the law, a difference between a settled custom and a passing vogue, and that some test of antiquity is therefore necessary. I am bound, however, to agree with Dr. Williams that the particular limit which English law has adopted—the year 1189—was not happily described by me in previous editions as 'arbitrary but convenient'. Arbitrary it obviously is; but it is true that in practice it is not convenient. I still hold, however—and Dr. Williams seems to agree, though for different and doubtless better reasons than mine—that *some* limit of time becomes imperative as the ages go on; and, short of some fiction such as was invented for prescription, it is questionable whether any limit which was adopted would not be arbitrary and to some extent inconvenient (though in practice, I think, not very often). With regard to Dr. Williams's criticism of my views on the reasonableness of custom, I have nothing to add to the supporting evidence which I have endeavoured to adduce in Appendix, *post*, p. 614.

period of limitation, fixed by the Statute of Westminster, 1275, for the bringing of Writs of Right. As time went on, the period dating back to 1189 became inconveniently long.[1] In the law of prescription, as is well known, a legal fiction was introduced that twenty years' uninterrupted user raised the presumption of a lost grant by the Crown.[2] This fiction, invented for prescription, did not apply to custom; for, as we have seen, custom involves a plurality of persons, and the notion of a grant therefore has no relevance, an indefinite number of persons not being 'capable grantees'.[3] If, then, a custom has existed for a long time (no uniform period can be specified for all cases) and there is no actual disproof of it since 1189, then there is a strong presumption that it has existed from time immemorial, and unless any other objection can be maintained against it, it will be upheld.[4] On the other hand, though the custom may have existed for centuries, yet on proof by fact or irresistible inference that it cannot have existed in 1189 it must be rejected. Thus in *Simpson* v. *Wells* (1872), L.R. 7 Q.B. 214, the appellant was charged with having obstructed a public footway by setting up a stall for the sale of refreshments. His defence was that he had done so by virtue of a custom existing at a 'statute sessions'—i.e. a fair held for the purpose of hiring servants and for proclamation of the current rate of wages. It was proved that the statute sessions were of great antiquity, having been held before the passing of the 5 Eliz., c. 4; and the custom of setting up stalls was proved to have been in force for at least fifty years. Statute sessions were, however, authorized by the Statutes of Labourers, the first of which was passed

[1] On the stages by which the prescriptive periods became established, see Holdsworth, *H.E.L.* vii. 343 ff.

[2] Lord Blackburn was of opinion that this doctrine did not finally establish itself till about the end of the eighteenth century: *Dalton* v. *Angus* (1881), 6 App. Cas. 740, 811 ff.

[3] *Constable* v. *Nicholson* (1863), 14 C.B.N.S. 230; Holdsworth, *H.E.L.* iii. 170.

[4] *R.* v. *Joliffe* (1823), 2 B. & C. 54; *Wolstanton, Ltd.* v. *Newcastle-under-Lyme Corpn.*, [1940] A.C. 860.

in the reign of Edward III. They therefore could not have existed in 1189, and the appellant's contention failed.

The onus of proof of antiquity is upon the person who sets up the custom. It may be a very considerable burden. 'Proof is required but it is hard to come by. The rules of evidence are liberal in matters of such antiquity, but they remain rules of evidence and, with every willingness to admit all such inferences as can properly be drawn, we must distinguish clearly between reasonable inference and plausible conjecture. The party setting up the custom must have the benefit of all legal presumptions, but he can take nothing by any resort to mere surmise, however ingenious, and his proof, though scanty, must still be "rational and solid".'[1]

Trade customs (usages)

A distinction is to be drawn between customs properly so called and *usages* of a particular trade, and also between customs and those local usages which are termed 'customs of the country'—e.g. those affecting the relations of landlord and tenant, and the reciprocal rights of incoming and outgoing tenants, and certain agricultural and mercantile customs. These are usually based on contract, express or implied, and the rule of immemorial antiquity does not apply to them; any long-established user, supported by notoriety, is sufficient.[2] On the other hand, the courts exercise a careful censorship over trade customs, which are frequently alleged. The courts must be satisfied of notoriety and acceptance among merchants, and this will not avail if the custom, even if proved, conflicts with a rule of law.[3] The custom must

[1] Per Lord Sumner, *Busby* v. *Avgherino,* [1928] A.C. 290, 294. See also *Iveagh* v. *Martin,* [1961] 1 Q.B. 232.

[2] *Dalby* v. *Hirst* (1819), 1 Br. & B. 224; *Goodwin* v. *Robarts* (1875), L.R. 10 Ex. 337; *Tucker* v. *Linger* (1883), 8 App. Cas. 508.

[3] Thus judges have repeatedly insisted on the delivery of the precise documents in a c.i.f. contract, as laid down in *Ireland* v. *Livingstone* (1872), 1 L.R. 5 H.L. 395: see *Manbre Saccharine Co., Ltd.* v. *Corn Products Co., Ltd.,* [1919] 1 K.B. 198; *Wilson, Holgate & Co., Ltd.* v. *Belgian Grain & Produce Co., Ltd.,* [1920] 2 K.B. 1; *Diamond Alkali Export Corpn.* v. *Fl. Bourgeois,* [1921] 3 K.B. 443.

also be reasonable—e.g., not contrary to natural justice.[1]

Continuance

Blackstone's next rule is that of *continuance*.[2] Interruption within legal memory defeats the custom. He draws a necessary distinction between the interruption of the *right* and of the mere *possession* of the thing over which the right is asserted.

> 'As if the inhabitants of a parish have a customary right of watering cattle at a certain pool, the custom is not destroyed though they do not use it for ten years; it only becomes more difficult to prove: but if the *right* be anyhow discontinued for a day, the custom is quite at an end.'

Thus discontinuance even for a long time will have no abrogative effect if the *right* has been confirmed by statute. In *Wyld* v. *Silver*, [1963] 1 Q. B. 169 1, a customary village right to hold a 'fair or wake' on the Friday in Whitsun week had not been exercised since 1875, but inasmuch as it had been confirmed as an 'ancient usage' by an Inclosure Act of 1799, it was held to have become a statutory right in perpetuity, which nothing short of an Act of Parliament could revoke. This test of continuity clearly goes to proof of existence. It is most improbable, almost inconceivable, that if a right truly exists by custom, it will be abandoned even for the shortest time by those who are entitled to the benefit of it. Hence we find Jessel M.R. saying that if the disturbance or interruption of an alleged custom has existed for any considerable period, a strong presumption arises that there never was any such custom at all[3]—a presumption, however, which, as we have seen, may be repelled by definite statutory provision to the contrary.

Peaceable enjoyment

The next rule is that the custom must have been enjoyed *peaceably*; and the right claimed must have been exercised *nec clam nec precario*—neither by stealth nor by revocable licence. It is sufficiently obvious that a 'custom'

[1] *London Export Corpn.* v. *Jubilee Coffee Roasing Co., Ltd.* (1958), 1 W.L.R. 661. On the whole subject of commercial usages, see Lord Devlin, 'Commercial Law and Commercial Practice', in *Samples of Lawmaking*, 28 ff.

[2] Co. Litt. 114b (s. 170): 'Continua dico ita quod non fit legitime interrupta': *ibid.* 113b.

[3] *Hammerton* v. *Honey* (1876), 24 W.R. 603.

which has only been wrested from the public by the strong hand is not a custom at all; for, as Blackstone observes, 'as customs owe their original to common consent, their being immemorially disputed, either at law or otherwise, is a proof that such consent is wanting'. A *secret* legal custom clearly cannot have any real existence, and so far as I can discover, no instance of such an anomaly has come before the courts.[1] The law is public, if it is anything. Nor can a 'custom' existing by mere revocable licence have any legal reality, since it depends on the will of an individual or group of individuals, not on public recognition or observance. In *Mills* v. *Mayor, &c., of Colchester* (1867), L.R. 2 C.P. 567, the owners of an oyster fishery had, since the time of Elizabeth, held courts at which they granted, on payment of a reasonable fee, licences to fish. Application might be made by any person within certain parishes who had been apprenticed for seven years to a licensed fisherman. The plaintiff possessed the necessary qualifications and was ready and willing to pay the fee, but the fishery court refused to grant him a licence. It was held that it could not be compelled to do so, since there had never been in the inhabitants of the parishes any enjoyment *as of right* so as to give rise to a custom.

Obligatory force

The three aspects of this rule therefore aim at determining whether the alleged custom has ever existed as a custom at all. It is further implied in the rule, and later expressly stated by Blackstone, that the custom must be supported by the *opinio necessitatis*. The public which is affected by the usage must regard it as obligatory, not as merely facultative. There is a difference between a habit and a legal custom. It is obligatory to wear clothes; it is not obligatory to wear flannels when playing cricket. On the other hand, it is more than a mere fashion which compels a barrister to wear wig and gown in court; the custom is legally compulsory, because if, without reason-

[1] *Barr* v. *Vandall* (1664), Ch. Cas. 30, cited in Vin. *Abr.* 188, for the rule that 'custom cannot be grounded upon fraud', refers to fiscal customs.

able excuse, the barrister ignores it, the court will not listen to him and he will be prevented from exercising his calling. Wig and gown are extremely irksome in certain temperatures, but counsel wear them in England before superior courts because they hold the opinion that it is *necessary* to do so. Again, says Blackstone, 'a custom that all the inhabitants shall be rated towards the maintenance of a bridge, will be good; but a custom that every man is to contribute thereto at his own pleasure, is idle and absurd, and indeed no custom at all'.

Certainty

Then the custom must be *certain*.[1] This is purely a rule of evidence. The court must be satisfied by clear proof that the custom exists as a matter of fact or legal presumption of fact. For the purpose of making and repairing grass-plots in their gardens and for the improvement thereof, all the customary tenants of a manor having gardens in their tenements claim a right by immemorial custom to carry away from the manorial wasteland 'such turf covered with grass fit for the pasture of cattle, as hath been fit and proper to be so used and spent every year, at all times in the year, as often and in such quantity as occasion' may require.[2] The Court rejects the custom. 'A custom,' says Lord Ellenborough C.J., 'however ancient, must not be indefinite and uncertain; and here it is not defined what sort of improvement the custom extends to. . . . There is nothing to restrain the tenants from taking the whole of the turbary of the common, and destroying the pasture altogether. A custom of this description ought to have some limit; but here there is no limitation to the custom as laid but fancy and caprice.'

[1] *Millechamp* v. *Johnson* (1746), Willes 205 *n.*; *Selby* v. *Robinson* (1788), 2 T.R. 758. In *Anon.*, Y.B. 12 & 13 Ed. III (R.S.), 236 (cited *Tanistry Case*, *ubi inf.*, at p. 33) a usage was set up that in Hereford a man could sell his land when he could measure an ell and count up to twelve pence; held void for uncertainty, 'for one person is twenty years old before he knows how to measure an ell, and another knows how when he is seven years old'. The Court was clearly unconvinced of the existence of any such custom as was alleged. Parker J. considered that in any case such a custom would be contrary to a fundamental rule of Common Law: *Johnson* v. *Clark*, [1908] 1 Ch. 303, 311 f.

[2] *Wilson* v. *Willes* (1806), 7 East, 121.

The Court clearly thinks it incredible that such a custom really exists. 'As laid', it is not a custom at all; those who claim the benefit of it have either misunderstood or exaggerated their rights. The true view is expressed by Willes C.J. in *Broadbent* v. *Wilkes* (1742), Willes 360, where he says that a custom must be certain 'because, if it be not certain, it cannot be proved to have been time out of mind, for how can anything be said to have been time out of mind when it is not certain what it is?' And to the same effect Jessel M.R. observes: 'When we are told that custom must be certain—that relates to the evidence of a custom. There is no such thing as law which is uncertain—the notion of law means a certain rule of some kind.'[1]

Consistency

'Lastly, customs must be *consistent* with each other; one custom cannot be set up in opposition to another. For if both are really customs then both are of equal antiquity, and both established by mutual consent: which to say of contradictory customs is absurd. Therefore, if one man prescribes that by custom he has a right to have windows looking into another's garden, the other cannot claim a right by custom to stop up or obstruct those windows: for these contradictory customs cannot both be good, nor both stand together. He ought rather to deny the existence of the former custom.'[2]

There does not seem to be much substance in this rule beyond the unquestionable truth that if two customs *in pari materia* (and presumably in the same locality or applying to the same persons) are manifestly incompatible, then one or the other is incorrectly called a custom. It

[1] *Hammerton* v. *Honey* (1876), 24 W.R. 603; see also *Blewett* v. *Tregonning* (1835), 3 A. & E. 554. In the *Tanistry Case* (1608), Dav. at p. 33, the reason given for the rule is that 'that does not lie in prescription which lies in the will of man, for the will of man is uncertain'.

[2] Bl. *Comm.* 78. 'When a man has a lawful easement or profit by prescription from time whereof, etc., another custom, which is also from time whereof, etc., can't take it away, for the one custom is as ancient as the other: as if one has a way over the land of A to his freehold by prescription from time whereof, etc., A can't allege a prescription or custom to stop the said way': *Aldred's Case* (1610), 9 Rep. 58, citing *Bland* v. *Moseley*. Cf. *Spooner* v. *Day* (1636), Cro. Car. 432.

remains for the parties concerned to prove by appropriate evidence which of the two really exists.

Reasonableness

The last and most difficult test is that of *reasonableness*. The true rule seems to be not that a custom will be admitted if reasonable, but that it will be admitted unless it is unreasonable.[1] This is not a mere distinction without a difference, for it seriously affects the onus of proof. The party who has proved the existence of a custom is not under the further necessity of proving its reasonableness; it is for the party disputing the custom to satisfy the court of its unreasonableness. The question of reasonableness is one of law for the court, not of fact for the jury.[2] The standard which the courts apply has been defined by a Divisional Court of the King's Bench as 'fair and proper, and such as reasonable, honest and fair-minded men would adopt'.[3] Brett J., with a characteristic leaning towards wide generalization, states the test still more broadly: 'Whether it is in accordance with fundamental principles of right and wrong.'[4]

Examination of the numerous cases in point leads to

[1] Co. Litt. s. 80. 'Every custom supposes a law, and if it be not irrational, and entertains no contradictions, it is good': per Vaughan C.J., *Collsherd* v. *Jackson* (1672), Freem. K.B. 63, 64. Cf. Keating J., *Paxton* v. *Courtnay* (1860), 2 F. & F. 131, and Parker J., *Johnson* v. *Clark*, [1908] 1 Ch. 303, 309, 311.

[2] Co. Litt. s. 80; 1 Bl. *Comm.* 77; *Bastard* v. *Smith* (1837), 2 Moo. & R. 129, 135.

[3] *Produce Brokers' Co.* v. *Olympia Oil and Coke Co.*, [1916] 2 K.B. 296, 298, following *Paxton* v. *Courtnay*, *ubi sup*. 'It seems to me that before the Court can say that a custom, not sought to be introduced against an ignorant purchaser, but known to both parties to the contract, is unreasonable, it has to say the custom outrages justice and common sense': per Rowlatt J., at p. 301. The matter in question was a commercial usage, but the same principle applies to all customs. For an example of a commercial usage which 'outrages justice and common sense', in the legal acceptation of *natural* justice, see *London Export Corpn., Ltd.* v. *Jubilee Coffee Roasting Co., Ltd.*, *ante*, p. 136. When a right existing by custom depends simply on supply and demand—e.g. a corporation's right to charge for 'stallages' in a market—no charge which is levied is *per se* unreasonable: *Att.-Gen.* v. *Colchester Corpn.*, [1952] Ch. 586.

[4] *Robinson* v. *Mollett* (1875), L.R. 7 H.L. 802, 817 (also a commercial usage).

the conclusion that the 'fundamental principles of right and wrong', upon which courts have held customs to be unreasonable, resolve themselves broadly into the following sets of circumstances:

1. On the facts of many cases, the question whether or not a custom is reasonable is indistinguishable from the question whether there is any evidence to go to the jury of its existence. Frequently the two aspects of the matter are treated as inseparable.[1] This is true when the custom or usage in question is alleged to be actually observed at the present time; it is also true when the courts have to determine whether a custom proved to have existed for some time past possesses the quality of immemorial antiquity. Its very nature, as alleged, may show that it cannot really have existed in the social and economic conditions of a distant age. Thus in *Bryant* v. *Foot* (1868), L.R. 3 Q.B. 497, the rector of a parish claimed that by custom a fee of 13*s*. was payable on the celebration of every marriage in the parish. The fee was shown to have been customary for forty-eight years, and it was argued that this raised a presumption of immemorial antiquity. But the Court, being at liberty to draw inferences of fact, had no difficulty in holding that in the reign of Richard I this fee would have been grossly unreasonable according to the value of money in the Middle Ages.[2] Here it is plain that the Court was really deciding that in the reign of Richard I the alleged custom did not in fact exist.

2. Sometimes the term 'unreasonable' is used of a custom or usage which is found to be contrary to statute or to a fundamental rule of Common Law.[3] In such a case it is really 'illegal' rather than unreasonable, and, as we have seen, is inadmissible.

[1] e.g. *Daun* v. *City of London Brewery Co.* (1869), L.R. 8 Eq. 155; *Nelson* v. *Dahl* (1879), 12 Ch. D. 568; *Gibbon* v. *Pease*, [1905] 1 K.B. 810.

[2] Contrast a case which followed that cited above, *Lawrence* v. *Hitch* (1868), L.R. 3 Q.B. 521, where the Court refused to apply the same reasoning to a toll of 1*s*. per cart-load levied on vegetables.

[3] e.g. *Perry* v. *Barnett* (1885), 15 Q.B.D. 388.

3. A custom or usage must be notorious, and cannot avail against a party who did not know, could not be expected to know, and was under no duty to know of its existence.[1] The courts constantly have to guard against the insinuation of usage into contracts for the benefit of one party only, especially in commercial causes. 'Customs of trade,' says Brett J.,[2]

'as distinguished from other customs, are generally courses of business invented or relied upon in order to modify or evade some application which has been laid down by the courts, of some rule of law to business, and which application has seemed irksome to some merchants. . . . When considerable numbers of men of business carry on one side of a particular business, they are apt to set up a custom which acts very much in favour of their side of the business. So long as they do not infringe some fundamental principle of right and wrong, they may establish such a custom; but if, on dispute before a legal forum, it is found that they are endeavouring to enforce some rule of conduct which is so entirely in favour of their side that it is fundamentally unjust to the other side, the courts have always determined that such a custom, if sought to be enforced against a person ignorant of it, is unreasonable, contrary to law, and void.'[3]

What is said of commercial usages (in which, however, this question most often arises) is true of all customs; hence the rule, already noted, that customs are to be regarded as requiring strict proof. A custom may be one-sided for the following reasons, aptly tabulated in Comyns's Digest:[4]

(*a*) If it be 'to the general prejudice, for the advantage of any particular person'.[5]

[1] Cf. the effect of custom on 'reputed ownership' in bankruptcy: *Re Horn* (1886), 2 T.L.R. 339; *Re Ford, Restall's Case*, [1929] 1 Ch. 134; *Re Ford, Powell's Case*, [1929] 1 Ch. 137.

[2] *Robinson* v. *Mollett* (1875), L.R. 7 H.L. 802, 817. Cf. *In re Goetz, Jonas & Co.*, [1898] 1 Q.B. 787; *Forres* (*Lord*) v. *Scottish Flax Co., Ltd.*, [1943] 2 All E.R. 366.

[3] See *Sagar* v. *Ridehalgh*, [1931] 1 Ch. 310; *Reardon Smith Line, Ltd.* v. *Black Sea &c. Insurance Co.*, [1938] 2 K.B. 730; *Forres* (*Lord*) v. *Scottish Flax Co., Ltd., ubi sup.*

[4] Tit. *Copyhold* (S), (s. 3), (ss. 13, 14, 15, 18).

[5] 'As, a custom that no commoner shall put his cattle on the common till

(*b*) If it be 'to the prejudice of any one, where there is not an equal prejudice or advantage to others in the same case'.[1]

(*c*) If it be 'that any one shall be judge for himself'; or, as it is more commonly put, 'that a man shall be judge in his own cause'.[2]

(*d*) If it 'imports a loss on one side, without a benefit in consideration'.[3]

These are elementary considerations of fairness; in applying them, and holding that a custom is unreasonable because it is one-sided, the court is saying in effect that it is not a custom at all, and there is a strong presumption against its ever having been a custom known and followed.[4]

4. It is well settled that the time to decide the reasonableness of a custom is the time of its origin.[5] Now it is said that if a custom has *not* a rational basis, but has 'resulted from accident or indulgence, and not from any right conferred in ancient times upon the party setting

the lord has put his cattle there; that no tenant shall marry his daughter till he pays a fine to the lord; that the lord shall take the cattle of a stranger levant and couchant upon the land, for his heriot; or shall take £3 of every stranger for a pound-breach; that a tenant shall be amerced if he does not put his cattle in the lord's pound.' All these examples are taken from the *Tanistry Case*, *loc. cit.* A few others are added from the Year Books.

[1] 'As, that the sheep of several owners upon the same tenement shall be counted *insimul*, and decimated; for one may pay all his lambs for tithes, and another nothing': *Barker* v. *Cocker* (1621), Hob. 329 (*post*, p. 616).

[2] 'As, that the lord shall detain a distress taken upon his demesnes, till fine made for the damage, at his will': *Tanistry Case*, *loc. cit.* Cf. Co. Litt. s. 212; *Wood* v. *Lovatt* (1796), 6 T.R. 511.

[3] 'As, that a lord of a manor shall have the best anchor and cable of every ship that strikes upon soil within his manor and perishes there, though it be not a wreck': *Geere* v. *Burkensham* (1683), 3 Lev. 85; *Simpson* v. *Bithwood* (1692), 3 Lev. 307. 'So, a custom that every ship which passes the river shall pay such a sum, because the City, etc., maintains a key for all goods unladen in the same city; for this does not extend to ships which do not unlade there': *Haspurt* v. *Wills* (1671), 1 Vent. 71. See, on these cases, *post*, pp. 619 ff.

[4] On the imposition of 'outrageous' tolls in the reign of Henry III, and the effect of the Statute Westminster I (1275) thereon, see Coke, 2 *Inst.* 220, and *Att.-Gen.* v. *Colchester Corpn.*, [1952] Ch. 586.

[5] *Tyson* v. *Smith* (1838), 9 A. & E. 406, 423; *Mercer* v. *Denne*, [1904] 2 Ch. 534, 557 (*post*, p. 616).

up the custom', there is then strong evidence that the custom is unreasonable and unenforceable.[1] It is not clear what is meant by 'indulgence' in this connexion, nor what is the relevance of 'conferring' (which presumably means granting) a right which arises by custom. As for 'accident', this cannot be considered a fatal objection to custom, for, as we have seen, it is impossible to find a specific and rational cause for every custom. These, therefore, do not seem to be valid grounds for rejecting a custom as unreasonable. The fact is that in the great majority of cases in which an ancient custom has been held to be unreasonable in its origin, it will be found that the real reason for rejecting it is that it was originally, or is now (or both), contrary to a well-established rule of law. When, for example, in the famous *Tanistry Case* (1608), Dav. 29, English judges, accustomed to the rule of primogeniture, had to consider the validity of the Irish Brehon law of succession, they were faced with the apparently barbarous rule that the property descended not to the eldest-born but to the *senior et dignissimus* of the blood and surname of the last owner. There was no doubt of the existence of the custom, the origin and purport of which, as Maine has shown,[2] the English judges did not fully understand. One of the chief reasons which they assigned for rejecting the custom as 'encounter the Commonwealth' was that in practice it destined the property not to the *senior et dignissimus* but to the 'most potent'—a moral argument against the triumph of might over right. But no modern reader can fail to detect in the case a deep seated prejudice against a custom which outraged feudal law by admitting a gap in the seisin, and by excluding daughters from the inheritance on the failure of heirs male; indeed, as Maine observes, 'the judges thoroughly knew that they were making a

[1] *Per* Lord Cranworth, *Salisbury* (*Marquis*) v. *Gladstone* (1861), 9 H.L.C. 692, 701, whereon see *Wolstanton, Ltd.* v. *Newcastle-under-Lyme Corpn.*, [1940] A.C. 860.

[2] *Early History of Institutions*, Lect. VII.

revolution, and they probably thought that they were substituting a civilized institution for a set of mischievous usages proper only for barbarians'.

Among the older precedents, the case just cited is the most authoritative, and is, indeed, the source of the chief learning in English law on the subject of custom. If we turn to a leading modern case on the same point, we find a similar view expressed in terms by an eminent Chancery judge. In *Johnson* v. *Clark*, [1908] 1 Ch. 303, a married woman, in order to secure a debt due upon a promissory note, purported to convey, by way of mortgage, to the creditor of the promissory note, certain property in which she had a life interest under her father's will. The conveyance was made with her husband's concurrence, but without any separate examination of the wife. The wife sought to have the mortgage set aside on the ground that without separate examination it was void in law. Against her it was contended that her estate was held in burgage tenure and that a local custom existed under which real property so held by a married woman could be disposed of by her with the consent of her husband without her separate examination and acknowledgement. Parker J. held that such a custom was repugnant to a principle of the Common Law vital at the time when the mortgage was made (though since abolished). Dealing with the question of reasonableness, he said:

'Looking at the matter apart from express authority, it is quite clear that for a custom to be good it must be reasonable or, at any rate, not unreasonable. The words "reasonable or not unreasonable" imply an appeal to some criterion higher than the mere rules or maxims embodied in the common law, for it is no objection to a custom that it is not in accordance with these rules or maxims. On the other hand, it is not the reason of the average human being to which appeal is made. Littleton says of customs: "Whatsoever is not against reason may well be admitted and allowed"; and on this Sir Edward Coke comments: "This is not to be understood of every unlearned man's reason, but of artificial and legal reason warranted by authority of law": Co. Litt. 62a. If this be so, it appears to follow that a custom to be valid must be such that, in the opinion of a trained lawyer, it is consistent, or, at any rate, not inconsistent, with those general principles which, quite apart from particular rules or maxims, lie at the root of our legal system.'

Conclusions as to tests of custom

The general effect of these tests of custom in English law, however they be classified, is a strict method of proof of a custom's existence. In the particular matter of reasonableness, the courts reserve to themselves a right to discountenance or abrogate a pernicious custom. 'Malus usus abolendus est' is an accepted maxim of our law.[1] But it is very rarely indeed that a court rejects a custom on the ground that it was unreasonable *in its origin*.[2] In holding the origin to have been unreasonable, the court nearly always doubts or denies the actual origin and continuance of the custom *in fact*. Further, the unreasonableness of a custom in modern circumstances will not affect its validity if the court is satisfied of a reasonable origin. 'A custom once reasonable and tolerable, if after it becomes grievous, and not answerable to the reason whereupon it was grounded, yet it is to be taken away by Act of Parliament'[3]—i.e. by nothing short of statute. But where the court finds a custom in existence which, either by aberration or by a change in law since its origin, not merely differs from but directly conflicts with an essential legal principle,[4] it has power in modern communities to put an end to the custom. In short, custom, once indisputably proved, *is law*; but the courts are empowered, on sufficient reason, to change the law which it embodies.[5]

[1] Co. Litt. s. 212.
[2] See Appendix, *post*, p. 614.
[3] 2 Inst. 664.
[4] Including a principle of public policy: *Johnson* v. *Clark*, *ubi sup.*
[5] See Excursus A, 'Custom as Law', *post*, p. 152. On judicial tests of foreign customs, see Excursus B, *post*, p. 157.

SUMMARY

To review our conclusions with regard to custom as a source of law: Legal custom is distinct from other social customs in that its obligatory sanction is complete and uniform. In early forms of society the conduct of men in forming legal relationships is governed by customary rules. These are recognized and followed as *law* independently of any 'sovereign' injunction or enforcement. It is a misunderstanding of the evolution of law and the conditions of primitive society to regard customs merely as 'positive morality' until they have been expressly ratified by some determinate law-making authority. The great majority of customs are non-litigious in origin, and depend for their rise and observance on *de facto* conduct and repetition. The importance of custom as a source of law is not entirely confined to the early stages of social growth; it has always been a primary factor in English law and is the basis of many of our most fundamental Common Law principles. It also repeatedly asserts itself in those foreign civilizations with which British administration of justice has to deal. Not only in English but in all civilized jurisprudence it has always been recognized as greatly influencing the development of legal institutions. Roman Law, though its theory in this respect was not entirely clear or consistent, attributed an important function to custom, constantly recognizing its effect both in substantive and in adjective law, though assigning to it a secondary position as compared with the supreme legislative instrument of the imperial régime. In modern jurisprudence, the Historical School of Germany found in custom the true source of all law, deriving it from the 'common consciousness of the people', or *Volksgeist*; and in the view of this school, law is valid and just only in so far as it makes known and embodies in concrete forms the inherent legal instincts of the community which it purports to govern. All law, therefore, according to this theory, should take its rise from, and so far as possible accord with, popular conviction; and the artificial manufacture of legal rules, without regard to popular consciousness, is based upon a fallacy which is certain to result in a breakdown of the practical workings of the law thus factitiously produced. This view needs modification, for it seems impossible to attribute all customs to a general conviction among the community of their necessity, rightness, and appropriateness. Customs are often the product not of a widespread conviction but of the convenience or interest of a ruling class which imposes its will on the majority of society. Many customs, again, are purely local in origin, and many are the result of mingled influences which cannot be called peculiarly popular or national. Further, it is necessary to distinguish between the inner and the outer manifestations of custom. In an embryonic state of social life it is not always possible to suppose that the concrete practice of certain customs is inspired by any conscious abstract feeling or motive. The *conduct* embodied in custom is the *corporate* action of an aggregation of individuals. In this corporate action rules and observances present themselves in tangible forms rather than as abstractions intellectually grasped and applied. Law is here a fact rather than an idea. In its earliest manifestations, therefore, custom grows by the force of practical example far more than by the impulse of reasoned conviction. The 'conviction', if any, which lies behind the majority of customs consists in the fact that there is usually some reason for them in practical necessity or convenience. This reason may not always be apparent at first sight, but can generally be discovered on closer investigation. But there are many customs which cannot be connected with any deliberate process of reasoned conviction and choice. Some consist of a selection between two indifferent alternatives: and the selection, once made, is followed and tends to become obligatory by repetition. Others, though originally prompted by some consideration of expediency, cannot become settled as rules without the establishment of some particular mode of observance, which is followed from motives of practical convenience rather than of rational apprehension. In these cases, and indeed throughout the whole operation of custom, a force of imitation, quite outside logical and utilitarian factors, exerts a powerful influence over men's minds, and is often responsible, fortuitously rather than deliberately, for the rapid and extensive adoption of particular customs. It is probable that the effect of this imitative fascination, which is of obscure psychological origin but is based upon the necessity for the individual to follow the line of least resistance in conforming to the ordinary circumstances of his environment, has been underrated in current theories of the compulsive force of custom.

Another perennial element in the consolidation of customary law is the effect upon it of judicial interpretation and application. As societies acquire recognized organs for the administration of justice, it is inevitable that an expert control should be exercised over real and alleged customary rules of law. History supplies abundant examples of a direct moulding influence on custom exercised by lawgivers, codifiers, jurists, and judges. This intervention of interpretation grows as society progresses; and it is impossible, on the evidence, to conclude that the interpreters are or should be merely mouthpieces of a popular instinct in the performance of their expert function. Interpretation becomes a technical, specialized science, and the personality of the interpreter is certain to invade and materially to affect the substance of the customary law with which he deals. The form, and often the content itself, of many customs which appear to spring from mere usage can in many cases be shown to be derived from technical rules evolved by interpreters and tribunals.

But custom must not be conceived as being purely a creation of judicial technique. The relation between indigenous customary law and technical treatment of it is one of action and reaction. The materials with which the interpreter has to deal are not manufactured by him; they grow spontaneously out of fundamental legal relationships and out of a certain characteristic habit of mind in the community towards law. The interpreter's task is to *find* these fundamental principles in the materials available to him. But in the process of 'finding' and applying, it is inevitable that he should impress his own personal cast of thought upon them; and in this way customs become radically affected, either by limitation or extension, in their treatment by expositors of law.

Yet, even in modern societies whose courts are the supreme interpreters of law, it is an essential characteristic of custom that it is not arbitrarily created by the jurisdiction of tribunals or any other determinate legal authority, but is scrutinized by them in order to test the actual observance and validity of the alleged custom as an existing rule of conduct. If satisfied by its scrutiny, the court recognizes the custom as being valid existing law obligatory for those who come within its ambit. In English law, which has a well-defined system of judicial examination in this matter, the tests established by Common Law precedents go to proof of the existence of the custom in dispute. As most, though not all, customs have a rational basis in utility and convenience, a custom satisfactorily proved to hold sway in fact is self-justified and recognized by the courts as good law.

Modern States, however, entrust their tribunals with a power of adjudging custom by standards of positive legality and public policy. No custom can be allowed to run counter to a fundamental principle of Common or Statute Law, though it may be an exception to it; and any custom which, though good in its origin, conflicts with a rule of law subsequently made, is thereby abrogated. Few if any customs are in this sense illegal, unreasonable, or mischievous in their origin; but, if a court should deem them to be so, or should hold them to be contrary to a legal principle later in origin than the custom itself, it has, and is bound to exercise, the power of suppressing the custom from thenceforth.

Existing custom is therefore law: if it is not called in question, it operates as part of the general law of the land: if it is challenged, and is proved to exist as a local variation of the ordinary law, and further is not shown to violate an essential general legal principle, it is recognized by judicial authority as good law. If it is not proved to exist, it is necessarily declared not to be law and to have no validity; and further, if, in rare cases, though proved to exist in fact, it is held to be mischievous in tendency, it is abrogated by the court and thenceforth is of no binding force.

EXCURSUS A

CUSTOM AS LAW

A learned critic, whose opinion carries great weight (Professor John Dewey, in *Columbia Law Review*, June 1928, p. 832), made the following comment on the view here advanced of the legal efficacy of custom:

'It might be retorted that while customs involving unity of social action precede dissensions and litigation, yet customs do not become laws in any juridical sense until they are authoritatively stated or formulated, and that the occasion of such statement is always a dispute. Customs themselves conflict, and the source of law may be in the need of adjudicating such conflicts rather than in the bare fact of customs themselves. In this case, a rule of law cannot be conceived as the *mere* reduplication in formal statement of antecedent custom, for it involves an element which is additive and in a sense, as viewed from the standpoint of prior custom, creative. To recognize a custom as authoritative and obligatory is to give the custom a new status; in a way it represents the beginning of a *new* custom. . . . The point of these remarks is that something happens when a custom becomes a law, and I do not find in Mr. Allen a clear statement of just what this something is.'

With the greatest respect for this very pertinent criticism, I am unable to see that the 'something' which happens when a custom is the subject of adjudication differs in any essential particular from what happens when any other rule of law is in question. We may consider two alternatives. First, a proposition of law may be rejected either because it is an incorrect formulation, or because, though correct, it is not applicable to the instant case. Similarly a custom may be rejected because it is not established as matter of fact, or because it is not applicable to the parties before the court, or because, though proved, it is held to be *malus usus*. Secondly, a proposition of law may be adopted as being both a correct formulation and applicable to the case in hand. Now this is seldom a '*mere* reduplication' of the rule, since its application to new circumstances always gives it a new facet: there is thus, in nearly every decision, 'an element which is additive and in a sense . . . creative'. The mere fact that a rule is reasserted in a fresh setting reinforces and clarifies it, or throws new light upon it, and this element is 'additive'. I regard all judicial interpretation as necessarily 'additive and creative' in this sense, though I think it misleading (see *post*, pp. 307 ff.) to call this, without qualification, 'judicial legislation'. What applies to the adoption and application of Common Law rules seems to me to apply with equal force—neither more nor less—to the adoption and application of custom. I do not think it is open to reasonable doubt that when a court accepts and applies a custom, it does so not in the belief that it is introducing a new rule into the law, but in the belief that it is declaring and applying what is already the law. The only substantial difference, so far as the judicial process is concerned, between the adoption of Common Law and customary rules is one of adjective law. Custom is subject to its own methods of proof, which long since have been rubricated under well-defined heads. There is an evident reason for this, in the nature of the case. Custom is not usually matter of record, and has to be proved from practice—frequently ancient practice, not easily demonstrable; whereas rules of Common Law, however general and 'immemorial', are always to be found in some kind of formulation, whether in decisions, dicta, or commentaries. Further, custom, being local and therefore an *exception* from the general law, is under a special onus of proof. A confirmatory judgement of a court is certainly, therefore, an added strength to any custom; it is 'additive' in the sense that it reinforces the custom by setting at rest any doubts which may arise, in the course of time, about its origin, extent, and practice; and hence it is not surprising to find that at an early date, when custom formed a considerable part of local law, the *utentes* were always glad to have their customs confirmed by judicial declaration.[1] But matters of evidence and 'tests' clearly relate to procedure only, and do not affect the substantive question of inherent validity.

A more serious difficulty, in my judgement, lies in the fact that a court, though satisfied of the existence of a custom, may nevertheless reject it as being mischievous or contrary to the general policy of the law. We have seen that the maxim *malus usus est abolendus* is of very limited scope: it is, indeed, difficult to find in our books clear examples of its application: nevertheless, it is certainly part of the doctrine of our law with regard to custom. It is no quibble to ask: Can a rule which the courts claim power to reject or suppress properly be described as a rule of *law*? It is the business of courts (it may be argued) to accept and apply actual rules of law whether they approve of them or not. It is true that in the course of ages rules of law, which were appropriate at one epoch, become so modified or attenuated by judicial interpretation that they cease, to all intents and purposes, to be operative at another epoch; but no court claims an explicit right of general censorship concerning the expediency

[1] This is well illustrated by a case in the Eyre of Kent in 1313 (Y.B. 6 & 7 Ed. II (S.S. v), 18), which shows that the inhabitants of Kent were anxious to settle any doubt about their customs of gavelkind:

'*Passeley*. Sir, these good people are in the County of Kent, and they have divers customs of Gavelkind which differ from the common law, which customs they have enjoyed from time immemorial; and they pray you that you will, if it so please you, confirm these their customs; which customs, indeed, are of such diverse kinds that a man may not bear them all in his mind, and so here we tender to you inscribed on an escrowet some part of these customs; and the rest of them we pray you to allow when any question concerning them shall arise, according to the testimony of those who shall appear before you.

'STAUNTON J. Hand us your bill, for we understand that all the customs are mentioned therein.

'*Passeley*. That is not so; but we pray you to allow those therein mentioned, and others when question concerning them shall arise.

'STAUNTON J. It is desirable that all of them should be certainly set out; so take back your escrowet, and, after full consideration of the matter, insert therein the whole of your customs; and such of them as we find you have actually enjoyed and have also been allowed in Eyre, we will freely confirm to you now; for you may rest assured that you will be shorn of nothing to which you are entitled; and of that you need entertain no doubt.'

of rules of Common Law, whereas our courts do claim (though they rarely exercise) a certain degree of censorship over customary rules, and even more over commercial usages. It is undeniable that to this extent customary law stands in a peculiar position, and possesses less than the full validity of Common Law rules. This being admitted, the matter then becomes one of definition. If we insist, as Austin did, that nothing is entitled to the name 'law' which does not possess *all* the attributes of State-created and State-enforced law, then it is true that we are bound, in logic, to say either that customary law is not law at all, or that it is 'imperfect' or 'inchoate' law. To my mind, this is pedantic and unprofitable. Law may be, in every reasonable sense of the word, law though it does not accord with every aspect of an *a priori* definition of law. Few jurists would deny that the term 'law' can properly be applied to International Law, or would insist, because of certain obvious deficiencies, on calling it mere 'positive morality'. The difference between customary law and ordinary Common Law is infinitely less than that between international and municipal law, and I do not believe that it is sufficient, either in quantity or quality, to warrant our confusing a comparatively simple issue by placing custom in a special category of 'imperfect' or 'inchoate' law. No contradiction or fallacy is involved in the use of the plain term 'customary law'—a body of law within the framework of the Common Law—if we remember that in one not very important particular (i.e. the limited censorship of the courts) it differs from the remainder of the Common Law. It differs also, I would repeat, in methods of proof, but that does not affect its substance.

It is further to be remembered that the rejection of a proved *usus* on the ground that it is *malus* is really an application of the doctrine of public policy (see *Johnson* v. *Clarke*, *ubi sup.*). It is now generally recognized, especially since the decision in *Nordenfelt* v. *Maxim-Nordenfelt Co.*, [1894] A.C. 535, that public policy is 'the policy of the day'—i.e. that its standards change from age to age in accordance with the prevailing notions and the social institutions of the time.[1] Consequently, there is nothing anomalous in the fact that an ancient custom may be declared inexpedient according to the public policy of a later age. The surprising thing, indeed, is that this happens so infrequently; in actual practice, policy can seldom be invoked with regard to customs, even the most ancient; for, as we have seen, a custom is not to be rejected merely because it is 'unreasonable' in the sense that, the original occasion for it having disappeared, it is inappropriate in modern conditions. It is not *malus* merely because it is an erratic exception to the general law, but only if it is so violent an exception, to the advantage of a small class of persons that it clashes irreconcilably with a principle which it is the policy of the law to apply to all persons whatsoever.[2] Indeed, there is much ground for saying that the control or censorship of the courts is far narrower in respect of customs, which sometimes have nothing to commend them but an accidental antiquity, than it is in respect of those many rules of the Common Law (especially in torts) which are constantly being adapted and developed by the judiciary in accordance with changing social needs.

[1] See *Fender* v. *Mildmay*, [1938] A.C. 1.

[2] See Littleton J. in *Grimesby's Case* (1456), Y.B. 35 H. VI. 25, Mich. pl. 33 (see *post*, p. 631): 'If writ of trespass of battery be brought against a man, who comes and says that the custom in the place where the trespass [was committed] is, and has been from time, etc., that if anybody comes on the land in such place, it will be legal for him to beat [the trespasser]: and [he says] that the plaintiff came there, and he beat him as much as he liked, and therefore he asks for judgement: this plea fails, for the custom is wholly against reason.'

EXCURSUS B

JUDICIAL TESTS OF FOREIGN CUSTOM

Some brief observations have been made (pp. 77 ff.) on the importance of Eastern custom to English lawyers. The judicial tests which have been frequently applied to such customs by English courts are substantially the same as those which have established themselves in the English Common Law,[1] and which are discussed above; and it is submitted that here too the tests all tend in the same direction—viz. proof of the actual existence of the custom *de facto*. 'What the law requires,' the High Court of Madras has laid down, 'before an alleged custom can receive the recognition of the Court, and so acquire legal force, is satisfactory proof of usage so long and invariably acted upon in practice as to show that it has by common consent been submitted to as the established governing rule of the particular family, class or district or country'; and the Judicial Committee adds, in the same case on appeal: 'Their Lordships are fully sensible of the importance and justice of giving effect to long-established usages existing in particular districts and families in India, but it is of the essence of special usages, modifying the ordinary law of succession, that they should be ancient and invariable; and it is further essential that they should be established to be so by clear and unambiguous evidence. It is only by means of such evidence that the Court can be assured of their existence, and that they possess the conditions of antiquity and certainty on which alone their legal title to recognition depends.'[2]

[1] Trevelyan, *Hindu Law* (2nd ed.), 28; J. D. Mayne, *Hindu Law and Usage* (8th ed.), 56 ff.; Roy, *Customs and Customary Law in British India*, 24, and cases there cited.

[2] *Sivanaranja Perumal Sethurayar* v. *Murthu Ramalinga Sethurayar* (1866), 3 Mad. H.C. 75, 77; S.C. on appeal, *sub nom. Ramalakshmi Ammal* v. *Sivanantha Perumal Sethurayar* (1872), 14 Moo. I.A. 570.

But it is clear that when a dominant people is dealing with the customs of a different civilization and of different religions, the tests of reasonableness, morality, and public policy must be looked at from an angle somewhat different from that which would be appropriate in the conditions of English society. In general, British administration has endeavoured to leave indigenous customs intact, however alien they may be to Western and Christian nations; but where they are considered to violate elementary considerations of humanity and decency, they are either rejected by the courts or, more frequently, suppressed by legislation. The best-known example is that of the *suttee* which, as early as 1829,[1] the British Government found it necessary to forbid. Similarly, the practice of adopting females under the age of sixteen as dancing-girls in pagodas was held to constitute the offence of procuring minors for prostitution under the Indian Penal Code, ss. 373 and 383.[2] In English society there is, as a rule, not much doubt about the accepted standard of morality; but for the European in Eastern communities it is sometimes difficult to determine what the true morality of the situation is—to preserve the balance between a wise tolerance and an insistence on axioms of civilized corporate life. On the whole, the British courts have applied only those principles of morality which they consider to be common to all civilized peoples, without giving them a dogmatically Occidental—and of course not necessarily a Christian—colouring.[3]

[1] By Reg. XVII of that year. See Vinogradoff, *Historical Jurisprudence*, i. 236.

[2] For other examples of customs which have been held immoral or contrary to public policy, see Trevelyan, *op. cit.* 31, Roy, *op. cit.* 556 ff., and J. D. Mayne, *op. cit.* 62 ff. They are chiefly concerned with marriage and prostitution.

[3] At first sight, some of the decisions in this matter seem to force English notions on foreign institutions, rather in the spirit of the *Tanistry Case* (*ante*, p. 144). Doubtless in England a contract by which a prospective bridegroom promised to pay a consideration to the father of the prospective bride would he held contrary to public policy; but there seems to be no reason why this interesting relic of marriage by purchase, as practised among some Hindus,

Again, it is clear that some of the more artificial tests recognized in English law would be quite inappropriate in other surroundings. A 'legal memory' dating from the first year of Richard I would have been meaningless in India; accordingly, judicial decisions established an equally arbitrary but more convenient period for the antiquity of Indian customs.[1]

As to the methods of proving custom, where local rules of evidence existed and were recognized by British courts, they were taken as valid in establishing the existence of custom, however greatly they might differ from English rules. Notable among these was the *Wajib-al-urz*, a collection of village administrative documents made in pursuance of Reg. VII of 1882, regularly entered up, kept in the office of the Collector, and authenticated by the signatures of the officers who made the entries. It served as a record of general customs as well as of individual proprietary rights in villages; it was admissible as evidence under the Indian Evidence Act, and was accepted by the courts as *prima facie* evidence of a custom: see Roy, *op. cit.* 97, 81, and *Musammat Lali* v. *Murli Dhar* (1906), 22 T.L.R. 460.

While these examples from our former jurisdiction in India belong to a régime now past, the principles which they illustrate are still, in the main, characteristic of our approach to exotic customs wherever they fall within the world-wide scope of our legal systems. While the Privy Council no longer has jurisdiction over Indian causes, problems of Hindu and Muslim law are among

should be shocking to the English conscience; but it was disallowed by the courts. However, the true ground for the rejection would seem to be that the alleged custom, even if proved, would be expressly contrary to the Manu Code itself (Roy, *op. cit.* 558 ff.). In one case at least, the Judicial Committee seems to have been prepared to apply the peculiar principles of English trusteeship to the guardians of a temple; but here again the principle involved appears to be that of common honesty rather than of technical equity: *Vurmah Valia (Rajah)* v. *Ravi Vurmah Mutha* (1876), L.R. 4 I.A. 76, 85.

1 *Doe d. Jagomohan Rai* v. *Srimati Nimu Dasi*, Montriou's Cases in Indian Law, 596; *Garurudhwaja Parshad Singh* v. *Saparadhwaja Parshad Singh* (1900), L.R. 27 I.A. 238.

the many which still arise in various dependencies. Over the whole extent of the Colonial Empire the variety of indigenous customs is enormous, and a complete survey of them, if the huge labour which it would involve could be accomplished, would be a unique contribution to comparative law. British Africa alone presents a vast miscellany of tribal customs which constantly engage the attention of judges, magistrates, and administrative officers. This, however, is a specialist field on which the present writer is not qualified to enter, but for guidance concerning the general principles which have established themselves in it, the reader is referred to a valuable article on 'The Judicial Ascertainment of Customary Law in British Africa', by Dr. A. N. Allott, 20 *M.L.R.* (1957), 244.[1]

[1] The literature at present is scanty, but see J. Lewin, 'The Recognition of Native Law and Custom in British Africa', 20 *J.S.C.L.* (1938), 16; 'R. C. T.' on *Mokhatle* v. *Minister of Native Affairs* (1926), 42 *L.Q.R.* 154 (an interesting case on the meaning of 'civilization' in relation to custom); and other references given by Dr. Allott. Max Gluckman, *The Judicial Process among the Barotse*, contains *passim* much valuable material and reflection on customary law in a part of Northern Rhodesia. Examples of the wide jurisdiction of the Privy Council over native African custom may be found in *Eshugbayi* v. *Government of Nigeria*, [1931] A.C. 662 ('barbarous' custom); *Tschekedi Khama* v. *Ratshosa*, [1931] A.C. 784 (custom 'contrary to peace, order, and good government'); and *Inasa* v. *Oshodi*, [1934] A.C. 99 (a 'border-line' custom).

III

PRECEDENT: NATURE AND HISTORY

I. THEORY OF JUDICIAL DECISION

THE process of judicial decision may be regarded as either *deductive* or *inductive*, and the function of the judge will differ widely according as the one or the other of these two views is adopted.[1]

1. Two opposing views—deductive and inductive methods

The first theory, associated principally with codified systems, assumes that the legal rule applicable to any particular case is fixed and certain from the beginning, and all that is required of the judge is to apply this rule as justice-according-to-law demands, without reference to his own personal view. His decision is deduced directly from general to particular—from the general legal rule to the particular circumstances before him. He is not necessarily influenced by the deductions of other tribunals; it is to the stable general principle that he owes his allegiance in all circumstances, not to the possibly unstable interpretations of others. It follows that no individual decisions contain any future authority in themselves. They are not, however, without value and it is no part of the judge's duty to ignore them. It has never been claimed, even in the most rigidly codified systems, that the judge should shut his mind to the reasoning of others in like circumstances. No intelligent system would so crudely paralyse the indispensable instruments of analogy and parity of reasoning. Hence in all systems some degree of judicial uniformity is certain to exist and even to be applauded. But great care is taken to 'save' the fundamental rule that uniformity, however

[1] But see Lord Wright, *Cambridge Law Journal*, 1943, p. 124. Lord Wright's objection to the term 'inductive' seems to be based on associating it (unnecessarily, as, with respect, it seems to me) with the technique of natural science rather than with that of logic. See hereon Paton, *Jurisprudence* (2nd ed.), 150 ff., and Cross, *Precedent in English Law*, 202 ff.

convenient, shall not degenerate into a line of least resistance; it must remain a guide, and never become a tyrant. In this theory, the magistrate can never dispense himself from his own individual duty, whatever the opinions of others, of applying the relevant rule of law and justice which is incumbent upon him.

The second theory, characteristic of English law, starts with the same primary object of finding the general rule applicable to the particular case; but its method is wholly different. It does not conceive the rule as being applicable *directly* by simple deduction. It works forward from the particular to the general. Where the French judge has to find his master principle in formulated propositions of abstract law, the English judge has to search for it in the learning and dialectic which have been applied to particular facts. Thus he is always reasoning inductively, and in the process he is said to be *bound* by the decisions of tribunals higher than his own. In the one theory, antecedent decisions are helpful only as illustrations of a general proposition; in the other, they are the very soil from which the general proposition must be mined.

Different though these two theories seem to be in conception, in application they are not, as I shall attempt to show, as widely divergent as might be supposed. In one common case they are not, or ought not to be, really different in conception at all. When the English judge has to apply a *statute*—and this nowadays is a great part of his task—he is, it would seem, in much the same position as the Continental judge who has to apply a code. But here too—so deeply rooted is our principle of judicial analogy—our judges are governed by precedents of interpretation. An English statute is not very old before it ceases to be a dry generalization and is seen through the medium of a number of concrete examples. The result is often startlingly different from what the enactment would seem to have intended.

There is some plausibility in the view that ideally

every judicial decision should be the direct deduction of rule to fact. Admit the unrestricted force of example, it is urged, and you open the door to all the vagaries of infinite circumstances. Detached theorists like Hobbes, Bentham, and Austin have therefore not been slow to expose what they deem to be the fallacy on which our judicial reasoning rests. The system is certainly less than ideal; but in greater or less degree, whatever austere critics may say, practice shows it to be inseparable from any efficient administration of justice. The English are peculiar only in that they have admitted it more frankly, deliberately, and fully than most other peoples. This is, perhaps, not a mere accident of legal history; those who are curious to speculate about such matters may see in it a characteristic national tendency to compromise between abstract logic and practical stability. The same poet who wrote impatiently of

> the lawless science of our law,
> That codeless myriad of precedent,
> That wilderness of single instances,[1]

also wrote of a land

> Where Freedom slowly broadens down
> From precedent to precedent.

2. Precedent in Roman Law

This is often thought to be one of the characteristic points in which we have parted company with Roman tradition. Though this is true in the main, we must not suppose that the influence of precedent was entirely foreign to Roman Law. It was a commonplace with the Orators, and especially with Cicero, that the *res iudicata*, or the *iudicatum*, was an integral part of the civil law, along with statues, *senatusconsulta*, *iurisperitorum auctoritas*, magisterial edicts, custom, and equity.[2] In the

The Orators

[1] Tennyson, 'Aylmer's Field'.

[2] *Top.* vi. 28. Cf. *De Inv.* ii. 22, 67–68, where *aequitas* becomes *par*, and is classed with *pactum* and *iudicatum* as a branch of *customary* law. Cf. *De Or.* ii. 27, 116 and *De Leg.* i. 16, 43. Collinet ('Le Rôle des juges dans la

Auctor ad Herennium,[1] *iudicatum* appears in a slightly different list of sources—*natura*, *lex*, *consuetudo*, *iudicatum*, *aequum et bonum*, *pactum*—and is defined as 'id de quo sententia lata est aut decretum interpositum'. We must not, however, understand *res iudicata* here as corresponding in any true sense with modern 'precedent'. It means a decision given in a particular case and conclusive as between the parties to that case—a source of law only in the sense that it lays down the law finally in regard to a specific matter in issue.[2] It was not conceived as a permanent contribution to the general body of law, and its inclusion, like that of *pactum*, with such sources as *lex*, *consuetudo*, and *aequum et bonum* is due to a confusion of thought. There is no suggestion, even in the Orators, of any strictly 'binding' principle; and the Auctor ad Herennium makes special reference to the disparities of decisions—'ut aliud alii iudici, aut praetori, aut consuli, aut tribuno plebis placitum est'—giving examples from actual cases. Much, then, he says, must depend on the personality and reputation of the judge, the circumstances of the time, and the number of decisions in the same sense. But while these reservations preclude the strict authority of precedent in the modern sense, they do not necessarily mean that individual decisions were quite without effect on subsequent practice.

And, indeed, they could hardly be so in a system in

formation du Droit romain classique', in *Recueil d'études sur les sources du Droit en l'honneur de François Gény*) takes *res iudicata* and *iudicatum* in these passages as equivalent to the modern 'precedent'; *sed quaere*.

[1] ii. 13, 19.

[2] In reference to the revocation of judgements and decrees once given, it is used by Cicero when he deprecates 'iudiciorum perturbationes, rerum iudicatarum infirmationes' (*De Leg. Agr.* ii. 4, 10; cf. *Verr.* v. 6. 12, and Mommsen, *Strafrecht*, 482), and when he pours scorn on the *ius Verrinum* of Verres: 'alias revocabat eos inter quos iam decreverat decretumque mutabat, alias inter aliquos contrarium sine ulla religione decernebat ac proximis paulo ante decreverat' (*Verr.* i. 46. 120). *Res iudicata* has this technical sense regularly in the Corpus Iuris: thus Ulpian's well-known 'res iudicata pro veritate accipitur' (D. 1. 5. 25), and cf. D. 42. 1. 1 and 44. 2, and the 'exceptio rei iudicatae' (Roby, *Roman Private Law*, ii. 388). The principle is what we should call 'estoppel by matter of record'.

Praetorian and juristic law

which the praetorian edict played so vital a part. There could be no more instructive example than this of a whole body of law built up by judicial practice. The exact stages of its development are hidden from us: it differed, we need hardly say, in many essential respects from what we now understand by case-law; but it could not have attained its maturity except upon a recognized principle of judicial uniformity—though subject, unlike English precedents, to periodical recension. The praetor's duty of adhering to the principles announced in his edict, though it probably began as a mere convention, became statutory after the Lex Cornelia of 67 B.C.;[1] and it ensured to the public not only consistency during the magistrate's own term of office but continuity in the whole *ius honorarium*. It may well be that the very system of formulary procedure, which eventually supplanted the archaic forms of action, grew up *de facto* by praetorian practice and passed, by confirmatory statutes, into *de jure* validity, with well-known and profound effect upon the civil law. Side by side with this elaborate system of judge-made law is an equally elaborate system of jurist-made law. Whereas the English law has been built up by the Bench, it has been well said that a great part of Roman Law was built up by the Bar.[2] Though this jurist-made law was couched in the form of opinions and succinct statements of principles, much if not most of it was probably based upon the facts of actual cases, and, having been first regulated by the *ius respondendi* and the Law of Citations, and then finally embodied in Justinian's codification, it was in essence a vast body of case-law made authoritative by the selection and revision of masters of the law. It goes without saying that the Emperor's own *responsa* were nothing but summarized 'leading cases'; and these again were in no small measure

[1] Though this statute may have been of merely temporary effect: see Krüger, *Gesch. der Quellen des röm. Rechts*, 32, n. 7.

[2] Maine, *Ancient Law*, 39. 'Bar' is, of course, only a loose analogy to the Roman jurists.

'built up by the Bar', since they were largely the product of the Emperor's expert *consilium* of jurists.

It is possible that the connexion between praetorian and juristic law was even closer than used to be supposed. It has been universally recognized, chiefly (though not solely) on the authority of Pomponius,[1] that in the archaic period the *legis actiones* were forms of procedure composed and interpreted by the earliest jurists, i.e. the *pontifices*. Joinder of issue—*litis contestatio*—under this system was essentially the act of the parties. There has been an almost equally general opinion that the establishment of the formulary system gradually introduced a complete revolution into the law: the formula granted by the praetor, it was generally thought, was essentially a judicial decree, granted upon the merits of the substantive case by the magistrate, and necessarily comprising the joinder of issue, which thus became the act of the Court rather than of the parties. Wlassak,[2] however, as against a school headed by Keller, argues with much force and a copious citation of authority that this supposed revolution has been greatly exaggerated. He contends that the influence of the jurists upon the forms of action was undiminished, if not actually intensified, under the formulary system. His main thesis is that the formula was not, as has been so generally supposed, really the work of the praetor and his staff, but essentially that of the plaintiff and his legal advisers. This meant in practice that it was the work of counsel who were 'at arm's length' rather than of the magistrate himself or the technical experts of his *consilium*. It was the plaintiff's business to discover, first, whether he had a cause of action, and, if so, then, second, what was his appropriate form of procedure. On both these points he would necessarily require the assistance of counsel. If his case fell within a

[1] D. I. 2. 2. 6. The words are very explicit: 'omnium tamen harum et interpretandi scientia et actiones apud collegium pontificum erant, ex quibus constituebatur, quis quoquo anno praeesset privatis'.

[2] *Die klassische Prozessformel*, I. Teil, 1924.

common type of action, there would be a well-established precedent of pleading; but if no 'common form' covered his case, it was for the advising jurist to draft, and submit to the court, a new formula for the particular circumstances.[1] Wlassak considers this function of pleading to have been an essential part of the *munus* of the patented jurists.[2] Thus the office of the praetor was not to *decree* or formulate the substance of the action; rather was he in the position of an umpire or critic who assented or refused to grant a trial upon the issue as framed, and who incidentally admitted or rejected proposed modifications of the pleadings, without prejudice to the ultimate decision *apud iudicem*. He was primarily not a judicial officer settling a conflict but, as Cicero calls him,[3] *iuris civilis custos*. In a word, the magistrate's function, under the formulary no less than under the *legis actio* system, was, in Wlassak's view, to bring the issue between the parties to a correct formal expression and so provide a direction or instruction for the actual trial. It is true that, technically, the formula, as finally settled, emanated from the jurisdiction of the praetor; it is also true, certainly by the time of Cicero, that typical formulae were published as precedents in the edict: none the less they were, Wlassak maintains, devised in the first instance by the jurists, and hence it was really to them, in the exercise of this characteristic function of their *munus*, that we owe that constant renovation of the system of legal remedies which made the praetorian law such an important social instrument.[4]

If these views be well founded, they would seem to contract the function of the praetor in proportion as they expand the creative influence of the jurists upon the development of Roman Law. Yet to an English lawyer there is nothing surprising in this picture of Roman

Presumably the defendant would receive the like assistance in his pleadings, though this aspect of the matter has less prominence in Wlassak's theory.

[2] *Op. cit.* 46 ff.

[3] *De Leg.* iii. 3. 8: cited Wlassak, *op. cit.* 142.

[4] *Op. cit.* 99.

litigation. A praetor controlling the formulation of issues will not seem to him very different from a modern Master of the Supreme Court or Judge in chambers. And if he looks back into the history of English procedure, and remembers how largely it depended on pleading: if he reflects how much must have depended on expert advice concerning the appropriate writ for the plaintiff's action:[1] he will have no difficulty in picturing the magistrate as umpire in a contest which was as much a battle of writs as a battle of wits. Indeed, the judge as umpire rather than as final deciding authority is a familiar figure in all ancient law. The truth is, as Wlassak points out,[2] that we cannot, without great reservations, ascribe to ancient law the modern doctrine that every citizen has a positive right to demand protection from the State and to call upon the judge to accord that protection, as in duty bound. It is only at a late stage of development that initiative passes from the disputants themselves to public authority. And when, as in Rome, legal science is so much identified with a consultant rather than with an arbitral class, it seems highly probable that that class must have been exceedingly influential in shaping the forms no less than the substance of the law. Indeed, in early law, the one thing necessarily involves the other.

The *iudices*

It is interesting to speculate, but difficult to know, whether in the proceedings *apud iudicem* under the formulary system the *iudices* showed any tendency to imitate each other. It has been suggested, upon interesting and persuasive evidence,[3] that the influence of these magistrates in the development of the classical law has been seriously underestimated, and, indeed, almost wholly neglected. We are apt to think of them as mere

[1] There is no evidence, however—so far as I am aware—that the actual invention of original writs was due to learned counsel, though it seems sometimes to have been attributable to judges. The Chancery clerks were responsible for this part of legal mechanism, though, as Pollock and Maitland observe (i. 196), 'the chancery had not yet fallen so far apart from the courts of law that the justices could not get new writs made if they wanted them'.

[2] *Op. cit.* 195 f., citing Mommsen in support.

[3] Collinet, *op. cit.*

'lay' judges, comparable to the modern juryman, or perhaps to the amateur Justice of the Peace. In reality, it is probable that they were seldom persons wholly untrained in the law. They might be chosen from the *album iudicum*, which was composed of persons of distinction, possessing the legal and administrative knowledge common to most educated Romans—senators, knights, *tribuni aerarii*, and the like; or the judge might be nominated by the parties; and litigants would not be likely to agree upon any casual, untrained person, but would naturally choose an arbitrator whose qualifications commended him to both parties. Indeed, the *iudex* might himself be a *jurisprudens;* and, in any case, there is abundant evidence from Cicero[1] that upon any point of law—and purely legal issues frequently fell within the scope of the judge's function—he had access to a *consilium* of jurisconsults. Collinet collects a number of extremely suggestive instances which seem to show not only that in the classical period the *iudices* were, in many cases, men of considerable legal attainment and experience, but that their decisions had at least a limited, *de facto* authority in several important branches of the law: for example, a decision of P. Mucius Scaevola, as *iudex*, in 133 B.C., upon a matter of a wife's dotal property, was cited by Javolenus in the Digest[2] as being still authoritative more than 700 years later. Continuity of doctrine was probably imperfect, since there is little ground for supposing that the *sententiae* (delivered orally) of the *iudices* were systematically recorded; but it may well have been that a consistent course of decisions by *iudices* materially influenced the development of doctrines such as good faith in contracts, degrees of *diligentia*, or the general standard of conduct expected of a *bonus paterfamilias.* Reviewing the evidence which he assembles, Collinet concludes that 'it seems to be proved that *res iudicatae*, if they were not one of the direct sources of Roman

[1] See Collinet, *op. cit.* 25.

[2] D. 24. 3. 66. pr. (following Servius, who followed Scaevola).

Law, were at least an indirect source, and it is perhaps for this reason that neither the jurisconsults nor Justinian reckoned them among the sources of law, whereas Cicero, who wrote as a philosopher rather than a jurist, included them among the sources of law'.

The study of papyri within recent years has disclosed much new and extremely interesting evidence that in at least one important Roman province, Egypt, during a period roughly corresponding to the classical era of Roman jurisprudence, there was abundant recourse, in the daily practice of the courts, to something very similar to the modern citation of precedents. Papyri ranging in date from A.D. 134 to 250 show that it was common practice to keep records of lawsuits, both arguments and judgements, and many of these records are vividly reminiscent of the informal style and 'human touch' of our own Year Book reports. It is beyond doubt that these 'reported' cases were constantly cited in order to influence the court's decision, though there is no suggestion that the judge was 'bound' by them. Summing up his illuminating discussion[1] of this material, the late Professor Jolowicz observed:

> 'There existed a definite practice of citing decided cases as authority in courts of law, judgements were sometimes expressly based on such authority, and practice was facilitated by the use of official diaries and collections made from the reports that they contained. But it is unlikely that there was much in the way of a theory of case law, though it was no doubt clear that judgements had to give way to "laws", including especially imperial enactments of any sort, and quite possibly some idea that a judge need not consider too carefully the decision of one whose rank was inferior to his own.'

It is controverted, and is bound to remain uncertain in the absence of similar documentary evidence from Rome and Byzantium, whether this system was peculiar to the province of Egypt or characteristic of court practice

[1] 'Case Law in Roman Egypt', *Journal of the Society of Public Teachers of Law*, 1937, 1.

in the whole Roman empire; and again it is open to speculation whether these papyri records were influenced by Roman or by Greek sources. A guess may be hazardous, but, since the instrument of analogy is indispensable to the judicial process in any age and in any system, it seems excessively cautious to suppose that what was familiar in one Roman province was not equally familiar in other provinces and in the metropolis. As for Greek influences, the whole conception of precedents appears to have been so vague and fluid in Greek law that the Egyptian practice seems much more likely to have been derived from the highly developed Roman system.

In the later Roman Law, however, it is probable that the influence of the individual judge and of the single decision became more restricted by the central imperial authority. As that authority matured and strengthened, the whole tendency was for the *iudex* to become a State functionary rather than an arbitrator selected by the parties. With the establishment of the procedure *extra ordinem* in the time of Diocletian, this process is finally consolidated. There is now a class of permanent professional judges and a system of courts with copious records. It is reasonable to suppose that these professional lawyers tended to rely on the examples of colleagues and predecessors. At all events, we shall see that there is sufficient evidence of a marked uniformity in adjective if not in substantive law. It is tempting to conjecture, though it is not advanced as more than a conjecture, that Justinian's famous prohibition of precedent as a creative source of law is itself evidence of a tendency among judges to *stare decisis*. This would plainly be antagonistic to the central conception of imperial sovereignty, especially after the codification. If any decisions were to be binding authorities, they must be the decisions of the Emperor himself, whether they concerned particular cases or the interpretation of enactments. The language of Justinian's constitution[1] is so emphatic that

Force of imperial decisions

[1] C. 1. 14.12.

it certainly seems to be aimed at an existing practice which was considered dangerous.

'If the Emperor's majesty has heard and determined a suit, be it known to all judges whatsoever within our realm that the decision is settled law (*legem*, i.e. with the force of statute) not only for that cause in which it was pronounced, but for all like causes. For what is higher or holier than the Emperor's majesty, and who is so puffed up as to think lightly of the royal judgement, when the jurists of the old law openly and most plainly lay down that constitutions issuing from imperial decree have the force of law? We further find it doubted in certain ancient statutes whether imperial interpretation of statute ought to have the supremacy of sovereign pronouncement. This doubt we hold in derision for a barren nicety and one necessary to be amended. Therefore we decree that every interpretation of statutes rendered by the Emperor, whether in respect of petitions or of causes in action or in whatever other manner pronounced, shall be of indisputable authority (*ratam et indubitatam haberi*). For if, at the present time, it is the prerogative of the Emperor alone to publish statutes, so the interpretation thereof should pertain to his dignity alone. Why otherwise, in special cases stated by magistrates (*ex suggestionibus procerum*), when the judge is in doubt upon a point arising at trial and deems the decision to be beyond his competence, is the matter referred to us? Why are difficulties in the interpretation of statutes submitted by judges to our own proper person (*aures accipiunt nostrae*) if interpretation proceeds not from our own proper judgement? . . . An end now made to these vain doubts, so shall the Emperor be justly esteemed not only as the sole author but also as the sole interpreter of statutes. But nothing herein contained shall derogate from the status of the jurists of the old law, for they too, by favour of the Emperor's majesty, enjoy this privilege.'

It is merely the corollary to this vigorous assertion of monopoly that authority is denied to any decisions other than those of the Princeps; and it would seem to be more than a coincidence that this corollary was enacted on the very same day as the constitution last quoted, and addressed to the same person:[1]

'No judge or arbitrator is to deem himself bound by juristic

[1] C. 7. 45. 13.

opinions (*consultationes*) which he considers wrong: still less by the decisions of learned prefects or other judges. For if an erroneous decision has been given, it ought not to be allowed to spread and so to corrupt the judgement of other magistrates. Decisions should be based on laws, not on precedents. (*Non exemplis sed legibus iudicandum est.*) This rule holds good even if the opinions relied upon are those of the most exalted prefecture or the highest magistracy of any kind. Our will is that all our judges adhere to the true meaning of laws and follow the path of justice.'

This we may take to have been the final 'official' Roman view of precedent, whatever the practice may have been;[1] and it is therefore not surprising that Cicero's inclusion of *res iudicatae* among the sources of law does not reappear in the later jurists. One passage only in the Corpus Iuris seems to conflict directly with Justinian's principle, and it has been the occasion of much controversy. Callistratus, in D. 1. 3. 38, says: 'Nam imperator noster Severus rescripsit in ambiguitatibus quae ex legibus proficiscuntur consuetudinem aut rerum perpetuo similiter iudicatarum auctoritatem vim legis optinere debere.' Even this statement is confined to the interpretation of *statute*; and if it correctly represents a rule laid down by Septimius Severus (of which nothing else is known), it is so directly contrary to Justinian's constitution quoted above that we must suppose it to have been repealed, if it ever existed. Indeed, it is not impossible that Justinian had it specially in contemplation in enacting his constitution, and that he indirectly refers to it in the phrase 'in veteribus legibus invenimus dubitatum'.[2] If this be so, it is doubtful whether the extract from Callistratus should have found a place in the Digest; but such inconsistencies are not unknown in the Corpus Iuris. In any case, Callistratus's dictum can

[1] In modern Roman-Dutch law, Justinian's principle, though acknowledged in theory, is subject to such modifications in practice that it can hardly be said to be operative: see R. W. Lee, 'Roman Law in the British Empire', in *Atti del Congresso Internazionale di Diritto romano*, ii (1935), 282.

[2] C. 1. 14. 12. 2.

scarcely be considered as representative of Roman theory.

Mos iudiciorum

If the full force of precedents was not admitted under the Empire, professional practice had an important influence on the development of legal forms. 'The custom of the court' (*mos iudiciorum*) is often referred to as a decisive factor in the form of the plaintiff's remedy. Thus a creditor on a pact with stipulation is not to proceed to execution *citra sollemnem ordinem*, but must obtain his remedy by judgement *more iudiciorum*.[1] The importance of this common phrase should not be exaggerated. It occurs only in imperial constitutions and seems to refer chiefly to points of procedure.[2] When, for example, the plaintiff is directed by a constitution of Antoninus: 'If you claim that you are entitled to the possession of certain things, you must recover possession *more iudiciorum*, for the onus of proofs is not on the defendant, and the dominium remains with him *te in probatione cessante*':[3] the reference is clearly limited to the procedural method of proof. At other times the expression seems to be little more than one of those catchwords so common in legal phraseology, and it might be translated as 'in due form', 'by due process of law', or 'by the appropriate form of action'. Thus in one case[4] we have the well-known rule asserted that the principal is not to be prejudiced by the agent's excess of his mandate. But suppose the agent, though invested with full discretion, has yet exceeded his authority to the extent of becoming involved in litigation. Ought the judgement in the action to be rescinded? The answer is that the judgement must stand, because the principal can bring action against the agent *more iudiciorum* if the agent has acted fraudulently. This seems equivalent only to saying that the principal has an ordinary *actio mandati*, and the known forms of action in such circumstances must be adhered to. Or again, suppose slaves have been bought in the names of yourself

[1] C. 2. 3. 14.
[2] Brie, *op. cit.* 52 ff.
[3] C. 4. 19. 2.
[4] C. 2. 12. 10.

and your brother, to whom you have now succeeded as heir, the fact (expressly mentioned in the instrument of sale) that the purchase-money was paid by your mother will not prevent you from suing *more iudiciorum*[1]—i.e. by whatever form of action fits the circumstances: perhaps an *actio ex empto*, perhaps an *actio quanti minoris* or *redhibitoria*, and so forth. These and similar constitutions[2] seem only to assure the plaintiff that he is not debarred from his remedy in the ordinary course of law though they say nothing about the merits of the action itself. They may have been in the nature of a preliminary opinion taken by a prospective litigant to ascertain his best method of procedure, or possibly of a decision, by way of appeal, on procedural objections raised in court against the plaintiff's claim. Sometimes the phrase is *more solito*, and it does not seem to differ from the meaning already suggested.[3] But in two cases there are hints that it may refer to some *local* rule of practice. A litigant is told[4] that she may proceed *more solito*, if she thinks she has a good cause of action, against one who has built so as to obstruct her lights; and Girard sees here a possible reference to local building regulations.[5] A clearer suggestion of purely provincial practice is contained in a passage[6] which lays down that a husband who alleges, under the *Lex Iulia de adulteriis*, the adultery of his wife must proceed *more solito* in the province where the offence was committed. Unless some local peculiarity of procedure is indicated, there seems to be little purpose in the regulation.[7] Other evidence is not wanting that provincial customs prescribed rules of form which were well known

[1] C. 4. 50. 3.
[2] C. 5. 62. 15; 7. 21. 4; 9. 2. 4.
[3] C. 7. 73. 3; 9. 35. 3.
[4] C. 3. 34. 1.
[5] *Manuel* (5th ed.), 360, n. 6, in support of the theory that the controverted *ius altius tollendi* was an exemption from local building restrictions. But it seems unsafe to lay too much stress on the phrase. The sting of the rescript lies in its tail, which insists that prescriptive possession must be 'nec vi nec clam nec precario'.
[6] C. 9. 9. 12.
[7] e.g. there would be nothing surprising or irregular in the fact that a particular jurisdiction required a certain form of *accusatio* with specified particulars in a statutory action of this kind.

and observed. In one case a local procedural rule is actually enjoined upon the magistrate, and he is told that in summoning witnesses he must have regard to the custom of the province in that respect.[1]

Provincial courts cannot have been peculiar in this matter. Any court must develop, as part of its routine, working rules of procedure which are not covered by any statute or code. It was not inconsistent with imperial authority that this kind of precedent should be both permitted and encouraged. Thus Justinian specifically ordains that the form of oaths, in all cases where procedure by oath is appropriate, shall be determined by the *observatio iudicialis*.[2] And although the express admission of precedent hardly travelled beyond the sphere of adjective law, this was by no means an unimportant element in Roman jurisprudence; for an established rule of adjective law, operating, as it must, on the remedies available to litigants, cannot fail to affect substantive principles. Of this we have a striking example in the Institutes,[3] where, after stating detailed rules for the giving of securities for litigation, Justinian observes: 'Quae omnia apertius et perfectissime a cottidiano iudiciorum usu in ipsis rerum documentis apparent.' As he has already told us that recent practice has developed new forms of securities—'alium (modum) novitas per usum amplexa est'—it seems plain that these important rules of litigation sprang from procedural precedent, and that this origin was recognized as unexceptionable.

We may, then, conclude that the later Roman jurisprudence, while unable to exclude altogether the operation of judge-made rules, admitted it only as an indirect and greatly restricted influence upon the substantive law.

[1] D. 22. 5. 3. 6: 'sed et divi fratres rescripserunt: "Quod ad testes evocandos pertinet, diligentiae iudicis est explorare, quae consuetudo in ea provincia, in quam iudicat, fuerit." '

[2] C. 4. 1. 12. 5. D. 4. 1. 7. pr. seems to give little warrant for the view that the practice of pronouncing judgement by default against an absent defendant sprang solely from judicial practice. *More* here seems to mean only 'as usual'.

[3] iv. 11. 6.

Judge-made principles were not placed even as high as custom, for the *mos iudiciorum* is nowhere mentioned as a department of *consuetudo*, except in the passage of Callistratus which has been mentioned.[1] In English law there may often be found a *mos iudiciorum* which grows up by practice, though not possessing the binding force of law—e.g. the rule that in certain offences the evidence of an accomplice must be corroborated.[2] The courts, however, hold themselves free to change or depart from such settled rules of practice if necessary.[3] A remarkable example of rules of practice, which may be termed semi-authoritative, are the so-called Judges' Rules concerning statements by persons suspected of crime or by prisoners in the custody of the police. The first of these were drawn up by the King's Bench Judges in 1912; they have been added to as new points of doubt have arisen, and they have been supplemented from time to time on matters of detail by Home Office instructions to the police, until they now form a code of some complexity. So far as they have been expressly approved by the courts (and some of them have repeatedly been so confirmed, especially in the Court of Criminal Appeal), they may be said to have the force of law; but they were in origin advisory only and were issued 'for the information and guidance of the police'. They constitute, nevertheless, a settled code of rules of evidence as between the police and suspected persons or persons in custody, and neglect of them may lead to quashing a conviction. (It may be added that they are rules which it is often difficult for the police to interpret and apply.) The law of evidence is full of rules which have grown up simply by the practice of the courts.[4]

[1] On precedent in Greek law see Vinogradoff, *Historical Jurisprudence*, ii. 78 ff. Its scope was vague, but there is evidence from the Orators that it had no small effect in settling certain doctrines, especially in commercial and testamentary law.

[2] See *R.* v. *Tate*, [1908] 2 K.B. 680, *Statham* v. *S.*, [1929] P. 131, and *Fairman* v. *F.*, [1949] P. 341.

[3] See *R.* v. *Morris*, [1951] 1 K.B. 394, and *R.* v. *Higgins*, [1952] 1 K.B. 7.

[4] See, for example, the observations of Lord Goddard C.J. in *Hollington* v. *Hewthorn*, [1943] K.B. 587, 593.

Professional usage in Chancery practice is perhaps even stronger than in the King's Bench.[1]

3. Precedent in modern Continental law

Justinian's 'non exemplis sed legibus iudicandum est' might be taken as the epitome of the deductive principle of judicial reasoning, widely accepted, in theory at least, at the present day on the Continent. We may take French law as characteristic,[2] and it may not be unprofitable to compare briefly the theory and practice of the French courts in this respect.[3]

Extra-judicial doctrine

An Englishman approaching the study of French law is at once struck by the seeming paradox that while the codified law is insisted on as supreme, a highly important part is played by extra-judicial and extra-legislative doctrine. The great commentaries on the Civil Code are an indispensable supplement to the Code itself, for without them the bare provisions of the Code are far from self-explanatory to the practitioner. He turns to great works like those of Aubry and Rau and of Beaudry-Lacantinerie for the true Pandects of his law, for here he will find not only the provisions of the law itself but the historical accretions which are inseparable from it.[4] So important is this great body of learning (*la doctrine*), together with judge-made law (*la jurisprudence*), that one

[1] See *In re Hillas-Drake*, [1944] Ch. 235; *In re Slee*, (1962) 1 W.L.R. 496.

[2] See Planiol, *Traité élémentaire de Droit Civil*, i. 45 ff.; Colin et Capitant, *Cours élémentaire de Droit Civil français*, i. 29 ff.; Ancel, 'Case Law in France', *J.S.C.L.*, Feb. 1934, 1; Lawson, *Negligence in the Civil Law*, 231 ff.; Amos and Walton, *Introduction to French Law* (2nd ed.), 9 ff.; F. P. Walton, 'Delictual Responsibility in Civil Law', 49 *L.Q.R.* 70.

[3] On the German view of *Praxis*, *Gerichtsgebrauch*, and *Juristenrecht* as sources of law, see Gierke, *DPR.* i. 176 ff., and J. C. Gray in 9 *H.L.R.* 27, where Stobbe, *DPR.*, is cited as the characteristic view: 'Practice is in itself not a source of law; a court can depart from its former practice and no court is bound to the practice of another. Departure from the practice hitherto observed is not only permitted but required, if there are better reasons for another treatment of the question of law.' Gierke (*op. cit.* 179 and n. 8) ranges himself with a numerous school in considering it as a subordinate part of customary law, with the same force as custom. See also Lipstein, 'Precedent in Continental Law', 28 *J.S.C.L.* (Pts. III and IV), 34 ff.

[4] On the great commentators on the Code and the different schools of interpretation, see Bonnecase, *La Pensée juridique française*, and 'The Problem of Legal Interpretation in France', 12 *J.S.C.L.* 79.

school of thought regards them as the most essentially creative elements in law, and pleads for a *libre recherche scientifique* which shall constantly adapt formulated rules to changing social needs. It is claimed that the formulated rule, as originally framed, soon detaches itself completely from the will and intention of its creator and assumes a different character in the hands of the interpreter. Without necessarily conceding so wide and, as the opposing school holds, so dangerous a function to doctrine, every French lawyer admits its vital importance in the legal system.

There are many reasons, both in history and in the constitution and hierarchy of the French courts, why it would have been impossible, even if it had been desired, for France to develop a 'binding' system of precedents in the same way that England has done.[1] Consequently, the opinions of jurists of high reputation enjoy far greater authority in France than they do in England. In strict theory, they are, like extra-judicial opinion in England, 'persuasive' only; no court would admit that they contain intrinsic, 'binding' authority. But they undoubtedly exercise a very real influence not only on professional opinion but upon judicial doctrine; they form an integral part of the teaching of law, and on occasion they do not hesitate to claim for themselves a greater accuracy than the judgements even of the highest tribunals. An eminent French authority informs us:[2]

'Writers are in the habit of giving their own interpretations of the law, which are sometimes contrary to the solutions of the courts, but which they nevertheless consider as the only real expression of French law. On many important points . . . there exists a doctrine of the courts and a doctrine of law writers. So you can find in France a law which is printed in books and taught in universities, and which yet differs much from, even when not contrary to, the law applied by the courts of justice. Writers

[1] See Lipstein, *loc. cit.* For similar reasons, a binding hierarchy of authority did not exist in England until the nineteenth century: see *post*, pp. 231 ff.

[2] Ancel, *loc. cit.*

nowadays take care to state not only their own opinion, but also the opinion of the *jurisprudence*, but yet they put forward their solution as the only legal one.'

To all this, and to the 'current of authority' in decided cases, no conscientious court can remain indifferent. But the Code itself insists that the French judge confine himself to the process of deduction of rule to case. Article 5 expressly inhibits magistrates from any pronouncement 'par voie de disposition générale et réglementaire sur les causes qui leur sont soumises'. The English reader will at once be struck by the contrast between this rule and the wide generalizations which are constantly to be found in English judgements. Sometimes the contrast may strike him as one between the embarrassing amplitude of English judgements and what he may think the somewhat cryptic curtness of French judgements. For the French judgement, at all events in the superior courts, to English eyes, is highly compressed, and not easily understood by anybody who is not familiar with the Code, with statute law, and with the method of their interpretation. A judgement of a French court is, as we should expect of the Gallic genius, a meticulously constructed piece of logic—a pared and polished judicial syllogism, as it were. The narrative is given in a series of concise premisses, and the judgement, by a succession of logical steps, states the main relevant facts and the statutory provisions which are applicable to them and which thus lead to the conclusion. Every French judgement must be, by law, *motivé* in this manner.[1] There is much to be read between the lines and this is, of course, largely a matter of habit and technique. Often, if the case is considered important, the report of the judgement is accompanied by a further exposition,

[1] In earlier editions of this book, a loose statement which implied the contrary (though it was not intended to do so) was properly criticized by Professor E. Lambert (Lambert and Wasserman, 'The Case Method in Canada', *Yale Law Journal*, Nov. 1929). To my general position with regard to *doctrine* and *jurisprudence* in French law I adhere, with the support of M. Ancel as against M. Lambert.

with abundant references to other decisions and authorities. This gloss, however, comes not from the court itself but from some accredited jurisconsult—often a distinguished practitioner, often an academic teacher or learned writer. Again, this is only of 'persuasive' authority, but it is frequently of great value and influence, and adds considerably, in practice, to the prestige of the decision.

Respect for decided cases is a growing element in modern French legal method, though, as we shall see, the decided case occupies a status different from what English lawyers understand by 'precedent'. The numerous and extensive collections of reports are now almost as much a part of the French as of the English lawyer's professional equipment.[1] Nobody can hope to understand the workings of French law without constant reference to standard reports, published periodically, like those of Dalloz and Sirey, or the *Gazette du Palais*. In the administrative sphere French lawyers have before them a striking example of 'judge-made law', for the whole remarkable jurisprudence of the Conseil d'État, never having been governed by a Code like the civil law, has been built up by case-law.[2] There is an increasing tendency to cite decisions in judgements.[3] What we should call 'case-books' (*espèces choisies*) have for many years past been published, often under distinguished editorship. It is now recognized that a strong and uniform line of decisions may modify or even completely reverse a rule of legislation, and that far-reaching principles may establish themselves quite independently of any enactment in that behalf. Thus Article 1554 of the Civil Code forbids (with certain exceptions mentioned in succeeding Articles) the alienation of immovable property forming part of a dowry. Nothing is said about

[1] The chief series of reports and commentaries are mentioned in Colin and Capitant, *op. cit.* i. 34, n. 2.

[2] See Berthélemy, *Traité élémentaire de Droit administratif*; M. A. Sieghart, *Government by Decree*.

[3] Ancel, *loc. cit.*

movable property; but the principle has been extended to movables by a series of decisions which are now recognized as embodying a rule of law. Articles 1119 and 1121 forbid the practice of entering into a stipulation on behalf of another, except under certain narrow conditions. This rule was found extremely inconvenient, especially in connexion with life insurance, a transaction unknown to the framers of the Code. Throughout the nineteenth century a long series of decisions gradually whittled away the rule, until it fell virtually into desuetude, and the *stipulation pour autrui* became legitimate and frequent. The matter is now regulated by codifying statutes.

Again, the motor-car, in France as in most other countries, has presented problems which it has been necessary to work out by 'common law' methods. As is well known, the general principle of delictal imputability in French law, embodied in Article 1382 of the Code, is based on fault or *culpa*. By an ingenious combination of this Article with Article 1384 (1) (which refers to liability for things in the defendant's custody), the French courts have established a principle that a presumption of liability, in case of damage, rests upon the person who has 'custody' of a motor-car. The result has been reached after a long and much-disputed series of decisions. A leading judgement of the Cour de Cassation in 1924 was resisted by a number of Courts of Appeal, and the doctrine was not finally established until 1930, when the Cour de Cassation affirmed it *toutes chambres réunies* (a form of judgement which will presently be explained).

In some instances, judicial practice seems even to have succeeded in defying, or at least in circumventing, the clear intention of the Code. Thus specific performance is unknown to the strict French law, since Article 1142 places all compensation for civil injury on a monetary basis. The courts, however, have developed, and frequently employ, an indirect form of specific performance known as *astreinte*. It consists in the simple but effective device of imposing on the defendant, *de die in diem*, such heavy penalties for non-performance that he is in effect compelled to perform.[1]

Despite these and other similar examples, French theory is far from conceding any 'binding' authority even to a consistent series of decisions, and it allows none at all to the isolated decision, even of the highest tribunal. The whole traditional doctrine of France insists on the supremacy and sufficiency of the *lex scripta*,[2] and this is not surprising, since France, even before that miracle of legislation, the Code Napoléon, had a long tradition of enacted law; whereas, as we shall see,[3] for centuries in England, while the Common Law was evolving, the nature and effect of statute-law were variable, uncertain, and unscientific. It is remarkable how the two systems, while both adopting similar methods in order to keep the law abreast of the times, have diverged in the ostensible operation of the method. Where the English judge introduces new law under the guise of old precedent, the French judge does so under the guise of a new interpretation of the *lex scripta*. An admirable apophthegm of R. Saleilles[4] neatly expresses the governing principle: 'Beyond the Code *through* the Code!' But it is the Code which theoretically remains supreme. Such authority as precedent possesses (but it is none the less powerful on that account) exists *de facto* and not *de jure*; and even so, it is not the authority of the single decision from the highest tribunal, but a current of decisions so strong that it has settled into 'judicial practice' or 'custom of the court'.[5] 'The theory of the law is that every judge is responsible for the interpretations which he

[1] Ancel, *loc. cit.*

[2] See Gény, *Méthode d'interprétation*, vol. i and *passim*. The whole of Gény's work, which has had a profound effect on legal thought and method in France, was directed against the rigidity of the 'traditional view' of written law, which has its counterpart in England in the old Coke-and-Blackstone dogma of the all-sufficiency of the immemorial Common Law.

[3] *Post*, Chapter VI.

[4] Introduction to Gény, *op. cit.* (2nd ed.).

[5] See A. L. Goodhart, 'Precedent in English and Continental Law', 50 *L.Q.R.* 40.

places upon the written texts. He may support his conclusion by invoking the settled practice of the courts and the opinion of accepted commentators, but he cannot, in theory, shelter himself behind any such extraneous authority.'[1] The Cour de Cassation allows no appeal from *jurisprudence*, but only from *the law*. It would seem, however, that this court, certainly when sitting *toutes chambres réunies*, hardly ever departs from its previous decisions.[2]

General theory of precedents in French law

Again and again it is insisted that every court must be at liberty to change its mind and therefore need not repeat its own previous decision; still less need it follow the decisions of other courts, of whatever degree.[3] As against the examples of uniformity which I have given, it would be easy to find many others of wide discrepancies. Conflicting decisions have caused no small embarrassment and in particular the absence of any definite hierarchy of authority has presented a problem. For more than a century France has been endeavouring to establish some final authority to ensure uniformity of doctrine; and the gradual steps by which it has arrived at the present arrangement show how reluctant it is to derogate from the complete independence of its inferior tribunals. The final appellate court on the civil and criminal (as opposed to the administrative) side of French jurisdiction is the Cour de Cassation, which hears appeals on points of law only. Its judgements are therefore the most authoritative in the land, but they are in danger of being undermined if the independence of the lower courts is carried to an extreme. The position becomes the more complex in view of the great

[1] Amos and Walton, *loc. cit.* See further H. W. Goldschmidt, *English Law from the Foreign Standpoint*, 39 ff., for an interesting comparison of English doctrine with that of other European countries. Professor Goldschmidt is strongly of opinion that the force of precedent in Continental systems has been underestimated by English lawyers.

[2] Lawson, *op. cit.* 234, who says that it has 'almost the authority of the House of Lords'.

[3] See *In re Annesley*, [1926] Ch. 692.

importance which French law attaches to the right of appeal in all but the most trifling causes. The first attempt, in 1790, to solve the difficulty, vested the final right of interpretation in the legislature. If the lower court persisted in its opinion despite *two* decisions in appeal to the contrary, it was for the legislature to state the true rule of law. The inconvenience of this device, and its incompatibility with the principle of the separation of powers, need hardly be pointed out. The second experiment, in 1807, was even more hesitating, and, in violation of traditional French doctrine, gravely confused the judicial with the administrative power. If, after one decision, the same matter came before the Cour de Cassation in its original form, the court, before affirming its previous decision, could apply to the Government for a ruling. The Government in its turn took the advice of the Conseil d'État (the final appellate court in purely administrative suits), and the only practical effect was that the responsibility of final decision was shifted from one forum to another and from one constitutional sphere to another. A further and even more unsatisfactory attempt was made in 1828 to divide the responsibility between the Cour de Cassation and the legislature; and it was not till 1837 that the present system was finally established and authority was fully vested in the ultimate court itself. As matters now stand, if the ordinary Cour de Cassation (i.e. one *chambre* or bench of that Court) has allowed an appeal, and the lower court to which the case is remitted (*tribunal de renvoi*) refuses to accept the ruling laid down, then if the same case goes a second time to appeal, an extraordinary or full Cour de Cassation (*toutes chambres réunies*)[1] hears the case, and its decision must be accepted by the inferior court.

Even this arrangement seems, to English eyes, strangely circuitous. It must be remembered that *cassation*

[1] Now consisting of four divisions, one *Chambre criminelle* and three *Chambres civiles*. Before 1947 an appeal had first to pass through the 'sieve' of the *Chambre des Requêtes*, but this is no longer necessary: Lawson, *op. cit.*

is not the same thing as reversal of judgement in the English sense. When the Cour de Cassation allows an appeal, it does not enter final judgement for the appellant, but sends the case back, not, it is true, to the same court which originally tried the case, but to another court of equal jurisdiction. It grants what we should call a new trial. At this second trial, the judge may adhere, despite the Cour de Cassation, to the view originally taken by the court of first instance. It is improbable that he will do so, since the Cour de Cassation is likely to reassert its previous view. But a sensitive legal conscience may make him desire a ruling from the Cour de Cassation *toutes chambres réunies*. Or he may be merely obstinate, in which case the parties to the suit, exposed to further litigation, become the *corpus vile* of his recalcitrance. The procedure is extraordinarily circuitous, for if the full Cour de Cassation is to be regarded as an appellate court from the ordinary Cour de Cassation (*chambre civile*), there seems little reason why the appeal should not lie direct, without the intervening stage of a second trial. However this may be, the final decision of the Cour de Cassation is authoritative only for the particular case before it: the system outlined above aims only at preventing multiplicity of actions on the same cause. There is no compulsion on lower courts to follow the ruling even of the full Cour de Cassation (*toutes chambres réunies*) *in pari materia*. Nor is the Cour de Cassation in theory bound by its own previous decisions, but in practice it is virtually so bound, and therefore these decisions of the highest tribunal do produce a substantial uniformity in the law. Not only is respect naturally and genuinely paid to so eminent a court, but inferior judges are hardly likely to give decisions with the certainty that they will be reversed on appeal, especially as there is in France a regular system of judicial promotion which necessarily depends in great measure on proved efficiency. Thus, in the words of M. Planiol, 'we may see the growth of unmistakable currents of jurisprudence which cannot be stemmed or diverted. We may then say that judicial doctrine (*la jurisprudence*) is fixed or complete (*faite*). ... Changes therein are dangerous by reason of their retroactive effect on private interest and contracts.'[1]

II. GROWTH OF PRECEDENT IN ENGLISH LAW

The growth of the authority of precedents in our own law is a study full of interest. Though it is difficult to determine precise stages of evolution, a gradual building up of tradition is discernible. It has been conjectured that reports existed 'digested in years and terms as ancient as the time of King William the Conqueror', but this speculation rests upon no authority. Its author,[2] however, calls attention to an interesting sidelight from literature on legal methods in the fifteenth century. When Chaucer says of his Serjeant:

> In termés hadde he caas and doomés alle,
> That from the tyme of kyng William were falle,

he at least indicates that a knowledge of decided cases was the mark of a learned lawyer in his own day though from what source such knowledge was derived we cannot tell. Citation of cases scarcely exists in our earliest institutional writers. In Glanvil one decision is referred to, in Fleta one, in Britton none, in Littleton eleven.[3] With Bracton the case is very different, and it is from him that our evidence begins to take shape. He lays down a

Bracton

[1] *Op. cit.*, § 124. In the United States, largely owing to the diversity of jurisdictions and the overwhelming mass of precedents, the principle of *stare decisis* has created great difficulties and has been the subject of much controversy: see A. L. Goodhart, 'Case Law in England and America', in *Essays in Jurisprudence*, 50; and see *ante*, p. 42. In recent years there has been a growing feeling, even in England, that the ever-increasing mass of precedents makes the consistent application of *stare decisis* a matter of difficulty; see *post*, pp. 340. ff.

[2] Sir John Davies, Introduction to his Reports (1604–12). See Horwood, Preface to Y.B. 30 & 31 Ed. I (R.S.), xvi. Blackstone (1 *Comm.* 69) quotes Selden (*Review of Tithes*, c. 8) as saying that the 'praeteritorum memoria eventorum' was reckoned, *even so early as the Conquest*, as one of the chief qualifications of those who were held to be 'legibus patriae optime instituti'.

[3] J. C. Gray, 'Judicial Precedents', *H.L.R.* ix. 27.

general principle, on Roman lines, but with an interesting addition concerning the English judicature.

'If any new and unwonted circumstances, hitherto unprecedented in the realm, shall arise, then if anything analogous has happened before, let the case be adjudged in like manner (*si tamen similia evenerint per simile iudicentur*), since it is a good opportunity for proceeding *a similibus ad similia*. But if nothing of the same kind has ever happened before, then let such matters be referred to the Magna Curia, that they be there determined by deliberation of the Curia. There be some who are so confident of their knowledge of every part of the law, that they are unwilling to seek the advice of anybody else; but in such a case it would be more meet and prudent of them to take advice than to come to a rash decision, since it is inexpedient to be in doubt on particular points of law.'[1]

It is consistent with this principle that his own treatise contains some 500 references to decided cases. Not all, but most, of these may be attributed to the author himself—enough certainly to show that he resorted frequently to decisions, taken from Court rolls and probably often from personal recollection, as part of his ordinary method of legal exposition. Bracton went far beyond his contemporaries in this respect, and cannot be regarded as representative of the judicial method of his day;[2] but there is respectable evidence that at least as early as the last quarter of the thirteenth century the practice of citation was frequent in the legal profession. It was well known to one of the foremost judges of this period, Ralph de Hengham, and Professor Woodbine has adduced interesting evidence to the same effect from manuscript tracts of about the same date.[3] But most

[1] *De Leg.*, f. 1b; Woodbine, ii. 21. Cf. D. 1. 3. 12: 'Non possunt omnes articuli singillatim aut legibus aut senatus consultis comprehendi: sed cum in aliqua causa sententia eorum manifesta est, is qui iurisdictioni praeest ad similia procedere atqua ita ius dicere debet.'

[2] As Professor Plucknett points out (*Concise History of English Law* (5th ed.), 342), he was unique in his use of the Plea Rolls, to which few had access; and his object (like Coke's) was to correct vices, which he believed to be current in the profession, in the use of case-law.

[3] Bracton, *De Leg.* i. 366 f. Judges are commonly mentioned by name as

striking of all is the evidence furnished by the celebrated *Note Book* which Bracton certainly used, if he did not compile it with his own hand. No lawyer would have been at the pains of making this collection of some 2,000 decided cases, or having it made for him, unless he laid great store by it as a 'practice book'.[1] Its utility can be the better appreciated when we remember how great a part pleading played in the medieval lawyer's business, and how important the practice of the courts must have been in this respect. Bracton's law, as Maitland has emphasized, was therefore 'case-law' in a very real sense, and 'in dealing with concrete matters he appeals not to Azo, nor to Ulpian, nor again to Reason or Nature, but to this and that case adjudged by Martin Pateshull or William Raleigh'.[2] More than this, some of Bracton's cases themselves carry us back a stage farther and show us that judges were seeking the guidance of precedent early in the thirteenth century. Thus in a case of 1234 in the Eyre of Essex[3] we find the judges asking 'si umquam tale factum fuit iudicium in praefata curia, et quod ostendunt exemplum' and (so it is to be inferred) refusing to lay down a new rule in the absence of any such *exemplum*. By 1237 that very British (and very human) argument, 'I never heard of such a thing!', has commended itself to judicial dialectic, and we seem to see the judges holding up their hands in horror when we read 'omnes dixerunt quod nunquam viderunt talem casum'.[4] In 1292 the settlement executed by Thomas of Weyland raised novel questions concerning the creation of

having laid down certain rules. Some of the cases collected by Professor Woodbine are of remarkable interest: see his note to p. 367. He points out that after Edward I it became the fashion to refer to clauses of statutes rather than to judges and cases. On Hengham, see further Vinogradoff, 'Ralph of Hengham as Chief Justice of the Common Pleas', in *Essays in Mediaeval History presented to T. F. Tout* (ed. Little and Powicke).

[1] Though doubtless his chief object was the preparation of material for his treatise.

[2] *Bracton's Note Book*, i. 11. But, in view of later evidence, Maitland probably exaggerated Bracton's singularity in this respect.

[3] *Ibid.* ii. 641, Case 834.

[4] *Bracton's Note Book*, iii. 242, Case 1227.

remainders and conditions in the devolution of land; the case was considered so important that it was argued before all the judges, the Barons of the Exchequer, the Council, and Parliament; and Parliament ordered the rolls to be searched for a precedent bearing on the case in hand.[1]

The Year Books

With the beginning of the Year Books we can form some notion of the practical workings of precedents in the courts. Decisions are cited often enough to show that both Bench and Bar consider them a relevant part of argument. At the beginning of the fourteenth century, counsel solemnly reminds the court that 'the judgement to be by you now given will be hereafter an authority in every *quare non admisit* in England'.[2] In proportion to the total number of cases contained in the Year Books, the amount of citation is small, though by no means inconsiderable; and it is not improbable that the recorded instances represent only a very small proportion of the citations actually employed in court, since most of the Year Book reports are highly compressed, and give us only fragments of the case as it was presented to the court.[3]

[1] Rot. Parl. i. 66 (19 Ed. I, no. 1); Holdsworth, *H.E.L.* iii. 104, and *Sources and Literature of English Law*, 87.

[2] Y.B. 32 Ed. I (R.S.), 32.

[3] On the other hand, the reporters occasionally add a note citing parallel cases: see *Anon.*, Y.B. 6 Ed. II (S.S. xiv (1)), 120; and note to *Abbot of St. Nicholas* v. *Prior of Nocton*, Y.B. 7 Ed. II (S.S. xvi), 120, 122. Sir Percy Winfield (*Chief Sources of English Legal History*, 145 ff.) laid emphasis on the fact that citations appear in only a small minority of Year Book cases. This is unquestionable, but, with all respect, I doubt whether it necessarily means that actual citation in court was the exception rather than the rule. Most of the Year Book cases, especially those of the thirteenth century, are cursive jottings, and do not pretend to record more than one or two points which struck the reporter's attention; the absence of citations in such telegraphic notes cannot be said to prove anything. What is significant is that when we get a more extended report of the argument, and when the reporter thinks the 'examples' sufficiently interesting and relevant to be recorded, we receive a strong impression that this was part of the ordinary forensic routine. In short, I am inclined to think that, even in the thirteenth and fourteenth centuries, citations were far more frequent in practice than their incidence in the Year Books would suggest, and that from about the middle of the fifteenth

The cases are sometimes, but comparatively rarely, cited by name in the course of counsel's argument, e.g. 'witness the plea of Richard the Fowler, where the *quid iuris clamat* was brought in a similar case', &c.;[1] or 'witness the Bishop of Hereford who made avowry upon Roger Mortimer', &c.;[2] or 'David of Fleetwick's case was just the same' (*Davyd de Flepwye' fut en mesme le cas*).[3] Sometimes the form of the reference suggests that the example cited was a 'leading case' well known to the profession—thus *le play bastard vous salve*, 'the Bastard's Case saves you' (followed by a short précis of the case).[4] A common formula is 'we have seen before now', or 'we saw in the time of such-and-such a Judge' (*nous avons vew, nous veymes*), followed by a summary of the case, which is sometimes given by name.[5]

The fascinating game of 'distinguishing' is already popular. *Non est simile* seems to have been the most effective retort to any citation by one's learned friend.

> '*Toudeby*. Moreover, we have seen that aid was granted in a case like this between Tybaud of Verdone, &c.
>
> '*Herle. Non est simile.* For in the case of Tybaud the tenements were given in frank-marriage, &c.'[6]

The Bench is prompt to find joints in learned counsel's harness. Sometimes a judge will distinguish a cited case in point of law,[7] sometimes 'on the facts'.[8] 'Not

century they became almost habitual. But this, as we shall see, is a very different thing from a 'system of precedents' in the sense in which it is understood today.

[1] *Waleys* v. *Eyuile*, Y.B. 6 Ed. II (S.S. xiv (1)), 81, 82.

[2] *Durant* v. *Cogan*, Y.B. 4 Ed. II (S.S. iv), 110, 111.

[3] *Tremur* v. *Giffard*, Y.B. 6 Ed. II (S.S. xiii), 211, 212.

[4] *Anon.*, Y.B. 2 Ed. II (S.S. i), 130.

[5] *Ibid.* 70, 72, *per* Toudeby (case not named); *Archbishop of Canterbury* v. *Percy*, Y.B. 3 Ed. II (S.S. iii), 31, 34, *per* Scrope, citing *Robert of Tattershall* v. *Prior of Wymondham*; *Beneyt* v. *Lodewyk*, *ibid.* 46, *per* Passeley: 'Sir, in the time of Sir John of Metingham we saw here that a sealed tally was denied.' Other forms of citation are: '*Homme ad souvent vu*', '*Il ad este adjudge avant ceo*', '*Il est tenu en nostres livres*', and the like; see T. Ellis Lewis, 'The History of Judicial Precedent', 46, 47, and 48 *L.Q.R.*

[6] *Anon.*, Y.B. 6 Ed. II (S.S. xiii), 189, 190.

[7] *De la More* v. *Thwing*, Y.B. 2 Ed. II (S.S. i), 176, 178, *per* Scrope J.

[8] *Whitacre* v. *Marmion*, Y.B. 7 Ed. II (S.S. xvi), 126, 127; *Inge J.* (to

similar' (*n'est pas semblable*) is again the appropriate repartee.[1] Citations seem to come more often from the Bench than from the Bar. The reporter will tell us that the Judge cited (*allega*[2]) a certain assize of novel disseisin which seemed to be in point; counsel perhaps replies with another case, giving its name: 'not similar', answers the Judge, for such-and-such reasons.[3] The following is a characteristic interchange:

'*Stanton J.* That the writ [of account] lies against strangers is shown by the case of John of Studley and the Bishop of Winchester.

'*Herle.* Yes, and I could find you others [against whom it has been brought].

'*Hunt.* No wonder! There [the bishop] assumed the wardship, saying that [Studley] held of him by a service that [gives wardship to the lord], and this was found to be untrue. Here, however, we are not guardians but the farmer of J., who leased to us these tenements for a hundred shillings, which naturally [must be regarded as] the issues of the land, and they came to his hand. So he, it seems, is the person to render the account.'[4]

In one case the Chief Justice is unkind enough to confront counsel with his own argument in a previous case, of which, as it happens, we have a report in the same Year Book.[5]

Except in rare instances where the case seems to be notorious, the impression conveyed is that counsel are drawing on their own memories. Thus 'Huntingdon said that he saw a fine levied before Sir Thomas of Weyland between two parties where it was declared by the fine that one of them should have the half towards the

Toudeby): 'You are not in the circumstances of William the Butler, for he was within age, etc.'

[1] *Anon.*, Y.B. 4 Ed. II (S.S. iv), 164; *Warthill* v. *Selby*, Y.B. 7 Ed. II (S.S. xvi), 110, 112.

[2] Cf. *Abbot of Barlings* v. *Paynel*, Y.B. 7 Ed. II (S.S. xvi), 162, 164.

[3] *Warthill* v. *Selby*, *ubi sup.*, argument between Inge J. and Denham.

[4] *Anon.*, Y.B. 2 Ed. II (S.S. i), 109.

[5] Bereford C.J. and Herle in *Walsham* v. *W.*, Y.B. 8 Ed. II (S.S. xviii), 52, 57.

south and the other the half towards the north. And this seemed strange to Bereford (C.J.).'[1] Probably owing to the reporters' laconic methods, the references are sometimes very vague; but they were doubtless mentioned with fuller detail in court, for opposing counsel seem to recognize the circumstances at once. When, for example, Scrope makes a citation in such general terms as 'a wife that sought to recover her inheritance was rebutted', &c., Denham answers, 'That case is still undecided' (*C'est unquore pendant*).[2] Sometimes, when counsel is relying on memory, the scepticism of the Bench is candid to the point of brutality. We find Stanton J. in 1311 using an expression which may be regarded as the medieval equivalent of 'If that is the law of England, I will eat my hat!' He asks Miggeley:

> 'Where have you seen a guardian vouch on a writ of dower?
>
> *Miggeley*. Sir, in Trinity term last past, and of that I vouch the record.
>
> *Stanton J.* If you find it, I will give you my hat (*jeo vous dorra mon chaperon*).'[3]

Miggeley's words remind us that ultimately the only authority cognizable by the court was the record of the case. Nevertheless, a great deal must have turned on the readiness of counsel in adducing precedents within their own experience.

This is even more true of the Bench. One cannot help being struck by the particularity with which judges recall the circumstances of preceding cases, many of them of no very recent date. In 1310 Stanton J. is relying confidently on a case decided by Sir John of Metingham,[4] who was appointed to the King's Bench in 1276 and died in 1301, so that Stanton must be carrying his memory back some distance. Inge J. in 1314 not only

[1] *Anon.*, Y.B. 2 Ed. II (S.S. ii), 5, 6.

[2] *Bordesdene* v. *B.*, Y.B. 7 Ed. II (S.S. xv), 190.

[3] *Anon.*, Y.B. 4 Ed. II (S.S. vi), 168. The *chaperon* was a hood attached to, and forming part of, the elaborate headgear of the period.

[4] *Kembeare* v. *K.*, Y.B. 4 Ed. II (S.S. iv), 153, 154.

cites an opinion of Sir Ralph of Hengham, which must have been at least ten years old and probably much older, but recalls a remark which Hengham made to Bereford.[1] But most conspicuous in this respect is Bereford himself. In the Year Books of Edward II, his is the dominating personality on the Bench. He is a Chief Justice in no mere titular sense. Time and again he supports his opinions, in the most emphatic manner, with citations. 'I have seen a case of' is his frequent expression, or 'Do you not remember the case of?' &c.,[2] and he unmistakably gives counsel to understand that unless they can 'distinguish' his precedent, they cannot succeed.[3] Occasionally he recalls not only decisions, but arguments before the court: 'and once I saw here a great master (*un graunt mestre*) wanting to aver in a writ of entry', &c.[4] His rejection of counsel's citations is sometimes very summary, not to say impatient. His only reply to Scrope's adduction of a named case is, 'Never will you see such an avowry received.'[5] His memory, if it be solely memory, is very tenacious. In 1312 he cites a decision of Sir John Lovetot, who was raised to the Common Pleas in 1275 and removed therefrom in 1289.[6] His statement of the facts of a case is usually clear and concise;[7] and, indeed, some of his *memorabilia* are as vivacious as they are instructive. The following is typical of his manner of narration, and is interesting in showing that what Bereford was doing with precedents, Hengham had done before him.

'In the time of the late King Edward a writ issued from the Chancery to the sheriff of Northumberland to summon Isabel

[1] *Kemston* v. *Ralph*, Y.B. 8 Ed. II (S.S. xviii), 24, 25.
[2] See Maitland, Y.B. 3 Ed. II (S.S. iii), Introd. x.
[3] See, for example, *Halstede* v. *Gravashale*, Y.B. 2 & 3 Ed. II (S.S. ii), 53, 54; *Bernake* v. *Montalt*, Y.B. 3 Ed. II (S.S. iii), 60.
[4] *Bassett* v. *Driby*, Y.B. 6 Ed. II (S.S. xv), 46, 47; *Walsham* v. *W.*, Y.B. 8 Ed. II (S.S. xviii), 52, 57.
[5] *Archbishop of Canterbury* v. *Percy*, Y.B. 3 Ed. II (S.S. iii), 31, 34.
[6] *Anon.*, Y.B. 6 Ed. II (S.S. xiii), 43, 44.
[7] See, for example, a model précis in *Walsham* v. *W.*, Y.B. 8 Ed. II (S.S. xviii), 52, 56, in the form of a note.

Countess of Albemarle to be at the next parliament to answer the King "touching what should be objected against her". The lady came to parliament, and the King himself took his seat in the parliament. And then she was arraigned by a justice of full thirty articles. The lady, by her serjeant, prayed judgement of the writ, since the writ mentioned no certain article, and she was arraigned of divers articles. And there were two justices who were ready to uphold the writ. Then said Sir Ralph Hengham to one of them: "Would you make such a judgement here as you made at the gaol delivery at C. when a receiver was hanged, and the principal [criminal] was afterwards acquitted before you yourself?" And to the other justice he said: "A man outlawed was hanged before you at N., and afterwards the King of his great grace granted the man's heritage to his heir because such judgements were not according to the law of the land." And then Hengham said: "The law wills that no one be taken by surprise in the King's court. But, if you had your way, this lady would answer in court for what she has not been warned to answer by writ. Therefore she shall be warned by writ of the articles of which she is to answer, and this is the law of the land." Then arose the King, who was very wise, and said: "I have nothing to do with your disputations, but, God's blood! you shall give me a good writ before you arise hence." So say I here.'[1]

The citations of Bereford, as well as of other judges of this period, are so circumstantial when we get anything like a full report of them, that one is tempted to wonder whether they were based solely on extemporary recollection. We know from modern experience that judges often have extraordinarily long and vivid memories of case-law; but if Bracton compiled a case-book, it is not unreasonable to suppose that other judges did the same. Certainly some of the judicial dicta have an air of being based on some kind of private jottings. In that matter, however, we can but conjecture; but I suspect that we may see here the beginnings of those 'private reports'

[1] *Goldington* v. *Bassingburn*, Y.B. 3 Ed. II (S.S. iii), 194, 196; also reported in Y.B. 5 Ed. II (S.S. xi), 42, 44; see Bolland, Introd. to this vol., xl. Cf. Bereford's graphic citations in *Toftes* v. *Thorpe*, Y.B. 3 Ed. II (S.S. iii), 71, 72, and *Scaldeford* v. *Abbot of Vaudey*, Y.B. 3 & 4 Ed. II (S.S. iv), 30, 33.

of which the Year Books, according to the prevailing modern view, are themselves examples, and which were common among judges of a later period.

There does not seem to have been any rule for the antiquity of precedents. Occasionally a decision is referred to as 'an ancient case',[1] but we seldom have means of knowing how ancient. Sometimes we know from other sources that the case referred to was quite recent,[2] and once or twice we have references to cases reported in the Year Books themselves.[3] In one case, already referred to, counsel in 1308 is citing a decision which cannot have been more recent than 1289.[4] But, for the most part, in these early years of the fourteenth century the judges do not seem to go back beyond the latter part of the thirteenth century, particularly to the decisions of Hengham and Metingham. This would seem to mean that they are drawing chiefly upon their own experience at the Bar.[5]

The following dicta, taken from cases ranging from the end of the thirteenth to the end of the fifteenth century, illustrate judicial opinion concerning the importance of relevant example and consistency of decision. This opinion unquestionably grew and strengthened, until, by the reign of Edward IV, it had become a settled and integral element of our Common Law.[6]

In 1294 Saham takes his stand upon tradition in these

[1] *Anon.*, Y.B. 2 Ed. II (S.S. i), 186, 187: 'et sur ces allegerunt un aunciene fet qe fut de un Sire Henri de Berkelee' (nothing else known of this).

[2] *Peter of Peckham's Case*, referred to by Stanton J. in *Bacon* v. *Friars Preachers*, Y.B. 3 Ed. II (S.S. iii), 198, 199.

[3] *Anon.*, Y.B. 3 & 4 Ed. II (S.S. iv), 164: Ingham J. cites *Boys* v. *Charles*, Y.B. 3 Ed. II (S.S. ii), 168. *Leighton* v. *Hegham*, Y.B. 4 Ed. II (S.S. vi), 42: the reporter cites *Wyke* v. *Coleshull*, *ibid.* 44.

[4] *Anon.*, Y.B. 2 Ed. II (S.S. ii), 5, 6, *ante*, p. 193, n. 1. The reference is to a decision of Weyland J., who was dismissed from the Chief Justiceship of the Common Pleas in 1289.

[5] Dr. T. Ellis Lewis (*op. cit.* 47 *L.Q.R.* 415) inclines to think that, on the whole, new cases were preferred to old, but admits that the matter is very uncertain.

[6] See T. Ellis Lewis (*op. cit.*), to whom I am indebted for some of these illustrations.

explicit words:[1] 'In whom are we to put trust, in ancient opinions and in the Justices who were before us and from whom we learned the law, or in your modern notions? I think in the ancient opinions; and we have learned from the Justices, etc.'

In 1327 Scrope is even more emphatic:[2] 'The King has commanded us that we do law and reason according to that which has been done in like case (*en semblable cas*); wherefore consider whether there is any case like to this matter.' [Basset then cited a case.]

In 1454 Prisot gives us[3] what is perhaps the most illuminating discussion of precedent to be found in the Year Books:

'. . . which is strange, as it seems to me, having regard to the many judgements which have been recorded a dozen times in our books, and often argued and adjudged, etc., whereas [there is] no judgement to the contrary. . . . And if we are to defer (*doner regard*) to the opinion of one or two Judges in opposition to so many judgements of various honourable Judges to the contrary, it will be strange, especially when we remember that the Judges who gave these decisions in ancient times were nearer to the making of the statute than we now are, and had more acquaintance with it (*notice dicel'*). . . . And, Sir, if this be now adjudged "no plea", as you vainly contend, it will be a bad example (*mal ensample*) for the young apprentices who are keeping their terms; for they will never be willing to trust their books (*doner credence a lour livres*), if a judgement like this, which has been so many times laid down in their books, is now to be reversed (*ajuge le contrary*).'

A few years later, a studied pronouncement of Yelverton[4] shows that by 1469 judges not merely accepted *stare decisis* as part of forensic routine but were building a kind of legal philosophy upon it. Yelverton's observations are equally interesting in their negative and their

[1] *Alice de C.* v. *Abbot of B.*, Y.B. 21 & 22 Ed. I (R.S.), 429.

[2] *Anon.*, Y.B. 1 Ed. III. 24 (Mich. pl. 21). Nothing else is known of the royal injunction to which this interesting reference is made.

[3] *Windham* v. *Felbridge*, Y.B. 33 Hen. VI. 38, 41 (Mich. pl. 17).

[4] *Anon.*, Y.B. 8 Ed. IV. 9 (Mich. pl. 9).

positive aspects. The question before the Court,[1] he says, has never arisen before. How should a judge approach such a *res integra*? Yelverton replies that he must do as the Canonists[2] and Civilians do 'when a novel case arises upon which there is no previous decision (*nul ley adevant*)'[3]—that is, they must 'resort to the Law of Nature, which is the ground of all laws'. Now, the first principle of the Law of Nature (according to Yelverton, though it may be doubted whether Civilians and Canonists would have agreed without reservation) is that it should be as beneficial as possible to the 'Common Weale'. If then the Court is to *lay down a settled rule* (*un positive ley*) on this new point, it must first of all consider the effect of the rule on the Common Weal, and it would be contrary to the Common Weal to compel men to fulfil judgements without notice, because the object of judgement is 'to appease disputes and wrongs between citizens (*appeser debates and tortes enter les peoplès*)—hence fines;[4] and if the judgement can charge the party with execution without notice, then people are likely to fear and hesitate to submit themselves to judgement'.

So far, Yelverton's reasoning may be considered somewhat casuistical, or, as would be said nowadays, 'wider than was necessary to the decision'; but the significant thing is the responsibility which he evidently felt in making a decision on a point of public importance, *which would be regarded as law in future*. This he expressly states in conclusion: '. . . for this case has never

[1] Briefly, it was whether a party should be held to the fulfilment of a judgement which it was impossible for him to fulfil, owing to lack of notice. The case is an early illustration of the principle *lex non cogit ad impossibilia*. It was evidently regarded as of special interest, and had a further hearing (reported in the same Y.B., f. 20b, Mich. pl. 35).

[2] Strangely printed in the black-letter edition as 'savonists'.

[3] *Ley* is, of course, in its broadest sense, a rule of law; but what Yelverton clearly has in mind is a rule laid down in a decided case; and this sense of *ley* is not uncommon in the Year Books of the period. Cf. the use of *un positive ley*—a very significant expression—which immediately follows.

[4] A fine being, by derivation, the *end* or *conclusion* of a judicial process—as, for example, in 'fine and recovery'. In other words, Yelverton's real point is *interest reipublicae ut sit finis litium*.

been seen before, and therefore our present judgement will be taken for a precedent (*un president*) hereafter.' There could be no clearer proof that by the middle of the fifteenth century judges were fully conscious of the effect of decided cases in moulding the Common Law; and Yelverton's view was certainly not peculiar to himself, though his opinions upon the Law of Nature and public policy might not have been universally accepted.

Two final examples may be taken from the end of the fifteenth century. In 1496 Hussey J. observes:[1] 'Our decision in this case will be shown hereafter as a precedent (*pur un precedent*). We therefore wish to consider our judgement (*estre avises, que nous ferons in le cas*).' In 1498 Fineux J. says, in a case of *quare clausum fregit*:[2] 'I apprehend that your decision (*agard*) in the case will be a precedent (*un precedent*) in similar cases on the statute from this day henceforth, and although the rule (*le Ley*) was against your opinion, yet it is not error for us to grant aid, even though aid did not lie'—which seems to mean that the Court was following 'authority' contrary to its inclination.

I must not give the impression that at this period there was any explicit doctrine that precedents were 'binding'. If, for example, Bereford did not like a precedent, he had no hesitation in saying so; and there are at least hints in the reports that whether he liked it or not depended to some extent on the state of his temper.[3] In *Berewyk* v. *Brembre*[4] a writ of debt was brought against B and C of forty pounds. B came to Court and acknowledged that

1 *Anon.*, Y.B. 11 Hen. VII. 10 (Mich. pl. 33).

2 For other examples from the same period, see T. Ellis Lewis, *op. cit.*, 47 *L.Q.R.* 412, who does not overstate the matter when he observes that 'the legislative aspect of the judicial process was not disguised'.

3 One can imagine the reporter's sly smile as he records Bereford's outburst against the learned Hengham: '*Bereford irascitur, dixit*: Do you think, John Hengham, to embarrass the court in this plea as you did in the case of Christian the widow of John Chaloner? *Par seint Jake*, you shall not!': *Anon.*, Y.B. 4 Ed. II (S.S. vi), 168, 169, referring to *Chaloner* v. *Conduit*, *ibid.* 18.

4 Y.B. 4 Ed. II (S.S. vi), 9.

he was bound by specialty for the debt. But C pleaded that she was a married woman on the day when the writ was purchased, and still was so. Counsel asked for execution as to a moiety, and damages. Stanton J., evidently *dubitans*, waited until the Chief Justice came, and put the matter before him. Bereford was clearly out of humour. 'A plague on your covenants!' he cried. 'They are a nuisance to the Court!'[1] Apparently there followed a discussion on the Bench; then:

> '*Stanton J.* said that he had seen a tenant make two attorneys in the time of Metingham J. One came and said nothing; the other denied [something]; and then the judge made the tenant come in his own person.
>
> '*Bereford C. J. That was a mistake.* We will not do so; but will enquire whether the woman was covert or not; meanwhile let execution against him who has acknowledged the deed remain in suspense, &c. And so the matter stood.'

In *Drinkstone* v. *Prioress of Markeyate*,[2] Hedon *arguendo* cites *Cooper* v. *Delegold*, a reported case to which Bereford was a party,[3] and urges that 'we have seen damages awarded in similar circumstances'. All the Chief Justice has to say is, 'You will never see them so long as I am here.' The judges seem sometimes to have taken a strong line of their own, even to the point of ignoring quite well-established doctrines.[4] They were not for a moment 'bound' by previous doctrines of which they did not approve; justice stood above all precedent and, as Sharshulle J. once declared emphatically, '*nulle ensaumple est si forte comme resoun*'.[5] A scientific search for precedents did not exist—indeed, in the nature of the case, it could not exist. There were no 'reports' as we understand the term. The Year Books themselves were certainly nothing of the kind; and if they had been

[1] 'Meschaunce aveigne a vos covenauntz; ils encombrent la court.'

[2] Y.B. 5 Ed. II (S.S. xi), 96, 98.

[3] *Ibid.* 84.

[4] See *Thornhead* v. *Salkeld*, Y.B. 5 Ed. II (S.S. xii), 69, and Bolland's observations thereon, *ibid.*, Introd., xviii ff.

[5] Y.B. 18 & 19 Ed. III (R.S.), 376; see *post*, p. 400, n. 3.

intended to be so, they would have been extremely defective guides as to *rationes decidendi*, for they concern themselves for the most part with points of pleading and with the discussion of the case rather than with the actual decision—indeed, the decision is often left to conjecture. As has been said, the only authoritative source of decisions was the Plea Rolls themselves.[1] But Plea Rolls were obviously not things which could be produced easily in court; it was no light matter to search them or have them searched; and there is ample evidence that they were very difficult of access even to prominent counsel.[2] Lawyers therefore had to rely, as we have seen that they did, on their own memories, doubtless assisted by current notes.

And if there is no reference to 'reports', because they did not exist, neither is there reference to what did exist —viz. learned treatises. To speak of a 'system of precedents' in connexion with the Year Books would be a complete anachronism. Nevertheless, the foundations of our case-law do most plainly exist in these medieval reports. Their very *raison d'être* was the instructive value of the decided case, or the arguments and pleadings leading to it. The judges were well aware, even from early times, that their decisions were shaping the law. In 1305 Hengham addresses counsel in these emphatic terms: 'Leave off your noise and deliver yourself from this account; and afterwards go to the Chancery and purchase a writ of Deceit; *and consider this henceforth as a general rule* (*e ceste reulle tiegnez desormes generale*).'[3] In 1310 Bereford declares that 'by a decision on this avowry we shall make a law throughout all the land'.[4]

[1] On the nature of the court records, see S. E. Thorne, 'Courts of Record and Sir Edward Coke', *University of Toronto Law Journal*, No. 1, 1937.

[2] Bolland, *Lectures on the Year Books*, 34; Holdsworth, *Sources and Literature of English Law*, 82 ff. Holdsworth also points out (42 *L.Q.R.* 254) that a great change was bound to come over the records of decisions when medieval oral pleadings gave place to written pleadings. The Year Books are, after all, only notes of *things said* in court.

[3] *Anon.*, Y.B. 33 & 35 Ed. I (R.S.), 4.

[4] *Venour* v. *Blount*, Y.B. 3 & 4 Ed. II (S.S. iv), 161.

In 1313 Stanton J. says 'that if judgement had been given against the claimant on this he would have been without recovery for all time; *and that you may safely put in your books for law.*[1] And Bereford C.J. said the same.' Whether or not Stanton was referring to a report which he knew was being taken of that particular case, it is impossible to say. The Year Books themselves may conceivably be referred to in the words 'your books'; but they were never adduced as actual authorities in court.[2] Yet they greatly affected the conception and application of precedent. By the middle of the fourteenth century Hillary J. says, 'We will not *and we cannot* change the ancient usages'.[3]

As time went on, respect for precedent steadily grew, and the somewhat arbitrary disposition of Bereford C.J. ceased to be characteristic: until, by the beginning of the sixteenth century, it is possible to say that Bracton's principle, *a similibus ad similia*, is playing an even greater part in the development of our law than he himself could have foreseen. It is true that judges continued to be in two minds—at one time they would say, like Hillary J., that they *could* not, even if they would, change the established law; at another they seemed disposed to hold that no amount of precedent could justify what they considered to be bad law; and certainly no medieval judge would have conceded that, merely because a doctrine had been laid down in previous cases, it was necessarily law which he was bound to follow. But this contradiction, as we shall see, was not peculiar to the medieval period; it persisted for centuries after the days of the Year Books. What seems certain is that from the earliest times of our legal records there was steadily growing a principle of judicial technique which was the exact opposite of Justinian's dogma, and which has been,

[1] 'Et que homme pout sauuement mettre le en son liuere pur ley': *Midhope* v. *Prior of Kirkham*, Y.B. 7 Ed. II (S.S. xv), 172, 178.
[2] Maitland, Y.B. 3 Ed. II (S.S. iii), Introd., ix ff.
[3] *Anon.*, Y.B. 16 Ed. III (R.S.), 88.

indeed, the master principle of the growth of the Common Law.[1]

Sixteenth- and seventeenth-century Reports

When we reach the sixteenth century, the Year Books end abruptly and in future are known to lawyers chiefly through the Abridgements. Now begin those series of 'private reports' which will continue to flow forth in extraordinary abundance until the middle of the nineteenth century. We have seen that the actual term 'precedent', or 'president', was already becoming common in the later Year Books. It reappears in Dyer, one of the pioneers of the private reports—e.g. in a case of the

[1] Numerous other examples both of the adoption and of the rejection of precedents in the Year Books are to be found in the works already cited of Sir Percy Winfield and of Dr. T. Ellis Lewis. In previous editions of this book evidence drawn from the earlier Year Books suggested the conclusion that precedent played an important part even in the thirteenth century—more important, I believe, than had been generally recognized. The researches of Dr. Ellis Lewis in the same period, and more especially in the later Year Books, have produced an overwhelming body of evidence, as it seems to me, to the same effect. It is therefore a little difficult to understand why Dr. Ellis Lewis warns us so anxiously and so often that there was no system of 'binding' precedents, that 'example' or 'ensample' was a different thing from 'authority' in the modern sense, and that 'consistency of judicial decision', rather than 'following authority', was the only significance of citation in the Year Books. The point, if one may say so with respect, is hardly worth labouring. As will appear in these pages, the whole conception of the hierarchy of judicial authority and the binding force of the case 'on all fours' is a comparatively modern notion, which took centuries to develop into its present form, and which would have been quite inconceivable in the judicial and governmental organization of medieval England. The important consideration is that at a very early stage our law took the line of the inductive method of judicial technique, and has ever since adhered to it. 'Consistency of judicial decision' is, after all, the basic principle of any method of employing precedents, and is no different in essence in the twentieth century from what it was in the fifteenth, though in form and operation it differs greatly, inasmuch as it has been systematized on certain well-defined principles. It was an historical impossibility for those systematic principles to exist in the Middle Ages; but the substance was already there, and nothing could be farther from the truth than the notion, once popular (chiefly on the supposed authority of Coke), but now discredited, that 'case-law' was practically unknown in the medieval period, and was suddenly invented in the sixteenth century (or even invented, as has been sometimes suggested, by Coke himself). Actually, the transition from the Year Books to the reports which began to abound in the succeeding centuries was perfectly natural, consistent, and, indeed, inevitable; and it would be difficult to account for it if the Year Books were as innocent of 'case-law' as we have sometimes been asked to believe.

year 1557. There it is said that a decision was given 'notwithstanding two presidents'.[1] The practice of citation is firmly established in these early reports. Dyer often refers to Year Book cases, as well as to Britton, Fleta, Littleton, and Fitzherbert.[2] Sometimes, as in the Year Books, counsel and judges seem to be relying on their memory: thus Willoughby cites a case of Lord Roos and Fitzherbert J. 'remembered this as Willoughby said'.[3] Some cases consist almost entirely of citations by judges, counsel, or the reporter himself.[4] In Plowden (Reports, 1550–80) the same method is followed, and here we have one interesting statement of the principle of judicial uniformity.

'For *Onslow* and *Gerard* said that the records of every court are the most effectual proofs of the law in relation to the things

[1] *Anon.*, 2 Dyer 148b. In the edition of 1588, which has been available to me (probably the second—Dyer's reports cover the period 1513–82), the words are: 'Et le briefe et judgement supra fuit rule per opinionem Curiae de Banco non obstante deux presidents, lun fur un nihil dicit lauter fur confession, monstre al contrary tempore E. Montague, S. que speciall judgement et briefe dexecution serra de lentier assets, quod est difficile ut credo, vide antea fol.', &c. The Montague referred to was Chief Justice of the King's Bench from 1539 to 1545 (Foss, *Judges*, 449), so that the precedent was not very old; but Dyer's caveat seems to indicate that he doubted the accuracy of the report.

[2] e.g. *Warren* v. *Lee*, 2 Dyer 126b. Typical examples of his method of reporting may be found in *Anon.*, 1 Dyer 7a, and *Wise's Case*, 2 Dyer 144b. In view of numerous examples to the contrary (including many cited by himself), I am at a loss to understand Dr. T. Ellis Lewis's observation (48 *L.Q.R.* 239) that 'with the exception of Coke, the reports down to the time of Burrow, by what seems a singular conspiracy of silence among their authors, rarely devote even a passing notice to the authority of judicial decisions.'

[3] *Abbot of Bury* v. *Bokenham*, 1 Dyer 7b, 11a.

[4] e.g. *Bold* v. *Molineux*, 1 Dyer 14a. In these early reports, unless one is fortunate enough to have access to a first edition, there is nothing except the dates of the cases (an insufficient guide) to show how many of the references are attributable to the reporter himself and how many were actually cited in court. It was the practice for subsequent editors to add great numbers of cases, and to announce this fact in title-page and preface as one of the chief attractions of the edition. At a later date, the habit of annotation grew up, so that the gloss sometimes became more bulky than the text. The classic example is Williams's Saunders. But it is indubitable that Dyer's method was largely based on precedent. His reports, like so many which followed them, were in inception and purpose simply a judge's notebook for his own guidance and, probably for that reason, were often laconic and obscure in form.

treated of in the same court; and that which is used in one court is law in all courts, and throughout all the realm. And therefore in matters of the Crown, as in appeals of felony, and indictments of murder and treason and such like, if a question arises what is the law in such things and what not, the records of the King's Bench are the most effectual proofs of it, and that which is used there ought to be taken as a proof of the law throughout the realm; for that court treats of such things, and has jurisdiction of them, and the records there are testimonies of the law in those points.'

And the same is said of the law of property in the Common Pleas and of the King's revenue in the Exchequer.[1]

In this passage it will be observed that the reference is not so much to the *ratio decidendi* of cases as to the *mos iudiciorum*. We read in Coke that 'the customs and courses of every of the King's Courts' (though not of local courts) 'are as a law, and the Common Law, for the universality thereof, doth take notice of them; and it is not necessary to allege in pleading any usage or prescription to warrant the same. . . . Every Court of Westminister ought to take notice of the customs of the other Courts.'[2] This is characteristic of most of the seventeenth-century reports, and indicates a tendency to lay stress on what we should nowadays call points of practice. When Hobart (Reports, 1603–25) speaks of precedent, he is generally thinking of the practice of the courts in matters of pleading and procedure.[3] The application of precedents of this kind is very rigorous, and the Court will follow them even when it disagrees with the rule which they embody. The sheriff of Norfolk's return to a writ for an inquiry of damages for slander

[1] *The Case of Mines*, Plow. 310, 320 (ed. 1791).

[2] *Lane's Case* (1588), Co. Rep. 15b.

[3] Thus in a writ of assize, the court will not amend *illum* to *illam* because in one case of 11 Hen. VII it has been so held: *Oglethorp* v. *Maud*, Hob. 128. Cf. *Blount's Common Recovery*, Hob. 196: *Bird* v. *Snell*, Hob. 249. The word 'precedent' has always been used in a special sense of model forms of pleading and conveyancing.

is held insufficient in law: 'but yet the Court would not reverse the judgement, because there were divers of the like, both in the King's Bench and Common Pleas, especially in Suffolk and Norfolk in later times'.[1] A new form of writ of waste is held to be 'wanting substance', yet is allowed 'because the Clerks of the Chancery affirmed and showed their books that they had used this form always in that case since the making of the statute'.[2] Something of the same kind is to be found in Yelverton (Reports, 1603–25);[3] here again 'precedents' seem generally to refer to matters of procedure.[4] However, the importance of substantive precedents is also constantly recognized. As early as Croke's Elizabethan Reports, it is laid down that 'being there is not any president found thereof, it is a good argument that the action is not maintainable';[5] and a little later that 'presidents are founded upon great reason and are to be observed',[6] and 'these things which have been so often adjudged ought to rest in peace'.[7] In Hobart, the Star Chamber lays down that 'presidents of Courts as well as laws are built upon reason and justice, and *tantum habent de lege quantum habent de Justitia*'.[8] Jenkins, in the preface to his Reports, which cover the period Charles I and the Commonwealth, deprecates 'variety of judgements and novelty of opinions (those two plagues of the Commonwealth)' and pays a tribute to the authority of Littleton,

[1] *Virely* v. *Gunstone*, Hob. 83. Note the reference to local practice.

[2] *Skeat* v. *Oxenbridge*, Hob. 84.

[3] '*Sed non allocatur*; for 1,000 precedents are contrary; and in respect of the continual use to lay the statute in this form as the plaintiff has declared, the Court said they would not alter it, for that would be to alter all the judgements that were ever given in this Court': *Oliver* v. *Collins*, Yelv. 126, 127.

[4] e.g. *Charnell* v. *Holland*, Yelv. 49, and *Weaver* v. *Clifford*, Yelv. 42, where occurs the interesting dictum that precedents in the Chancery do not 'close the mouths of the Judges of the Common Law'.

[5] *Damport* v. *Sympson*, Cro. Eliz. 520, 521.

[6] *Robins* v. *Sanders*, Cro. Jac. 386, though here the point is purely one of form—whether judgement should be entered as *concessum est* or *consideratum est*.

[7] *Spicer* v. *S.*, Cro. Jac. 527.

[8] *Courteen's Case*, Hob. 270.

whose treatise, he says, is filled with resolutions of the courts, and 'the learned from his time to ours have constantly adhered to these resolutions, and not departed from them in the least'. Indeed, it seems that the courts had come to depend so habitually on 'authority' that they were in some embarrassment when there was no authority to guide them; and in the great case of *Manby* v. *Scott* in 1659[1] the Court of Exchequer Chamber felt it necessary to state explicitly that when no precedent existed the Court was perfectly at liberty to create one.

Coke

The imperishable landmark, in this aspect of the development of the Common Law, was Coke himself. Naturally of a conservative temperament, he believed ardently in the force of example and tradition in all things legal and constitutional. 'Our book cases', he says, 'are the best proof what the law is; *argumentum ab auctoritate est fortissimum in lege*':[2] and the principle reappears in many different forms throughout his writings. But, while he had great faith in precedent, he believed in it only if it was used intelligently. He was profoundly dissatisfied with the indiscriminate and pretentious citation, which seems to have come into vogue in his day, which has not ceased since his death, and of which, it must be confessed, he was himself not always innocent. He tells us[3] that in Year Book days it was the custom to cite general principles which were to be found 'in our books', but without reference to particular instances;[4] whereas in his own day, the tendency was to cite multitudinous instances, without sufficient regard to principle or to relevance; 'and now in so long arguments with such a farrago of authorities, it cannot be but there is much refuse, which ever doth weaken or lessen the weight

[1] 2 Sm. L.C. (13th ed.) at p. 428.

[2] Co. Litt. 254a.

[3] 10 Rep., Preface, xiib.

[4] For reasons which we have seen; but Coke's statement is perhaps too wide, for, as we have noted (*ante*, p. 187), cases were occasionally cited by name in the Year Books. Coke's statement in this well-known Preface has sometimes been interpreted as an assertion that citation was unknown in the Year Books—which Coke neither said nor meant.

of the argument'. Further, he was of the decided opinion that the usefulness of case-law was being undermined either by inaccurate reporting or by the absence of any definitive reporting at all. His blunt words on this subject are worth recalling:

'I have often observed that for want of a true and certain report, the case that hath been adjudged standing upon the rack of many running reports (especially of such as understood not the state of the question) hath been so diversely drawn out, as many times the true parts of the case have been disordered and disjointed, and most commonly the right reason and rule of the Judge utterly mistaken. Hereout have sprung many absurd and strange opinions, which being carried about in a common charm, and fathered on grave and reverend Judges, many times with the multitude, and sometimes with the learned, receive such allowance as either beguile or bedazzle their conceits and judgements.'[1]

His object, therefore, in publishing his Reports (which, he tells us, he was for long reluctant to do) was twofold—first, to provide a permanent record of cases which he regarded as illuminating different branches of the law; and second, to furnish a model of accurate and learned reporting. Despite his prolixity and the asperities of his style, he succeeded eminently in both objects and exercised a profound influence upon the annals of the Common Law. After him, the 'unwritten' law of England could no longer remain unwritten, and judicial records, which he had called the *thesauri absconditi* of the law[2] and which were not preserved in a well-ordered treasure-house, could no longer be 'carried about in a common charm'. With his great erudition Coke combined sensible practical precepts for the use of case-law—as when he advised the student (whom, in his solicitude for the future of his profession, he always had in mind) to sharpen his wits on recent judgements before he attempted the more recondite learning of the Year Books.[3]

[1] 1 Rep., Preface.

[2] *The Marshalsea Case* (1613), 10 Rep. 75a.

[3] Co. Litt. 249b.

Unfortunately, the better elements of Coke's doctrines were not taken to heart immediately and his influence was to be somewhat delayed, for the very success of his Reports carried with it its own penalty. In the troubled days of constitutional crisis, and especially during the Commonwealth period, he was followed by many inferior imitators, not a few of whom, falling into the very vices which he condemned, would have incurred his robust disdain. Throughout the remainder of the seventeenth century, and, indeed, until the appearance of Sir James Burrow's reports in the mid-eighteenth century, the whole theory and practice of precedent was in a highly fluctuating condition. It is interesting, therefore, to find, seventy-three years after Coke published the first volume of his Reports, John Vaughan, who was Chief Justice of the Common Pleas from 1668 to 1674, attempting to develop a systematic theory of the authority of precedents, and of the relative validity of *rationes decidendi* and of *dicta*.

Vaughan's principles

In the case of *Bole* v. *Horton* (1673), at p. 382 of Vaughan's Reports, the following principles are laid down:

'An extra-judicial opinion given in or out of Court is no more than the *prolatum* or saying of him who gives it, nor can be taken for his opinion, unless everything spoken at pleasure must pass as the speaker's opinion.

'An opinion given in Court, if not necessary to the judgement given of record, but that it might have been as well given if no such, or a contrary opinion had been broached, is no judicial opinion, nor more than a *gratis dictum*. But an opinion, though erroneous, concluding to the judgement, is a judicial opinion, because delivered under the sanction of the judge's oath, upon deliberation, which assures it is, or was, when delivered, the opinion of the deliverer. Yet if a Court give judgement judicially, another Court is not bound to give like judgement, unless it think that judgement first given was according to law. For any Court may err, else errors in judgement would not be admitted, nor a reversal of them. Therefore, if a judge conceives a judgement given in another Court to be erroneous, he being sworn to judge according to law, that is, in his conscience, ought not to give the like judgement, for that were to wrong every man having a like cause, because another was wronged before, much less to follow extra-judicial opinions, unless he believes those opinions are right.'

In the same strain he declares: 'Presidents are useful to decide questions, but in such cases as these which depend upon fundamental principles, from which demonstrations may be drawn, millions of presidents are to no purpose.' Therefore procedural precedents of process issued by Sheriffs of Wales are not necessarily to be accepted, without a judicial decision confirming them: 'many things may be done several ways (as Bonds) though they have regularly one common form, yet they may be in other forms as well.'[1]

Vaughan's principles might well be adopted by any French court at the present day. They constitute a reaction against the austerity of the *mos iudiciorum* exemplified by the cases cited above from Hobart. To the same effect is Hale. 'It is true', he says,

> 'the decisions of courts of justice, though by virtue of the laws of this realm they do bind as a law between the parties thereto, as to the particular case in question, till reversed by error or attaint, yet they do not make a law properly so-called (for that only the King and Parliament can do); yet they have a great weight and authority in expounding, declaring and publishing what the law of this kingdom is, especially when such decisions hold a consonancy and congruity with resolutions and decisions of former times, and though such decisions are less than a law, yet they are a greater evidence thereof than the opinion of any private persons, as such, whatsoever.'[2]

The eighteenth century

In the middle of the eighteenth century, the operation of precedent had become an integral part of the Common Law system. The period of Lord Mansfield is one of the turning-points of our legal history, and in order to understand the development and final establishment of case-law in the nineteenth century, we must

[1] *Concerning Process into Wales*, Vau. 419.

[2] *Hist. Com. Law*, iv. 67 (ed. 1739).

consider the part which it played in Lord Mansfield's great constructive work.

Two distinct and complementary principles are discernible in his judicial method.

Lord Mansfield

On the one hand, he insisted on the principle of certainty and consistency of decision. By his critics, not only in his own day but even at the present time, he has sometimes been charged with an iconoclastic disregard of tradition and example. This is a grave exaggeration. A reformer he was, and sometimes his reforming zeal outran the restraints of time and circumstance; but there is a world-old difference between the reformer and the revolutionary, and, with a few notable exceptions, Mansfield's method was that of moulding and adapting, rather than destroying and replacing, the existing material of the law, to which his learning and his training made him profoundly respectful, even if his natural sympathies sometimes inclined him to be impatient with it. To say that he played fast and loose with precedent is to belie many of his own most deliberate utterances.

On the other hand, he, like Coke, had a deep impatience of the unintelligent and mechanical use of precedent merely for its own sake and without any true relevance to the underlying principles involved in a legal issue. For this reason he frequently insisted, as many judges have done before and since, that the only proper use of precedents was to illustrate and ascertain pertinent principles, not to regard them, as the baser sort of pleaders do, as a machine which will deliver convenient decisions by the mere turning of a handle.

It is worth while to consider in some further detail each of these elements in the philosophy of one of the greatest of English judges, and to observe how they were reconciled and applied.

Many dicta might be quoted to illustrate Mansfield's insistence, even against some of his own contemporaries, on the necessity of adhering to settled principles, *provided that they were established by clear evidence* (we shall see that this was an important qualification) in the form of reliable precedents or well-known practice. I will content myself with one quotation, which crystallizes Mansfield's general attitude to this matter, after he had been on the Bench for eleven years:

'Certainty is one great object of all legal determinations, and peculiarly to be wished for in that branch of the law which concerns corporations, because such questions are often agitated with a heat and spirit not to be satisfied by the best reasons of the soundest discretion, and only to be checked by the authority of rules and precedents, deliberately settled upon former occasions.'[1]

This principle, in one form or another, he again and again asserted, by no means always (as has sometimes been assumed) when it accorded with his own sympathies; for there are not a few instances of his having reached a decision with unconcealed reluctance, solely because 'the authorities are too strong', or 'the cases cannot be got over'.[2] But perhaps the best and clearest example of Mansfield's general position is furnished by the case of *Bishop of London* v. *Ffytche* (1782), wherein a pitched battle was fought between Lord Mansfield and Lord Thurlow upon this very issue of the sanctity of authority and practice. The case is not very well known, being reported in full only in a now forgotten book, Cunningham's *Law of Simony* (p. 56);[3] but it is of particular interest, since it is one of the few comprehensive reports at this period of an appeal to the House of Lords on a matter which was regarded as of great public importance to all the clergy and to certain of the laity.

[1] *R.* v. *Dawes and Marten* (1767), 4 Burr. 2120.

[2] See, for example, *Ingle* v. *Wordsworth* (1762), 3 Burr. 1284; *Swan* v. *Broome* (1764), 3 Burr. 1595; *Doe d. Baynton* v. *Wotton* (1774), Cowp. 189; *Pistol d. Randal* v. *Riccardson* (1784), 3 Doug. 361; *O'Neil* v. *Marson* (1771), 5 Burr. 2812; all of which are cited by C. H. S. Fifoot, *Lord Mansfield*, 208 ff. and elsewhere.

[3] It is also reported, inadequately and with a flatly erroneous headnote, in 1 Brown P.C. 211. The first appeal, to the King's Bench in error from the Common Pleas, is reported in 3 Douglas, 142, and (much better and more fully) in 1 East, 487.

It was, in reality, a test case upon the validity of an ingenious device known as the 'resignation bond', whereby a patron presented to an ecclesiastical living on condition that the incumbent should resign when called upon, or otherwise forfeit the penalty named in the bond (which was often so severe as to be, in effect, compulsory). There is little doubt that the expedient was commonly used as an evasion of the law of simony, for it allowed the patron, by means of a purely fictitious presentation, followed by the incumbent's resignation under bond, to sell a vacant presentation.[1] Nevertheless, it had been in common use for about 150 years, and had been repeatedly held by the courts not to be technically contrary to the Elizabethan statute against simony. Whatever the objections, therefore, on grounds of public policy—and they were considerable—the contrivance had a great weight of precedent to support it; but it was, of course, open to the House of Lords to reverse the current of authority. The judges were summoned, and seven of them, including Lord Mansfield and Skynner C.B., gave their opinions in favour of upholding the bond and dismissing the appeal. They based themselves solely on the unbroken line of authority. One judge only (Eyre B.) was for allowing the appeal, and was prepared to sweep aside all the precedents, on the ground that they had been misinterpreted. Several of the Bishops urged that the legal authorities were of no account as against the strong considerations of policy. Lord Thurlow, who ultimately obtained a narrow victory by 19 votes to 18, was in his most pugnacious mood. In effect, he told their Lordships that he was prepared to ignore the whole body of judicial opinion, and that nothing which had been laid down by other legal authorities would influence his

[1] As was said in argument in the King's Bench: 'The parson has only to refuse to resign, when the patron may sue him on his bond and recover the price of the presentation.' Or the presentee, a man of straw, might resign (as was intended by the parties) in favour of the concealed purchaser. Bishop Stillingfleet had inveighed against the practice in a treatise which was much canvassed in the House of Lords.

own judgement; 'he was not to waive his own opinion upon the general arguments of judges'. These heresies (for which Lord Thurlow, somewhat vaguely, claimed the authority of Lord Hardwicke), together with the revolutionary suggestions of the bishops, deeply shocked Lord Mansfield.[1] His dignified protest may be regarded as his confession of faith concerning the force of authority in law. He said:

'They had heard very strongly upon the other side arguments to the contrary; and certainly it might have admitted of a difference of opinion; but since it has been judicially established, there is a period when it is wiser, better and safer not to go back to arguments at large. He did not know where it would lead to. Were any man to go back to argue at large upon the system of law that has been built upon the Statute De Donis, he did not know that it could be maintained upon arguments; and were any man to go back and argue upon the general reasoning and system of law upon the Statute of Uses, he did not know they could be supported upon general reasoning; but being once established, it is better they should stand erroneous, than by contrary judgements to overturn what has passed. . . . The object of the law is certainty, especially such parts of the law as are of extensive and general influence, which affect the property of many individuals, and which inflict pecuniary penalties; which create personal disabilities; and which work forfeitures of temporal rights. It was of vast consequence *stare decisis*; no man could perceive the mischief of a contrary practice; it was an object of importance to that judicature for many reasons. In the first place, because they were under no control. In the next place, if a wrong rule of law had crept in, they could rectify it in their legislative capacity; and he could by no means agree to what dropped from some of the reverend prelates, that they were not to judge by rules laid down by the Courts below; and that they had a judgement and rules

[1] In the King's Bench, he had already said (3 Doug. 146): 'We are bound by the decisions, if we thought them ever so wrong.' Buller J. was even more emphatic (1 East, 495): 'The rule *stare decisis* is one of the most sacred in the law: and if not adhered to in such a case as this, it would be very difficult to say that it ought to weigh in any. If the law be thought to be improper or inconvenient, application to correct it must be made elsewhere, and not to those who are bound by the repeated and solemn judgements of their predecessors.'

of their own. That he held to be quite unconstitutional. They were to give that judgement which the Courts below ought to have given in their opinions. . . . They were not to be governed by any other rules but the rules of law, equally belonging to the Courts below and that judicature; and the judgement they pronounced must be that which the judges of the Courts of law, properly informed, *ought* to have given.'

There could scarcely be a more energetic assertion of the duty of judicial 'loyalty', and such pronouncements amply justify Mr. Fifoot, in his valuable study of Lord Mansfield (p. 201), in saying that 'he assumed as the foundation of his technique the validity of judicial decisions'. Indeed, some of the expressions in *Bishop of London* v. *Ffytche* venture even farther than a modern lawyer would go, for they seem to deny to the House of Lords the right to reverse a line of authorities. It must be added, however, that Lord Mansfield was not always faithful to the principle which he affirmed so explicitly in this case. His premature attempts (to which lawyers, two hundred years later, are now returning) to expel from the law of contract certain anomalies of the doctrine of consideration; and his effort (which had to wait a century for fulfilment by the legislature) to break down the more artificial barriers between law and equity; these are too well known to need description here. An even bolder heterodoxy was his revolt against those technicalities of conveyancing which he regarded (not without reason) as an elaborate cult for defeating intention. Once again he was two hundred years before his time, and his assault on the Rule in Shelley's Case in *Perrin* v. *Blake* (1770), 4 Burr. 2579, however much it may have been justified by 'reasons at large' which the legislation of the twentieth century was to vindicate, was a sophistical defiance of authority, and was doomed to failure—rightly, upon Lord Mansfield's own professed principles. This he was later to acknowledge with the most creditable candour,[1] and the longer he remained upon the Bench,

[1] In *Hodgson* v. *Ambrose* (1780), 1 Doug. 337. For the whole story of Mansfield's epic battle with the conveyancers, see Fifoot, *op. cit.*, ch. vi.

the more disposed he became to submit with resignation to the exigencies of *stare decisis*.[1] His departures from it are not to be regarded as renunciations, or even as evidence that his mind wavered about it, but rather as the rationalizations of a 'strong' judge to escape a discipline which sometimes was none the less irksome in practice because he acknowledged its necessity in theory.

But, while Mansfield thus consolidated and reaffirmed the doctrine of 'judicial consistency' which, as we have seen, had been gathering momentum since the beginnings of the Common Law, he was equally insistent upon an intelligent technique in the use of precedent. He frequently protested against the shallow notion that there is any magic in *mere* citations, without regard to their true significance as embodiments of principle. His warning in *Jones* v. *Randall* (1774), Cowp. 37, has often been quoted, and often misunderstood.

> 'The law of England would be a strange science if indeed it were decided upon precedents only. Precedents serve to illustrate principles and to give them a fixed certainty. But the law of England, which is exclusive of positive law, enacted by statute, depends upon principles, and these principles run through all the cases according as the particular circumstances of each have been found to fall within the one or the other of them.'

Similarly in *Fisher* v. *Prince* (1762), 3 Burr. 1363, he said: 'The reason and spirit of cases make law, not the letter of particular precedents.' And again in *Rust* v. *Cooper* (1777), Cowp. 629: 'Perhaps there is no case exactly parallel to this in all its circumstances. . . . But the law does not consist in particular cases, but in general principles, which run through the cases and govern the

[1] In one respect he remained impenitent, and did not hesitate to reverse 'erroneous points of practice . . . when found to be absurd or inconvenient', because having no far-reaching consequences in unsettling the law, or affecting any 'rule of property', such departures from precedent did not violate the principle of 'certainty': see *Robinson* v. *Bland* (1760), 1 W.Bl. 256.

decision of them'; and in *R.* v. *Bembridge* (1783), 3 Doug. 327: 'The law does not consist of particular cases, but of general principles, which are illustrated and explained by these cases.'

'*The reason and spirit of cases make law, not the letter of particular precedents.*' This was as fundamental a tenet with Lord Mansfield as the doctrine of consistency and authority which he enunciated so earnestly in cases like *R.* v. *Dawes and Marten* and *Bishop of London* v. *Ffytche.* There is no real contradiction between the two principles: indeed, the one is the necessary counterpart of the other. What Lord Mansfield was emphasizing was the fundamental—indeed, the self-evident—canon that a case is of value as a precedent only for what it *means.* In and of itself, it means nothing; before it can have any relevance to the matter in hand, it must be interpreted; the principle which it embodies, or which it is said to embody, must be brought into logical correlation with the principle on which the decision of the instant case is to depend. In this sense, every precedent is, and can only be, an 'illustration of principle'. There is no other possible basis upon which it can be used as a dialectical instrument. This is as true today as it was in the eighteenth century; it is what we really mean when we say that the only part of a precedent which is authoritative is its *ratio decidendi*: for what else is the *ratio decidendi* than 'the general principle, which runs through the case and governs the decision of it'? It is only by this analysis and synthesis of recorded decisions, in their bearing upon legal principles, that precedents can be of any true illumination; and there is no greater snare in the use of case-law than the mere 'letter of particular precedents' unaccompanied by the interpretative process. Many warnings, besides those of Lord Mansfield, have been uttered from the Bench against this fatal misconstruction of the doctrine *stare decisis.* Lord Hardwicke denounced it with vigour: 'Neither law nor equity consists merely of casual precedents, but the general rules and principles by the reason of which, the several cases coming before the courts of justice, are to be governed.'[1] Similar words were used by Parker C.B. in the great case of *Omychund* v. *Barker* (1784), 2 Eq. Cases Abr. 401.[2] One of the greatest equity lawyers of the nineteenth century affirmed the principle in terms of which Lord Mansfield would have heartily approved.[3] In our own day, another Master of the Rolls warns students of the law that 'cases are decided in accordance with a principle applicable to their own particular facts. The task of the judge to whom a case is cited is to ascertain the principle which was expressly or tacitly applied to those facts by the court which decided it. This leads to misuse of authority and is a not infrequent source of error. The desire for simplification is a perennial weakness of the human mind, even the mind of judges.'[4] This is a matter of daily observation in the courts, and the 'abuse of authority', which becomes a constantly greater danger as precedents grow in volume, can be avoided only by due attention to both

[1] *Gorton* v. *Hancock*, Harg. MSS. 353, f. 122, cited Holdsworth, *H.E.L.* xii. 156.

[2] Cited *ibid.*

[3] Sir George Jessel M.R. in *In re Hallett's Estate* and in *Osborne to Rowlett*, cited *post*, p. 269, n. 1.

[4] Sir Wilfrid Greene M.R. in his Presidential Address (*The Judicial Office*, p. 12) to the Holdsworth Club of the Faculty of Law in the University of Birmingham, 1938. Cf. du Parcq L.J. in *Petrie* v. *Mac Fisheries*, [1940] 1 K.B. 258, 265 and in *Easson* v. *L.N.E.Ry.*, [1944] K.B. 421, 426; *Sparks* v. *Ash*, [1943] K.B. 223, 237; *Maitland* v. *Raisbeck*, [1944] K.B. 689, 692. In *Scott* v. *Seymour*, [1942] 1 K.B. at p. 415 (a case on the Workmen's Compensation Act, 1925), MacKinnon L.J. observed: 'I think it would be possible, owing to the industry which reporters and text-book writers have bestowed on this Act, to find some case or some sentence in support of the most obviously fallacious argument which could ever be adduced during the hearing of cases under the Act.' In *Qualcast* (*Wolverhampton*) *Ltd.* v. *Haynes*, [1959] A.C. 743, both Lord Somervell and Lord Denning protested against the citation of findings of *fact* in particular cases of negligence as precedents of *law*, 'lest we be crushed under the weight of our own reports'. There is a distinction, however, between a *specific* fact found at first instance, and an *inference* drawn from it, which an appellate court may legitimately review; *Benmax* v. *Austin Motor Co. Ltd.*, [1955] A.C. 370. On the logical fallacy involved in reasoning 'from one particular to another particular', see Max Radin, 'The Trail of the Calf', *Cornell Law Quarterly*, Nov. 1946.

of Lord Mansfield's principles, and by regarding them as complementary, not antagonistic.

To this extent, then, we can say that the doctrine of precedent had reached an advanced stage of development in the eighteenth century; all the foundations had been laid; but the process which was to establish the theory, in its full modern acceptation, was not yet complete, and, in the nature of things, could not be complete until a good many more years had passed.[1] Several factors, which have almost entirely disappeared today (though new difficulties have appeared in our own age), made the whole operation of precedent much more unstable than it is at the present time, or has been for nearly a hundred years past.

The whole system of authority nowadays depends upon

[1] There has been some controversy upon this point: see two articles, 'Precedent in English and Continental Law' and 'Case Law: a Short Replication' (A. L. Goodhart, 50 *L.Q.R.* 40 and 196); 'Case Law' (50 *L.Q.R.* 180, now incorporated in *H.E.L.* xii. 102 ff.) and 'Precedents in the Eighteenth Century', 51 *L.Q.R.* 440, by Sir William Holdsworth; and 'Case Law: an Unwarrantable Intervention', by the present writer, 51 *L.Q.R.* 333. Sir William Holdsworth maintained that the 'modern' doctrine of precedent was settled in the latter half of the eighteenth century. The term 'modern' is relative, and no doubt in proportion to the whole span of our legal history the eighteenth century may be regarded as 'modern', but I hardly think that most people so consider it in view of the vast legal transformations of the nineteenth century. At all events, I believe the evidence is convincing that the principle of *stare decisis*, as accepted and practised at the present time, was not, and indeed could not be, settled until the nineteenth century. Sir William Holdsworth explained that the 'modern' doctrine in the eighteenth century was subject to certain 'reservations', and that in the course of the nineteenth century these reservations were either wholly removed or modified to vanishing-point. But he cannot 'have it both ways'. The answer given (*H.E.L.* xii. 157) is a few scattered instances, intended to show that modern courts still exercise some 'censorship' over what they will or will not accept as authority. There must, of course, always be *some* discrimination and scrutiny in the acceptance of any printed material; but if Sir William Holdsworth's rejoinder is intended to mean that the 'reservations' are the same today as in the eighteenth century, it is not only unsustainable on the manifest facts, but is in contradiction of his own thesis. Surely the truth is that in the eighteenth century the doctrine of *stare decisis* was recognized and applied as fully as the circumstances of the time permitted; but that it did not and could not reach its final 'modern' development until certain important changes had taken place in the succeeding age. Otherwise, we seem to be inevitably involved in anachronism.

Judicial hierarchy in the eighteenth century

a clear and unchallengeable hierarchy of courts. The pattern was far more confused in the eighteenth century, and it was by no means easy to say that decisions were 'binding' solely by reason of the source from which they emanated. The complexity which resulted from the co-existence of three jurisdictions in Common Law, a jurisdiction in Equity which often diverged from that of the Common Law, and of two superior courts in the Exchequer Chamber and the House of Lords, made it extremely difficult to distinguish degrees of authority; and this complexity was not thoroughly reformed, though there had been several previous modifications, until 1876. Perhaps the most striking contrast with the modern system is to be found in the authority and jurisdiction of the highest tribunal of all. Today, it is an axiom of the whole legal system that the decisions of the House of Lords, which for this purpose is now an exclusively 'legal' tribunal and is largely recruited from the most distinguished members of other courts, have the last word, unassailable by any other court. Moreover, these decisions are elaborately reported in easily accessible form. It was far different in Mansfield's time. Reliable reports of proceedings in the House of Lords were almost wholly lacking, for the excellent reason that it was a breach of privilege to publish them.[1] Constitutionally,

[1] In 1698 Sir Bartholomew Shower published some indifferent reports of House of Lords cases, in the ingenuous hope 'that these reports may probably convince the young Nobles of this realm, and all who are employed in and about their education, that some general knowledge of the laws of England, and some acquaintance with history and other learning, cannot be unworthy the ambition of every nobleman's son, who has any hopes to sit as judge in that august assembly'. The broad hint, though highly reasonable, was evidently tactless, and the affronted peers, far from seizing the means of grace, voted Shower's volume a breach of privilege. Under this threat, no other reporter dared reveal the mysteries for nearly a century. Brown's Parliament Cases, in eight volumes, covering the greater part of the eighteenth century, did not appear until 1784. Though conscientiously done and of good reputation, they are tantalizing to the modern reader, since they give only the narrative, arguments, and decision, without any of the speeches or reasons. The first adequate House of Lords reports were those of Dow (1812–18), followed, with steady improvement, by Bligh and by Clark & Finnelly.

the House of Lords was, as it now is, the ultimate and absolute Court of Appeal, but it was impossible, for several reasons, for the profession to treat it with the respect which was theoretically due to it. Apart from the mystery with which it surrounded itself, and which made it extremely difficult for anybody to know what exactly it had decided and why, the fact that it might contain a predominant element of peers and churchmen who had no knowledge of law, and did not even pretend to base their decisions on legal considerations, necessarily detracted from its authority in the eyes of all professional lawyers. Further, the practice of 'summoning the judges' was not only extremely cumbrous and burdensome, but had an air of ironical futility when (as happened as late as 1853)[1] a great volume of elaborate judicial opinion might be assembled only to be rejected. The result was that, in practice, the decisions of the Exchequer Chamber, which had a long tradition of authority behind them and which represented the cream of judicial deliberation, carried far more weight than those of the House of Lords. If the reader will consider how completely subversive it would be if the Court of Appeal and the House of Lords occupied the same relative positions today, he will realize how great a difference existed between the eighteenth and nineteenth centuries in this respect alone.

Reports and reporters

An even more marked contrast is to be found in the whole system of reports and reporting; and I doubt whether many lawyers today, accustomed as they are to a comparatively limited number of workmanlike reports (many of them revised by the judges themselves), realize how great this difference was, and how much it affected the whole citation of authority. Douglas, in the introduction to his admirable reports of Mansfield's time,

[1] *Egerton* v. *Brownlow*, 4 H.C.L. 1. Another example may be found in *Bishop of London* v. *Ffytche*, *supra*, pp. 212 ff. The practice, which had long been falling into disuse and disrepute, was abandoned after *Allen* v. *Flood*, [1898] A.C. 1.

expresses astonishment at what has always been one of the most remarkable of our legal anomalies—namely, that although our Common Law has for many centuries drawn much of its life-blood from recorded precedents, it has never had any settled and scientific system of recording them. Similarly, Foster, in the middle of the eighteenth century, observed in the introduction to his *Crown Cases*: 'Imperfect reports of facts and circumstances, especially in cases where every circumstance weigheth something in the scale of justice, are the bane of all science that dependeth upon the precedents and examples of former times.' Attempts at regularization which have been made in earlier times—for example, by Bacon—have never been successful; and even today some substance remains in Douglas's criticism, for though we have abundant and competent reports, their selection depends upon the discretion of individual editors and reporters. In the eighteenth century the situation was entirely different from anything which exists today. A precedent was by no means accepted as an authority merely because it was adduced from a volume of reports; a great deal depended upon the reporter, and judges not only considered themselves at liberty to attach different degrees of weight to different authorities, but could not do otherwise, so great were the variations. Lord Mansfield has often been charged with 'blaming the reporter' when he did not like an inconvenient decision. It is true that he was sometimes a little arbitrary in his preferences, and that later generations did not always concur in his more severe strictures. But in reality he was only doing what every judge of his period had to do, though, with the great authority which he wielded, no doubt he did it, on occasion, somewhat imperiously. For reasons which I have given, I do not believe that he ever deliberately brushed aside an authority, provided that he was satisfied that it *was* an authority. That, however, was a preliminary question which was constantly before the court when cases were cited. The necessity for it will be more clearly appreciated if we consider what material was available.

The Year Books had by this time become, for the most part, antiquarian learning. Between the last of the Year Books and the time of Mansfield there had been a copious production of reports, and nearly a hundred well-known volumes or series were in existence.[1] Among all these, three masterpieces stood by themselves, two belonging to the sixteenth and one to the seventeenth century. These were Coke, Plowden, and Saunders. Their authority was unquestionable, though it is unnecessary to observe that much of the learning in Coke and Plowden was already venerable to the point of obsolescence. Coke, with his enormous superstructure of commentary, was a *thesaurus* of English law rather than a mere set of reports. Saunders was pre-eminently a book of pleading, and was the Bullen and Leake of its age. It enjoyed successive lusty reincarnations at the hands of Serjeant Williams and of his descendants down to Vaughan Williams L.J.

The other reports it is possible to distinguish roughly into three classes. There were upwards of a dozen which were generally recognized as of high authority, though they were by no means of even quality; they were always treated with respect, but it did not follow that they were invariably accepted without question. Most of them were the work of distinguished and learned men, and their imperfections were due not so much to the lapses of their authors as to the fact that they were originally intended only for private use and edification, and that they had been published (in some cases reluctantly) as a protection against plagiarism or importunity. (This had been true even of Plowden, as he tells us himself.) Of these 'superior' reports, about four belonged to the older

[1] There were also manuscript collections, many of which were unknown to posterity. One of them, by John Spelman, a Judge of the King's Bench from 1532 to 1544, seems to have been well known to the profession and was used by Coke: see A. W. B. Simpson, 72 *L.Q.R.* 334.

order (Dyer, Moore, Leonard, and Croke), while the remainder were of the seventeenth and eighteenth centuries.[1] Even the best of these, however, could not be received, and still are not received, without question, and in recent years a case in Croke, which has been constantly cited in connexion with trespassing pigeons, has been rejected for unsatisfactory reporting.[2]

These were sheep, with fleeces not as white as snow, but as white as could be expected in the strange pastures through which some of them had strayed. But there was also a class of goats, not to say scapegoats. Though some judges might regard them more leniently than others, the profession as a whole was agreed that they were of little value, and any counsel who relied on them might elicit from the Bench not attention and sympathy but a satirical smile, or even Olympian wrath. Some of them, like Barnardiston, Bunbury, and Atkyns, Lord Mansfield forbade to be cited to him. This may have been rather harsh, but nobody was greatly surprised at it. Probably the worst reputations were, and are, those of Siderfin, Gilbert, Keble, Carter, Ambler, Comberbach, and (a little after Mansfield's time) Espinasse: while the curious medley known as the Modern Reports,[3] though not without valuable matter, and though greatly improved by the labours of Leach, was notoriously unreliable. Of this undistinguished company, some four dated (in publication) from the sixteenth and early seventeenth centuries (Benloe and Dalison, Keilway,[4] Noy, and Owen), and there were upwards of twenty dating from the seventeenth and eighteenth centuries.[5] Some of the

[1] Yelverton, Rolle, Hobart, W. Jones, T. Raymond, Orlando Bridgman, Vaughan, Salkeld (vols. i and ii only), Wilson, Foster's *Crown Cases*.

[2] See *Hamps* v. *Darby*, [1948] 2 K.B. 311, on *Dewell* v. *Sanders* (1618), Cro. Jac. 490.

[3] See *Hollington* v. *Hewthorn*, [1943] K.B. 587, 598.

[4] On the dubious authorship of his reports, see A. W. B. Simpson, 'Keilwey's Reports', 73 *L.Q.R.* 89.

[5] Latch, Hetley, Style, Siderfin, Levinz, Keble, Freeman, Modern, Kelyng, Carter, Comberbach, Carthew, Skinner, Carey, Barnardiston, Bunbury, Barnes, Atkyns, Espinasse, Select Cases in Chancery, Cases temp. Talbot,

older ones, like Noy, were merely cursive notes, and it was hardly fair to regard them as reports at all. Lord Mansfield and other judges were very free in their comments on some of these weaker brethren[1] and adopted a tone which would be highly unusual in our own day with regard to modern reports.

Finally, there was a large company of reporters—not less than fifty—who might be said to stand in a midway

Ambler, Vesey Senior, Sayer, Anstruther. Occasionally some of these reporters receive thrusts even in modern cases: see, e.g., *Woolmington* v. *Director of Public Prosecutions*, [1935] A.C. 462, 478 on Kelyng; *Wessex Dairies* v. *Smith*, [1935] 2 K.B. 80, 84, and *Hersom* v. *Bernett*, [1955] 1 Q.B. 98, on Espinasse; and *Aglionby* v. *Cohen*, [1955] 1 Q.B. 558, 563, on Siderfin. For criticisms of more modern reports, see *Baylis* v. *Bishop of London*, [1913] 1 Ch. 127, 134, 140 on *Peto* v. *Blades* (1814), 5 Taunt. 657; *Smith* v. *Bailey*, [1891] 2 Q.B. 403, 406 on *Stables* v. *Eley* (1825), 1 C. & P. 614; *In re Adams*, [1922] P. 240, 242 and 39 *L.Q.R.* 12. The *Law Times* and *Law Journal* reports were criticized by Roxburgh J. in *In re Thirlwell*, [1958] Ch. 146, 153. A clear case of misreporting occurs in *Re Swain* (1908), 99 L.T. 604; see 'R.E.M.' in 76 *L.Q.R.* 203, on *Re Levy*, [1960] Ch. 346. On misreporting in the well-known cases of *Williams* v. *Carwardine* (1833), 4 B. & A. 621 and *Dickinson* v. *Dodds* (1876), 2 Ch.D. 463, see Goodhart, 'Determining the *Ratio Decidendi* of a Case', in *Essays in Jurisprudence*, 1, 11. See further C. K. Allen, 'Case Law: an Unwarrantable Intervention', 51 *L.Q.R.* at p. 341.

[1] See, e.g., *Wilson* v. *Greaves* (1757), 1 Burr. 244 (on Ventris); *Cooper* v. *Chitty* (1756), 1 Burr. 20, 35, 36 (on Siderfin, Comberbach, and Lord Raymond); *Lowe* v. *Joliffe* (1762), 1 W.Bl. 365 (on Siderfin and Keble); *Denn d. Burges* v. *Purvis* (1757), 1 Burr. 326 (on Levinz, *per* Denison J.); *Heylyn* v. *Adamson* (1759), 2 Burr. 669, 677 (again on Lord Raymond); *R.* v. *Benfield and Saunders* (1760), 2 Burr. 980, 984 (on Strange); *Soulsby* v. *Hodgson* (1764), 3 Burr. 1474 (on Bulstrode); *Lowe* v. *Peers* (1768), 4 Burr. 2225, 2229 (on a case in Rolle's Abridgement); *R.* v. *Inhabitants of Witney* (1770), 5 Burr. 2634, 2636 (again on Lord Raymond); *Tinkler* v. *Poole* (1771), 5 Burr. 2657 (on Bunbury); *Pillans* v. *Van Mierop* (1765), 3 Burr. 1663, 1671 (on Strange, *per* Wilmot J.); *Woolston* v. *W.* (1761), 2 Burr. 1136 (on Barnardiston); *Le Grew* v. *Cooke* (1798), 1 B. & P. 332 (on Barnes, *per* Buller J.: 'that case is *felo de se* ... unsupported by authority and contradicted by reason'); *Borrowdale* v. *Hitchener* (1802), 3 B. & P. 244 (on Barnes, *per* Heath J.); *Quantock* v. *England* (1770), 5 Burr. 2628 (on Moseley). These examples have been chosen at random: many others might be found. Some of the observations were very severe. In *Bishop of London* v. *Ffytche*, *ubi sup.*, several of the judges referred with unconcealed contempt to Noy, and drew from Lord Thurlow a spirited, but purely rhetorical, reply. Even Lord Kenyon, who professed his determination to stand '*super antiquas vias*', as against the innovations of Lord Mansfield, was, according to Espinasse, sometimes highly impatient of precedent: see Campbell's *Lives of the Chief Justices*, iv. 93, which, however, is hostile evidence.

position.[1] Many of them were very uneven and not highly regarded, but did not occupy so low a status as those who were last named. Others, like Strange, Lord Raymond (whom, however, Lord Mansfield frequently criticized), Lutwyche, the two Blackstones, and perhaps Fortescue and Bulstrode, were, on the whole, listened to with respect but not necessarily with acquiescence, since they were all far from uniformly accurate and intelligible. Not one of them was accepted as being *ex facie* 'binding' on the Court in the same way that modern authorized reports are, with negligible exceptions, received today.

The reasons for the disparities in the reports were many. In the sixteenth century, despite the example of Coke and Plowden, there was no uniform standard of reporting, and, as we have seen, many of the reports, collected for private use and instruction, were not intended for publication at all. Matters did not improve greatly in the seventeenth century, and, indeed, sharply deteriorated during the Commonwealth period, in which reports of the most variable quality proliferated. There seems to have been an almost unlimited appetite for them, but few of them were of any accuracy or repute. The literary history of these sixteenth- and seventeenth-century reports is extraordinary—and depressing.[2] Many,

[1] The list is long and tedious, but it is well to remind ourselves how extensive it was. I would place in this class: (sixteenth century) Bellewe, Little Brooke, New Benloe, Brownlow & Goldsborough, Godbolt, Saville, Popham, Jenkins; (seventeenth century) Davies, Lane, Ley, Calthrop, Bulstrode, Hutton, J. Bridgman, Palmer, Winch, Littleton, Clayton, Aleyn, Hardres, T. Jones, Ventris, Shower P.C., Lutwyche, Godbolt, Goldsborough, March, Popham, Tothill, Anderson, Lord Raymond, Strange; (eighteenth century), Comyns, Fitzgibbon, W. Kelynge, Lee, Cunningham, Fortescue, Cooke, Parker, W. Blackstone, H. Blackstone, Wilmot, Kenyon, Pollexfen, Shower K.B., Moseley, Andrews. A few of these slightly post-date Mansfield.

[2] See Holdsworth, *H.E.L.* v. 355 ff., vi. 551 ff., and xii. 102 ff.; and Veeder, 'The English Reports', *Select Essays in Anglo-American Legal History*, ii. 124. On different degrees of 'authority', see 1 Bl. *Comm.* 72. The principal source for this interesting subject is Wallace, *The Reporters*, which unfortunately takes us only to the end of the eighteenth century. Though full of valuable information, this work is too fragmentary and garrulous to be quite satisfactory.

if not most, were posthumous, and given to the world by irresponsible hands; some of the older ones, already terse and obscure, were further darkened by indifferent translation from Law French; they sometimes purported to cover absurdly long periods of the law; not a few were filched and pirated, and at least one (Freeman) is said to have been hashed up from a stolen manuscript. The attempt to regulate the matter by means of the judges' *imprimatur* degenerated into an empty form and effected no real change. Subsequent editors made considerable improvements in some cases, but the Commonwealth reports, as a whole, remained at best a motley collection, and by the middle of the century they were already drawing strong comments and warnings from those who were concerned for the welfare of the Common Law. In 1657, in an 'Address to the Students of the Common Laws of England', prefixed to the third volume of Croke's Reports, Sir Harbottle Grimstone declared:

'A multitude of flying reports (whose authors were as uncertain as the times when taken, and the causes and reasons of the judgements as obscure, as by whom judged) have of late surreptitiously crept forth. . . . We have been entertained with barren and unwanted products, *infelix lolium et steriles avenae*, which not only tends to the depraving of the first grounds and reason of our students at the Common Law and the young practitioners thereof, who by such false lights are misled, . . . but also to the contempt of our Common Law itself and divers of our former grave and learned Justices and Professors thereof, whose honoured and reverend names have in some of said books been abused and invocated to patronize the indigested crudities of those plagiaries; the wisdom, gravity and justice of our present justices not deeming or deigning them the least approbation in any their courts.'

In the same year, Bulstrode, in the Epistle Dedicatory to his Reports, referred indignantly to

'these late and flying reports, most of them being *incerti temporis* and of late published, not by the authors themselves (who were well known to be profoundly learned), nor yet by them during their lives fitted and prepared for the press, but after their deaths, thus published by others, yet not known by whom, having not named themselves, and these reports not without many gross mistakings in them, whereby they do rather cherish than extinguish law suits'.

Style, also in his Epistle Dedicatory, says quaintly:

'There is not a father alive to own many of them, and they speak so plain in the language of Ashdod, that a knowing man cannot believe they ever sprung from Israelitish parents, but by their pronunciation of Siboleth instead of Shiboleth, may easily collect of what extract they are.'

In 1704 Holt C.J. protested against 'these scrambling reports', which 'will make us to appear to posterity for a parcel of blockheads'.[1] There was marked improvement throughout the eighteenth century, but no radical change until the appearance of the reports of Burrow, Douglas, and Cowper, which, after so much dross, were like pure gold, and indeed constituted the most important event since Coke and Plowden in the history of our law-reporting. Lord Mansfield was far more fortunate in this respect than some of his predecessors—for example, Sir Matthew Hale, who had no better Boswell than Keble: and yet Burrow, in his introduction, expresses the utmost diffidence in his own handiwork, and gives us an instructive insight into the difficulties of accurate reporting in his day. If Burrow, with all his immense industry, and with the exceptional opportunities which he enjoyed as an officer of the Court (he was Master of the Crown Office from 1733 to 1782), was conscious of these deficiencies, how much greater must they have been in his less conscientious predecessors and contemporaries.

I dwell at some length on this subject, because I think it is important for the modern lawyer to realize how utterly different the whole 'state of the authorities' in

[1] *Slater* v. *May*, 2 Ld. Raym. 1072, referring to 4 Mod.

former ages was from the system to which he has become accustomed, and which he is inclined to take for granted. Anybody who has the curiosity to read through Wallace's volume will realize what very diverse opinions were held about the value of the different reports. Nowadays it is perfectly open to a court to question the accuracy or value of a report, but the number of cases in which this is a serious issue is infinitesimal. For Mansfield and Blackstone the position was far otherwise. When Blackstone tells us[1] that 'it is an established rule to abide by former precedents', except when they are 'contrary to reason', or 'unless flatly absurd and unjust', the modern lawyer is apt to regard the reservation either as a mere historical oddity or as a doctrine no less heretical than the same writer's half-hearted doctrine that not only precedents but even statutes are invalid 'if clearly contrary to the divine law'.[2] Blackstone's statement—although it was substantially repeated as late as 1833 in what is generally regarded as a classic enunciation of the doctrine of *stare decisis*[3]—would not be accepted today without considerable qualification, and indeed, his own editor, Christian, entered a caveat against it; but it must be remembered that in Blackstone's day there were many cases in the books which, *as reported*, were indeed 'flatly absurd or unjust'. It is probable that this was what Blackstone had in mind, rather than any theory (which would have been quite contrary to well-recognized judicial principles) that the 'reason' or 'convenience' of each case was a matter for the individual discretion of the judge. Similarly, Blackstone is sometimes suspected of heresy when he tells us (in common with Coke and Hale) that precedents are the best *evidence of the law*, instead of saying that they *are law*. Too

[1] 1 *Comm*. 69.

[2] See *ante*, p. 225.

[3] Parke J. in *Mirehouse* v. *Rennell*: see *post*, p. 232; and cf. Lord Tenterden C.J. in *Selby* v. *Bardons* (1832), 3 B. & A. 17, where he says that precedents must be followed 'unless we can see very clearly that they are erroneous' (cited Holdsworth, 50 *L.Q.R.* 184).

much may be made of this distinction.[1] Remembering, as we always must, that the authority of a decided case lies not in the mere words and phrases which compose it but in the principle which is to be extracted from it, every precedent is, in a sense, only 'evidence' of the law, and not (like a statute) 'the law itself'. This is as true today as it ever was, though the body of precedents is now so highly systematized that it would merely cause confusion and misunderstanding to describe them as 'evidence'. We think of them rather as 'material', though we should still be guilty of misconception if we thought of them as 'the law itself'. But there was another sense, which has now almost entirely disappeared, in which cited cases were 'evidence' in the eighteenth century. The first and most important problem of evidence is its credibility, and the eighteenth-century judge, when an 'authority' was cited to him, had to exercise a preliminary function of which his modern successor is almost wholly relieved—he had to decide whether the witness (i.e. the reporter, or the particular report) was both competent and credible. It is, I think, safe to say that the same difficulty would exist in our own time if the old reports, especially of the 'inferior' class, were in current professional use. As it is, the citation of cases older than the nineteenth century is now rare,[2] but whenever they do make a shy and diffident appearance in court, it is impossible to say that (unless they are among the great 'classics') they usually receive the same respect as modern cases. This is partly because the whole legal system has so greatly changed, but also because in many cases it is extremely difficult to extract from them either an adequate statement of the facts or a *ratio decidendi* on which a modern lawyer feels that he can rely.[3]

[1] I have myself been an offender: 51 *L.Q.R.* 333 ff.

[2] Taking, as fair specimens, the two volumes of Queen's Bench Reports for 1961, I find that out of 167 cases cited or referred to, only 5 were older than the nineteenth century.

[3] They are not therefore valueless. Mr. Veeder (*op. cit.*) very truly observes that 'their historical value can hardly be over-estimated. Reports that are

General view of precedent to end of eighteenth century

It is needless to pursue further the story of the Law Reports.[1] Burrow and his fellow workers had laid the foundations well and truly, and rendered inestimable service to the annals of our law. The Term Reports of Durnford and East, at the end of the century, also marked an auspicious change; they inaugurated a system of recent reports, whereas most of the earlier reports covered cases decided long before publication. From the end of the eighteenth century to 1865, when the semi-official series of the Incorporated Council of Law Reporting was instituted, a very large number of reports—well over 300 different series, covering every jurisdiction—appeared in a continuous stream. They are a storehouse of extraordinary wealth and a wonderful record of the development of the law at a singularly constructive period of our history. They are not all of equal quality, and some few have never commanded great respect;[2] but the average is incomparably higher than in the preceding ages, and the least distinguished of them is not so bad as the worst of the seventeenth century. Among the reporters were the names of not a few who afterwards became famous on the Bench, and at least one great lawyer (Blackburn) was elevated straight from the pedestrian labours of a reporter to the judicial seat. The slipshod work of the seventeenth century would not have been tolerated. There is some evidence that, by 'editing', some learned reporters formulated better law than the judges whom they were reporting. Thus Lord Campbell professed, by 'editing' the reports which he published in youth, to have corrected many 'blunders' of Lord Ellenborough.[3] Nowadays it is customary for judges to

almost worthless as judicial records often throw valuable side-lights upon early practice and procedure'.

[1] See Holdsworth, 'Law Reporting in the Nineteenth and Twentieth Centuries', *Anglo-American Legal History Series*, No. 5 (1941).

[2] e.g. Taunton (1808–19) and Hare (1841–53); while Nisi Prius cases, though well reported in the mid-century by Carrington & Payne, Carrington & Kirwan, and Foster & Finlason, seldom carry as much weight as decisions in Bank. Best & Smith are criticized in *Cotterill* v. *Penn.* [1935] 1 K.B. 53, 61.

[3] See Lord Devlin, *Samples of Lawmaking*, 68.

revise the reports of their own judgements, and sometimes substantial alterations are made on second thoughts.[1]

And so the whole structure of case-law, which we have seen steadily mounting from its deep-laid foundations throughout the centuries, was at last entire—a mixture of styles, perhaps, but a remarkable piece of architecture. The finishing touch was given when the whole system of judicature was simplified. I doubt whether it is possible to fix, or whether it is profitable even to try to fix, an exact moment of time when the 'modern' doctrine of precedents may be said to have established itself once for all. The substance of it, which had evolved gradually but upon organic laws of growth, had reached a high state of development by the end of the eighteenth century, but needed the continually improving mechanism of the succeeding age to give it final and definitive form. In 1833 one of the greatest common lawyers of his age propounded, in terms which have been accepted as a *locus classicus*, the contemporary theory of case-law, though indeed it only reaffirmed what had been said many times before in the more sonorous tones of earlier ages:

'Our Common Law system consists in the applying to new combinations of circumstances those rules of law which we derive from legal principles and judicial precedents; and for the sake of attaining uniformity, consistency and certainty, we must apply those rules, where they are not plainly unreasonable and inconvenient, to all cases which arise; and we are not at liberty to reject them, and to abandon all analogy to them, in those to which they have not yet been judicially applied, because we think that the rules are not as convenient and reasonable as we ourselves could have devised. It appears to me to be of great importance to keep this principle of decision steadily in view, not merely for the determination of the particular case, but for the interests of law as a science.'[2]

[1] See *R.* v. *Agricultural Land Tribunal, Exp. Bracey*, [1960] 1 W.L.R. 911, 914.

[2] *Per* Parke J., *Mirehouse* v. *Rennell*, 1 Cl. & F., 527, 546. It is interesting

Modern doctrine of English law

No judge at the present time would need any reminder to keep this principle 'steadily in view'. The duty of judicial 'loyalty' is now beyond question, and is regulated by principles which we must consider in the next chapter. A few minor points of doubt still remained to be resolved in the later nineteenth century. Thus, in a number of cases it was still debated whether the House of Lords was bound by its own decisions,[1] and as late as 1898[2] the Lord Chancellor thought the matter still sufficiently uncertain to require definite settlement. We shall see (*post*, p. 253) that the principle is, however, subject to growing doubt. The authority of decisions by the Privileges Committee of the House of Lords even now remains in some doubt.[3] While the House of Lords is certainly not bound by decisions of the Judicial Committee of the Privy Council, there is still some theoretical doubt whether the converse is true,[4] since the jurisdiction of the Privy Council is not, like that of the House of Lords, confined to the law of England and Scotland; but on any question of English law it is difficult to imagine the Privy Council rejecting the authority of the House of Lords. There has been some conflict of judicial opinion concerning the relative degrees of authority of

to observe, however, that this celebrated *dictum* was not merely an enunciation of *stare decisis*, but was another assertion of the doctrine that cases must be decided on principle and not on mere citations. Parke J. began by saying that there was no exact authority for the case in hand, and then made his point that it must be decided 'on principle', as *illustrated* by analogous precedents.

[1] *R.* v. *Millis* (1843), 10 Cl. & F. 534; *Bright* v. *Hutton* (1852), 3 H.L.C. 341; *Beamish* v. *B.* (1859), 9 H.L.C. 274; *Att.-Gen.* v. *Dean etc. of Windsor* (1860), 8 H.L.C. 369; *Caledonian Railway Co.* v. *Walker's Trustees* (1882), L.R. 7 App. Cas. 259. See Pollock, *First Book of Jurisprudence* (6th ed.), 334 ff.

[2] *London Street Tramways Co.* v. *L.C.C.*, [1898] A.C. 375. For the history of the controversy, see Lord Wright, 'Precedents', *Cambridge L.J.*, 1943, 1. Previous decisions on questions of foreign law, being regarded as matters of fact, are not binding: *Lazard Bros.* v. *Midland Bank*, [1933] A.C. 289.

[3] *St. John Peerage Claim*, [1915] A.C. 282, 308, *per* Lord Parker; *Viscountess Rhondda's Claim*, [1922] 2 A.C. at p. 376, &c.

[4] See Lord Wright, *loc. cit.*

the Court of Appeal and the Court of Criminal Appeal;[1] and although the general question is not expressly decided in the only relevant House of Lords case,[2] it seems probable that in view of that decision the Court of Criminal Appeal will not readily feel at liberty to resist the conclusions of the Court of Appeal. The doubt in this matter arose out of the fact that under the present system of judicature the Court of Appeal has no direct jurisdiction in criminal matters; and a kindred question, of some importance, is whether expressions of opinion in the Court of Appeal on points of criminal law (which often arise incidentally in civil cases, and may even be essential to the issue) are binding on criminal courts. Probably they are not, in strict theory: but in practice it would be a bold judge who would direct a jury in defiance of an opinion of the Court of Appeal.[3] There is no explicit rule, so far as the present writer knows, about the hierarchy of authority for County Court Judges. While they owe obedience to all appellate divisions of the Supreme Court, it is open to question whether they are actually bound by decisions of individual High Court Judges, though there is no doubt that they will differ from them only with great hesitation.[4]

[1] *Ware & de Freville* v. *Motor Trade Assocn.*, [1921] 2 K.B. 40, *R.* v. *Denyer*, [1926] 2 K.B. 258, and *Hardie* v. *Chilton*, [1928] 2 K.B. 306. On authority in the Court of Criminal Appeal see W. H. D. Winder, 'Precedent in Criminal Courts', *Journal of Criminal Law*, v. 242 (1941).

[2] *Thorne* v. *Motor Trade Assocn.*, [1937] A.C. 797.

[3] See C. K. Allen, 54 *L.Q.R.* 201. At least one modern decision of the Court of Appeal in tort is authoritative in the law of false pretences and of larceny by a trick: *Folkes* v. *King*, [1923] 1 K.B. 282. In *Mead* v. *Chelmsford R.D.C.*, [1953] 1 Q.B. 32, a submission that on an appeal, by case stated, from summary jurisdiction in a criminal matter decisions of the Court of Appeal were not binding was rejected by the Divisional Court of the Queen's Bench.

[4] Whether County Court decisions will be accepted as precedents seems to be in some doubt: see *Rogers* v. *Hyde*, [1952] 2 K.B. 923, 926, 931, and *Morcom* v. *Campbell-Johnson*, [1956] 1 Q.B. 106, 111. A difficulty here is that County Court proceedings are not reported in any published series. Nor is there any full transcript of them, and in case of appeal the superior court usually has to rely on the judge's note, which varies in scope and quality.

These unsettled questions, if they can be so considered, are of comparative unimportance beside the general principle of uniformity, which is now indubitable. It remains to consider its operation in the work of the courts.[1]

[1] On precedent in Equity see Excursus D, *post*, p. 380, and W. H. D. Winder, 57 *L.Q.R.* 245.

IV

PRECEDENT: AUTHORITY AND OPERATION

I. GENERAL RULES FOR APPLICATION OF PRECEDENTS IN ENGLISH LAW

THERE are certain general rules which are now recognized, though with qualifications which will appear, as governing the application of precedents in English law.

Judges of first instance and magistrates' courts

Each court is bound by the decisions of courts above it, and the degrees of authority in the judicial hierarchy are well understood and observed, except that, as we have seen (*ante*, pp. 233 f.), some doubt still exists concerning the relative status of the Court of Appeal and the Court of Criminal Appeal.

Individual judges are not bound by each other's decisions,[1] though judicial courtesy naturally requires that they do not lightly dissent from the considered opinions of their brethren. Courts of summary jurisdiction are bound by the decisions of the High Court, whether appellate or of first instance; but on all questions of law the final court of appeal for magisterial courts is, by the

[1] *Forster* v. *Baker*, [1910] 2 K.B. 636, 638, *per* Bray J.; *Green* v. *Berliner*, [1936] 2 K.B. 477, 493, *per* du Parcq J.; *Police Authority for Huddersfield* v. *Watson*, [1947] K.B. 842, 848, *per* Lord Goddard C.J.; *Alma Shipping Co.* v. *Salgaoncar*, [1954] 2 Q.B. 94, 104, *per* Devlin J. In *Receiver for the Metropolitan Police District* v. *Croydon Corpn.* [1956] 1 W.L.R. 1113, and *Monmouthshire C.C.* v. *Smith*, [1956] 1 W.L.R. 1132, a head-on collision between Slade J. and Lynskey J. was resolved by the Court of Appeal in *Receiver for the Metropolitan Police District* v. *Croydon Corpn.*, [1957] 2 Q.B. 154. A similar difference of view in *Ross Smith* v. *R.S.* was not settled until the case reached the House of Lords, [1963] A.C. 280. It is not surprising that on the perennially difficult question of the measure of damages for personal injury there has been great difference of opinion between judges of equal degree: see *Hultquist* v. *Universal Pattern and Precision Engineering Co., Ltd.*, [1960] 2 Q.B. 467, and *Pope* v. *Murphy*, [1961] 1 Q.B. 222.

Summary Jurisdiction Act, 1879, the Divisional Court of the Queen's Bench Division.[1] Consequently, although a magisterial court may consider itself bound by a High Court decision, it cannot refuse the right of appeal, by way of case stated, if the point is still open for consideration by the Divisional Court.[2]

Tribunals

There are now a number of tribunals rendering judgements on different points of law. Sometimes there is, by statute, an appeal from them to the High Court, in which case it may be presumed that the High Court will consider itself bound by its previous decisions *in pari materia*. Sometimes there is no such appeal expressly provided by statute, and then the High Court can exercise control only by means of its prerogative orders (see *post*, pp. 572 ff.). The question remains unsettled whether a tribunal is bound by *its own* antecedent decisions. *Merchandise Transport Ltd.* v. *British Transport Commission*, [1962] 2 Q.B. 173, would seem to indicate the contrary, but there were particular features in that case which leave the general question uncertain. One difficulty is that the system of recording the determinations of many tribunals is variable and incomplete.

The Divisional Court of the Queen's Bench

As for the Divisional Court itself, it certainly recognizes the authority of the Court of Appeal in all civil matters and, of course, the House of Lords, and though

[1] Except in matrimonial causes, from which appeal on law and fact from courts of summary jurisdiction lies to the Divisional Court of the Probate, Divorce & Admiralty Division. The jurisdiction of these two appellate courts overlaps at many points and there has sometimes been an unfortunate conflict between them: see *Naylor* v. *N.*, (1962) P. 253.

[2] *R.* v. *Watson, Ex p. Bretherton*, [1945] K.B. 96. The sequel to this case is to be found in *Bretherton* v. *United Kingdom Totalisator Co., Ltd.*, [1945] K.B. 555, where the Divisional Court overruled the decision of Eve J. in *Elderton* v. *United Kingdom Totalisator Co., Ltd.* (*No. 1*), [1935] Ch. 373, by which the magistrate, in refusing to state a case, had held himself to be bound. The tangle of precedents, however, did not end here, because in *Elderton* v. *United Kingdom Totalisator Co., Ltd.* (*No. 2*), [1946] Ch. 57, the Court of Appeal followed *Bretherton* v. *United Kingdom Totalisator Co., Ltd.*, *ubi sup.*, but in *Zeidman* v. *Owen*, [1950] 1 K.B. 593, while also overruling Eve J. in *Elderton's Case, No. 1*, it declined to follow, in other respects, its own decision in *Elderton's Case, No. 2*!

it is arguable whether in criminal matters it is strictly bound by the Court of Criminal Appeal, that question seems to be merely academic and in no case known to the present writer has it been seriously debated. Whether or not the Divisional Court is bound by its own decisions has, in the past, been the subject of much doubt and confusion. This may have been due principally to the fact that this court, being one of constantly shifting personnel and varying numbers, has not had the same stability of authority as the Court of Appeal. At all events, for many years the distinction was drawn that in civil matters in which the final appeal lay at a higher level, the Divisional Court was bound by its own previous decisions, whereas in those criminal matters, especially of summary jurisdiction, for which the Divisional Court was by statute the final appellate authority, the same consistency need not be preserved. In strict theory, this doctrine may still hold good, but the tendency of recent years has been for the Divisional Court to stand by its own decisions, save where it feels at liberty to choose between plainly conflicting authorities,[1] and this has now been clearly laid down in *Police Authority for Huddersfield* v. *Watson*, [1947] K.B. 842 and *Younghusband* v. *Luftig*, [1949] 2 K.B. 354, 361.[2] The latter case also lays down that a full Divisional Court 'has no greater powers' of overruling itself than a court of three or even of two judges. Whatever the theoretical 'powers' of the court may be, it can hardly be doubted that a decision of the full court, especially after reargument, carries more weight than that of the ordinary court, and in practice an inconvenient or dubious previous decision will have great difficulty in standing against it. And in spite of the positiveness of the principle established in the two cases last cited, the doctrine of *stare decisis* in the Divisional

[1] The history of the matter is set forth, and the authorities assembled, by W. H. D. Winder, 'Divisional Court Precedents', 9 *M.L.R.* 257. See also O. M. Stone, 'Stare Decisis in the Divisional Court', 14 *M.L.R.* 219.

[2] See also *Moore* v. *Hewitt*, [1947] K.B. 831, and *Jeffery* v. *Johnson*, [1952] 2 Q.B. 8.

Court seems to be subject to the same flexible exceptions as those which, as we shall see, apply in other courts, for in *Nicholas* v. *Penny*, [1950] 2 K.B. 466 the Court did not hesitate to dissent from its previous majority decision in *Melhuish* v. *Morris*, [1938] 4 All E.R. 98, which must now be considered as of no authority.[1]

The Court of Criminal Appeal

The Court of Criminal Appeal is a newcomer in our law, having been established only in 1907,[2] and in the main it has adopted the ordinary principles of the application of precedents. It has, for example, held itself bound by decisions of its ancestor, the Court of Crown Cases Reserved.[3] There have, however, been some notable exceptions. The remarkable case of *R.* v. *Norman*, [1924] 2 K.B. 315, of great importance in the law relating to habitual criminals, was argued three times: first before three judges, then before five, and finally before thirteen. In the result, a majority of eight to four rejected the decision, only four years old, of the Court of Criminal Appeal in *R.* v. *Stanley*, [1920] 2 K.B. 235.[4] *R.* v. *Taylor*, [1950] 2 K.B. 368 opens a still wider door

[1] The grounds given *per* Lord Goddard C.J. were that in the earlier case the respondent had not been represented and that important authorities had not been cited. According to the report in [1950] 2 All E.R. at p. 91, the Lord Chief Justice went farther, and said: 'We can . . . always differ from a case on the ground that it has not been argued on both sides.' This wide statement, however, is modified in the report in [1950] 2 K.B. at p. 372, where we read: 'Without necessarily saying that we can always differ from a previous decision of the Divisional Court merely because it has not been argued on both sides, the court is not obliged to follow' *Melhuish* v. *Morris*, because of the rules in *Young* v. *Bristol Aeroplane Co.* (*post*, pp. 241 ff.). In his criticism of *Nicholas* v. *Penny*, in 'Stare Decisis in the Court of Appeal' (19 *M.L.R.* 136), Mr. G. F. Peter Mason has relied only on the report in [1950] 2 All E.R. His general criticism, however, seems to be justified by *Morelle* v. *Wakeling*, [1955] 2 Q.B. 379, especially at p. 406.

[2] With regard to the treatment of authorities in the earlier forms of criminal appeals, especially the Court of Crown Cases Reserved, see W. H. D. Winder, 'The Rule of Precedent in the Criminal Courts', *Journal of Criminal Law*, July 1941.

[3] *R.* v. *Cade*, [1914] 2 K.B. 209, 211, 212.

[4] Here, too, stress was laid on the fact that the prisoner was unrepresented, and that the authorities on which the Court had relied were unsatisfactory (one of them being unreported).

to exceptions, not only in the Court of Criminal Appeal but generally. This appeal, which involved a crucial point in the law of bigamy, was argued before seven judges, and in effect the decision overruled *R.* v. *Treanor*, [1939] 1 All E.R. 330.[1] Lord Goddard C.J., having observed that 'the Court of Appeal in civil matters usually considers itself bound by its own decisions or by decisions of a court of co-ordinate jurisdiction', and that 'in civil matters this is essential in order to preserve the rule of stare decisis', continued:

> 'This court, however, has to deal with questions involving the liberty of the subject, and if it finds, on reconsideration, that, in the opinion of a full court assembled for that purpose, the law has been either misapplied or misunderstood in a decision which it has previously given, and that, on the strength of that decision, an accused person has been sentenced and imprisoned, it is the bounden duty of the court to reconsider the earlier decision with a view to seeing whether that person had been properly convicted. The exceptions which apply in civil cases ought not to be the only ones applied in such a case as the present.'

If this be the correct principle—and, so far as we are aware, it has never before been laid down in terms—there seems to be no reason why it should not apply equally to the Divisional Court of the Queen's Bench, and indeed to the House of Lords in the limited criminal jurisdiction which is assigned to that tribunal by the Administration of Justice Act, 1960.[2] There is ground for thinking that the principle is at least implicitly

[1] *R.* v. *Taylor* is all the more remarkable because the appellant at his trial had pleaded guilty, and applied only for leave to appeal against his sentence; but the Court took the view that the whole basis of *R.* v. *Treanor* (on the authority of which he clearly had no defence) needed to be reconsidered by a full Court, and not only the sentence but the conviction was quashed. See on this case Glanville Williams, 'Bigamy and the Third Marriage', 13 *M.L.R.* 417.

[2] Courts of Quarter Sessions have appellate jurisdiction, both on law and on fact, from courts of summary jurisdiction, but it would be, we conceive, impracticable (even if desirable) to apply the principle here, since the decisions of these courts are seldom reported.

recognized by the Judicial Committee.[1] *R.* v. *Taylor* also seems to put it beyond doubt that a decision of the full Court of Criminal Appeal has more authority than that of the ordinary court of three judges.[2]

The Court of Appeal

The Court of Appeal has, by almost universal consent and practice, considered itself bound by its own previous decisions.[3] Not infrequently this Court has bowed to decisions which it has openly disliked, even expressing a hope that it might be overruled by the House of Lords.[4] On the other hand, equally often it has writhed under earlier decisions which it has clearly disapproved and has performed some valiant feats of 'distinguishing' in order to escape from them.[5] At least an academic doubt remained until 1944, when the question was raised 'nakedly' in *Young* v. *Bristol Aeroplane Co.*, [1944] K.B. 718 (affirmed, though not on this point, [1946] A.C. 163), in which the Court was invited to dissent from its previous decisions in *Selwood* v. *Townley Coal Co.*, [1940] 1 K.B. 180 and *Perkins* v. *Stevenson & Sons, Ltd.*, [1940] 1 K.B. 56.

This decision, given by a full Court of Appeal of six members, laid it down that the Court of Appeal is bound

[1] See *Gideon Nkambule* v. *R.*, [1950] A.C. 379, *post*, p. 251, though Lord Goddard's generalization was not explicitly stated in that case.

[2] Doubted by Avory J. in *R.* v. *Norman, ubi sup.*

[3] There have been some exceptions. In *Wynne-Finch* v. *Chaytor*, [1903] 2 Ch. 475, the Court of Appeal rather summarily 'overruled' one of its earlier decisions. See also *Re Shoesmith*, [1938] 2 K.B. 637, 644. An Election Court is bound by decisions of the Court of Appeal: *In re Parliamentary Election for Bristol South East*, [1961] 3 W.L.R. 577.

[4] See, for example, *Adair* v. *Birnbaum*, [1938] 4 All E.R. 775, *In re Morgan*, [1942] Ch. 345, *Fibrosa Société Anonyme* v. *Fairbairn, Lawson, Ltd.*, [1942] 1 K.B. 12. In the latter case the hope was fulfilled ([1943] A.C. 32) and the long-discredited rule in *Chandler* v. *Webster*, [1904] 1 K.B. 493, was overruled and destined to be given its *coup de grâce* by the Law Reform (Frustrated Contracts) Act, 1943.

[5] See, for example, *Chisholm* v. *London Passenger Transport Board*, [1939] 1 K.B. 426, in which *Bailey* v. *Geddes*, [1938] 1 K.B. 156, was ingeniously distinguished (rightly, as was later held in *Wilkinson* v. *Chetham-Strode*, [1940] 2 K.B. 310 and *London Passenger Transport Board* v. *Upson*, [1949] A.C. 155); and *Lancaster Motor Co.* v. *Bremith*, [1941] 1 K.B. 675 (distinguishing *Gerard* v. *Worth of Paris, Ltd.*, [1936] 2 All E.R. 905).

by its own decisions, and rejected the suggestion made by Greer L.J. in *Newsholme Bros.* v. *Road Transport and General Insurance Co.*, [1929] 2 K.B. 356, 384 that the full Court of Appeal had greater power than a single division of the Court to overrule itself. At the same time, the Court defined certain exceptions, which are thus summarized in the headnote:

'(1) The court is entitled and bound to decide which of two conflicting decisions of its own it will follow; (2) the court is bound to refuse to follow a decision of its own which, though not expressly overruled, cannot, in its opinion, stand with a decision[1] of the House of Lords; (3) the court is not bound to follow a decision of its own if it is satisfied that the decision was given *per incuriam*, e.g., where a statute or a rule having statutory effect[2] which would have affected the decision was not brought to the attention of the earlier court.'

These rules do not purport to cover all possible cases of conflict, for later (at p. 729) in the judgement of Lord Greene M.R., which was the judgement of the Court, it is said:

'Two classes of decisions per incuriam fall outside the scope of our inquiry, namely, those where the court has acted in ignorance of a previous decision of its own or of a court of co-ordinate jurisdiction which covers the case before it—in such a case a subsequent court must decide which of the two decisions it ought to follow; and those where it has acted in ignorance of a decision of the House of Lords which covers the point—in such a case a subsequent court is bound by the decision of the House of Lords.'

These formulations have been helpful in 'removing doubts', which the Court was surprised to find existing as late as 1944. According to one school of thought, to which the present writer humbly subscribes, they are opportune in relaxing the bonds of precedent when they

[1] An ambiguity, as we shall see, arises out of this expression.

[2] This does not apply to every *interpretation* of a statute, even when that interpretation (held to be erroneous) appears to have been adopted by a later enactment: *Royal Court Derby Porcelain Co., Ltd.* v. *Russell*, [1949] 2 K.B. 417; *Mucklow* v. *I.R.C.*, [1954] 2 All E.R. 508.

threaten to stop the circulation of the law's life-blood; while to another school of thought they have already introduced, and are likely to accentuate, an element of 'uncertainty' in our case-law, and have created certain problems,[1] the solution of which remains to be worked out. I will endeavour to summarize as briefly as possible what seem to me to be the principal of these open questions.

(1) Whether or not preceding cases which are cited to the court are in conflict or are consistent with each other, is clearly a matter of individual interpretation. For example, in *Rothwell* v. *Caverswall Stone Co., Ltd.*, [1944] 2 All E.R. 350, a workman's compensation case, a great many authorities were cited, and the majority of the Court of Appeal held that they were not irreconcilable. The dissenting member, Scott L.J., held that they divided themselves into two opposing 'lines', and in an exhaustive judgement he felt himself under the necessity of choosing between them. In *Hogan* v. *Bentinck West Hartley Collieries, Ltd.*, [1948] 1 All E.R. 129, the Court of Appeal, differently constituted, without itself examining all the earlier authorities, held itself bound to accept the majority view in *Rothwell's Case*, though it did so 'with distaste' and 'with regret'. Similarly, in *Holman* v. *Elliott*, [1944] K.B. 591, on a point of practice, the relevant authorities were cited to a Court consisting of MacKinnon L.J. and Morton J., and their decision was followed by two Judges on separate occasions; but in *Battersby* v. *Anglo-American Oil Co.*, [1945] K.B. 23, the Court of Appeal held that *Holman* v. *Elliott* was in fact inconsistent with the earlier cases, and refused to follow it. It remains to be seen whether, on the interpretation of the common 'fair wear and tear' clause in a lease, the Court of Appeal will hold *Taylor* v. *Webb*, [1937] 2 K.B. 283, to be irreconcilable with *Brown* v. *Davies*, [1958]

[1] See A. L. Goodhart, 'Precedents in the Court of Appeal', *Cambridge Law Journal*, 1947, 349, R. N. Gooderson, *ibid.*, 1950, 432, and G. F. Peter Mason, 'Stare decisis in the Court of Appeal', 19 *M.L.R.* 136.

1 Q.B. 117, and therefore subject to a choice between them, or whether the later case will hold the field by a process of 'distinguishing'.[1] In plain terms, it seems that the Court may take a different view of the authorities from its predecessors and thus refuse to submit to an apparently 'binding' recent decision of its own. There is, and there will probably continue to be, a certain element of fiction in this process, but it may be a somewhat less disingenuous fiction than 'distinguishing' what is, in substance and in truth, indistinguishable (see *post*, pp. 297 ff.). We shall see also that there has emerged a process of 'overruling by implication' which is not free from doubt and uncertainty.

(2) A decision need not be followed if the court is of opinion that it cannot stand with 'a decision of the House of Lords'. Does this mean *any* decision of the House of Lords, whenever it may be given? If the case in the superior tribunal is subsequent to the Court of Appeal decision which is impugned, then the situation is clear, and the earlier case is discredited. But if the House of Lords case was already in existence and was (as is subsequently contended) misinterpreted or misapplied by the lower court, is that sufficient to discredit the Court of Appeal's decision? The answer given in *Young* v. *Bristol Aeroplane Co.* itself (at p. 722), and again in *Williams* v. *Glasbrook*, [1947] 2 All E.R. 270, is emphatically no; for to say that the Court of Appeal misinterpreted an existing decision from higher authority is merely to argue that it made a mistake, and that is not sufficient ground for rejecting a decision of co-ordinate jurisdiction. This distinction, however, has not been consistently maintained, for in several instances the Court of Appeal has preferred *pre-existing* decisions of the House of Lords to decisions of its own in which the House of Lords authorities were before the Court.[2]

[1] See Megarry, 74 *L.Q.R.* 33, and Diamond, 21 *M.L.R.* 292.

[2] See *Fitzsimmons* v. *Ford Motor Co., Ltd.*, [1946] 1 All E.R. 429, and *Wilson* v. *Chatterton*, [1946] 1 All E.R. 431, and on these cases Gooderson,

The confusion has arisen partly because throughout the judgement in *Young* v. *Bristol Aeroplane Co.* it is clear that the Master of the Rolls was referring to *subsequent* decisions of the House of Lords, but in his summary of rules he refers merely to 'a decision' of the House of Lords, and this form of words is reproduced in the head-notes to most reports of the case.[1]

(3) Do the rules enunciated in *Young's Case* apply only to the Court of Appeal or to all courts?[2] The impression left by the whole judgement in *Young's Case*, and in the rules formulated, is that the Court was dealing specifically with its own decisions in relation to decisions of the only court superior to it, i.e. the House of Lords. But in *R.* v. *Northumberland Compensation Tribunal*, [1951] 1 K.B. 711, the Divisional Court of the King's Bench held itself at liberty to disregard the decision of the Court of Appeal in *Racecourse Betting Control Board* v. *Secretary of State for Air*, [1944] Ch. 114, on the grounds that in that case two decisions, one of the House of Lords and one of the Privy Council, had not been cited. This appears to be a very important extension of the rules in *Young's Case*, for it opens the application of those rules to any court of any degree. If the Divisonal Court can renounce the authority of the Court of Appeal because it holds that that Court has acted in

loc. cit., and G. A. Forrest in 10 *M.L.R.* 68. One cannot but agree with Mr. Forrest that in these cases the court merely adopted 'a polite and rather circuitous way' of saying that it had changed its mind. See also *Lyus* v. *Stepney B.C.*, [1941] 1 K.B. 134, Lord Wright's observations in *Noble* v. *Southern Railway*, [1940] A.C. 583, and Mr. Gooderson hereon. In *R.* v. *Northumberland Compensation Appeal Tribunal*, *ubi sup.*, the reference seems to be to an *earlier* decision of the House of Lords which was not cited to the Court, and this is stated in the headnote, but not expressly in the judgement of Lord Goddard C.J.

[1] See Gooderson, *loc. cit.*

[2] At p. 729 Lord Greene M.R. refers to 'decisions of its own' (i.e. of 'the court') 'or of a court of co-ordinate jurisdiction'. If, as seems to follow from the context, he is referring to the Court of Appeal, it is not clear what other court is nowadays of co-ordinate jurisdiction with the Court of Appeal—unless the Court of Criminal Appeal can be so regarded, which is very doubtful. The reference, however, may be to former decisions of the Court of Exchequer Chamber, whereon see *ante*, p. 221.

ignorance of superior decisions, there seems to be no reason why a judge of first instance should not do the same with regard to any appellate tribunal, if he is convinced that he has the same grounds for doing so. Here, presumably, common sense and judicial comity must come to the rescue; but it is difficult to resist the conclusion that the interpretations placed on *Young's Case* carry it, for better or for worse, much beyond its original intent. We shall see that judges of first instance sometimes have to make a difficult choice between conflicting decisions of higher courts; but, up to the present time of writing, no judge sitting alone seems to have rejected an appellate court's ruling on any of the grounds afforded by *Young's Case*; nor, it is believed, is this likely to happen.

(4) What is *incuria* and what are its limits? Although the difficulties of this problem have increased with the growth of reports, they are by no means new. Thus, at the beginning of this century, there arose a very important question whether the King's Bench had power to punish contempt of petty sessional and other inferior courts, and it is clear that until the error was corrected in *R.* v. *Parke*, [1903] 2 K.B. 432, and *R.* v. *Davies*, [1906] 1 K.B. 32, a misunderstanding of the Judicature Act, 1873, had led to a series of erroneous decisions that no such power existed.

Incuria means literally 'carelessness', which apparently is considered less uncomplimentary than *ignorantia*; but in practice *per incuriam* appears to mean *per ignorantiam*. It would almost seem that *ignorantia juris neminem excusat* —except a court of law. Ignorance of what? The example given in the actual rules in *Young's Case* is ignorance of a statute, or of a rule having statutory effect (such as a Rule of the Supreme Court),[1] which would have affected the decision if the court had been aware of it. Later in his judgement Lord Greene M.R. expressly says that two classes of decision 'fall outside the scope of

[1] See *Lancaster Motor Co., Ltd.* v. *Bremith, Ltd.*, [1941] 1 K.B. 675.

our inquiry'—namely, when the court is unaware of a previous decision of its own 'or of a court of co-ordinate jurisdiction', or is unaware of 'a decision of the House of Lords which covers the point'. Paradoxically, however, the judgement, while saying that these contingencies lie outside its scope, does not refrain from expressing an opinion about them; on the contrary, it plainly says that in the first class of cases the court will choose which decision or decisions it prefers to follow, and in the second class it will be bound by the House of Lords. In decisions subsequent to *Young's Case* it has been assumed that the rule concerning *incuria* applies to overlooked precedents as much as to overlooked statutes. Thus in *Moore* v. *Hewitt*, [1947] 2 All E.R. 270, 272, Lord Goddard C.J. said that one of the exceptions laid down in *Young's Case* is 'where the court gives a decision *per incuriam* because the provisions of a statute *or the authority of a case*' (my italics) 'have not been brought to their attention'. Again, in *Nicholas* v. *Penny*, [1950] 2 K.B. 466, 473, Lord Goddard C.J. said that it had been laid down in *Young's Case* 'that where material cases or statutory provisions, which show that a court has decided a case wrongly, were not brought to its attention the court is not bound by that decision in a subsequent case'.[1] Whether or not *Young* v. *Bristol Aeroplane Co.* ever intended to go as far as this, and to extend the principle to all courts as well as to itself, it is difficult to say; but it may be assumed (it is submitted) that this interpretation of it is likely to be accepted in the future. If so, it is clear that a wide scope is given to *incuria* and that courts of all degrees will enjoy much more freedom than formerly in rejecting authorities which are *prima facie* binding, if they are of opinion that all relevant considerations were not before the court. This principle cannot work mechanically, however, and difficulties of interpretation remain; for, manifestly, a decision is not necessarily

[1] See also *Melias, Ltd.* v. *Preston*, [1957] 2 Q.B. 380. In *Berkeley* v. *Papadoyannis*, [1954] 2 Q.B. 149, the Court of Appeal left the question open.

erroneous *per incuriam* merely because every possible precedent has not been prayed in aid. It still remains to be determined whether, if the omitted authority had been cited, it would have gone to the root of the *ratio decidendi*; and on that question opinions may greatly differ.[1]

The whole question came under the review of the Court of Appeal in *Morelle* v. *Wakeling*, [1955] 2 Q.B. 379.[2] Sir Raymond Evershed M.R. (as he then was) limited the *incuria* rule to 'decisions given in ignorance or forgetfulness of some inconsistent statutory provision or of some authority binding on the court concerned'; and such instances, he added, should be 'of the rarest occurrence'. This does not greatly help to solve the conundrums which have been mentioned, and it may, with respect, be questioned whether the cases in which these points of doubt arise have been, or are, 'of the rarest occurrence'. The main purport, however, of *Morelle* v. *Wakeling*, in this aspect of it, is a restraint upon the notion, which was growing and which was suggested by the Crown's argument, that because an antecedent case has not been presented as well and as fully as it might have been, that amounts to *incuria*. The Master of the Rolls said (at p. 406):

> 'It is . . . impossible to fasten upon any part of the decision under consideration or upon any step in the reasoning upon which the judgments were based and to say of it: "Here was a manifest slip or error." Acceptance of the Attorney-General's argument would necessarily involve the proposition that it is open to this court to disregard an earlier decision of its own or of a court of co-ordinate jurisdiction (at least in any case of significance or complexity) whenever it is made to appear that the court had not upon the earlier occasion had the benefit of the best argument that

[1] See further on *Noble* v. *Southern Railway Co.*, [1940] A.C. 583, *post*, p. 320. In 'Some Aspects of the Work of the Court of Appeal', *Journal of the Society of Public Teachers of Law*, 1950, 350, 362, Asquith L.J. (as he then was) set an ingenious 'examination' on *Young* v. *Bristol Aeroplane Co.* The present writer is happy to leave the correct answers to those students of the law who, unlike himself, are young enough to be able to pass examinations.

[2] See also *Att.-Gen.* v. *Parsons*, [1955] Ch. 664 and [1956] A.C. 421.

the researches and industry of counsel could provide. Such a proposition ... would open the way to numerous and costly attempts to re-open questions now held to be authoritatively decided.

To the same effect is *Bryers* v. *Canadian Pacific Steamships, Ltd.*, [1957] 1 Q.B. 134, in which it was held (see especially Singleton L.J. at p. 147) that when a point, which is later represented to be vital, was not taken in an earlier case, this does not amount to an invalidating *incuria*. Similarly, in *Critchell* v. *Lambeth B.C.*, [1957] 2 Q.B. 535, the Court declined to reject a recent decision of its own on the contention that a point of importance had not been fully argued. Imperfection in the presentation of a case is, of course, quite distinct from the 'authority' of a case as explained by Lord Goddard C.J. in *Moore* v. *Hewitt*, *ubi sup.*, and *Nicholas* v. *Penny*, *ubi sup.*

This is a timely warning against pushing *incuria* to lengths which would make it possible to attack almost any decision, for of what case can it be said that it has been presented and considered with perfect cogency and completeness? In sum, it may be said (it is submitted) that the rules laid down in *Young* v. *Bristol Aeroplane Co.*, though carried somewhat beyond their original compass, have proved of advantage in the application of precedent, but that they need to be cautiously prayed in aid and that they place a heavy onus on any court or counsel relying on *incuria*.[1]

The Privy Council

The Judicial Committee of the Privy Council, being in theory only an advisory body to the Sovereign, occupies a peculiar position in the hierarchy. Though most of its appellate jurisdiction from the Dominions has now gone, it remains a final court of appeal from various British colonies and dependencies, where its decisions are binding; but it is not an appellate tribunal from the ordinary courts of England and Wales, other than ecclesiastical and Admiralty, nor, of course, from Scotland. English courts, therefore, of whatever degree,

[1] See G. F. Peter Mason, *loc. cit.* 143, citing *Gibson* v. *South American Stores, Ltd.*, [1949] 2 All E.R. 985.

theoretically reserve to themselves independence in respect of Privy Council decisions.[1] In at least one important principle of civil liability, namely, the question whether damages can be recovered for 'nervous shock', the courts have refused to follow a principle laid down by the Judicial Committee in 1887.[2] The House of Lords has sometimes treated Privy Council decisions with scant respect,[3] and strong dissent from them has been expressed even in the Court of Appeal.[4] Lower courts, however, in practice dissent only with grave hesitation from a tribunal which, in its judiciary if not in its jurisdiction, is almost an *alter ego* of the House of Lords.[5] However, in *Port Line Ltd.* v. *Ben Line Steamers Ltd.*, [1958] 2 Q.B. 146, Diplock J., with notable 'judicial valour', declined to follow the decision of the Privy Council in *Lord Strathcona Steamship Co. Ltd.* v. *Dominion Coal Co. Ltd.*, [1926] A.C. 108, a case which had been under constant adverse criticism. On the other hand, as will be mentioned later (*post*, p. 343), in *Overseas Tankship (U.K.) Ltd.* v. *Mort's Dock and Engineering Co. Ltd.* (*The Wagon Mound*), [1961] A.C. 388, the Privy Council refused to follow, and in effect overruled, *Re Polemis*, [1921] 3 K.B. 560, and a doubt arose whether this decision would be binding on English

[1] *Venn* v. *Tedesco*, [1926] 2 K.B. 227; *Lynn* v. *Bamber*, [1930] 2 K.B. 72, 81; *Dulieu* v. *White*, [1901] 2 K.B. 669.

[2] *Victorian Railway Commissioners* v. *Coultas* (1887), 13 App. Cas. 222; see *Coyle* v. *Watson*, [1915] A.C. 1.

[3] See *Absalom* v. *Talbot*, [1944] A.C. 204 (followed in *Bristow* v. *Dickinson*, [1946] K.B. 321), on *Gleaner Co., Ltd.* v. *Assessment Committee of Jamaica*, [1922] 2 A.C. 169. In the important case of *Duncan* v. *Cammell, Laird & Co.*, [1942] A.C. 624, the equally weighty decision of the Judicial Committee in *Robinson* v. *State of South Australia* (*No. 2*), [1931] A.C. 704, was very summarily treated.

[4] In *Fanton* v. *Denville*, [1932] 2 K.B. 309, Greer L.J. described *Toronto Power Co.* v. *Paskwan*, [1915] A.C. 734, as 'inconsistent with the whole trend of the English decisions'.

[5] 'In . . . mercantile or admiralty law, where the same principles are . . . followed in the colonies as in this country, it is . . . highly undesirable that there should be any conflict between the decisions of the Judicial Committee and those of the High Court or Courts of Appeal in this country': *The City of Chester* (1884), L.R. 9 P.D. 182, 207.

courts.[1] In the subsequent case of *Smith* v. *Leech Brain & Co.*, [1962] 2 Q.B. 405, Lord Parker C.J. expressly said that he accepted the authority of *The Wagon Mound*, though with a qualification which possibly still leaves room for argument and appeal. For reasons advanced by Professor Goodhart[2] it seems to the present writer extremely unlikely that English courts in future will cause further confusion on a vital principle of the law of negligence and damages by rejecting the doctrine of *The Wagon Mound*, but it cannot be said that the situation, as between 'persuasive' and 'binding' authority, is yet free from doubt.

Whether the Privy Council is bound by its own decisions has been the subject of some doubt. It seems certain that the Judicial Committee is reluctant to reverse a longstanding decision of its own which has established a well-recognized constitutional principle. Thus in *Attorney-General for Ontario* v. *Canada Temperance Federation*, [1946] A.C. 193, the Board was strongly pressed to 'reconsider' *Russell* v. *Reg.* (1882), 7 App. Cas. 829, which had been doubted or qualified in previous cases, but it declined to do so on the ground that this decision established a principle which was 'deeply embedded in the constitutional law of Canada'. At the same time the Board, *per* Viscount Simon, observed: 'Their Lordships do not doubt that in tendering humble advice to His Majesty they are not absolutely bound by previous decisions of the Board, as is the House of Lords by its own judgements.' There have been some striking examples of this freedom of decision,[3] and the case of *Gideon Nkambule* v. *R.*, [1950] A.C. 379, makes it clear that in criminal matters at least, where life and liberty are at stake,[4] the Privy Council will not hesitate to reject even a recent decision of its own,[5] if it is satisfied that all

[1] See Goodhart, 77 *L.Q.R.* 175. [2] *Ibid.*

[3] Thus in *Mercantile Bank of India* v. *Central Bank of India*, [1938] A.C. 287, the Board refused, with little ceremony or apology, to follow its own decision in *Commonwealth Trust* v. *Akotey*, [1926] A.C. 72.

[4] See *ante*, p. 240. [5] *Tumahole Bereng* v. *R.*, [1949] A.C. 253.

relevant considerations and historical circumstances were not before the Court in the earlier case.

The Privy Council also has power, in effect, to rehear and reconsider its own previous decisions. This comes about because, under s. 4 of the Judicial Committee Act, 1833, a question may be referred by the Crown to the Privy Council for opinion, and by this means the Board has an opportunity of rehearing and, in effect, reversing a previous decision of its own which has been based on an error of fact.[1] It is always to be remembered that, constitutionally speaking, a 'decision' of the Judicial Committee is merely advice to the Sovereign, and there is no actual judgement, conclusive between the parties, until an Order in Council, based on the Committee's report, has been made. In other courts, when final judgement has once been entered, the whole cause of action *transit in rem judicatam* and in most cases creates an 'estoppel by matter of record'; there is, therefore, so far as we are aware, no power to recall a final judgement in a civil action, even if it is later discovered to have been based on an error of fact—though this, of course, may be a strong ground of appeal.[2]

The Privy Council also has appellate jurisdiction in certain Admiralty Prize and Ecclesiastical causes, and from determinations of the Disciplinary Committee of the General Medical Council (by the Medical Act, 1950), together with certain default powers under the Professions Supplementary to Medicine Act, 1960. There seems to be little authority on the question

[1] *In re Transferred Civil Servants (Ireland) Compensation*, [1929] A.C. 242.

[2] See *Dollfus Mieg et Cie.* v. *Bank of England*, [1950] Ch. 333. See, however, the curious case of *Hedger* v. *Shutler*, cited *post*, pp. 373 ff. It is not clear whether, in that case, judgement had actually been entered before it was revoked—presumably not. *In re Waring*, [1948] Ch. 221, seems to show that parties to the original suit cannot be subsequently released from the judgement, even if it should appear, according to later and higher authority, to have been erroneous, though parties who were not originally before the Court may claim the benefit of the later overruling authority. *In re Koenigsberg*, [1949] Ch. 348, which distinguished *In re Waring* on the facts, does not dissent from this principle, harsh and inconvenient though it seems to be.

whether in such matters it is bound by its own previous decisions, but that would seem to be the rule.

The House of Lords

The House of Lords, as we have seen nowadays considers itself bound by its own decisions. The principle is now so well recognized that if, as sometimes happens, an even number of peers are sitting, and they are equally divided in opinion, then, by the practice of the House, the appeal is deemed to have failed and the resultant negative is regarded as a precedent for the future.[1] This cannot be regarded as a satisfactory rule, except perhaps on the ground that *interest reipublica ut sit finis litium*.[2]

In recent years there has been a growing volume of protest against the rigidity of precedent in the House of Lords. The chief revolutionary (if the term may be used without disrespect) has been Lord Denning, whose views are expressed in his Romanes Lecture, *From Precedent to Precedent* (1959).[3] His Lordship's appeal for greater freedom of decision in the highest tribunal was graphically put in *Ostime* v. *Australian Mutual Provident Society*, [1960] A.C. 459, 489: 'The doctrine of precedent does not compel your Lordships to follow the wrong path until you fall over the edge of the cliff. As soon as

[1] *Beamish* v. *B.* (1859), 9 H.L.C. 274; *Smith* v. *Lion Brewery Co.*, [1911] A.C. 150, and *Usher's Wilts. Brewery* v. *Bruce*, [1915] A.C. 433; *Lumsden* v. *I.R.C.*, [1914] A.C. 877, and *I.R.C.* v. *Walker*, [1915] A.C. 539. The rule in the Court of Appeal is more doubtful: see Cross, *Precedent in English Law*, 91 ff. Interlocutory appeals may be, and generally are, heard by two Lords Justices, who may also, by preliminary agreement of the parties in writing, hear final appeals; but if the two members of the Court then disagree, the appeal is dismissed (*Packer* v. *P.*, [1954] P.15), but the unsuccessful party may demand a rehearing before a fully constituted Court. For further discussion of equally divided courts, see R. E. Megarry and Dr. Glanville Williams, 70 *L.Q.R.* 318, 469, 471.

[2] An anomalous position of authority is occupied by answers given by the judges in reply to hypothetical questions put to them by the House of Lords. This practice has always been rare, and may now be regarded as obsolete. On the authority of the celebrated answers given in *McNaghten's Case* (1843), 10 Cl. & F. 200, see Stephen, *Hist. Cr. L.* ii. 153 ff.

[3] Lord Denning appears to be of opinion that English law would gain in wisdom and development if the House of Lords reverted to its pre-1850 practice of hearing appeals with mixed legal and lay peers.

you find you are going in the wrong direction, you must at least be permitted to strike off in the right direction, even if you are not allowed to retrace your steps.' In *London Transport Executive* v. *Betts*, [1959] A.C. 213, 247, he protested against following a precedent which, in his view, conflicted with a 'fundamental principle' of English law.[1] In *Close* v. *Steel Co. of Wales Ltd.*, [1962] A.C. 367, 388, he said: 'The doctrine that your Lordships are bound by a previous decision of your own is . . . limited to the decision itself and to what is necessarily involved in it. It does not mean that you are bound by the various reasons given in support of it, especially when they contain "propositions wider than the case itself required".'

Lord Denning has not lacked support for his view. As long ago as 1943 Lord Wright favoured a relaxation of the strict rule in the House of Lords.[2] One of the most trenchant critics of it has been Dr. Glanville Williams.[3] In 1952 Lord Reid, striving to distinguish the instant case from *Usher's Wiltshire Brewery Ltd.* v. *Bruce*, [1915] A.C. 433, observed: 'It is very unsatisfactory to have to grope for a decision in this way, but the need to do so arises from the fact that this House has debarred itself from ever reconsidering any of its own decisions. It matters not how difficult it is to find the *ratio decidendi* of a previous case, that ratio must be found.'[4] If there be any doubt about this difficulty of discovering the ratio of preceding cases, it is only necessary to read the judgement of Lord Radcliffe in *Unit Construction Co. Ltd.* v. *Bullock*, [1960] A.C. 351, and the speeches of all the peers in attempting to find the ratio of *Elder, Dempster &*

[1] Viz., that courts could not read into a statute words which were not there —a somewhat surprising orthodoxy from this source, since Lord Denning has always favoured a liberal interpretation of statutes.

[2] (1943) 8 *Camb. L.J.* 144.

[3] Salmond, *Jurisprudence*, 11th ed., 175 ff. and App. IV.

[4] *Nash* v. *Tamplin & Sons*, [1952] A.C. at p. 250. See also his observations in *London Transport Executive* v. *Betts*, *ubi sup.*, at p. 232, and cf. the observations of Lord Dunedin in *The Mostyn*, [1928] A.C. 57, *post*, p. 291.

Co., Ltd. v. *Paterson, Zachonis & Co. Ltd.*, [1924] A.C. 522, in *Scruttons Ltd.* v. *Midland Silicones Ltd.*, [1962] A.C. 446. In the latter case Lord Reid, bred in Scots law, where the same ridigidity of precedent does not prevail, said this (at p. 199):

> 'I would certainly not lightly disregard or depart from any *ratio decidendi* of this House. But there are at least three classes of case where I think we are entitled to question or limit it: first, where it is obscure, secondly, where the decision itself is out of line with other authorities or established principles, and thirdly, where it is much wider than was necessary for the decision so that it becomes a question of how far it is proper to distinguish the earlier decision.'

If these exceptions were admitted, they would seem to give the House of Lords something of the same latitude as the Court of Appeal now possesses under *Young* v. *Bristol Aeroplane Co.* Such suggestions, however, were sternly rejected by Lord Simonds and other notably 'orthodox' peers. It remains to be seen whether in future they will bear any fruit. Whether they do or not, there is little doubt that the rule in the House of Lords is occasioning more and more restiveness, which is not likely to diminish as precedents multiply.[1]

Recently, by the Administration of Justice Act, 1960, the criminal jurisdiction of the House of Lords has been considerably enlarged. An appeal by defence or prosecution now lies by leave of the Court of Criminal Appeal on a point or points of *general* public importance (which may be specifically limited by the Court)—not, as previously, only on a certificate of the Attorney-General on a point of *exceptional* public importance. Of the appeals which have been heard up to the present date of writing, it is only necessary to say that *D.P.P.* v. *Smith*, [1961] A.C. 290, *Shaw* v. *D.P.P.*, [1962] A.C. 220, *Sykes* v. *D.P.P.*, [1962] A.C. 528, and *Jones* v. *D.P.P.*, [1962], A.C. 635, have all caused acute

[1] See G. Dworkin, 'Stare decisis in the House of Lords,' 25 *M.L.R.* 163, who suggests some possible future means of modifying the rule.

doubt and controversy in the profession.[1] It is to be questioned whether this appeal to the highest tribunal has succeeded in illuminating our criminal law. The previous practice, similar to that of the Judicial Committee, of one leading judgement being delivered in which the other peers (no doubt after discussion) concurred, has been abandoned in favour of separate and often lengthy speeches. This embarrassment of riches does not conduce to clarity in matters of life and liberty; the criminal law—perhaps all law—can suffer from 'too much of a good thing'.

The House of Lords is the final interpreter of the law for the United Kingdom and its decisions are absolutely binding on all lower courts. But within the sphere of its jurisdiction are two distinct legal systems, the English and the Scottish, which part company at many points. Scottish appeals from decisions of the Inner House are frequent, and for many years past it has been customary for the Lords of Appeal in Ordinary to contain a certain number of peers bred in the law of Scotland. There has not been universal satisfaction north of the Border with all decisions of the House of Lords, especially when constituted of a majority of English peers, upon points of pure Scots law,[2] and it is a nice question how far House of Lords decisions are automatically authoritative for both countries. It is said that pronouncements 'of general jurisprudence' are binding on both, but, as Professor T. B. Smith has pointed out,[3] it begs the question to talk of 'general jurisprudence' unless the possible differences between the two systems have been fully canvassed, as they frequently are not. It seems to be self-evident that when a decision turns on a point peculiar to Scots law, it can have no relevance for English courts; and it now seems to be settled by *Glasgow Corpn.* v. *Central Land*

[1] See Cross, 'The Criminal Evidence Act, 1898, and the House of Lords as a Court of Criminal Appeal', 78 *L.Q.R.* 407.

[2] See Prof. D. M. Walker, 'Some Characteristics of Scots Law', 18 *M.L.R.* 321; and *contra*, 'R. E. M.', 19 *M.L.R.* 95.

[3] 19 *M.L.R.* 427, 428.

Board, [1955] S.L.T. 155 and [1956] S.L.T. 41, that a decision on an English appeal does not override a different, pre-existing rule of Scots law. In that case it was held that a rule concerning the court's discretion as to so-called privileged Crown documents, laid down in *Duncan* v. *Cammell, Laird & Co.*, [1942] A.C. 624, did not apply to Scotland; and this is all the more interesting because (confirming Professor T. B. Smith's point) Viscount Simon L.C. had erroneously assumed, with the concurrence of the other (including Scottish) peers, that the law of the two countries was the same. *Quaere*, whether this was *incuria*; or is *incuria* unthinkable in the House of Lords? On the possibility of *incuria* through an overlooked statute, see *post*, p. 295, n. 3.

Principles of interpretation

Certain well-recognized principles of interpretation apply throughout.

1. Any relevant judgement of any court is an argument entitled to careful consideration.

2. Antiquity does not necessarily derogate from a precedent, but rather strengthens its authority: unless the law has been definitely altered since the decision was given.

3. *Per contra*, it is well recognized that the law gradually adapts itself to changing social conditions and that very ancient precedents are often inapplicable to modern circumstances. For this reason they are cited with comparative infrequency. Precedents may be compared to wine which 'improves with age', up to a certain point, and then begins to 'go off'.[1] A venerable precedent

[1] A precedent must of course, be interpreted in the light of its contemporary law and of the interpretation, which may since have changed, placed upon it at the time; see *per* Denning L.J., *Richardson* v. *L.C.C.*, [1957] 1 W.L.R. 751, 756, and see *Winchester* v. *Fleming*, [1958] 1 Q.B. 259. If, however, circumstances have not changed, antiquity does not derogate from authority: *Triefus & Co. Ltd.* v. *Post Office*, [1957] 2 Q.B. 352. In *Rawlence* v. *Spicer*, [1935] 1 K.B. at p. 435, Lord Wright refers to a case of Lord Mansfield's time (*Hutchins* v. *Chambers*, 1 Burr. 579) as having been 'held up to general obloquy on the ground of its antiquity'. For examples of this 'obloquy' see *Cochrane's Case* (1840), 8 Dowl. 630, *apud Reg.* v. *Jackson*, [1891] 1 Q.B. 671; and *Cole* v. *Hawkins* (1736), Andrews 275, *apud R.* v.

which has been long overlooked is apt to fall into what Sellers L.J., in *Mathews* v. *Kuwait Bechtel Corpn.*, [1959] 2 Q.B. 57, 69, called 'the limbo of lost causes'.

4. There is no one sovereign system of recording precedents. They may be drawn from any source which the court considers reliable—besides the regular and periodical series of reports, from newspapers, manuscripts, historical documents, or even the personal recollection of judges.[1] Anybody may publish reports of cases heard in open court, though they will not be accepted as authorities for citation unless sponsored by a member of the Bar. But since 1865 there has been a series of reports in all courts, recognized as of peculiar

Jones, [1931] 1 K.B. 664. There are, however, cases in which exhaustive researches into ancient precedents may be necessary; see, for example, *In re Diplock*, [1948] Ch. 465; *Minister of Health* v. *Simpson*, [1951] A.C. 251; *Williams* v. *Linnitt*, [1951] 1 K.B. 565; *In re Green, decd.*, [1951] Ch. 148; *Iveagh* v. *Martin*, [1961] 1 Q.B. 232.

[1] Thus Lord Eldon in *Bulkley* v. *Wilford* (1834), 2 Cl. & F., 102, 177: 'I have in my possession at this moment the manuscript of that decree, which was quoted at the bar. I am sure it is genuine; I know the handwriting of Sir Anthony Hart, the then Lord Chancellor of Ireland. This manuscript which I now have shows the diligence and accurate attention which he gave to the subject, having corrected and recorrected it, in order that the principle might be understood upon which the decree was made.' Cf. the same Lord Chancellor in *Sidney* v. *Shelley* (1815), 19 Ves. 352, 359, and Sir Cresswell Cresswell in *In the Goods of Alexander* (1860), 29 L.J. (P. & M.) 93: 'A gentleman, who is publishing a book on the practice of the Court of Probate, has kindly furnished me with a copy of the actual report made to Her Majesty by the Judicial Committee [in *Tatnall* v. *Hankey* (1838), 2 Moo. P.C. 342] which gives an express opinion on this very point. . . . This express opinion of the Judicial Committee is conclusive.' In *R.* v. *Labouchere* (1884), 12 Q.B.D. 320, 328, Lord Coleridge C.J. cited a newspaper report which had been brought to his attention by a member of the Bar and himself cited two unreported cases from personal memory. See also an important manuscript authority relied on in Foster's *Crown Cases*, Disc. II, ch. v, p. 292 (ed. 1762); Lord Campbell in *Johnstone* v. *Beattie* (1843), 10 Cl. & F. at p. 136; *Gibbon* v. *Pease*, [1905] 1 K.B. 810, 812; *Palgrave* v. *The Turid*, [1922] 1 A.C. 397, 413; Lord Blanesburgh in *Barras* v. *Aberdeen Steam Trawling Co.*, [1933] A.C. at p. 434. 'According to modern custom', says Sir Frederick Pollock, 'any report vouched for at the time by a member of the bar may be used in court for what it is worth, although the citation of an unpublished report is not at all common nowadays' (*Essays in the Law*, 243). But on the danger of abbreviated reports, especially in newspapers, see *Mahon* v. *Osborne*, [1939] 2 K.B. 14.

authority by the profession,[1] though not in any sense sanctioned by the State. With regard to cases decided since 1865, these reports possess more authority than any series (of which there are many) published by private enterprise, especially as the judgements recorded in them are almost invariably revised by the judges themselves before publication.

The present system, or lack of system, in reporting decided cases has grown up at haphazard, and although proposals have been made from time to time for putting it on a more stable basis, they have not so far borne fruit. We shall see[2] that certain inconveniences result which gravely threaten the efficacy of the whole system of case-law and that the time may have come when the question needs a more thoroughgoing examination than it has yet received.

5. Any judgement of any court is authoritative only as to that part of it, called the *ratio decidendi*, which is considered to have been necessary to the decision of the actual issue between the litigants. Many attempts have been made to define the *ratio decidendi*.[3] In its simplest form it may be said to be the principle or principles, deduced from authority, on which the Court reached its decision; or, negatively, the principle or principles *without which* the Court would not have reached the decision that it did reach. But simplicity, as in most definitions, is deceptive, and it disappears when we add, as we are

[1] Except the *Weekly Notes*, which are merely current précis, not to be cited as 'reports' in the strict sense: *In re Loveridge*, [1902] 2 Ch. 859, 865 (Buckley J.). They will, however, be accepted in the absence of any fuller report: see, for example, *In re Hooper*, [1932] 1 Ch. 28. Unreported cases, if well attested, are not infrequently relied on and followed: see *post*, pp 372 f. In *In re Boyer*, [1935] Ch. 382, an unreported decision going back as far as 1856 was followed. The *Estates Gazette* was not admitted as an authority in *Birtwistle* v. *Tweedale*, [1954] 1 W.L.R. 190, nor *Current Law in Rivoli Hats, Ltd.* v. *Gooch*, [1953] 1 W.L.R. 1190. But on the *Estates Gazette* see R. E. Megarry, 'Reporting the Unreported', 70 *L.Q.R.* 246.

[2] Excursus C, *post*, p. 367.

[3] See Cross, *Precedent in English Law*, for a full discussion of the various theories. Mr. Cross's 'description' of it, at p. 75, though ingenious, is perhaps a little too complicated to be really illuminating.

bound to add, that the governing principle may be derived, or believed to be derived, from a number of different sources—from a single preceding case 'on all fours', from a series of preceding cases which are believed to lay down a consistent principle, from analogy from preceding cases, from the common law, or perhaps from natural justice as conceived by the common law. Deductive decision from authorities is never, and cannot ever be, a mechanical process. Every *ratio* is an *interpretation* of authorities in the light of the facts of the instant case; and every interpretation, save in the House of Lords, is subject (when appeal is available) to review by a higher court, which may or may not agree with the interpretation of the lower court; and even in the highest tribunal its members may differ in their interpretation of the *ratio* of anterior cases.[1] Indeed, it is for a court, of whatever degree, which is called upon to consider a precedent, to determine what the true *ratio* was. The difficulties which attend this process will be considered later. The *ratio* is thus in a constant state of flux, and I venture to agree with Mr. Cross that it is not susceptible of any precise and comprehensive definition.

Ratio and Dicta

One of the greatest difficulties in its conception is the distinction which is constantly drawn between *ratio* and *dictum*, the essential and the inessential. In the course of the argument and decision of a case, many incidental considerations arise which are (or should be) all part of the logical process, but which necessarily have different degrees of relevance to the central issue. Judicial opinions upon such matters, whether they be merely casual, or wholly gratuitous, or (as is far more usual) of what may be called collateral relevance, are known as *obiter dicta*, or simply *dicta*, and it is extremely difficult to establish any standard of their relative weight. We have already seen (*ante*, p. 209) that, as early as 1673, Vaughan C.J. attempted to define their place in the judicial process, but the task of assessing their nature

[1] As in *Close* v. *Steel of Wales*, *ante*, p. 254.

and value is seldom easy and always, in great measure, subjective. Many protests against arguments founded on irrelevant *dicta* have come from the Bench;[1] on the other hand, it is a mistake to regard all *dicta* as equally otiose and therefore equally negligible. Much depends on the source of the *dictum*, the circumstances in which it was expressed, and the degree of deliberation which accompanied it. Lord Sterndale M.R. observed in *Slack* v. *Leeds Industrial Co-operative Society*, [1923] 1 Ch. 431, 451 (reversed [1924] 2 Ch. 475 and [1924] A.C. 851):

> 'Dicta are of different kinds and of varying degrees of weight. Sometimes they may be called almost casual expressions of opinion upon a point which has not been raised in the case, and is not really present to the judge's mind. Such dicta, though entitled to the respect due to the speaker, may fairly be disregarded by judges before whom the point has been raised and argued in a way to bring it under much fuller consideration. Some dicta, however, are of a different kind; they are, although not necessary for the decision of the case, deliberate expressions of opinion given after consideration upon a point clearly brought and argued before the Court.[2] It is open, no doubt, to other judges to give decisions contrary to such dicta, but much greater weight attaches to them than to the former class.'

These distinctions sound admirably clear-cut in the abstract; but how apply a qualitative standard in the concrete? How distinguish between 'deliberate expressions of opinion given after consideration' and mere 'statements by the way'?[3] By what test is an expression of judicial opinion a mere 'aside' or 'one of the links in the chain of reasoning'?[4] A judgement, especially in

[1] See, e.g., Lord Mansfield in *Miller* v. *Race* (1758), 1 Burr. 452, Buller J. in *Moss* v. *Gallimore* (1779), 1 Doug. 279 *ad fin.*

[2] Expressions of opinion on points not made or argued before the Court are to be regarded as *dicta* only: *Rahimtoola* v. *Nizam of Hyderabad*, [1958] A.C. 379.

[3] *Flower* v. *Ebbw Vale Steel &c. Co.*, [1934] 2 K.B. 132, 154. In *National Assistance Board* v. *Tugby*, [1957] 1 Q.B. 506, magistrates were pardonably misled by *dicta*.

[4] See Denning L.J. (dissenting) in *Korner* v. *Witkowitzer*, [1950] 2 K.B. 128 (affirmed [1951] A.C. 869).

higher courts where there is more time and opportunity for consideration—and sometimes for prolixity—is not always a chain; it is more like a fabric woven out of all kinds of different materials, and it is frequently difficult to determine exactly what ingredients were essential to its warp and woof. Whoever is called on to make the analysis must exercise his individual faculty of discrimination and no stereotyped rules can dispense him from that delicate task. Here, however, the discipline of our judicial hierarchy helps to some extent. Though it may be true to say that, in strict theory, a judge of the lowest degree ought to disregard a mere *dictum*, even from the most exalted authority, if he considers it to be inessential, yet this is a counsel of perfection and in practice it requires exceptional hardihood for a lower court to brush aside pronouncements of a higher court as being irrelevant.[1] This is well illustrated by *Adams* v. *Naylor*, [1946] A.C. 543. In that case the House of Lords expressed disapproval of the long-established device of the 'nominal defendant' by which Government departments, with the laudable intent of giving an aggrieved person a *locus standi in foro*, sometimes evaded the old rule that no action in tort lay against the Crown. All that was said in this connexion in *Adams* v. *Naylor* was entirely (and avowedly) *obiter*, since the actual decision turned on another point. When the same issue came before the Court of Appeal in *Royster* v. *Cavey*, [1947] K.B. 204, the Court felt that, in view of the explicit and considered *dicta* in the House of Lords, it could not entertain the action in the form in which it was presented. Consequently, persons who had been injured by Crown servants were left without even a fictional remedy, and the glaring light thus thrown on an ancient anomaly hastened the overdue enactment of the Crown Proceedings

[1] In *Kruse* v. *Questter*, [1953] 1 Q.B. 669, Pilcher J. preferred *dicta* of the House of Lords in *Heyman* v. *Darwin's, Ltd.*, [1942] A.C. 356, to the decision of the Privy Council in *Hirji Mulji* v. *Cheong Yue Steamship Co., Ltd.*, [1926] A.C. 497, by which, of course, he was not bound.

Act, 1947. An even more striking example is *Duncan* v. *Cammell, Laird & Co.*, [1942] A.C. 624, in which Viscount Simon L.C. laid down a series of rules concerning the privilege of Crown documents. Most of these rules were unnecessary to the main issue, which was one of public security; but they have been accepted as a statement of the law for England, though not without much doubt and dissatisfaction.[1] As against cases of this kind, in *In re Hastings (No. 2)*, [1959] 1 Q.B. 359 and *In re Hastings (No. 3)*, [1959] Ch. 368, many *dicta* of the House of Lords, and a supposed rule of practice in *habeas corpus*, were rejected as being based on a misunderstanding of statute. It is very seldom that a *dictum* of Lord Macnaghten has been questioned or dissented from; but in *Public Trustee* v. *I.R.C.*, [1958] Ch. 865 and [1960] A.C. 399, a *dictum* of his, dating from 1899, which had been accepted by the Court of Appeal and which had seemed to be the basis of settled practice, was renounced by the House of Lords. Age cannot wither nor custom stale the fallibility of a mere *dictum*!

And yet it is remarkable how sometimes a *dictum* which is really based on no authority, or perhaps on a fallacious interpretation of authority, acquires a spurious importance and becomes inveterate by sheer repetition in judgements and textbooks. Nobody has ever discovered the origin of Lord Abinger's dogma in *Priestley* v. *Fowler* (1837), 3 M. & W. 1, which remained for more than a century the basis of the whole irrational and unjust law of common employment, and finally had to be uprooted by legislation. Sixty-eight years passed before the House of Lords held, in *United Australia, Ltd.* v. *Barclays Bank, Ltd.*, [1941] A.C. 1, that a supposed rule (and an extremely inconvenient one) laid down by Bovill C.J. in *Smith* v. *Baker*, [1873] L.R. 8 C.P. 350, was not a rule at all, but a mere *dictum* based on a misunderstanding of *Buckland* v. *Johnson* (1854), 15 C.B. 145. *Dicta* of Kennedy L.J. in *Hillyer* v. *St. Bartholomew's Hospital*,

[1] See the present writer's *Law and Orders* (2nd ed.), pp. 369 ff.

[1909] 2 K.B. 820, purported to lay down in wide terms a principle of the greatest importance in the liability of hospitals to their patients, and it was not until the decision in *Gold* v. *Essex County Council*, [1942] 2 K.B. 293, that the mischief of this *dictum* was restrained to a more reasonable principle.[1] There is always a danger that a *dictum*, as was said in *Cavanagh* v. *Ulster Weaving Co.*, [1960] A.C. 145, may degenerate into a mere 'formula of words', a supposed generalization without due regard to the particular circumstances to which it related.

The whole position with regard to *dicta* has undoubtedly become confused, and, as authorities multiply, it is increasingly difficult to determine what is essential and what is merely incidental to a decision.[2] We hear more and more protests from the Bench against the citation of *dicta* for what they do *not* decide;[3] but those whose duty it is to assist the court with the best material which they can find should not be blamed too severely if, in the present state of our authorities, they sometimes discover mares' nests. And indeed, in some important branches of the law, it has not been easy for anybody to know what is authoritative and what is not. Until recently, the law governing the liability for negligence of an occupier to persons upon his premises, which was based on distinctions originally drawn in *Indermaur* v. *Dames* (1866), L.R. 1 C.P. 274, had involved themselves in such a tangle of authority that it was wellnigh impossible to discover a path through them. Cases like *Miller* v. *Hancock*, [1893] 2 Q.B. 177, *Fairman* v. *Perpetual Investment Building Society*, [1923] A.C. 74,

[1] The fallacy had previously been exposed by Professor A. L. Goodhart, 54 *L.Q.R.* 553. See also *Collins* v. *Hertfordshire C.C.*, [1947] K.B. 598; *Cassidy* v. *Minister of Health*, [1951] 2 K.B. 343; *Roe* v. *Minister of Health*, [1954] 2 Q.B. 66.

[2] See Paton and Sawer, 'Ratio Decidendi and Obiter Dictum', 43 *L.Q.R.* 461. *Armstrong* v. *Strain*, [1952] 1 K.B. 232, provides ample material for this form of mental gymnastics.

[3] See, for example, Lord Atkin in *London Brick Co.* v. *Robinson*, [1943] A.C. 341, 349, and Evershed M.R. in *In re McGreavey*, [1950] Ch. 269, 278.

Jacobs v. *L.C.C.*, [1950] A.C. 361, and many others which might be cited, had surrounded this important subject with such a fog of doubt as between *ratio* and *dictum* that the law had become largely guesswork. So the Law Reform Committee thought, and as the result of its recommendations the Occupiers Liability Act, 1957, was passed. Of course the Act still leaves problems unsolved,[1] as all questions of negligence must do eternally, but by establishing one Common Law standard of care for all persons (with necessary exceptions) lawfully upon premises, it has at least cleared the law of confusing and unnecessary distinctions which had lasted for nearly a hundred years.

We certainly seem to have reached the extreme of obfuscation when a single judge, attempting to thread his way through a labyrinth, says that expressions of a higher court were *obiter* and therefore not binding, and is then told by the higher court that his criticisms were themselves *obiter*, and both are told by a learned commentator that the criticism of the criticism was *obiter*![2] Hard indeed will be the lot of Bench and Bar who in the future may have to dissect into *ratio* and *dictum* the three cases (with many others which they touch at one point or another) of *Pickavance* v. *P.*, [1901] P. 60, *Hopkins* v. *H.*, [1914] P. 282, and *Land* v. *L.*, [1949] P. 405. The last-mentioned case appears to lay down that however weighty a *dictum* may seem to be, if in the opinion of the Court it has been misinterpreted in subsequent cases, the latter are of no authority. This seems to add the last refinement to the process of judicial ordeal-by-*dictum*.

A judgement is made up of many different elements, and in our law it has no uniform pattern, since it is the product of an individual mind and personality. It is therefore very difficult to formulate any rule which can distinguish automatically between *ratio* and *dictum*. In

[1] See Payne, *The Occupiers Liability Act*, 21 M.L.R. 359.

[2] See *Goss* v. *G.*, [1948] P. 15, and note thereon in 64 *L.Q.R.* 15.

Behrens v. *Bertram Mills Circus Ltd.*, [1957] 2 Q.B. 1, Devlin J. put the matter thus (at p. 24):

'It is well established that if a judge gives two reasons for his decision, both are binding.[1] It is not permissible to pick out one as being supposedly the better reason and ignore the other one; nor does it matter for this purpose which comes first and which comes second. But the practice of making judicial observations *obiter* is also well established. A judge may often give additional reasons for his decision without making them part of the *ratio decidendi;* he may not be sufficiently convinced of their cogency as to want them to have the full authority of precedent, and yet may wish to state them so that those who later may have the duty of investigating the same point will start with some guidance. This is a matter which the judge himself is alone capable of deciding, and any judge who comes after him must ascertain which course has been adopted from the language used and not by consulting his own preference.'

Unfortunately, however, it is not always true that 'the judge himself is alone capable of deciding' whether he is giving expression to *ratio* or *dictum*. He may easily mistake one for the other, and then the responsibility rests on 'any judge who comes after him'—or, more commonly, an appellate court which comes after him—to decide what he really intended. This is well illustrated by the curious history of *Atkinson* v. *Bettison*, [1955] 1 W.L.R. 1126, a case which concerned the true purpose of a landlord, under the Landlord and Tenant Act, 1954, in refusing to grant a new lease of business premises, on the ground that he required possession himself, but with an 'ancillary purpose' of reconstruction. Statements of Denning L.J. seemed to indicate that one at least of the *rationes* was that a merely ancillary purpose could not be allowed as a ground for the refusal of a new lease. In *Fisher* v. *Taylor's Furnishing Stores Ltd.*, [1956] 2 Q.B. 78, the Court of Appeal, constituted, as to two-thirds, of the same members as before, put quite a

[1] So held in *Jacobs* v. *L.C.C.*, [1950] A.C. 361, followed in *Cane* v. *Royal College of Music*, [1961] 2 Q.B. 89.

different interpretation on the *ratio* of *Atkinson* v. *Bettison* and distinguished it. Confusion, however, remained, especially in the County Courts, and in *Craddock* v. *Hampshire C.C.*, [1958] 1 W.L.R. 202, the Court of Appeal, differently constituted, was faced with the real or apparent conflict between the two decisions of its own court.[1] It decided in favour of *Fisher* v. *Taylor's Stores*, rejecting the view that an 'ancillary purpose' necessarily defeated the landlord's refusal. Finally, in *Betty's Cafés Ltd.* v. *Phillips Furnishing Stores Ltd.*, [1959] A.C. 20, the same point, among others, came before the House of Lords, which approved *Fisher* v. *Taylor's Stores* and distinguished *Atkinson* v. *Bettison*. Lord Denning himself said (at p. 53) that the Court of Appeal had 'virtually overruled one of the grounds of decision in *Atkinson* v. *Bettison*, leaving the decision to rest on its other ground'. This seems to mean that while two distinct *rationes* may be right and binding,[2] if one is right and the other wrong, the wrong one is to be treated as merely *obiter* (and erroneous), while the right one stands in full force and virtue. The position for anybody who has to advise a client becomes curiouser and curiouser.

The line between *dictum* and *ratio* therefore remains indistinct and in each case must be a matter of delicate discrimination. On the whole, it may be said that when a superior tribunal, and especially the ultimate appellate court, devotes much thought and dialectic to discussing a controversial issue, it is unreal to brush the fruit of its labours aside as 'not necessary to the decision', and no court is likely to do so. In *Adams* v. *Naylor*, [1946] A.C. 543, we have seen an example of opinions which were manifestly and avowedly *obiter*, but which had an authoritative effect not only in the Court of Appeal but in legislation. In that case, however, as in *Duncan* v.

[1] This case was heard on 23 January 1958, and *Betty's Cafés Ltd.* v. *Phillips Furnishing Stores Ltd.* in the House of Lords on 28 January 1958. Owing to its recency it was not cited in the House of Lords.

[2] *Jacobs* v. *L.C.C. ubi sup.*

Cammell, Laird & Co., [1942] A.C. 624, the *dicta* were clear and calculated, and it would have been impossible to disregard them (though in the case last mentioned they were quite gratuitous and in at least one respect mistaken). But all this assumes that there must be unanimity or at least a clear preponderance of opinion; and this does not always exist. Thus in *Cricklewood Property and Investment Trust* v. *Leighton's Investment Trust*, [1945] A.C. 221, which touched on, but left open, the important and unsettled question whether the doctrine of frustration applies to a lease, the *dicta* were so conflicting that they clearly leave a controverted issue still open in the lower courts. In sum, if the eminence of the tribunal, the consensus of judicial opinion, and the degree of deliberation all combine to lend a special weight and solemnity to *dicta*, then, and only then, they become for all practical purposes authoritative.

II. AUTHORITY OF PRECEDENT

Authoritative and unauthoritative precedents

These rules are the alphabet of his study to any modern English lawyer, and none of the observations which here follow is intended to cast the slightest doubt on their validity as an essential part of our legal technique. But it is unfortunate that in our extra-judicial doctrine, though certainly not in the practice of the courts themselves, a number of scholastic and, as it seems to me, unprofitable dogmas have grown up which tend to obscure the real function of precedent in our legal reasoning. So many arbitrary distinctions are drawn as to what precedents may be admitted and what may not, that we are in danger of regarding mere decisions *in themselves* as settling disputed points, and of forgetting the fundamental principle which governs the whole employment of precedent. That principle, as we have seen, was insisted upon by Lord Mansfield, and it was reaffirmed by Sir George Jessel with his usual clarity, when he said:[1] 'The only use of authorities or decided cases is the establishment of some principle which the Judge can follow out in deciding the case before him.' Simple and self-evident though this *dictum* may sound, it is not always kept in view. The result is that the form tends to be confused with the substance. Precedents, as has been observed by a distinguished judge of our own time, should be 'stepping-stones, and not halting-places'.[2]

It is, of course, beyond doubt that existing decisions by courts of higher authority, or generally (though not always) of co-ordinate authority, are 'binding', whether the judges like them or not, if the principle which they lay down is clear and definite and plainly applicable to the facts of the instant case. In that sense actual pertinent decisions are, by an established rule of judicial technique, *legal* authorities. We have seen, however, that often it is difficult, because it is a matter of subjective interpretation, to determine exactly what principle the *legal* authorities embody. So it is with statutory interpretation, which forms such a large part of the business of the courts nowadays. Nobody can deny that the language of a statute is a binding legal authority, but we shall see that here again there is often difficulty in deciding to what conclusion it binds—in short, what it means! In their search for the governing principle, our courts do not hesitate to turn to sources other than the legal-binding. These are often called 'historical' or 'material' sources of law. It is true that our courts are not *obliged* to accept them, but in fact they have so often done so when they are relevant that the rigid distinction

[1] *In re Hallett's Estate* (1879), 13 Ch.D. at p. 712. Cf. the same judge in *Osborne to Rowlett* (1880), 13 Ch.D. 774, 785: 'I have often said, and I repeat it, that the only thing in a Judge's decision binding as an authority upon a subsequent Judge is the principle upon which the case was decided; but it is not sufficient that the case should have been decided on a principle if that principle itself is not a right principle, or one not applicable to the case; and it is for a subsequent Judge to say whether or not it is a right principle, and, if not, he may himself lay down the true principle.' On the whole subject see Austin, *Jurisprudence*, Lects. XXXVIII and XXXIX.

[2] Lord Macmillan in *Birch* v. *Brown*, [1931] A.C. at p. 631.

between the 'binding' and the 'persuasive' becomes very shadowy and insubstantial.

It is submitted, therefore, that it is an exaggeration to say that

> 'the precedent is the legal source of the rule, and the others are merely its historical sources. The precedent is its source not merely in fact, but in law also; the others are its sources in fact, but obtain no legal recognition as such. Our law knows well the effect of precedent, but it knows nothing of Pothier, or of Tribonian, or of the Urban Praetor. The proposition that every principle embodied in a judicial decision has for the future the force of law is not merely a statement of historical fact as to the growth of English law; it is itself a rule of law. But the proposition that much of the law of Rome has become incorporated into the law of England is simply a statement of fact, which has in law no relevance or recognition. . . . We are here concerned solely with the legal sources of law. Its historical sources pertain to legal history, not to legal theory. Hereafter, when we speak of the sources of law, we shall mean by that term the legal sources exclusively'.[1]

Foreign jurists

All this sounds very clear and exact, but when we come to apply it in the courts, its precision becomes blurred.[2] We find the judges disobligingly oblivious of these stern distinctions. For example, Pothier is a particularly unfortunate illustration of the theory advanced. As it happens, this foreign jurist has been treated as an authority by our judges on several very important points of law. In 1822 Best J. speaks of him in the following terms:

> 'The authority of Pothier is expressly in point. That is as high as can be had, next to the decision of a court of justice in this country. It is extremely well known that he is a writer of acknowledged character; his writings have been constantly

[1] Salmond, *Jurisprudence*, 11th ed., 133 f. The passage as originally written has been considerably modified by the Editor, Dr. Glanville Williams.

[2] Professor Hart, *The Concept of Law*, p. 246, defends the distinction between 'legal' and 'historical' sources, but agrees that the distinction 'may be blurred'. He suggests a dichotomy between 'permissive' and 'mandatory' sources. But if a non-obligatory source is 'permissive' to a decision, why is it not an 'authority'?

referred to by the court and he is spoken of with great praise by Sir William Jones in his *Law of Bailments*, and his writings are considered by that author equal in point of luminous method, apposite examples, and a clear manly style, to the works of Littleton on the laws of this country. We cannot, therefore, have a better guide than Pothier on this subject.'[1]

Sixty years later Lord Blackburn refers to him in the House of Lords with no less respect.[2] These are no mere empty compliments, as is shown by the series of cases based upon *Smith* v. *Wheatcroft* (1878), 9 Ch.D. 223. In that case Fry J. had to consider a difficult point concerning *error in persona* of a contracting party. For the true principle to be applied this very learned Judge turned to Pothier's *Traité des Obligations*. The passage which he cited from that work, not as mere illustration, but as decisive authority, has become a *locus classicus* in our law, and there is scarcely a modern case on the same point in which it is not applied as the proper test.[3] The

[1] *Cox* v. *Troy* (1822), 5 B. & Ald. 474, 480.

[2] 'We constantly in the English Courts, upon the question what is the general law, cite Pothier, and we cite Scotch cases where they happen to be in point; and so in a Scotch case you would cite English decisions, and cite Pothier, or any foreign jurists, provided they bore upon the point': *McLean* v. *Clydesdale Banking Co.* (1883), 9 App. Cas. 95, 105.

[3] See *Nash* v. *Dix* (1898), 78 L.T. 445; *Gordon* v. *Street*, [1899] 2 Q.B. 641; *Phillips* v. *Brooks*, [1919] 2 K.B. 243; *Said* v. *Butt*, [1920] 3 K.B. 497; *Lake* v. *Simmons*, [1927] A.C. 487, 501; *Sowler* v. *Potter*, [1940] 1 K.B. 271; *Dennant* v. *Skinner*, [1948] 2 K.B. 164. There is, however, no little irony in the fact that the reference to Pothier has constantly been given wrongly, that an important part of his statement has been omitted, and that in consequence the interpretation put upon him is disputable: see J. F. Wilson, 'Identity in Contract and the Pothier Fallacy', 17 *M.L.R.* 515, and J. C. Smith and J. A. C. Thomas, 'Pothier and the Three Dots', 20 *M.L.R.* 38. As long ago as 1941 Professor Goodhart (57 *L.Q.R.* 228) attacked the Pothier doctrine, ending his article with the words 'it is certainly time . . . that Pothier's statement was firmly and finally buried'. In *Ingram* v. *Little*, [1961] 1 Q.B. 31, the whole problem came under review. Slade J., at first instance, adopted the reasoning of Professor Goodhart. In the Court of Appeal Sellers and Holroyd Pearce L.JJ., Devlin L.J. dissenting, without actually holding that *Phillips* v. *Brooks*, which followed Pothier, had been wrongly decided, distinguished it on the facts. It is difficult to say, therefore, whether Pothier is now 'firmly and finally buried', or has one foot in the grave, or is still alive and kicking. Only the House of Lords can tell us. Whatever view is taken, the fact remains that, rightly or wrongly, Pothier has repeatedly been accepted as an authority.

gist of the matter is whether it will be so applied, and not whether we dub it 'binding' on the one hand, or 'persuasive', 'legal', or 'literary' on the other. Thus, of recent years various American and Dominions decisions have been examined and followed with such respect that it is little more than a fiction to say that they are not regarded as 'authorities'.[1]

Roman Law

It is true that the voice of Justinian is heard once in our Courts where the voice of our own legal authorities is heard a thousand times; and any counsel who based his argument solely on the Digest would occasion depression, if not a certain irritation, on the Bench.[2] But it is going much too far to say that our law 'knows nothing' of Tribonian and the Urban Praetor, or indeed of any weighty exposition of a principle relevant to the case in hand. Some departments of our law have been settled almost entirely on the authority of the Digest. The most conspicuous example is the right to flowing or percolating water. On this point we find Tindal C.J. declaring that the authority of Marcellus in the Digest is not merely in favour of the defendant but 'appears decisive'.[3] In *Bechervaise* v. *Lewis* (1872), L.R. 7 C.P. 372, the defendant had made himself a party to a joint and several promissory note, but as a surety only. Action being brought against him for the amount of the note, the question was whether the surety could avail himself, by way of equitable defence, of a set-off which his principal had against the payee (plaintiff). In the judgement of the Court, delivered by Willes J., not a single English case is cited, and the sole authority relied upon is a passage of the Digest (16. 2. 4). In 1863, with *Taylor* v. *Caldwell*, 3 B. & S. 826, began a series of modern cases

[1] See *post*, pp. 280 ff.

[2] See characteristic remarks of Lord Halsbury L.C. in *Keighley, Maxsted & Co.* v. *Durant*, [1901] A.C. 240, 244.

[3] *Acton* v. *Blundell* (1843), 12 M. & W. 324, 353. Cf. arguments in this case, and judgement of Denman C.J. in *Mason* v. *Hill* (1838), 5 B. & A. 1, which settled similar questions with regard to water flowing in defined channels.

which have greatly restricted the scope of that severe principle of contract known as the rule in *Paradine* v. *Jane* (1647), Aleyn 26. The celebrated judgement of Blackburn J. was based very largely on Roman doctrines;[1] and indeed it may be said generally that in case after case this very learned lawyer, who, perhaps more than any other judge, exercised a notable creative influence on the development of the Common Law in the nineteenth century, showed himself a disciple of Roman principles. We even find modern judges turning to Roman Law for guidance in solving the problem whether, on failure of a promise to marry, the engagement ring and gifts must be returned, and testing an old problem in the English law of sale by the Roman Law of *emptio venditio*.[2] There is still much work to be done in investigating the influence of the Corpus Juris upon the general development of our law: but it seems certain that that influence has been powerful and continuous from the earliest times, even though there was never any actual 'reception'.[3] How far Roman Law directly inspired the beginnings of our equitable jurisdiction is still an open question.[4] To this day our highest tribunal contains judges who have been trained in Roman doctrines, to which they frequently and without hesitation have recourse. Anybody uninfluenced by dogmatic classifications would indeed be surprised, on

[1] Cf. Lord Shaw in *Horlock* v. *Beal*, [1916] 1 A.C. at p. 512.

[2] McCardie J. in *Cohen* v. *Sellar*, [1926] 1 K.B. 536 (see 43 *L.Q.R.* 156), and Slesser L.J. in *Robinson* v. *Graves*, [1935] 1 K.B. at p. 589. In *Nugent* v. *Smith* (1875), 1 C.P.D. 19, Brett J.'s attempt to base the liability of carriers by sea on Roman principles was rejected by the Court of Appeal (1 C.P.D. 423). See also *The Tubantia*, [1924] P. 78, and *In re Knapton*, [1941] Ch. 428.

[3] For the whole story, see P. & M. i, chs. i and v, *et passim*; Holdsworth, *H.E.L.* ii. 133 ff., 145 ff., iv. 217 ff.; Lévy-Ullmann, *Éléments d'introduction générale à l'étude des sciences juridiques*, vol. i, part i, ch. vi; Scrutton, *The Influence of Roman Law on the Law of England*; Jolowicz, *Roman Foundations of Modern Law*. On Blackstone's fanciful account of the authority of Roman Law in English courts, see Holdsworth, *loc. cit.*, Lévy-Ullmann, *loc. cit.*, and Pollock *apud* Maine, *Ancient Law*, Note G. See further W. Senior, 'Roman Law MSS. in England', 47 *L.Q.R.* 337.

[4] See Kerly, *History of Equity*, 189.

reading the judgement of Holt C.J. in *Coggs* v. *Bernard* (1703), 2 Ld. Raym. 909, or of Collins L.J. in *Durant* v. *Keighley, Maxsted & Co.*, [1900] 1 Q.B. 629, or of all the Peers in *Cantiare San Rocco* v. *Clyde Shipbuilding Co.*, [1924] A.C. 226, to learn that the Digest has no recognition in our courts.[1] Of our law of sale, Chalmers, the draftsman and annotator of the Sale of Goods Act, 1893, observed in his Introduction: 'There is hardly a judgement of importance on the law of sale in which reference is not made to the Civil Law.' There is still no better approach for the student to this important branch of our law than the Digest. Roman Law profoundly affected the whole development of the Law Merchant, and has had a marked influence on such departments of English Law as easements,[2] waste,[3] and various aspects of succession, especially *donatio mortis causa*.[4] It is quite artificial to condemn it to the irrelevance of the 'unauthoritative'.

Private International Law

Something has been said already concerning the creative influence of *Juristenrecht* as compared with customary law.[5] If we compare it in modern law with the

[1] Cf. *Sinclair* v. *Brougham*, [1914] A.C. 398. In ecclesiastical and Admiralty jurisdiction, Canon and Roman Law have always been authoritative: but on the position of Canon Law in our courts after the Reformation, see Lord Hardwicke in *Middleton* v. *Crofts* (1736), 2 Atk. 650. The influence is most notable in testamentary law—a good example will be found in the rules governing soldiers' wills (now embodied in the Wills Act, 1837, s. 2, and extended by the Wills (Soldiers and Sailors) Act, 1918): see *Drummond* v. *Parish* (1843), 3 Curt. 522, *In re Wernher*, [1918] 1 Ch. 339 (affirmed [1918] 2 Ch. 82); *In re Booth*, [1926] P. 118; *In re Wingham*, [1949] P. 187. Every reader of the Law Reports will also be aware that there are many cases before the Privy Council in which Roman doctrines in the Dominions have to be considered; see, for example, *Galliers* v. *Rycroft*, [1901] A.C. 130, where the judgement of the Judicial Committee turned almost entirely on the interpretation of passages of the Digest concerning *fideicommissa*. Cf. the large number of juristic authorities examined in *Abeyawardene* v. *West*, [1957] A.C. 176.

[2] See *Dalton* v. *Angus* (1881), 6 App. Cas. 740, and *Gale on Easements*, *passim*.

[3] See *Dashwood* v. *Magniac*, [1891] 3 Ch. 306.

[4] On the whole subject, see Mackintosh, *Roman Law in Modern Practice*, and Oliver, 'Roman Law in Modern Cases', in *Cambridge Legal Essays*, 243.

[5] *Ante*, pp. 116 ff.

influence of precedents, we find that its creative work is by no means exhausted and that it is not always possible to put it in the second rank as 'persuasive' merely. At least one great department of modern law, International Law, has been built up very largely on the researches and opinions of learned writers. I leave aside Public International Law, since its development is not complete, and its exact nature and authority as law are still open to controversy. But well-defined rules of Private International Law constantly have to be applied in our courts. Now this is a comparatively recent growth in English jurisprudence. 'Down to the middle of the eighteenth century in England', wrote Frederic Harrison in 1879,[1]

'I cannot find a single opinion or decision which seemed to show the consciousness on the part of English lawyers that there was any branch of law such as we are now considering. . . . . Our insular position, our complete detachment from the civil law, and our complete indifference to any systematic treatment of legal theory, apart from cases of practice, explain the fact that down to the beginning of the nineteenth century Private International Law was absolutely unknown in this country.'

It could not remain indefinitely in this condition. The nineteenth century had to construct a whole system of Private International Law. To what sources did it turn? Let me quote Harrison again,[2] reminding the reader that his words were written in 1879:

'And yet when a question of this class arises, it is seldom decided off-hand with reference merely to English decisions. Books are cited as authorities which are usually foreign; the decisions of foreign tribunals have frequently to be reviewed. An author such as Huber, a Dutch professor of the seventeenth century, is constantly quoted. American decisions, the codes of foreign countries, public treaties, old civilians, old and modern treatises on International Law, are continually appealed to. Story, Foelix and Boullenois are in constant requisition, and the court will seriously attend to dicta of foreign lawyers writing

[1] *Jurisprudence and the Conflict of Laws*, 118. [2] *Op. cit.* 102.

under systems widely different from our own and from each other, whose notions of jurisprudence rest upon theories entirely contrary to our own.'

These authorities are appealed to not only in difficult and extraordinary cases; we have no separate jurisdiction for questions of Private International Law; the problems may arise in any court at any time and in connexion with almost any kind of action, great or small. It goes without saying that at the present day, this branch of our jurisprudence having now been elaborated for upwards of a century and a half, our courts do not rely solely on foreign jurists and foreign decisions. When Professor Dicey published the first edition of his *Conflict of Laws*, seventeen years after Harrison had written the words which have been quoted, he made it his endeavour to pursue a positive rather than a theoretical method of analysis, and placed the sources of Private International Law in the order (1) statutes, (2) decisions, (3) 'such general principles as may be elicited from the judgements of foreign courts, the opinions of distinguished jurists, and rules prevalent in other countries'.[1] By 1896 the amount of available English precedent had grown very considerably: it has continued to grow since that date, so that at the present time decisions can usually be relied on in any question of conflict of laws. It still remains true, however, that English decisions are much fewer in this branch of the law than in most others, and there is hardly a case in which the opinion of learned writers, such as Story, Westlake, Cheshire, or Dicey himself and his later editors, is not cited as authority. In particular, the influence of Story has been predominant in both England and America, in regard to particular doctrines as well as to the whole foundation of this branch of the law. Story himself is a vast repository of the opinions of foreign jurists, who, through him, have unmistakably influenced our

[1] *Conflict of Laws* (1st ed.), 22.

doctrine. Indeed, it is not too much to say that the true and recognized course of this new department of English law—at all events, in most of its essential components—is a stream of foreign juristic writing beginning in the fourteenth century; and that when judges follow the precedents of our own courts in this domain, they are often really affirming principles enunciated by Continental jurists of the sixteenth and seventeenth centuries.[1]

Real Property

In another and complex branch of our law, the opinions of learned practitioners and commentators have had great influence with the courts, and to dismiss them as 'unauthoritative' is to do them less than justice. Large and important parts of the law of Real Property have been developed almost entirely by the practice of conveyancers. To take the most prominent example, the Statute of Uses itself became a plaything in the hands of conveyancers, energetically seconded by the Court of Chancery. The widow could be barred from her Common Law right to dower by the ingenious manipulation of uses, the express provisions of statutes could be nullified by the employment of such devices as bargain and sale and lease and release; and the modern settlement, on which the rights of so many owners of real property depend, is almost wholly the work of practitioners. When statute regulated the matter, as it did repeatedly in the nineteenth century, it followed the lines laid down by conveyancers in essentials. Much of real property law *is* conveyancing and nothing else. It is not surprising,

[1] What is true of Private is even more true of Public International Law. 'The consensus of authors of good repute', writes Sir Frederick Pollock (*Essays in the Law*, 65), 'or even the clear statement of one eminent author, may be taken as evidence of the accepted practice where practice is not shown to be otherwise.' 'Vattel', said Lord Stowell in *The Maria* (1799), 1 C. Rob. 373, 'is here to be considered, not as a lawyer merely delivering an opinion, but as a witness asserting the fact—the fact that such is the existing practice of modern Europe.' The subject is discussed at length, and with much learning, by Sir R. Phillimore in *Reg.* v. *Keyn* (1876), 2 Ex. D. at pp. 69 ff., and in the judgement of Lord Evershed M.R. in *Ex p. Mwenya*, [1960] 1 Q.B. 241, 301. See further Harrison, *op. cit.*: and on the limitations of this principle, Lord Alvestone C.J. in *West Rand Central Gold Mining Co.* v. *R.*, [1905] 2 K.B. at pp. 401 ff.

therefore, that the courts have consistently heeded weighty expositions of the practice of conveyancers coming from extra-judicial sources, and have not hesitated to treat them, in fact if not in name, as 'authority'. 'For the exposition of our very complicated real property law', says Byrne J., 'it is proper in the absence of judicial authority to resort to text-books which have been recognized by the courts as representing the views and practice of conveyancers of repute';[1] and he proceeds to make reference, among other works, to Challis on Real Property—a book which has been constantly cited with approval in the Chancery Division.[2] Nor is this principle confined to any particular jurisdiction. In a very different branch of the law—Admiralty—we find a modern Lord Justice paying this compliment to extra-judicial doctrine:

'This is one of those cases dealing with damages which in my experience I have found to be a branch of law on which one is less guided by authority laying down definite principles than on almost any other matter that one can consider. I think the law as to damages still awaits a scientific statement which will probably be made when there is a completely satisfactory text-book on the subject.'[3]

[1] *Hollis's Hospital and Hague's Contract*, [1899] 2 Ch. 540, 551.

[2] See also *Bain* v. *Fothergill* (1874), L.R. 7 H.L.158, and *Smith* v. *Earl of Jersey* (1821), 2 Br. & B. 473, cited Pollock, *First Book of Jurisprudence*, 321. Cf. Jessel M.R., *London & South Western Railway Co.* v. *Gomm* (1882), 20 Ch. D. 562, 581. 'No doubt the practice of conveyancers is not law in the same sense as a statute or a judgement is law; and if it is founded on an erroneous view of the law it will be disregarded. But provided that it is unanimous, and provided that it is not contrary to any ascertained rule of law, it will be such cogent evidence of the law that it will rarely be disregarded by the courts': Holdsworth, *H.E.L.* vii. 386, q.v., also iii. 219 ff., and vii. 384 ff. on the whole subject. *Contra*, see *Newman* v. *N.* (1885), 28 Ch. D. 674 and Sargant L.J. in *In re Ryder and Steadman's Contract*, [1927] 2 Ch. 62, 84.

[3] *Per* Atkin L.J., *The Susquehanna*, [1925] P. 196, 210. On books of authority in general, see 1 Bl. *Comm.* 72 ff.; and, for a bitter indictment of them, Bentham, *A Comment on the Commentaries*, 204. By a well-known professional convention, living writers are not cited as authority, but Bench and Bar may 'adopt' their statements as correct expositions of the law. This is in many cases little more than a polite fiction. In *R.* v. *Sandbach, Ex p. Williams*, [1935] 2 K.B. 192, Blackstone was followed, and Humphreys J.

In *Bastin* v. *Davies*, [1950] 2 K.B. 579, Lord Goddard C.J. said that 'this court would never hesitate to disagree with a statement in a text-book however authoritative or however long it had existed, if it thought right to do so'; but he added:

'It would be unfortunate if doubt had to be thrown on a statement which has appeared in a well-known textbook for a great number of years without being judicially doubted and after it had been acted on by justices and their clerks for many years.'

Not without reason did John Stuart Mill write:[1]

'Whatever definiteness in detail, and whatever order or consistency as a whole, has been attained by any established system, has in almost all countries been given by private writers on law. All the generalizations of legal ideas, and all explicit statements of the meaning of the principal legal terms, have, speaking generally, been the work of these unauthorized persons—have passed from their writings into professional usage, and have ended by being either expressly, or oftener by implication, adopted by governments and legislatures.'

And to governments and legislatures we may add judges. Sometimes the converse process is to be observed. Judges do not hesitate to differ from statements even in the most respected practice-books, if they consider them ill founded.[2] A statement of dubious authority may be made by one text-writer and repeated by others until it comes to be accepted as a commonplace of the law; whereas if its origins are examined, it may be found to rest on little or no basis in actual judicial decision. Thus it has long been stated in textbooks as a well-established principle of the royal prerogative that the Crown may take advantage of a statute by which it is not bound: in other words, that it may have the benefit without

went so far as to say: 'It is too late, in 1935, to attempt to show that Blackstone was wrong.'

[1] *Dissertations*, iii. 214.

[2] See, e.g., *Pavlides* v. *Jensen*, [1956] Ch. 565, 572, and *In re H. L. Bolton Engineering Co., Ltd.*, [1956] Ch. 577, 584, on *Buckley on Companies*; *In re a Debtor*, [1951] Ch. 612, 621, on *Williams on Bankruptcy*; and *Beevis* v. *Dawson*, [1957] 1 Q.B. 195, 207, on *Gatley on Libel and Slander*.

the burden of a statute. The interesting suggestion has been made that these extra-judicial statements really rest upon no authority; and although the matter has not been expressly decided, there seems to be much force in the contention.[1] Again, it was for long believed, and constantly stated in textbooks, that at Common Law statements made between husband and wife during marriage were privileged; but in *Shenton* v. *Tyler*, [1939] Ch. 620, the Court of Appeal, after an elaborate examination of the authorities and of the textbooks, came to the conclusion that no such rule had ever existed at Common Law and that so far as it was valid it was entirely the creation of statute.[2] Similarly in *In re a Debtor*, [1950] Ch. 282, the Court of Appeal rejected the statement to be found in textbooks of authority, that an infant cannot in any circumstances be made bankrupt. We shall see (*post*, pp. 326 ff.) that in the development of case-law ideas sometimes grow up and earn credence by the mere force of uncritical repetition; and it must be confessed that the same thing sometimes happens in books and commentaries even of the highest authority and reputation. It is not always easy in the study and application of law, and yet it is necessary, to remind oneself that nothing can be taken for granted.[3]

Foreign judgements

These may be called indirect but powerful influences on the development of English law; even more important is the readiness with which English judges turn to the decisions and reasons of 'foreign' courts—by

[1] See *Cayzer* v. *Board of Trade*, [1927] 1 K.B. 269 (affirmed [1927] A.C. 610), and cf. 43 *L.Q.R.* 157.

[2] The principle was affirmed by the House of Lords in *Rumping* v. *D.P.P.*, [1962] 3 W.L.R. 770.

[3] On the whole question of textbooks and juristic writings see Paton, *Jurisprudence* (2nd ed.), 199 ff., where the valid point is made that of recent years increasing deference seems to have been paid by the courts to extra-judicial writings and opinions. There could be no better example than *In re Egerton's Will Trusts*, [1956] Ch. 593, in which Roxburgh J. based his judgement largely on deciding between two rival theories of Dr. G. C. Cheshire and Dr. J. H. C. Morris. Danckwerts J. was referee in a similar contest of authorities in *In re Waite's Settlement Trusts*, [1958] Ch. 100.

which, of course, I mean only English-speaking courts in countries beyond this realm. Such decisions are not technically 'binding', but in recent years there has been noticeable an increasing respect for them; and frequently there seems to be little real difference between praying them in aid to support a *ratio decidendi* and actually 'following' them as authoritative statements of the law.

This is especially true when the matter under consideration has an international aspect. Thus The Hague Rules, which were the product of conferences on Maritime Law held in 1922 and 1923, have been substantially embodied by most civilized nations in municipal Carriage of Goods by Sea Acts. In both *Midland Silicones Ltd.* v. *Scruttons Ltd.*, [1962] A.C. 446[1] and *Riverstone Meat Co. Ltd.* v. *Lancashire Shipping Co. Ltd.*, [1961] A.C. 807,[2] on points arising out of bills of lading, the need for maintaining the 'prevailing harmony', as Viscount Simonds called it, in these maritime matters was much emphasized, and American and Australian decisions were freely cited—indeed, Viscount Simonds went out of his way to pay a special tribute to a judgement of the late Fullagar J. in one Australian case.

Similarly when a statute is common to both England and Scotland it is highly desirable, to avoid confusion, that antecedent Scottish decisions should if possible be followed,[3] even though the Court does so somewhat sceptically, as Lord Goddard C.J. seems to have done in *Cording* v. *Halse*, [1955] 1 Q.B. 63. In *Abbott* v. *Philbin*, [1960] Ch. 27, the Court of Appeal, evidently for the sake of comity, but with unconcealed doubt, followed the Scottish case of *Forbes Trustees* v. *I.R.C.* (1958), S.C. 177, but the doubts were vindicated by the House

[1] See at p. 471.

[2] See at p. 840.

[3] See *Daley* v. *Hargreaves*, [1961] 1 W.L.R. 487. In *Minister of Pensions* v. *Higham*, [1948] 2 K.B. 153, Denning J. followed a decision of the Court of Session which was at variance with one of his own previous judgements, so as to avoid a conflict of view on an important point concerning the nature of a 'war risk injury'.

of Lords, which overruled the Scottish case ([1961] A.C. 352). The principle of uniformity, of course, cannot be maintained when there is a fundamental difference of judicial opinion. Thus in *Kahn* v. *Newberry*, [1959] 2 Q.B. 1, the Divisional Court of the Queen's Bench declined to follow two Scots decisions on the perpetually elusive meaning of the word 'place', and in *Lyle* v. *Rosher*, [1959] 1 W.L.R. 8, Lord Reid issued a warning against attempting to apply English equitable principles to Scottish cases, since Scotland has never had a separate equitable jurisdiction.

It goes without saying that decisions in Scots law may be decisive in appeals from Scottish judgements to the House of Lords, just as in appeals to the Privy Council the decisions of superior courts in the Commonwealth are of high relevance: see, e.g., *Commonwealth of Australia* v. *Bank of New South Wales*, [1950] A.C. 235. In special circumstances, our courts show no hesitation in borrowing from the law of Scotland. Thus, when after the passing of the Homicide Act, 1957, the first English case arose of the interpretation of 'diminished responsibility', Lord Goddard C.J. said that the doctrine had been borrowed from Scots law, and he accepted as the governing pronouncement on a notoriously difficult question the Scottish case of *H.M. Advocate* v. *Braithwaite* (1945), S.C. (J.) 55.

The same principle of the 'homogeneous development' of the law in the Commonwealth—in this instance the measure of damages for negligence—was emphasized by Lord Parker C.J. in *Smith* v. *Leech Brain & Co. Ltd.* (*ante*, p. 251). Again, in *R.* v. *Patents Appeal Tribunal, Ex p. Swift & Co. Ltd.*, [1962] 2 Q.B. 647, he said (at p. 664): 'Finally, one cannot shut from one's mind the desirability of having a homogeneous development of the law in all countries which have adopted our system of patent legislation. That desirability must result in a tendency of our courts to follow those decisions if it is possible to do so.' In the absence of any express English authority on the point at issue, the Court followed without apology an Australian and a New Zealand decision. Again, in *Att.-Gen.* v. *Clough*, [1963] 1 Q.B. 773, at p. 792, Lord Parker C.J. said:

'Not only do I treat that decision [*McGuiness* v. *Att.-Gen. of Victoria* (1940), 63 C.L.R. 73] as most persuasive authority, but I confess that I should hesitate very long if in a matter which pertained to the common law of England, this country should differ, unless it had to, with another Commonwealth country. It is surely of importance, to say the least, that the common law should develop homogeneously throughout the Commonwealth.'

Sometimes it may happen that there is no English authority directly covering the circumstances of the instant case. The Court will then avowedly rely on rulings in foreign jurisdictions. A conspicuous example of this process is *Wood* v. *W*., [1957] P. 254. The question was whether a matrimonial order for maintenance, made in England during the residence of the spouses, survived a subsequent *ex parte* Nevada decree of divorce granted at the husband's suit, on the ground that, without any matrimonial offence being alleged, the parties had not lived together for three years. The question of jurisdiction which arises in such a case is well known in the United States as 'divisible divorce'. There was no English authority on all fours, but Professor Goodhart had called attention in 73 *L.Q.R.* 9 to two American cases which were directly in point. These were fully discussed by the Court, and though not the sole authority relied on, were 'applied' in the decision, which was that the maintenance order not only continued in force but was subject to variation.[1]

Similarly *Wise* v. *Kaye*, [1962] 1 Q.B. 638. Here the question was the measure of damages recoverable by a plaintiff who, through the negligence of the defendant,

[1] See further, on the force of foreign judgements in the absence of English authority, *Hasham* v. *Zenab*, [1960] A.C. 316, and *Randolph* v. *Tuck*, [1962] 1 Q.B. 175.

had been rendered unconscious for 3½ years and, though still alive, had no prospect except bare existence as a helpless patient. There was much argument as to whether the test to be applied to her condition was 'objective' or 'subjective'. Curiously enough, there was no English precedent directly on this difficult and vital point, but Upjohn and Sellers L.JJ. (*dissentiente* Diplock L.J.) were content to accept the *ratio* of two Australian cases that the test must be objective. In *Tursi* v. *T.*, [1958] P. 54, a large part of the judgement of Sachs J. was founded entirely on Australian precedents. There is no doubt that Australian decisions are regarded with growing deference by English courts, not least by the House of Lords. In the *Wagon Mound* (*ante*, p. 250) much reliance was placed on the reasoning of Australian cases, and in *Sykes* v. *D.P.P.*, [1962] A.C. 528, on the question whether misprision of felony was still an offence known to English law, the decision of the High Court of Victoria in *R.* v. *Crimmins* was unhesitatingly approved and 'applied'. In *Hughes & Vale Proprietary Ltd.* v. *State of New South Wales*, [1955] A.C. 241, Lord Morton, delivering the judgement of the Judicial Committee, said:

> 'Their Lordships have adopted the unusual course of answering this important question not in language of their own but in the language of judges of the High Court of Australia. They do so . . . because they are in agreement with this language and see no reason to suppose that they can improve upon it.'

The examples which have been chosen here are all of recent date at this time of writing, and they indicate, in my submission, a growing disposition in our courts to recognize pertinent foreign judgements as somewhat more than merely 'persuasive', and to regard the line between 'persuasive' and 'binding' as thin and shadowy, or at least as technical and artificial. In the search for a ruling principle, our judges take their good where they find it. This tendency has been marked of late, but it is by no means new. For other examples of the influence of foreign judgements, the reader is referred to the following cases, among many which might be cited: *Scaramanga* v. *Stamp* (1880), 5 C.P.D. at p. 303; *The Gas Float Whitton*, [1896] P. at pp. 59 ff.; *Haynes* v. *Harwood*, [1935] 1 K.B. 146, 156; *Beresford* v. *Royal Insurance Co. Ltd.*, [1937] 2 K.B. 197, 216 ff., and [1938] A.C. 586, 600; *Biberfeld* v. *Berens*, [1952] 2 Q.B. 770; *Broom* v. *Morgan*, [1953] 1 Q.B. 597; *Stafford Allen & Sons Ltd.* v. *Pacific Steam Navigation Co. Ltd.*, [1956] 1 W.L.R. 629; *Longden* v. *Minister of Pensions*, [1956] 1 Q.B. 587.

III. WORKING OF LEGAL INDUCTION

There is a danger in any mechanical dichotomy of 'legal' and 'historical' sources; for to divorce the history from the theory of the law is to court error. Let us remind ourselves of Sir George Jessel's simple principle, that precedents are employed *in order to establish principles*. Throughout the whole application of the law, the principles are primary and the precedents are secondary, and if we lose sight of this fact, the precedents become a bad master instead of a good servant. The business of a court in deciding any particular issue is to work its way by the inductive principle which I have mentioned to a relevant *rule*. To this end the arguments of counsel are directed, and the process from first to last is one of logical development. Any material of logical relevancy, whether it be 'legal' or 'historical' or 'literary', is legitimate and germane. Doubtless the best possible instrument of demonstration is the exact analogy of a previous case. But analogies are seldom exact, and counsel is rarely fortunate enough to be able to checkmate, so to speak, in one move. Almost invariably he has to justify or amplify his analogy from other sources, and it matters not what those sources are provided that they are material to his main purpose. If he betakes himself to the opinions of reputable writers, to decisions of other countries, to

At the Bar

history, to common sense, to natural justice, to convenience and utility, to the etymology and interpretation of words, he will never be stopped by the Court because the sources on which he is drawing are not 'legal'. He ceases to convince only when his argument, whatever its source, is beside the main purpose. This is as true of a legal argument as of any other kind of argument; and a legal argument is not governed by any peculiar magic of its own. Lawyers do not possess, and do not claim to possess, a monopoly of the art of dialectic. They have to deal in argument more frequently than other people, and they naturally develop a special facility in doing so, but the principles of reason and logic upon which their arguments are based are the common property of mankind. The only reason why precedent figures so largely in the method which they employ is because the analogy of precedent is a forcible method of demonstration in any and every argument. Parity of reasoning is as natural to logic as reasoning itself. It is more convincing than most other methods of demonstration simply because a close analogy is more convincing than a far-fetched illustration. Consequently the pleader relies on precedents as the most convincing arguments he can adduce, and the judge, with faculties specially trained to this end, becomes adept at distinguishing between the stronger and the weaker of the analogies presented to him.

On the Bench

The judge himself addresses his task in much the same way as counsel. His decision is given in the form of a structure of logic, in which he may use *any* material which he considers *ad rem*. If the matter is governed by the clear and unambiguous provision of a statute, his task is simplified. In a great many cases, no statute is applicable, and even if it is applicable, it is frequently the reverse of clear and unambiguous. The judge must then proceed, as Bacon laid down long ago,[1] either by *parity of reasoning* ('vel per processum ad similia') or by *the use of examples*, though they have not been embodied

[1] *De Aug.*, Lib. VIII, cap. iii, Aph. 10.

in any statute ('vel per usum exemplorum, licet in legem non coaluerint'), or by rules of natural reason and discretion ('vel per iurisdictiones quae statuunt ex arbitrio boni viri et secundum discretionem sanam'). The method of his reasoning may take innumerable forms, and no rule of law limits and controls those forms, provided that they achieve a logical conclusion. It would, of course, be grossly inaccurate to say that a judge who has to decide whether a wild duck is a bird of warren is 'bound' by the evidence of literature; yet he will not hesitate to turn to literature if it assists him in determining whether Coke's statement of the law on this point be correct or not.[1]

As an example of the mechanism of judicial logic I will take a case in which, though the point at issue was 'naked' and uncomplicated, the decision could be reached only by an intricate logical progression. Two persons were in treaty for the sale of a certain brewery. There were two typed copies, one the original and one a carbon copy, of a document in which it was stated, among other terms, that 'I agree to purchase' the premises in question for £2,000, paying £50 deposit. Stokes, the prospective purchaser, signed the original; Whicher, the prospective vendor, did not himself sign the carbon copy, but it was signed by his agent duly appointed in that behalf, which amounts to much the same thing. Stokes gave a cheque for the deposit, and Whicher's agent appended a receipt therefor to the carbon copy given to Stokes.

Whicher refused to complete, and Stokes brought action for specific performance.

[1] See Parker J. in *Fitzhardinge* (*Lord*) v. *Purcell*, [1908] 2 Ch. 139, citing (p. 164) Drayton's *Polyolbion* and Madden's *Diary of Master William Silence*. Cf. *In re Orbit Trust*, [1943] Ch. 144, 151, in which Uthwatt J. drew upon Pepys's Diary in discussing, by way of analogy to modern enactments, the legislation passed to deal with leaseholds after the Great Fire of London. In *Corkery* v. *Carpenter*, [1951] 1 K.B. 102, counsel in argument did not hesitate to appeal, on a point of 'popular meaning', to the deathless ballad of 'Daisy Bell'.

Main question. This, being a contract for the sale of real property, requires a memorandum in writing. Legislation—the Statute of Frauds—imposes this main requirement and judicial decisions have added that the memorandum must contain, *inter alia*, a description or identification of the parties to the contract. Does this document, the carbon copy exhibited by Stokes, comply with these requirements?

Let us see by what stages the learned Judge arrived at his answer to this question—the sole question in the case.

First subsidiary question. Does this document, if valid in other respects, constitute an agreement by the defendant to sell? Is it intended to impose, and does it impose, a contractual liability?

Answer. The true construction of the document is that Whicher means that he thereby agrees to sell, *to some individual*, the property comprised in the document and upon the terms therein stated.

Second subsidiary question. But does the document comply with the requirement that it must contain a description of the parties? The signature of Whicher's agent describes Whicher as 'Vendor', so that there is no doubt in his case; but there is no description or identification of the purchaser. The purchaser is somebody who simply describes himself as 'I'. Is the judge entitled to resort to evidence outside the document itself to discover who 'I' is?

First answer. *Long* v. *Millar* (1879), 4 C.P.D. 450, lays down that 'if you can spell out of the document a reference in it to some other transaction, you are at liberty to give evidence as to what that transaction is'. To the same effect is another relevant decision.[1] Now the receipt shows on the face of this document that on a certain date £50 was paid by cheque to the vendor as the agreed deposit. A cheque of the same date for an amount which includes this £50, signed by Stokes, has been

[1] *Pearce* v. *Gardner*, [1897] 1 Q.B. 688.

produced. Connecting these two documents, in accordance with the principle of *Long* v. *Millar*, the judge is entitled to conclude that 'I' is Stokes.

Second answer. 'The document is, as is quite obvious to the eye, a carbon copy of another document. It is called a contract.[1] The parties to the contract are the vendor who signs that particular document and someone else who is there mentioned as "I". That involves that "I" has contracted, for otherwise there would be no contract. "I" must have bound himself, otherwise the document could not be called upon its face a contract. Therefore, in the document itself I think I get a reference to some agreement or transaction binding "I". That being so, a document is produced before me bearing the same date, in the same words, with the same alterations in the body of it, also called a contract. It is obviously the original of which this document is the duplicate. The verbal evidence in the case proves that to be so, and that they were executed and exchanged at the same time; but, apart from that evidence, I am of opinion, finding as I do a reference in the document to some other transaction which is a transaction binding upon "I", that I am at liberty to inquire what that transaction was, and I find that it was a transaction evidenced in a written document which contains the purchaser's name; and so, in my opinion, I may connect those two documents and read them together as one.'

Third answer. The document is a complete memorandum except that it does not contain the purchaser's name. But the memorandum need not contain the *name* of the party: it is sufficient if it contains something which describes or identifies him. 'Does this document sufficiently identify "I"? I think it does. Taking the document as a whole, it shows that "I" is the person who has undertaken and discharged the obligation to pay £50, and it has been proved that the person who paid the £50 was Mr. Stokes; I am entitled to take that verbal evidence

[1] It was so headed.

and so identify the person who is described as "I" as the person who has undertaken to discharge and has discharged that obligation.' Authority for that reasoning is *Carr* v. *Lynch*, [1900] 1 Ch. 613.

Conclusion. The memorandum is complete: therefore the vendor is bound: therefore there must be a decree of specific performance.[1]

In what sense is the judge 'bound'?

In this typical example of judicial reasoning it will be seen that there is a blend of pure logic based on the facts of the case, and logic based on the analogy of authorities: both are subservient to the principal purpose of 'subsuming' the case under a general rule. It must never be forgotten that the judge has to review every precedent cited to him, not as a precise formulation of a general, abstract rule of law (like an article of a code), but as a concrete application of, or as an argument in favour of, some real or supposed rule of law. We say that he is bound by the decisions of higher courts; and so he undoubtedly is. But the superior court does not impose fetters upon him; he places the fetters on his own hands. He has to decide whether the case cited to him is truly apposite to the circumstances in question and whether it accurately embodies the principle which he is seeking. The humblest judicial officer has to decide for himself whether he is or is not bound, in the particular circumstances, by any given decision of the House of Lords.[2] His task is often exceedingly difficult. Not only is it true that the circumstances of two cases are seldom exactly identical, but sometimes it is by no means

[1] *Stokes* v. *Whicher*, [1920] 1 Ch. 411 (Russell J., later Lord Russell of Killowen). The reasoning was approved in *Fowler* v. *Bratt*, [1950] 2 K.B. 96. A case, different on the facts in one essential particular, was *Timmins* v. *Moreland Street Property Co. Ltd.*, [1958] Ch. 110, in which *Stokes* v. *Whicher* was distinguished. An excellent example of the stages in a long process of judicial reasoning, though unfortunately it is concerned with one of the most artificial doctrines of the law, may be found in the series of decisions affecting the acknowledgement of statute-barred debt; see *Spencer* v. *Hemmerde*, [1922] 2 A.C. 507, especially the speech of Lord Sumner.

[2] See the very interesting observations of Roxburgh J. in *In re House Property & Investment Co., Ltd.*, [1954] Ch. 576, 601.

easy to discover the true reasons which led the superior court to its conclusion. This is particularly observable in the highest tribunal of all, in which the number of separate judgements delivered, and of reasons assigned, often leads to great complexity.[1] We have already seen the difficulties which sometimes arise in distinguishing between *dicta* and *ratio* in superior courts. In the case of *The Mostyn*, [1927] P. 25, the Court of Appeal confessed its despair of discovering the true *ratio decidendi* in *River Wear Commissioners* v. *Adamson* (1877), 2 App. Cas. 743, a case of great importance to harbour authorities.[2] With little conviction, and not without dissent, it selected one *ratio* from a bewildering variety. In such a case, it would seem that the subordinate judge is at least trying to do his duty in difficult circumstances; and it is perhaps a little hard on him to be told by superior authority that he must not find a *ratio decidendi* where no *ratio decidendi* exists. For in the same case on appeal,[3] Viscount Dunedin, in his dissenting speech, said (at p. 73):

'If from the opinions delivered it is clear—as is the case in most instances—what the *ratio decidendi* was which led to the judgement, then that *ratio decidendi* is also binding. But if it is not clear, then I do not think it is part of the tribunal's duty to spell out with great difficulty a *ratio decidendi* in order to be bound by it. That is what the Court of Appeal has done here. With great hesitation they have added the opinion of Lord Hatherley to that of Lord Cairns and then, with still greater difficulty, that of Lord Blackburn, and so have secured what they think was a majority in favour of Lord Cairns's very clear view. I do not think that the respect which they hold and have expressed for the judgements of your Lordships' House compelled them to go through this difficult and most unsatisfactory performance.'

[1] See, e.g., *Blane Steamships, Ltd.* v. *Minister of Transport*, [1951] 2 K.B. 965, and *St. Aubyn* v. *Att.-Gen.*, [1952] A.C. 15.

[2] See *post*, pp. 504 ff. The Court of Appeal was in much the same difficulty in *Dickson* v. *Flack*, [1953] 2 Q.B. 464, a case which, after much judicial doubt and hesitation, was eventually overruled (but by a majority only) in *Close* v. *Steel Co. of Wales Ltd.*, [1962] A.C. 367.

[3] *Sub nom. Great Western Ry. Co.* v. *Owners of S.S. Mostyn*, [1928] A.C. 57.

Nothing therefore remains, continues Viscount Dunedin, of *Wear* v. *Adamson* except the actual judgement and a number of weighty opinions. But—the subordinate judge may well ask—what is the value of the judgement unless we know on what basis it rests, and what is the 'authority' of a decision of the highest tribunal if it is merely opinion, or a mosaic of opinions? The law stands greatly indebted to the copious treatment which cases receive in our final appellate court; but it cannot be concealed that the very wealth of learning and discussion in that exalted assembly sometimes embarrasses rather than assists the task of subsumption. It is only necessary to refer in this connexion to the amount of ingenuity which has been expended on reconciling, or attempting to reconcile, the two cases of *Allen* v. *Flood*, [1898] A.C. 1, and *Quinn* v. *Leathem*, [1901] A.C. 495.[1] Much doubt and controversy still exist as to what the House of Lords really decided in the important case of *Minister of Health* v. *R., Ex p. Yaffé*, [1931] A.C. 494;[2] and the effect of *Baxter* v. *B.*, [1948] A.C. 274, which raises crucial questions in the modern law of nullity of marriage, is far from clear.[3] When an appeal is made on a number of separate grounds, which may be viewed in different ways by the members of the court, it is not always easy to determine which grounds have been decisive even when the appeal succeeds. Indeed, it is possible that when a party to an appeal, before a court of three or five judges, relies on a number of different submissions, he may win by a unanimous decision and yet not have a majority in his favour on any single one of his contentions.[4] What then has the case decided? It

[1] Cf. *Sorrell* v. *Smith*, [1923] 2 Ch. 32, at first instance, On the whole subject see Goodhart, 'Determining the *Ratio Decidendi* of a Case', *Essays in Jurisprudence*, 1.

[2] See Paton and Sawer, 'Ratio Decidendi and Obiter Dictum', 63 *L.Q.R.* 461, 473, and C. K. Allen, *Law and Orders* (2nd ed.), 297 ff.

[3] See *Grimes* v. *G.*, [1948] P. 323, *White* v. *W.*, [1948] P. 330, and *Cackett* v. *C.*, [1950] P. 253.

[4] See 66 *L.Q.R.* 298, where reference is made to an observation on this point by Lord Simonds during the argument in *Commonwealth of Australia*

is manifest that if the same issue arises later, a lower court can only select at its discretion from the reasoning of its superiors, and it is little more than a fiction, in such circumstances, to say that it is 'bound'. What it really does is to discuss, with every customary tribute of respect, all the different *rationes* in the higher court—and then decide the question for itself *de novo*.

Again, it may sometimes happen that opinions expressed even in the House of Lords lose much of their authority because, in the view of the judge who has to consider them later, they were founded upon issues inadequately presented to the court. 'The opinions', said Romer J.,[1] 'of such high authorities as Lord Cranworth, Lord Wensleydale, and Lord Chelmsford must naturally be received with the greatest respect. I may, however, be pardoned if I venture to criticize their opinions, seeing that the point was never argued on the part of the respondents, and that the argument on the part of the appellants, so far as this point is concerned, does not appear to have been supported by the citation of any reported case or authority.'[2]

It is therefore fallacious to regard the application of precedents in the courts as a mere functioning of machinery. It is a complex process, depending greatly upon the faculties of individual judges, and it is dangerous arbitrarily to exclude any element from it simply by dubbing it 'unauthoritative'.

Precedent as against governing principles of Common Law

For underneath the whole elaborate structure of precedents in our courts lies a permanent foundation of fundamental legal doctrine. 'It is a dangerous thing',

v. *Bank of New South Wales*, [1950] A.C. 235. See, to the same effect, Lord Justice Asquith, 'Some Aspects of the Work of the Court of Appeal', *Journal of the Society of Public Teachers of Law*, 1950, at p. 358.

[1] *In re Mason*, [1928] Ch. 385, 400.

[2] The reference is to *Att.-Gen.* v. *Kohler* (1861), 9 H.C.L. 54. The learned judge was, of course, here dealing with opinions which he treated as *dicta*, and therefore not binding on him. There was no question of *incuria* merely because a relevant point had not been taken (see *ante*, p. 248). His decision was upheld ([1929] 1 Ch. 1) and in the Court of Appeal *Att.-Gen.* v. *Kohler*, *ubi sup.*, was not even referred to.

says Coke, 'to alter or shake any of the fundamental rules of the common law, which in truth are the main pillars and supporters of the fabrick of the commonwealth'.[1] The isolated example which 'alters or shakes a fundamental rule of the common law' will itself soon fall to the ground and become neglected as a worthless ruin. I have already called attention to a significant reservation made by Parke J. in his classic *dictum* concerning the authority of precedents: they are binding, he says, 'where they are not plainly unreasonable and inconvenient'.[2] Nobody in his senses would imagine this to mean that an inferior judge is at liberty to reject a principle laid down by the House of Lords merely because he does not consider it in the best interests of justice and convenience. What it does mean is that there are certain cardinal rules of English law which are more important than the decisions of any tribunals, and more 'binding' upon judges than any individual cases. For all practical purposes, a precedent which ignores or misconceives a clear and positive rule of law is no precedent. In the last analysis, the judge follows 'binding' authority only if and because *it is a correct statement of the law*.[3] In almost all cases it is,

[1] 1 Inst. 74.

[2] *Ante*, p. 232. Cf. Blackstone's qualification, cited *ante*, pp. 229 ff. Cf. Lord Ellenborough C.J. in *Vere* v. *Lord Cawdor* (1809), 11 East 568, 570: 'The question is whether the plaintiff's dog incurred the penalty of death for running after a hare in another's ground? And if there be any precedent of that sort, which outrages all reason and sense, it is no authority to govern other cases.' Cf. observations of Lord Denning in *London Transport Executive* v. *Betts*, *ante*, p. 254.

[3] In *Dugdale* v. *D.* (1872), L.R. 14 Eq. 234, Malins V.C. went so far as to say: 'The Court is not bound to follow a decision even of the Court of Appeal if clearly erroneous.' The observation was made in connexion with *Hansman* v. *Fryer* (1867), L.R. 3 Ch. 420, in which Lord Chelmsford, on appeal from Kindersley V.C., had decided a point in the marshalling of assets directly contrary to well-settled practice. Stuart V.C. in *Collins* v. *Lewis* (1869), L.R. 8 Eq. 708, and Hall V.C. in *Farquharson* v. *Floyer* (1876), 3 Ch. D. 109, besides Malins V.C., declined to follow him. Malins V.C. said that he remembered three occasions on which Stuart V.C. had refused to follow Lord Westbury. One of these occasions was *Drummond* v. *D.* (1866), L.R. 2 Eq. 335, where the Vice-Chancellor felt the less scruple in his insubordination because Lord Westbury's decision, in two cases which were relied upon, had been given in ignorance of a statute. There is, however, a

to him, a correct statement of the law because it is not open to him to set up his own opinions against a higher authority; but where it is plainly and admittedly founded on error, his obligation disappears. He owes a higher obligation to his mistress, the law. We need not resort to

great difference, in respect of Chancery appeals, between the present position and that which existed before the Judicature Act; it was notorious that the Vice-Chancellors were often more familiar with Chancery practice than the Chancellors who heard appeals from them; and I do not think that any judge today would go as far as Malins V.C. with regard to decisions of the modern Court of Appeal. In *A.* v. *A.* (1875), L.R. 3 P. & D. 230, however, Sir James Hannen, in holding that the Probate and Divorce Division had power to hear a matrimonial suit in camera, declined to follow *H., falsely called C.* v. *C.* (1859), 1 Sw. & Tr. 606, in which Sir Cresswell Cresswell, Williams J., and Bramwell B. had held that the Court had no power to hear a nullity suit except with open doors. Sir James Hannen's reason for his decision was that the rule had not been acted on, and a contrary practice had established itself. Twenty-eight years later, Sir Francis Jeune took the same view in *D.* v. *D.*, [1903] P. 144, though neither of the two cases above-mentioned seems to have been cited to him. This was overruled, and the principle of *H., falsely called C.* v. *C.* restored, in *Scott* v. *S.*, [1913] A.C. 417, where Lord Halsbury said (at p. 443): 'I confess I am amazed to find three such learned judges as Sir Cresswell Cresswell, Williams J. and Bramwell B. . . . overruled by any single judge, and especially when it is remembered that this was a judgement given after consultation upon this very point—after consultation with the Judge Ordinary.'

The possiblity that a House of Lords decision might be given in ignorance of a statute was considered by Lord Halsbury L.C. in *London Street Tramways Co.* v. *L.C.C.*, [1898] A.C. 375. The Lord Chancellor's answer was that this would be a mistake of fact, and that the decision based upon it would certainly not be binding (i.e. on the House of Lords, and presumably not on any court). This is a point not covered by the rules in *Young* v. *Bristol Aeroplane Co.* A very curious position arose in *Rudd* v. *Elder Dempster & Co.*, [1933] 1 K.B. 566. If the interpretation placed in that case (by the Court of Appeal) on *Groves* v. *Wimborne (Lord)*, [1898] 2 Q.B. 402, was correct, it followed that a number of Workmen's Compensation cases in the House of Lords had been based on a misconception (to be regarded as a mistake of fact?) of that case in its relation to the Workmen's Compensation Act, 1897. Unfortunately, the question was never settled in the House of Lords, where an appeal was lodged but compromised (see [1934] A.C. 244). But it is a nice point—unsettled, as far as I know—what the duty of inferior courts would be if it appeared that a line of House of Lords decisions had been based upon a manifest misinterpretation of a statute—e.g. a mistake about the date of its coming into operation, which may easily happen nowadays. I am inclined to think that a cautious judge would adopt and follow the erroneous decisions, in the hope that on appeal the House of Lords would reverse itself. Clumsy though this would be, and unfortunate for the litigants, it would be the safest way of settling the law.

extreme hypothetical cases to find illustrations of this principle. It is constantly to be observed that a precedent, of whatever origin, which is based on error, has the greatest possible difficulty in fighting against the current of legal doctrine. If it be derived merely from a strained or fanciful interpretation, it may succeed in perpetuating an anomalous, or, so to say, an eccentric doctrine; but if it offends against one of the axiomatic precepts of law or reason, it may maintain itself for a short and harassed existence, but the collective displeasure of the profession will kill it in the end: and usually the end will not be long in coming. Every now and then, by one of those aberrations of which even the keenest minds are capable, an absurd and unreasonable principle like 'the doctrine of identification' creeps into our law. That particular anomaly managed to subsist for thirty years, which was a surprisingly long life for so sickly a creature; but it was doomed from birth, and when its time came, it was dispatched without scruple or apology.[1] Doubtless there are other doctrines of the Common Law which many think absurd and unreasonable,[2] but which have so far proved indestructible;[3] but none, I believe, which is a flagrant violation of reason and utility, indefensible on any rational ground. Lord Esher once observed: 'Any proposition the result of which would be to show that the common law of England is wholly unreasonable and unjust, cannot be part of the common law of England.'[4] The *communis opinio doctorum* seldom fails to get its own way in the end. Bad cases sometimes become so emaciated by ingenious methods of 'distinguishing' or 'not following' that they

[1] *Thorogood* v. *Bryan* (1849), 8 C.B. 115; *Waite* v. *North Eastern Ry. Co.* (1858), E.B. & E. 719; *Mills* v. *Armstrong* (*The Bernina*) (1887), 12 P.D. 58; *Oliver* v. *Birmingham and Midland Motor Omnibus Co.*, [1933] 1 K.B. 35.

[2] See *post*, pp. 327 ff.

[3] 'The rule in *Andrews* v. *Partington* (1791), 3 Bro. C.C. 401, is a somewhat battered veteran, but it still remains on its feet after upwards of 200 years': *per* Jenkins L.J., *In re Bleckly*, [1951] Ch. 740, 751.

[4] *Emmens* v. *Pottle* (1885), 16 Q.B.D. 354, 357. But Lord Esher was somewhat given to such wide generalizations.

cease to have any vitality.[1] When, for example, the House of Lords, in 1923, definitely overruled *Miller* v. *Hancock*, [1893] 2 Q.B. 177,[2] it merely set the seal on a process which had been going on for twenty years, and which had 'distinguished' this case out of any real authority.

It is, indeed, often difficult to see the difference between 'distinguishing' and outright overruling.[3] For example, it is only by straining language that we can say that *Bailey* v. *Geddes*, [1938] 1 K.B. 156, was merely 'distinguished' in *Chisholm* v. *London Passenger Transport Board*, [1939] 1 K.B. 426 (and du Parcq L.J. felt that he could not carry ingenuity so far), or that *Jackson, Stansfield & Sons* v. *Butterworth* [1948] 2 All E.R. 558, was merely 'distinguished' in *Falmouth Boat Construction Co., Ltd.* v. *Howell*, [1951] A.C. 16, or *Oliver* v. *Goodger*, [1944] 2 All E.R. 481, in *Challand* v. *Bartlett*, [1953] 1 W.L.R. 1105; what seems certain is that nobody in future will regard the earlier case as authoritative. A decision, to be binding, must not only emanate from high authority, but must be 'good law': if it once earns the reputation of being 'not law',[4] it perishes, sometimes by express disapproval, more often by cold disregard. If all else fails, the blame for its defects may be laid at the door of the reporter—sometimes not without cause.[5]

[1] See Professor J. L. Montrose, 'Distinguishing Cases and the Limits of Ratio Decidendi', 19 *M.L.R.* 525, discussing *Pound* v. *Hardy*, [1956] A.C. 588, and *Brandt* v. *Morris*, [1917] 2 K.B. 784.

[2] *Fairman* v. *Perpetual Investment Building Society*, [1923] A.C. 74.

[3] See Max Radin, 'The Trail of the Calf', *Cornell Law Quarterly*, Nov. 1946, 137, 143, and the present writer, 'Road Traffic Precedents', 72 *L.Q.R.* 516.

[4] e.g. *Gibbons* v. *Proctor* (1892), 64 L.T. 594, or *Wilson* v. *Lady Dunsany* (1854), 18 Beav. 293, on which see Pearson J., *In re Kloebe* (1884), 28 Ch.D. 175, 180. 'There is', said Lord Coleridge C.J. in *R.* v. *Labouchere* (1884), 12 Q.B.D. 320, 324, 'the leaning of the Courts for a certain time in a particular direction, balanced at least if not reversed by the leaning of the Courts for a certain time in a direction opposite. The current of legal decisions runs often to a point which is felt to be beyond the bounds of sane control; and there is danger sometimes that the retrocession of the current should become itself extreme.'

[5] See *ante*, pp. 221 ff. and *post*, pp. 373 ff.

Precedent and justice

If it is true that precedents are employed only to discover principles, so it is true that principles are employed only to discover justice. We speak of the judge's function as 'the administration of justice', and we are sometimes apt to forget that we mean, or ought to mean, exactly what we say. Popular catchwords are too fond of distinguishing between the administration of law and the administration of justice, as if they were two different things. Nobody claims that the law always achieves ideal moral justice, but whatever the inevitable technicalities of legal science may be, they exist for the prosecution of one aim only, which is also the aim of the judge's office: to do justice between litigants, not to make interesting contributions to legal theory. This dominant purpose all precedents, all arguments, and all principles must subserve; and when precedents do not help, enlightenment must be found elsewhere. Hence arise those cases 'of first impression' which are by no means uncommon in the courts, even at this day when so many permutations and combinations of circumstances have been considered and recorded. To what, then, do the judges turn? To those principles of reason, morality, and social utility which are the fountain-head not only of English law but of all law. The judge is not embarrassed by the absence of 'authority' in clear cases of this kind, for no authority is needed for the affirmation of the very essence of law. A husband connives at his wife's adultery and then turns her out of doors; she pledges his credit for necessaries, and the husband disclaims liability. The Court makes short work of the matter.[1] 'There is no direct authority', says Fry L.J. 'In my opinion to say that such circumstances justify the husband in turning his wife out of doors would be *morally and socially wrong*.' 'Nothing', says Lord Esher M.R., 'would induce me to declare that such was the law except a superior authority which would bind me.' An alien enemy is made a defendant in an

[1] *Wilson* v. *Glossop* (1888), 20 Q.B.D. 354.

action before an English Court. It is held that the action properly lies against him. 'The next question is, Can he appear and defend either personally or by counsel? I think', says Bailhache J., 'he certainly can. To allow an action against an alien enemy to proceed and to refuse to allow him to appear and defend himself would be opposed to the fundamental principles of justice. No state of war could, in my view, demand or justify the condemnation by a Civil Court of a man unheard.'[1] An infant pays for something which is not a necessary, consumes or uses it, and then demands his money back. The Court holds without hesitation that 'it is contrary to natural justice that he should recover back the money which he has paid'.[2] A husband claims the right to imprison his wife and treat her as a chattel; the Court says that, apart from any authority, English law will not countenance such a claim.[3] 'But in the end', said Lord Simonds in *National Bank of Greece* v. *Metliss*, [1958] A.C. 509, 525, 'and in the absence of authority binding this House, the question is simply: What does justice require in such a case as this?' It is these guiding rules of right and reason which are constantly moulding the law to social conditions. Consciously or unconsciously, judges are primarily and perpetually furthering them.[4]

The process of expansion and adaptation of the law goes on constantly, and the student a hundred years hence will be able to discern equally distinct currents of legal theory in this age as we can now discern in the nineteenth century.[5] Not only changed social circumstances, but changes and developments in human knowledge, may greatly affect the application of precedent. An

[1] *Robinson* v. *Continental Insurance Co. of Mannheim*, [1915] 1 K.B. 155 (view upheld in *Porter* v. *Freudenberg*, [1915] 1 K.B. 857).

[2] *Valentini* v. *Canali* (1889), 24 Q.B.D. 166.

[3] *Reg.* v. *Jackson*, [1891] 1 Q.B. 671, *ante*, p. 257, n. 1

[4] See the speeches of Lord Atkin and Lord Macmillan in *Donoghue* v. *Stevenson*, [1932] A.C. 562.

[5] Whereon see Sir Frederick Pollock, *The Expansion of the Common Law*, 123 ff.

interesting question, for example, is opened up by a case like *M.-T.* v. *M.-T.*, [1949] P. 331. Here the issue was whether a child born 340 days after the last possible opportunity of intercourse between the spouses could be legitimate. There were previous cases, including a recent one in the Court of Appeal,[1] in which the courts had declined, either on medical evidence or on the doctrine of judicial notice, to hold that so long a period of gestation was a physical impossibility. The medical evidence, however, brought before Ormerod J. in *M.-T.* v. *M.-T.* in 1948 convinced him that in recent years there had been great advances in the science of gynaecology which justified him in refusing to follow earlier cases based on more imperfect scientific knowledge. Science, we are told, is always extending its boundaries, and what is true of a comparatively limited field like gynaecology doubtless applies equally to many other and perhaps larger fields. It is a matter for speculation how far judges in the distant future will consider themselves free to disregard precedents in the light of what they believe to be larger and superior knowledge.

Law is the product of its own period and environment and it cannot remain static. We shall see (*post*, pp. 479 ff.) that there are statutes still in our books which have little or no relevance to the circumstances of this age. Similarly ancient doctrines of the Common Law are constantly undergoing adaptation. Thus, in the fundamental matter of domestic relations, we have recently seen restrictions placed on traditional ideas of matrimonial consortium[2] and on the notion of 'service' as it appeared for centuries in the action *per quod servitium amisit.*[3] But

[1] *Hadlum* v. *H.*, [1949] P. 197. See further on this question *Preston-Jones* v. *P.-J.*, [1951] A.C. 391.

[2] *Best* v. *Fox*, [1951] 2 K.B. 639, and [1952] A.C. 716; *Lampert* v. *Eastern National Omnibus Co., Ltd.*, [1954] 1 W.L.R. 1047; *Winchester* v. *Fleming*, [1958] 1 Q.B. 259.

[3] *Inland Revenue Commissioners* v. *Hambrook*, [1956] 2 Q.B. 641. Yet, by a fiction, the old doctrine remains the basis of the (now rare) action for seduction of a daughter.

the process is slow and uneven, and it would be an exaggeration to suppose that the Common Law always keeps abreast of changing conditions. Sometimes, out of excessive deference to precedent, it singularly fails to do so. Whether or not the doctrine of common employment was reasonable in its day (see *post*, p. 329), it became more and more manifestly unreasonable throughout the nineteenth and twentieth centuries; but nothing except legislation could uproot it. 'Loyalty' in the Chancery Division attached for over 200 years an immutable meaning to the word 'money', until the House of Lords came to the rescue.[1] The law relating to domestic animals is still strangely antiquated in some respects. Study of *Cresswell* v. *Sirl*, [1948] 1 K.B. 241, will show that there have been continuous changes in the extensive case-law concerning dogs; but it is still a Common Law principle today that 'the owner of a field abutting on the highway is under no *prima facie* legal obligation to users of the highway so to keep and maintain his hedges and gates along the highway as to prevent his animals from straying on to it. Nor is he under any duty as between himself and users of the highway to take reasonable care to prevent any of his animals, not known to be dangerous, from straying on to the highway'.[2] While this may have been a reasonable principle in days of slow-moving traffic, it hardly seems to be so in the Machine Age, when straying animals may be of the greatest possible danger to rapid motor vehicles.[3] Yet none of the modern Road Traffic Acts, nor yet the most recent Act affecting highways (Highways (Miscellaneous Provisions) Act, 1961), has dealt with this nuisance, which is the occasion of

[1] *Perrin* v. *Morgan*, [1943] A.C. 399.

[2] Headnote to *Searle* v. *Wallbank*, [1947] A.C. 341. See also *Wright* v. *Callwood*, [1950] 2 K.B. 515, and *Brock* v. *Richards*, [1951] 1 K.B. 529.

[3] This view is confirmed by the fact that under the Highway Act, 1864, it is an offence of summary jurisdiction to allow cattle to stray on the highway. The penalty, however, is limited to 5*s*. per head (with a maximum of 30*s*.), and the present writer knows of one offender—a serious menace to his neighbourhood—with eighty-four convictions, punishable each time at the rate of 5*s*. only.

frequent litigation. In the same spirit of the ancient Common Law, it is, apparently, not *per se* negligent to drive sheep along a highway at night without a light[1]—though nothing could be more dangerous to motorists.

Nevertheless, in general the forces which produce the streams of 'prevailing doctrine' are deeper and subtler than the mere practice of courts and the officers of courts. It is possible to find in every legal system certain elemental principles which seem to be permanent, others which perpetually adapt themselves to environment. Both are vital, as they are in all organisms, and together they constitute a body of doctrine which is the primary preoccupation of every court. Precedent and example are at once the most convenient and the most reliable means for discovering them; but they form only one, though the chief, among many such means. The difference between the authoritative and the so-called 'persuasive' sources is one of degree, not of kind.

How far do judges make law?

To what extent are these underlying legal principles independent and pre-existent, to what extent are they the product of judicial reasoning? We have seen that the English judge exercises a function more avowedly creative than a Continental judge; and that at its early formative period much of our Common Law took its shape from doctrines consciously evolved by the royal courts. If we examine the great legal tendencies of the nineteenth century, we shall find the hand of the judge equally active in moulding the doctrines of the law. A great deal of controversy has centred on this question of how far the judge can and does legitimately 'make' law. We must use this word 'make' with caution; and I think we shall find that, in one sense of it at least, judges are not merely resorting to what Bentham called 'a childish fiction' when they disclaim the capacity to create new law.

There are, as I have mentioned, a number of cases, by no means inconsiderable, in which judges have to lay down a rule for the first time without any assistance

[1] *Catchpole* v. *Minster* (1913), 30 T.L.R. 111.

from express enactment or previous decision. It is seldom that a judge cannot find guidance of some kind, direct or indirect, in the mass of our reported decisions —by this time a huge accumulation of facts as well as of rules.[1] But in an appreciable number of cases he cannot find this guidance. The thousands of volumes of reports are silent on this one point. This happens more frequently than one might suppose possible in view of the dimensions of our case-law. To take one matter alone— in the greatly changed structure of modern, and especially post-war, society, judges may at any moment be faced with quite unprecedented questions of public policy, and these they must sometimes decide not only without express authority but, what is far more irksome, without evidence to help them.[2] Again, great changes in the economic order of society cannot be ignored, as may be seen from *British Transport Commission* v. *Gourley*, [1956] A.C. 185, which (with that distracting variety of judicial reasoning which we have noted, *ante*, p. 291) has

[1] Even Bentham, the relentless enemy of judge-made law, could not withhold a tribute from the comprehensiveness (even in his day) of our precedents. 'Traverse the whole Continent of Europe—ransack all the libraries belonging to the jurisprudential systems of the several political states—add the contents all together—you would not be able to compose a collection of cases equal in variety, in amplitude, in clearness of statement—in a word, all points taken together, in instructiveness—to that which may be seen to be afforded by the collection of English reports of adjudged cases': 'Papers on Codification' in *Works*, iv. 461.

[2] e.g. *Rawlings* v. *General Trading Co.*, [1921] 1 K.B. 635; *Neville* v. *Dominion of Canada News Co.*, [1915] 3 K.B. 556; *Montefiore* v. *Menday Motor Co.*, [1918] 2 K.B. 241. It has been much controverted, as the result of observations by Lord Halsbury L.C. in *Janson* v. *Driefontein Consolidated Mines*, [1902] A.C. 484, whether the Courts can now create any new 'heads' of public policy. The notion, however, of 'heads' or categories, settled once for all, in a matter like this, is quite artificial and, it is submitted, unprofitable, except for convenience of arrangement and exposition. Whatever classificatory terminology we use, it is in the very nature of public policy that it should constantly pass through new transformations—as was recognized in *Nordenfelt* v. *Maxim-Nordenfelt Co.*, [1894] A.C. 535. If *Neville* v. *Dominion of Canada News Co.*, *ubi sup.*, *Montefiore* v. *Menday Motor Co.*, *ubi sup.*, and *Parkinson* v. *College of Ambulance*, [1925] 2 K.B. 1, were not new 'heads' or interpretations of public policy, it is difficult to explain them. See further Stone, *The Province and Function of Law*, 494 ff.

probably had a more profound effect on the law of damages than any other case in our reports.

It is often remarkable that questions which, one would have thought, must have arisen repeatedly in everyday dealings, have never been the subjects of judicial decision. Judges sometimes express their pained surprise at this embarrassing fact.[1] The words of a distinguished and lamented American judge, writing of his everyday experience, are instructive on this point. He confesses to

> 'a mounting sense of wonder that with all our centuries of common law development, with all our multitudinous courts and still more multitudinous decisions, there are so many questions, elementary in the sense of being primary and basic, that remain unsettled even now. If they were propounded to you suddenly, you would say that of course there must be authorities in abundance for anything so fundamental. You might feel some pricks of conscience at your own ignorance in being unable to repeat the proper answer out of hand. You would have your self-respect restored in some degree if you came to survey the field, and found that the answer, if there was any, was at best uncertain and obscure. I have noticed this particularly in connexion with the law of torts. Rights and privileges at the root, it would seem, of life in civilized society, are discovered to be involved in doubt. One wonders how one has attained maturity without getting oneself in trouble when one has been so uncertain all along of the things that one might do in affairs of primary concern. Take such fundamental privileges or claims of privilege as these—the privilege to employ force against another who threatens one with bodily harm; the privilege to employ force to effect a recaption of chattels taken from one's custody; the privilege to employ force to effect an entry upon land. It is astonishing how obscure and confused are the pronouncements upon these fundamental claims of right.'[2]

What more common source of strife among neighbours than the predatory habits of domestic animals? Yet, if we exclude cattle and dogs, there is remarkably little authority on this subject, and it was not until 1926 that

[1] e.g. *Hartley* v. *Hymans*, [1920] 3 K.B. 475; *Gayler* v. *Davies*, [1924] 2 K.B. 75; *Aktieselskabet Reidar* v. *Arcos, Ltd.*, [1927] 1 K.B. 352, 362.

[2] Cardozo, *Paradoxes of Legal Science*, 76 f.

the Courts considered,[1] apparently for the first time in their history, whether a man is liable for the depredations of a cat which hunts and kills his neighbour's birds. What more ready form of fraud for the plausible rogue than to walk into a jeweller's shop and say, 'I am Sir Somebody Something, the well-known millionaire: here is my cheque, kindly let me have these diamonds'? When the cheque turns out to be that not of a millionaire but of a common cheat, is the contract of sale void or voidable? Upon that question will turn the rights of third parties who have since *bona fide* acquired the goods. This fraud must have been practised time out of number, yet when the point arose in a very well known case[2] there was not a single English decision upon it and the judge had to turn to the American courts for guidance. What more common accident than that a tree growing on premises which adjoin a highway should, without negligence on the part of the occupier of the premises, fall and injure a passer-by? Yet there was no authority governing this case when it arose.[3] Any lawyer who, in the course of his reading, has the curiosity to collect cases in which a court says that it has no authority to guide it, will be astonished at the number of specimens which he can assemble. Let me, without going into excessive detail, give a few random examples, for the most part arising within a very limited period, of these new and unsettled problems of the law.

Whether a deviation by a ship in order to save life or property is justifiable as against a goods owner or insurer.[4] Whether when a husband is charged with personal injury to his wife the wife is a competent and compellable witness for the Crown.[5] Is a dog a domestic animal?[6] What and whose is the liability when a piece of roof-guttering, in the control of the landlord, falls and

[1] *Buckle* v. *Holmes*, [1926] 2 K.B. 125 (see 42 *L.Q.R.* 146).
[2] *Phillips* v. *Brooks*, [1919] 2 K.B. 243.
[3] *Noble* v. *Harrison*, [1926] 2 K.B. 332.
[4] *Scaramanga* v. *Stamp* (1880), 5 C.P.D. 295.
[5] *R.* v. *Lapworth*, [1931] 1 K.B. 117.
[6] *Ellis* v. *Johnstone*, [1963] 2 Q.B. 8.

injures a sub-tenant in a block of flats?[1] What is meant by 'procuring' instruments for purposes of abortion?[2] When a daughter marries, do the 'dominion' and influence of her parents cease?[3] Whether a pilot's official report to Trinity House is admissible in evidence in a collision case.[4] Whether the personal representative of a suicide can recover upon a policy of life insurance.[5] The meaning of the expression 'fair wear and tear' in a lease.[6] The duties at Common Law of a buoyage and beaconage authority.[7] Is a master entitled to recover damages for the loss of services of an employee who has been injured by the tort of a third person?[8] Is a window part of a wall?[9] Does a report in an English newspaper of legal proceedings in a foreign court enjoy qualified privilege?[10] If you allow your dog to escape on to the highway, and it collides with a motor-car [*qy.* or a person?] are you liable for the damage?[11] What is the duty of care (if any) owed by players in a game to the spectators?[12] What is an 'organ' of the human body?[13] Can a blind person witness a will?[14] The last is a very striking

[1] *Cunard* v. *Antifyre, Ltd.*, [1933] 1 K.B. 551.

[2] *R.* v. *Mills*, [1963] 1 Q.B. 522.

[3] *Lancashire Loans, Ltd.* v. *Black*, [1934] 1 K.B. 380.

[4] *The Prinses Juliana*, [1936] P. 139.

[5] *Beresford* v. *Royal Insurance Co.*, [1938] A.C. 586.

[6] *Taylor* v. *Webb*, [1937] 2 K.B. 283 (see *ante*, p. 243).

[7] *The Neptun*, [1938] P. 21. For other examples see *Nelson* v. *Cookson*, [1940] 1 K.B. 100; *Butler* v. *Standard Telephones*, [1940] 1 K.B. 399; *France Fenwick Co.* v. *Procurator-Gen.*, [1942] A.C. 667, 689; *In re Gess*, [1942] Ch. 37; *In re Clarke*, [1942] Ch. 434; *Kerr* v. *Kennedy*, [1942] 1 K.B. 409; *Smythson* v. *Cramp*, [1943] 1 All E.R. 322; *D. & L. Caterers* v. *d'Ajou*, [1945] K.B. 364; *In re Rushbrook's Will Trusts*, [1948] Ch. 421; *The Sobieski*, [1949] P. 313, 323; *Boguslawski* v. *Gdynia-Ameryka Linie*, [1950] 1 K.B. 157; *China* v. *Harrow U.D.C.*, [1954] 1 Q.B. 178; *Hersom* v. *Bernett*, [1955] 1 Q.B. 98; *Milner* v. *Staffs. Congregational Union*, [1956] Ch. 275; *In re Callaway*, [1956] Ch. 559; *In re Kilvert, decd.*, [1957] 1 Ch. 388.

[8] *Mankin* v. *Scala Theodrome*, [1947] K.B. 257.

[9] *Holiday Fellowship* v. *Hereford*, [1959] 1 W.L.R. 211.

[10] *Webb* v. *Times Publishing Co. Ltd.*, [1960] 2 Q.B. 535.

[11] *Gomberg* v. *Smith*, [1963] 1 Q.B. 25.

[12] *Wooldridge* v. *Sumner*, [1963] 2 Q.B. 43.

[13] *R.* v. *Medical Appeal Tribunal, Ex p. Burpitt*, [1957] 2 Q.B. 584.

[14] *In the Estate of Gibson*, [1949] P. 434.

example, for it is remarkable that in more than a century since the passing of the Wills Act, 1837, the point should never have arisen expressly for decision. It seems almost incredible that throughout the ages it had never been settled, until the question arose in *Wormald* v. *Cole*, [1954] 1 Q.B. 614, whether the owner of straying cattle was liable for personal injury done by his animals to the occupier of the land on which they trespassed; or that until *R.* v. *Sharp and Johnson*, [1957] 1 Q.B. 552, it had never been settled whether self-defence was an answer to a charge of being a party to an affray.

A judge, in laying down a rule to meet these situations, is certainly making a new contribution to our law, but only within limits, usually well defined. If he has to decide upon the authority of natural justice, or simply 'the common sense of the thing',[1] he employs that kind of natural justice or common sense which he has absorbed from the study of the law and which he believes to be consistent with the general principles of English jurisprudence. The 'reason' which he applies is, as Coke said, not 'every unlearned man's reason', but that technically trained *sense of legal right*—we need not follow Coke so far as to call it 'the perfection of reason'—with which all his learning imbues him. The public policy which he will apply to a new point is what he understands public policy to be from studying it in other legal connexions. The phrase commonly used is that he decides 'not on precedent, but on principle'. The difference is that in the one case he is applying a principle illustrated by previous examples, in the other case he is applying a principle not previously formulated, but consonant with the whole doctrine of law and justice. Although, therefore, he is making a definite contribution to the law, he is not importing an entirely novel element into it.[2]

Still less, in that overwhelming majority of cases where

[1] *Pearce* v. *Gardner*, [1897] 1 Q.B. 688.

[2] See, on the 'inarticulate major premiss' of Holmes, and on the use of analogy in cases of first impression, Paton, *Jurisprudence* (2nd ed.), 168.

precedent is cited and adopted, is the judge seeking to import anything novel into the law. His whole effort is to find the law, not to manufacture it. He is always working with materials which exist *in the present or the past*; his concern is not with the future effect of the rule which he is laying down, but with the application of what he conceives to be an existing rule to a concrete case before him. He cannot, however much he may wish to do so, sweep away what he believes to be the prevailing rule of law and substitute something else in its place. In this sense it is no 'childish fiction' to say that he does not and cannot 'make' law, and it was not without reason that Lord Esher M.R. said: 'There is in fact no such thing as judge-made law, for the judges do not make the law, though they frequently have to apply existing law to circumstances as to which it has not previously been authoritatively laid down that such law is applicable.'[1] 'This Court', said Scrutton L.J.,[2] 'sits to administer the law; not to make new law if there are cases not provided for.' 'It may be', said Lord Denning M.R. in *Att.-Gen.* v. *Butterworth*, [1963] 1 Q.B., 696, 719, 'that there is no authority to be found in the books, but if this be so all I can say is that the sooner we make one the better.' But how did the Master of the Rolls 'make' this authority? By reference to 'many pointers to be found in the books in favour of the view which I have expressed'. Judges in this way are constantly reasoning not by explicit authority 'on all fours', but *by analogy* with principles extracted from precedents if not precisely *in pari materia*, at least *in consimili casu*.

Compare now the function of the legislature in 'making' law. It is at once apparent that it has an entirely different opportunity: it is not confined to law in the present or the past, but may do as it wills with the future.

[1] *Willis* v. *Baddeley*, [1892] 2 Q.B. 324, 326. Cf. Farwell L.J., *Baylis* v. *Bishop of London*, [1913] 1 Ch. at p. 137: 'It is in my opinion impossible for us now to create any new doctrine of the Common Law.'

[2] *Harnett* v. *Fisher*, [1927] 1 K.B. 402, 424 (affirmed, [1927] A.C. 573).

Though it is true that it frequently works upon existing and even ancient material (e.g. in codifying statutes) it can 'make' new law in a sense which is quite precluded to the judge. It *legislates* where the judge *interprets*. By no possible extension of his office can a judge introduce new rules for the compensation of injured employees, for national health insurance, for the rate of taxation, for the appropriation of public money, for the franchise, for summer time, for the supply of gas, water, electricity —to take at random instances which affect everybody's daily affairs. The legislature can project into the future a rule of law which has never before existed in England. The courts can do nothing of the kind. And while it is true, as has already been pointed out, that a decision founded on plain error does not usually survive for long, the courts cannot, like the legislature, at their pleasure abrogate a settled doctrine which they think would be better expunged from the law. To take one example, before the year 1891 many judges did not disguise their strong disapproval of the rule that a woman could not recover damages for an oral imputation of unchastity without proving special damage. But they were powerless to change the rule, and what they were unable to do Parliament did with a stroke of the pen.[1]

Thus there are two distinct senses in which we may speak of 'making' law. In applying the expression to the judge, we use it only in a derivative or secondary sense. Otherwise we are in danger of obscuring his essentially interpretative function. *In this secondary sense*, but only so, the judge does undoubtedly 'make' law. It is not an original act of creation. Every act of interpretation shapes something new, in a secondary sense.[2] A man who chops a tree into logs has in a sense 'made' the logs. A man who annotates a code has 'made' a learned work, but he has not 'made' a system of law. Mankind, with all its resource and inventiveness, is limited in its creative power by the physical material vouchsafed to it. Similarly

[1] Slander of Women Act, 1891. [2] See *ante*, Excursus A, p. 152.

the creative power of the courts is limited by existing legal material at their command. They find the material and shape it. The legislature may manufacture entirely new material.

Nevertheless, this limited creative power of the courts is of the utmost importance to the development of law. If we compare the work done by the courts and by the legislature, we find that they are usually operating in two quite distinct spheres of law. With regard to the substance of English law as a system of jurisprudence—the underlying principles of right and duty—it is the courts which take the lead. It is comparatively seldom that the legislature interferes in this domain, except to gather up loose ends, to resolve a doubt, or to abrogate a principle which has become inexpedient or mischievous. It may regulate when doctrine has become obscure or static, and when it does so, it usually takes its cue from the judges: it may codify a part of the law which, though well settled, has become scattered and unwieldy in form; but it seldom lays hands on any of those principles which lawyers have come to regard as fundamental. It is difficult, for example, to imagine a statute enacting that hearsay evidence should be admissible at the discretion of the court, or that an accused person should be presumed guilty until proved innocent, or that trespass should be actionable only on proof of wilful intent. The legislature *may* enact any of these things—for all that we can predict, conditions may some day arise which will make these changes necessary: settled doctrines have from time to time been radically changed by statute —e.g. Common Law doctrines of the relationship between master and servant, and of the common crime of larceny, have been revolutionized in some respects: to take a minor illustration, when the ancient doctrine of liability for domestic animals is found insufficient to protect cattle against marauding dogs, a Dogs Act is passed; or to turn to Equity, many cherished doctrines of conveyancing are swept away by the Law of Property Acts,

1925. But a glance at any yearly volume of statutes will show that enactments of this kind are in a very small minority. The great bulk of legislation is concerned with public law. It is for the most part of a social or administrative character, defining the reciprocal duties of State and individuals, rather than the duties of individuals *inter se*. This indifference of the layman politician to 'lawyer's law' is a far greater impediment to legal reform and progress than the alleged conservatism of the legal profession. It is the reverse of the truth to say that the reforms of the law (e.g in the nineteenth century) have come from outside the profession. Both Bench and Bar frequently desire and advocate and even plead for changes in the law which they, better than the layman, know to be urgently necessary. Such demands from the Bench are often emphatic—and equally often unheeded. The difficulty is to obtain interest (let alone unanimity) from laymen politicians who, having power to remove anomalies, are content either to scoff at them or to regard them as the mere hobby-horse of 'cranks'.

In the domain, then, of private law, it is the courts which are still predominant, both in affirming settled principles and in gradually adapting them to changing conditions. The position is well stated by Byrne J.:

'Mr. Challis is right of course when he says that "when any part of the common law is found to require amendment, the Legislature alone is competent to apply the remedy". But the Courts have first to find what is the common law—that is, the principle embodied in what is called the common law—and to apply it to new and ever-varying states of facts and circumstances. The common law is to be sought in the expositions and declarations of it in the decisions of the Courts and in the writing of lawyers.[1] New statutes and the course of social development give rise to new aspects and conditions which have to be regarded in applying the old principles.'[2]

[1] The remark is noteworthy as a comment on 'unauthoritative' sources.

[2] *Hollis's Hospital and Hague's Contract*, [1899] 2 Ch. 540, 552. Cf. Lord Esher M.R. in *Cochrane* v. *Moore* (1890), 25 Q.B.D. 57, 74.

IV. PRACTICAL WORKING OF PRECEDENTS

So long as we keep in view the main purpose for which the method of precedents exists, and do not allow it to become a mechanical expedient divorced from the living content of law, it is, and has proved itself to be in England, a most valuable instrument of jurisprudence. The Benthamite criticisms of it miss its purport. But it is far from perfect, for it does not operate without certain practical inconveniences and inconsistencies, which do not diminish as time goes on.

Reports A precedent is not a precedent unless it is accurately reported. Attention has already been called[1] to the difficulties which arose out of the older reports. They are enormously less than they were, though even now judges do not always conceal their scepticism concerning certain contemporary series;[2] but we are not yet independent of ancient reports, and here the value of precedents may vary greatly, as we have seen, with the skill and reputation of the reporter. Even in Coke, a turn of phrase, a small omission, in his crabbed diction may lead to unfortunate misconceptions: for example, it would seem that the so-called Rule in *Pinnel's Case* (1602), 5 Co. Rep. 117—an artificial and groundless rule which has been consistently condemned[3]—arose out of just such a verbal ambiguity in Coke. This inconvenience may be considered as diminishing with the improvement of reports, but it is by no means negligible even in modern times. The chief complaints which are heard today are not so much about inaccurate reports as about their complete absence. In spite of the various concurrent series of reports which now exist, from time to time important cases seem to elude the vigilance of all reporters and

[1] *Ante*, pp. 221 ff.

[2] See *In re Canadian Oil Works Corporation* (1875), L.R. 10 Ch. 593, 600; Bankes L.J., *Moore* v. *Landauer*, [1921] 2 K.B. 519, 523; 37 *L.Q.R.* 403; *Brentnall* v. *L.C.C.*, [1945] K.B. 115, 120; *Younghusband* v. *Luftig*, [1949] 2 K.B. 354, 365; *In re Thirlwell*, [1958] Ch. 146, 152; *In re Levy*, [1960] Ch. 346, 367, whereon see 76 *L.Q.R.* 203.

[3] See *post*, p. 337.

editors. Examples of this mischief call for separate treatment,[1] and their unfortunate effect is to bring the law into discredit, for it has always to be remembered that courts of law exist not to adorn learning by the elaboration of legal subtleties, but to do justice between citizens on concrete issues; and it is a blemish on the administration of justice that litigation should be protracted and parties put to expense because courts have not all the relevant material before them. A patient who was unsuccessfully treated by a surgeon would find it a singularly unsatisfying excuse that the specialist did not have at his command all the necessary apparatus of his craft.

Accidents of litigation

Nor is it an entirely unjust criticism that precedents tend to make the development of the law depend on accidents of litigation. Important points may remain at large simply because nobody happens to have brought action upon them. An erroneous judgement may stand, and acquire an undeserved authority, merely because the losing party does not appeal against it—usually for the excellent reason that he cannot afford any further costs of litigation.[2] Similar circumstances may arise many years later, and an appeal is brought which is in effect an appeal against the earlier decision; meanwhile, the profession has been following what turns out to be an incorrect rule.[3] In the case of a statute, it may not occur to anybody until many years after it has been passed to raise a point which may entirely alter its effect. There was a striking example of this when the whole law of gaming and wagering was thrown into confusion by a new and ingenious point taken, in 1920, upon the

[1] See Excursus C, *post*, p. 367.

[2] Thus the well-known decision on gaming and wagering, *Hyams* v. *Stuart-King*, [1908] 2 K.B. 696, though constantly doubted and criticized, stood its ground until overruled by *Hill* v. *William Hill, Ltd.*, [1949] A.C. 530, and its predecessor, *Bubb* v. *Yelverton* (1870), L.R. 9 Eq. 471, was 79 years old before it was given its quietus by the same decision of the House of Lords.

[3] e.g. *In re Tringham's Trusts*, [1904] 2 Ch. 487 and *In re Bostock's Settlement*, [1921] 2 Ch. 469; *Bourne* v. *Keane*, [1919] A.C. 815; *In re Constable's Settled Estates*, [1919] 1 Ch. 178, and *Parr* v. *Att.-Gen.*, [1926] A.C. 239; *The Fibrosa Case*, [1943] A.C. 32; *Perrin* v. *Morgan*, [1943] A.C. 399.

Gaming Act of 1835.[1] For many years the profession laboured under a misapprehension about the procedure in *habeas corpus*, until *In re Hastings (No. 3)*, (1959) Ch. 368, corrected the error. For nearly a century it was commonly supposed that, under the Hackney Carriages (London) Act, 1853, the driver of a hackney carriage (i.e. in modern times, a taxi-cab), when travelling along the road, or 'cruising', was legally bound to pick up any pedestrian who hailed him, until the Divisional Court of the King's Bench decided otherwise in *Hunt* v. *Morgan*, [1949] 1 K.B. 233. So firmly was this error rooted that many taxi-drivers had been prosecuted for failing to comply with the supposed rule, and after the decision in *Hunt* v. *Morgan* it was necessary to grant them all free pardons. It would seem that a putative father's right to guardianship of his illegitimate child has been frequently misinterpreted and misapplied under the Guardianship of Infants Act, 1886, and its amending legislation.[2] Two hundred and thirty years passed before the profession learned that levying distress for poor rates was possible under the Landlord and Tenant Act, 1709.[3] It is difficult to say how many years had gone by—possibly centuries—before it was laid down (and it is still open to question by higher courts) that a judge of the Queen's Bench Division has no inherent jurisdiction to grant bail to a convicted person pending appeal.[4] The Rent Restriction Acts had been in operation for thirty years before their effect was fundamentally altered by the doctrine of 'sharing' established by *Neale* v. *Del Soto*, [1945] K.B. 144.[5]

[1] *Dey* v. *Mayo*, [1920] 2 K.B. 346; *Sutters* v. *Briggs*, [1922] 1 A.C. 1; Gaming Act, 1922. Cf. *Brown* v. *Allweather Mechanical Grouting Co., Ltd.*, [1954] 2 Q.B. 443.

[2] *In re C.T. (an Infant)*, [1957] 1 Ch. 48.

[3] *Hickman* v. *Potts*, [1940] 1 K.B. 29 (reversed, but not on this point, [1941] A.C. 212); see *post*, p. 333.

[4] *Ex p. Blyth*, [1944] K.B. 532 (Hallett J.).

[5] See Denning L.J., *Paisner* v. *Goodrich*, [1955] 2 Q.B. 353, 357. In *Att.-Gen. for Australia* v. *Reg.*, [1957] A.C. 288, the Privy Council held unconstitutional an Australian statute which had stood unchallenged for 25 years.

Over-looked authorities

Another difficulty, and one likely to increase in future with the ceaseless growth of recorded cases, is that exact and comprehensive citation cannot be ensured. If the judge is to be bound by precedents, he should have all the relevant authorities at his command. But he cannot carry them all in his head, nor is it always easy to find them, in spite of the many modern devices for facilitating the search. In 1930, McCardie J.[1] called attention to 'the confusion which so often arises in English law either because counsel do not raise the necessary points or because the courts do not receive a sufficient citation of the relevant authorities'. There has always been danger of these oversights: for example, as long ago as 1813, the case of *Hodgson* v. *Temple*, 5 Taunt. 181, turning on the point whether a sale of goods is vitiated by a known illegal destination of the goods, gave a negative answer to that vexed question, in ignorance of the fact that precisely the reverse had been decided, only a few months before, by the King's Bench in *Langton* v. *Hughes*, 1 M. & S. 593. Search would doubtless discover similar examples in the past; but it is manifest that as precedents multiply year by year, litigants run increasing risk from this source. Counsel, who are primarily responsible for putting the court in possession of the material for decision, are between Scylla and Charybdis. They incur reproach and tax the patience of the Bench if they waste time and money on precedents of dubious relevance[2] (there are loud complaints on this score in the United States, where the welter of precedents from different jurisdictions is truly overwhelming): on the other hand, compression of citation may be false economy when it is so easy for something of importance to be overlooked. In the press of a busy practice and of overcrowded judicial lists strange things may happen. *Fisher* v. *Oldham*

[1] *Fisher* v. *Oldham Corporation*, [1930] 2 K.B. at p. 373.

[2] 'Counsel appearing before us', said Scrutton L.J. caustically in *Reckitt* v. *Barnett*, [1928] 2 K.B. at p. 258, 'each of whom said his case was too plain for argument, and took a long time in arguing it, buried the Court under authorities, to a few of which I must refer.'

Corporation, [1930] 2 K.B. 364, illustrates how a 'line of authorities' may gradually grow in the wrong direction because one important precedent has escaped attention. The question at issue in that case was one of great importance to the public. If a man is falsely imprisoned by a constable, he knows that it is fruitless to bring an action for heavy damages against the constable personally; formerly he was also aware that he had no action against the Crown; but if he learned that the constable was appointed and, in large measure, controlled by a borough corporation, he had some ground for thinking that he might be able to sue the corporation on the ordinary principles of master and servant. In fact, he could not, if the decision of McCardie J. in this case was correct (and it has not been challenged); but the decision rests upon a somewhat intricate interpretation of a number of statutes, and there seems to be much substance in the complaint of McCardie J. that in some of the preceding cases[1] it was impossible to discover the *ratio decidendi*, owing to inadequate reports, and that in one leading case[2] an important authority[3] had been wholly omitted from consideration.

The decision of the Judicial Committee in the now discredited case of *Commonwealth Trust* v. *Akotey*, [1926] A.C. 72 (see *ante*, p. 251), might have been different if *London Joint Stock Bank* v. *Macmillan*, [1918] A.C. 777, had not been overlooked. *Toronto Power Co., Ltd.* v. *Paskwan*, [1915] A.C. 734, a decision of the Judicial Committee, is very difficult to reconcile with *Fanton* v. *Denville*, [1932] 2 K.B. 390, and with *Cole* v. *Trafford (No. 2)*, [1918] 2 K.B. 523. This decision of the Privy Council was not actually binding on the Court of

[1] *Goff* v. *Great Northern Ry.* (1861), 3 E. & E. 672; *Edwards v. Midland Ry. Co.* (1880), 6 Q.B.D. 287.

[2] *Lambert* v. *Great Eastern Ry. Co.*, [1909] 2 K.B. 776.

[3] *Stanbury* v. *Exeter Corporation*, [1905] 2 K.B. 838. It is probable that this case would not have affected the decision in *Lambert* v. *Great Eastern Ry. Co.*, which depended on special statutory considerations, but the principle involved was certainly important and relevant.

Appeal, but possibly more respect would have been paid to it in the very important case of *Fanton* v. *Denville* if authorities of considerable weight had not been omitted from the consideration of the Court.[1]

Instances of this grave defect in our system of precedents are numerous, and of recent years they seem to have increased to such an extent that detailed consideration of them seems more suitable for separate treatment[2] than for discussion at this point. For the present, I will content myself with two illustrations which seem somewhat startling. *Penrikyber Navigation Colliery Co.* v. *Edwards*, [1933] A.C. 28, was the last stage in a protracted battle between a miner and his employers concerning liability to compensate for miner's nystagmus. The short point was whether a medical referee's certificate of complete recovery (for so the House interpreted the document) was, under the special procedure of the Workmen's Compensation Acts, conclusive against the claimant, or whether an arbitrator could consider further evidence produced in contradiction of the referee's report. The Court of Appeal, relying on one of its own previous decisions, held that the certificate was not conclusive. Upon this decision it is sufficient to quote the observations of Viscount Dunedin:

> 'My Lords, it is much to be regretted that neither the county court judge nor the Court of Appeal had their attention directed by the Bar before them to two more recent cases in this House: *Wilsons and Clyde Coal Co.* v. *Burrows*, [1929] A.C. 651, and *Connor* v. *Cadzow Coal Co.*, [1932] A.C. 1, without a consideration of which it is impossible to determine the present question. Indeed, this omission is so grave as to make it useless to canvass the judgement of the Court of Appeal as it stands. Had these cases been before the Court of Appeal I am quite unable to say what their judgement would have been.'

If such an omission, vital to the litigants, can occur in

[1] See *per* Scrutton L.J., *Fanton* v. *Denville*, *ubi sup.*, at p. 327.
[2] See Excursus C, *post*, p. 367.

respect of recent House of Lords cases, directly and unmistakably in point, it is not difficult to imagine how easily they may happen in less obvious circumstances.

In *King* v. *K.*, [1943] P. 91, the question at issue was whether, having regard to the Common Law rule that a husband is liable for his wife's necessaries, the Court had jurisdiction to order the husband to find security for his wife's costs when he appealed from the dismissal of his petition for divorce. The matter was considered to be so important in divorce practice that it was ordered to be argued before a full Court of Appeal of seven members. At first it appeared that the sole apposite authority was a decision of the Court of Appeal which had found its way into only one series of reports—*Shufflebotham* v. *S.* (1923), 128 L.T. 642. This case was strongly against the wife's application for security for costs; but her counsel had discovered a decision, also of a full Court of Appeal (presided over by the Earl of Birkenhead L.C.), which had never been reported anywhere except in *The Times*. This was *Vidal* v. *V.*, *The Times*, 13 October 1921, and in it the Court had ordered security to be given for the wife's costs, though the abbreviated newspaper report did not give full reasons for the judgement. This decision, though quite recent at the time of *Shufflebotham* v. *S.*, was never before the Court in that case, and indeed Lord Sterndale M.R. seems to have based his judgement largely on the fact that there was no precedent for the respondent's application. It is truly remarkable that a judgement of a full Court of Appeal (a comparatively rare event) in so important a matter of practice was never reported more adequately.

Conflicting binding authorities

Sometimes, again, a judge is in a dilemma between what he conceives to be conflicting decisions in courts of superior jurisdiction. Suppose the House of Lords has given a decision, and the same or a similar point subsequently comes before the Court of Appeal. Then it arises again before a single judge and he is of opinion that the Court of Appeal has not truly 'followed' the

House of Lords. The decisions in both cases are ostensibly binding on him. Which is he to follow?[1]

Only too often nowadays is a court faced with what Lord Goddard C.J. described in *Younghusband* v. *Luftig*, [1949] 2 K.B. at p. 371, as a 'complete fog' of authorities, or what Upjohn J. called in *Smeaton* v. *Ilford Corpn.* [1954] Ch. 450, 478, a 'rough sea of contradictory authority'.[2] Nothing but sympathy can be felt for a judge who is constrained to say, as Humphreys J. said in *Lyus* v. *Stepney Borough Council*, [1940] 2 K.B. at p. 663: 'I find myself confronted with authorities all of which I should like to follow and all of which are binding on me, but with regard to which I have the greatest possible difficulty in understanding how they can all be right.' Sympathy is not diminished when it is found that the learned judge is reversed by the Court of Appeal ([1941] 1 K.B. 134), that this decision of the Court of Appeal is followed by that Court itself in *Fox* v. *Newcastle Corporation*, [1941] 2 K.B. 120, but that both

[1] e.g. Russell J. in *Sorrell* v. *Smith*, [1923] 2 Ch. 32. In *Osgood* v. *Sunderland* (1913), 30 T.L.R. 530, Bailhache J. based his judgement on a case which, unknown to him and apparently to counsel, had been reversed by the Court of Appeal: see *Lynn* v. *Bamber*, [1930] 2 K.B. 72, 78. Cf. *Commissioners of Inland Revenue* v. *Lawrence, Graham & Co.*, [1937] 2 K.B. 179, where the Judge of first instance found himself in a maze of authorities from which only the Court of Appeal could extricate him. Scrutton L.J. was sometimes very outspoken in his criticisms of conflicting authorities. See, e.g., his observations in *Mourton* v. *Poulter*, [1930] 2 K.B. at pp. 188 ff., on the decisions of the House of Lords in *Addie* v. *Dumbreck*, [1929] A.C. 358, and *Excelsior Wire Rope Co.* v. *Callan*, [1930] A.C. 404 (two cases which certainly are not easy to reconcile). See Scrutton L.J. also on *May and Butcher* v. *R.*, [1934] 2 K.B. 17, and *Hillas* v. *Arcos* (1932), 147 L.T. 503, in *Foley* v. *Classique Coaches Ltd.*, [1934] 2 K.B. 1; on *Glossop* v *Ashley*, [1922] 1 K.B. 1, and *Dufty* v. *Palmer*, [1924] 2 K.B. 35, in *Phillips* v. *Copping*, [1935] 1 K.B. 15; and on a 'chaotic and contradictory' clash of authorities in *Hill* v. *Aldershot Corporation*, [1933] 1 K.B. 259.

[2] For equally inspissated 'fogs', see *Rothwell* v. *Caverswall Stone Co.*, [1944] 2 All E.R. 350; *Colebrook* v. *Watson Investment Co.*, [1944] Ch. 387; *Dixon* v. *D.*, [1953] P. 103; *In re Brown, decd.*, [1954] Ch. 39; *Solomons* v. *Gertzenstein*, [1954] 2 Q.B. 243; *Hughes and Vale Proprietary, Ltd.* v. *State of New South Wales*, [1955] A.C. 241; *Pinnick* v. *P.*, [1957] 1 W.L.R. 644. 'In this labyrinth it is obvious that it is not easy for a judge of first instance to find his way': *per* Wilberforce J., *In re Howard's Will Trusts*, [1961] Ch. 507, 517.

decisions of the Court of Appeal are later disapproved by that Court itself (*Fisher* v. *Ruislip–Northwood U.D.C.*, [1945] 1 K.B. 584)!

It seems, however, now to be an established principle in the Court of Appeal, in accordance with the interpretation placed on *Young* v. *Bristol Aeroplane Co.*, [1944] K.B. 718, that if a case is deemed to be inconsistent with a later decision of higher authority, the earlier case should not be accepted. The principle is thus stated by Lord Goddard C.J. in *R.* v. *Porter*, [1949] 2 K.B. at p. 132:

> 'When you find that a case, whether it has been expressly overruled or not by the final Court of Appeal, has been dealt with, or the facts, which were the governing facts in a particular case, have been regarded in a totally different manner by the final Court of Appeal, so that it is obvious in the opinion of the final Court of Appeal that the cause was wrongly decided, then whether they have in terms said they overrule the case or not, I think this court ought to treat the case as overruled.'

The same principle appears from *Noble* v. *Southern Railway Co.*, [1940] A.C. 583, in which the House of Lords held that the Court of Appeal ought not to have considered itself bound by one of its own decisions which (so it was held) was at variance with later decisions of the House of Lords. It would almost seem that the Court of Appeal sometimes prefers a clear statement of the law by a single judge to a series of conflicting decisions and *dicta* by itself.[1] At other times the Court, confronted with an overwhelming bulk of fluctuating decisions, prefers to 'cut through' the mass—in effect declining to add further confusion by considering and balancing all the components—and settles the law once for all (or so it is hoped!) by a clear formulation of principle.[2]

[1] See, e.g., *Law* v. *Dearnley*, [1950] 1 K.B. 400.

[2] A notable example is *Baindail* v. *B.*, [1946] P. 122, where a comparatively short and simple judgement takes the place of what might have been an immensely long and complicated one. This heroic method seems to be more frequent in the United States than in England: see Max Radin, 'The Trail of the Calf', *Cornell Law Quarterly*, Nov. 1946, 137, 158.

There appears to be a growing freedom among judges of first instance in applying the same principle as the Court of Appeal when a case is deemed to be inconsistent with a subsequent decision of higher authority,[1] and even when a doubtful point has been left open by higher authority.[2] A strong example of this freedom is *Colman* v. *Croft*, [1947] K.B. 95, in which Hilbery J. felt himself able to reject the well-known and long-standing decision of the Exchequer Division in *Degg* v. *Midland Railway Co.* (1857), 1 H. & N. 773, because he considered it to be inconsistent with *Radcliffe* v. *Ribble Motor Services*, [1939] A.C. 215.

These modifications certainly mitigate any tendency towards unintelligent rigidity in the working of precedent, but they still leave problems of individual interpretation which cannot be escaped. There is inevitable doubt and ambiguity whenever a case is said to be overruled 'by implication' only. Thus in *Noble* v. *Southern Railway Co.*, *ubi sup.*, though the House of Lords took a clear view of the duty of the Court of Appeal, a study of the contentions and judgements in that Court (reported in [1939] 2 All E.R. 817) leaves the impression that it was at least highly arguable whether the case by which the Court held itself bound (*Clarke* v. *Southern Railway Co.* (1927), 20 B.W.C.C. 309) was really untenable in view of *Thomas* v. *Ocean Coal Co.*, [1933] A.C. 100, and *Harris* v. *Associated Portland Cement Manufacturers*, [1939] A.C. 71—the more so because the main question turned on the interpretation of a notoriously difficult section of the Workmen's Compensation Act, 1925. Again we see that no rule of thumb can relieve the judge of his own personal responsibility not merely for applying the law but for finding the law which he must apply.

Communis error facit ius

But to the uncompromising critic like Bentham, all these objections are trivial compared with the main indictment that, out of respect for precedent, a principle

[1] See Denning J. in *Minister of Pensions* v. *Chennell*, [1947] K.B. 250.
[2] See Hodson J. in *Cackett* v. *C.*, [1950] P. 253.

of law may be followed which is known to be wrong, and that a judge may be compelled to apply an established rule contrary to his own sense of justice. It is against this possibility that Continental systems particularly guard themselves; and it must be admitted that in strict theory it is difficult to justify the doctrine *communis error facit ius*. Our courts do, however, admit this doctrine, though with caution, in the belief that unless the erroneous rule is working some manifest hardship, it is better not to interfere with it when it has been adopted as the basis of frequent transactions. 'If', said Jessel M.R.,[1]

> 'I find a long course of decisions by inferior Courts acquiesced in, which have become part of the settled law, I do not think it is the province of the Appeal Court after a long course of time to interfere, because most contracts have been regulated by those decisions. . . . There is another consideration which always has weight with me. When the law is settled it gets into the text-books, which are a very considerable guide to practitioners.'

The same eminent judge extends the principle even to erroneous interpretations of statute.

> 'Where a series of decisions of inferior Courts have put a construction on an Act of Parliament, and have thus made a law which men follow in their daily dealings, it has been held, even by the House of Lords, that it is better to adhere to the course of the decisions than to reverse them, because of the mischief which would result from such a proceeding. Of course, that requires two things, antiquity of decision, and the practice of mankind in conducting their affairs.'[2]

The 'mischief' in such cases is apparent enough, but it is questionable whether it is not a greater mischief that error should become inveterate merely by antiquity; and

[1] *Wallis* v. *Smith* (1882), 21 Ch.D. 243, 265.

[2] *Ex p. Willey* (1883), 23 Ch.D. 118, 127. 'I protest', said Lord Esher M.R. in *Robins* v. *Gray*, [1895] 1 Q.B. 501, 503, 'against being asked, upon some new discovery as to the law of innkeeper's lien, to disturb a well-known and very large business carried on in this country for centuries.'

it is difficult to set precise limits to the doctrine, for if it were carried to its logical conclusion, no long-standing precedent would ever be overruled, whereas, as we shall see, this is sometimes done without scruple, and in recent times with increasing frequency, whatever the 'daily dealings' of men have been.

As an example of the awkward complexities which sometimes arise out of the doctrine of *communis error*, I will take a point which fluctuated in a curious manner in our Court of Probate for some seventy years. An Englishwoman marries a foreigner and lives with him abroad. She makes a will while domiciled in her foreign country of residence. According to a rule of Private International Law,[1] if this will is to be admitted to probate in England, it must be made in accordance with the law of the country of domicil. But now suppose that the woman has a power of appointment, by deed or by will, over property in England. Purporting to act in execution of the power, she makes a will, while still domiciled abroad, in the manner prescribed by the Wills Act, 1837, appointing the English property to certain uses. The question is whether this will can be admitted to probate. On the face of it, it cannot, inasmuch as it has not been made in accordance with the law of the country of domicil; but will it be saved from the operation of this rule by the fact that it is an execution of a power of appointment in accordance with English law? The Court of Probate merely has to decide the question of probate: whether or not the power has been properly executed is for the Court of Chancery. It is interesting to follow the different stages of the rule throughout the nineteenth century.

1. In 1838 the point came before the Judicial Committee in *Tatnall* v. *Hankey*, 2 Moo. P.C. 342. The Court of Probate had decided that it had no jurisdiction in such a case, as it could not consider questions of powers of appointment, which were for the Chancery. The Judicial Committee, as reported by Moore, held

[1] *Bloxam* v. *Favre* (1884), 9 P.D. 130.

that the Court of Probate had jurisdiction, without giving any final opinion on the substantive point.

2. In 1846, in *Barnes* v. *Vincent*, 5 Moo. P.C. 201, Lord Brougham in the Judicial Committee expressed the opinion that probate ought not to be granted in such circumstances.

3. In 1859, in *Crookenden* v. *Fuller*, 1 Sw. & Tr. 441, the point came before Sir Cresswell Cresswell, though it was not the principal matter for decision. By way of *dictum*, the learned judge said that probate ought not to be granted, despite the power of appointment, unless the will conformed to the law of domicil.

4. In the following year, Sir Cresswell Cresswell had to decide the point expressly in *In the Goods of Alexander*, 29 L.J. (P. & M.) 93. He revoked what he had said in *Crookenden* v. *Fuller*, on the ground that the judgement of the Judicial Committee in *Tatnall* v. *Hankey* was not correctly reported by Moore. He preferred to rely upon the headnote to that case, and on a copy of the Judicial Committee's actual report made to the Crown, which was shown to him privately.[1] According to these statements of *Tatnall* v. *Hankey*, he held that the will ought to be admitted to probate and he granted the application as prayed.

5. In 1865, the decision in *In the Goods of Alexander* was supported by a *dictum* of Lord Romilly in *D'Huart* v. *Harkness*, 34 Beav. 324, 328.

6. In 1866, the point arose before Sir J. Wilde (Lord Penzance) in *In the Goods of Hallyburton*, L.R. 1 P. & D. 90. The judge there gave it as his opinion that Sir Cresswell Cresswell was right in his first decision in *Crookenden* v. *Fuller*, 'and that the note upon which he acted in the case of *Alexander*, of the decision of the Judicial Committee, which does not appear in the report in Moore, is at variance with the subsequent case of *Barnes* v. *Vincent*. Both *Tatnall* v. *Hankey* and *Barnes* v. *Vincent* appear to me to decide that where a will was

[1] *Ante*, p. 258, n. 1.

executed under a power, the Court of Probate must determine whether or not there is a will.' This amounts to a clear opinion that the case of *Alexander* was wrongly decided. Nevertheless, the learned judge followed the erroneous decision; for, he said, 'great injustice might arise if I were to do otherwise, because, for aught I know, the attorney who drew the will in this case may have acted on the authority of that very decision'.

7. So the matter stood for the next thirty years, until it arose again in 1896 in *In the Goods of Huber*, [1896] P. 209. The learned President (Sir F. H. Jeune) was clearly of opinion that Lord Penzance's criticism of *In the Goods of Alexander* was justified, and that that case could not be supported on principle or authority. But he took the same view of his duty as his predecessor, and declined to dissent from a decision which, though in his opinion plainly mistaken, had stood and had been acted on for thirty-six years.

8. Finally, in *Murphy* v. *Deichler*, [1909] A.C. 446, the point was brought for the first time before the House of Lords. A strenuous attempt was made to induce the House to overrule a decision of such doubtful antecedents. Lord Loreburn L.C. dealt with the matter very shortly.

> 'I think this case falls within the rule that it is not necessary or advisable to disturb a fixed practice which has been long observed in regard to the disposition of property, even though it may have been disapproved at times by individual judges, where no real point of principle has been violated.'

The result is that a decision given by a judge on second (and worse) thoughts, based on a misapprehension of a report and contrary to two rulings of a higher tribunal, becomes ineradicably settled in the law.[1]

[1] Another interesting example may be found in the chequered career of *Newton* v. *Harland* (1840), 1 M. & G. 644, whereon see Scrutton L.J. in *Hemmings* v. *Stoke Poges Golf Club*, [1920] 1 K.B. 720, 739. On the strange descent of the unsatisfactory rule in *Simpson* v. *Crippen* (1872), L.R. 8 Q.B. 14, from *Pordage* v. *Cole* (1669), 1 Wms. S. 319, see Williston, *Some Modern*

Turning to another branch of the law, we find that conveyancing precedents sometimes establish rules of interpretation which are difficult to justify in logic and which are regrettably effectual in defeating intention unless restrained by statute. One conspicuous instance is the multitude of complex distinctions which have arisen in connexion with remainders limited 'on failure of issue'. When a man by his will makes a gift to A for life, but if 'he die without' issue, or 'without having' issue, or 'before he has any' issue, then to B: it is difficult to doubt that he means that if A has no issue living at the time of his death, then the property is to go over to B. Now this was perfectly well recognized in the case of personal property, for the obvious reasons stated by Lord Macclesfield in 1719 in the leading case of *Forth* v. *Chapman*, 1 P. Wms. 663.[1] With regard to *leaseholds* he said:

> 'If I devise a term to A, and if A die without leaving issue, remainder over, in the vulgar and natural sense, this must be intended if A die without leaving issue at his death, and then the devise over is good; that the word "die", being the last antecedent, the words "without leaving issue", must refer to that. Besides, the testator who is *inops consilii*, will, under such circumstances, be supposed to speak in the vulgar common and natural, not in the legal sense.'

It was unfortunate for the testator that in respect of *freeholds*, his words were not deemed to be 'vulgar common and natural'; for out of a solicitude for the issue of the first taker of the freehold, there grew up a number of precedents which held that the words 'die without issue' might mean 'if he die *and his issue fail at any time after his death*'. This is one of the most remarkable instances in our law of the misuse of language, and its effect was, in the majority of cases, unless a clear contrary intention

Tendencies in the Law, 82. On the history of the anomalous rule in *Lawes* v. *Bennett* (1785), 1 Cox 167, see 48 *L.Q.R.* 458.

[1] A great many of the cases are collected in the note to *Forth* v. *Chapman*, *ubi sup.*, in Tudor's *Leading Cases in Real Property*.

made this construction impossible, to give the first taker an estate tail and so to nullify the wishes of the testator. Precedent confirmed precedent to this effect, until s. 29 of the Wills Act, 1837, reversed the position and attached the natural meaning to the words unless it was excluded by a contrary intention.[1]

As a final example, I will take a rule which seems to be strangely at variance with the reasonableness underlying most Common Law principles of liability. Whence and by what means we acquired the doctrine *actio personalis moritur cum persona*, nobody has succeeded in discovering. We need not discuss the various theories of its origin, since none of them so far has progressed beyond the stage of speculation;[2] whatever that origin may be, the rule itself has little to commend it, even in its restricted sense as applied to the transmissibility of actions to and against executors. In the secondary meaning which had become attached to it, viz. that damages could not be recovered for the death of a human being, it reached an even higher degree of unreason. This interpretation of it did not follow logically from the main rule, even if the main rule could have been justified: and attention was often called to the absurdity in which it resulted, namely, that a plaintiff could recover damages for harm wilfully or negligently done to his servant, but not if the harm resulted in death. The principle seemed to be, the greater the damage, the less the compensation. The manner in which this anomaly rooted itself in our law is very curious. There is little doubt that after the time of Coke the maxim *actio personalis moritur cum persona*, whether or not it had existed before, or was invented by Coke, became commonly accepted.[3] It may be that the secondary meaning of the rule also gained currency: possibly we are dealing here with one of the not uncommon cases

[1] See *Jarman on Wills* (7th ed.), 1914 ff., 1932 f.

[2] See Goudy, 'Two Ancient Brocards', in *Essays in Legal History, 1913* (ed. Vinogradoff).

[3] Goudy, *loc. cit.* 226.

of a rule known to the profession long before it receives judicial formulation. But there is no positive evidence that any rule that damages could not be recovered for death was ever laid down in terms until the case of *Higgins* v. *Butcher* (1606), Noy 18.[1] Nor is it heard of again for more than two centuries, when Lord Ellenborough states it categorically in the well-known case of *Baker* v. *Bolton* (1808), 1 Camp. 493. This was a case at nisi prius, and Lord Ellenborough's judgement occupies only a few lines of print; and the whole report is meagre to a degree.[2] Never was an important principle of liability founded on such slender authority. The doctrine does not appear to have been raised again until 1873 in *Osborn* v. *Gillett*, L.R. 8 Ex. 88. It was vehemently attacked by Bramwell B., and it is not disrespectful to say that his reasoning carries far more conviction than that of the two other members of the Court, who upheld Lord Ellenborough's real or supposed principle on the unsatisfactory ground that there was no authority to the contrary. They were, however, also influenced by the fact that the doctrine had been indirectly recognized by Lord Campbell's Fatal Accidents Act. If the Court of Exchequer had taken a decided line in this case, the doctrine would probably have died there and then; but after a long interval, it again received express recognition from the Court of Appeal in *Clark* v. *London General Omnibus Co.*, [1906] 2 K.B. 648. The whole matter was reopened before the House of Lords in 1917 in *Admiralty Commissioners* v. *S.S. Amerika*, [1917] A.C. 38. The House refused to disturb a rule of such long, though insecure, standing. Their Lordships gave historical reasons for their decision, which, however, have been gravely doubted by eminent authority;[3] and the truth is that the law could thank nothing but a vicious antiquity

[1] It is not without significance that Noy misunderstood the maxim and erroneously attributed it to Bacon: Goudy, *loc. cit.* On the general nature of Noy's reports, see *ante*, p. 225. The case is also reported in Yelverton, 89.

[2] See Bramwell B., *Osborn* v. *Gillett*, *ubi sup.*, at p. 96.

[3] Holdsworth, *H.E.L.* iii, App. VIII.

for a rule which constituted a serious anomaly in our law of civil wrongs. It had perforce to be mitigated by a series of exceptions, introduced by the Fatal Accidents Act, 1846 (Lord Campbell's Act), the Workmen's Compensation Acts, and the Law Reform (Miscellaneous Provisions) Act, 1934. Even so, the law remains in a far from satisfactory condition[1] and now confronts the courts with problems in the assessment of damages which it seems almost impossible to place on a practicable basis, and which possibly were never contemplated by the legislature.[2]

Other examples of irrational doctrines, almost universally condemned, which have come into the law by a side-wind, but have defied all assaults upon them, are the doctrine of common employment—a groundless fiction apparently invented by Lord Abinger in *Priestley* v. *Fowler* (1837), 3 M. & W. 1, which robbed many a deserving plaintiff of his manifest rights until it was abolished by the Law Reform (Personal Injuries) Act, 1948;[3] and the artificial and barren learning which has grown up round the acknowledgement and revival of statute-barred debts.[4]

All these are examples of what Lord Denman once called[5] the *cantilena* of lawyers—a kind of incantation which becomes magical by mere repetition. The origin

[1] See Winfield, *Law of Tort* (6th ed.), 224 ff.

[2] *Flint* v. *Lovell*, [1935] 1 K.B. 354; *Rose* v. *Ford*, [1937] A.C. 826; *Roach* v. *Yates*, [1938] 1 K.B. 256; *Morgan* v. *Scoulding*, [1938] 1 K.B. 786; *Bailey* v. *Howard*, [1939] 1 K.B. 453; *Benham* v. *Gambling*, [1941] A.C. 157; *Bishop* v. *Cunard White Star Co., Ltd.*, [1950] P. 240.

[3] See Scrutton L.J. in *Fanton* v. *Denville*, [1932] 2 K.B. 309, 315; *Radcliffe* v. *Ribble Motor Services*, [1939] A.C. 215; and cf. Goodhart, 'Determining the *Ratio Decidendi*', *Essays in Jurisprudence*, at p. 2.

[4] See *Spencer* v. *Hemmerde*, [1922] 2 A.C. 507. On the history and present mischiefs of the 'order for ship's papers' in marine insurance, see *Leon* v. *Casey*, [1932] 2 K.B. 577, and especially the judgement of Greer L.J.

[5] In *O'Connell* v. *Reg.* (1844), 11 Cl. & F. 373 (cited by Max Radin, *loc. cit.*, at p. 144). Lord Denman said: 'When, in pursuit of truth, we are obliged to investigate the grounds of the law, it is plain . . . that the mere statement and re-statement of a doctrine—the mere repetition of the *cantilena* of lawyers, cannot make it law, unless it can be traced to some competent authority.'

of these eccentricities is sometimes obscure, and may go back to very distant and primitive sources: this, perhaps, is the explanation of the rule in *Baker* v. *Bolton;* of the curious Common Law rule that not only the burden but even the benefit of a contract could not be assigned; of the strange and irrational rule, established in 1799 by Lord Kenyon in *Merryweather* v. *Nixan*, 8 T.R. 186, that there could be no contribution between joint tort-feasors;[1] or, to take an example which was long since consigned to the 'cabinet of legal curiosities', the strange law of deodand in our earlier criminal law. These are survivals, and in the same class we may put the 'earnest', or Roman *arrha*, which is still a living, though unimportant and harmless, part of our law of sale. But sometimes legal aberration arises from more insidious causes and particularly from that perennial hood over the lamp of reason, the false premiss. For example, Lord Abinger's reasoning in *Priestley* v. *Fowler* was based on the assumption that a workman, when he accepts employment, also accepts ('impliedly', it was said) the risk of suffering injury at the hands of careless fellow-workmen. Granted the assumption, an imposing structure of logic will rapidly arise; but the assumption itself does not correspond with any reality, and nobody now supposes that it does, or ever did. The Workmen's Compensation Acts (now superseded by National Insurance) not merely rebutted the false premiss (though unfortunately still leaving it available in some cases), but imposed liability on the employer for accidents which were in no way due to his fault. The false premiss, and the misdirected ingenuity which flows from it, are endemic diseases in the law and, indeed, in any system of ratiocination. I have referred several times to the so-called doctrine of 'identification'. As a piece of logic, it will not bear a moment's analysis; and yet it is easy to guess the confusion of thought which gave rise to it. When two 'free agents' are concerned together in the same act or course of conduct—if, for

[1] See Goddard L.J. in *Ettenfield* v. *E.*, [1940] P. 96, 110.

example being both of responsible age, they link arms and recklessly cross a crowded street with traffic—it is eminently reasonable to say that they are both subject, in equal degree, to a defence of contributory negligence. The doctrine of identification, however, took account only of the fact that two persons were jointly concerned in the same physical conduct and paid no attention to the vital element of their relative *responsibility* for the action; and thus, by a transparent fallacy, it 'identified' the child with the negligence of the adult person who was guiding it, and the passenger with the negligence of the driver over whom the passenger had no control. This is an example of false reasoning due to laying the emphasis in the wrong place, or focusing attention only on one element of a situation; and that, too, is a danger which may sometimes engender unreasonable and obstinate doctrines in the law as it descends from case to case.

It is very easy, in the forest of precedents, not to see the wood for the trees. Tests of liability which may be useful in *some* circumstances become artificial and unsound when applied rigidly to *all* circumstances. For many years we saw a kind of suffocating fog spread round the subject of contributory negligence, until it became extremely difficult for a judge to direct a jury, upon what should be a comparatively simple issue, in any manner which was comprehensible to the average lay intelligence.[1] Most of this gratuitous intricacy resulted from the attempt to apply the so-called doctrine of 'last opportunity' as a universal and infallible test of responsibility for accident. No lawyer, nor indeed anybody who thought for a moment about the infinite variations of mishap and miscalculation in human affairs, really felt satisfied with this test: it broke down again and again, and indeed was either extended[2] or limited[3] out

[1] See *Swadling* v. *Cooper*, [1930] 1 K.B. 403 and [1931] A.C. 1.

[2] *British Columbia Electric Railway Co.* v. *Loach*, [1916] 1 A.C. 719; Greer L.J. in *The Eurymedon*, [1938] P. 41.

[3] *Admiralty Commissioners* v. *S.S. Volute*, [1922] 1 A.C. 129.

of all likeness to its original self: but it lived on and continued, in its more rigid manifestations, to embarrass a branch of the law which is of great and daily importance and which in essence ought not to be one of excessive complexity.[1] Lord Atkin, in *Donoghue* v. *Stevenson*, [1932] A.C. at p. 579, issued a timely reminder of the difference between the wood and the trees, when he said:

'The courts are concerned with the particular relations which come before them in actual litigation, and it is sufficient to say whether the duty exists in those circumstances. The result is that the courts have been engaged upon an elaborate classification of duties as they exist in respect of property, whether real or personal, with further distinctions as to ownership, occupation or control, and distinctions based on the particular relations of the one side to the other, whether manufacturer, salesman or landlord, customer, tenant, stranger and so on. In this way it can be ascertained at any time whether the law recognizes a duty, but only whether the case can be referred to some particular species which has been examined and classified. And yet the duty which is common to all the cases where liability is established must logically be based upon some element common to the cases where it is found to exist. . . . There must be, and is, some general conception of relations giving rise to duty of care, of which the particular cases found in the books are but instances.'[2]

Communis error sometimes creeps in not so much by positive doctrine or assertion as by mere assumption which is treated, and continues to be treated, as well founded only because it is not challenged. There are many principles of law which are regarded as so elementary that they need no demonstration by argument

[1] The law was altered, on much the same principles as for liability in Admiralty, by the Law Reform (Contributory Negligence) Act, 1945. On the decline and fall of the doctrine see Denning L.J. in *Davies* v. *Swan Motor Co., Ltd.*, [1949] 2 K.B. 291, and *Harvey* v. *Road Haulage Executive*, [1952] 1 K.B. 120.

[2] Contrast Lord Buckmaster at p. 567: 'Now the common law must be sought in law books by writers of authority and in judgements of the judges entrusted with its administration.' This is a perfect expression of the 'mechanical' view of precedent.

in court; but it sometimes happens that propositions which seem to be elementary, and thus grow into a *communis error*, are found, under criticism, to be disputable. Lord Denman, in *O'Connell* v. *Reg.* (1844), 11 Cl. & F. 155, which was a political *cause célèbre* of its day, observed (at p. 372):

> 'A large portion of that legal opinion which has passed current for law, falls within the description of "law taken for granted". If a statistical table of legal propositions should be drawn out, and the first column headed "Law by Statute" and the second "Law by Decision"; a third column, under the heading of "Law taken for granted", would comprise as much matter as both the others combined.'

These *assumptions* of the legal profession were doubtless more numerous in former times, when the field covered by printed precedent was smaller, than they are today; but they still exist, and must always be regarded with caution. Even when they cannot be shown to be actually erroneous, mere assumptions *sub silentio* are not to be taken as authoritative, but, at the best, as merely persuasive.[1] Error may also lurk in tacit and repeated assumptions of a negative kind—for example, that because a point has not been taken before, therefore it is not a point at all. We have seen (*ante*, p. 314) that it is not uncommon for a new situation to arise out of a statute many years after it has been passed. Thus it was not until two hundred and thirty years had passed that the point was first taken[2] that the levying of distress for poor rates was an 'execution' under s. 1 of the Landlord and Tenant Act, 1709. Not only had the question never arisen in any reported case, but it had been omitted from consideration by nearly all writers of textbooks. It was therefore argued that the point could not be valid, but the Court

[1] See Viner's *Abridgement*, Tit. *Precedents* (A) 2; *R.* v. *Warner* (1661), 1 Keb. 66; *R.* v. *Bewdley* (1712), 1 P. Wms. at p. 223. See further Cross, *Precedent in English Law*, 144, and Glanville Williams, *Salmond's Jurisprudence*, 11th ed., 212 f.

[2] *Hickman* v. *Potts*, [1940] 1 K.B. 29.

of Appeal rejected the contention. Delivering the judgement of the Court, Goddard L. J. said (at p. 45):

'Even if we assume that those whose business it is to levy distress for rates have long been of opinion that the Act does not apply, this affords no ground for perpetuating the error. "Communis error facit jus" is a maxim of very limited application; it is truer to say "Communis opinio is evidence of what the law is"—per Lord Ellenborough C.J. in *Isherwood* v. *Oldknow* (1815), 3 M. & S. 382, 396, but here there is no trace of a communis opinio among lawyers. And if there has been prevalent an erroneous view of the Act, it is clear that no one has acquired rights in consequence. . . . We are bound to decide the case according to what we believe to be the true view of the law.'[1]

It must not be supposed, however, that the absence of a relevant precedent is without significance. If a point of substance has, for a long period of time, never succeeded, it is not likely to do so when raised afresh. Thus in *Hargreaves* v. *Bretherton*, [1959] 1 Q.B. 45, the claim was for civil damages for perjured evidence. The fact that for some 300 years attempts to bring actions of this kind had repeatedly failed was one which was bound to weigh heavily with the Court (Lord Goddard C.J.).[2]

Over-ruling

These are but some of the ways—many others might be discussed—in which *communis error* creeps into a legal system based on the necessarily empirical method of case-law. If we ask to what extent *error* is deliberately permitted to create *jus*, and to what extent it is corrected and modified by those higher tribunals which alone have the power to exercise censorship, it is difficult to find a consistent answer. The proposition that error must be perpetuated merely because it is of long standing is extremely unsatisfying to the intelligence.

[1] Although the case was reversed (*Potts* v. *Hickman*, [1941] A.C. 212), the House of Lords did not dissent from these principles, but allowed the appeal on a different interpretation of the controverted section.

[2] See also the observations of Viscount Simonds L.C. in *Bromley* v. *Tryon*, [1952] A.C. 265, 275. And cf. *R.* v. *Chancellor of St. Edmundsbury, Ex p. White*, [1947] K.B. 263 and [1948] 1 K.B. 195.

The argument usually advanced in support of it—that it is better to let things alone, however muddled they may be, than to introduce uncertainty into rights of property or principles of liability—is also unconvincing in many circumstances; for when an established doctrine is reversed by a competent tribunal the position for the future does not differ from that which follows upon a statutory change of the law. It may not always be easy, but it is perfectly possible, for lawyers—and, indeed, it is a considerable part of their business—to adapt themselves to these changes as they occur. It is clear, therefore, that there must be some limits to the doctrine of *communis error*, for otherwise the law would never progress at all. In actual fact, the limits exist, but they are extremely ill defined. Superior tribunals, especially the House of Lords (which, of course, has greater opportunities than any other court), will sometimes boldly remove the ancient landmark, and at other times cautiously declare that it would be impious and dangerous to do so. It cannot be said that there is any consistent policy in the matter, or that anybody can tell which view will be taken when an established doctrine is attacked in the House of Lords or the Court of Appeal. In *Westminster Council* v. *Southern Railway Co.*, [1936] A.C. at p. 563, Lord Wright M.R. said:

'There is no rule which debars your Lordships from doing justice even at the cost of reversing an old authority, that is, an authority of a Court inferior to this House. In *West Kent Main Sewerage Board* v. *Assessment Committee of Dartford Union*, [1911] A.C. 171, 177, this House did depart from the old rule in regard to the rateability of underground sewers. . . . In *West Ham Union* v. *Edmonton Union*, [1908] A.C. 1, 4, Lord Loreburn admirably stated the general principle: "Great importance is to be attached to old authorities, on the strength of which many transactions may have been adjusted and rights determined. But where they are plainly wrong, and especially where the subsequent course of judicial decisions has disclosed weakness in the reasoning on which they were based, and practical injustice in the consequences that must flow from them, I consider it is the duty of this House to overrule them, if it has not lost the right to do so by itself expressly affirming them." '

And in *Robinson Bros.* v. *Houghton Assessment Committee*, [1937] 2 K.B. at p. 462, Greer L.J. said:

'It was argued by the respondents that it is too late for the Court to reverse the decision in the *Bradford* case [*Bradford-on-Avon Union* v. *White*, [1898] 2 Q.B. 630], because it was decided in the year 1898, and year after year assessments have been based on the assumption that the decision was right. *West Ham Union* v. *Edmonton Union*, [1908] A.C. 1, and *Hamilton* v. *Baker* (1889), 14 App. Cas. 209, are cases in which previous decisions were held to be plainly wrong and were overruled by the House of Lords after more years than have passed between the date of the decision in the *Bradford* case and the present date.'

The Lord Justice then cited the observations, which have been already quoted, of Lord Wright in *Westminster Council* v. *Southern Railway Co.*, and concluded that 'practical injustice must follow' unless the decision of 1898 were overruled. This reasoning was adopted, and the decision affirmed, by the House of Lords ([1938] A.C. 321).

Contrast with these *dicta* the expressions which have been mentioned *ante*, pp. 322 and 325, and the following *dictum* of Lord Sumner:

'If[a] maxim expresses a positive rule of law, once established, though long ago, time cannot abolish it nor disfavour make it obsolete. The decisions which refer to such a maxim are numerous and old, and although none of them is a decision of this House, if they are in agreement and if such is their effect, I apprehend they would not now be overruled, however little Reason might incline your Lordships to concur in them.'[1]

Again, in *Admiralty Commissioners* v. *S.S. Valverda*, [1938] A.C. 173, Lord Wright himself observed, at p. 194:

'I have given reasons for the view that the true construction of the clause [s. 557, sub-s. 1, of the Merchant Shipping Act,

[1] *Bowman* v. *Secular Society*, [1917] A.C. at p. 454. For numerous other expressions of the conservative view, see Lord Wrenbury, *Bourne* v. *Keane*, [1919] A.C. at pp. 922 ff.

1894] is to exclude all claims whatsoever for salvage by the Admiralty, but even if I were wrong in this it would, I think, be too late for this House to set aside the consistent and unbroken authority of the Admiralty Court and the Court of Appeal, and depart from the established rule and practice, even though the question has not been determined by this House. This House has no doubt power to overrule even a long-established course of decisions of the Courts, provided it has not itself determined the question. It is impossible to lay down precise rules according to which this power will be exercised. But in general this House will adopt this course only in plain cases where serious inconvenience or injustice would follow from perpetuating an erroneous construction or ruling of law.'

It is not easy to reconcile either these statements of principle or some of the decisions in which they appear. It has already been mentioned that in *Admiralty Commissioners* v. *S.S. Amerika*, [1917] A.C. 38, the House of Lords was invited to exorcize a doctrine which, though a century old, had lived a most precarious existence, under constant criticism. The House declined to take the opportunity. In 1884, in *Foakes* v. *Beer*, 9 App. Cas. 605, the House of Lords was pressed to dispose finally of the absurd rule that part-payment of a debt can never be a satisfaction of the whole debt. Lord Blackburn was of opinion that this whole anomalous law of accord and satisfaction had sprung from a mistake in Coke's report of *Pinnel's Case* (1602), 5 Rep. 117a,[1] made inveterate by *Cumber* v. *Wane* (1719), 1 Str. 426. This great authority on the Common Law concluded his speech with these words:

'What principally weighs with me in thinking that Lord Coke made a mistake of fact is my conviction that all men of

[1] See *ante*, p. 312. Although Coke's report does state the principle as it has since been received into the law, the actual decision in *Pinnel's Case* seems to have turned not on the substance of the claim, but on a point of pleading—viz. the defendant pleaded only that the plaintiff had accepted the part-payment and not that he had accepted it in full satisfaction: see Max Radin, 'The Trail of the Calf', *Cornell Law Quarterly*, Nov. 1946, 153.

business, whether merchants or tradesmen, do every day recognize and act on the ground that prompt payment of a part of their demand may be more beneficial to them than it would be to insist on their rights and enforce payment of the whole. Even where the debtor is perfectly solvent, and sure to pay at last, this often is so. I had persuaded myself that there was no such long-continued action on this dictum as to render it improper in this House to reconsider the question. I had written my reasons for so thinking; but as they were not satisfactory to the other noble and learned Lords who heard the case, I do not now repeat them nor persist in them.'

In this case, too, the House refused to disturb a rule of such long but lame standing,[1] and it is still the law today.[2] Four years after the passing of the Married Women's Property Act, 1882, the curt decision of a Divisional Court in *Seroka* v. *Kattenburg*, 17 Q.B.D. 177, placed upon s. 1, subsec. 2, of that Act a construction which it is very difficult to believe was ever the intention of the legislature, and which resulted in a perpetuation of the old rule that a husband was liable for his wife's torts.[3] It would have been difficult to find anybody who was prepared to defend this state of the law on grounds of either reason or expediency. It was, however, reaffirmed fourteen years later in *Earle* v. *Kingscote*, [1900] 2 Ch. 585. In 1924 the whole matter was reopened before the House of Lords,[4] which, however, declined (by a narrow majority) to disturb *Seroka* v. *Kattenburg*. This indefensible anomaly had to wait another eleven years to be suppressed by legislation.[5]

[1] Another leading case in this branch of the law, *Fitch* v. *Sutton* (1804), 5 East 230, was, on the admission of Lord Ellenborough, based on a misunderstanding of the facts: see *per* Lord Blackburn, *Foakes* v. *Beer*, *ubi sup.*, at p. 621.

[2] *Vanbergen* v. *St. Edmunds Properties, Ltd.*, [1933] 2 K.B. 223. The Sixth Interim Report of the Law Revision Committee recommended the abolition of the rule. In *Central London Property Trust, Ltd.* v. *High Trees House, Ltd.*, [1947] K.B. 130, Denning J. suggested that the current of authority since the fusion of law and equity had undermined *Foakes* v. *Beer*, *ubi sup.*, but this is unsettled: see Cheshire and Fifoot, 63 *L.Q.R.* 283.

[3] See *post*, p. 497.

[4] *Edwards* v. *Porter*, [1925] A.C. 1.

[5] Law Reform (Married Women and Tortfeasors) Act, 1935.

On the other hand, in *Bowman* v. *Secular Society*, [1917] A.C. 406, the House of Lords, in upholding a bequest to a company formed for the purpose of opposing Christian dogma, was prepared to overrule decisions going back for more than fifty years.[1] Still stronger was the line which the House took in *Bourne* v. *Keane*, [1919] A.C. 815, where it held that masses for the dead were not 'superstitious uses' under the Chantries Act, 1547. With the dissent of Lord Wrenbury, who vigorously reasserted the orthodox doctrine of *stare decisis*, the majority overruled a whole line of cases going back to Lord Cottenham's decision in 1835 in *West* v. *Shuttleworth*, 2 My. & K. 684—or even going back (as it is possible to argue) to the Chantries Act itself. Again, in *Woolmington* v. *Director of Public Prosecutions*, [1935] A.C. 462, the House was prepared to reverse an old-established principle concerning the onus of proof in homicide. It is true that this principle was not very well supported by decided cases, but it had been uniformly accepted since its enunciation by Sir Michael Foster in 1762, and had been repeated without question in every work of authority on criminal law since that date. In *Woolmington's Case* there was no question of disturbing expectations or rights of property, but rather of reinforcing the presumption of innocence; but this could not be said of *Bourne* v. *Keane*, for the rule there reversed had affected many dispositions and bequests for at least eighty-five years.

The fluctuations in this matter of overruling may be observed in the Court of Appeal as well as in the House of Lords; for example, in the Chancery reports for 1932 there will be found two cases, decided before a Court constituted of the same members, in one of which the Court refused to reverse a doctrine of which it heartily disapproved, dating from 1785, while in the other it unhesitatingly overruled a decision of Lord Romilly in

[1] *Briggs* v. *Hartley* (1850), 19 L.J. (Ch.) 416; *Cowan* v. *Milbourn* (1867), L.R. 2 Ex. 230.

1863.[1] In *Brownsea Haven Properties Ltd.* v. *Poole Corpn.*, [1958] Ch. 574, which mainly involved the interpretation of the *ejusdem generis* rule, the Court did not hesitate to reject five previous decisions, dating from 1914. In *St. Marylebone Property Co. Ltd.* v. *Fairweather*, [1962] 1 Q.B. 498,[2] it showed no greater tenderness towards a Divisional Court decision sixty years old (*Walter* v. *Yalden*, [1902] 2 K.B. 304). On the other hand, in *In re Neeld*, [1962] Ch. 643, being faced with much conflict of authority on the validity of the 'name and arms clause', it preferred to cling to old doctrine and precedents, dating from 1787, rather than bow to the unmistakable tendency of a number of comparatively recent decisions.

On the whole, it may be said that of late the superior courts have shown less compunction towards *communis error* and unfortunate decisions than they formerly displayed. In recent years the House of Lords has taken a strong line in several matters which were a serious embarrassment, not to say reproach, to the law. Thus in the *Fibrosa Case*[3] it expelled (with necessary qualifications) the so-called Rule in *Chandler* v. *Webster*, [1904] 1 K.B. 493,[4] which throughout its thirty-nine years of life had had few champions, and this salutary reform was promptly followed by the necessary supplement of the Law Reform (Frustrated Contracts) Act, 1943. In *Lissenden* v. *C.A.V. Bosch, Ltd.*, [1940] A.C. 412, the Lords had no hesitation in overruling the decision of the Court of Appeal in *Johnson* v. *Newton Fire Extinguisher Co.*, [1913] 2 K.B. 111, which had been frequently criticized and about which some very frank

[1] *In re Carrington*, [1932] 1 Ch. 1, and *Re Duncombe*, [1932] 1 Ch. 622: see further hereon 48 *L.Q.R.* 458. Cf. *Oakley* v. *Lyster*, [1931] 1 K.B. 148, and *R.* v. *Harding* (1929), 46 T.L.R. 105, cited Goodhart, 50 *L.Q.R.* at p. 54.

[2] Affirmed [1963] A.C. 510.

[3] *Fibrosa Spolka Akcyjna* v. *Fairbairn Lawson Combe Barbour, Ltd.*, [1943] A.C. 32.

[4] The rule that 'the loss lies where it falls' when money has been paid in advance, e.g. by way of deposit, on a contract which is subsequently frustrated by uncontrollable events.

things were said in the House;[1] thereafter the harsh and unjust rule no longer prevailed that because a workman had accepted an award by way of weekly payments, he was debarred from afterwards claiming that his total award under the Workmen's Compensation Act was inadequate. *Perrin* v. *Morgan*, [1943] A.C. 399, at last emancipated the law from the absurd rule that 'money' still meant only cash, as it had meant in the eighteenth century, according to *Shelmer's Case* (1725), Gilb. 200. *Hill* v. *William Hill (Park Lane) Ltd.*, [1949] A.C. 530, put an end to the ingenious method which bookmakers and others had found, with the assistance of *Hyams* v. *Stuart-King*, [1908] 2 K.B. 696, of enforcing gambling debts; and *National Anti-Vivisection Society* v. *Inland Revenue Commissioners*, [1948] A.C. 31, overruling *In re Foveaux*, [1895] 2 Ch. 501 (as the Court of Appeal had done by a majority), repudiated the long-held belief that anti-vivisection was a charitable purpose. Lord Wright observed (at p. 46): 'One of the most important aspects of the judicial functions of this House is to harmonize or correct the decisions of the lower courts, even though, as Lord Birkenhead L.C. said,[2] it would be "overruling decisions which have been treated as binding for generations".' While it is true that *In re Foveaux* was the decision of a single judge only, it is difficult to see how the attitude of the majority of the House of Lords and of the Court of Appeal can be reconciled with the doctrine that long-standing decisions will not be rejected if they have affected rights and expectations, for the opponents of vivisection had had every reason to suppose for over half a century that their funds were exempt from income tax. In *Galloway* v. *G.*, [1956] A.C. 299, the House of Lords held, contrary to the generally accepted view and to several express decisions of lower courts, that the word 'children', as employed in various clauses of the Matrimonial Causes Acts, 1857–1950, included

[1] See, e.g., Lord Atkin at p. 424.

[2] In *Bourne* v. *Keane*, [1919] A.C. 815, 830.

illegitimate children. This construction is of great and (as some think) of revolutionary importance to the custody of infants. But perhaps the most interesting and most controversial recent example of overruling in the House of Lords is *Ross Smith* v. *R.S.*, [1963] A.C. 280. The question, briefly, was this: when a marriage has been solemnized in England but one of the spouses is domiciled and resident abroad, has the English court jurisdiction to pronounce a decree of nullity, and if so, can it do so with regard only to a marriage void *ab initio* or also to one voidable by subsequent cause (such as incapacity or wilful refusal to consummate)? There had been much conflict of judicial opinion, and the answer to the problem depended largely on the authority of *Simonin* v. *Mallac*, [1860], 2 Sw. & Tr. 67. That case, a century old, was overruled, but in a somewhat curious and inconclusive manner. Three peers were for banishing it outright, two for limiting its operation to void marriages, and one dissented. In the result it was held that an English court had no jurisdiction to entertain the suit (since the marriage was alleged to be voidable only), but a question may remain—though improbably—whether jurisdiction would be valid, on the authority of *Simonin* v. *Mallac*, if the marriage were alleged to be void. It is to be observed that *Simonin* v. *Mallac* had been followed for a century in many cases, but, as Lord Reid observed (at p. 399):

> 'It would have been a compelling reason against overruling that decision if it could reasonably be supposed that anyone has regulated his affairs in reliance on its validity, but it would be fantastic to suppose that anyone has married, or indeed entered into any kind of transaction, on the faith of being able to obtain a decree of nullity in a particular jurisdiction. And no decree of nullity already pronounced could be affected.'

While the House of Lords in these cases seems to have had no doubt of its duty, in *Wolstanton, Ltd.* v. *Newcastle-under-Lyme Corporation*, [1940] A.C. 860, it declined to overrule *Hilton* v. *Lord Granville* (1845),

5 Q.B. 701, which is discussed *post*, p. 624. Though this latter decision has been constantly under fire, there is still room for two opinions about it, and the case for overruling it was by no means as clear as in the other decisions which have been cited.

A similar disposition to overrule when necessary has been observable in the Privy Council. A conspicuous recent example is *Hughes and Vale Proprietary Ltd.* v. *State of New South Wales*, [1955] A.C. 241 (followed in *Commissioner for Motor Transport* v. *Antill Ranger & Co. Proprietary Ltd.*, [1956] A.C. 527), in which, after much conflict of opinion, a number of decisions, dating back to 1933, of the High Court of Australia were overruled.[1] And in *Overseas Tankship (U.K.) Ltd.* v. *Morts Dock & Engineering Co. Ltd. (The Wagon Mound)*, [1961] A.C. 388, the Judicial Committee has been responsible for what is perhaps the most dramatic (some would say revolutionary) reversal of a legal principle in modern times. Whether, when negligence is alleged, liability depends on the 'foreseeability' of the damage actually caused has been hotly controverted for many years past, and is indeed a fundamental problem of the law of tort. It is well known that *In re Polemis and Furness Withy & Co.* (known with either affection or aversion as *Polemis*), [1921] 3 K.B. 560, appeared to reject the 'foreseeability' test, but this has now been reversed by the *Wagon Mound*, and the law of negligence takes on a new aspect. It has already been considered (*ante*, p. 250) whether this decision, though not binding, is likely to be followed in English courts.

In the Divisional Court of the Queen's Bench, and in the Court of Criminal Appeal, there has also been evident a disposition to chafe at the shackles of precedent. The latter has shown a certain resolution in attempting to cut Gordian knots—see, for example, *R.* v. *Hudson*, [1943] K.B. 458, though it is to be feared that in the branch of the law with which that case was concerned

[1] See also *Dun* v. *D.*, [1959] A.C. 272.

(larceny and *animus furandi*) loose ends will remain, however many knots are slashed. The Court of Appeal has also shown some justifiable impatience with decisions, old and new, which seemed to have little to commend them; thus in *Minister of Supply* v. *British Thomson-Houston Co.*, [1943] K.B. 478, it would have none of the startling rule, laid down by several judges of first instance, and in particular by Farwell J. in *Gilleghan* v. *Minister of Health*, [1932] 1 Ch. 86, that when a statute empowers a Minister to 'sue and be sued', he cannot be sued, not even by way of counterclaim, except with his own consent.[1] On the other hand, in *Adair* v. *Birnbaum*, [1938] 4 All E.R. 775, it held itself bound to follow a precedent which led to 'extraordinary results', and in *Sorrel* v. *Paget*, [1950] 1 K.B. 252, we find the same Court upholding a rule, laid down in 1845, which, in the opinion of at least one member of the Court,[2] might well be considered harsh and unreasonable in modern conditions.

In Chancery matters a more conservative spirit is still maintained (see Excursus D, *post*, p. 380). A striking example of this tendency is *Perrin* v. *Morgan*, *ubi sup.*, from which it appears that if Chancery judges had applied not merely a more liberal, but more correct, principle to the interpretation of wills, they would never have affixed for so long an obviously inappropriate meaning to the word 'money'. When a superior court is composed partly of Common Law and partly of Chancery members, it is generally to be observed that judges who have been trained in the principles and practice of Equity are disposed to show a greater deference to the ancient landmark (however much it may disfigure the landscape) than their more irreverent brethren of the Common Law.[3]

[1] For other examples of unceremonious overruling by the Court of Appeal, see *Bell Property Trust* v. *Hampstead Assessment Committee*, [1940] 2 K.B. 543, and *The Cheldale*, [1945] P. 10.

[2] See Asquith L.J. at p. 266.

[3] But see, *contra*, *In re Lambton's Marriage Settlement*, [1952] Ch. 752, in which the Court of Appeal unhesitatingly overruled *Att.-Gen.* v. *Glossop*, [1907] 1 K.B. 163.

From these contrasted examples, is it possible to extract any general principles which will tell us, with some measure of probability, when a superior court will rid the law of what are generally agreed to be errors or blemishes? It seems impossible to predicate anything very definite, and much appears to depend on the constitution of the court which is faced with the problem. What Sir Frederick Pollock called 'judicial valour' is ever an uncertain quantity; some judges will always 'play safe' and some will be astute to mitigate the *rigor juris* in accordance with common sense, justice, and social requirements. The former earn the respectable reputation which always accompanies orthodoxy; the latter run the risk of being considered 'unsound', and sometimes undoubtedly they allow good intentions to outrun prudence and they then have to be called to order. Both represent necessary aspects of the judicial office; but our legal history shows that all our greatest judges have been those of the more adventurous type, whatever errors they may have committed and however much criticism they may have incurred. Those who have insisted merely on standing *super antiquas vias* have usually stood nowhere at all, and have been soon forgotten.

Attempts at generalizations in this matter have not been very successful. *Dicta* sometimes suggest[1] that mere antiquity or inveteracy should never be a protection for bad law; but we have seen that unfortunately this is by no means always true. Some of the *dicta*, indeed, seem to state such contrary principles that it is difficult to reconcile them.[2] Perhaps the nearest attempt at a rubric is to be found in the speech of Lord Buckmaster in *Bourne* v. *Keane*, [1919] A.C. at p. 874:

'Firstly, the construction of a statute of doubtful meaning, once laid down and accepted for a long period of time, ought not

[1] See, e.g., Viscount Simon in *The Fibrosa Case, ubi sup.*, at p. 44.

[2] e.g. contrast Lord Wright in *Westminster Council* v. *Southern Railway Co.*, [1936] A.C. 511 (*ante*, p. 335), and in *Admiralty Commissioners* v. *S.S. Valverda*, [1938] A.C. 173, 193.

to be altered unless your Lordships could say positively that it was wrong and productive of inconvenience. Secondly, decisions upon which title to property depends or which by establishing principles of construction or otherwise form the basis of contracts, ought to receive the same protection. Thirdly, decisions that affect the general conduct of affairs, so that their alteration would mean that taxes had been unlawfully imposted, or exemption unlawfully obtained, payments needlessly made, or the position of the public materially affected, ought in the same way to continue.'

It must be confessed, however, that to every one of the principles thus formulated exceptions so conspicuous can be found that they seem to leave little basis for the tentative rule. The plain truth is that in this important matter our judicial technique does not seem to have developed any consistent principle; *quot judices tot sententiae*. On the other hand, the balance of evidence seems to show that there is now a somewhat more liberal tendency in superior courts towards correcting and harmonizing the law than was apparent in the nineteenth century.

'Certainty' in law

Thus there exist in our law today two differing theories of the censorship or control which superior courts can exercise over precedent, in order to preserve a balance between organic development and stunted growth. The competition of these two influences has led to no little discussion of the relative merits of 'certainty' and 'flexibility' in our Common Law.[1] This, however, is to approach the subject from the wrong angle, for the argument rests upon a false antithesis. 'Certainty' and 'flexibility' are not natural opposites, either in logic or in language. The true antithesis is between certainty and uncertainty, or between rigidity and flexibility. Which, if any, of these terms is aptly descriptive of our case-law?

[1] See Holdsworth, *H.E.L.* xii. 159 ff., and Goodhart, 'Precedent in English and Continental Law', 50 *L.Q.R.* 40. On the whole subject of 'certainty', see Max Radin, 'The Trail of the Calf', *loc. cit.*, Paton, *Jurisprudence* (2nd ed.), 169 ff., and H. W. R. Wade, 'The Concept of Legal Certainty', 4 *M.L.R.* 183; and *ante*, pp. 42 ff.

Startling though the proposition may sound, every law is rigid. A rule is a rule, and it ceases to be so if it is flexible, just as a manufactured foot-rule would cease to be a measure of distance if it could be bent at the pleasure of the user. A law which can be bent at discretion in order to make exceptions from its generality is not a law at all, but an arbitrary exercise of will. It is for this reason that, as we shall see, many systems of law have had recourse to a separate body of equitable or discretionary jurisdiction in order to make exceptions to the uniform operation of law. Equity in this wide and unrestricted sense is called equity for the very reason that it is *not law;* but, as we shall also see, with the passage of time this 'free', indefinite sense of equity disappears and in its place there grows up a code of rules just as 'inflexible' as those of law, so that in the result there are two complementary bodies of rules working together to mutual advantage. At that stage neither the one nor the other is 'flexible'. But (it may be said) there are exceptions to most rules of law. True, but they are exceptions to the rule which the rule itself allows and specifies. They cannot be exceptions made merely at the will of the judge, because then they are not exceptions, but simply violations of the rule. Then what of judicial discretion? This forms a considerable part of every system of law; in particular, it is a very important element of criminal law, since the great majority of punishments are at the discretion of the court. But discretion is itself governed by rule, because it cannot exist unless it is permitted, expressly or implicitly, by a rule of law; and there are further rules of law which control its exercise, the principal of them being that discretion must be used after proper consideration of evidence and with reference to the relevant considerations—in short, not at will or at whim, but 'in a judicial manner'; and there is a mass of law concerned with determining what is and what is not a 'judicial manner'. Again, discretion is seldom completely at large; usually, it can be exercised only within certain prescribed limits. Thus, to take again the illustration of punishment, the upper limit of the penalty which can be inflicted is usually prescribed by law—or at least this is true of the very numerous crimes which nowadays are governed by statute.[1]

Every law, then, is rigid; but no law is certain. The only laws which are certain and invariable in their operation are those which we call, by analogy only and, as Austin said, 'improperly', the 'laws' of nature. By this term we mean no more than that, so far as scientific observation can determine, certain natural forces operate in a uniform and invariable manner. All such generalizations are tentative only, and no reputable scientist would claim for them eternal verity. Increasing knowledge may cause them to be modified or even reversed; in one age it is a law of nature that the sun moves round the earth, and in another that the earth moves round the sun. Nevertheless, there is in the operation of natural forces, so far as we can observe them with our limited means, a degree of certainty which cannot be attributed to human laws. Setting aside the controversial question whether they can be 'suspended' by miracles (and even so, they are none the less laws because they are suspended), the laws of nature cannot admit of any exceptions. If Sir Isaac Newton had watched not one, but a thousand or a million apples, he could not have found one which, when it broke from the tree, did not fall to the ground. It is inconceivable that the earth should not rotate or that the sun should shine in the tropics at night. No such certitude, even of a tentative kind, can ever be attached to a man-made law; and the reasons are very plain. Every law, or rule, is an attempt at a comprehensive generalization; and it has to be expressed in words, written or spoken. In both aspects it is doomed

[1] There is no fixed limit of imprisonment for misdemeanours at Common Law, but excessive and cruel punishments are forbidden by Magna Carta and the Bill of Rights, and in any case are subject to appeal as an improper use of judicial discretion: *R.* v. *Morris*, [1951] 1 K.B. 394; *R.* v. *Higgins*, [1952] 1 K.B. 7; *R.* v. *Pearce*, [1953] 1 Q.B. 30.

from birth to be imperfect. No generalization is ever completely comprehensive, because it is beyond the wit of man to foresee all the permutations and combinations of circumstances to which it may have to be applied; and this is particularly true of law, which is concerned not with abstractions for their own sakes, but with human relationships. As for words, hard things have been said about them—not least by those who themselves have been the greatest masters of them. Shakespeare, through the mouth of Hamlet, compared them to a 'windy suspiration of forced breath'. Voltaire said that they were given to us in order to conceal our thoughts. Perhaps Tennyson came nearer to the truth when he said that words

> like Nature, half reveal
> And half conceal the Soul within.

But we need not appeal to poets or philosophers; common experience tells us that it is impossible to devise any combination of words, especially in the form (which all laws must take) of a wide generalization, which is absolutely proof against doubt and ambiguity. So long as men can express their thoughts only by the highly imperfect instrument of words, an automatic, irrefragable certainty in the prescribed rules of social conduct is not to be attained. 'Certainty', said Mr. Justice Holmes long ago,[1] 'generally is illusion and repose is not the destiny of man.'

This does not mean, of course, that all laws are unintelligible or completely erratic and unpredictable in their operation. The 'uncertainty' of law can be greatly exaggerated. In actual practice, in the common daily dealings of men, the simpler rules of law which regulate their conduct towards each other are plain enough and certain enough for all ordinary purposes. It may well be that the law is never absolutely indubitable or beyond the ingenuity of subtle argument; it is true, as we

[1] 'The Path of the Law' (1897), 10 *H.L.R.* 457, 466, cited Stone, *op. cit.* 376.

have seen (*ante*, p. 47), that propositions of law which have been accepted as self-evident sometimes turn out to be vulnerable; but over much the greater part of human behaviour, the law governing a given situation is at least sufficiently clear to warn any wise person against the risk of a 'hopeless case'. For this reason the vast majority of differences and disputes between men never come to litigation at all, and those which do come to *litis contestatio* are those 'marginal' cases, which, because of the inevitable imperfections which have been mentioned, raise at least an arguable doubt. Because the cases in our books are usually only those which concern such debatable points, they are apt to give the impression that law is far more variable in its meaning and operation than it actually is in daily life.

We cannot, then, look for more 'certainty' in case-law than is afforded by as much consistency as judges, faced with problems and circumstances of kaleidoscopic variety, can reasonably achieve; and lest, expecting too much, we suffer disappointment, we should be warned that this degree of certainty is limited and inconstant. It cannot be otherwise when, as we have seen, the whole system of precedent must inevitably operate through the fluctuating, subjective medium of *interpretation*. It is necessary to enter this caveat because the claims made for the 'certainty' of precedent are sometimes extravagant and therefore misleading to students.[1] On the other hand, it is equally fallacious to conclude that, because precedent does not possess all the certainty which its more hyperbolical admirers claim for it, there is no such thing as judicial consistency, and that cases are decided solely by the 'hunches', prejudices, idiosyncrasies, or sophistries of individual judges.[2] The judge who administers law by means of 'hunches' (as some, like the

[1] See Holdsworth, *H.E.L.* xii. 159 ff., and *contra* Goodhart, 'Precedent in English and Continental Law', 50 *L.Q.R.* at p. 58.

[2] See *ante*, p. 47, and cf. Scrutton L.J. in *Hill* v. *Aldershot Corporation*, [1933] 1 K.B. 259, whereon see 51 *L.Q.R.* 338.

notorious Serjeant Arabin, doubtless have done) is certain to be a very bad judge. It is sometimes said that a good judge arrives at his decision first, and finds the reasons afterwards. This only means that a judge who is steeped in the law can often discern the principle which governs the situation before he can cite the exact authorities which support it; and, indeed, this is an experience common not only to judges but to all well-trained lawyers. But this is not to say that the judge is dependent on 'hunch', in the sense of inspiration or supra-rational intuition; his mind is working in accordance with long training and experience, and there is nothing at all remarkable in the fact that he can see the picture before he has filled in all the details.

I repeat that no law, and no source of law, is certain. It is impossible to exclude a large degree of variation and even of conflict. Statute aims at being a final, accurate, 'watertight' formulation of law. As we shall see—and, indeed, this is a matter of the commonest knowledge—no statute has ever yet succeeded in being watertight, and some statutes (in England, at all events) are so full of holes that they can be kept afloat only by a most exhausting process of baling and pumping. Not even the highly scientific codes of Continental countries have proved flawless: the Code Napoléon itself has sprung its leaks: and Justinian's ambition to say the last and infallible word in codified law proved to be a vain hope. In this matter of 'certainty', then, case-law is no better and no worse off than any other source of law; but we shall merely darken counsel if we claim for it a degree of certitude or predictability which, in its very nature, it cannot possess.

There is a manifest inconsistency in claiming for case-law, with one breath, a large measure of certainty, and, with the next breath, a large measure of flexibility.[1]

[1] See, for example, Holdsworth, *loc. cit.* For some examples of 'flexibility', see 51 *L.Q.R.* 337.

It is claimed[1] that, by virtue of its flexibility, the Common Law has kept abreast of the needs of society, and that when it has been prevented from doing so by the restrictions of precedent, legislation has been easily able to remedy its defects. It is true that the Common Law, and especially the law of torts, has adapted itself progressively and that it has passed through enormous transformations in the course of centuries. To say this, however, is not to pay it any very high compliment, for, obviously, the utmost conservatism of which the law was capable could not wholly put the clock back and keep modern England in thrall to medievalism. Any system of law which is not merely barbarous or superstitious *must*, in some measure, progress—or perish. It is true, therefore, that the Common Law, through the medium of precedents, has profoundly changed in many departments; but it is also true that again and again the process of adaptation has been painfully slow and visibly reluctant. Under a system of *stare decisis*, in which a court frequently has to say, 'Whatever the anachronism or inconvenience, we must abide by the established rule', it is extremely difficult for changing social needs to be met promptly and systematically; and this is not because (as is frequently suggested) judges are naturally and incorrigibly obscurantist, but because the system with which they have to work compels them to be 'behind the times', though they may be, and frequently are, as anxious and as well-qualified as their voluble critics to look ahead of the times. This 'time-lag' of the law, in relation to changing social circumstances, is notorious—perhaps too notorious, for it is often the object of ill-founded criticism. Nevertheless, it is a real and serious factor in the system of case-law, and it is inevitably antagonistic to 'flexibility'.

Nor is it adequately compensated by the corrective influence of legislation. If the self-imposed adaptations of the Common Law are slow, the reforms of legislation

[1] Holdsworth, *loc. cit.*

are even slower. Again and again the most obvious and urgent corrections of the law have to wait for many years before they can be achieved, or before they can even claim interest and attention; and this is more than ever true today, when the press of 'social' legislation is such, and the time of Parliament is so crowded, that mere 'lawyers' law' has little appeal for the legislator.[1] The nineteenth century was an age of extraordinary legislative activity and reform, and yet most of its reforms were not only long overdue but were bitterly resisted by a section of opinion which regarded (and always regards) any change in the law as the prelude to social disruption. Maine has suggested[2] that the legal status of women is a fair general test of the 'progressiveness' of societies. It is not too much to say that until the late nineteenth century the proprietary rights of married women in England, and in some respects their whole status, were less enlightened than those of a Roman matron in the time of Cicero. Equity had done what it could to protect the property of a limited class of 'well-off' women, but the rank and file of English wives remained under Common Law rules worthy only of an Oriental community.[3] Yet no radical legislative change was made until 1882, and even then it was accompanied by the most melancholy prophecies of disaster. 'At a time', said Greer L.J. in *Leon* v. *Casey*, [1932] 2 K.B. at p. 488, 'when the criminal law of this country was in a state to disgrace a half-civilized country, judges of high authority and writers of textbooks had been brought up to regard it as the "perfection of reason".' They ceased so to regard it during the nineteenth century, and set to work vigorously, if unsystematically, to reform it. But even now the process has not gone far enough. The ferocities and absurdities of the old criminal law have gone one by one, and in substance it is thoroughly cleansed; but in form it remains a sprawling and

[1] *Ante*, p. 311.

[2] *Ancient Law*, ch. v.

[3] See Dicey, *Law and Opinion in England*.

unwieldy mass, and it still contains a number of anachronisms and anomalies—such as the now valueless and inconvenient distinction between felonies and misdemeanours—which hardly a lawyer in the land would be prepared to defend. For more than half a century eminent authorities and experts have urged, and have even prepared, its codification, for which the time and the material have long been ripe. There is no real reason, except inertia, why this task, heavy though it is, should not be undertaken. Despite the constant excuses about the overtaxed time of Parliament, it has been shown again and again that when somebody in a position of influence really makes up his mind to carry a reform of the law through Parliament, the thing can be done, and often done much more easily and quickly than was supposed—witness the Law of Property Acts, 1925, the Criminal Appeal Act, 1907, the Matrimonial Causes Act, 1937, the Law Reform (Miscellaneous Provisions) Act, 1934, and the Crown Proceedings Act, 1947. It is not time or opportuntiy, but initiative, which is lacking in these humdrum matters of legal reform; and so long as interest and initiative continue to be wanting, the 'time-lag' will be a clot in the arteries of case-law.

Our system of precedents, then, is full of imperfections, and no good purpose is served by pretending that they are perfections. Voltaire's Dr. Pangloss is a type as well known in law as in philosophy, and on the whole he has done infinitely more harm than good. But when we have candidly acknowledged the defects, we have then to ask whether they are too heavy a price to pay for the merits which our Common Law, built upon precedents, has so well established that they have unquestionably commanded the respect of the whole world. I think the answer must be that the gods sell all things at a price, and that the price in this case, though high, is not too high. Legal systems cover the whole range of private and public life, and in so vast an area they cannot be expected to work without inconveniences or even injustices. When all has been said in criticism of our case-law, it remains true, as I believe, that the amount of error, injustice, and perverse doctrine which have resulted from adherence to precedent is a small proportion of an enormous legal system; and it is also true that the records of our law form one of the world's great monuments not only of legal science but of human intelligence—a monument none the less imposing because it has been slowly and sometimes painfully built up stone by stone with sweat of the brow and strife of the spirit. Nor must we 'regard history as a blank page', as it was said that Jeremy Bentham was willing to do in his reforming zeal. Were there a thousand reasons of cold logic and utility for rejecting the principle of strict judicial consistency (has not that quality been scornfully described as 'the hobgoblin of little minds'?), it would be madness to ignore the fact that precedent is the evolutionary principle on which the Common Law has grown; and laws of growth are laws of life, which cannot be suddenly arrested or eliminated without committing murder. English law, therefore, is never likely to abandon the working principle of *stare decisis*, but because it adheres to it, it need not enter into abject bondage to it. Freedom can coexist with discipline, and may even be strengthened by it; and progressive adaptation is not inconsistent with caution and deliberation. The 'liberal spirit' which has been shown by all our greatest judges, and is, indeed, the quality above all others which has made them great, is the strongest safeguard against the 'time-lag'. With this sentinel at the gate, corrective and vigilant legislation should stand side by side. Nor need it be impulsive or premature. If the choice should be necessary—though I see no reason why it should—between tardy and hasty legislation, Englishmen would probably continue to prefer the more leisurely kind; for nothing that has happened in recent years in countries where law is made overnight by decree and proclamation and ordinance has disposed them to covet mass-produced law. But legislation may and should maintain a steady if measured stride, without running or stumbling, and, at such a gait, it may help the pace of the Common Law when it tends to falter or, as the phrase is, to 'stick in the mud'.

The theory of precedents in transition

So safeguarded and so assisted, our case-law can still be in the future, as it has been in the past, a strength rather than a weakness of our jurisprudence. I believe it to be, with all its defects, a great and successful legal instrument, not because it is either certain or flexible, and assuredly not because there is any sacramental magic in mere precedent as opposed to principles of reason and justice; but because for England at least there seems to be no better way of applying legal principles to infinitely variable facts, and because our reports constitute an incomparable treasury of legal reasoning, exposition, analogy, and learning, which provide a better basis for dialectic and adjudication than more abstract, even if more scientific, formulations of law. At the same time, there is a growing consciousness in the present age of the imperfections of the system and a strengthening desire to correct them; and, as a result, it seems that the whole system of case-law is now passing through a critical stage in its history. No English lawyer is likely to advocate the abandonment of the general principle of *stare decisis* in favour of 'free law-finding'; to do so would be to revolutionize, and possibly to arrest, the whole development of our Common Law. Nevertheless, there are many evidences of a certain restiveness when the discipline of precedent becomes a mere tyranny and 'loyalty' degenerates into perpetuating blindly what a court believes to be bad or outworn law. The difficulties inherent in the system are certain to grow *pari passu* with the continuous accumulation of recorded cases. It is obvious that the task of finding a way through a labyrinth of decisions is infinitely greater today than it was two hundred or a hundred years ago, and even if ancient authorities are cited less and less frequently until they fall virtually into oblivion, still as the years go on the mass of authority will become more formidable. Those 'fogs' and 'tangles' of precedent of which we have seen examples are not likely to diminish, and the attempt to take a short cut through them is always attended by the risk of overlooking authorities which are really important. For the avoidance of this peril the court, which cannot be omniscient, is largely dependent on the skill and care of counsel—and all counsel are not equally skilled and careful.

There are many indications that a compromise is being gradually worked out between a slavish subjection to precedent on the one hand and a capricious disregard of consistency on the other hand. There seems to be less reluctance than formerly in superior courts either to overrule previous, and sometimes old, precedents, or else to sterilize them by the semi-fictions of 'distinguishing' them on tenuous grounds of fact or law by recourse to the doctrine of *incuria*. With the help of a certain degree of 'judicial valour', new opportunities seem to be opening up of escaping from bondage which carries 'consistency' or 'loyalty' to unprofitable extremes —as when it is held that a court which is concerned with life and liberty must give greater consideration to them than to mere formal authority,[1] especially when an accused person has not been professionally represented or his case has not been fully argued,[2] or when a superior court will *mero motu* both grant and allow an appeal on a point of law which a convicted person himself has not raised,[3] or when a judge of first instance is prepared to hold that in the light of new scientific knowledge 'binding' precedents have lost their force,[4] or when a judge of first instance is able to renounce a long-standing decision of the Exchequer Division, in view of a more recent decision of the House of Lords.[5] The *Wagon*

[1] *Gideon Nkambule* v. *R.*, [1950] A.C. 379 (*ante*, p. 251); *R.* v. *Taylor*, [1950] 2 K.B. 368 (*ante*, p. 240f).

[2] *Nicholas* v. *Penny*, [1950] 2 K.B. 466 (*ante*, p. 247).

[3] *R.* v. *Taylor*, *ubi sup.*

[4] *M.-T.* v. *M.-T.*, [1949] P. 331 (*ante*, p. 300).

[5] *Colman* v. *Croft*, [1947] K.B. 95 (*ante*, p. 321).

Mound, which has been discussed *ante*, p. 343, is particularly significant as indicating a readiness, at least in the Privy Council, to reconsider fundamental principles which might well have been thought to be rooted in our law beyond hope of deracination.[1] The rules in *Young* v. *Bristol Aeroplane Co.*, [1944] K.B. 718, though not free from ambiguity, have been so interpreted that they have undoubtedly opened doors, and may yet open others, which for long were shut or, at most, only ajar.

There still remains the rule, however, that the two most authoritative courts in our hierarchy—the House of Lords and the Court of Appeal—are bound by their own previous decisions, and up to the present time the House of Lords has allowed itself no such exceptions as the Court of Appeal has rubricated in *Young* v. *Bristol Aeroplane Co.* There can be no doubt that apparently conflicting opinions, and especially *dicta*, in the House of Lords, present courts below it with puzzling problems of interpretation, the more so because in a House generally consisting of at least five members, with ampler argument and more time for consideration than are usual in lower courts, there is almost an embarrassment of riches in the opinions expressed. Some are of opinion[2] that the ultimate tribunal should be free, in clear cases, frankly to dissent from its own previous decisions. This is the practice in the Supreme Court of the United States, and authorities like Professor A. L. Goodhart, who have the advantage of knowing both English and American law, hold the view that the system has not led to the inconveniences which most English lawyers would expect in it. That opinion, however, is not universal among American lawyers, and from time to time we hear complaints that conflicting decisions of the Supreme

[1] If it may be suggested without blasphemy, the decision gains in clarity and authority by being a single collective pronouncement instead of a mosaic of five separate speeches.

[2] See Paton, *Jurisprudence* (2nd ed.), 162 ff.; Lord Wright in *University of Toronto Law Journal*, 1942, 275–7; A. L. Goodhart, 'Precedents in the Court of Appeal', *Cambridge Law Journal*, 1947, 349.

Court have left the law in a state of bewildering uncertainty.[1] The present writer has not sufficient acquaintance with American law to express an opinion upon this question, but he thinks it unlikely that the majority of English lawyers would look with favour on a similar freedom in the House of Lords. There is still enough faith, right or wrong, in the 'certainty' of case-law to offer formidable, and probably insuperable, objection to so novel a doctrine. For the present, then, the advocates of a more liberal theory of precedent must repose their hopes in what seems to be the prevailing disposition of the House of Lords to overrule the decisions of lower courts when necessary, and for the rest to apply to its own decisions, when occasion so demands, that process of 'distinguishing' which, however unsatisfying it may be to perfect logic, often (though not always) succeeds, in the long run, in purging the Common Law of its more glaring anomalies. It is not impossible, however, that some day our highest tribunal may find for itself a counterpart to *Young* v. *Bristol Aeroplane Co.*; but that, for the present, must remain matter of conjecture—startling to the orthodox and hopeful to the latitudinarians.[2]

[1] See, for example, T. R. Powell, 'The Judiciality of Minimum-Wage Legislation', 37 *H.L.R.* 545.

[2] In 'The Court of Appeal in England', Lord Evershed M.R. seems to be of opinion that a self-corrective power already exists in the House of Lords. He observes (at p. 17): 'In the House of Lords, the principle of *stare decisis* has no such rigid application—as Lord Watson observed in the famous *Nordenfelt* case' [*Nordenfelt* v. *Maxim-Nordenfelt Co.*, [1894] A.C. 535, 553] 'the House can, and on occasions must, modify its previous pronouncements when they cease to conform to the social philosophy of the day. So long as such revising discretion remains in the highest tribunal in the land there is wisdom in the practice that cobblers in less exalted places should stick to their lasts and should leave to the supreme tribunal the task of making such modifications as the times may require to previously established rulings.' With respect, it is submitted that Lord Watson's observations are not an authority for the wide discretion here claimed. It is well settled that public policy is 'the policy of the day' and may alter from time to time; but the same general relativity is not acknowledged—explicitly, at all events—in other branches of the law; and, indeed, Lord Watson himself (at p. 553) draws a distinction between questions of public policy and 'principles which are purely legal'.

SUMMARY

To review our conclusions concerning precedent as a source of law: The process of judicial decision may be regarded as either deductive or inductive. In one view, the function of the magistrate is to deduce from a formulated general rule of law the principle applicable to the case before him. In the other view, the magistrate is called upon to reason from particular cases to a general principle appropriate to the matter in hand. The former principle is characteristic of codified systems, the latter of English Common Law. In Roman jurisprudence, though the Orators include *res iudicata* among the sources of law, this is not precedent in the modern sense; there is no theory of 'binding' case-law. The law of the praetors and of the jurisconsults was largely built up on cases, and the Bar did for the development of Roman case-law and procedure much the same as the Bench has done for English Common Law. It is possible that under the formulary system the non-professional *iudices* tended to develop a principle of judicial uniformity in some doctrines; probable that after the establishment of the *extraordinaria cognitio* the professional *iudices* did this in many departments of the substantive law; and certain that they did it in procedural law. Justinian expressly discountenanced the obligatory force of any decisions except those which emanated from the Emperor himself. He strongly asserted, as a general principle of decision, 'Non exemplis, sed legibus iudicandum est.' This was the general rule in regard to substantive law; but there is much evidence that a body of adjective law was influenced by, and even founded on, a *mos iudiciorum* or *observatio iudicialis*. Apart from this law of procedure, Roman jurisprudence admitted judicial precedent only as an indirect and limited influence on substantive rules, and not as a primary source of law.

In modern Continental systems, as exemplified by French law, there is a great deal of extra-judicial or jurist-made doctrine which is recognized as a necessary and constant factor in legal theory. The judge is limited strictly to the issue before him, and it is not part of his function to lay down any 'general disposition'. In practice, recorded precedents exert a considerable influence, which may be said to be on the increase. In some cases, express provisions of the Code have been virtually nullified by a line of decisions. But there is no absolute uniformity; and though there is a marked tendency thereto in practice, French theory insists strongly on the independence of all courts, of whatever degree, in deciding cases according to principle and not necessarily according to example. After a number of experiments, the final Court of Appeal, the Cour de Cassation, has been given a jurisdiction of last resort in certain circumstances, but even the final judgements of this court, though greatly respected in practice, are not in theory binding on any courts for future cases.

In English law, the habit of noting decisions seems to have arisen very early in the legal profession. Bracton lays down certain principles for judicial uniformity, and was himself an industrious collector of cases, many of which served as material for his institutional treatise, though they were not 'reports' in the modern sense. By the thirteenth century, the judges show a distinct desire to tread the beaten path. In the Year Books, although citation of specific cases by name is infrequent (being at this period difficult and nearly impossible), there is considerable evidence that both judges and counsel frequently reasoned by the analogy of previous decisions, for the most part drawing upon their personal recollection or possibly upon private notes. But there is no trace of a doctrine in the Middle Ages that precedents were 'binding', and if a court considered an alleged decision to have been ill founded, it had no hesitation in rejecting it. At the same time, there is an unmistakable consciousness on the part of judges that their decisions are helping to settle the law for the future; and on occasion they said so in plain terms. In the sixteenth century, with Dyer's reports, a system of citations begins to be consolidated on well-recognized lines, and this technique may be said to have been finally established by Coke. Many of the 'precedents' of the sixteenth and seventeenth centuries are precedents of pleading and practice rather than of substantive law; and these possessed a peculiar stringency. But the importance of substantive precedents is well established. In the latter half of the seventeenth century, Vaughan C.J., C.P., lays down certain principles concerning the relative values of different kinds of precedents. While fully conscious of the importance of case-law, he is clear that 'if a Court give judgement judicially, another Court is not bound to give like judgement, unless it think that judgement first given was according to law'. He even denies the force of procedural precedents unless they are 'according to law'. Sir Matthew Hale was of much the same opinion. Nevertheless, throughout this period the influence and authority of precedent are steadily growing. In the eighteenth century, precedent forms a regular and integral part of judicial technique. In the time of Lord Mansfield, the duty of judicial 'loyalty' was fully recognized and repeatedly asserted, though Lord Mansfield himself, while remaining a firm believer in *stare decisis*, did not himself always adhere faithfully to it. By the end of the eighteenth century, all the foundations of the modern doctrine of precedent were laid, but it could not reach its final development until certain changes, especially in the system of judicature and in the nature of the law reports, had been fulfilled. By 1833 it is recognized that the decisions of higher tribunals are binding on lower tribunals, unless 'plainly unreasonable and inconvenient', and that no judge is at liberty to depart from a principle once laid down merely on the ground that it is not 'as convenient and reasonable as he himself could have devised'. In the latter half of the nineteenth century the system of judicature is simplified, the reports are regularized, the hierarchy of authority becomes settled, and the general rules for the application of precedents are well defined and observed.

These rules are that: (1) Each court is bound by the decisions of courts above it, and the House of Lords and the Court of Appeal are bound by their own decisions, though with certain defined exceptions in the Court of Appeal. (2) Any relevant judgement of any court is a strong argument entitled to respectful consideration. (3) A judgement is authoritative only as to its *ratio decidendi*. (4) A precedent is not abrogated by lapse of time. (5) But very ancient precedents are not in practice commonly applicable to modern circumstance. (6) A precedent may be cited from any source which the court considers reliable, but the reports of the Incorporated Council of Law Reporting for England and Wales enjoy peculiar authority.

The only proper use of precedents is to establish principles. A distinction is sometimes drawn between 'legal' and 'historical' precedents, but it is misleading and unnecessary in the actual working of precedents in the courts. The judgements of English courts stand in a special position as the most decisive authorities which can be cited; but other decisions and opinions are integral parts of forensic dialectic if relevant to a general proposition of law. Thus French writers and Roman Law have had an important influence on some branches of our law. English rules of Private International Law have been constructed largely on the opinions of jurists. The law of Real Property has been greatly affected by the practice of conveyancers. Some textbooks have enjoyed high esteem in our courts. There has been an increasing tendency of recent years for English courts to pay regard to, and even to 'follow', judgements in the Commonwealth and the United States. The technique of legal argument is not some esoteric magic peculiar to a particular profession, but is a system of strict logical demonstration. In order to arrive at the appropriate principle, counsel may use any material which is *ad rem*; but among this material the analogy of decided cases is the most convincing. This is as true of judgements as of argument, for judgements are logical expositions of principles, based in the same way on any relevant material. The judge is 'bound' by authority only according to his own lights, i.e. according as he himself considers the precedent cited to him to be applicable to the circumstances in issue. Hence the use of precedents can never be merely mechanical. Over and above all particular precedents stand certain cardinal principles of the Common Law, and decisions, however deliberately made, which run counter to these principles, possess at best an ostensible authority and are likely to lose it either by the process of 'distinguishing' or by being expressly overruled. The essential function of the judge is to find and uphold not only these fundamental technical principles of law, but the general administration of justice. Therefore in cases to which no specific decisions apply, he has recourse to natural justice, reason, morality, and social utility. These general ethical principles, though they cannot avail against express decisions (which do not commonly conflict with them) have played a large part in the development of our Common Law, and are still indispensable to it.

The English system of precedents, being so deeply rooted in our law, is often referred to as 'judge-made law'. This term, though it contains a partial truth, is misleading. There are some cases 'of first impression' in which the judge can find no specific authority to guide him, and here he has to 'make' a rule for the first time. But even in these cases the judge decides upon considerations which his professional training lead him to believe are consistent with general principles of English law. He applies a technically trained sense of right. In the vast majority of cases which are directly or indirectly governed by decisions, the judge does not 'make' a rule as an act of original creation. He is limited in his material; he can work only upon that which exists in the present or the past; he does not consciously project a rule into the future, but applies what he conceives to be an existing rule to a concrete case. In this respect his powers are quite different from those of the legislator, in the proper sense of that term. His function is to interpret, not to legislate; but in the process of interpretation he inevitably affects the development of the law. He 'makes' law only in a secondary or derivative sense; but the formative effect of his interpretation on all the most essential principles of law is of the highest and most lasting importance.

Precedent, restrained to its proper use and understood as an instrument of logic, has proved itself one of the most valuable factors in our legal reasoning. But it has certain disadvantages and inconveniences. The variety and sometimes the deficiencies of the reports of cases may lead to ambiguities or serious errors. Case-law is irregular in its operation, since it must depend on the accidents of litigation. There is no certainty that the judge, in arriving at his decision, has considered all the relevant authorities; and, with the increase of reports, it becomes more and more difficult for him to do so. Sometimes a conflict, or supposed conflict, between two higher authorities places a single judge in a dilemma. Erroneous decisions, though indefensible on principle, may sometimes establish themselves in the law either by uncritical acquiescence, or because they are never challenged in superior courts; and the principle *communis error facit ius*, while it is the line of least resistance, is open to grave dangers. The corrective powers of the legislature and of the highest tribunals are sporadic and uncertain. The handicap of case-law is its rigidity and the 'time-lag' from which it suffers in relation to changing social conditions. Although the Common Law is constantly, but in many cases very slowly, passing through transformations, its inherent rigidity is inconsistent with the claim of 'flexibility'. But these weaknesses, though considerable, and not to be minimized by the complacency to which many lawyers are prone, do not outweigh the substantial merits of the system of precedents as practised in our law; and the amount of irrationality introduced into the law by certain inevitable difficulties of application is inconsiderable beside the solid and rational jurisprudence which the Common Law, built up on example and analogy, has erected to so high a position in European civilization. There is, however, at the present time, a marked disposition to mitigate, by various devices, the severity of precedent when it tends merely to perpetuate error, and the whole system seems to be passing through a critical phase in its long history.

EXCURSUS C

THE SEARCH FOR AUTHORITY

It has been observed above (*ante*, pp. 315 ff.) that the omission of relevant authorities, which would sometimes be decisive if they were known to the Court, is a serious defect in the system of precedents and one which seems to be growing. In support of this statement, I select, from a large variety, a number of examples, all within comparatively recent years, and it will be convenient to mention them in chronological order.

R. v. *Crewe (Earl)*, *Ex p. Sekgome*, [1910] 2 K.B. 576, is a leading case upon the status in the British Empire of protectorates and their inhabitants; one of the authorities to which the Court of Appeal attached primary importance (see per Farwell L.J. at pp. 614 ff.) was an unreported decision of the Privy Council, *Staples* v. *Reg.* (1898).

In 1931 the Divisional Court of the King's Bench was called upon to decide the burning question whether a dog-race was a 'game or pretended game of chance' within the meaning of the Vagrant Act Amendment Act, 1873, and whether the keeping of a public totalisator in connexion with a dog-race was an offence under the Act[1] (*Everett* v. *Shand*, [1931] 2 K.B. 522). In holding that no offence had been committed, the Court followed *Att.-Gen.* v. *Luncheon and Sports Club, Ltd.*, [1929] A.C. 400, in so far as that case held that in gambling on a totalisator the bets are made between the individual gamblers themselves and not between the gamblers and the keeper of the machine. In *Tollett* v. *Thomas* (1871), L.R. 6 Q.B. 514, the contrary principle was laid down (or rather assumed) by a strong court of the Queen's Bench. Possibly that case would not have affected the decision of the House of Lords, but it is

[1] Totalisators on horse-races were specially authorized by the Racecourse Betting Act, 1928.

strange that, so far as the report shows, it was never cited or considered.[1] It was held to have been overruled, so to say, *in absentia*.

In *Barker* v. *Mumby*, [1939] 1 All E.R. 611, one of the numerous cases which have had to wrestle with the legal definition of a lottery, Charles J. expressed emphatic surprise that the parallel case of *Challis* v. *Newman* (1937), a decision of the Divisional Court, had never been reported.

In *Daponte* v. *Schubert*, [1939] Ch. 958, Morton J. found himself in a labyrinth of conflicting authorities, and eventually relied on two cases, one of which had been mentioned only in the *Weekly Notes*[2] and the other had not been reported at all (*D'Auvergne* v. *Cooper* (1899), W.N. 256, and *Attwood* v. *Gibbons* (1927), A. 344). In *Mahon* v. *Osborne*, [1939] 2 K.B. 14, the trial judge was criticized for having relied on an incomplete newspaper report of *James* v. *Dunlop* (1931), and a new trial was ordered principally on this ground.[3]

Before the passing of the Law Reform (Miscellaneous Provisions) Act, 1949, which abolished the so-called

1 For the later guerrilla warfare about the totalisator, see *Shuttleworth* v. *Leeds Greyhound Association*, [1933] 1 K.B. 400, and *Streatham Cinema, Ltd.* v. *McLauchlan*, [1933] 2 K.B. 331.

2 For other cases in which the court had to rely only on the *Weekly Notes*, see *In re Derham and Allen*, [1946] Ch. 31, and *Preston* v. *Norfolk C.C.*, [1947] K.B. 775, 787.

3 This example is taken from the Minority Report to the Report of the Committee on Law Reporting (see *post*, p. 377) by Professor A. L. Goodhart, who continues: 'In *Re Cawston's Conveyance*, [1939] Ch. 784, counsel for the plaintiff having cited an unreported decision of Eve J. in *Dixon* v. *Rackham* (1913), Simonds J. said: "The only note I have of it is in a publication called *The Local Government Chronicle*, which does not give me any guidance at all as to the arguments, at least on one side, which were addressed to the learned Judge or the reasons for his decision." In *Worthy* v. *Lloyd*, [1939] 2 K.B. 612, it was pointed out that the case was "a great hardship on the landlord", for if he had known of *Langley* v. *Wood* (1926) and *London County General Real Property Co.* v. *Randle* (1930), he could have avoided his error. (These cases can only be found in the *Estates Gazette Digest*.) In *Galene* v. *G.*, [1939] P. 237, the authority directly in point was *De Massa* v. *De M.*, which can only be found in *The Times* newspaper. In *Parkinson* v. *P.*, [1939] P. 346, Bucknill J. referred to the unreported case of *Jones* v. *J.*, which counsel cited from memory.'

Rule in *Russell* v. *R.*, [1924] A.C. 687 (concerning evidence of marital access tending to bastardize a child born in wedlock), *Ettenfield* v. *E.*, [1940] P. 96, was an important decision upon the applicability of that rule to spouses separated by agreement. In this case the Court of Appeal, applying the full rigour of *Russell* v. *R.*, refused to follow *Stafford* v. *Kidd*, [1937] 1 K.B. 39, and *Mart* v. *M.*, [1926] P. 24, because, among other reasons, in those cases an old and authoritative decision (*Inter the Parishes of St. George and St. Margaret* (1706), 1 Salk. 123) was not cited to the Court.

In *Hulme* v. *Brigham*, [1943] K.B. 152, before Birkett J.—one of the perennial series of cases on the nature of landlord's fixtures—the hearing was far advanced before the industry of counsel discovered an authority which was exactly 'on all fours', and which had been reported only in the *Solicitors' Journal* (*Northern Press and Engineering Co.* v. *Shepherd* (1908), 52 S.J. 715).

Leivers v. *Barber, Walker and Co.*, [1943] K.B. 385, turned on the applicability of the Statutes of Limitation to workmen's compensation. Two important authorities, which the majority of the Court (Scott and du Parcq L.JJ.) considered supported their view, were not discovered until after the judgements had been prepared (*Fry* v. *Cheltenham Corporation* (1911), 81 L.J. (K.B.) 41, and *Tuckwood* v. *Rotherham Corporation*, [1921] 1 K.B. 526). The dissenting member of the Court, Goddard L.J., also remembered, after he had prepared his judgement, that certain questions relevant to the decision had been discussed by Lord Atkin in *Lissenden* v. *C. A. V. Bosch, Ltd.*, [1940] A.C. 412, 415.

In *Gregory* v. *Cattle* (1943), 107 J.P. 122, which involved technical issues too complex for full discussion here,[1] the relevant and possibly decisive case of *Hughes* v. *Wavertree Local Board* (1894), 58 J.P. 654, was not before the Court.

[1] See further on these cases 59 *L.Q.R.* 309; 60 *ibid.* 22; 63 *ibid.* 417.

In *Pickford* v. *Mace*, [1943] K.B. 623, the decision in *Knight* v. *Winter* (1942) was held to be exactly in point and therefore binding, and yet, while the case and the principle which it embodied were well known to agricultural authorities, it had never found its way into any of the reports. In *Garcia* v. *Harland and Wolff, Ltd.*, [1943] K.B. 731,[1] the judge had before him no report of the relevant case of *Fitzpatrick* v. *Crichton* (1941), except a shorthand note of the judgement, presumably taken by counsel or solicitors in court, and not from any official source.

Fisher v. *Ruislip–Northwood U.D.C.*, [1945] K.B. 584, presented the Court of Appeal with the all too familiar task of attempting to reconcile a number of contradictory decisions. The main issue was the liability of local authorities for damage suffered by motorists through collisions with air-raid shelters. This was a vexed question during the 'black-out' period of the war, and probably no issue of negligence, except pedestrian crossings, caused so much confusion in the courts at that time. The Court of Appeal took the only course possible by rejecting certain decisions and accepting others, in a manner which does not make easy of interpretation the rules in *Young* v. *Bristol Aeroplane Co.*, [1944] K.B. 718. In his judgement Lord Greene M.R. called attention (at p. 609) to the fact that in two of the cases which were disapproved the important decision of *Morrison* v. *Sheffield Corporation*, [1917] 2 K.B. 866, had not been brought to the notice of the Court.

The question in *M.* v. *M.*, [1946] P. 31, was whether the Court had power to grant to a successful petitioner for divorce the custody of a child legitimated *per subsequens matrimonium* by operation of the Legitimacy Act, 1926, though no decree of legitimacy had ever been obtained. Denning J., in making an order for custody, had no scruple in declining to follow three cases, *Bednall* v. *B.*, [1927] P. 225, *Green* v. *G.*, [1929] P. 101, and

[1] See 60 *L.Q.R.* 325.

Jones v. *J.* (1929), 45 T.L.R. 292, because in none of these, being decisions of individual judges, was the long-standing decision of the Court of Appeal in *Langworthy* v. *L.* (1886), L.R. 11 P.D. 85, put before the Court. In this view the learned judge was later confirmed by the Divisional Court of the Probate, Divorce, and Admiralty Division, which in *Colquitt* v. *C.*, [1948] P. 19, overruled the three discredited cases.

Gott v. *Measures*, [1948] 1 K.B. 234, raised the interesting question whether a person who has sporting rights over land is entitled to shoot and kill a dog which is pursuing game on the land. In allowing an appeal, by case stated, against acquittal, Lord Goddard C.J. sympathized with the justices for not having had 'all these reports from East downwards' before them, and Croom-Johnson J. observed that the justices might not have followed the cases on which they relied if their attention had been called to *Miles* v. *Hutchings*, [1903] 2 K.B. 714. Here it may be observed that magistrates are frequently in this difficulty, since in summary jurisdiction, though arguable questions of law often arise, the citation of authorities is usually, and almost inevitably, inadequate.[1]

Few cases have raised more important issues in the law of divorce and nullity of marriage than *Cowen* v. *C.*, [1946] P. 36, and *Baxter* v. *B.*, [1948] A.C. 274, which concern the effect of contraceptives on the technical meaning of consummation of marriage. The House of Lords in the latter case overruled *Cowen* v. *C.*, and Viscount Jowitt L.C. observed (at p. 288) that neither in that case nor in *J.* v. *J.*, [1947] P. 158, was the relevant decision in *L.* v. *L.* (1922), 38 T.L.R. 697, considered (though it would not have been actually binding on the Court of Appeal).

Nicholas v. *Penny*, [1950] 2 K.B. 466, has cleared up a point, of equal importance to the public and to the police, concerning evidence of the speed of a motor vehicle as

[1] See 66 *L.Q.R.* 167.

registered by a speedometer. In holding that a policeman's evidence of a speedometer reading does not necessarily require either human or mechanical corroboration, if the Court is otherwise convinced by it, the Divisional Court had to reject its own previous decision in *Melhuish* v. *Morris*, [1938] 4 All E.R. 98, and one of its grounds for doing so was that in the case two important authorities had not been cited (see *ante*, p. 239).

In *Smith* v. *Morris Motors, Ltd.*, [1950] 1 K.B. 194,[1] the decision turned on two unreported cases which were not known, and could not be expected to be known, to the justices from whom appeal was made, and Lord Goddard C.J. described it as an 'impossible task' even for the Government department which was immediately concerned to be aware of them.

With *Worthy* v. *Lloyd* and *Pickford* v. *Mace*, *ubi sup.*, should be compared *Minister of Agriculture* v. *Matthews*, [1950] 1 K.B. 148, before Cassels J. If in *Worthy* v. *Lloyd* there was a hardship on the landlord, in *Matthews's Case* there was an even greater hardship on the tenant, for it was held that he was not a tenant at all (though he had been given every reason by the Ministry to think that he was), and was therefore liable to summary dispossession. In reaching this conclusion the learned judge relied, as he was bound to do, on the unreported case of *Minister of Agriculture* v. *Hulkin*. This was a case of great importance to agricultural tenants under the Defence (General) Regulations, 1939, and it was a decision of the Court of Appeal. It is difficult to understand why it was never reported.

In *Simpson* v. *S.*, [1951] P. 320, the Divisional Court relied strongly on the unreported judgement, of which a transcript was obtained, of Evershed M.R. in *Allen* v. *A.*, and in *Richards* v. *R.*, [1953] P. 36, it attached importance to an unreported case of *Jones* v. *J.* In *Harling* v. *Eddy*, [1951] 2 K.B. 739, Denning L.J. relied on *Lee* v. *Gray*, an unreported case in which he had been of

[1] See 66 *L.Q.R.* 16 and 166.

counsel. In *Davis Contractors, Ltd.* v. *Fareham U.D.C.*, [1956] A.C. 696, the decision turned largely on a case, *Bush* v. *Whitehaven, &c. Trustees*, which was to be found only in *Hudson on Building Contracts.*[1]

The decision of the House of Lords in *Glasgow Corpn.* v. *Central Land Board*, [1956] S.L.T. 41, is extremely important for the modifications which it makes of the rules laid down in *Duncan* v. *Cammell, Laird & Co., Ltd.*, [1942] A.C. 624, concerning the privilege of Crown documents in Scots law. The case has not found its way into the English reports.

Other examples may be found in *Re Waldron's Settlement*, [1940] 3 All E.R. 442 (see 56 *L.Q.R.* 453); *Bowring-Hanbury's Trustee* v. *Bowring-Hanbury*, [1942] Ch. 276 (see 58 *L.Q.R.* 461); *Broughton* v. *Whittaker*, [1944] K.B. 269 (*Bowker* v. *Woodroffe*, [1928] 1 K.B. 217, not cited to justices); *Jones* v. *Amalgamated Anthracite Collieries, Ltd.*, [1944] A.C. 14 (*S.S. Raphael (Owners)* v. *Brandy*, [1911] A.C. 413, not cited in the Court of Appeal); *R.* v. *I.C.R. Haulage, Ltd.*, [1944] K.B. 551 (*Chuter* v. *Freeth*, [1911] 2 K.B. 832, not cited in *R.* v. *Cory Bros.*, [1927] 1 K.B. 810); *Lane* v. *L.*, [1952] P. 34, 41; *National Assistance Board* v. *Wilkinson*, [1952] 2 Q.B. 648, 659; *Thompson* v. *Ward*, [1953] 2 Q.B. 153, 163; *In re Banque des Marchands*, [1954] 1 W.L.R. 1108, 1114; *Taylor* v. *National Assistance Board*, [1958] A.C. 532; *Morley* v. *M.*, [1961] 1 W.L.R. 211; *Prophet* v. *Platt Bros.*, [1961] 1 W.L.R. 1130; *David* v. *Commissioner of Metropolitan Police*, [1962] 2 Q.B. 135. On the whole subject see R. E. Megarry, 'Reporting the Unreported', *loc. cit.*, and O. M. Stone, *Knowing the Law*, 24 M.L.R. (July 1961), 475.

A curious, not to say comic, example of the situation which may arise when a relevant authority is overlooked is provided by *Hedger* v. *Shutler*, which has not found its way into any 'full-dress' report, but was noted in the

[1] On cases reported only in textbooks, see R. E. Megarry, 'Reporting the Unreported', 70 *L.Q.R.* 246.

Estates Gazette,[1] 1942, 369, 453 (see also 86 S.J. 264, 285, and 61 L.N. 164). This was an appeal from a County Court on a point of rent restriction, and on the second day of the hearing judgement was delivered for the respondent. One member of the Court of Appeal, however, felt uneasy about the decision, and after the rising of the Court he discovered an authority (*Tibber* v. *Upcott*, [1940] 1 K.B. 613) for which his memory had been searching; it was flatly at variance with the judgement to which he had just been a party. The Court of Appeal expunged its first judgement, and, a week later, gave exactly the contrary decision, on the authority of *Tibber* v. *Upcott*. Meanwhile, conscientious commentary had been offered in learned periodicals on the first and revoked judgement in *Hedger* v. *Shuttler*. It is not always that a court is provided, through the vigilance and learning of one of its members, with so swift a *locus poenitentiae* when it has committed a sin of ignorance.

It is impossible, in the light of these and similar examples, to be satisfied that our system of citations works with anything like the smoothness and accuracy which, *ex hypothesi*, might be expected of it. The paradox which, hundreds of years ago, surprised and discomfited conscientious reporters like Douglas and Foster (*ante*, pp. 221 f.) has lost none of its force today; if the Common Law principle is to be *exemplis iudicandum est*, then the *exempla* should manifestly be as complete and accurate as system, skill, and care can make them. That they fall short of that ideal is due to two principal causes: (1) that every important case is not reported, or at all events not reported in those places where we might reasonably expect to find it; and (2) that even when important decisions are reported, they not infrequently escape the attention of Bench and Bar.

There has been much debate about the whole existing system of recording decisions and about the principles

[1] On Rent Restriction and other cases which seem to be reported only in this periodical, see R. E. Megarry, 66 *L.Q.R.* 255.

on which the selection should be made of 'reportable' cases. It is unnecessary to discuss in detail here the history of the matter, the experiments which have been made, and the suggestions which have been offered.[1] Suffice it to say that among the various series of reports which are issued by private enterprise today, in addition to the semi-official *Law Reports*, the great majority of valuable cases appear in one publication or another, and are duly noted in indexes and digests. On the other hand, there are not a few surprising, and indeed inexplicable, exceptions. It is astonishing that a case so important as *Vidal* v. *V.* (*ante*, p. 318) had never been reported except in a newspaper, and that its predecessor, *Shufflebotham* v. *S.* (*ibid.*), had appeared only in one series of reports. The two cases of *May and Butcher* v. *R.* and *Hillas* v. *Arcos Ltd.* are now recognized as leading authorities on the difficult subject of 'contract to make a contract'.[2] The former was a decision of the House of Lords, and it was entirely unreported until it made a belated appearance as a note in [1934] 2 K.B. 17. The latter was reported in 43 Ll.L. Rep. 359, 38 Com. Cas. 23, and 147 L.T. 503, but not in the *Law Reports*. *McLean* v. *Bell* is a well-known case on contributory negligence: it is to be found only in 147 L.T. 262. *Blacker* v. *Lake* is a case on dangerous chattels familiar to every student and noted in every textbook on torts; it appears only in 106 L.T. 533. *Williams* v. *Glasbrook*, [1947] 2 All E.R. 270 (*ante*, p. 244), is an important decision on the rules in *Young* v. *Bristol Aeroplane Co.*; it is surprising that, although included, very properly, in the *All England Reports*, it has not found its way into the *Law Reports*. Other examples will be found in the preceding chapter.

The task of any editor of reports is difficult, and we should not be too severely critical if he sometimes nods.

[1] For full discussion see *Report of the Committee on Law Reporting* (H.M.S.O., Lord Chancellor's Office, 1940), A. L. Goodhart, 'Reporting the Law', 55 *L.Q.R.* 29, and C. G. Moran, *The Heralds of the Law.*

[2] See 48 *L.Q.R.* 312; 49 *ibid.* 316; 51 *ibid.* 277.

Apart from the problem of selection, there were for some years after 1939 certain physical limitations; everybody responsible for publications of any kind had to consider the purely material restrictions of print and paper. Again, the growing exigencies of statutory interpretation have complicated this and other questions. Every reader of the *Law Reports* is impressed, and not a few are irked, by the amount of space occupied by two irrepressible classes of cases—those concerned with Inland Revenue and with Rent Restriction—even though only a comparatively small proportion of these cases are considered 'reportable' in the major series. These cases certainly raise questions of importance for the public, and for those who have to advise clients, but from a purely legal point of view they are of a highly specialized nature, and it is difficult to resist the impression that they sometimes crowd out cases which have a bearing on more general and more illuminating problems of legal liability.[1]

Omissions and oversights of reported authorities, of which many examples have been given, are impossible to control, since, as has been said, they must depend on the individual skill and memory of counsel, and sometimes of judges. In this matter not even the most learned lawyer or the most retentive memory can do without mechanical aids, in the form of indexes, digests, and works of reference. It is said[2] that in this respect England lags behind the United States, where the vast and intricate body of authority in different jurisdictions demands a highly scientific and comprehensive apparatus of aids to memory. On this subject the present writer is not qualified to express an opinion; but the difficulties which he has often experienced in searching for a half-forgotten authority leave him with the impression that in this

[1] The Committee on Law Reporting recommended that the *Law Reports* might 'take a more generous view of what is reportable, particularly in the range of cases which exemplify the application of legal principle'.

[2] See Goodhart, *loc. cit.*

important instrument of technique we have much to learn. Even standard works of reference often seem to contain indexes which are exasperatingly elusive at moments of need.

In 1939 the Lord Chancellor (Viscount Maugham) appointed a representative committee to consider the whole question of law reporting. Its report, published in 1940, contains a concise account of the history of the subject and discusses, and in large measure concurs in, the main criticisms which have been made of the present system. Its recommendations are almost entirely negative, and the majority of members are unable to suggest any cure for the weaknesses which are acknowledged to exist. There is, however, a vigorous dissenting report by Professor A. L. Goodhart, which recommends that 'official shorthand writers should be attached to all Courts of record to take and transcribe all judgements. The transcripts should then be sent to the judges for such revision as they might consider it desirable to make in them. After a reasonably short period, not exceeding if possible a week, these transcripts should be returned to a central office at the Law Courts, where copies could be obtained by reporters and by any other persons on payment of a fee. All judgements would be filed in the central office, and would be indexed by an official specially appointed for the purpose.' The proposal had the weighty support of the late Sir William Holdsworth in one of his last papers.[1]

The recording of judgements in different Courts has been strangely unsystematic. Official shorthand notes are taken in the House of Lords and the Privy Council (where nearly all judgements are printed and immediately available to reporters), in the Court of Criminal Appeal, in witness actions, summonses, and motions in the Chancery Division and the Queen's Bench Division or at Assizes (this includes all oral evidence, summing

[1] 'Law Reporting in the Nineteenth and Twentieth Centuries', *Anglo-American Legal History Series*, No. 5, 1941.

up, and judgement),[1] in the Probate, Divorce, and Admiralty Division, and in all examinations in bankruptcy.[2] Curiously enough, there are no such official transcripts in the Divisional Court of the Queen's Bench, nor, until recently—most strangely of all—in the Court of Appeal. In *Gibson* v. *South American Stores*, [1950] Ch. 177, the Court found it necessary to consider the unreported case (1935) of *In re Laidlaw*, decided by the Court of Appeal, and Sir Raymond Evershed M.R. observed (at p. 195): 'It has before been observed to be a peculiar and unfortunate characteristic of our system that, although in the great majority of cases which come before it, this court is the final court of appeal for England, no provision whatever is made for taking a note or making a record of the judgements of the court.' In considering *In re Laidlaw*, therefore, the Court had to be content 'with such material as the vagaries of our reporting system have left for posterity'.[3] This anomaly was corrected in 1951, and transcripts of judgements in the Court of Appeal are now available in the Bar Library and are resorted to not infrequently by both Bench and Bar.[4]

It seems elementary that there should be, in all decided cases, especially in superior courts, an official record for future reference not only of the actual judgement as between the parties but of the reasons for it when reasons have been given. This improvement, however, would not in itself settle all the problems of the search for authority. Much must still depend on the

[1] Unless the judge otherwise directs: R.S.C., Order LXVI A, r. 2.

[2] See Moran, *op. cit.* 51. Shorthand notes are also taken at Quarter Sessions, and usually notes of some kind are taken by the Clerk to the Justices at petty sessions in all but the simplest cases. This is particularly important in matrimonial causes, since, if they are taken to appeal, the Divisional Court of the Probate, Divorce, and Admiralty Division, in the absence of the parties, relies solely on the Clerk's summary of evidence at Petty Sessions, especially for findings of fact.

[3] As supplied by counsel. On the importance of the unreported case in this instance, see 66 *L.Q.R.* 14. See further Lord Justice Asquith, 'Some Aspects of the Work of the Court of Appeal', *Journal of the Society of Public Teachers of Law*, 1950, 350, 356.

[4] But on the limitations of this privilege, see O. M. Stone, *loc. cit.*

knowledge and industry of counsel, aided by the best mechanical means which can be devised; and even these adventitious aids are of limited utility, for in the last resort the decisive factor is individual memory, or, more often, that kind of instinct which comes from long training and which frequently supplies the clue to what seems to have been lost in the maze of memory. A maze, however, it is likely to remain and it will not become less intricate as authorities constantly multiply with the passage of time. On the whole, study of our age-old reports causes less surprise at the shortcomings of legal erudition than admiration for its range and resourcefulness both on the Bench and at the Bar.

EXCURSUS D

PRECEDENT IN EQUITY

Selden's celebrated raillery of the 'length' of the Chancellor's conscience has sometimes been interpreted to mean that our early Chancellors were indifferent to uniformity of practice and decision. This view is emphatically repudiated by our leading historians of Equity. Spence[1] contends strenuously that 'there is an uninterrupted chain in the influence of precedent, from the earliest times, in the application of the principles of equity and conscience, *positively*, that is, where they ought to be applied, and *negatively*, that is, where the law ought to be left to its own operation'; and supports his thesis by strong examples. No less convinced is Kerly[2] that 'until the retirement of Lord Eldon equity was developed wholly by judicial legislation, it was entirely constructed upon precedent'. Holdsworth[3] takes the same view. Lord Eldon throughout his long chancellorship undoubtedly felt himself bound by authority and expressly said so in *Gee* v. *Pritchard* (1818), 2 Swanst. 402 (see *post*, p. 410). It is only necessary to look at the great cases in a collection like *White and Tudor* to realize that this statement is not too wide. No doubt until the time of Lord Nottingham the application of precedents was uncertain, owing largely to the scarcity of reliable reports;[4] but successive Chancellors were zealous in following the practice of the court as closely as possible. There was an impression among common lawyers to the

[1] *History of Equitable Jurisdiction*, i. 415 ff.

[2] *History of Equity*, 185.

[3] *H.E.L.* xiii. 627 ff.

[4] Some attempt at systematic reporting of Chancery decisions begins in the middle of the sixteenth century with Lambert's (so-called Carey's) Cases (1557–1604), the Choyce Cases in Chancery (1557–1606), and Tothill's Digest (1559–1646), but they are all extremely inadequate. There are no really reliable and thorough Chancery reports until Peere Williams (1695–1736). On the whole subject see Veeder, 'The English Reports', in *Select Essays in Anglo-American Legal History*, ii. 148 ff.

contrary, but that it was resented by Chancery practitioners is well shown by a discussion reported in *Fry* v. *Porter* (1670), 1 Mod. 300, 307. As was not uncommon at the time, the Chancellor in this case called upon the Common Law Chief Justices to assist him in his decision. In the course of the argument, Kelynge C.J. referred to several cases reported in Coke and Plowden. He was thus rebuked by Vaughan C.J., whose somewhat latitudinarian view of precedents we have already had occasion to remark (*ante*, p. 209): 'I wonder to hear of citing precedents in matter of equity, for if there be equity in a case, that equity is an universal truth, and there can be no precedent in it, so that in any precedent that can be produced, if it be the same with this case, the reason and equity is the same *in itself*; and if the precedent be not the same case with this, it is not to be cited.' But Lord Keeper Bridgeman, answering for the Chancery, said: 'Certainly precedents are very necessary and useful to us, for in them we may find the reasons of the equity to guide us; and besides, the authority of those who made them is much to be regarded. We shall suppose they did it upon great consideration and weighing of the matter, and it would be very strange and very ill if we should disturb and set aside what has been the course for a long series of time and ages.'

By the time of Lord Hardwicke, Equity lawyers were extremely averse from altering settled doctrine, even though it might not entirely commend itself to contemporary practice. In the well-known case of *Chesterfield* v. *Janssen* (1750), 1 Atk. at p. 353, Lord Hardwicke declared himself to be 'under an indispensable obligation of following' his predecessors Lord Nottingham, Lord Cowper, Lord King, and Lord Talbot. It is true, as is pointed out in a well-known judgement of Jessel M.R.,[1] that a number of equitable doctrines are of comparatively

[1] *In re Hallett's Estate* (1879), 13 Ch.D. 696, 710. The examples he cites are: the separate estate of married women, the restraint on alienation, the modern Rule against Perpetuities, and the rules of equitable waste.

recent origin and may be considered as the handiwork of individual Chancellors. But once established, they have been loyally followed; indeed, it may be said of the modern practice of Equity that it has depended even more than the Common Law on uniformity of decision, sometimes with the result that inelegant doctrines have perpetuated themselves to the prejudice of 'equity' in the broader sense. Thus in *In re Compton*, [1945] Ch. 123, the Court of Appeal found it 'quite impossible' to overrule what is frankly called the old 'anomalous' cases (concerning charitable bequests for 'poor relations') of *Isaac* v. *De Friez* (1754), 2 Amb. 595, *White* v. *W.* (1802), 7 Ves. 423, and *Att.-Gen.* v. *Price* (1810), 17 Ves. 571. Again, in *In re Morgan*, [1942] Ch. 347, the Court of Appeal, while commenting severely on the absurdity in modern conditions of the rule that in a will 'money' meant only 'cash', felt itself bound to follow authorities dating back to 1725, and was doubtless relieved when it was reversed by the House of Lords *sub nom. Perrin* v. *Morgan*, [1943] A.C. 399.

On the whole, extra-judicial opinion, especially in matters of conveyancing practice, may be said to have more influence in Chancery than in the Common Law. See *ante*, p. 326, and further, Spence and Kerly, *locc. cit.*

V

EQUITY

I. LAW AND JUSTICE

The idea of law

It is only since rules of law have become multiform through long processes of synthesis that law and justice have been conceived, as they are still sometimes conceived, as belonging to two distinct spheres. It would never have occurred to a political theorist in the Middle Ages to doubt that the whole aim of law was approximation to ideal justice, or to regard particular laws merely as rules of thumb for the mechanical regulation of society.[1] It was because they found in human law an aspiration towards ideal justice that the men of the Middle Ages were so deeply concerned with the Law of Nature. It has become the fashion to treat their speculation as chimerical fantasy; that it was much more than that is sufficiently shown by the influence which, as we have seen,[2] the Law of Nature exercised on subsequent theory and practice. If former doctrines in this kind were vague and mystical, yet they contemplated an ideal with which the world cannot yet dispense. Our methods today are more empirical and less abstract; but if modern lawyers rightly distrust generalizations about natural justice and 'justice as between man and man',[3] that is only because in the process of time most of our rules of law have shaped themselves as justice and utility demand, and it is not usually necessary to travel beyond settled doctrine into unsettled hypothesis. But in the past the conscious striving after principles of natural fairness has played a supremely important part in legal

[1] Carlyle, *Mediaeval Political Theory in the West*, ii. 1 f., iii. 183.

[2] *Ante*, pp. 26 ff.

[3] See, e.g., Lord Sumner (then Hamilton L.J.) in *Local Government Board* v. *Arlidge*, [1941] 1 K.B. 160, 199 ff., and in *Sinclair* v. *Brougham*, [1914] A.C. 398.

evolution. Equity has been, as Maine called it, a kind of 'supplementary or residuary jurisdiction' without which law would have been fatally stunted.

But since justice is the aim of law, why should not law be sufficient unto itself? Whence the necessity for any supplementary or residuary jurisdiction?

Necessity for a jurisdiction supplementary to law

As we have already seen, a legal rule, like every kind of rule, aims at establishing a generalization for an indefinite number of cases of a certain kind. Uniformity and universality are essential characteristics of it. To the quality of uniformity there can be no exception; a rule cannot be expressed in different forms having different meanings, for then it ceases to be a rule; though it may be expressed, as legal rules often are, in different forms having the same meaning. The essential meaning and intention of the rule must be uniform. To the quality of universality there may be apparent exceptions; many laws seem at first sight to apply only to a limited section of the community. In reality, their application is universal, for though they may not affect the interests of all citizens equally, they are binding comprehensively upon all lieges. A mariner's legal duties while on the high seas may seem to have little application to a landsman; but should the landsman happen to be a passenger on a ship, maritime law may at any moment have a very real meaning to him, either if his safety be imperilled by the mariner's neglect of duty, or if he attempt to interfere with the proper execution of that duty.

But no generalization can be completely general. The trite phrases that there are exceptions to every rule, or that the exception proves the rule, are only different ways of saying that human calculation is imperfect and human reason limited. In a great many of our rules the exceptions do not gravely disturb us: we are not shaken in our conviction that the dog is a four-footed animal because one dog happens to be born with three legs. Nor are we seriously disconcerted because many of our working conventions are imperfect approximations; the science of geometry is not thrown into confusion because no straight line can be perfectly straight and no parallel lines absolutely parallel. But in the domain of law the effect of exceptions may be more detrimental. Law and justice exist for the regulation of actual rights and duties; and the incompleteness of the generalization, which is certain to make itself felt at some point or other, may produce results which are antithetic to the very purpose of the generalization.

In many legal systems, therefore, a discretionary or moderating influence has been superadded to the rigour of formulated law. It has assumed different names at different times, but we may consider it under the general description of equity. It has exhibited itself in two principal forms: (1) a liberal and humane interpretation of law in general, so far as that is possible without actual antagonism to the law itself—this we may call *equity in general*; (2) a liberal and humane modification of the law in exceptional cases not coming within the ambit of the general rule—this we may call *particular equity*.[1]

How far can legal rules admit exceptions?

It is the latter aspect of equity which raises the most difficult problems. Where a rule works hardship in a particular case, it is not only permissible but it is necessary to ask, Is it not *eo ipso* a bad rule? Not infrequently it is proved to be so, and in the light of the 'glaring case' it stands self-condemned. A change must then be made, and it is by this somewhat painful process of trial and error that a great many necessary reforms in all legal systems have been effected—formerly by fiction, when legislation was less sensitive to social needs than it is today; in modern times by legislation, in so far as an overworked legislature can be stimulated into action.

But there are many circumstances in which, though the lot of the individual litigant seems hard, it is neither

[1] Cf. Cic. *Partit.* 37, 130: 'Aequitatis autem vis est duplex: cuius altera directa et veri et iusti, et, ut dicitur, aequi et boni ratione defenditur; altera ad vicissitudinem referendae gratiae pertinet.' Cf. Pollock, 'The Transformations of Equity', *Essays in Legal History, 1913* (ed. Vinogradoff), 287.

possible nor desirable to abrogate the general rule. It is impracticable to avoid such unfortunate incidents without abandoning uniformity in favour of mere caprice. In such circumstances the law and lawyers often have to bear hard words. Too frequently the layman, loud in his condemnation of 'flagrant injustice', will not attempt to look beyond the particular to the general, which it is exactly the business of the lawyer to do, and which must be done by somebody, if society is to maintain its discipline. Repeatedly law is denounced in the same manner as the whole science of surgery might be denounced because a single patient died under the knife. It must be admitted—and it is a source of genuine regret to every lawyer who respects his profession—that the law, like surgery, 'loses' a certain number of patients; but its instrument is not, as some seem to think, that of the butcher, but of the healer.

Yet the lawyer cannot afford to be contemptuous of the average instinct of justice in the ordinary man; for if he has a sense of proportion, the lawyer is aware of the peculiar danger to which he himself is liable—that in the honest pursuit of scientific logic he may forget the true proportion between form and content. The history of law shows only too clearly and too often how easy it is for the man of law to succumb to his besetting sin of formalism.

The natural sense of justice

He is sceptical of the over-confident sense of justice in the uninstructed mind because his training has made him aware that the theory and practice of justice are not acquired solely by the light of nature. No riddle is more difficult to solve, none has more persistently engaged the attention of thoughtful minds; and those who ignore the difficulties do so out of the abundance of their ignorance. 'But how can you love justice', asks Fortescue,[1] 'unless you first have a sufficient knowledge in the laws, whereby the knowledge of it is won and had, for the Philosopher saith, that nothing can be loved except it be known. . . ?

[1] *De Laud.*, ch. 5.

As for that which is unknown, it is wont not only not to be loved, but also to be despised.

Omnia quae nescit dicit spernenda colonus.'

'He alone', says Rudolph Sohm,[1] 'can claim to have obtained a real vision of law, of justice and of injustice, to whom life has revealed itself in its fullness. It is, of course, true of jurisprudence as it is of other sciences that the knowledge it commands is, and will remain, fragmentary. But it has a lofty aim in view to which it must strive, with unremitting endeavour, to approach as nearly as may be.' If truth lies at the bottom of a well, so does justice, and it will be found only by those who know how to swim, not by those who throw themselves in at a venture. Nothing is more treacherous than popular justice in many of its manifestations, subject as it is to passion, to fallacy, and to the inability to grasp general notions or to distinguish the essential from the inessential.

Nevertheless, the 'natural sense of justice'—or what has been called *vulgaris aequitas*[2]—is not a meaningless term. All law must postulate some kind of common denominator of just instinct in the community. There is no meaning in any legal system unless this foundation exists. Incalculable though the variations of subjective opinion may be, it needs no subtle dialectic to demonstrate that there is in man at least an elementary perception of justice, as a form of the right and the good, which no law, save under an irresponsible tyrant, dare flagrantly transgress.

It is upon some such primary sense of justice that a great deal of early law—not merely what we have come to recognize as equity in a special sense—is founded. Customary law can do no more than establish the

[1] *Institutes of Roman Law* (2nd ed.), 31.

[2] For examples see Voigt, *Ius Naturale, Aequum et Bonum u. Ius Gentium*, i. 37 ff. The adjective appears as *rudis*, as opposed to *constituta*, in Martinus's gloss on C. 2. 1. 1; see Savigny, *Gesch. des röm. Rechts im Mittelalter*, iv. 486 f.

general rule: it necessarily leaves many contingencies unprovided for. When the lawgiver begins to interpret custom, he must be guided by a native sense of justice in the actual application of the law; and he is a lawgiver exactly because he possesses this sense, or instinct, in a higher degree than the majority of his fellows. One of the first necessities imposed upon him is to administer law in that spirit of humane interpretation which has been called *equity in general*.

II. PHILOSOPHICAL CONCEPTION OF EQUITY

1. Equity in Greek Law

This conception found full and repeated expression in the Greek philosophers and orators. To consider the Greek view of justice in general, especially as discussed by Plato and Aristotle, would take us too far afield;[1] we may, however, make a brief reference to the general principle of fairness or equity (ἐπιείκεια), which is highly characteristic of Greek philosophy and law. The essence of the conception is expressed in a well-known passage in Plato's *Statesman*:[2]

Plato

'*Stranger*. There can be no doubt that legislation is in a manner the business of a King, and yet the best thing of all is not that the law should rule, but that a man should rule, supposing him to have wisdom and royal power. Do you see why this is?

Young Socrates. Why?

Stranger. Because the law cannot comprehend exactly what is noblest or most just, or at once ordain what is best, for all. The differences of men and actions, and the endless irregular movements of human things, do not admit of any universal and simple rule. No art can lay down any rule which will last for ever—that we must admit.

Young Socrates. Certainly.

Stranger. But this the law seeks to accomplish; like an obstinate and ignorant tyrant, who will not allow anything to

[1] A thorough but somewhat prolix examination of the theory of *ius naturale*, with which *aequitas* and ἐπιείκεια are intimately connected in Greek philosophy, is to be found in Voigt, *op. cit.*

[2] 294 a. Jowett's translation.

be done contrary to his appointment or any question to be asked —not even in sudden changes of circumstances, when something happens to be better than what he commanded for someone.

Young Socrates. True; that is just the way the law treats us.

Stranger. A perfectly simple principle can never be applied to a state of things which is the reverse of simple.'

Plato is here perhaps a little hard on the *ius strictum*, but expresses the root idea of ἐπιείκεια—that it is a necessary element supplementary to the imperfect generalizations of legal rules.

Aristotle

The notion was more fully examined by Aristotle in the tenth chapter of the fifth book of the *Ethics*, and as this is the most important surviving discussion of ἐπιείκεια in ancient philosophy, I venture to quote it almost in full:[1]

'Our next subject is equity and the equitable,[2] and their respective relations to justice and the just. For on examination they appear to be neither absolutely the same nor generically different; and while we sometimes praise what is equitable and the equitable man (so that we apply the name by way of praise even to instances of other virtues, meaning by ἐπιεικέστερον that a thing is better), at other times, when we reason it out, it seems strange if the equitable, being something different from the just, is yet praiseworthy; for either the just or the equitable is not good, if they are different; or, if both are good, they are the same.

'These, then, are pretty much the considerations that give rise to the problem about the equitable; they are all in a sense correct and not opposed to one another; for the equitable, though it is better than one kind of justice, yet is just, and it is not as being a different class of thing that it is better than the just. The same thing, then, is just and equitable, and while both are good the equitable is superior. What creates the problem is that the equitable is just, but not the legally just but a correction [ἐπανόρθωμα] of legal justice. The reason is that all law is universal but about some things it is not possible to make a universal

[1] Ross's translation.

[2] ἐπιείκεια and τὸ ἐπιεικές throughout. The reader need not be reminded that 'equity' is not here used in the purely technical sense which it has acquired in English law. 'Justice' and 'the just' are δικαιοσύνη and τὸ δίκαιον throughout.

statement which shall be correct. In those cases, then, in which it is necessary to speak universally, but not possible to do so correctly, the law takes the usual case, though it is not ignorant of the possibility of error. And it is none the less correct; for the error is not in the law nor in the legislator but in the nature of the thing, since the matter of practical affairs is of this kind from the start. When the law speaks universally, then, and a case arises on it which is not covered by the universal statement, then it is right, when the legislator fails us and has erred by over-simplicity, to correct the omission—to say what the legislator himself would have said had he been present and would have put into his law if he had known. Hence the equitable is just, and better than one kind of justice—not better than absolute justice but better than the error that arises from the absoluteness of the statement. And this is the nature of the equitable, a correction of law where it is defective owing to its universality.'

Here Aristotle was conscious of a difficulty which was not present to Plato, a difficulty in logic and a danger in practice. Logically—if law is justice, as it ought to be, why is any further element of justice necessary as a supplement? Practically—how reconcile the general authority of a law with individual relaxations of it? The answer is found in this, that the supplementary equitable interpretation should be *in the spirit of the law itself*, doing that which the law would have done if it had envisaged this particular case. Thus we have an early anticipation of the principle 'Equity follows the law': we shall observe the same principle at work in the interpretation of statutes;[1] and we may remark at once that the principle leaves many doubts open and has sometimes led to refinements which border very closely on fiction. We are on slippery ground when we speak of doing that for the law which the law has not done for itself; and the principle of equity following the law has, in common experience, sometimes meant that equity follows at such a respectful distance that the law is quite lost to view, or else strides out so boldly that it outstrips, not to say outwits, the law.

[1] *Post*, pp. 451 ff.

Aristotle's view centres in *particular equity*, and he finds the chief function of ἐπιείκεια to consist in supplying the deficiencies of νόμος. He epitomizes his doctrine in the last phrase of the passage cited: καὶ ἔστιν αὕτη ἡ φύσις ἡ τοῦ ἐπιεικοῦς, ἐπανόρθωμα νόμου, ᾗ ἐλλείπει διὰ τὸ καθόλου. Elsewhere he speaks in more general and idealistic terms of the nature of ἐπιείκεια as *equity in general*. In the *Rhetoric*,[1] after advancing the same general observations as in the *Ethics*, he continues:[2]

> 'It is equity to pardon human failings, and to look to the lawgiver and not to the law; to the spirit and not to the letter; to the intention and not to the action; to the whole and not to the part; to the character of the actor in the long run and not in the present moment (μηδὲ ποῖός τις νῦν, ἀλλὰ ποῖός τις ἦν ἀεὶ ἢ ὡς ἐπὶ πὸ πολύ); to remember good rather than evil, and good that one has received rather than good that one has done; to bear being injured (τὸ ἀνέχεσθαι ἀδικούμενον); to wish to settle a matter by words rather than by deeds[3]; lastly, to prefer arbitration to judgement, for the arbitrator (διαιτητής) sees what is equitable, but the judge only the law, and for this an arbitrator was first appointed, in order that equity might flourish.'

A little later,[4] equity is described as eternal and immutable: τὸ μὲν ἐπιεικὲς ἀεὶ μένει καὶ οὐδέποτε μεταβάλλει. So, above all the inelegances of positive law, 'The one remains, the many change and pass'.[5]

Practical application of equity in Greek Law

These doctrines were by no means unpractical abstractions in Greek law. The division of law into the written and unwritten (τὸ γεγραμμένον and τὸ ἄγραφον) was an axiom of Greek jurisprudence, and ἐπιείκεια was a definite, recognized, and operative part of the ἄγραφον. It is a little difficult for the modern lawyer to reconcile

[1] i. 13. 1374 a.

[2] *Ibid.* 1374 b; Grant's translation, *apud Eth. Nic.*, note to v. 10. 1.

[3] A somewhat dark saying, and, some may think, a reflection of the peculiar genius of the Greeks for talking; but λόγος here seems to mean 'openness to persuasion' as opposed to ἔργον, standing on one's rights without listening to the voice of sweet reasonableness.

[4] i. 15. 1375 a.

[5] On ἐπιείκεια in Aristotle see further Voigt, *op. cit.* iv. 2, 372 ff.

himself to the Orators' continual vague appeals to the unwritten law; the dangers of subordinating positive law to a moral principle, which must partake largely of the subjective, are self-evident. The pleader who relies on natural equity is always open to the suspicion that he does so because he has nothing more substantial to assist him. Equity may easily become a *pis aller;* and it is difficult to resist the belief that in the hands of the Orators forensic exigencies frequently lent it an undue elasticity. But it is a mistake to judge a system of law by forensic exigencies. We pride ourselves in England that our law is strict and impartial; but if half the speeches addressed to juries were recorded and read by a foreigner, he would form a very strange idea of our jurisprudence. Making all allowances for that emotionalism which more than one incident in the history of Athens revealed in startling manner, it is unreasonable to suppose that Athenian courts regarded all the excesses of pleaders as a sober statement of legal principles; otherwise a very elaborate and complex structure of law, such as the Attic system undoubtedly was, becomes an inexplicable contradiction. Despite rhetorical hyperbole, equity remained a real, indispensable factor in the Greek conception of the administration of justice.[1] Its practical sphere of operation was found chiefly in the interpretation of wills, in the preservation of good faith in contracts, and in the liberal interpretation of archaic or obscure statutes. Over and above these special departments of law there was a general residuary justice, or prerogative, in the sovereign people of which the higher Athenian courts were in theory and in practice the representatives *ad hoc.*[2]

2. *Equity in Roman Law*

To what extent Roman jurisprudence was influenced by Greek philosophy and rhetoric has been much debated. It is no longer doubted by modern students of Roman Law that the influence of Greece from the time of the Twelve Tables was, to put it at the lowest, real

[1] Vinogradoff, *Historical Jurisprudence*, ii. 66.
[2] *Ibid.*

and considerable.[1] It is equally clear not only that some knowledge of Greek culture and thought was an indispensable part of the equipment of every well-educated Roman, but that it attracted the particular attention of the *veteres* who founded the tradition of classical Roman jurisprudence; and we have the evidence of Cicero that some of the more distinguished of this 'old school' studied under Stoic teachers.[2] That this early philosophic attitude towards jurisprudence maintained its influence throughout the classical period is sufficiently shown by the fact that some of the standard conceptions of law and justice in the Corpus Iuris still bear the unmistakable stamp of Greek philosophical commonplaces.[3]

Influence of Greek philosophy

It is as easy as it is unwise to exaggerate Greek influence, especially in the development of the praetorian *ius gentium*, for there is no reason to suppose that the Romans were incapable of forming a conception of *aequitas* for themselves. Yet it is not a little surprising to find, in a system so absolute, comprehensive, and explicit as the Roman, especially as codified by the authority of the supreme lawgiver, the conception of *aequitas* or *aequum et bonum* so firmly embedded. To regard it as a mere vague counsel of perfection, with little practical application, is entirely inconsistent with the evidence of the Corpus Iuris.[4] Nor was it introduced by a side-wind through the practice of the Courts as against the strict theory of the imperial law. Not only is it not discountenanced, as future juristic interpretation and 'judge-made law' were discountenanced,[5] by the sovereign, but in the fourth century A.D. it is

Equity a practical element in Roman Law

[1] Cuq, *Institutions juridiques*, 10, etc., represents the characteristic modern view.

[2] *Ibid.*; see references there cited, 40 (4). Cf. *Brut.* xli. 152. See also Schulz, *Roman Legal Science*, 62 ff., and *Principles of Roman Law*, 129 ff.

[3] e.g. the dichotomy of written and unwritten law, the famous *tria praecepta iuris*, the definitions of *sapientia*, *iurisprudentia*, and *iustitia*, and (perhaps more doubtfully) the delimitation of *infantia* and *pubertas*: Voigt, *op. cit.* i. 257.

[4] Cuq, *op. cit.* 44.

[5] *Ante*, p. 172.

expressly enjoined by imperial legislation[1] as a positive duty of the judge: 'Placuit in omnibus rebus praecipuam esse iustitiae aequitatisque quam stricti iuris rationem.' It is impossible to imagine a wider charter for equity than this. Nor were the doctrines of *aequitas* expressed only in sweeping generalities. Our English system of equity has developed many doctrines of a particular technical rather than a general moral significance; yet not a few surprising affinities exist between Roman and English technical principles of this kind, as was shown by Professor Buckland in the numerous instructive parallels which he instituted between the two systems.[2]

Chief equitable principles of Roman Law

Beyond these technical rules it is possible to distinguish certain general doctrines of equity which profoundly influenced Roman Law in many of its branches. Under the various titles of *aequitas*, *aequum et bonum*, *utilitas*, *humanitas*, *benignitas*, *ratio naturalis*, and in a great measure *bona fides*, it appears almost everywhere; but it may be said to have exerted its chief influence in the following principles of Roman jurisprudence:

1. In the triumph of the natural idea of blood relationship over the artificial idea of agnation. This principle, it may be thought, was almost inevitable in the natural evolution of Roman society; but when one considers how profoundly patriarchal that society was in its origin and structure, the victory of cognation, based on a principle variously called *sanguinis ratio*,[3] *caritas sanguinis*,[4] or *humana interpretatio*,[5] appears as no mean achievement of juridical development. Its scope and effects are too well known to need comment: it was the source of the whole system of praetorian succession, of such enactments as the SC. Orphitianum and SC. Tertullianum,

[1] Constantine and Licinius, A.D. 314: C. 3. 1. 8; cf. C. 3. 38. 12.

[2] *Equity in Roman Law, passim.*

[3] D. 38. 8. 2.

[4] D. 25. 3. 5. 2.

[5] D. 38. 17. 1. 6. Other leading passages are: D. 37. 1. 6. 1, 5. 1. pr., 11. 2. pr.; D. 38. 16. 1. 4, 17. 5. pr.; D. 48. 20. 7. pr., 23. 4. Cf. Gai. *Inst.* iii. 7, 18–24.

and of Justinian's final settlement of the law of succession. It affected the law of testate as well as intestate succession, as the Lex Falcidia and the *querela inofficiosi testamenti* bear witness.

2. The development of the principle of *good faith* in contractual obligations. The whole conception of a pact is based by Ulpian on *aequitas naturalis:* 'quid enim tam congruum fidei humanae, quam ea quae inter eos placuerunt servare?'[1] The tendency throughout the whole history of Roman contract is from the formalistic towards the consensual; and the recognition of a large and important class of agreements, common in daily life, of which *bona fides* is a necessary element, opens up a wide discretion to the judge. The same discretion is exercised in applying the *exceptio doli* to *actiones stricti iuris*, *aequitas* being the natural antithesis of *dolus*.[2] The *naturalis obligatio* is also a well-established conception, and the obscure doctrine of *causa civilis* becomes artificial and almost fictitious beside the fundamental requirement of good faith. Further, the praetor travels outside the *ius strictum* to find new and necessary forms of obligation where the civil law supplies none.[3] The governing principle becomes *grave est fidem fallere*.[4]

3. Akin to the principle last mentioned is a dogma of interpretation that wherever possible the intention rather than the form should be looked to. This is not only inherent in consensual obligations,[5] in the same degree as the requirement of good faith, but is to be regarded in the performance of any juristic act—e.g. the transfer of property:[6] it is a safeguard against inadvertence and innocent mistake—e.g. in verbal contract[7] or in the release of a debt.[8] If it may be prayed in aid by those who are living and able to explain themselves, *a fortiori* it must be applied in interpreting the

[1] D. 2. 14. 1. pr.; cf. D. 46. 3. 95. 4.
[2] D. 44. 4. 12; cf. D. h.t. 1. 1.
[3] e.g. *actiones adiecticiae qualitatis*: see Gai. *Inst.* iv. 71.
[4] D. 13. 5. 1. pr.
[5] Gai. *Inst.* iii. 537.
[6] D. 41. 1. 9. 3.
[7] D. 45. 1. 36.
[8] D. 20. 6. 8. 16.

intentions of the dead. Hence, as in Greek law and to a large extent in modern law, we find the principle invoked chiefly in the interpretation of testaments.[1]

4. There is no principle of equity which appears more frequently in Roman Law, and in more diverse connexions, than the prohibition of unjust enrichment at the expense of another. He who has come into possession of property not his own, even though the acquisition may have been made accidentally or by mistake and without deliberate fraud, is under a strict obligation to return it or its value to the true owner. This was the foundation of the important action of *condictio indebiti* and in the main of the praetor's wide discretionary remedy of *in integrum restitutio*. Among innumerable statements of the principle in the Corpus Iuris, the most succinct and characteristic is that of Pomponius:[2] 'Iure naturae aequum est neminem cum alterius detrimento et iniuria fieri locupletiorem.' Cicero[3] regards the principle as essential to the very existence of society, and the negation of it as more subversive than any other detriment which could befall body or estate. It was, indeed, the natural corollary of *suum cuique tribuere*.

5. Repeatedly the spirit of *aequitas* is opposed to *dolus malus*, and one form of *dolus malus* is *subtilitas*, or adherence to the strict letter of the law, in order to make it the means of an unscrupulous advantage. The essence of the wrong complained of is not that it is illegal, but that it is too legal. Undoubtedly the judge here looks beyond legal right to *motive*, and it was not questioned that it was his duty as well as his right to do so. This principle of the *abuse of right* is expressed in modern Continental systems as *chicane*, and is a perfectly well-recognized form of civil wrong. Except for certain somewhat hesitating doctrines of equity, modern English

[1] D. 28. 2. 13. pr., 3. 17; D. 35. 2. 88. 1; C. 6. 24. 6.

[2] D. 50. 17. 206. Other general statements are to be found in D. 23. 3. 6. 2 and D. 47. 4. 1. 1. Cf. D. 12. 1. 32, D. 22. 1. 38. 7, and D. 47. 2. 63. 5.

[3] *De Off.* iii. 5. 21 (somewhat rhetorically stated).

law is unable to carry judicial discretion so far.[1] In Roman Law, it was the *nimia subtilitas* of the old *legis actiones*, and the uses to which they were put, which brought about their downfall,[2] and it was the doctrine of liberal interpretation which gave rise to the praetor's *utilis actio*. That it was immensely important in the general discretion of Roman courts is shown by the abundance of references to it throughout the Corpus Iuris.[3]

6. It follows from these principles that the responsibility of the judge is high and his task extensive. Maitland has compared the judge in a primitive system of law to an umpire whose function it is to give 'Out' or 'Not out' to the 'How's that?' of the players in the game of pleading.[4] Such, doubtless, was the whole duty of the umpire—the *praetor*—in the *subtilitas* of the archaic Roman Law; but in the maturity of Roman jurisprudence, a new kind of umpire—the *iudex*—plays a much more individual role with a greatly extended discretion. Instead of merely regulating the game, he has the important duty of assessing damages: he has his ductile *exceptio doli;* in personal actions, he has a wide field of *bona fides;* in real actions, he has his adaptable *formula petitoria*.[5] And throughout, he is expected to behave not like a machine, but like a *vir bonus*.[6]

It is not to be supposed that these principles of equity in Roman Law always passed unchallenged. We may

[1] See C. K. Allen, 'Legal Morality and the Ius Abutendi', *Legal Duties*, 95.

[2] Gai. *Inst.* iv. 30.

[3] The terms in which it is described vary considerably: thus *benignius*, D. 8. 3. 11, D. 12. 1. 20, D. 39. 5. 25; *humanius*, D. 28. 5. 29, D. 29. 2. 86; *humanitatis ratio*, D. 4. 6. 38. 1, D. 49. 5. 12. 5; *ex bono et aequo*, D. 11. 7. 14. 6, D. 39. 2. 19. pr.; *aequitas et officium viri boni*, D. 46. 6. 12; *quam rationem bonus paterfamilias reciperet*, D. 40. 4. 22. No exact definition can be given of the cases in which the principle may arise; 'multi casus . . . nec singulatim enumerari potuerunt', D. 4. 6. 26. 9 (of *in integrum restitutio*). The references are very numerous, but the following are also characteristic: D. 11. 7. 43, D. 41. 1. 7. 5, D. 41. 3. 32. 2, C. 8. 16. 5, C. 3. 42. 8.

[4] P. & M. ii. 671.

[5] Cuq, *op. cit.* 46.

[6] D. 45. 1. 137. 2; cf. D. 4. 6. 26. 9, C. 5. 13. 7, C. 7. 71. 3.

Criticisms of equity in Roman Law

be sure that disingenuous appeals to *naturalis aequitas* were no more unknown in the Roman than in the Greek courts; and sometimes we hear vigorous protests against taking liberties with the express provisions of the law. For example, one of Quintilian's speeches[1] throws an interesting light on the methods which were sometimes adopted to evade the very clear provision of the Lex Voconia that a wife could not take more than half her husband's property on his death by way of legacy. It was an old statute, probably passed about the middle of the second century B.C., and though unrepealed, it had evidently been attacked as obsolete and inelegant. 'Nowadays', says the orator,

> 'there is a tribe of ingenious pleaders who would have us "interpret" this statute. It does not, they claim, mean what it says. I greatly admire the subtlety of these advocates: they are much more acute than our ancestors—those mere founders of the law, mere framers of our legal system: they must be more acute, or they would not attempt to show that these ancestors of ours lacked both speech and sense. Now, before I deal with the purpose of this particular statute, I have just this one remark to make to the Court, that this kind of so-called "interpretation" is thoroughly mischievous. For if the Court is always to be spending its time turning statutes inside out to discover what is just and what is equitable and what is expedient: well, then, there might as well be no statutes at all. No doubt there was a time when law was nothing but a kind of native justice. But because justice appealed to different minds in different ways, and it was therefore impossible to decide with certainty what it ought to be, a definite form of law was established to govern our lives. That form the framers of statutes expressed in explicit words: and if everybody is to be allowed to change it and twist it to his own purposes, the whole force and purpose of the law is gone. We might just as well have no laws at all as uncertain laws.'

Such protests, expressed with as much common sense as vigour, were no doubt sometimes necessary as a counterblast. But in reality there was no fundamental

[1] *Decl.* cclxiv.

antinomy between safe, certain law and a humane interpretation of it; and it cannot be doubted that in the Roman system the two principles were equally settled and equally salutary.

III. EQUITY IN ENGLISH LAW

1. Relation between Common Law and Equity

Equity in royal jurisdiction

In the English system 'equity' has acquired a technical connotation and we are accustomed to think of it as a whole jurisdiction distinct from Common Law principles. But the general conception of equity as a moderating and humane influence was inherent in our jurisprudence long before it became specialized first by the King's Council and then by the Chancellor himself apart from the Council. The Anglo-Saxon and early Norman and English kings were 'fountains of justice' in the very real sense that they themselves dispensed justice. Their jurisdiction was not confined to the ordinary course of litigation, but a prerogative of *mercy* and *equity* was an essential part of their regal office.[1] In this respect they embodied a principle which is invariably associated with the early conception of kingship,[2] and which, whether or not it be actually derived from Roman doctrines,[3] is clearly formulated in the principal pattern of European sovereignty, that of Byzantium.[4] It is characteristic that in the so-called Laws of Henry I the king is described as the defender of the poor and defenceless,[5] and it is in the same spirit that in all our records of the Council and the Chancery, so far as they have been investigated, the 'common form' of petition is the appeal *ad misericordiam*.

Equity of royal courts

In the course of time the royal jurisdiction has been converted from a fact to a constitutional fiction; and the process which brought about this result—the *imperium*

[1] Spence, *Equitable Jurisdiction*, i. 77 ff.; Kerly, *History of Equity*, 13 ff.

[2] Maine, *Early Law and Custom*, ch. vi; Pollock, *The Expansion of the Common Law*, 67 ff., and *First Book of Jurisprudence* (6th ed.), 258.

[3] Allen on *The Prerogative*, 94.

[4] C. 1. 14. 1. 9.

[5] Spence, *op. cit.* 78.

in imperio of the royal courts of justice—began very early in our legal history and has been many times described. In the gradual erection of the great edifice of the Common Law, natural equity is not the least important of the foundation-stones. To Bracton,[1] following Roman precepts, equity is 'rerum convenientia quae in paribus causis paria desiderat iura et omnia bene coaequiparat'. It is *equality*: and the virtue of a court of justice is to be *equal*, while the virtue of a *man* of justice is to be just. This borrowed[2] distinction is somewhat academic, but it sufficiently expresses the notion that a spirit of equity is inherent in any court of justice worthy the name. Such undoubtedly was the accepted principle during the critical period of the thirteenth century. It is well summarized by Maitland, writing of the age of Henry III:[3]

'We must . . . remember, first, that a contrast between *aequitas* and *rigor iuris* is already a part of what passes as philosophical jurisprudence, and secondly, that our King's court is according to very ancient tradition a court that can do whatever equity may require. Long ago this principle was asserted by the court of Frankish Kings and, at all events since the Conquest, it has been bearing fruit in England. It means that the royal tribunal is not so strictly bound by rules that it cannot defeat the devices of those who would use legal forms for the purposes of chicane; it means also that the justices are in some degree free to consider all the circumstances of those cases that come before

[1] F. 3 (Woodbine, ii. 25).

[2] From Azo; Maitland, *Bracton and Azo*, S.S., vol. viii. 27.

[3] P. &. M. i. 189 f. A good example is Y.B. 18 & 19 Ed. III (1345), R.S. 376, cited by Dr. T. Ellis Lewis, 46 *L.Q.R.* 220: 'Sharshulle J. dissented from a previous decision and said, "One has often heard speak of that which Bereford and Herle JJ. did in such a case . . . but nevertheless no precedent is of such force as that which is right (*mes nepurquant nulle ensaumple est si forte comme resoun*)." R. Thorpe argued that unless the judges did as others had done in the same case no one would know what the law was. Hilary J. said, "It is the will of the Justices." . . . Stonor J. said, "No, law is that which is right." The decision finally went against Thorpe. Sharshulle J. after a logical argument rejected the opinion of Bereford and Herle—two Judges whose views were usually treated with respect—and by a majority the Court, whilst denying law to be subjective whim, agreed that right, reason or justice outweighs all precedents.'

them and to adapt the means to the end. In the days of Henry II and Henry III the King's court wields discretionary powers such as are not at the command of lower courts, and the use of these powers is an exhibition of "equity". Often on the plea rolls we find it written that some order is made "by the counsel of the court" (*de consilio curiae*). It is an order that could not be asked for as a matter of strict right; the *rigor iuris* does not dictate it—would perhaps refuse it; but it is made in order that the substantial purposes of the law may be accomplished without "circuity of action". The need of a separate court of equity is not yet felt, for the King's court, which is not as yet hampered by many statutes or by accurately formulated "case law", can administer equity.'

Equity through Common Law forms

This does not mean that in the English courts of the thirteenth century justice was no more than 'justice as between man and man'. Procedure and technical rules were strict, and could not be ignored with impunity; but the courts were endeavouring to find the compromise—always difficult—between substantial justice and a proper discipline of form.[1] Further, although the Common Law jurisdiction grew up on a framework of writs, even within that inflexible system there were not a few important remedies which later would have been considered typically 'equitable', inasmuch as they aimed rather at the 'specific relief' characteristic of the Chancery than the damages characteristic of the Common Law.[2] Thus we find the enforcement of what were virtually uses or trusts of chattels or money by writs of detinue and account;[3] at least until the time of Edward I, the enforcement of gages of property, with relief to the gagor very much in the nature of an equity of redemption; the specific enforcement of contractual obligations, aimed unmistakably *in personam* and not, as we expect of the Common Law, *in rem;* writs of prohibition and

[1] Holdsworth, *H.E.L.* ii. 250 ff.

[2] Hazeltine, 'The Early History of English Equity', in *Essays in Legal History, 1913* (ed. Vinogradoff).

[3] Hazeltine, *op. cit.*, following Ames, 'History of Parol Contracts Prior to Assumpsit', *Select Essays in Anglo-American Legal History*, iii. 340 ff.

estrepement which are for all practical purposes injunc tions, prohibitory and mandatory, interlocutory and perpetual; and writs called by Coke '*brevia anticipantia*, writs of prevention', of some half-dozen kinds,[1] which are strongly analogous to the later bills of *quia timet* in Chancery.

A striking example of the kind of equitable relief which is given as early as the beginning of the fourteenth century is a case to which Maitland has called attention.[2]

> 'A man has bound himself to pay a certain sum if he does not hand over a certain document on a certain day. Being sued upon his bond, he is unable to deny that he did not tender the document on the day fixed for the transfer; but he tenders it now, excuses himself by saying that he was beyond the sea, having left the document with his wife for delivery, and urges that the plaintiff has suffered no damage. The plaintiff relies upon the words of the bond, and we must confess to having thought that in and about the year 1309 judgement for the plaintiff would have followed as a matter of course. But to our surprise Bereford C.J., after remarking that what is sought to be recovered is not properly speaking a debt (*purement dette*) but a penalty (*une peine*), exclaims, "What equity would it be to award you the debt when the document is tendered and you cannot show that you have been damaged by the detention?" In the end the plaintiff is told that he will have to wait seven years for his judgement. Here certainly we seem to see "relief against penalties" and relief that is granted in the name of "equity", though it takes the clumsy form of an indefinite postponement of that judgement which is dictated by the rigour of the law.'

This, and a case of the same year, *Prior of Coventry* v. *Grauntpie*,[3] a clear example of a 'perpetual injunction', Maitland characterizes as 'premonitions of Equity', and observes: 'In divers quarters much evidence seems to be collecting which tends to show that the number of

[1] *Mesne, warrantia cartae, monstraverunt, audita querela, curia claudenda, ne iniuste vexes*: Co. Litt. 100 a; Hazeltine, *op. cit.*

[2] *Umfraville* v. *Lonstede*, Y.B. 2 & 3 Ed. II (S.S. ii), 58, and Introd. xiii.

[3] Y.B. 2 & 3 Ed. II (S.S. ii), 71.

thoroughly new ideas introduced by the Chancellors of the later Middle Ages was by no means large.'[1]

Equity in the Eyre

These words, printed in 1904, proved prophetic, for the later researches of Bolland into the procedure in Eyre, of about the same date as the cases last mentioned, showed conclusively that equity, wide though it was at Westminster, was even wider before the itinerant justices.[2] The bills in Eyre of the early fourteenth century are indeed a remarkable example of the King's vicarious justice.[3] We cannot better describe their general characteristics than in Bolland's own words:[4]

'So far as we have gone we find that these bills are addressed to the Justices of the King "who are put in the place of the King to do justice". They are largely used by very poor people. No rules as to form affect them, so that, no expert knowledge being necessary, they can be framed and presented by anyone who can write or can get another to write for him. There is no evidence that any fee was payable on presentation of a bill, as it was on the purchasing of a writ, but there is conclusive evidence that the way of a very poor man to the ear of the King's Justices was made easy for him. Now to what does all this point? Surely to the immemorial belief that inherent in the King are the right and the power to remedy all wrongs independently of common

[1] Y.B. 2 & 3 Ed. II (S.S. ii), xiv.

[2] Bolland, *Eyre of Kent* (S.S., vols. xxiv, xxvii, xxix); *Select Bills in Eyre* (S.S., vol. xxx).

[3] That the judges specifically claimed a wider jurisdiction in Eyre than in Bank seems to be sufficiently shown by an emphatic remark of Spigurnel J. in *Bruce* v. *Horton*, Y.B. 6 & 7 Ed. II (Eyre of Kent), S.S., vol. xxix. 198:

'Maud that was wife of William Bruce brought the *scire facias* against John of Horton calling upon him to show whether he had aught to say why execution should not be done of the judgement given between this same Maud and John of Horton, father of the aforesaid John, &c., before the Justices in Bank; and note that John of Horton said that he ought not to answer unless he had notice by a writ from the King as was the rule before the Justices in Bank.

Westcote. That is not so. If a man be within the jurisdiction it is sufficient if he have notice by precept. You are within the jurisdiction, and therefore you have had sufficient notice.

Malmerthorpe. You ought not to be in a better position than the Justices in Bank.

Spigurnel J. You are talking idly. We can do many things which they cannot do. And so answer.'

[4] S.S., vol. xxvii, p. xxviii.

law or statute law and even in the teeth of these; the right and the power, in fact, to do as he likes whatever hard law and still harder practice may dictate; and the hope and the trust that, his own personal interests being in no way concerned, he will right the wrong and see that justice is done. And the Justices in Eyre were in a very special sense impersonations of the King who had received from the King not only authority to hold all pleas, but, further than that, authority to hearken to and to give amends for any complaint that should be brought by any against any other.'[1]

Among many examples of this kind of jurisdiction in the Eyre of Kent we may take a case in which the justices, through pure considerations of hardship (*duresse*), abate a writ of debt, perfectly good in law, against an executor:[2] and the pitiful story of John Fesrekyn, a poor man who had deposited a sum of six marks as perpetual security for board and lodging. The landlord not only failed to give value in bed and board, but with a startling reversion to *manus iniectio*, imprisoned his guest and loaded him with a chain, 'and gave me a scrap of bread as though I had been but a pauper begging his bread for God's sake, and through him I all but died of hunger'. John protests that, owing to the conspiracy of the rich to oppress the poor, he cannot afford counsel's fee, and begs that he may have his money back before the Judge leaves the town: in return for which favour he will go to the Holy Land and pray for the Judge, 'by your name, Sir John de Berewick'. Apparently John got his money, 'and', adds Bolland with a piety which every reader of this moving tale must share, 'if he afterwards reached the Holy Land I hope he did not forget his promise to Sir John Berewick'.[3]

Whether these doctrines of the Eyre were, as Bolland suggests,[4] 'the very beginning of the equitable

[1] Cf. S.S., vol. xxx, pp. xv f.

[2] *Anon.* v. *Anon.* (S.S., vol. xxvii. 42). Cf. Y.B. 6 Ed. II (S.S. xiii. 226 f.), cited Holdsworth, *H.E.L.* ii. 335.

[3] S.S., vol. xxvii, pp. xxiii f. Cf. Pollock, 'The Transformation of Equity', *Essays in Legal History, 1913* (ed. Vinogradoff), 292.

[4] S.S., vol. xxvii, p. xxix.

jurisdiction'—meaning the jurisdiction of Chancery—is open to question;[1] but there can be no doubt that they represented a frame of mind which was deeply characteristic of justice as conceived by the ordinary courts of the King.

Continuous relation between Common Law and Equity

Yet they did not remain, at all events in full, with the ordinary courts of the King, but were destined to pass to the special cognizance of the Chancellor. The *rigor iuris*, in the form of a very elaborate writ-procedure, triumphed over the *humana interpretatio*, and the principles of equity passed to other hands. It is no part of our present purpose to describe how English equity became divided from the Common Law, and through what historical causes, being once separated, it developed. That curious tale has been sufficiently told by legal historians, though important parts of it are still obscure.[2] For better or for worse, the stream of English law bifurcated into two channels, not without considerable disturbance of the soil and some turbidity of the waters. But the interdependence of law and equity has never wholly disappeared; the waters in both channels have come from the same stream. 'We ought', as Maitland said,[3] 'to think of equity as supplementary law, a sort of appendix added on to our code, or a sort of gloss written round our code. . . . We ought not to think of common law and equity as of two rival systems. Equity was not a self-sufficient system, at every point it presupposed the existence of common law.' It is true that once the divergence had taken place, it was impossible to ignore it. Attempts at a complete *rapprochement*, especially the well-known attempt of Lord Mansfield, failed, though not ignobly. But to this day there are many doctrines in the Common Law which are essentially equitable in character, if we use the word 'equitable'

[1] Holdsworth, *H.E.L.* ii. 342 ff.

[2] *Ibid.* ii. 341, 524, 554, 591 ff., etc.; Spence, *op. cit.* i. 322 ff., etc.; Baldwin, *The King's Council*, 246 ff.

[3] *Equity*, 18 f.

in its wider sense. Whether or not quasi-contract in English law can be based on a principle of natural justice is still hotly disputed;[1] Lord Mansfield's broad statement of principle in *Moses* v. *Macferlan* (1760), 2 Burr. 1009, has, beyond doubt, been greatly modified, if not actually rejected, by later decisions; but there is much ground for thinking that a restraint on unjust enrichment—though much narrower than the praetorian doctrine of Roman Law—runs through our whole law of quasi-contract. An equitable spirit is also conspicuous in the Common Law treatment of voidable contracts, of subrogation,[2] of contribution between co-sureties and between debtor and surety, and of bailment.[3] Nor is it to be imagined that 'natural justice', however much it may be distrusted as against a positive rule of law, is by any means a mere phrase in our courts of Common Law.

2. Equity and morality in English law

Con-science

If we look for one general principle which more than any other influenced equity as it was developed by the Chancery, we find it in a philosophical and theological conception of *conscience*. The term was from an early date familiar to English lawyers. In the Common Law courts of the thirteenth and fourteenth centuries, we hear a good deal, in many connexions, about 'conscience', 'good faith', 'reason', 'conscience and law', 'the law of conscience', 'law and right', 'law, right, and good conscience', 'right and reason', 'reason and good faith':

[1] See 53 *L.Q.R.* 302, 447, 449, 54 *ibid.* 24, 29, 201, and 55 *ibid.* 37. 'The whole modern doctrine of . . . quasi-contract rests on a bold and timely application . . . of principles derived from the Law of Nature': Pollock, *Essays in the Law*, 68 f. See Winfield, *The Province of the Law of Tort*, ch. vii; Lord Wright, *Legal Essays and Addresses*, 1; Cheshire and Fifoot, *Contracts* (5th ed.), 553 ff., where the principal authorities are cited; Winfield, 'Equity and Quasi-Contract', 64 *L.Q.R.* 46; C. K. Allen, 'Fraud, Quasi-Contract and False Pretences', 54 *L.Q.R.* 201.

[2] See Buckland, *Equity in Roman Law*, 47 ff.

[3] S. G. Fisher, 'Equity through Common Law Forms', 1 *L.Q.R.* 462; and see on *brevia anticipantia*, *ante*, p. 402. Even a constitutional remedy like the Petition of Right is said to be founded on 'moral equity and conscience': Tindal C.J. in *Gibson* v. *East India Co.* (1839), 5 Bing. N.C. at p. 274 (*scil.* before the passing of the Petition of Right Act, 1860).

of 'equity' we hear very little.[1] In the practice of the Chancery, when it diverged from the Common Law, we hear still more about *conscience* from an angle of view which attempts, though with only partial success, to be scientifically dialectical.

St. Germain

For this is the ambitious aim of the remarkable treatise of St. Germain, *Doctor and Student*, which appeared early in the sixteenth century. It attempts to approach our whole system of law from the standpoint of moral philosophy. A Doctor of Divinity, professing ignorance of technical rules of law, seeks enlightenment from a student of law concerning the attitude of our jurisprudence towards conscience. The ensuing discussion is not always very clear; it wanders into many by-paths, interesting enough in themselves, but bearing a somewhat tenuous relation to the main inquiry. It is only by nimble acrobatics that the writer brings all his various topics back to his central theme, and for this reason the treatise as a whole leaves the impression of being amorphous. But the attempt is highly instructive, if over-ingenious.

What does St. Germain mean by conscience? Naturally the reply lies in the mouth of the Doctor of Divinity. He treats us to an academic account of *sinderesis*,[2] reason, and conscience, all plainly canonical and somewhat pietistic in conception. Then he proceeds to discuss the elements of equity. It is a righteousness which considers all the particular circumstances of the deed, tempering justice with mercy. This is a necessary element in every law, 'for the extreme righteousness is extreme wrong: as who saith, if thou take all that the words of the law give thee, thou shalt sometimes do against the law'. It is impossible to frame any general rule of law which will not fail in some cases; and it is an implied reservation in every law that it is not to operate

[1] Baildon, *Select Cases in Chancery* (S.S., vol. x), xxix f.

[2] A crude anglicization of συντήρησις: Vinogradoff, 'Reason and Conscience in Sixteenth-Century Jurisprudence', *Collected Papers*, ii. 190.

against the law of God and the law of reason. Any law without this limitation is doomed to failure: 'for such causes might come, that he that would observe the law should break both the law of God and the law of reason'. Thus equity follows the intent rather than the words. The Student supports this view by legal examples, citing as an instance, among others, a statute of Edward III which forbids, on pain of imprisonment, the giving of alms to any valiant beggar. If, he says, a man were to meet a beggar actually perishing for want of succour, and give him assistance, he would be excused from the statute by the law of reason. Yes, says the Doctor, but would he be excused at Common Law, or, for the matter of that, in the Chancery? The Student is very doubtful; but thinks he would be excused on the ground that the statute must have intended such an exception.[1] Some discussion follows on various rules of the Chancery, and the Student makes the important point that the Chancery acts *in personam* by means of the subpoena, and this is its characteristic mark. We learn from a reply to one of the Doctor's questions that the technical jurisdiction of the Chancery was not as yet known by the general term 'equity', that word being understood in its broad meaning of natural justice.

Canon Law

St. Germain's preoccupation is with *equity in general*, the faculty, sublimated in conscience, of discerning between good and evil and inclining towards the good; it 'is not occasional and overriding interference, but enlightened scientific interpretation'.[2] Sir Paul Vinogradoff has shown[3] that St. Germain derived many of his ideas and practically all his method from John Gerson (1363–1429), the famous 'Doctor Christianissimus' and 'Doctor Consolatorius' and Chancellor of the University of Paris. In effect, therefore, *Doctor and Student*,

[1] One would have supposed that the simple answer was that a beggar dying of starvation was not 'valiant' (i.e. 'able-bodied')!

[2] Pollock, 'The Transformation of Equity' (*loc. cit.*), 294.

[3] *Op. cit.*

which came at a most opportune time in the development of the Chancery and was very widely known,[1] expounded canonical doctrines for the benefit of English readers and particularly of English lawyers. Not only did the book itself exercise a considerable influence, but it was symptomatic of a tendency big with important consequences for English equity; it meant that 'the common lawyers of the fifteenth century joined the ecclesiastics seated in the Chancery in framing views about the administration of equity, which, though Decretals and Summae Confessorum were not quoted, strongly savoured of the principles and distinctions of the Canon Law. The marked differences on particular points are hardly sufficient to obliterate the impression that we have to reckon not only with the stress of business requirements and with a spontaneous growth of English doctrines, but also with a process of indirect reception of Canon Law.'[2]

Systematization of equity

Thus English equity begins to be systematized under the guidance of a governing moral principle. Not that we can suppose that all the Chancellors were assiduous and consistent in the pursuit of that principle. Under the Tudors some of them behaved with an arbitrariness worthy of their royal masters, going far beyond the proper function of a Court of Conscience in imposing all kinds of extra-legal duties on litigants. These occasional aberrations may have inspired Selden's oft-quoted, but probably only half-serious, quip about the length of the Chancellor's foot. But they were not typical; the 'conscience' which the Chancellor set before him was normally something more constant and enduring than mere caprice. A 'hardening' process sets in. In 1609 appeared a volume (now rare) entitled *Epieikeia*, by a barrister named Thomas Ashe. It is a somewhat pedestrian work, consisting chiefly of tabulations, but it contains an interesting definition of equity, quoted from West's *Symboleography*. Equity is here described as '*a ruled kind*

[1] Holdsworth, *H.E.L.* v. 266 ff. [2] Vinogradoff, *op. cit.*

of justice'. Though 'ruled', it is 'allayed with the sweetness of mercy, and may well be compared to a shoemaker's shop, that is furnished with all manner and sorts of lasts for men's feet, where each man may be sure to find one last or other that shall fit him, be he great or small'.[1] By 1676 we find Lord Nottingham expressly repudiating the notion that the conscience of the Chancellor is merely *naturalis et interna*,[2] and in 1818 Lord Eldon summarily repudiates any notion that mere individual discretion is open to an Equity judge.[3]

3. Forms of English equitable jurisdiction

Let us remind ourselves briefly of the principal forms which this settled system of conscience has taken in English law. Each one of the doctrines of the Chancery has a history of its own, and many accidental elements have entered in during the course of development; but we may distinguish certain leading principles. Sir Thomas More summarized them aphoristically as 'fraud, accident, and things of confidence'.[4] That classification still covers no small part of the ground, but in modern equity it may be expanded as follows:

'Things of confidence'

1. '*Things of confidence.*' The enforcement of obligations dictated rather by conscience than by a positive *vinculum iuris*—sometimes, indeed, dictated in direct opposition to the law. Here we must place uses and trusts, still the most important part of Chancery jurisdiction. Here, too, the equity of redemption in mortgages, and equitable obligations between principal and surety, partners and co-adventurers (including general average contribution). In these cases equities are enforced in bilateral obligations: a unilateral obligation is imposed on the executor and administrator, with a peculiarly

[1] The similarity between this figure of speech and Selden's may be pure coincidence, but is striking, and it is difficult to resist the conclusion that there has been a borrowing. West's book was published in 1605, Selden's *Table Talk* in 1689.

[2] *Cook* v. *Fountain*, 3 Swanst. 385, 600.

[3] *Gee* v. *Pritchard*, 2 Swanst. 402, 414; see Spence, *op. cit.* i. 413 ff., and Excursus D, *ante*, p. 380.

[4] 1 Roll. *Abr.* 374; Spence, *op. cit.* i. 413.

stringent fiduciary duty both to the quick and the dead. 'Confidence' is also the starting-point of technical doctrines such as conversion, joint ownership, assignment of choses in action, and powers of appointment.

Fraud

2. *Fraud*. Unconscionable dealing short of actionable deceit at Common Law. Here the Chancery had to proceed with caution. It would have been going much too far to repudiate a legal bond merely because one of the parties to it had not acted up to the highest standards of honour or conscience. Equity did not pose as pure morality. It could not, for example, reject a defence based on a strict statutory rule merely because it was morally unmeritorious.[1] It could sometimes find a way round technical Common Law rules in the interests of conscience—e.g. it could refuse to make a debtor pay twice over solely because he had lost the written acquittance of his first payment. But for the most part equitable fraud came within the domain of 'things of confidence', resolving itself into cases—generically, undue influence and catching bargains—where there was some special relationship of trust or confidence between the parties.

Accident

3. *Accident*, or, as it used to be called, 'extremity'. The doctrine cannot be precisely formulated, since of

[1] None the less, equity has, even in modern days, sometimes come very near to abrogating the provisions of statutes. It was only by a transparent fiction that the 'equitable doctrine of part performance' could be said to 'follow' s. 1 of the Statute of Frauds and s. 3 of the Real Property Act, 1845: in reality, it could and did render those sections nugatory for all practical purposes. Similarly, the doctrine of equitable mortgage by deposit of deeds was invented in the teeth of the Statute of Frauds: *Russell* v. *R.* (1783), 1 Brown Ch. 269, and 2 *White and Tudor* (9th ed.), 69 ff. On the question whether it is proper for a trustee in bankruptcy to press to the point of hardship a strictly statutory right, see *Scranton's Trustee* v. *Pearse*, [1922] 2 Ch. 87, and preceding cases there cited; 38 *L.Q.R.* 402, and the present writer's 'Legal Morality and the Ius Abutendi', *Legal Duties*, 95. 'Where there is an apparent fraud, or a case dubious in the law of which the party could not have knowledge, this will be aided in equity encounter the statute': Roll. *Abr.* 378 (S.), 4, 6; an extremely vague doctrine, which is, however, apparently the basis of the equitable evasions of the Statute of Frauds: *Rochefoucauld* v. *Boustead*, [1897] 1 Ch. 196. The situation does not seem to be affected by the Law of Property Act, 1925, s. 52. On the 'equity of a statute', see *post*, pp. 451 ff.

its very nature it contemplates the undefined case: the case where, through the happening of some unforeseen event, or through the omission or misstatement of some term, an obligation good in its essence stands in danger of being thrown away. The cause of the defect must be purely accidental, in the sense that it could not have been foreseen by reasonable prudence. Equity is not a *procurator fatuorum*[1] and no man has a claim to be relieved from his own weakness, unless he was from the first at a disadvantage or his disability was deliberately exploited. Out of this doctrine grow the equitable jurisdiction in regard to mistake, and, as a corollary, the rectification and rescission of documents.

Giving effect to intentions

4. *Giving effect to intentions*, more especially those intentions which are dubiously or imperfectly expressed. This is, or ought to be, the guiding principle in the interpretation of wills, settlements, and other documents. In practice, artificial rules of construction have in great measure overlaid the central notion of penetrating to the actual intention behind the words.

Tutelary jurisdiction

5. *Tutelary jurisdiction* in respect of those who, through special circumstances, are particularly in need of protection: infants, married women, mariners, borrowers, those who are subject to harsh penalties, and formerly the poor and the insane. The principle here is humanity amounting, at its highest, to actual tutelage in the case of infants; at its lowest, to a very present help in time of trouble. In the same spirit, Chancery exercises a special jurisdiction over public charitable objects. There is no more characteristic instance of this spirit of enlightened benignity than the example set to the legislature in the protection of married women's property from 'kicks and kisses'.[2]

Supplementary remedies

6. *Remedies supplementary to the Common Law*: specific performances, specific restitution, and formerly discovery

[1] This was, however, the function which the Chancellor, Bishop Stillington, ascribed to the Deity in 1467! See Vinogradoff, *op. cit.* 199.

[2] Dicey, *Law and Opinion in England*, Lect. XI.

of documents; injunctions mandatory and prohibitory, interim and perpetual.

Throughout these several departments of jurisdiction runs the common principle that the Chancellor addresses himself directly to the conscience of the individual, acting *in personam* by means of the subpoena and being therefore independent of territorial limits of jurisdiction.[1]

IV. EQUITY AS A SOURCE OF LAW

Common Law and Equity not necessarily distinct branches of jurisdiction

These principles and their many subsidiary departments have, for a century at least, been established in our law as a stable system, and from the beginning of our legal studies we are accustomed to think of law and equity as sharply divided. The distinction has certainly been modified by the Judicature Acts, but the policy of those statutes, so often referred to as a 'fusion', in no sense meant the merger of one system in the other. There is still a frontier between the Common Law and the Chancery. The training is different, the habit of thought is different, the subjects of jurisdiction are different; and the English Bar is still divided into two kinds of practitioners who deal with quite distinct kinds of material and may be said without impiety to stand to each other in a state of friendly neutrality. Nobody supposes nowadays that equity is purely matter of conscience and Common Law purely matter of *ius strictum*. They are simply different branches of legal science; but the boundary between them is so clearly drawn that we in England are apt to think of the duality as juristically inevitable. It is not so today in Continental systems. In France and Germany, for example, equity has been a

[1] For a more detailed discussion than is here possible of the nature of equitable rights and the classification of equitable remedies, see Maitland, *Equity*; Lévy-Ullmann, *Éléments d'introduction générale à l'étude des sciences juridiques*, ii, Part III; Hohfeld, 'The Relations between Equity and Law', *Fundamental Legal Conceptions*, 115; H. G. Hanbury, 'The Field of Modern Equity', *Essays in Equity*, 23, and *Modern Equity*, ch. iii.

clearly recognized element in the administration of justice, and enjoined upon the judge, but assigned to no special jurisdiction.[1] Austin rightly insists that the cleavage which occurred in the Roman and English systems is to be attributed to historical causes and not to any necessity in the nature of the case. We have seen that the general spirit of equity was inherent in our medieval courts, and that certain doctrines which we have come to regard as peculiarly equitable, in the technical sense, were anticipated by Common Law writs and by the practice of the itinerant justices. It has been contended by writers of authority that the separation which eventually took place was bound to happen in the natural order of things, and that it was fortunate for our jurisprudence that it did happen;[2] but while we must admit the practical inconveniences which might have arisen in respect of procedure, it is difficult to doubt that had things fallen out differently, and had the Chancellor's separate jurisdiction never been recognized, our Common Law would have found that a vigorous element of equity was indispensable to its existence.

But equity a necessary source of law

We must not, then, regard a self-contained, separate system of technical equity as a necessarily characteristic source of law. But, on the other hand, we cannot regard equity, as some writers would have us do, as merely 'a frame of mind in dealing with legal questions, and not a source of law'.[3] It is a frame of mind so essential as an adjunct to strict law that we cannot rule it out as a source of legal institutions. Many other 'frames of mind' are, in a sense, sources of law, simply because law is a product of human reason: morality, religion, logic, convenience, economic necessities, and many similar factors all exert

[1] *Code. Civ.*, Arts. 565, 1135, 1845. See further Gény, *Méthode d'interprétation*, ii. 109, 112. The provisions of the *Burgerliches Gesetzbuch* as to good faith are wide and far-reaching; e.g. Arts. 133, 155, 242. See further Schuster, *German Civil Law*, 104 ff., 144.

[2] Kerly, *op. cit.* 11 ff.; Fisher, 'Equity through Common Law Forms', 1 *L.Q.R.* 462.

[3] J. C. Gray, *The Nature and Source of the Law*, 308.

a formative influence. But these are sources only indirectly, whereas legal notions and rules are perpetually derived directly from equity. Doubtless the ultimate source is the natural sense of justice inherent in conscience; but the lawyer is concerned to discover the concrete forms which are derived, in known systems of law, from this source of formal justice. The main lines of English equity which I have endeavoured to sketch are no mere casual phenomena. An intelligible principle of justice runs through them all, and their analogies are to be found in all systems where liberal interpretation has been at work.[1] Law cannot be conceived apart from interpretation, and one of the most important interpretative factors is a trained sense of *discretionary* justice. This remains true whether this part of the judicial function is assigned to a separate jurisdiction, as it is in England, or is part of the common property of all judges, as it is on the Continent.

The *rigor aequitatis*

In England equity has had a social as well as a juristic value. Its greatest invention, the trust, has been, in Maitland's phrase,[2] 'a most powerful instrument of social experimentation.

To name some well-known instances:—It (in effect) enabled the landowner to devise his land by will until at length the legislature had to give way, though not until a rebellion had been caused and crushed. It (in effect) enabled a married woman to have property that was all her own until at length the legislature had to give way. It (in effect) enabled men to form joint-stock companies within limited liability, until at length the legislature had to give way. The case of the married woman is specially instructive. We see a prolonged experiment. It is deemed a great success. And at last it becomes impossible to maintain (in effect) one law for the poor and another for the rich, since, at least in general estimation, the tried and well-known "separate use" has been working well. Then on the other hand let us observe how impossible it would have been for the most courageous Court of Common Law to make or to suffer any experimentation in this

[1] As, for example, in Roman technical doctrines of equity: *ante*, pp. 394 ff.
[2] 'The Unincorporate Body', *Coll. Papers*, iii. 278.

quarter. . . . The trust has given us a liberal substitute for a law about personified institutions. The trust has given us a liberal supplement for a necessarily meagre law of corporations.'

For the valiant part which it has played in matters of such high social importance as these our debt to equity is great and our acknowledgement should be unstinted. At the same time it is matter of regret that in certain respects our system of equity, springing from such liberal principles, should have developed on lines which sometimes seem to be the opposite of natural justice. It is a fact only too observable that while the litigant in the Queen's Bench has some rudimentary notion of his rights and his prospects, the litigant in the Chancery Division frequently cannot see a step ahead on his dolorous way. This is partly the heritage of our feudal land law, with the most tortuous intricacies of which the Chancery has had to wrestle. A person of ordinary intelligence can understand a simple contract and will not be entirely baffled even by a complicated contract; but put in his hands a strict settlement of real property, and were he the greatest genius born, he could not understand two consecutive sentences of it without some initiation into the mysteries of the Chancery.

And not all the artificiality of equity comes from the land law. It is a curious paradox that in its anxiety to respect conscience, Chancery has gone to extremes which sometimes paralyse conscience. Bramwell L.J. once observed[1] that the result of a good many doctrines of Courts of Equity was 'a disregard of general principles

[1] *Greaves* v. *Tofield* (1880), 14 Ch.D. 563, 578 (one of the rare occasions on which a decision of Jessel M.R. was reversed by the Court of Appeal, though with great reluctance so far as Bramwell L.J. was concerned). This was not the only time that this outspoken judge tilted at the Chancery. In *Salt* v. *Marquess of Northampton*, [1892] A.C. at p. 19, (as Lord Bramwell) he referred sardonically to certain aspects of the doctrine of 'clog' as the result of 'the piety or love of fees of those who administered equity'; and observed that 'the borrower was such a favourite with courts of equity that they would let him break his contract, and perhaps, by disabling him from binding himself, disable him from contracting on the most advantageous terms to himself'.

and general rules in the endeavour to do justice more or less fanciful in certain particular cases'. With all respect, it would seem that the besetting sin of equity is rather an insistence on artificial doctrines to the prejudice of that substantial justice 'in certain particular cases' which the spirit of equity was originally intended to promote. There is an 'over-righteousness' of equity as unfortunate in its consequences as the 'over-righteousness' of law, a *rigor aequitatis* as austere as the *rigor iuris*.[1] Thus the anxiety to interpret intention has led to the establishment of rules which, degenerating into shibboleths, have merely succeeded in defeating intention; and this is particularly true of the interpretation of wills, where it is specially important (but apparently specially difficult) for intention to be fulfilled.[2] In this respect the Chancery has been far more deeply in bondage to precedent than has the Common Law. 'In hearing case after case cited', said James L.J.,[3] 'I could not help feeling that the officious kindness of the Court of Chancery in interposing trusts where in many cases the father of the family never meant to create trusts, must have been a very cruel kindness indeed.' 'The doctrine of precatory trusts', said Lopes L.J.,[4] 'is a creature of equity, by whose aid the intentions of testators, in my judgement, have too frequently been defeated.' The fantastic results of the Rule against Perpetuities are thus described by a modern Lord of Appeal trained in the principles of equity:

'We have in this case, my Lords, an extreme but by no means uncommon illustration of the stringency—I might even describe it as the penal character—of this rule. At no time was there here any practical possibility that a perpetuity could eventuate as a result of the complete fulfilment of the terms of the gift in

[1] See *contra* H. G. Hanbury, 'The Field of Modern Equity', *Essays in Equity*, 23.

[2] See, for example, Lord Cairns L.C. in *Sykes* v. *S.* (1868), L.R. 3 Ch. at p. 302, and cf. *In re Forrest*, [1931] 1 Ch. 162. See further H. A. Smith, 'Interpretation in English and Continental Law', *J.S.C.L.* (3rd ser.), ix. 153.

[3] *Lambe* v. *Eames* (1871), L.R. 6 Ch. 597, 599.

[4] *Hill* v. *H.*, [1897] 1 Q.B. 483, 488.

question; while, by the time any contest as to the validity of the gift arose, it had become, by reason of the death of the testator's father, inconceivable that any infraction of the rule could be involved in it. . . .

'In its application to the present case, the rule has been really a snare, useless so far as its legitimate purpose is concerned, but operative . . . to produce an intestacy under which certainly one person would greatly benefit whose interests it was the permissible and express purpose of the testator by his codicil to circumscribe and reduce.

'In my experience nearly all modern manifestations of the rule are of this character, and have this result . . . . So far as the Courts are concerned, the existence of the rule in these days is usually made manifest only in cases where nothing of the kind having been desired or suspected, and where by nothing short of a miracle could a perpetuity at any time have supervened, even that possibility has, by the time of the contest, ceased to be existent. All the same in these cases the rule is fatal even to gifts so innocuous, and I cannot doubt that such a result is both mischievous and unfortunate, in many directions—in this notably, that it brings a sound principle into entirely gratuitous discredit.'[1]

At one period the 'conscience' of the trustee was so severely scrutinized that ordinary honest execution of a trust became a matter of considerable difficulty; and it was not till 1887 that doctrines of this kind were tempered with common sense, not to say mercy.[2] The doctrine of the ademption and the satisfaction of debts by legacies has been pushed to a severe and, in some circumstances, unreasonable extreme, and there it still remains.[3] The doctrine of consolidation of mortgages has reached a degree of questionable utility which only statute can cure;[4] and until 1914[5] the doctrine of 'collateral

[1] Lord Blanesburgh in *Ward* v. *Van der Loeff*, [1924] A.C. 653, 677. Cf. Lord Buckmaster, *Portman* v. *P.*, [1922] 2 A.C. 473, 506.

[2] *Learoyd* v. *Whiteley*, 12 App. Cas. 727.

[3] *In re Carrington*, [1932] 1 Ch. 1, whereon see *ante*, p. 340.

[4] It is left practically untouched by the Law of Property Act, 1925, s. 93. On the undesirable elements of the doctrine, see observations of all the Lords in *Pledge* v. *White*, [1896] A.C. 187.

[5] *Kreglinger* v. *New Patagonia Meat Co.*, [1914] A.C. 25.

advantages' in mortgages bade fair to go the same road. Modern legislation, by reforming our troublesome dual system of devolution, may, in course of time, straighten out the intricacies of conversion and reconversion; but that, too, is an equitable principle which has caused more frustration of purpose than it has ever brought enlightenment to obscure intentions. The whole law relating to charitable trusts has been well described as a 'wilderness',[1] and it provides one of the worst examples in our law of endless technical distinctions which have no relation to reality or common sense, and which again and again succeed only in frustrating the intentions, to the prejudice of the public interest, of benevolently minded testators. Faith and Hope are highly necessary virtues in all courts of law, but in the Chancery Division Charity is the least, and not 'the greatest of these'. When it is remembered how much of the early jurisdiction of conscience was 'in the way of charity', there is something peculiarly ironical in these words of a Master of the Rolls:

'I, at any rate, am unable to find any principle which will guide one easily and safely through the tangle of the cases as to what is and what is not a charitable gift. . . . The whole subject is in an artificial atmosphere altogether. A large number of gifts are held to be charitable which would not be called charitable in the ordinary acceptation of the term, and when one takes gifts which have been held to be charitable and compares them with gifts which have been held not to be charitable, it is very difficult to see what the principle is on which the distinction rests. I confess I find considerable difficulty in understanding the exact reason why a gift for the benefit of animals, and for the prevention of cruelty to animals generally, should be a good charitable gift, while a gift for philanthropic purposes, which, I take it, is for the benefit of mankind generally, should be bad as a charitable gift. The gift for the benefit of animals, apparently, is held to be valid because it is educative of mankind, it being good for mankind that they should be taught not to be cruel but kind to animals, and one would quite agree with that. But if the benefit

[1] N. Bentwich, 'The Wilderness of Legal Charity', 49 *L.Q.R.* 520.

of mankind on that particular side makes that a good charitable gift, it is a little difficult to see why any philanthropic purpose to benefit mankind on all sides is a bad one. But it is so; it has been so decided, and therefore the present case is made very difficult, as every case is where there is no governing principle which can be applied.'[1]

While, therefore, Equity (in the technical sense) has made important contributions to our law, there is another and a darker side of the picture. The history of the Court of Chancery is one of the least creditable in our legal records. Existing nominally for the promotion of liberal justice, it was for long corrupt, obstructive, and reactionary, prolonging litigation for the most unworthy motives and obstinately resisting all efforts at reform. At no period was the Common Law open to the same charges in the same degree. About a century ago a cleansing process had to be undertaken for the sake of public health, which was suffering severely. Charles Dickens did not exaggerate the desolation which the cold hand of the old Court of Chancery could spread among those who came to it 'for the love of God and in the way of charity'. All that is gone, and we breathe again a healthy atmosphere; but even today it is not in a spirit of cynicism, but of cold truth, that a modern Chancery judge is able to say, 'This Court is not a Court of conscience'.[2] Our scepticism of 'conscience' is commensurate with our veneration for

[1] Lord Sterndale M.R. in *In re Tetley*, [1923] 1 Ch. at p. 266 (affirmed *sub nom. Att.-Gen.* v. *National Provincial Bank*, [1924] A.C. 262), cited Bentwich, *op. cit.* A striking example of the incongruity to which Lord Sterndale refers will be found in the contrast between this same case (*In re Tetley*) and the subsequent decision of the Court of Appeal in *In re Smith*, [1932] 1 Ch. 153. Within recent years it has been held that an Anti-Vivisection Society is not a charity exempt from income tax (*National Anti-Vivisection Society* v. *Inland Revenue Commissioners*, [1948] A.C. 31) and that the 'prayer, contemplation, penance and self-sanctification' of an order of cloistered nuns are not charitable purposes (*Gilmour* v. *Coats*, [1949] A.C. 426); but that a bequest 'for the welfare of cats and kittens needing care and attention' serves a good charitable purpose, as being 'calculated to develop the finer side of human nature' (*Re Moss*, [1949] 1 All E.R. 495).

[2] Buckley J., *In re Telescriptor Syndicate*, [1903] 2 Ch. 174, 195.

prescriptive formula; perhaps both need to find a more tolerant basis of coexistence.

SUMMARY

To review our conclusions concerning equity as a source of law: Until recent times, when the technical elaboration of law has reached an advanced stage of development, a sharp line between the formal administration and the ethical ideal of justice has not been drawn. In the growth of legal systems a conscious aspiration toward a 'constant' of fairness in legal relationships has played a large part in shaping substantive rules. Equity has stood to strict law as 'supplementary or residuary jurisdiction'. This has been necessary because legal rules are formulated generalizations and as such are necessarily incomplete. Absolute uniformity cannot be achieved in the operation of any law, however well expressed in itself, and unless a margin is left for extraordinary cases it will be found that *summum ius* is *summa iniuria*, and the essential purpose of *ius* is thereby thwarted. This margin of discretionary interpretation may take the form either of *equity in general*—a general disposition towards a humane and liberal interpretation of law; or *particular equity*—a discretionary modification of the strict law in individual exceptional cases which are not covered by the general rule. The former, as an habitual judicial attitude of mind, is comparatively easy to maintain and is essential to every rational system of justice; the latter is more difficult, for though hard cases are in themselves a reflection, not to be ignored, upon the rule which causes them, it is not always possible or desirable to relax a necessary rule out of compassion for an unfortunate individual. In this sense, what is popularly called 'injustice' is inevitable in certain cases. Popular ideas of justice and injustice are not always to be trusted, being too much influenced by the particular and too little aware of the general. Nevertheless, the popular or natural sense of justice cannot be altogether disregarded; it has a real meaning in law, since it represents an average element in the community with which it is necessary that law should harmonize; and most of the equitable or discretionary ingredients which are constantly found in legal systems are based upon this primary sense of justice inherent in the average moral sense of the community.

The necessity for a supplementary and benevolent jurisdiction was insisted on by the Greek philosophers. Plato emphasizes the point that legal generalizations, if unmodified by a liberal spirit, become 'like an obstinate and ignorant tyrant', and that equity is therefore indispensable to any intelligent administration of justice. Aristotle holds that justice and equity are 'neither absolutely the same nor generically different'—i.e. the difference between them is not one of kind, but of degree, and equity is the higher degree. Its function is that of a *corrective* of legal justice, again because the 'universality' of law cannot be completely universal. But in exercising this corrective function, equity must as far as possible follow the spirit of the law which it seeks to apply benevolently, and it must do that which presumably the legislator himself would have done had he contemplated the exceptional case. Thus equity embodies a moral ideal, and it is constant and immutable while positive law is inevitably subject to many imperfections and inconsistencies. These principles of equity were not mere counsels of perfection in Greek law. It is probable that pleaders, for their own purposes, made disingenuous appeals to equity when more solid resources failed them; but there is ample evidence that, despite all rhetorical exaggerations and forensic artifices, the general principle of equity was an integral and valuable part of the Athenian administration of justice.

Roman jurisprudence was influenced in some measure by Greek philosophical ideas; and it is probable that this influence is to be traced in the Roman conception of *aequitas* and *aequum et bonum*, which is very prominent in Roman Law. It was commended and enjoined by imperial authority as a general principle of judicial interpretation; and it is to be found not only as an abstraction of speculative jurisprudence, but in many substantive doctrines of the Roman system. It is recognized by a number of different titles in many various contexts, but it may be said to have been particularly active in the supersession of agnation by the claims of natural kinship, in the development of a governing principle of good faith as against strict form in contractual obligations, in the endeavour to discover and carry out the true intentions of those who purport to effect acts-in-the-law, in the discouragement of all unjust enrichment at the expense of another, in the discountenancing of super-subtle interpretation of the letter of the law and of the unmeritorious or malicious use of strict legal right; and finally, in a general discretion of good faith and common sense which was inherent in the office of the magistrate. These principles were doubtless sometimes appealed to, as in Greek law, to bolster up a case otherwise weak; hence we hear protests against their indiscriminate use; but kept within proper limits, and maintained without prejudice to a firm application of the general law, their effect on Roman Law was strong and beneficent.

In English law, Equity has become, in the course of time, a technical system distinct from the Common Law; but its origin is not to be found exclusively in the jurisdiction of the Chancellor. A prerogative of mercy and equity was from the earliest times deemed to be inherent in the royal office. In the thirteenth century the jurisdiction of the King's Court is that of a 'court that can do whatever equity may require'. Under Henry II and Henry III 'the King's court wields discretionary powers such as are not at the command of lower courts, and the use of these powers is an exhibition of "equity"'. Much is done purely *de consilio curiae*.

The rules of substantive law are strict, those of adjective law even stricter; but the Court retains a general humane discretion. Further, a number of Common Law writs are directed towards remedies which later would have been considered essentially 'equitable' in character. The discretionary powers of the King's Justices were even wider and more vigorous in their jurisdiction in Eyre, and the itinerant judges were regarded as representing the kingly office in doing not what strict law only, but what right and justice also demanded. It is probable that these Common Law methods 'on circuit' influenced importantly the equitable principles which were subsequently developed by the Chancellor.

For historical and procedural reasons, the general principle of equity in England was destined to pass from the control of the Common Law to that of the Chancellor's Court. But the vital connexion between the two jurisdictions has always been maintained, and they are not to be thought of as two rival systems. Many doctrines of the Common Law are still 'equitable' in their nature and intent, and 'natural justice' is by no means an unreal element of our law today, though it must be regarded with jealousy and applied with caution.

In the jurisdiction of the Chancellor, the governing moral principle was that of conscience, an idea of theological origin, patiently expounded and much popularized by St. Germain in the early sixteenth century. It meant the partial acceptance by English Courts of doctrines of the Canon Law; and it was viewed not as a charter for mere caprice, but as a foundation for enlightened scientific interpretation. The Chancellors were not invariably consistent or conscientious in basing their jurisdiction on a uniform principle of this kind; but on the whole they strove steadfastly to do so, and the result was a consolidation of well-recognized principles of equity which reached a stage of approximate completenesss under Lord Eldon. The main departments of equity have separated themselves into fiduciary relationships, fraud less than actionable deceit at Common Law, accidental and unforeseen cases of hardship, tutelary jurisdiction of those under permanent or temporary disability, and remedies supplementary to the Common Law. These principles and their many reticulations are now a separate and almost entirely technical system of law, and it is no longer possible to think of the distinction between Common Law and Equity in England as identical with the distinction between *ius strictum* and *aequitas*. But it is not to be supposed that the bifurcation of a legal system into these two branches is a juristic necessity. It is perfectly possible, and is the existing fact in most systems other than the English, that the two principles may be comprised within one body of law and administered by the same courts. But it does not follow that equity is not in itself a distinct source of law. An element of discretionary justice is and always has been essential to the efficient interpretation and application of law. Equity is therefore the source of a vital ingredient in law, none the less necessary because it is supplementary.

It is doubtful whether the general spirit and utility of equity in English law have gained by being detached in a separate jurisdiction. English equity has developed a rigour and artificiality of its own which have sometimes resulted in the denial rather than the furtherance of natural justice. The desire to respect conscience has sometimes led to such an austerity that the dictates of conscience have become impracticable. Moreover, Equity has shown some over-anxiety to follow and maintain artificial rules when they have reached extremes of questionable utility. The nineteenth century has, however, done much to reform these defects.

VI

LEGISLATION

I. PLACE OF LEGISLATION AMONG SOURCES OF LAW

Relation between legislation and public opinion

Legislation and 'popular consciousness'

IF the relation between the State and the individual is regarded as nothing more than that of superior to inferior, the sovereign will, as expressed in legislation, may be arbitrary, despotic, and irrational. It need possess no social or moral content: that is a consideration lying outside its validity as law. It is merely the exercise of power, and the end to which the power is directed is not relevant to its authority as a command. Such was the Hobbesian view, and the danger which it threatened largely inspired Savigny's distrust of legislation. The conception of law as being imposed by external will, instead of growing of its own strength, was repellent to his whole theory of legal evolution. The apprehensions which he felt were to be vindicated in no small measure, more than a century later, by the legislative methods of totalitarian systems—and, ironically enough, not least in his own country. Savigny could not, however, get rid of legislation or even codification by merely dismissing them from the field of law. He lost his fight against them, and they were destined to develop even more rapidly than he could have imagined. But to justify it at all, he had to consider legislation as one of the tributaries of the great stream of popular law; and the conclusion was irresistible that if it was opposed to the main tendencies of native law, to that extent it deserved no recognition. Whether or not this view was justified in doctrine, it was clearly perilous in practice, since it raised insoluble problems between constituted authority and subjective judgement. Some of Savigny's followers escaped the dilemma by the same kind of reasoning which they applied to the supposed relationship between judicial interpretation and popular law. Enacted law, it was said, is the creature of the legislator's thought and will. But once the law is put in circulation, it begins to live a life of its own, a life quite independent of sovereign will, and essentially in harmony with popular consciousness. Something of the same kind is held in France by those who find it difficult to reconcile the strict authority of the Code with the effect of judicial interpretation upon it. Here, however, the 'separate life' of the enacted law takes its rise not from 'popular consciousness' but from the creative activity of tribunals.

Social elements in legislation

In modern democratic communities, the formula 'superior and inferior', or 'sovereign and subject', expresses only one aspect, and that not the most important, of the relationship between State and individual. The notion of a social contract, so far as it contains the idea of a mutuality of rights and duties between governor and governed—so far, too, as it expresses a compromise of individual liberty for the common weal—has not been without its lesson for the modern world; and in striving increasingly to realize this principle of mutuality, the nineteenth and the twentieth centuries have reverted to the idealistic political theories of the ancient world. The spirit which dominates modern doctrine is observable in the trend of legislation. At least in democratic countries, it is not a process solely of command and obedience, but of the action and reaction between constitutionally authorized initiative on the one hand and social forces on the other. Which creates the other, where one begins and the other ends, it is often very difficult to say. It is, however, certain that the great mass of 'inferiors' or 'subjects' are not nowadays simply passive recipients of orders.

Initiative of the legislature

This is not to say that democratic government means the automatic reproduction of the wishes of a majority in all circumstances or indeed in most. Legislators are representatives of the electors who invest them with authority, but nobody today cherishes the doctrine which has sometimes been heard in the past—that 'representation' means the mechanical carrying out of a 'mandate'. The mandate of any representative body, or any single member of it, can only be given in the most general terms and cannot exist at all without a very wide discretion and initiative. It needs but a glance at any volume of statutes to realize that a very great deal of the work of the legislature cannot be related to 'popular consciousness' or 'the will of the people' in any accurate sense of those terms. The plain fact is that there is *no* consciousness or will in the people about innumerable enactments which, both in their subject-matter and in their very language, would convey nothing to the enormous majority of the free and independent electors. It is not only in the technical minutiae of the law that the legislature does and must assume the initiative, being elected for the express purpose that it shall do so: the same is true of great matters of social and national policy. There have been long periods in English history when Parliament has been sluggish and unproductive, and has left it almost entirely to the courts to work out the principles of law. At other times its activity has been catholic and unceasing, and it has affected every domain of private and public life. The difference will be sufficiently realized by a comparison of the output of the age of Edward I[1] or the Tudor period with that of the eighteenth century. But nowhere is it more conspicuous than in the comparison between the eighteenth and early nineteenth centuries and the period of reform which began in 1832.

Public opinion

This latter period has been the special study of A. V. Dicey, and it is needless to traverse again the ground which he so brilliantly explored in his *Law and Opinion in England*. The effect of legislative industry he epitomizes in the terse phrase, 'Laws foster or create

[1] Holdsworth, *H.E.L.* ii. 299 ff., and 'The Reform of the Land Law: an Historical Retrospect', 42 *L.Q.R.* 158.

law-making opinion'; and in connexion with one of his most fully expounded examples of reformative legislation—the status of women in England—he sums up: 'Law and opinion are here so intermixed that it is difficult to say whether opinion has done most to produce legislation or laws to create a state of legislative opinion.' Since these words were written the movement to which they refer has been carried farther than Professor Dicey can have imagined in 1905, and infinitely farther than the framers of the Married Women's Property Acts could ever have conceived possible. Whether or not laws 'created a state of legislative opinion' in the eighties about the so-called 'emancipation' of women, there can be no doubt that opinion produced the most recent developments of this course of legislation. It was not, perhaps, a very representative opinion; it probably aroused, among the majority of the nation, more opposition than sympathy; yet it was sufficiently persistent, however grotesque its methods, to prevail in the end. Here, then, we have an example of the converse process to that which we have been considering. The 'popular consciousness' with which legislation must always stand in harmony—at least in societies with representative government—is the code of prevailing convictions which we call public opinion. To quote Professor Dicey again:

> 'There exists at any given time a body of beliefs, convictions, sentiments, accepted principles, or firmly-rooted prejudices, which, taken together, make up the public opinion of a particular era, or what we may call the reigning or predominant current of opinion, and, as regards at any rate the last three or four centuries, and especially the nineteenth century, the influence of this dominant current of opinion has, in England, if we look at the matter broadly, determined, directly or indirectly, the course of legislation.'

Today the current phrase to describe these general sentiments is the 'climate of opinion'. It is true that these prevailing convictions are usually traceable to the influence of individual dominant minds; it is true that in any age the main stream of opinion is often rendered turbid by cross-currents; but the main stream grows and flows, though it may sometimes run underground and become difficult for contemporaries to trace. They are, indeed, frequently mistaken about public opinion; the politician himself, who is most concerned to gauge it, is sometimes startlingly wrong in his calculations; but if it does not always manifest itself in palpable forms, it is no less a propelling force because it is unseen. The historian, viewing it in a more just perspective, is often able to see its form and intent where the men of its own generation are able to *feel* it driving them in a certain direction towards a destination which they cannot discern. So urgent is its impulse, so all-pervading its influence, and so momentous its achievements that we are warned to see in Savigny's People-Spirit something more than a mystical figment. Lacking sustained harmony with this public sentiment, sovereign legislation is sovereign only in name, and will soon cease to be even that. Other legislators must be found to restore the harmony, and silence any lingering echoes of discord.[1]

It will be apparent that these observations apply only to the democratic type of modern State. It is easy enough to imagine societies, or to find examples of them in the ancient and modern worlds, in which either there is no articulate public opinion, or such opinion as exists is terrorized into silence, is starved of impartial information, and is kept in bondage to perpetual, powerful, and highly organized emotional influences. It has been reserved for modern civilization to devise the thorough and scientific destruction of free thought; and the world does not yet know what the effect of these processes will be on spirit and action, private and public. With the legislation of absolutist systems of government we are not now concerned, though it may well be questioned

[1] The conception of the *Zeitgeist* or *Zeitbestimmung* in law has been elaborated by Ihering, *Geist des römischen Rechts*, i, Introd., and especially pp. 58 ff.

whether any government, however despotic, has ever been able to dispense, in the long run, with the vital support of public recognition. We are to consider statute as a source of law in the conditions of English society.

But what *is* public opinion and how does it reflect itself in the law of the land? The answer has never been simple at any period, and today, in populous communities with a highly ramified social organization, it is peculiarly difficult. There are experts who profess to be able, by various technical devices of 'polls', questionnaires, and 'cross-sections', to ascertain the trend of public opinion at any given moment on any given question. This is not the place to discuss the value of these expedients or the role—by no means negligible—which they may assume in the working of democratic institutions; but, whatever their merits or demerits, we should note one modern constitutional development which vitally affects the relationship between law and public opinion.

It is probable that in all societies at all times the principal initiative in creating formulated (as opposed to customary) law has rested with those who have had the power of direction, or what in modern terminology we call 'the government of the day'. The ordinary representative of current opinion—the 'private member' of our own time—obviously has never had as much scope for influencing the law as the actual wielders of power, whether they have been secular or sacerdotal, military or aristocratic, hereditary or popularly elected. Yet throughout the history of our own country, and doubtless of most others, a great deal of legislation which ostensibly has emanated directly from authority, often after long struggle and delay, has in fact been moulded by the persevering efforts of individuals or of groups. Even in the Middle Ages, many of our most famous ordinances and constitutional charters—the Great Charter itself not least among them—were the product of these unofficial and often anonymous influences.

Though in their final form they wore the vestments of sovereign pronouncement, they were in reality the off-spring of a kind of public opinion which a learned writer has called a sense of 'the community of the realm'.[1] In more recent times, the influence exerted by individuals like Bentham, Romilly, and Shaftesbury, or of groups like the Anti-Slavery Society, immediately spring to the mind.

Today, however, in England and in most other countries the business of legislation is almost entirely monopolized by the Government, of whatever political complexion it may be. Loud complaints are heard that the private member has less and less opportunity for advocating causes or effecting reforms which he believes respond to public opinion or need, and which sometimes he is pledged to espouse when he is elected. Government, however, claims its pre-emption on the grounds of lack of time and press of business; and it was only after a vote adverse to the Government of the day that in 1950 the private member of the House of Commons recovered his right, which had been suspended for ten years and which in any case is severely restricted, of introducing legislation. Even so, private members' Bills have little chance of success if the Government frowns upon them, and at the most they can represent only a very small fraction of legislative actitivity. The main responsibility must rest upon the Government not only for financial measures, in which constitutional convention grants it a monopoly, but for general legislation.

The danger of this system is that a Government, in pursuit of a preconceived policy, may impose upon the country a course of legislation with little regard to public opinion and especially the opinion of minorities. If that happens, government, by becoming arbitrary and bureaucratic, has clearly lost its democratic character. This danger must always be kept in view and guarded

[1] Helen Cam, *The Legislators of Medieval England*, Proceedings of the British Academy, 1945.

against, the more so when debate upon far-reaching and complicated measures is abridged by devices like the 'guillotine'; but up to the present time Government predominance in legislation does not necessarily negative, though it sometimes diminishes, the force of public opinion. The elements which contribute to the framing of much modern legislation are numerous and diverse. They are bound to be so in crowded communities where 'public opinion' is not usually one collective and unanimous sentiment, but is fragmented among many different sections and interests. It is doubtless possible to distinguish public opinion into many kinds and degrees, but we content ourselves here with one broad though by no means exhaustive classification.

At one end of the scale there are subjects of so technical a nature—such as a change in conveyancing law—that, as we have seen, there is really no general opinion about them at all except among a very limited class. At the other end of the scale there are questions of such immediate import to every individual—such as national defence or survival—that it is possible to discern an overwhelming majority of general sentiment. In between these two extremes there is a vast number of day-to-day concerns less obviously vital to individual and collective existence, but of importance to different sections of the community. Thus in innumerable matters in the modern State public opinion is not one, but many.

This diversity necessarily reflects itself in both the character and the process of law-making. A measure of any considerable range and importance is seldom introduced without a great deal of preparation and research of which the general public, and indeed many legislators, are scarcely aware. Numerous expert and representative interests are consulted, and many data assembled, often over a long period of time, so that a contemplated measure may pass from one administration to another before it is finally in shape for debate and enactment. The conception or framing of 'policy' comes in the main from the Cabinet, and in theory it is only formulated and carried into effect by the Executive—though in fact today not only the operation but even the genesis of policy often comes from the administrative departments; but there are many other sources, less easily definable, from which the impulse to legislation may be said to arise. The busy bees of Westminster and Whitehall pollinate plants of many different species which otherwise would bear no fruit. If the statutes for any year are traced back to their true origins, it will generally be found that innumerable influences have contributed to their inception. Besides the Cabinet, the individual Ministries, the Dominions and Colonies, and private members, there are Royal Commissions, Government Committees, local authorities, trade and professional unions and organizations representing employers, employees, and consumers, not to mention an enormous variety of charitable, religious, and many other kinds of voluntary organizations for the furtherance or the protection of causes, interests, and projects. Probably in no country in the world are there as many organizations of this kind as in England; we are, even more than the Americans, a nation of 'joiners'. All these societies form what are called in the United States 'pressure-groups', and they have a powerful influence on law-making by means of advocacy and negotiation which often extend over many years.[1] No less than Oxford is the lobby of the House of Commons the home of lost causes, but also of many victorious causes. There are, of course, more direct and vehement manifestations of public opinion than these. Sometimes it will flare up suddenly over an 'incident', or over some indiscretion, injustice, or scandal, which gains notoriety in the press and touches excitable susceptibilities; this is particularly true in England of any real or supposed infringement of personal liberty or any

[1] A full and interesting study of some of them may be found in Sir Ivor Jennings, *Parliament*, ch. vii.

arbitrary action by the police. Sometimes public opinion is reflected in that vague but unmistakable 'feeling of the House', which no Government can afford to ignore. Sometimes a judicial decision concentrates attention upon a glaring anomaly of the law, and a demand for immediate reform proves irresistible. These are the more obvious manifestations; but for the most part in the modern State the forces of public opinion, or of sections of it, are more subtle and less discernible than these loud and clear voices of sentiment or conviction. They make themselves felt through many and devious channels, so that their exact course and their degrees of efficacy are not easy to trace. But they are always trickling or flowing, and sometimes flooding.

We must turn now to consider the operation of the legislative function, and we cannot understand its place in our legal system without first glancing at (1) the forms of statute law and (2) the manner in which statute has established its peculiar authority. These aspects, then, we now proceed to discuss.[1]

II. FORMS OF LEGISLATION

Forms of ancient enactments

We are accustomed to think of statute, according to the classic definition of Coke, as that which has received the 'threefold assent' of King, Lords, and Commons. Anything less than this, whatever its persuasive force, has not the absolute authority of enactment; and it has happened even in modern times that the courts have refused to recognize deliberative 'measures' of Parliament less than statutes—e.g. resolutions of the House of Commons.[2] But the 'threefold assent' cannot refer to a time earlier than that of Parliamentary government based on modern constitutional theory. If we go back

[1] On the whole subject, see further S. E. Thorne, Intro. to the *Discourse upon the Statutes*, and S. B. Chrimes, *English Constitutional Ideas in the Fifteenth Century*.

[2] *Stockdale* v. *Hansard* (1839), 9 A. & E. 1; *Bowles* v. *Bank of England*, [1913] 1 Ch. 57.

to the twelfth century we cannot, of course, expect any such clear-cut conception of statutory forms and authority. So-called ancient statutes resemble modern statutes in that they are documents of public authority and governmental importance, but they are not necessarily legislative enactments, as we understand the term today. 'A statute in the reign of Edward I', writes Professor Plucknett,[1]

> 'simply means something established by royal authority; whether it is established by the King in Council, or in a Parliament of nobles, or in a Parliament of nobles and commons as well, is completely immaterial. It is equally immaterial what form the statute takes, whether it be a charter or a statute enrolled and proclaimed, or merely an administrative expression of the royal will notified to the judicial authorities. . . . The great concern of the government was to govern, and if in the course of its duties legislation became necessary, then it was effected simply and quickly without any complication or formalities.'

These governmental acts go by a bewildering variety of names—*carta*, *assisa*, *constitutio*, *provisio*, *ordinatio*, *statutum*, *isetnysse*, *établissement*: 'statute' is a less frequent term than most of the others, and seems to have meant 'something decided on', a *provision* of a public document, rather than the whole document itself.[2] Often they are declaratory and imperative in form,[3] but almost as often are in the nature of grant, or confirmation,[4] rather than of command, and not infrequently they take the form of solemn agreement among magnates of the realm.[5] It has been a subject of controversy whether the different names which were given to legislation represented any substantial distinction in nature and effect. Coke, for

[1] *Concise History* (5th ed.), 322. See, more fully, the same author's *Legislation of Edward I*, ch. i.

[2] Plucknett, *Statutes and their Interpretation in the Fourteenth Century*, 11. The word does not seem to have come into common use until the end of the thirteenth century: Richardson and Sayles, 'The Early Statutes', 50 *L.Q.R.* 201.

[3] e.g. Constitutions of Clarendon, 1164, Stubbs, *Sel. Ch.* (9th ed.), 161 ff.

[4] e.g. Statute of Merton, 1235, *Statt. R.* i. 1.

[5] e.g. Provisions of Oxford, 1258, Stubbs, *Sel. Ch.* 369 ff.

example, was positive enough about the distinction between a 'statute' and an 'ordinance', and his view has been upheld by some modern constitutionalists; but the better view seems to be that if any such distinction existed, it was shadowy, not consistently maintained, and not of great practical importance.[1] The key to the position is that in the government of medieval England there is no conscious doctrine of separation of powers. What we should now call the legislative and administrative functions frequently overlap. Law comes from the king himself as the sole proper source of sovereign control, but it comes in the shape not only of general decree, but of particular instructions given to judges and other public officers, and thus passes into the Common Law. This is specially noticeable in the far-reaching formative work of Henry II.[2] In the thirteenth century the king is still theoretically the fountain of all law, but by the time of Henry III we may observe at least the beginnings of an understanding that he shall not legislate for the whole realm without the advice and concurrence of his magnates.[3] Even in the fourteenth century, when the constitutional form of Parliament has become settled in essentials, there is no invariable line of demarcation between the legislative, judicial, and administrative functions.[4] It is probable that the Parliament of Oxford in 1285 marked an important change both in the form and in the peculiarly authoritative nature of statutes.[5] From the time (1285) of the Statue of Westminster II we begin to recognize something like a 'common form' of enactment, but subordinate rules, amounting in effect to legislation, continue to exist. 'It is not', says Sir William Holdsworth, 'till nearly the close of the Middle

[1] Co. Litt. 159 b; 4 Inst. 25; McIlwain, *High Court of Parliament*, 313, and *Magna Carta*, 145; Plucknett, *Statutes and their Interpretation*, 32, and *Concise History* (5th ed.), 322; Introd. to *Statt. R.*, ch. iii, s. 1. Richardson and Sayles, *op. cit.* 556, regard *permanency* as the distinguishing mark of a statute at this period.

[2] P. & M. i. 136.

[3] *Ibid.* 181.

[4] Plucknett, *op. cit.* 20.

[5] Richardson and Sayles, *op. cit.* 203 ff.

Ages that we can clearly distinguish between statutes and legislative acts less solemn than statutes.'[1]

Their uncertainty

It follows inevitably from this indistinctness of legislative theory that our early records of statute law are highly imperfect. In 1800, when a Select Committee of the House of Commons reported on the public records, it was stated that 'many statutes and ordinances in the rolls of Parliament are not inserted in the printed statute-book; and it is certain that many Acts and matters not found in any statute roll, nor contained in any printed edition of the statutes, are found on the Parliament Rolls, which appeared to have received the threefold assent of King, Lords, and Commons, or to have such qualities as have been allowed by courts of law to imply that assent'.[2] Our first statute roll dates from 1278, our first Parliament roll from 1290.[3] The statute rolls came to an end in 1468, or possibly 1489;[4] their place was taken by Enrolments of Acts of Parliament, and by engrossed copies of the original Acts, which have been continued until the present time. It is only since 1887 that a volume containing the annual statutes has been printed each year by authority.[5] But printed collections of statutes, entirely unofficial in character, began to appear from 1481 onwards, the first being the *Vieux Abridgement des Statutes*, printed by Letton and Machlinia.[6] No official

[1] *H.E.L.* ii. 220. Cf. Barraclough, 'Legislation in Medieval England', 56 *L.Q.R.* 75.

[2] Introd. to *Statt. R.*, *apud Select Essays in Anglo-American Legal History*, ii. 178. On the various forms of the official records, see Richardson and Sayles, *op. cit.* 206 ff., and Lévy-Ullmann, *Éléments d'introduction générale*, ii, ch. v.

[3] 'So far at least as its earlier portions are concerned, the statute roll makes no attempt at completeness, and certainly before 1299 its texts cannot be relied upon as strictly contemporary or authoritative. . . . The original basis of the roll was not a collection of authentic texts preserved in the chancery but a private collection of statutes such as was circulating among the legal profession in the late thirteenth century. To this collection little was added from other sources and even after 1299 those responsible for keeping the roll did not regard it as necessary to enter every statute upon it': Richardson and Sayles, *op. cit.* 215.

[4] Holdsworth, *H.E.L.* ii. 426.

[5] Ilbert, *Legislative Methods and Forms*, 26.

[6] *Statt. R.* i, App. A.

edition existed, with the result that we may see again the influence of jurist-law even in the domain of omnipotent sovereign legislation; for, as Sir William Holdsworth observes,

'lawyers were dependent for their knowledge of the contents of the Statute Book upon judicial dicta, books of authority and the work of private persons, such as Pulton, Cay, Hawkins, and Ruffhead. In the absence of official publications, the learning of the bar and the enterprise of the law publisher employed upon the Statute Book and the reports have exercised a very real censorship upon the sources of English law.'[1]

No official collection of enactments was undertaken until the beginning of the nineteenth century, when the Record Commission published the great series of Statutes of the Realm. They derived their material from many different sources beside the statute rolls and the official Exemplifications and Enrolments, their object being to include all those instruments which had been 'for a long series of years referred to, and accepted as statutes in the courts of law'.[2] They found it impossible to assign degrees of authority to all these instruments, and expressly disclaimed any intention of doing so.[3] The fact is that the true authority for a great many of our early statutes is what Hale called the 'general received tradition' of the

[1] *H.E.L.* ii. 427. 'The authority these texts command is the authority of tradition, the tradition of the courts coming to accept without verification documents which—if it would be a hard saying to call them spurious—are certainly often garbled and mutilated. But the tradition was of gradual growth: there was a stage when the courts relied upon no statute book': Richardson and Sayles, *op. cit.* 544.

[2] *Select Essays in Anglo-American Legal History*, ii. 177.

[3] *Ibid.* Even in the selection of texts, and in the translations of some of the statutes, the Record Commission was far from impeccable: see Plucknett, *Statutes and their Interpretation*, ch. ii. It is certain that some of the texts reproduced as 'statutes' cannot properly be called so. Thus the *Circumspecte Agatis* of 1285 (?) (Stubbs, *Sel. Ch.* (9th ed.), 469) appears in the first volume of the *Statt. R.* (p. 101), but having long been suspected to be of mixed origin and in the nature of a writ *ad hoc* rather than a general statute (see P. & M. ii. 200 ff., Stubbs, *Const. Hist.* ii. 124, and *post*, p. 453), it has now been proved so to be: see E. B. Graves in 43 *E.H.R.* 1.

profession[1]—a tradition largely founded and fostered by learned editors and commentators.

This question of the source and authority of ancient statutes—the question, in short, of what *is* a statute in English law—is not of merely antiquarian interest. It may sometimes be of decisive importance in a modern action, especially an action concerned with real property. Thus in *Merttens* v. *Hill*, [1901] 1 Ch. 842, the lord of the manor of Rothley in Leicestershire claimed a customary fine of one shilling in the pound on the purchase-money paid by the defendant for certain property within the manor. The manor was of ancient demesne, and among other issues raised, the learned judge (Cozens-Hardy J.) decided that the freehold of land held in socage in a manor of ancient demesne was in the tenant, not in the lord. One of the remaining questions which then arose was whether a fine of this kind could be imposed on a freeholder. In deciding that it could not, Cozens-Hardy J. relied partly on the Statute Quia Emptores, and partly on a statute of 8 Ed. II (1315). This latter was not printed in any collection, but was found in a Parliament Roll. It was held to be of full statutory authority, and inasmuch as it enacted 'that from henceforth none should demand or take any fine from freemen for entering upon the lands and tenements which are of their fee, so always that by such feoffment they be not losers of their services nor that their services be denied', the plaintiff's claim was adjudged inadmissible, even if proved as a custom (which it was not), as being contrary to statute.[2]

[1] *Hist. Com. Law*, ch. i *ad fin.*

[2] See also the very interesting discussion of the statute 51 Hen. III, stat. 4 ('Les Estatuz del Eschekere') in *Swaffer* v. *Mulcahy*, [1934] 1 K.B. 608. Here MacKinnon J. held that whether or not an alleged 'statute' could be proved historically to have had full legislative force, it was binding, in the sense of being *declaratory of the Common Law*, if it had been consistently recognized as authoritative. This principle will apply to many old statutes of which the exact origin and form may be in dispute. The form of the so-called statute was remarkable, and well illustrated the nature of our early records. MacKinnon J. (himself a keen antiquarian) observed at p. 627: 'The earliest

Disorder of statutory records and attempts to reform it

Uncertainty about its authority cannot exist in regard to a modern Act of Parliament; but when we speak glibly of the 'statute-book' we do not always realize what a curiously formless document it is. Until the Statutes of the Realm were published, our enacted law was disorderly to an almost incredible degree. There were many projects for reforming it. It is said that the infant King Edward VI showed his precocity by a scheme for eliminating a great deal of matter which even in the sixteenth century had become redundant.[1] In 1557 Sir Nicholas Bacon, Lord Keeper, 'drew up a short plan for reducing, ordering, and printing the Statutes of the Realm' on the following general principles:

> 'First, where many lawes be made for one thing, the same are to be reduced and established into one lawe, and the former to be abrogated.—Item, where there is but one lawe for one thing, that these lawes are to remain in case as statutes.—Item, where part of one acte standeth in force and another part abrogated, there should be no more printed but that that standeth in force.'

Similar schemes were advocated by James I and Francis Bacon, and the latter asisted in a commission for reform, besides outlining the principles on which it should be conducted.[2] The project was again canvassed during the Commonwealth and Restoration, but came to nothing. No serious effort seems to have been made during the eighteenth century. Bentham[3] attacked the

document in which [the statute] appears is an extremely interesting volume which was brought here yesterday from the Record Office and which I looked at with enthusiasm. In that, this supposed statute is written out in the middle of another statute of the Exchequer, which is commonly called 51 Henry 3, stat. 5. It is not only in the middle of it, but it is in the middle of one section of it, and there appears to be a note by the scribe in that ancient volume to the effect that he has made a mistake and written it out in the wrong place.' Professor Plucknett gave expert evidence that the alleged date, 51 Henry 3, was almost certainly wrong and ascribed the document to the reign of Edward I.

[1] Ilbert, *op. cit.* 43.

[2] See *Select Essays in Anglo-American Legal History*, ii. 169, and 170, n. 5, for references to Bacon's proposals.

[3] *Passim*: see especially 'Of Nomography', *Works* (ed. Bowring), iii. 234; 'Justice and Codification Petitions', v. 438.

inconveniences of the existing system, and in this, as in so many other departments of the law, his criticisms were not without effect. The work of revision was seriously taken in hand in 1810, and between that date and 1822 the Record Commission published the statutes up to the end of the reign of Anne. But little attempt had been made so far to discard the accumulated lumber of centuries, and in the intricate maze of statutes repealed, partially repealed, and re-enacted in whole or in part, it was sometimes almost impossible to ascertain what the true statute law was on any uncertain point. The most absurd results were sometimes produced. A statute, 21 & 22 Vict., c. 26, was solemnly passed to repeal 6 Anne, c. 5, and 33 Geo. II, c. 20, both of which had been repealed by 1 & 2 Vict., c. 48.[1] In 1842, in the case of *Reg.* v. *G.W. Railway Co.*, 3 Q.B. 333, the Court of Queen's Bench carefully considered the statute 2 & 3 Ed. VI, c. 24, which had been repealed fourteen years previously. Counsel not infrequently went into court relying on Acts which neither they nor the judge knew, nor could reasonably be expected to know, had been abrogated.[2] At last a move was made for extensive revision. A number of commissions sat from 1834 onwards, and though many of their recommendations never progressed beyond the stage of pious wishes, one result was a series of Statute Law Revision Acts which began in

[1] Holland, *Forms of the Law*, 122.

[2] *Ibid.* 154. Even in recent times there have been instances of attempts to enforce non-operative statutes, but these have been the result of an over-complex system of making rather than of unmaking law. In *R.* v. *Kynaston* (1927), 19 Cr. App. R. 180, a doctor had been fined for an offence under a section of the Dangerous Drugs Act, 1925. The conviction was quashed by the Court of Criminal Appeal on the very sufficient ground that the section on which it depended was not to come into force until an Order in Council had been made, and no such Order in Council had ever been made! 'This prosecution', remarked Lord Hewart C.J., 'resembles nothing so much as pulling a bell handle without a bell at the other end.' See *post*, p. 471, n. 2. In *Meek* v. *Powell*, [1952] 1 K.B. 164, a man was charged under a section of an Act which had been repealed, and the conviction was quashed although the section had been re-enacted by a later statute. Lord Goddard C.J. referred to a similar case at assizes in 1929, *R.* v. *Tuttle* (1929), 140 L.T. 701.

1861 and got rid of an enormous quantity of obsolete matter. One Act of 1867 alone repealed 1,300 statutes.[1] This salutary process of expurgation has gone on more or less continuously up to the present time.[2] The Revised Statutes were published 1870–85, and the second edition 1888–97. We now have reasonably manageable collections of legislation.[3] But we are still far off perfection, and much might yet be done to reduce the statutes to a more systematic form.[4]

[1] Holland, *op. cit.* 137.

[2] Seven hundred and forty-seven statutes, passed since 1900, were repealed in whole or in part by the Statute Law Revision Act, 1927. Hundreds of statutes were repealed by the Law of Property Act, 1925, and the Judicature Act, 1925. The Statute Law Revision Acts, 1948 and 1950, repealed many hundreds of Acts dating from the reign of Henry III to 1945. Similar laws have been passed in 1953, 1958, and 1959. On the whole subject see Sir Cecil Carr, 'Revised Statutes', 45 *L.Q.R.* 168, and 'The Statutes Revised', 67 *L.Q.R.* 482; Sir Granville Ram, 'The Improvement of the Statute Book', *Journal of the Society of Public Teachers of Law*, 1951, p. 442; Viscount Jowitt L.C., *Statute Law Revision and Consolidation* (Presidential Address to the Holdsworth Club, University of Birmingham, 1951); and *post*, pp. 476 ff., on consolidation. The edition of 1950 is the best which has yet been issued, and it reduces to thirty-two volumes the whole 'living' English statute-law up to 1948.

[3] The following are the principal editions: *The Statutes of the Realm*, 1011–1713; *The Public General Acts*, 1714 to present day; *The Revised Statutes*, published under the direction of the Statute Law Committee, 1870–85, and second edition of the same, 1888–97, and the third edition, 1950, with a foreword by Viscount Jowitt L.C. (whereon see a valuable article in *The Justice of the Peace*, 1950, p. 704); the annual volumes of statutes published with the Law Reports by the Incorporated Council for Law Reporting. Of the various series of *Statutes at Large*, the best known are those of Pickering, continued by Tomlin and Raithby to cover the period Magna Carta to 1870; another edition by Tomlin and Raithby in 39 vols. covering the same period; Ruffhead's edition, Magna Carta to 1801, and Runnington's edition of Ruffhead for the same period. To these must now be added Halsbury's *Statutes of England*. Of abridged or annotated editions 'of practical utility' the most popular are *Chitty's Statutes*, *The Yearly Statutes*, and *The Annotated Acts*. A general guide and reference index is supplied by the *Chronological Table and Index to the Statutes*. For the best known of the sources of the statutes from the earliest times see Winfield, *The Chief Sources of English Legal History*, 84 ff.

[4] On various projects for reform, and especially on the recommendations of the Select Committee of 1875, see Sir William Graham Harrison, 'Criticisms of the Statute Book', *Journal of the Society of Public Teachers of Law*, 1935, p. 9.

III. FORCE OF LEGISLATION

1. *Growth of principle of binding force of statutes*

The variety of legislative forms in the Middle Ages necessarily produced uncertainty with regard to the binding authority of statutes or reputed statutes. In the early part of the fourteenth century it is not uncommon to find the judges evading the provisions of statutes and sometimes refusing outright to apply them, either for purely arbitrary reasons or at least for reasons of which the Year Book reports do not fully inform us.[1] Bereford C.J. seems to have taken as independent a line in this matter as in most others. Sometimes the Court doubted, not whether the statement was binding if proved, but whether it existed at all in valid form; for example, great importance was attached to the question whether or not it had been sealed. Bereford declares that he 'knows nothing' of a certain statute of 20 Ed. I,[2] and 'if, indeed, the King should send us word that we are to take this ordinance for law, we will accept it, but never else'.[3] Apart from questions of authenticity, there seems to be little doubt that at this period, and certainly before it, the judges reserved to themselves a discretion in the application of statutes. An Act or ordinance was undoubtedly of high authority, but was entitled to no extraordinary sanctity unless it amounted to direct royal command. This general attitude towards statute has led to a theory that the only law recognized as 'sovereign' was the fundamental Common Law, a body of unwritten tradition recognized as authoritative by judges and by the profession generally; and that the sole aim

[1] A number of striking examples are collected by Professor Plucknett, *Statutes and their Interpretation*, 66 ff.; and see S. E. Thorne, 'The Equity of a Statute and Heydon's Case', *Illinois Law Review*, xxxi. 202. Professor Thorne aptly observes, of the medieval judges, that 'their great preoccupation was to apply the best law they knew as courageously as they could'.

[2] The so-called 'Statute of William Butler', *Statt. R.* i. 109.

[3] *Cayley* v. *Tattershall*, Y.B. 8 Ed. II (S.S. xvii), 116 and xlii ff. The question of the exact forms of statutes and ordinances was still matter of controversy in the early seventeenth century, and much learning on the subject is collected in *The Prince's Case* (1605), 8 Rep. 1.

and effect of medieval enactment was to strengthen, interpret, or regulate this fundamental law, but not to abrogate it or import novelties into it.[1] This theory goes too far and is not generally accepted.[2] There is every reason to believe that in the fourteenth century the Courts recognized a pre-eminent right in the king in Parliament to introduce 'special law' and 'novel law'.[3] Nevertheless, it is only gradually that the judges feel themselves to be bound strictly by the precise terms of an enactment and compelled to apply them without recourse to their own discretion. By the reign of Edward III there is a noticeable tendency to interpret statutes strictly and to bow to their superior authority;[4] but it is probably not till the end of the fifteenth century that anything like the modern doctrine of the absolute, literal authority of statute has settled itself in our law.

2. Supposed and real limitations on the force of statutes

Even so, it is not 'absolute' in the sense of being unrestricted by any moral, social, or religious considerations and therefore obligatory upon the individual in all circumstances. It is an axiom of modern English law that the scope of legislation is 'legally unlimited'. Our institutional writers lay down the principle in the widest terms. 'Of the power and jurisdiction of the Parliament for making of laws,' says Coke,[5] it is so transcendent and absolute as it cannot be confined either for causes or persons within any bounds.' Or again, Blackstone:[6]

The unlimited power of the legislature

'An act of parliament is the exercise of the highest authority that this kingdom acknowledges upon earth. It hath power to bind every subject in the land, and the dominions thereunto belonging; nay, even the King himself, if particularly named therein. And it cannot be altered, amended, dispensed with, suspended or repealed, but in the same forms and by the same authority of parliament.'

[1] McIlwain, *op. cit.*

[2] Holdsworth, *H.E.L.* ii. 442, and *Sources and Literature of English Law*, 41 ff.; Plucknett, *Statutes and their Interpretation*, 26 ff.

[3] In 1310 Ingham says *arguendo*: 'For one canon annuls divers *leges*, so also the Statute annuls divers things which were by the common law': *Venour* v. *Blount*, Y.B. 3 & 4 Ed. II (S.S. iv), 162.

[4] S. E. Thorne, *op. cit.* 207 ff. [5] 2 Inst., Proem. [6] 1 *Comm.* 185.

Modern exponents of our constitutional law state the principle in equally unqualified terms. It goes without saying that we do not recognize the distinction, which exists in countries like France and the United States, between 'organic' or 'constitutional' and 'ordinary' laws; nor can any English statute be unconstitutional in the legal sense—the courts have not the power, as they have in the United States, to refuse to apply it on the ground of unconstitutionality.

Law of God

But the absolutely unlimited sovereignty of statute has not been admitted in the theory of our law until comparatively recent times. In the sixteenth and seventeenth centuries it would have required considerable audacity on the part of any lawyer to deny that the only ultimate, supreme authority lay in a law higher than any man-made ordinance—the eternal dictates of natural justice, reason, or equity; or, in its theological aspect, the law of God.[1] 'There is no law in England', said Keble J. in 1653,[2]

> 'but is as really and truly the law of God as any Scripture phrase, that is by consequence from the very texts of Scripture: for there are very many consequences reasoned out of the texts of Scripture: so is the law of England the very consequence of the very Decalogue itself: and whatsoever is not consonant to Scripture in the law of England is not the law of England . . .: whatsoever is not consonant to the law of God in Scripture, or to right reason which is maintained by Scripture, whatsoever is in England, be it Acts of Parliament, customs, or any judicial acts of the Court, it is not the law of England, but the error of the party which did pronounce it; and you, or any man else at the bar, may so plead it.'

The theological doctrine is represented here, as everywhere, by St. Germain, who distinguished between the law of reason and the law of God, giving the latter, curiously enough, as the *second* 'ground of the law of England'. 'If any general custom', he says,[3] 'were made

[1] From the earliest times it is a rhetorical commonplace to regard law as 'the gift of God': see the famous definition of Demosthenes (*Aristogeiton*) cited D. 1. 3. 2.

[2] *R.* v. *Love,* 5 St. Tr. 43, 172.

[3] Ch. vi.

directly against the law of God, or if any statute were made directly against it: as if it were ordained that no alms should be given for no necessity, the custom and statute were void.' But the only examples he gives are those of statutes which do preserve 'the intent of the law of God': he produces no instance of a statute being overridden for violating that law. He is, in fact, thinking, in his characteristically canonical manner, of the connexion between common law and ecclesiastical law, and the rest of the discussion in this part of his treatise is concerned with that point.[1] The theological element disappears in Coke in favour of 'common right and reason', and statute law becomes subject to that kind of fundamental, governing Common Law which has been already discussed. Coke's words in *Bonham's Case* (1610), 8 Rep. 114, 118, go to a remarkable length.

'Right and reason' and 'control of the Common Law'

'And it appears in our books, that in many cases the Common Law will control Acts of Parliament and sometimes adjudge them to be utterly void: for when an Act of Parliament is

[1] The law of God was formerly much spoken of in connexion with incest. This offence, since it depended on the Levitical degrees rubricated by the Church, was purely ecclesiastical (see Stephen, *Hist. Cr. L.* ii. 430, where it is mentioned as 'the only form of immorality which in the case of the laity is still punished by ecclesiastical courts'), and was not made a misdemeanour until 1908 (Punishment of Incest Act, 1908). It was therefore constantly described as being 'prohibited by God's law' in the old statutes and in the learning thereon: see, for example, 25 Hen. VIII, c. 22, and 28 Hen. VIII, c. 7 (afterwards repealed, 28 Hen. VIII, c. 16, 32 Hen. VIII, c. 38). The first-mentioned statute (s. 3) declares: 'No man, of what estate, degree or condition soever he be, hath power to dispense with God's laws, as all the clergy of the realm in the said convocations, and the most part of all the famous universities of christendom, and we also, do affirm and think.' The same words occur in the statute 28 Hen. VIII, c. 7, s. 12. These statutes were considered in *Brook* v. *B.* (1861), 9 H.L.C. 193, and the modern view was stated by Lord Cranworth at p. 226: 'We do not hold the marriage to be void because it is contrary to the law of God, but because our law has prohibited it on the ground of being contrary to God's law. It is our laws which makes (*sic*) the marriage void, and not the law of God.' See also *Reg.* v. *Chadwick* (1847), 11 Q.B. 205. Unnatural offences were punishable by ecclesiastical courts until 1533 and bigamy until 1603 (see Stephen, *Hist. Cr. L.*, *loc. cit.*). The offence which, in the phraseology of our old books, 'is not to be named among Christians' was regarded as a violation of Divine Law. Its very long history in canon law can, I am inclined to think, be traced back to the Old Testament.

against common right and reason, or repugnant, or impossible to be performed, the Common Law will control it and adjudge such Act to be void.'

For this proposition he relies upon *Tregor's Case*, Y.B. 8 Ed. III, 26, and not only misquotes an *obiter dictum* of Herle J. but seems to have entirely misunderstood the case; it is no authority whatever for the principle which he states so positively. All his remaining examples are cases merely of strict interpretation which seem to have produced a result other than that which was intended by the legislator, but none of them can be considered as in any way supporting a general doctrine that the courts have any power to 'adjudge an Act to be void'.[1] Coke seems to have been the first to lay it down in terms, but it appears also in Hobart in the form that 'even an Act of Parliament, made against natural equity, as to make a man judge in his own cause, is void in itself, for *iura naturae sunt immutabilia*, and they are *leges legum*'.[2] The *dictum*, however, was not relevant to the decision, since it had been expressly decided that the custom alleged in the case did not fall within the customs of London which were confirmed by the Act in question.

In 1701 Lord Holt is reported as describing the *dictum* in *Bonham's Case* as a 'very reasonable and true saying', on the point that no statute can make a man judge in his own cause; and he is said to have added, somewhat inconsequently, that 'an act of parliament can do no wrong, though it may do several things that look pretty odd.... An act of parliament may not make adultery lawful, that is, it cannot make it lawful for A to lie with wife of B, but it may make the wife of A to be the wife of B and

[1] On these cases see Plucknett, *Statutes and their Interpretation*, 68 ff., and 'Bonham's Case and Judicial Review', *H.L.R.* xl. 30; Holdsworth, *H.E.L.* ii. 442; Pound, 'Common Law and Legislation', *H.L.R.* xxi. 383.

[2] *Day* v. *Savadge* (1615), Hob. 85, 87; *post*, p. 622. Similarly, in *Sheffield (Lord)* v. *Ratcliffe* (1615), Hob. 334, 346, he referred to 'that liberty and authority that Judges have over laws, especially over statute laws, according to reason and best convenience, to mould them to the truest and best use'. There are many rhetorical generalities of the same kind in the famous but obscure judgement of Vaughan C.J. in *Thomas* v. *Sorrell* (1674), Vau. 330.

dissolve her marriage with A'.[1] It is difficult to guess why Coke suddenly injected his sweeping proposition into *Bonham's Case*, for its terms were far wider than were necessary to the decision.[2] It may be that, feeling the increasing pressure of royal censorship and displeasure, he made a deliberate attempt to recapture for the judiciary the 'free interpretation' of the medieval period, when, as we have seen, statute differed materially in form and effect from the enactments of Coke's day. This, at all events, seems to have been the light in which his *dictum* was viewed at Court, for after he had been removed from office he was called upon, in 1616, to explain and justify his words.[3] He replied by merely reasserting the doctrine and citing the same apocryphal authorities. He found little following among his successors and contemporaries, except Hobart, and although his generalization was revived with the Restoration as a charter for the reborn Stuart prerogative (especially in *Godden* v. *Hales* (1686), 11 St. Tr. 1165), it died with the Revolution and thereafter was several times repudiated in express terms from the Bench.[4]

[1] *City of London* v. *Wood* (1701), 12 Mod. 669, 687. This is, however, a bad example of the 'scrambling reports' in Modern to which Holt himself referred so scathingly (see *ante*, p. 228). The whole judgement, as reported, is so confused that it is impossible to believe that it represents what a great judge really said. It is, presumably, by similar misreporting that Holt is made to say, gratuitously and nonsensically, in *R.* v. *Banbury* (*Earl*) (1695), Skinner 517, 527, that it is part of the daily business of judges to declare statutes to be void. No importance can be attached to these alleged *dicta*.

[2] He had also said that 'if any statute be made to the contrary of Magna Carta, it shall be holden for none': 3 Inst. 111.

[3] Plucknett, *op. cit.*, *H.L.R.* xl. 50. See also S. E. Thorne, 'Dr. Bonham's Case', 54 *L.Q.R.* 543. Professor Thorne maintains that the *dictum* was meant to refer to inherent *repugnancy*, and that a far wider meaning has been attributed to it than Coke intended. His analysis of the case certainly lends colour to this contention; but if Coke had (as any judge may do) used wider language than he intended, it is difficult to understand why he did not qualify it when he was given the opportunity. I agree with Professor Thorne that Coke was not necessarily appealing to a 'natural law', as has often been suggested, but he seems indubitably to have been claiming for the judiciary a greater power than it possessed.

[4] Plucknett, *op. cit.*, *H.L.R.* xl. 51 ff. Some doubt seems to be cast on it in *Mercers' Co.* v. *Bowker* (1726), 1 Str. 639, but the report is obscure.

In the eighteenth century some shadow of the doctrine still lives on in juristic theory, and is stated somewhat perfunctorily by Blackstone,[1] though not without protest from his editor, Christian; it is, indeed, inconsistent with the whole tenor of Blackstone's precepts concerning legislation, and seems to be added as a kind of pious afterthought.[2] All these statements in reality amount only to affirmations of the fundamental justice and reasonableness which should underlie all law, statutory or other; there is not, so far as I am aware, a single example in our books of the courts rejecting the plain and express provisions of a statute on the ground that it was contrary to any ethical principle.[3] It is not, however, until 1871 that the Bench, taking the common example of a statute which makes a man judge in his own cause, is prepared to deny expressly any right in the courts to question the authority of such an enactment. The Common Law no longer—if, as is highly doubtful, it ever did so—claims any power to 'control' statute. 'It was once said', says Willes J.,[4]

[1] 1 *Comm.* 40.

[2] It is to be noted that he confines himself to the theological commonplace; the *dicta* of *Bonham's Case* he expressly rejects, and though he says that 'if there arise out of [statutes] collaterally any absurd consequences, manifestly contrary to common reason, they are, with regard to those collateral consequences, void', his subsequent explanation shows that he uses the word 'void' in Coke's somewhat loose sense. What he says does not go to the authority and validity of the statute, but merely means that the Court will be astute to avoid interpretations which result in absurdity. He is, in fact, in two minds, and the passage shows clearly that in 1765 English jurisprudence had not reached a clear conclusion on this point: 1 *Comm.* 90–91. He does, however, say in another place (*ibid.* 43) that 'if any human law should allow or enjoin us to commit it [i.e. murder], we are bound to transgress that human law, or else we must offend both the natural and the divine'.

[3] But it seems to have been sincerely believed by many in former times that there were definite divine limitations on the legislative power of Parliament. Thus 'the debate on the Septennial Act of 1716 shows that many members of the House of Commons thought that the Legislature had no power to modify that Act; and that they denied the proposition that there were no legal restrictions on its power': Holdsworth, *Some Lessons from our Legal History*, 129, citing Cobbett, *Parl. Hist.* Cf. Dicey, *Law of the Constitution* (10th ed.), 44 ff.

[4] *Lee* v. *Bude, &c., Ry. Co.* (1871), L.R. 6 C.P. 576, 582.

'that if an Act of Parliament were to create a man judge in his own cause, the Court might disregard it. That dictum, however, stands as a warning, rather than an authority to be followed. We sit here as servants of the Queen and the legislature. Are we to act as regents over what is done by parliament with the consent of the Queen, lords, and commons? I deny that any such authority exists. . . . The proceedings here are judicial, not autocratic, which they would be if we could make laws instead of administering them.'

The 'equity of a statute'

In the sixteenth and early seventeenth centuries there was a theory of a special 'equity' which controlled statutes, both by extending and restricting them. The classic exposition of this doctrine is to be found in the pages of Plowden, in his note on *Eyston* v. *Studd* (1574), Plow. 459, 465. We read:

'It is not the words of the law but the internal sense of it that makes the law, and our law (like all others) consists of two parts, viz. of Body and Soul; the letter of the law is the body of the law, and the sense and reason of the law is the soul of the law. . . . And it often happens that when you know the letter, you know not the sense, for sometimes the sense is more confined and contracted than the letter, and sometimes it is more large and extensive. And Equity . . . enlarges or diminishes the letter according to its discretion, which Equity is in two ways. The one Aristotle defines thus . . .: *Equitas est correctio legis generatim latae qua parte deficit*, or as the passage is explained by Perionius, *Equitas est correctio quaedam legi adhibita, quia ab ea abest aliquid propter generalem sine exceptione comprehensionem.*'

This, then, is Aristotle's general principle of ἐπιείκεια (see *ante*, p. 290) given a particular application to statute (which, needless to say, was far less than Aristotle meant, his doctrine being of general relevance to *ius* rather than *lex*). Plowden gives a great number of examples of this extensive interpretation, and continues:

'Experience shows us that no lawmakers can foresee all things which may happen, and therefore it is fit that if there is any defect in the law, it should be reformed by equity, which is no part of the law, but a moral virtue which corrects the law. . . . From whence the reader may observe how convenient a thing this equity is, and the wise Judges of our law deserve great commendation for having made use of it where the words of the law are rigorous, for thereby they have softened the severity of the text, and have made the law tolerable.'

He then goes on to consider the second kind of statute-equity, which is

'in a manner of a quite contrary effect, and may well be thus defined: *Equitas est verborum legis directio efficacius* (sic), *cum una res solummodo legis caveatur verbis, ut omnis alia in aequali genere eisdem caveatur verbis.*'[1]

In short, the equity of a statute extends its provisions either (1) to *casus omissi* which the legislator never had in mind, or (2) to cases similar to those which the legislator had in mind, and which, though he has not expressly specified them, he may be supposed to have intended by implication. How are we to arrive at and to fulfil his intention? The answer given by Plowden (again following Aristotle) may seem naïve, and yet it is not an altogether fantastic description of the feat of imagination which courts still have to perform in endeavouring to 'carry out the intention of the legislature'.

'And in order to form a right judgement when the letter of a statute is restrained, and when enlarged, by Equity, it is a good way, when you peruse a statute, to suppose that the lawmaker is present, and that you have asked him the question you want to know touching the equity; then you must give yourself such an answer as you imagine he would have done, if he had been present. . . . And if the lawmaker would have followed the equity, notwithstanding the words of the law . . . you may safely do the like. . . . And so the Judges did in the principal case here, by following Epichaia (*sic*).'

All this is an elaboration of doctrines which had already appeared in *Doctor and Student* and in Coke,[2] to both of whom Plowden makes frequent reference. A certain amount of learning grew up round the 'equity of a

[1] The same exposition, with the same mistranslations of Greek into Latin, is reproduced in Ashe's *Epieikeia* (1609), whereon see *ante*, p. 409.

[2] Co. Litt. 24 b, 2 Inst. 401, 487.

statute', and it is included in some of the Abridgements[1] as a recognized aspect of statute law. When Sir Fortunatus Dwarris published his *Construction of Statutes* in 1830, although he regarded Plowden's principles as dangerous in themselves, and in any case as obsolete in the nineteenth century, he nevertheless thought it necessary to devote a good deal of space to the old learning about the equity of a statute, and he divides the subject into different headings illustrating the judicial extension of statutory provisions to 'other cases, other persons, other things, other remedies, times not mentioned, other places, later provisions of subsequent statutes', and so forth. When his examples are examined, however, they amount to little more than an array of various unexpected sets of circumstances which have arisen under certain statutes, and which have therefore raised problems, by no means extraordinary in themselves, of interpretation.

And indeed, except in early times, Plowden's grandiloquent principles crystallize merely into a general doctrine of liberal and intelligent interpretation, having the double aspect that a 'remedial' statute is to receive an 'equitable' interpretation, while a penal statute, or a statute in derogation of the Common Law, is to be construed strictly.[2] There is no doubt that in the medieval period judicial interpretation sometimes extended the scope of statute in a manner which seems startling to modern notions; perhaps the most famous example is that of the *Circumspecte Agatis* which, having forbidden judicial interference with the Bishop of Norwich in his spiritual jurisdiction, was extended to furnish the same protection to all prelates and ecclesiastics.[3]

[1] See, e.g., Bacon, Abr., *Statute*, i. 6; Viner, Abr., *Statutes* (E. 6), 32; Comyns, Dig., *Parliament*, R. 13.

[2] For the development of these rules, see S. E. Thorne, *op. cit.*

[3] 2 Inst. 487; *Platt* v. *Sheriffs of London* (1550), Plow. 35, 36; Maxwell, *Interpretation of Statutes* (11th ed.), 246. Another remarkable instance of the same kind is the construction placed by Bereford C.J. on the statute *De Donis* in *Belyng* v. *Anon.*, Y.B. 5 Ed. II (S.S. xi), 176. As is well known, before the passing of the statute, where land was given to a man and the heirs of his body, the donee was free to alienate the land as soon as an heir was born. Now the

Possibly 'equitable' extension was made necessary because, as Coke says,[1] 'it was the wisdom of ancient parliaments to comprehend much matter in few words'. As we shall see, the diction of statutes has varied greatly at different periods of our legal history, and has swung from a telegraphic brevity to 'exuberant verbosity'. It would not have been easy to give effect to some of the early statutes unless the courts had been prepared, and indeed had been expected, to amplify some of their curt provisions. But apart from this question of language, we have seen that statutes of the twelfth and early thirteenth centuries were conceived in a wholly different spirit from modern legislation. They were not so much exact formulas emanating from a supreme Parliamentary authority, as broad rules of government and administration, intended for guidance rather than as meticulous instruction, and meant to be applied on elastic principles of expediency. It is doubtful whether the judges of this period, whatever liberties they seem to have taken with statute, were conscious of performing anything more than an ordinary, routine function of judicial technique.[2] The doctrine of statutory 'equity' was a later invention, and seems to have arisen from two principal causes—first, a reaction against the much stricter principles of statutory interpretation which set in during the latter half of the fourteenth century; and second, the influence

operative words of the statute seem to provide no more than this, that in future *the original feoffee* (and only he) shall be restrained from alienating the land on the birth of issue. This Bereford held to be the literal provision of the statute; but he went on: 'He that made the statute meant to bind *the issue in fee tail* as well as the feoffees until the tail had reached the fourth degree; and it was only through negligence that he omitted to insert express words in the Statute to that effect.' It may very well be, as Bolland suggests, that this decision, rather than the statute itself, made the fee tail inalienable by both feoffee and issue in tail, until the device of fine and recovery was invented: see Y.B. 5 Ed. II (S.S. xi), Introd. xxv ff. Holdsworth suggests that Bereford's interpretation was based on a not unnatural, but decidedly audacious, analogy to descent to issue in frank-marriage: *H.E.L.* iii. 115. See also Plucknett, *Concise History* (5th ed.), 331.

[1] 2 Inst. 401.

[2] S. E. Thorne, *op. cit.*, *Illinois Law Review*, xxxi. 207.

of the growing Chancery jurisdiction, and, in particular, its philosphical rationalization by St. Germain. We have already seen that *Doctor and Student* had an immediate and a powerful influence;[1] it evidently made a great impression upon Plowden, whose Reports were published about fifty years (1578) after the appearance of St. Germain's treatise. Although Plowden was himself trained on the Common Law side, this newly expounded philosophy of the Chancery seems to have had a peculiar fascination for him, for it is a persistent theme throughout his volume, either in the cases which he reports or in his commentary upon them.[2] Yet, when we scrutinize his examples, we find either that they go back to the period of 'free interpretation' of statutes, or that they are merely instances of what we should now call liberal interpretation, or of *casus omissi* not very remarkable in themselves. In short, Plowden's attempt to build round statutes, in the manner of St. Germain, an Aristotelian ἐπιείκεια analogous to the *sinderesis* of the Chancery, was artificial and unfruitful.

So, at least, later generations seem to have considered. In the seventeenth and eighteenth centuries, the 'equity of a statute', so far as I have been able to trace the doctrine, rapidly shrinks; the phrase itself lives on in legal terminology, but the elaborate system which Plowden attempted to build upon it seems to be almost entirely forgotten. As early as 1639, Sir William Jones criticized and discredited it as 'too general a ground' for the construction of statute.[3] Few important references to it, and no systematic analysis of it, are to be found in later reports and abridgements.[4] In 1758 Lord Mansfield summarily described the equity of a statute as 'synonymous

[1] And see Holdsworth, *H.E.L.* v. 268.

[2] See especially *Stradling* v. *Morgan* (1560), Plow, 199; *Stowel* v. *Lord Zouche* (1564), Plow. 353; *Wimbish* v. *Tallboys* (1551), Plow. 38, 59.

[3] *James* v. *Tintney*, Wm. Jo. 422.

[4] There are traces, but hardly more than that, in *New River Co.* v. *Graves* (1701), 2 Vern. 431, *Hammond* v. *Webb* (1714), 10 Mod. 282, and *Briant's Case* (1794), 5 T.R. 509.

to the meaning of the legislator'.[1] In the nineteenth century the very term 'equity' in connexion with statute has become an archaism.[2] So far as it survived as a pretext for circumventing the express provisions of statutes, it was several times denounced by high authority,[3] and it may now be considered to have disappeared as a term of art or as an element of our jurisprudence.[4] Whether or not this is an advantage, and whether any relic of statutory 'equity' still descends to us from *Heydon's Case*, we shall consider presently.

The true 'control of the Common Law'

A general 'control' of the Common Law over statute is not, however, entirely meaningless even at the present time, though it certainly does not amount to a right to resist even the most Draconic statute, provided that it be clear in its intention. But there is a constant 'control' exercised by the interpretation of the courts—to this we shall advert presently; and there is the dominant principle, never absent from the minds of judges, that the Common Law is wider and more fundamental than statute, and that, wherever possible, legislative enactment should be construed in harmony with established Common Law principles rather than in antagonism to them. A general intention is presumed in the legislature to fit new enactments into the general structure of the law and to effect no more change than the occasion strictly demands. In Coke's words, 'The surest construction of a statute is by the rule and reason of the common law.'[5] This principle has been criticized as conducing to a narrow and jealous interpretation, and as being entirely a modern innovation,[6] and doubtless it has sometimes led

[1] *R.* v. *Williams*, 1 W. Bl. 95.

[2] Thus Byles J. in *Shuttleworth* v. *Le Fleming* (1865), 19 C.B.N.S. 687, 703: 'I suppose "within the equity" means the same thing as "within the mischief" of the statute' (which, *scilicet*, was not Plowden's meaning).

[3] Lord Tenterden in *Brandling* v. *Barrington* (1827), 6 B. & C. 467, 475; Pollock C.B. in *Miller* v. *Salamons* (1852), 21 L.J. (Ex.) 161, 197.

[4] Maxwell, *op. cit.*; Craies, *Statute Law* (3rd ed.), 95.

[5] Co. Litt. 272 b. Cf. *Stowel* v. *Lord Zouche* (1564), Plow. 353.

[6] Pound, 'Common Law and Legislation', *ubi sup.* The principle, though not, of course, the exact form of Coke's statement of it, seems to be older than

to strained and grudging constructions; but in reality it is an essential guiding rule, for without it the continuity of legal development would be gravely imperilled. In modern law the principle is expressed in the familiar rule that statutes 'in derogation of the Common Law' are to be construed strictly. 'The general words of an Act are not to be so construed as to alter the previous policy of the law, unless no sense or meaning can be applied to those words consistently with the intention of preserving the existing policy untouched.'[1] Difficult though it may be to reconcile with the supreme dignity of the sovereign legislature, our judges do not hesitate to assume—to put it plainly—that they know more about the law than Parliament! Though to a Continental lawyer it would sound impertinent, we feel no incongruity when an English judge says, 'We ought, in general, in construing an Act of Parliament, to assume that the legislature knows the existing state of the law.'[2] But sometimes it is perfectly plain that the legislature does *not* know the existing state of the law, or at all events states it in a singularly inaccurate manner. In a statute of 1873[3] the following surprising statement will

Professor Pound allows, as will be gathered from what has been already said. In 1314 Staunton J. says: 'A statute does not alter common law unless it expressly purports to do so': *Bakewell* v. *Wandsworth*, Y.B. 6 & 7 Ed. II (*Eyre of Kent*) (S.S. viii), iii. 78. Mr. J. M. Landis, 'Statutes and the Sources of Law', *Harvard Legal Essays* (1934), 213, Note 11, follows Professor Pound in holding that 'the doctrine that statutes in derogation of the common law are to be strictly construed was a product of eighteenth-century thought'. *Contra* see S. E. Thorne, 'The Equity of a Statute and Heydon's Case', *Illinois Law Review*, xxxi. 202, and 'Statuta in the Post-Glossators', *Speculum*, xi. 452. With all respect to Messrs. Pound and Landis, I think that Professor Thorne has shown conclusively, with abundant examples, that the principle of strict interpretation was at least as old as the time of Edward III. Mr. Landis, *loc. cit.*, citing this page, credits me with 'attempting to date the attitude back to the origin of the common law'. I look in vain for any such statement in what I have written.

[1] *Per* Romilly M.R., *Minet* v. *Leman* (1855), 20 Beav. 269, 278, cited and adopted in *National Assistance Board* v. *Wilkinson*, [1952] 2 Q.B. 648, 659.

[2] *Per* Lord Blackburn, *Young* v. *Leamington Spa* (1883), 8 App. Cas. 517, 526. Cf. Lord Halsbury L.C., *Ex p. Council of Kent, &c.*, [1901] 1 Q.B. 725, 728.

[3] Extradition Amendment Act, 36 & 37 Vict., c. 60, s. 3, amended by

be found: 'Whereas a person who is accessory *before or after the fact*, or counsels, procures, commands, aids or abets the commission of any indictable offence, *is by English law liable to be tried and punished as if he were the principal offender*', etc.—a statement of the law which needs great modification so far at least as accessories after the fact are concerned. There are abundant examples of errors either of law or of fact contained in statutes,[1] or of statutes which are inconsistent with each other.[2] How are the courts to treat them? The Judicial Committee unequivocally affirms the discretion which is reserved to the judge in such cases. 'The enactment is no doubt entitled to great weight as evidence of the law, but it is by no means conclusive; and when the existing law is shown to be different from that which the legislature supposed it to be, the implication arising from the statute cannot operate as a negation of its existence.'[3] It will be observed that the *dictum* is restrained to an *implication* arising from a statute; the courts will not, if they can help it, allow any enactment to overrule existing Common Law *by inference* merely. It is quite otherwise when the provision of the statute is express, or when there is a general clear intention to change the law, even though the legislature has chosen language which involves an erroneous statement, by way of recital, of the law.[4]

It is not to be disguised, however, that when there is any reasonable pretext to justify them, the courts will

58 & 59 Vict., c. 35; cited Maxwell, *Interpretation of Statutes* (11th ed.), 308. It must be said in extenuation that the statement is by way of preamble only.

[1] See Maxwell, *op. cit.* 303 ff.; and cf. *Ormond Investment Co.* v. *Betts*, [1928] A.C. 143. By s. 45 (6) of the Law of Property Act, 1925, recitals, statements, and descriptions *of facts* in Acts of Parliament, if twenty years old at the time of a contract for sale of property, are sufficient evidence of the truth of such facts, *unless and except so far as they may be proved to be inaccurate*.

[2] See, e.g., *Taylor* v. *Parry*, [1951] 2 K.B. 442; *Beck* v. *Newbold*, [1952] 2 Q.B. 732.

[3] *Mollwo* v. *Court of Wards* (1872), L.R. 4 P.C. 419, 437.

[4] *Reg.* v. *Mayor of Oldham* (1868), L.R. 3 Q.B. 474.

not carry out the probable intention of the legislature if to do so would be to confirm a misconception of the law. This may be seen in the questions of sporting rights which have arisen under various Inclosure Acts. There existed for a long time 'a very mistaken notion'[1] that the lord of a manor had sporting rights over the waste lands of the manor by virtue of his seigniory. It was a common practice in Inclosure Acts, when vesting the freehold of the allotted lands in the allottees, to introduce a saving clause which reserved to the lord a number of his manorial rights, including various sporting rights. The question then arose whether, after the inclosure, the lord had the right of shooting over the allotments which had now passed to other hands. It is difficult to doubt, though judicial opinion was somewhat divided on the point, that the intention of the legislature was to reserve this right among others; but that intention was founded on a misconception—a 'blunder', it is freely called in the cases—and the judges refrained from carrying it out, holding that the right in question was territorial and not seigniorial, i.e. had been vested in the lord by virtue of his ownership of the soil in the waste, and did not pass with the seigniorial rights reserved.[2]

International Law

There is another kind of 'fundamental law', akin to the law of reason or of nature, which has sometimes been believed to impose positive limits on the scope of legislation. I refer to International Law. A *dictum* of Lord Mansfield seems to suggest that in his opinion Parliament had no power to legislate in direct opposition to an established principle of the Law of Nations: 'The privileges of public Ministers and their retinue depend upon the Law of Nations, which is part of the Common Law of England. And the Act of Parliament 7 Anne, c. 12,[3] did not intend to alter, *nor can alter*, the Law of

[1] *Per* Bayley J., *Pickering* v. *Noyes* (1823), 4 B. & C. 648; cf. Martin B., *Bruce* v. *Helliwell* (1860), 5 H. & N. 609, 620.

[2] *Sowerby* v. *Smith* (1874), L.R. 9 C.P. 524; *Devonshire* (*Duke of*) v. *O'Connor* (1890), 24 Q.B.D. 468; *Ecroyd* v. *Coulthard*, [1898] 2 Ch. 358.

[3] The Act imposed a penalty on anybody who infringed the rule of

Nations.'[1] In the great case of *The Franconia*[2] two judges, Sir R. Phillimore and Kelly C.B., seemed to incline to the opinion that legislation could not override a rule of International Law, and the Chief Baron said:

> 'I hold that no one nation has the right to exercise criminal jurisdiction over the ships of other nations, or the subjects of other nations within such ships, navigating the high seas . . . unless by treaty, or express agreement, or unless by some uniform, general and long-continued usage, evidenced by the actual exercise of such jurisdiction acquiesced in by the nation or nations affected by it';

which would seem to exclude the validity of statute in such a case.[3] There have undoubtedly been cases in which the courts have greatly restrained the effect of widely expressed statutes in order to preserve consistency with International Law. Perhaps the strongest example is the construction put upon the Acts of 1807 and 1811 prohibiting the slave-trade.[4] These enactments, as is well known, were passed as the result of a strong humanitarian movement, and were expressed in very general and emphatic language which might have been construed to mean that Englishmen could with impunity prevent the slave traffic even if carried on by the subject

International Law concerning the immunity of the servants of ambassadors. Its curious political history is related by Lord Mansfield in *Triquet* v. *Bath* (1754), 3 Burr. 1478 (whereon see Lord Phillimore in *Engelke* v. *Musmann*, [1928] A.C. 433, 453). As to waiver of the privilege, see *Reg.* v. *Madan*, [1961] 2 Q.B. 1.

[1] *Heathfield* v. *Chilton* (1767), 4 Burr. 2015, 2016. Too much, however, has been made of the *dictum* (see Pound, *op. cit.*). Lord Mansfield seems only to mean that whatever municipal legislation might be, the rule of International Law would remain the same: he does not suggest that the municipal law would be invalid and unenforceable. The *dictum* is in any case very casual, as it was held that the Act in question, far from being contrary to International Law, was declaratory of it.

[2] *Reg.* v. *Keyn* (1876), 2 Ex. D. 63.

[3] The headnote to the case represents the view of these two judges as follows: 'That, by the principles of international law, the power of a nation over the sea within three miles of its coasts is only for certain limited purposes; and that *Parliament could not*, consistently with those principles, apply English criminal law within those limits.' But this is not stated in terms in either of the judgements.

[4] 47 Geo. III, c. 36, 51 Geo. III, c. 23.

of a State which recognized the traffic as lawful. This, however morally commendable, would have violated an elementary principle of International Law; and in *Madrazo* v. *Willes* (1820), 3 B. & Ald. 353, the Court of King's Bench, with regret but without hesitation, so narrowed the statutes that a Spaniard was enabled to recover very large damages in an English court for interference at Havana with his slave ship and traffic.[1] On the other hand, in questions of jurisdiction over crimes committed in English ships, whether in British waters or abroad, our courts have not hesitated to depart from a well-recognized rule of International Law; and this they are prepared to do on the authority not only of statute but even of a Common Law rule.[2] It cannot now be seriously contended that the so-called restrictive force of International Law goes farther than this, that 'every statute is to be so interpreted and applied, as far as its language admits, as not to be inconsistent with the comity of nations, or with the established rules of international law'.[3] It cannot, of course, be disputed', said Lord Parker, delivering the judgement of the Judicial Committee in *The Zamora*, [1916] 2 A.C. at p. 93, 'that a Prize Court, like any other Court, is bound by the legislative enactments of its own sovereign State. A British Prize Court would certainly be bound by Acts of the Imperial Legislature. But', he adds (and the qualification is important), 'it is none the less true that if the Imperial Legislature passed an Act the provisions of which were inconsistent with the law of nations, the Prize Court in giving effect to such provisions would no longer be administering international law.'

Apart from these supposed limitations, which modern doctrine has reduced to very slender proportions, certain principles, now well recognized, do in effect limit the scope of legislation, though they cannot be said to

[1] Cf. *Forbes* v. *Cochrane* (1824), 2 B. & C. 448; *Santos* v. *Illidge* (1860), 8 C.B.N.S. 861.

[2] *Reg.* v. *Anderson* (1868), L.R. 1 C.C.R. 161; *Reg.* v. *Keyn, ubi sup.*

[3] Maxwell, *op. cit.* 142.

derogate from the strict constitutional theory of the absolute authority of Parliament.

Impossibility

1. It 'neither requires nor is capable of proof' that a statute cannot decree what is physically impossible. Somewhere in the interstices of our statute-book there may be an example of an Act ordering that which, at the time of enactment, was impossible to be performed; it is not difficult to imagine such circumstances, but I do not know of any instance of this *antecedent* or *contemporaneous* impossibility.[1] *Subsequent* impossibility is another matter. A statutory rule may be perfectly reasonable and practicable in its general application, but in a particular instance, owing to inevitable circumstances, it may be impossible for an individual to comply with it. The maxim *lex non cogit ad impossibilia* then applies. A statute will not be construed as imposing on an individual a duty which it was not reasonably possible for him to perform. Thus, under the Metropolis Local Management Act, 1855, a vestry or local board was bound to cleanse sewers which were vested in them by the Act; but the liability did not extend to obstructions of which they did not know and which they could not have discovered by reasonable care and inquiry.[2] Similarly, under the Housing, Town Planning, &c., Act, 1909, a tenant of a certain kind of house enjoyed the benefit of an implied condition that the house should be and be kept reasonably fit for human habitation. He had to give notice to the landlord of repairs required in accordance with the provision; but if damage was caused by a defect which he could not have observed by reasonable care and vigilance, he did not lose the benefit of the implied condition because he had not given notice.[3]

[1] Something not unlike it occurred in the Newspaper Libel and Registration Act, 1881, which by its 9th section required printers to make certain returns before 31 July 1881. The Act was not passed until 27 August of that year.

[2] *Hammond* v. *Vestry of St. Pancras* (1874), L.R. 9 C.P. 316. It is otherwise when the liability is clearly expressed by the statute to be absolute, i.e. independent of negligence: see *Makin, Ltd.* v. *L.N.E.R.*, [1943] K.B. 467.

[3] *Fisher* v. *Walters*, [1926] 2 K.B. 315.

Retrospective and *ex post facto* legislation, and *privilegia*

2. There is in English jurisprudence a leaning against, though no actual constitutional limitation upon, legislation which is made *ex post facto* or is retrospective in its effect. These two kinds of legislation are usually classed together, but a distinction exists between them. In his classic judgement in *Phillips* v. *Eyre* (1870), L.R. 6 Q.B. 1, Willes J. appears to regard the term *ex post facto* as properly applied only to statutes designed to make unlawful, and to penalize by criminal sanctions, acts which were lawful when they were done; whereas retrospective legislation he considers to be of a more general nature, as affecting rights and duties of different varieties. Both kinds, of course, have a retroactive effect, but the one attaches to past events penalties which did not previously apply to them, and thus creates an entirely new situation, while the other merely alters a situation arising from pre-existing circumstances. The distinction, however, is one of degree rather than of kind and affects the strength, rather than the existence, of the rule of construction which we must now consider.

The maxim of the law, as stated by Coke,[1] is: *Omnis nova constitutio futuris formam imponere debet, et non praeteritis*. But it is clear that new law cannot always be *solely* prospective in its operation; it is almost certain to affect existing rights and, still more, existing expectations. It may be intended to operate in the future, but the mere fact that it operates at all inevitably, in the long run, impinges upon rights and duties which existed long before it came into being. This is particularly true of laws concerning property of a permanent and continuing nature, such as real property, which at some time or other must come within the ambit of every change in the law relevant to it. Case-law too, like statute, frequently places a new complexion on accepted rules, and sometimes, as we have seen, reverses a long line of decisions on which many transactions have been founded; while it may also give a new and unexpected meaning, after a long interval,

[1] 2 Inst. 95, 292.

to a statutory provision. Indeed, it is often impossible to say of a statute exactly what its effects will be on existing law until it has fallen to be interpreted by the courts. It cannot, therefore, be laid down as an invariable rule that all new law must project itself solely into the future without any influence upon the past, for there is a wider principle at work in human affairs—namely, that past, present, and future are all part of the same stream of consciousness and event.

The rule of construction, therefore, is limited to this, that 'a retrospective operation is not to be given to a statute so as to impair an existing right or obligation,[1] otherwise than as regards matter of procedure,[2] unless that effect cannot be avoided without doing violence to the language of the enactment. If the enactment is expressed in language which is fairly capable of either interpretation, it ought to be construed as prospective only.'[3] A great number of judicial expressions might be cited to the same effect; but the problem is, What are the rights and obligations to which the presumption applies? Attempts have been made to limit the doctrine to purely penal statutes, i.e. to those which concern crime and punishment.[4] But this is to place too narrow a construction on the principle. It is true that, for obvious reasons, the objection is felt far more strongly in respect of *ex post facto* imposition of novel penalties, and of the arbitrary creation of new crimes, than of any other form of retroactive legislation, for it shocks the most elementary sense of justice to punish anybody, as an afterthought,

[1] The same presumption exists against the restrospective conferment of rights and privileges: see *Smith* v. *Callender*, [1901] A.C. 297, 303.

[2] It is repeatedly laid down that alterations in procedure cannot be limited to a prospective effect, and there is obviously no hardship in this exception. See *Barber* v. *Pidgen*, [1937] 1 K.B. 664; *Brooks* v. *Brimecome*, [1937] 2 K.B. 675; *National Real Estate and Finance Co.* v. *Hassan*, [1939] 2 K.B. 61; *Craxfords Ltd.* v. *Williams & Steer Manufacturing Co., Ltd.*, [1954] 1 W.L.R. 1130; *In re Vernazza*, [1960] A.C. 965.

[3] *Per* Wright J., *In re Athlumney*, [1898] 2 Q.B. 547, 551. Cf. *Sunshine Porcelain Potteries, Ltd.* v. *Nash*, [1961] A.C. 927, and Kennedy L.J., *West* v. *Gwynne*, [1911] 2 Ch. 1, 15.

[4] See 'A. L. G.', 66 *L.Q.R.* 314.

for doing that which was lawful when he did it.[1] It is true also that the prohibition of *ex post facto* legislation contained in Art. I, s. 9 (3) of the Constitution of the United States has been applied principally to penal statutes,[2] though on the other hand there are many famous *dicta*, of long standing, from American judges of the highest eminence enunciating the same *rule of construction* (which of course is not the same thing as a constitutional prohibition) as is accepted in English courts; and the constitutional rule in America extends, in any case, beyond penal statutes to any enactment which 'impairs the obligation of contracts'.[3] The true rule of both English and American law, it is submitted, is stated by Maxwell:[4] 'It is chiefly where the enactment would prejudicially affect vested rights, or the legality of past transactions, or impair contracts, that the rule in question prevails. Every statute, it has been said, which takes away or impairs vested rights acquired under existing laws, or creates a new obligation, or imposes a new duty, or attaches a new disability in respect of transactions or considerations already past, must be presumed, out of respect to the legislature, to be intended not to have a retrospective operation.'[5] *A fortiori* the presumption is against the imposition of novel penalties for wrongs invented *ex post facto*, and it is matter for regret that in several cases in recent years this salutary principle, though not actually repudiated, has been endangered by decisions which have held that a man may be liable, through *ex post facto* legislation, for heavier penalties than those which existed when he committed his offence.[6]

[1] See 1 Bl. *Comm.* 46.

[2] See 'A. L. G.', *loc. cit.*, who in this respect seems to attribute to some of his opponents a misunderstanding which they never entertained.

[3] See the American authorities cited by Willes J. in *Phillips* v. *Eyre*, *ubi sup.*, and in Maxwell, *Interpretation of Statutes* (11th ed.), 206.

[4] *Op. cit.* 206.

[5] With regard to the effect of a change in the law on pending actions (from the time of plaint to the time of judgement), see *Hutchinson* v. *Jauncey*, [1950] 1 K.B. 574, and *Jonas* v. *Rosenberg*, [1950] 2 K.B. 52.

[6] See *Director of Public Prosecutions* v. *Lamb*, [1941] 2 K.B. 89; *Buckman*

It must be emphasized, however, that we are dealing here only with a presumption, or rule of construction, in the interpretation of statute. There is, in English law, no *constitutional* restraint upon retroactive legislation, and if an enactment is unequivocally expressed to operate retrospectively, there is no power in the courts to derogate from it. There are many examples in our books of statutes of this kind, and sometimes they bear hardly on vested rights,[1] though for the most part their retroactive effect is of limited scope and involves no intolerable hardship on individuals.[2] Whether or not Parliament chooses to legislate retroactively is therefore a question not of the validity of statute law, but of policy and statesmanship; and consequently the only *de facto* restraints which exist upon this kind of law are those which apply to all legislation—namely, wise government and public opinion.

Wise government will not lightly resort to retrospective legislation for the mere sake of expediency, since it realizes, or should realize, that in the last analysis justice itself is the highest form of expediency. At its peril, therefore, will it violate the average sense of justice, which is undoubtedly hostile, in England at least, to retroactive law. At the same time, there may be occasions when public exigency compels a departure from the general principle, and it is impossible therefore to say that retrospective legislation is in all circumstances unjustifiable. To quote Willes J. again:[3]

'Allowing for the general inexpediency of retrospective legislation, it cannot be pronounced naturally or necessarily unjust.

v. *Button*, [1943] K.B. 405; *R.* v. *Oliver*, [1944] K.B. 68; whereon see 59 *L.Q.R.* 199. With regard to liability under an expired statute for acts previously done, see *R.* v. *Wicks*, [1946] 2 All E.R. 529.

[1] See, for example, *Colonial Sugar Refining Co.* v. *Melbourne Harbour Trust*, [1927] A.C. 343.

[2] For examples, see Maxwell, *op. cit.* 222 ff., and cf. *Fairey* v. *Southampton C.C.*, [1956] 2 Q.B. 439. Various provisions of modern nationalization Acts have retrospective effect, under certain safeguards, on antecedent transactions: see, e.g., Electricity Act, 1947, ss. 18 and 29, and Transport Act, 1947, s. 15.

[3] *Phillips* v. *Eyre*, *ubi sup.*, at p. 27.

There may be occasions and circumstances involving the safety of the state, or even the conduct of individual subjects, the justice of which prospective laws made for ordinary occasions and the usual exigencies of society for want of prevision fail to meet, and in which the execution of the law as it stood at the time may involve practical public inconvenience and wrong—summum jus summa injuria.'

This is a 'matter of policy and discretion fit for debate and decision' in Parliament, 'as to which a court of ordinary municipal law is not commissioned to inquire or adjudicate'. While these exceptions must be admitted, wise government will treat them with great caution, for experience has often shown that *commodum populi* is even more treacherous than *salus populi* as a *suprema lex*.

As for public opinion, in this as in all other matters of legislation, it is impossible to generalize for all times and circumstances, but it is fairly safe to say that at least in democratic communities arbitrary legislation of retroactive effect is likely to offend the average sense of fairness and justice and to arouse opposition.

The objection is to laws which impose an undue or unforeseeable *detriment* on individuals; and the extreme form of this is the *privilegium*, or Act aimed specifically at a single person or group of persons. Such was the nature of the old Bills of Attainder and Bills of Pains and Penalties; but these have disappeared from our law and it is almost inconceivable that they should ever be revived. The same objection can hardly be felt to Acts which are passed *for the protection* of an individual or individuals, save in the improbable event of a Government providing absolution for wrongdoing which has no reasonable excuse. Indemnifying legislation of this kind has been fairly frequent. Perhaps the most famous instance of it in our constitutional history was the 4 Hen. VIII, c. 8, which was passed to annul the conviction in *Strode's Case* (1512)[1] and which is usually regarded

[1] See Holdsworth, *H.E.L.* IV. 91; May, *Parliamentary Practice* (16th ed.), 49.

as the charter of free speech in Parliament. Acts of Indemnity to validate measures for public safety in time of emergency have often been passed, though it is still debated whether they add anything to Common Law rules concerning martial law.[1] Sometimes they are passed to correct mere procedural oversights or mistakes,[2] or to protect an individual from the consequences of an innocent and inadvertent breach of some technical rule of law, such as sitting in the House of Commons when disqualified.[3] In 1932 it was found necessary to pass an Act, the 22 Geo. V, c. 21, to indemnify all Presidents of the Board of Trade since 1909, because it was discovered that the Board of Trade Act, 1909, by repealing an Act of 1826 and thereby reviving the provisions of the Succession Act, 1707, might have exposed every President to heavy penalties for sitting in Parliament. This example illustrates the fact that despite the leaning against retrospective laws, statute does sometimes have a completely unexpected retroactive effect, which is highly inconvenient and occasionally borders on the comic. The same, as we have seen, is from time to time true of case-law. A decision of the courts, even if it does not hark back to vested rights or duties, may have a grave effect upon status. Thus the decision in *Keyes* v. *K.*, [1921] P. 204, had the consequence that a number of persons who had been divorced in India were not really divorced at all, and those who had subsequently married were therefore technically guilty of bigamy. Parliament at once intervened to validate all such divorces retrospectively.[4] No sensible private or public

[1] See Willes J. in *Phillips* v. *Eyre, ubi sup.*, 23 ff., and for modern examples the Indemnity Act, 1920, and the Restoration of Order in Ireland (Indemnity) Act, 1923.

[2] e.g. the National Fire Service Regulations (Indemnity) Act, 1944.

[3] e.g. the William Preston Indemnity Act, 1925, the Arthur Jenkins Indemnity Act, 1941, the Niall Macpherson Indemnity Act, 1954, and the Charles Beattie Indemnity Act, 1956.

[4] Indian Divorces (Validity) Act, 1921. The matter was subsequently regulated by the Indian and Colonial Divorce Jurisdiction Acts, 1926 and 1940, whereon see *Buckle* v. *B.*, [1956] P. 181.

opinion, and certainly no rule of law, could possibly object to such remedial legislation; on the contrary, the common sense of fairness would be violated if it were not enacted.

Non-repeal

3. No statute can make itself absolutely secure against repeal. There is nothing to prevent any Parliament from enacting that a particular statute shall never in any circumstances be altered or abrogated, and at certain troubled periods of history this seems to have been the intention of the legislators.[1] But it is equally clear that there is nothing to prevent any subsequent Parliament from treating such a provision as *pro non scripto*. In any enlightened government, an unrepealable statute is a contradiction in terms, striking as it does at the very root of legislative theory. Its practical dangers are also manifest, for it turns the ordinary process of legislation into a constitutional issue so grave as to involve the danger of disorder or even revolution. Yet laws of this kind have not been unknown in some countries even in modern times. Thus in 1884 the Assemblée Nationale enacted that the republican form of government could not be made the subject of a proposal for revision. It is noteworthy that one of the earliest and most uncompromising advocates of unlimited sovereignty, Bodin, deprecated any attempt to make laws unrepealable.[2]

IV. SCOPE AND DURATION OF LEGISLATION

From these general considerations of the subject-matter of statute, we must next turn to the scope of its operation.

1. *Promulgation*

As early as 1365 it is laid down judicially that 'every one is bound to know what is done in Parliament, even although it has not been proclaimed in the country; as soon as Parliament has concluded any matter, the law presumes that every person has cognizance of it, for

[1] See Dicey, *Law of the Constitution*, ch. i, and 1 Bl. *Comm.* 90.
[2] See Pollock, *History of the Science of Politics*, 50.

Parliament represents the body of the realm'.[1] In days when communication was difficult and writing the privilege of few, this rule was one which might work hardship, and the promulgation of statutes was a problem of no small difficulty. Down to the reign of Henry VII, the statutes passed in a session were sent to the sheriff of every county with a writ requiring him to proclaim them throughout his bailiwick and to see to their observance.[2] Soon after the introduction of printing, statutes began to be promulgated in print, the first dating from 1484.[3] But their distribution and publicity were extremely defective, and gave rise to severe strictures. Hobbes, for example, waxed indignant at the difficulties which confronted the layman in ascertaining the law,[4] and he concluded that there ought to be as many copies of statutes abroad as of the Bible! Blackstone[5] lightly passes over the difficulty by the transparent sophistry that the people are present 'by their representatives' at the passing of the Acts, and must therefore be taken to know them. It was not until the end of the eighteenth century that any attempt was made at systematic promulgation. In 1796 it was ordered that the printed statutes should be distributed throughout the realm as speedily as possible after enactment. Soon after the Act of Union, it was resolved by the Commons that the King's Printer should publish not less than 5,000 copies of each Public General Act, and 300 copies of such local and personal Acts as were printed.[6] Until 1793[7] the position was made worse by what Christian calls the 'flatly absurd and unjust rule'[8] that every statute, unless another date was fixed for its operation, took effect from

[1] Thorpe C.J., *R.* v. *Bishop of Chichester*, Y.B. 59 Ed. III, 7; cited in abridged form, 4 Inst. 26.

[2] 4 Inst. 26, 28; 1 Bl. *Comm.* 184.

[3] Record Commission, *Select Essays in Anglo-American Legal History*, ii. 203.

[4] See *Works* (ed. Molesworth), vi. 27.

[5] 1 *Comm.* 184.

[6] Record Commission, *op. cit.* ii. 205.

[7] 33 Geo. III, c. 13 (Acts of Parliament Commencement Act).

[8] Note to 1 Bl. *Comm.* 70.

the first day of the session in which it was passed; and it might therefore result, in contravention of the rule against retrospective penalties, that 'all who, during a long session, had been doing an act, which at the time was legal and inoffensive, were liable to suffer the punishment prescribed by the statute'.[1]

Present rules as to promulgation

The present rule is that, as soon as a statute has received the royal assent, unless a future date is fixed for its operation,[2] (1) the courts will at once take judicial notice of it;[3] (2) it is binding on all the Queen's subjects at once. This application of the rule *ignorantia iuris neminem excusat* at first sight seems harsh, and it is indubitable that in some cases strange consequences follow from it. In *Tomlinson* v. *Bullock* (1879), 4 Q.B.D. 230, the Court had to consider the effect of the Bastardy Laws Amendment Act, 1872, which enabled any

[1] Christian, *loc. cit.* See *R.* v. *Thurston* (1662), 1 Lev. 91; *Att.-Gen.* v. *Panter* (1772), 6 Bro. P.C. 486; *Latless* v. *Holmes* (1792), 4 T.R. 660.

[2] It is a very common practice in modern statutes, especially those of extensive design connected with social services, for the Act to come into force on an 'appointed day'—i.e. a date to be fixed, under the authority of the Act itself, either by an Order in Council or by a Ministerial order. This is often necessary because a good deal of preparatory work has to be done by Departments, especially in framing consequential Statutory Instruments, before the Act can operate effectively. There can be no objection in principle to the method, but it is not without inconveniences, because insufficient publicity is sometimes given to 'pressing the button' (as it is called), and it is not always easy to know exactly when a statute has taken effect. Still more inconvenient, and much to be deprecated, is the practice of bringing different parts of an Act into operation at different times. This again is generally due to the necessity of drafting Statutory Instruments under different parts of the Act. The practice seems to be growing. It is believed that there are on the statute-book portions of Acts which have never been brought into operation at all: see *R.* v. *Kynaston* (1927), 19 Cr. App. R. 180. On the whole subject see Carr, *Delegated Legislation*, 10 ff., and cf. Ilbert, *Legislative Methods and Forms*, 213 ff.; and on the complications which sometimes arise from this legislative device, see *R.* v. *Minister of Town and Country Planning, Ex p. Montague Burton, Ltd.*, [1951] 1 K.B. 1, and *Usher* v. *Barlow*, [1952] Ch. 255. As to the nice calculations which sometimes have to be made about an Act's commencement, see *Hare* v. *Gocher*, [1962] 2 Q.B. 641.

[3] Interpretation Act, 1889, s. 9, which further provides that every Act passed since 1850 is a public Act, unless the contrary is provided by the Act itself.

unmarried woman who should be delivered of a bastard child 'after the passing of this Act' to apply for an affiliation order. The Act received the royal assent on 10 August 1872, and came into immediate operation. The appellant's bastard child was born on 10 August 1872, and it was held that the affiliation order might be granted in respect of a child born at any time on that day.[1] But in practice the rule of *ignorantia iuris* is plainly necessary as a matter of utility, and it may be doubted whether many substantial hardships result from it. Most people become acquainted with the elements of the statutory or Common Law which affect them specially in their particular vocations or circumstances. It is also questionable whether any artificial expedients would increase the public taste for the reading of statutes. It is, however, a serious inconvenience at the present time that a great deal of subordinate and local legislation is in forms which are by no means easy of access.[2]

2. *Repeal*

Once having come into operation, the statute remains effectual until repealed or, if it is a temporary statute, until it has expired. The repeal may be express or implied.

Express repeal

Express repeal seems at first sight to be simple enough, but we have seen that until a systematic effort was made to revise the statute-book, it was not always easy to be certain what statutes still remained in force when there had been a long course of legislation on the same subject. With respect to all Acts passed before 1850,[3] the position was greatly complicated by the Common Law rule[4] that when an Act was repealed, and the repealing statute itself was subsequently repealed, the first Act was revived as from the original time of its commencement. The effect of repeal, cross-repeal, and

[1] The classic example, too well known to need repetition here, is *R.* v. *Bailey* (1799), R. & R. 1.

[2] *Post*, pp. 549 ff.

[3] Interpretation Act, 1889, s. 11.

[4] 2 Inst. 686, 4 Inst. 325. Coke, at 4 Inst. 25, cites the remarkable case of the repeals and revivals, extending over about a century, in the legislation affecting the Spencers.

revival has sometimes created a legal maze through which judges have had the greatest difficulty in picking their way. A good illustration is afforded by the curiously anachronistic law which still governs the duty of attendance at the parish church. The Act of Uniformity, 1552 (5 & 6 Ed. VI, c. 1), provided that

'all and every person and persons inhabiting within this realm, or any other the King's majesty's dominions, shall diligently and faithfully (having no lawful or reasonable excuse to be absent) endeavour themselves to resort to their parish church or chapel accustomed; or upon reasonable lett thereof, to some usual place where common prayer and such service of God shall be used in such time of lett, upon every Sunday, and other days ordained and used to be kept as holydays, and then and there to abide orderly and soberly during the time of the common prayer, preaching or other service of God there to be used and ministered; upon pain of punishment by the censures of the Church.'

This Act, together with others of an ecclesiastical nature, was repealed by Mary, but was re-enacted by 1 Eliz., c. 2, with the addition that anybody who failed to comply with it was to be fined one shilling for each unexcused absence from divine service. By the Toleration Act of 1689 (1 Wm. & Mary, c. 18) the penalties of the previous legislation were not to be imposed on dissenters (except Roman Catholics), provided that they went through certain forms on Sunday. In 1846 came the Religious Disabilities Act (9 & 10 Vict., c. 59), which repealed the statute of Elizabeth, *but did not repeal the Statute of Edward VI*; and provided that nobody dissenting from the Church of England should be liable to *any penalties at all*. The result at the present time is that dissenters are not liable to any penalties for non-attendance at the Established Church, but Laodicean members of the Church of England, though relieved of Elizabeth's shilling fine, are liable to spiritual censures for every unjustified absence from divine service on Sundays and other appointed days; i.e. they may be admonished by an

Ecclesiastical Court and made to pay the cost of the proceedings.[1] In 1953, owing to a whole network of repeals and cross-repeals, it was in great doubt whether a right of appeal from the Transport Tribunal subsisted after the passing of the Transport Act, 1947, and the complexity of the question was shown by the fact that in *British Transport Commission* v. *L.C.C.*, [1953] 1 Q.B. 736, all three members of the Court of Appeal gave different reasons for holding that the right of appeal survived.[2]

Repeal by implication

Repeal by implication is a matter of construction, and is a very striking instance of 'control' exercised by the courts over the operation of statute. It is a Common Law rule that *leges posteriores priores contrarias abrogant.*[3]

> 'If two inconsistent Acts be passed at different times, the last must be obeyed, and if obedience cannot be observed without derogating from the first, it is the first which must give way. Every Act of Parliament must be considered with reference to the state of the law subsisting when it came into operation, and when it is to be applied; it cannot otherwise be rationally construed. Every Act is made either for the purpose of making a change in the law, or for the purpose of better declaring the law, and its operation is not to be impeded by the mere fact that it is inconsistent with some previous enactment.'[4]

It is the invariable practice at the present time, and has been for many years past, for an Act to contain a schedule of the statutes, or parts of statutes, which it repeals.[5] These schedules nowadays are reasonably complete, though sometimes a great deal of research is

[1] See *Taylor* v. *Timson* (1888), 20 Q.B.D. 671. Another curious example is to be found in the complex of legislation and counter-legislation which results (it would seem) in the rule that a promissory note for less than £5 payable to bearer on demand is void in England: see Chalmers, *Bills of Exchange* (11th ed.), 269.

[2] For another example of complicated repeals and cross-repeals, see *Eton College* v. *Minister of Agriculture*, [1962] 3 W.L.R. 726. On the whole subject, and especially on the technique of draftsmanship in this connexion, see further D. B. Murray, 'When is a Repeal not a Repeal?' 16 *M.L.R.* 50.

[3] 2 Inst. 685. For an example of repeal by construction, see *Smith* v. *Benabo*, [1937] 1 K.B. 518.

[4] *Per* Lord Langdale, *Dean of Ely* v. *Bliss* (1842), 5 Beav. 574, 582.

[5] On the statutory effect of this, see D. B. Murray, *loc. cit.*

necessary to discover every portion of preceding legislation which *may* be affected, apart from those provisions which it is intended expressly to cancel; thus, when the Common Informers Act, 1951, was passed, it was necessary to search the statute-book from 1332 to 1949 to discover all the repealable Acts. In the criminal law, a great many monetary penalties prescribed by old statutes are totally inadequate in existing economic conditions. The project for their revision has, at this date of writing, been in hand for over five years, but apparently the research is not yet complete. In the complexity of our statute-book it can never be guaranteed, when a long and far-reaching statute is in question, that the schedule is wholly exhaustive. Thus a new enactment cannot be fitted into the whole framework of legislation with infallible consistency; and the process of logical reconciliation constantly employed by the courts is a very real supervision over the operation of statute law.

Expiring laws

A distinction is to be drawn between repealed and *expiring* statutes. A certain number of Acts are, for one reason or another—e.g. to meet a special emergency—valid only for a limited period, and are known as *temporary Acts*. The most familiar example is the Army (Annual) Act, which, as every student of constitutional law knows, has a long history behind it; it dates back to the Mutiny Act of 1689 and is an echo of the great controversies which grew out of 'keeping a standing army in time of peace'. It is now, in effect, a permanent enactment, but by constitutional convention it is re-enacted every year. Other less fundamental statutes, being chiefly of an experimental nature, are given effect for a year only; if their usefulness is exhausted at the end of that time, they lapse automatically; otherwise they are renewed by an Expiring Laws (Continuance) Act, and each year a rather curious assortment of laws is given a fresh lease of life in this manner. Some statutes, again, such as Emergency Powers Acts, may be expressed to lapse, unless renewed, on a future date; others, again, to continue in force until the occasion or 'emergency' which gave rise to them is declared by Order in Council to be at an end.[1] The difference in effect between these two kinds of laws is that repealed statutes, 'except so far as they relate to transactions already completed under them, become as if they never had existed, but with respect to temporary statutes, the extent of the restrictions imposed by them becomes a matter of construction'.[2] The question sometimes arises whether a temporary statute which has lapsed still applies to acts or things done—e.g. to offences committed—before it ceased. This can be determined only by reference to the exact language of the enactment, which should be clear and unambiguous on such a vital point, but unfortunately is not always so.[3]

Codifying and consolidating Acts

The recension of statute law is not only destructive but constructive when it takes the form of *codifying* and *consolidating* Acts. There is a distinction between these two forms of enactment, though it is one which is not always easy to preserve with precision. A codifying Act is in the nature of what is called in the United States a 'restatement' of the law in a particular field, and it embraces not only previous statutory provisions but formulations of Common Law doctrines derived from case-law. Perhaps the two best-known examples are the Sale of Goods Act, 1893, and the Bills of Exchange Act, 1882, which gathered together in statutory form principles, many of them ancient, based very largely on the customs of merchants as developed in practice and interpreted by the courts. Acts of this kind are not 'codes' in the Continental sense, not being works of premeditation, but resemble them in so far as they shape the law into compact and authoritative form and so assist its ready application. They are not slavishly bound by pre-existing law, but in the main are declaratory of it.

[1] See *Willcock* v. *Muckle*, [1951] 2 K.B. 844.

[2] *Per* Parke, B., *Steavenson* v. *Oliver* (1841), 8 M. & W. 234, 241.

[3] See *R.* v. *Wicks*, [1946] 2 All E.R. 529.

A consolidating statute, on the other hand, is an expedient of convenience to assemble and re-enact a number of antecedent statutory provisions. It often happens that a long course of legislation on a particular subject, involving many repeals, amendments, and supplements, is scattered in unwieldy fashion over the so-called statute-book, until the time comes when it is necessary to 'tidy it up'. For example, since we are a maritime nation, it was natural that with the expansion of our trade in the nineteenth century and with the change from sail to steam, there should be constant legislation about the mercantile marine, and it was not until 1894 that all this was consolidated into a Merchant Shipping Act, which runs to 748 sections and covers 228 pages of print. But perhaps no more massive consolidation has ever been undertaken in our law than the series of Real Property Acts which began in 1922. The work of consolidation has been carried on very actively in the post-war period, and since 1947 over thirty consolidation Acts have been passed. Recent examples of this reconstructive process, which is necessarily accompanied by a great many repeals, are the Magistrates' Courts Act, 1952, the Matrimonial Causes Act, 1950, and the Sexual Offences Act, 1956.

The principle of interpretation which has always been applied to consolidating statutes is that they are presumed not to change the law but only to re-enact it.[1] Where there is a difference, or an apparent difference, between the terms of a consolidating statute and interpretations *in pari materia* which have been made in the absorbed precedents or enactments, it would seem that the phraseology of the consolidating statute must be

[1] With a few minor exceptions, Consolidating Bills are not subject to amendment in the ordinary way during their passage through Parliament: see Erskine May, *Parliamentary Practice* (15th ed.), 534, where, however, it is mentioned that a Bill may be designed not merely to consolidate, but to *consolidate and amend*. The example given is the Local Government Act, 1933, which is intituled 'to consolidate with amendments'. This is comparatively rare.

given its ordinary and natural meaning without regard to previous constructions.[1] It seems a pity, however, that in the process of amalgamation the opportunity should not be taken of resolving doubts and ambiguities which have arisen, and, in general, of smoothing rough edges. This limited kind of revision is now authorized by the Consolidation of Enactments (Procedure) Act, 1949, but it is restricted to 'corrections and minor improvements', which are defined with some particularity in the interpretation clause. When such alterations are proposed, they must be set forth by the Lord Chancellor in a memorandum which is laid before Parliament and is referred to a joint committee of both Houses, which reports to Parliament. Representations may be made by persons interested, and it is specially provided that alterations shall not be sanctioned if, in the opinion of the committee or the Lord Chancellor and the Speaker, they are more suitable for separate enactment.

3. *Desuetude*

Age cannot wither an Act of Parliament, and at no time, so far as I am aware, has it ever been admitted in our jurisprudence that a statute might become inoperative through obsolescence.[2]

[1] *Vagliano* v. *Bank of England*, [1891] A.C. 107 (especially *per* Lord Herschell); *Grey* v. *I.R.C.*, [1960] A.C. 1.

[2] It is true, however, that some statutes have been so persistently disregarded that for all practical purposes they have been of little or no effect; see examples given by J. C. Gray, *The Nature and Sources of the Law*, 194 ff. There was also at one time a theory, which, under the name of 'non-observance', came very near to a doctrine of desuetude, that if a statute had been in existence for any considerable period *without ever having been put into operation*, it might be treated as null. Coke (Co. Litt. 81 b) acknowledged the principle, explaining it obscurely, and it was accepted in not a few cases up to the end of the eighteenth century; but it may now be considered to be wholly discarded. Coke's cryptic rule that 'if a statute in the negative be declarative of the ancient lâw, that is, in affirmance of the Common Law, there as well as a man may prescribe or allege a custom against the Common Law, so a man may do so against such a statute, for as our author saith, *Consuetudo etc. privat communem legem*' (Co. Litt. 115 a), and indeed the whole of his distinction between statutes 'in the negative and in the affirmative', has met with such general disfavour that it seems hardly profitable to discuss them. The rule concerning desuetude is otherwise in Scotland. 'Custom, as it is equally

'The doctrine that, because a certain number of people do not like an Act and because a good many people disobey it, the Act is therefore "obsolescent" and no one need pay any attention to it, is a very dangerous proposition to hold in any constitutional country. So long as an Act is on the statute book, the way to get rid of it is to repeal or alter it in Parliament, not for subordinate bodies, who are bound to obey the law, to take upon themselves to disobey an Act of Parliament.'[1]

Nothing but repeal and revision can disembarrass the law of the considerable quantity of matter which nobody nowadays would dream of putting into effect. We have just seen that a parishioner (a term including nearly all inhabitants of the kingdom) is liable to punishment for not attending church. As late as 1923 a case of great political importance reminded the public that the savage penalties of *praemunire* were still in existence, and nothing short of a *privilegium*, in the shape of an Act of Indemnity, was able to save two Cabinet Ministers from those penalties.[2] Until recently, unlicensed persons who slaughtered horses or cattle were liable to flogging.[3] The 'ducking-stool' (or, more correctly, cucking-stool) is still a legal punishment for a common scold.[4] 'To this day', writes Stephen,[5] 'there is no legal reason why any Ecclesiastical Court in England should not try any person for adultery or fornication and enjoin penance upon them, to which they must submit under pain of six months' imprisonment.'[6] In criminal law, a number of Acts of the

founded in the will of the lawgiver with written law, has therefore the same effects; hence, as one statute may be explained or repealed by another, so a statute may be explained by the uniform practice of the community, and even, at least if it is a Scots Act, go into disuse by a posterior contrary custom. This power of custom to derogate from prior statutes is not confined to statutes concerning private right, but extends to those which regard public policy': Erskine, *Principles of the Law of Scotland*, 6. Cf. Stair, *Inst.* 12. On desuetude in Roman Law, see *ante*, p. 86.

[1] *Per* Scrutton L.J., *R.* v. *London County Council*, [1931] 2 K.B. 215, 226; and cf. Slesser L.J. at p. 242.

[2] *R.* v. *Sec. of State for Home Affairs, Ex p. Art O'Brien*, [1923] 2 K.B. 361.

[3] Knackers Act, 1786.

[4] 1 Hawk., c. 75, s. 14.

[5] *Hist. Cr. Law*, ii. 428.

[6] By 53 Geo. III, c. 127, ss. 1–3.

thirteenth century (these appear to be the most ancient) are still operative, though for the most part they refer to rare offences, such as champerty, abduction, and extortion by public officials;[1] and it is needless to say that Magna Carta itself belongs to that century. Many statutes of the fourteenth century are still in force in criminal law, notably the Treason Act of 1351 and the statutes of Richard II relating to forcible entry.[2] The statute 21 Hen. VIII, c. 5 (appointing the widow as administrator of the estate of an intestate person) and the Statute of Distribution, 1670, are still in force, and have recently been applied in Ghana.[3] A person who wantonly discharges firearms on a highway may still be indicted under an Act of 1328,[4] and it has become fairly common to prosecute for 'blemishing the peace' under the Justices of the Peace Act, 1360.[5] Antiquated statutes may sometimes be perpetuated very inconveniently—thus there have been, in modern times, many prosecutions by common informers under the Sunday Observance Act, 1780;[6] sometimes, on the other hand, it is as convenient as it is ingenious to resort to them—thus, when all modern legislation about road traffic had failed to provide for the very common offence of opening the off-side door of a motor-car without regard to the safety of passers-by, it was necessary to pray in aid (with somewhat surprising results) the Highways Act, 1835.[7] Perhaps the most striking example of incongruous survival in recent times is afforded by the disabilities which, despite the various Roman Catholic Relief Acts, still rested upon members of that faith until very recently. By the 3 & 4 Ed. VI, c. 10 (repealed by 1 Mar. St. 2, c. 2, but restored by

[1] See Archbold, *Criminal Pleading*, for the ancient statutes relating to these offences.

[2] See *Hemmings* v. *Stoke Poges Golf Club, Ltd.*, [1920] 1 K.B. 720.

[3] *Coleman* v. *Shang*, [1961] A.C. 481.

[4] The 2 Edw. III, c. 3; see *R.* v. *Meade* (1903), 19 T.L.R. 540.

[5] In practice, these prosecutions generally relate to offences of the 'Peeping Tom' type.

[6] But see now the Common Informers Act, 1951.

[7] See *Shears* v. *Matthews*, [1948] 2 All E.R. 1064; *Watson* v. *Lowe*, [1950] 1 All E.R. 100; *Eaton* v. *Cobb*, [1950] 1 All E.R. 1016.

1 Jas. I, c. 25) all books used for church services except the Book of Common Prayer (of that date), and all 'images of stone, timber, alabaster or earth, graven, carved or painted', were to be destroyed or defaced, and if those persons (mayors, bishops, &c.) who were made responsible by the Act for destroying them failed to do so, they were liable to a fine of £40. By the 1 Geo. I, c. 50, the estates of 'popish recusants', and estates given to superstitious uses, were forfeited and vested in the Crown for the use of the public. By the 11 Geo. II, c. 17, s. 5, every grant of an ecclesiastical living made by any Papist, unless to a Protestant purchaser for valuable consideration, and every devise of an ecclesiastical living made by a Papist, were void. The establishment or endowment of any Roman Catholic order in England was illegal, being (s. 17) specially excepted from the relief given to Roman Catholics by the 31 Geo. III, c. 32. By the 10 Geo. IV, c. 7, s. 26, any Roman Catholic ecclesiastic officiating, or wearing the habits of his order, except in the usual places of worship of the Roman Catholic religion, or in private houses, was liable to a penalty of £50. By the same Act, all Jesuits or members of other Roman Catholic orders and communities were bound to register themselves, any foreign Jesuit, &c., coming into the realm from abroad, except by licence, was liable to be banished, and any proselytizing by Jesuits, &c., was made a misdemeanour punishable (for both missionary and convert) by banishment or transportation for life. These disabilities, though long obsolete, were not removed by legislation until 1926.[1]

In all these cases the balance is preserved between Common Law and common sense, and between statute and public opinion. Disuse, though it may not abrogate it legally, renders the obsolete rule of little or no practical efficacy. Occasionally, as in the celebrated case of trial by battle,[2] outworn institutions are revived in a

[1] Roman Catholic Relief Act, 1926.

[2] *Ashford* v. *Thornton* (1818), 1 B. & Ald. 405.

startling manner, and the legislature then has to step in; but society does not suffer seriously from obsolete rules of law. While, however, ancient Common Law rules always have the capacity to adapt themselves gradually to new forms, a statutory rule, once reduced to an inelastic form of words, remains unadaptable for all time.

V. GENERAL PRINCIPLES OF STATUTORY INTERPRETATION

The operation of statute is not automatic, and can never be so. Like all legal rules, it has to take effect through the interpretation of the courts. The interpretation of statute is a science by itself, and it would be far beyond the scope of this book to attempt anything like an exhaustive survey of it. Some more general considerations will be discussed later; for the present, we will merely glance at the leading principles and their general effect on this source of law.

1. *Literal interpretation*

In their task of *literal* or *grammatical* interpretation judges are constantly reminded, to their unfeigned chagrin, of the imperfections of human language. The 'style' of statutes has differed greatly from age to age. From the laconic and often obscure terseness of our earliest statutes, especially when in Latin, we swung in the sixteenth, seventeenth, and eighteenth centuries to a verbosity which succeeded only in concealing the real matter of the law under a welter of superfluous synonyms. Nowadays the ideal aimed at is the minimum of words consistent with clearness, explaining themselves, so far as possible, one step at a time without involutions and cross-references. It is difficult to lay down any invariable scientific principles for legislative diction. Probably nothing more sensible has been said on the subject than by Montesquieu.[1] His rules may be epitomized as follows:

'Style' of statutes

[1] *L'Esprit des Lois,* xxix, ch. 16.

Montesquieu's principles

1. The style should be both concise and simple: grandiose or rhetorical phrases are merely distracting surplusage.

2. The terms chosen should, as far as possible, be absolute and not relative, so as to leave the minimum of opportunity for individual differences of opinion.

3. Laws should confine themselves to the real and the actual, avoiding the metaphorical or hypothetical.

4. They should not be subtle, 'for they are made for people of mediocre understanding; they are not an exercise in logic, but in the simple reasoning of the average man'.

5. They should not confuse the main issue by any exceptions, limitations, or modifications, save such as are absolutely necessary.

6. They should not be argumentative; it is dangerous to give detailed reasons for laws, for this merely opens the door to controversy.

7. Above all, they should be maturely considered and of practical utility, and they should not shock elementary reason and justice and *la nature des choses*; for weak, unnecessary, and unjust laws bring the whole system of legislation into disrepute and undermine the authority of the State.[1]

Drafting

Whether or not these admirable principles are observed depends on the particular draftsman; and drafting is a matter which we have treated in an extraordinarily casual manner. Until 1869 every Government department employed its own draftsmen, and the result was a great deal of overlapping and confusion.[2] Nowadays practically the whole work is done by the remarkably small staff of the Parliamentary Counsel Office.[3] Their task is not enviable;[4] apart from the technical

[1] Some useful principles concerning the languages of statutes are to be found in Craies, *Statute Law* (3rd ed.), 18 ff.

[2] Ilbert, *op. cit.*, ch. v.

[3] Hereon see Sir Granville Ram, 'The Improvement of the Statute Book', *Journal of the Society of Public Teachers of Law*, 1951, 442.

[4] The complex processes preliminary to any legislation—processes of which

difficulties of the Parliamentary process, anybody who has ever attempted it knows how extremely difficult it is to frame not only legal rules, but rules of any kind, in completely unambiguous terms. To demand perfection of expression and sense is to expect infallibility not only of human foresight but of human language; and the fact that this is unattainable is one of the most serious drawbacks of statute law. This defect may be inevitable, but that only makes it all the more inherent in the very nature of legislation. Judges have suffered much, and continue to suffer much, from bad drafting. In 1857 we find Lord Campbell commenting severely on 'an ill-penned enactment, like too many others, putting Judges in the embarrassing situation of being bound to make sense out of nonsense, and to reconcile what is irreconcilable'.[1] In 1835 the First Report of the Statute Law Commissioners was equally frank:

> 'The imperfections in the statute law arising from mere generality, laxity or ambiguity of expression, are too numerous and too well known to require particular specification. They are the natural result of negligent, desultory and inartificial legislation; the statutes have been framed extemporaneously, not as parts of a system, but to answer particular exigencies as they occurred.'

At the present time, judicial complaints increase in proportion as legislation grows. 'No one can be certain about the meaning of a section like the one we have to construe,' said Lord Sterndale M.R. of one enactment,[2] 'and I do not profess to feel certain about it.' Of the Income Tax Acts, which engross so much of the time of the courts, judges speak with undisguised despair. 'I do not pretend', said Lord Buckmaster,[3]

> 'that the opinion I hold rests on any firm logical foundation. Logic is out of place in these questions, and the embarrassment

the general public, and even judges, are scarcely aware—are admirably described by Sir Granville Ram, *loc. cit.*

[1] *Fell* v. *Burchett*, 7 E. & B. 537, 539.

[2] Agriculture Act, 1920: *In re Arden and Rutter's Arbitration*, [1923] 2 K.B. 865, 869; and cf. Warrington L.J. at p. 874.

[3] *G.W. Ry. Co.* v. *Bater*, [1922] 2 A.C. 1, 11.

that I feel is increased with the knowledge that my views are not shared by other members of the House, but this fact is not surprising. It is not easy to penetrate the tangled confusion of these Acts of Parliament, and though we have entered the labyrinth together, we have unfortunately found exit by different paths.'

And in the same strain Lord Carson:

'I think it is open to comment that the learned judge who heard this case was of one opinion and in the Court of Appeal two of the three Lords Justices were of a different opinion, whilst in your Lordships' House two noble and learned Lords differ from the other three! That shows how unfortunate the Legislature has been in its attempt to clearly impose a tax upon the subject.'[1]

The Schedule to the Stamp Act, 1891, Lord Reid has recently described as 'a mere conglomeration of uncoordinated provisions': *Inland Revenue Commissioners* v. *Ansbacher & Co.*, [1963] A.C. 191.

Harsh words have fallen from the Bench about certain modern enactments, such as the Shops (Sunday Trading Restriction) Act, 1936,[2] the Agricultural Holdings Act, 1923,[3] the Trade Marks Act, 1938,[4] the Rent and

[1] *Wankie Colliery Co.* v. *Inland Revenue Commissioners*, [1922] 2 A.C. 51, 71. Cf. MacKinnon L.J. in *Inland Revenue Commissioners* v. *Cull*, [1938] 2 K.B. at p. 137, and in *Asher* v. *London Film Productions, Ltd.*, [1944] K.B. 133, 141; and see observations and suggestions of Viscount Simon in *Nugent-Head* v. *Jacob*, [1948] A.C. 321, 322. See also Scrutton L.J. in *R.* v. *Secretary of State for Home Affairs, Ex p. Art O'Brien*, [1923] 2 K.B. 361, 384, *Inland Revenue Commissioners* v. *Pakenham*, [1928] 1 K.B. at p. 145 (affirmed [1928] A.C. 252), *Roe* v. *Russell*, [1928] 2 K.B. at p. 123, and *Hill* v. *Aldershot Corporation*, [1933] 1 K.B. at p. 272; *Ocean Coal Co.* v. *Davies*, [1927] A.C. 271; and Lord Radcliffe on 'the many minor mysteries of the law', *Sanderson* v. *I.R.C.*, [1956] A.C. 491, 501. With regard to revenue Acts, it is only fair to the draftsman to remind ourselves of Aristotle's *dictum* that it is not possible to express in simple language that which is not simple in itself.

[2] 'It might be possible, but I doubt if it would be easy, to compress in the same number of lines more fertile opportunities for doubt and error': per Lord Hewart C.J., *London County Council* v. *Lees*, [1939] 1 All E.R. 191, which contains a scathing analysis and criticism of the whole Act. See also *Binns* v. *Wardale*, [1946] K.B. 451.

[3] Referring to s. 12 (8) of the Act, Lord Goddard C.J. said in *Bebb* v. *Frank*, [1939] 1 K.B. at p. 568: 'For myself, I am not ashamed to admit that I have not the least idea what sub-s. 8 means. I cannot give any meaning to it in the least satisfactory in my own mind.'

[4] 'I doubt if the entire statute-book could be successfully searched for a

Mortgage Interest Restrictions Act, 1939,[1] the Factory and Workshop Act, 1901,[2] and the statutes concerning the guardianship and custody of infants.[3] So unintelligible is the phraseology of some statutes that suggestions have been made that draftsmen, like the Delphic Oracle, sometimes aim deliberately at obscurity, as a disingenuous means of passing a Bill quickly through Parliament. If a Bill is in plain language, anybody can pick holes in it, and consequently debate may be prolonged; if it is sufficiently technical and obscure, nobody likes to admit that he does not understand it, but is content to trust to the skill and experience of the draftsman—which is very convenient for the promoters of the measure. Whether this be true or not, there is something in the very form of a statute which invites, and indeed demands, a gloss. Except for the bare bones of its long and short titles—for nowadays even the preamble is virtually mute—a statute does not *explain itself*. It does not inform the reader of its policy and purport. It leaves these things to be extracted, as a kind of essence, from the raw material of the words which it employs. There is always a veil behind which the reader has to penetrate; the form of the enactment provides little clue to its real content. This is what Lord du Parcq meant when he said, in *Cutler* v. *Wandsworth Stadium Ltd.*, [1949] A.C. 398, 410:

'To a person unversed in the science or art of legislation it may well seem strange that Parliament has not by now made it a rule to state explicitly what its intention is in a matter which is often of no little importance, instead of leaving it to the courts to discover, by a careful examination and analysis of what is expressly said, what the intention may be supposed probably to be. There are no doubt reasons which inhibit the legislature from

sentence of equal length which is of more fuliginous obscurity': *per* MacKinnon L.J., referring to s. 4, in *Bismag* v. *Amblins*, [1940] Ch. at p. 687.

[1] See MacKinnon L.J., *Davies* v. *Warwick*, [1943] K.B. 329, 333.

[2] See Viscount Maugham, *Smith* v. *Cammell, Laird & Co.*, [1940] A.C. 242, 250.

[3] See Evershed M.R., *In re Dankbars*, [1954] Ch. 98, 106.

revealing its intention in plain words. I do not know, and must not speculate, what those reasons may be. I trust, however, that it will not be thought impertinent, in any sense of that word, to suggest respectfully that those who are responsible for framing legislation might consider whether the traditional practice, which obscures, if it does not conceal, the intention which Parliament has, or must be presumed to have, might not safely be abandoned.'

Something, then, lies at the door of the 'traditional practice' of Parliament, and we must not too readily blame the well-intentioned draftsman when an unexpected crux of interpretation suddenly appears.[1] As Denning L. J. observed in *Seaford Court Estates, Ltd.* v. *Asher*, [1949] 2 K.B. 481, 499,[2] 'it must be remembered that it is not within human powers to foresee the manifold sets of facts which may arise, and, even if it were, it is not possible to provide for them in terms free from all ambiguity. The English language is not an instrument of mathematical precision. . . . This is where the draftsmen of Acts of Parliament have often been unfairly criticized. . . . It would certainly save the judges trouble if Acts of Parliament were drafted with divine prescience and perfect clarity. In the absence of it, when a defect appears a judge cannot simply fold his hands and blame the draftsman.'[3] And that, as we shall see (*post*, p. 524), is what some judges are apt to do.

In all cases of statutory obscurity, it is a sound principle of construction that ambiguous words should not be interpreted to the detriment of the individual. 'If an Act of Parliament is so drawn as to make it really difficult to say what the legislature intended and what facts come within it, the benefit of that obscurity should be given to the accused person'[4]—or, we conceive, to any person

[1] See Mr. Justice Frankfurter, 'Some Reflections on the Reading of Statutes', *Record of the Association of the Bar of the City of New York*, vol. 2, 1947, 214 ff.

[2] Affirmed [1950] A.C. 508.

[3] On the draftsman's problems, see further *post*, p. 516.

[4] *Per* Humphreys J., *Binns* v. *Wardale*, [1946] K.B. 451, 457.

who is liable to suffer a detriment or disability or incur an obligation, though the general policy of the Act may sometimes reverse the presumption.[1] But if the statute, as printed, 'leads to an unintelligible result', it will be construed intelligibly, even to the extent of substituting 'or' for 'and', and even though the effect is detrimental to the individual.[2] If statutory language makes no sense whatever, *semble* it can be treated as *pro non scripto;* but the Court cannot escape the duty of interpretation merely because the language is difficult or ambiguous.[3]

Difficulties of literal interpretation

It is self-evident that no invariable rule can be established for literal interpretation. A number of statutes have laid down a few primary principles and have precisely defined certain terms of frequent occurrence. Eight such statutes were repealed by the Interpretation Act, 1889, which consolidates the main principles and supplies standing definitions for the most ordinary stock-in-trade of the draftsman. This, however, amounts only to general guidance. So long as words are different, interpretations of them will be different. Some statutes have given rise to an almost illimitable amount of minute literal interpretation. The Statute of Frauds will occur to every lawyer as a conspicuous and a melancholy example.[4] A single phrase in the Workmen's Compensation Act, 1906, 'an accident arising out of and in the course of his employment', had been the parent of many hundreds, possibly thousands, of cases. After the passing of the Increase of Rent and Mortgage Interest (Restriction) Acts, 1920–39, the courts almost every day were hearing actions which turned on the construction of words and phrases in the Acts. For example, quite a number of cases in the County Courts, and at

[1] *Contra,* see Friedmann, 'Statute Law and its Interpretation in the Modern State', *Law and Social Change,* ch. 2.

[2] *Reg.* v. *Oakes,* [1959] 2 Q.B. 350. For a bold reconstruction of a statute 'to avoid a capricious result', see *In re Lockwood,* [1958] Ch. 231, and cf. *Fry* v. *I.R.C.,* [1959] Ch. 86.

[3] *Fawcett Properties Ltd.* v. *Buckingham C.C.,* [1961] A.C. 636.

[4] See 43 *L.Q.R.* 1 ff.

least one in the Court of Appeal,[1] were concerned with the problem whether linoleum could be considered as furniture. It is often found that the more commonplace a word is, the more difficult it is to arrive at its exact meaning—and for a very good reason, since it is commonplaces which are used most vaguely and with the least attention to precise significance. An elaborate, but probably a confusing, essay might be written on the innumerable shades of meaning of the word 'place' in different branches of English law. A draftsman may well think that he has expressed himself clearly enough when he uses a phrase like 'an open space of land'; he little knows what problems he has left for the judge to solve.[2] He will hardly anticipate doubts when he uses the expression 'an electrically-propelled vehicle'; he little guesses what feats of logic and what sharp differences of judicial opinion may arise from the apparently unambiguous description.[3] He would indeed have required 'divine prescience' to foresee, when he used a simple word like 'vessel' in a shipping Act, that some day the question would have to be anxiously debated whether a 'rum-tum' was a 'vessel'.[4] What modern Solon would ever ask himself whether the term 'loudspeaker' would include an amplified chime of bells, and whether or not it

[1] *Wilkes* v. *Goodwin*, [1923] 2 K.B. 86. 'Whatever confidence I may have in my own judgement in other branches of the law, I never give a decision upon the Rent Restrictions Act with any confidence': *per* Scrutton L.J., *Dunbar* v. *Smith*, [1926] 1 K.B. 360, 364; and cf. the same outspoken Lord Justice in *Haskins* v. *Lewis*, [1931] 2 K.B. at p. 9, and in *Skinner* v. *Geary*, [1931] 2 K.B. at p. 558. The impenetrable maze which resulted from these Acts may be studied in the decision of the Court of Appeal in the cases consolidated *sub nom. Lloyd* v. *Cook*, [1929] 1 K.B. 103. These cases, and the preceding judgements which fell to be considered therein, form a monument in modern law of the conflict of judicial opinion—conflict, however, for which nobody but the legislator can be held responsible. See also *Capital and Provincial Property Trust, Ltd.* v. *Rice*, [1952] A.C. 142.

[2] See *In re Bradford City Premises*, [1928] Ch. 138. Cf. the difficulties of interpreting 'open land': *Stephens* v. *Cuckfield R.D.C.*, [1960] 2 Q.B. 373.

[3] *Tilling-Stevens Motors, Ltd.* v. *Kent County Council*, [1929] 1 Ch. 66, and [1929] A.C. 354—an instructive case on literal interpretation.

[4] *Edwards* v. *Quickenden*, [1939] P. 261. Similarly, much learning surrounds the word 'ship': see *The Gas Float Whitton (No. 2)*, [1896] P. 42.

must be 'electrically operated'.[1] Even a preposition may be an enigma: the whole decision in *R.* v. *Agricultural Land Tribunal, Exp. Graham*, [1955] 2 Q.B. 140, turned upon a patent or latent 'of', and *Takim* v. *Velji* [1955] A.C. 617, on the meaning, in time (there are similar problems about its meaning in space), of 'at'. Much may turn on the presence or absence of a comma.[2] In all such cases, which are constantly arising, the great danger is that strict literal interpretation may produce a result which is manifestly contrary either to common sense or to the general intention of the statute;[3] and we shall see that our law has not yet succeeded in finding a perfect balance between the *ratio verborum* and the *ratio legis*—indeed, with the predominance of legislation in modern times, equilibrium becomes increasingly difficult to attain.

Context

Words are meaningless in isolation, and their context must always be taken into account. Hence the well-known rule of *eiusdem generis*—i.e. that when 'general words' are used in a summarizing or comprehensive manner, they must be taken as referring only to those kinds of things with which the context deals explicitly or implicitly.[4] We have seen that the courts will correct a mistaken view of the law on the part of the legislature: *a fortiori* they will correct words used wrongly or unintelligently in a statute, provided that the error be patent and not latent.[5] These are simple rules for the reasonable use of language. They do not constitute any peculiar legal cult; the method of interpretation is the same as is used by any intelligent person in the construction of written words.

[1] *Reynolds* v. *John*, [1956] 1 Q.B. 650.

[2] *R.* v. *Governor of Brixton Prison, Ex p. Singh*, [1962] 1 Q.B. 211.

[3] A conspicuous example is *Inland Revenue Commissioners* v. *Hinchy*, [1960] A.C. 748.

[4] Maxwell, *op. cit.*, ch. 9. For a famous modern example, see *Att.-Gen.* v. *Brown*, [1920] 1 K.B. 773 (the 'Pyrogallic Acid Case') (reversed, owing to legislative change, [1921] 3 K.B. 29).

[5] Maxwell, *op. cit.*, ch. 9. For examples in French law, see Gény, *Méthode d'interprétation*, i. 252.

2. *The* ratio legis

As precedent is only an instrument of judicial reasoning, and serves as a means to the ascertainment of a principle, so literal construction is only an instrument of the same process, and serves, or should serve (though, as we have seen, the effect is often the reverse), for the ascertainment of the *general purport* of the statute, or *ratio legis*. This is the so-called 'golden rule' of all statutory interpretation, formulated in a very well known *dictum* of Parke B.:

The 'golden rule'

'It is a very useful rule in the construction of a statute to adhere to the ordinary meaning of the words used, and to the grammatical construction, unless that is at variance with the intention of the Legislature to be collected from the statute itself, or leads to any manifest absurdity or repugnance, in which case the language may be varied or modified so as to avoid such inconvenience, but no further.'[1]

Another great Common Law judge says:

'The only rule for the construction of Acts of Parliament is that they should be construed according to the intent of the Parliament which passed them. If the words of the statute are in themselves precise and unambiguous, then no more can be necessary than to expound these words in their natural and ordinary sense. The words themselves alone do in such case best declare the intention of the lawgiver.'[2]

Time and again the courts reiterate this principle, that the expression of the will of the legislator must be considered not only by itself, *but with the natural consequences flowing from it*,[3] and it would merely weary the reader to cite the many *dicta* in this sense.

But the apparent simplicity of the principle is deceptive. In practice, no doctrine of interpretation is more elusive. Everybody admits that the *ratio legis* must be kept steadfastly in view. Even Austin, whose oft-repeated

[1] *Becke* v. *Smith* (1836), 2 M. & W. 191, 195. Cf. 1 Bl. *Comm.* 59.

[2] *Per* Tindal C.J., *Sussex Peerage Case* (1844), 11 Cl. & F. 85, 143. Hereon see Lord Macnaghten, *Vacher* v. *London Society of Compositors*, [1913] A.C. 107, 118, and Buckley L.J., *In re Vexatious Actions Act, 1896*, [1915] 1 K.B. 21, 26; and cf. *S.S. Ruapehu* v. *Green*, [1927] A.C. 523.

[3] Korkunov, *General Theory of Law*, 476.

theme is that the subject's sole duty towards sovereign legislation is to accept it, cannot escape the extreme importance of the *ratio legis*. He defines it as 'the scope or determining cause of a statute law: that is to say, the end or purpose which determines the lawgiver to make it, as distinguished from the intent or purpose *with which* he actually makes it'.[1] The 'end or purpose' must not only be ascertained, but must be interpreted as reasonably as possible. Between two antagonistic principles—the authority of the printed word and the dictates of lega reasonableness—it is necessary, but often very difficult, to preserve a nice balance. If the printed word irresistibly leads to an anomaly, then judges must regretfully allow it to do so: they take the view that the responsibility is not theirs.[2] But if reason and convenience can do it, this result will be avoided. It is always to reason and convenience that the court should lean, and to that extent the reason of the Common Law 'controls'—though, it must be confessed, imperfectly—the rigour of statute.[3]

The policy of a statute

A dilemma of the same kind confronts the courts in dealing with what Austin calls the end or purpose *with which* the legislator acts; for this also cannot be ignored. It is repeatedly affirmed that it is not open to the courts to regard a statute in the light of its social or Parliamentary history. In the Middle Ages, judges, as members of the King's Council, were generally themselves legislators and not infrequently interpreted an enactment according to their personal knowledge of its occasion and purport.[4] But in modern times it has become an accepted rule of interpretation that the Parliamentary history of a statute is not to be considered by the court.[5]

[1] Lect. XXXVII.

[2] See again *Inland Revenue Commissioners* v. *Hinchy, ubi sup.*

[3] See Brett J. in *Hammond* v. *Vestry of St. Pancras* (1874), L.R. 9 C.P. 316, 322, and Jessel M.R. in *In re Bethlem Hospital* (1875), L.R. 19 Eq. 457, 459.

[4] Plucknett, *Statutes and their Interpretation*, 49 ff. For a modern contrast, see *Hilder* v. *Dexter*, [1902] A.C. 474, where Lord Halsbury L.C. declined to deliver judgement on the interpretation of a statute for the drafting of which he had been largely responsible.

[5] *Vacher* v. *London Society of Compositors*, [1913] A.C. 107; *R.* v. *West*

It is difficult to say exactly when this rule established itself. Professor Plucknett[1] finds the first explicit statement of it in 1769 in the judgement of Willes J. in *Millar* v. *Taylor*, 4 Burr. 2303; and he calls attention to a severe application of the rule in 1848, when Pollock C.B., in *Salkeld* v. *Johnson*, 2 Exch. 256, refused to admit the report of the Real Property Commissioners to elucidate the legislation based upon it. Yet in the nineteenth century there seems to have remained some uncertainty about the limits of 'extraneous' evidence in the interpretation of enactments. As late as 1879, in *Reg.* v. *Bishop of Oxford*, 4 Q.B.D. 525, the Court of Appeal was in doubt whether it should admit, in order to construe s. 3 of the Church Discipline Act, 1840, an opinion thereon delivered by Lord Cairns L.C. in the House of Lords on the occasion of the Public Worship Regulation Act, 1874. The Court decided to do so, Baggallay L.J. *dubitante* but not *dissentiente*. Bramwell L.J. said (at p. 549):

> 'I really do not know that there is any definite rule as to what may or may not be cited and acted on as authority. No doubt, we must act on general principles, and I suppose they would exclude what is said in debate in either House of Parliament. But to reject the opinion of the head of the law as to what is the law, given to advise the highest court of judicature in the country, sitting indeed in its legislative capacity, and at the same time admit the *obiter dictum* of a judge at nisi prius either in our own or an American court seems somewhat strange, more especially as it is certain that if it ought to be excluded, any judge knowing of it and excluding it, would as soon as he left the court consult the Hansard he had before rejected. I cannot think it was wrong to admit it.'

But even in this case it was conceded that while the Lord Chancellor's opinion might be admitted to explain *the state of the law* when a certain Act was passed, it could not have been admitted to explain the actual phraseology

Riding of Yorkshire C.C., [1906] 2 K.B. 676 (reversed, but not on this ground, [1907] A.C. 29).

[1] *Concise History* (5th ed.), 335.

of the Act itself. The rule has been severely criticized, on the ground that it opposes an unnecessary obstacle to the essential purpose of the court—i.e. to discover the real meaning of a statute taken as a whole. It is certainly difficult to reconcile with the principle of considering the 'policy' of a statute. Yet there is something to be said on both sides of this thorny question.[1]

Again, it is not permitted to determine the scope of statute by considering it in relation to a real or supposed general *social* policy. 'I am bound to say', says Lord Sterndale M.R.,

> 'I think that it is an extraordinarily dangerous and mischievous doctrine to hold that a Court, in considering whether it can give effect to an Act of Parliament or not, is to examine the Act and see whether it considers it is the kind of legislation which is consistent with the general policy of the realm. Such an attitude . . . is one which might lead to extraordinary results. In my opinion all this Court can do is to say: Is that what is enacted by the statute? and, if it is, it must give effect to it.'[2]

On the other hand, it is common to find judges referring to the 'policy' of a statute, and the reason for which it was passed. No judge, for example, would hesitate to say that the various Bills of Sale Acts have been enacted to prevent the secret and fraudulent conveyance of property; or to keep that main purpose clearly in view in interpreting the provisions of the codifying Act. 'Although', says Jessel M.R.,

> 'the Court is not at liberty to construe an Act of Parliament by the motives which influenced the Legislature, yet when the history of law and legislation tells the Court, and prior judgements tell this present Court, what the object of the Legislature was, the Court is to see whether the terms of the section are such as fairly to carry out that object and no other, and to read the section with a view of [*sic*] finding out what it means, and not with a view to extending it to something that was not intended.'[3]

[1] See *post*, pp. 510 ff.

[2] *Scranton's Trustee* v. *Pearse*, [1922] 2 Ch. 87, 123.

[3] *Holme* v. *Guy* (1877), 5 Ch.D. 901, 905. On the limitations of this principle, especially in regard to codifying statutes, see observations of Lord

The leading principles here are summarized in the celebrated resolutions in *Heydon's Case* (1584), 3 Rep. 7a:

'It was resolved by the Barons of the Exchequer that for the sure and true interpretation of all statutes in general (be they penal or beneficial, restrictive or enlarging of the Common Law) four things are to be discussed and considered: 1st, What was the Common Law before the making of the Act; 2nd, What was the mischief and defect for which the Common Law did not provide; 3rd, What remedy the Parliament hath resolved and appointed to cure the disease of the commonwealth; and 4th, The true reason of the remedy; and then the office of all the judges is always to make such construction as shall suppress the mischief and advance the remedy, and to suppress subtle inventions and evasions for continuance of the mischief, and *pro privato commodo*, and to add force and life to the cure and remedy according to the true intent of the makers of the Act *pro bono publico*.'[1]

These propositions, though they have an archaic flavour, are still constantly recognized by the courts as rules of practical importance;[2] and their consideration will often be decisive in interpreting the effect of a statute. They are nowhere better illustrated than in the modern decisions which determine the extent of civil liability arising from a breach of statutory duty. At one time, there were the beginnings (hardly more) of a doctrine that when a person had committed a breach of a statutory duty, any member of the public who was injured in any way as the result of the breach might maintain an action for damages.[3] It is now well established that in such circumstances the intentions of the legislature must be carefully examined before the

Herschell in *Bank of England* v. *Vagliano*, [1891] A.C. 107, 144 ff., and *Derby Territorial Army Assocn.* v. *Derby (S.E. Area) Assessment Committee*, [1935] 2 K.B. 373. Further on the judicial approach to 'policy', see Stone, *The Province and Function of Law*, 193 ff.

[1] On the significance of this case in the history of our statutory interpretation, see S. E. Thorne, 'The Equity of a Statute and Heydon's Case', *Illinois Law Review*, xxxi. 202, 215.

[2] See *In re Mayfair Property Co.*, [1898] 2 Ch. 28, 35; *Hickman* v. *Peacey*, [1945] A.C. 304, 315.

[3] *Couch* v. *Steel* (1854), 3 E. & B. 402; though the doctrine appears to reside in *dicta* rather than in the actual decisions.

plaintiff can succeed. Was the statute intended for the benefit and protection of all the Queen's subjects, or only of a certain class of persons in certain circumstances; and, in the latter case, does the plaintiff fall within that class? Has the legislature imposed a special penalty for the breach of duty, and, if so, did it or did it not intend thereby to exclude other remedies? Has the legislature prescribed a special form of procedure, and, if so, has it thereby debarred other and ordinary forms of procedure? These are nice questions of construction, and they can be answered only by a careful scrutiny of the whole purport of the Act under consideration. The governing principle, in close accord with that of *Heydon's Case*, has been well summed up by a reporter in a head-note:[1]

> 'When a statute creates a duty with the object of *preventing a mischief of a particular kind*, a person who, by reason of another's neglect of the statutory duty, suffers *a loss of a different kind*, is not entitled to maintain an action in respect of such loss.'

The case-law surrounding the subject cannot be examined here in detail, but it forms an instructive study in the judicial interpretation of legislative intentions.[2]

Casus omissi

It is one thing, however, to gather the intention of a statute from a consistent course of legislation, and quite another to apply it to circumstances concerning which an Act is silent. There was never any statute so far-sighted that it did not have its *casus omissi*; and there are some statutes in which the *casus omissi* seem to exceed the cases expressly provided for. The courts cannot

[1] *Gorris* v. *Scott* (1874), L.R. 9 Ex. 125.

[2] The principal authorities are considered in *Cutler* v. *Wandsworth Stadium, Ltd.*, [1949] A.C. 398. Cf. *Badham* v. *Lambs*, [1946] K.B. 45, and see Clerk and Lindsell, *Torts* (12th ed.), 1406 ff., and Winfield, *Law of Tort* (6th ed.), 192 ff. For other examples of judicial interpretation of the 'policy' of statutes, see *Edgington* v. *Swindon Corpn.*, [1939] 1 K.B. 86; and two cases on the Courts (Emergency Powers) Act, 1939—*Butcher* v. *Poole Corpn.*, [1943] K.B. 48, and *Watkinson* v. *Hollington*, [1944] K.B. 16. In the last case, as in *Pratt* v. *Cook*, [1939] 1 K.B. 364 (reversed, [1940] A.C. 437), Goddard L.J. laid special emphasis on 'mischief and remedy'.

escape the responsibility of considering these unforeseen contingencies. Two kinds of *casus omissi* may be distinguished. (1) Sometimes a case arises, or a right is claimed, which is not dealt with by the statute either directly or indirectly. It has not been unknown in former times that judges have extended the provisions of statutes in such a way as virtually to add a clause to them;[1] but in modern times courts are bound to take the view that if a case is entirely unprovided for by a statute, either directly or indirectly, then it must remain nobody's child—a luckless orphan of the law.[2] Very inconvenient results may sometimes follow, but that is not the fault of judges. A statute of 1959 (Restriction of Offensive Weapons Act) was intended to prohibit the sale, manufacture, &c., of flick knives. It was unfortunately overlooked that exhibiting one of these dangerous weapons in a shop window is, on many precedents in the Sale of Goods, not 'offering for sale' but merely soliciting an 'invitation to treat'. Amending legislation had to come to the rescue.[3] There have been some curious examples of draftsmen's oversights of this kind in the nineteenth-century legislation affecting married women. Thus the Act of 1870 (33 & 34 Vict. c. 93) made a married woman's separate earnings 'property held and settled to her separate use, independent of any husband'; and s. 11 of the same Act gave her power to maintain an action in her own name in respect of her separate property; but it was nowhere expressly stated that she might be *sued* in respect thereof, and it was consequently held that her husband must be joined with her as defendant in any action against her *quoad* separate earnings.[4] The

[1] See *ante*, p. 453.

[2] See *In re Leicester Permanent Building Society*, [1942] Ch. 340; *Ex p. Blyth*, [1944] K.B. 532; *Isle of Wight C.C.* v. *Warwickshire C.C.*, [1953] 1 Q.B. 553; *Barnsley Corpn.* v. *Lancashire C.C.*, [1957] 1 Q.B. 123. 'We cannot legislate for *casus omissi*': Devlin L.J. in *Gladstone* v. *Bower*, [1960] 2 Q.B. 384, 396.

[3] *Fisher* v. *Bell*, [1961] 1 Q.B. 394.

[4] *Hancocks* v. *Lablache* (1878), 3 C.P.D. 197.

Act of 1882 gave a married woman power to dispose as a feme sole of real estate being separate property of which she was legal owner, but did not expressly enable her to alienate lands of which she was an active trustee; and for this latter kind of disposition she therefore had to obtain the concurrence of her husband.[1] This inconsequence, surely never intended by the framers of the Act of 1882, was not remedied until 1907.[2] The same Act showed a hiatus, or at the least an ambiguity, on which the opinion of the profession was for many years sharply divided. Inasmuch as the statute merely said that a husband *need* not be joined in an action of tort against the wife, the House of Lords rejected the interpretation that the husband *shall* not be joined;[3] with the result, universally admitted to be illogical and inconvenient, that the husband was not liable for his wife's independent contracts but was liable for her independent torts.[4] In these and many similar cases a strict construction refuses to attribute to the legislature an intention which is not either explicit or implicit in the words of the statute. Sometimes judges can merely express regret for a statutory *lacuna*, and a hope that it will be remedied by legislation; and occasionally the hope is fulfilled, even if tardily.[5] (2) It is often a very impalpable line which distinguishes these cases from others in which the legislature has given a general indication but has not specifically included the particular case which arises for decision. Sometimes the omission is due to the most cogent of reasons—namely,

[1] *Re Harkness & Allsopp's Contract*, [1896] 2 Ch. 358.

[2] Married Women's Property Act, 1907.

[3] *Edwards* v. *Porter*, [1925] A.C. 1.

[4] The law was altered by the Law Reform (Married Women and Tortfeasors) Act, 1935. Strange fissures are already beginning to appear in the long-considered and carefully drafted Criminal Justice Act, 1948; see *R.* v. *Middlesex Quarter Sessions*, [1950] 2 K.B. 589.

[5] See, e.g., Denning L.J. in *Littlewood* v. *Wimpey and B.O.A.C.*, [1953] 2 Q.B. 501 (affirmed, [1955] A.C. 169) at pp. 514 and 520. The inequitable distinction, there mentioned, between limitation of actions against public authorities and other defendants was remedied by the Law Reform (Limitation of Actions, &c.) Act, 1954. And see *Fisher* v. *Bell, ubi sup.*

that the circumstances which gave rise to the case could not possibly have existed at the time when the statute was passed. The growth of inventions like the motor-car, the aeroplane, broadcasting, and many others, has occasioned enormous changes both in common and in statute law; many of the problems thus created have been dealt with by new legislation, but not infrequently the interpretation of a statute anterior to these inventions has to take account of their *ex post facto* existence and development. The court cannot, without doing injustice, ignore them merely because the statute did not mention them and could not have mentioned them. Thus we find the Judicial Committee holding, without great hesitation, that 'broadcasting falls within the description of "telegraphs"'.[1] There are many other cases in which a statute, though laying down a general policy, is silent upon a particular point, not because it was impossible for the situation to arise, but simply because it was not foreseen by the framers of the statute, or was insufficiently defined. Suppose, for example, that a statute[2] says that a drunken driver of a motor vehicle shall be disqualified from holding a driving licence unless there are 'special reasons' to the contrary. What kind of reasons did the legislature contemplate? The Court holds that they must be reasons special to the offence and not to the offender—i.e. that there must be some exceptional extenuation of the illegal act, but that mere personal considerations affecting the defendant, such as previous good character or hardship resulting from disqualification, are irrelevant.[3] Was this the 'implied will of the legislator', or was it a rather striking example of 'judge-made law'?

In such circumstances the court is resorting to what is really a fiction. It is often entirely uncertain not only what the intention of the lawgiver was, but what it would

[1] *In re Radio Communication in Canada*, [1932] A.C. 304, 315; cf. *In re Aeronautics in Canada*, [1932] A.C. 54.

[2] Road Traffic Act, 1930, s. 15.

[3] *Whittall* v. *Kirby*. [1947] K.B. 194.

have been if the particular question had been considered. In the example just cited, who can say whether Parliament would or would not have wished to limit 'special reasons' as the court did? There is no more self-evident reason for the one view than the other. It is obvious, from studying the leading case,[1] that some distinguished judges considered that the legislature in 1882 did intend a husband to be liable for his wife's torts, others that it did not. In innumerable instances the fate of the *casus omissus* lies entirely in the hands of the judges, and in no real sense depends on the will of the legislator. The courts lay down a rule exactly because the legislature has not done so, and has not intended to do so. Judges must and do carry out the express will of the legislature as faithfully as they can; but there is a very wide margin in almost every statute where the courts cannot be said to be following any will except their own. The statute then becomes, as to a great part of it, not a direct 'command', but simply part of the social and legal material which judges have to handle according to their customary process of judicial logic.[2] It is in the process of filling in these gaps, more than anywhere else, that the Common Law may be called, with some plausibility, 'judge-made law'. To assert, as is sometimes done,[3] that judges do not in fact cement these interstices in statutes is to run counter to a thousand instances.

These gaps and inadvertences in enacted law are only one, though perhaps the most conspicuous, example of the difficulties of attempting to penetrate the mind of the legislator. It was one thing to discover 'intent' in the time of Coke, when statutes were comparatively few and when they explained their purposes, often in verbose and grandiloquent terms, by their preambles. It is quite another thing today, when statutes are far more extensive and infinitely more complex. It is, indeed, a very differ-

[1] *Edwards* v. *Porter*, *ubi sup.*

[2] Gény, *Méthode*, i. 304 ff.

[3] See, e.g., Lord Simonds, *Magor and St. Mellons R.D.C.* v. *Newport Corpn.*, [1952] A.C. 189, 191.

ent situation today from that which existed even when Parke B. and Tindal C.J. laid down the doctrines which have already been quoted. Consequently, most modern judges are extremely chary of the principle of statutory 'intent', for they feel that it asks of them more than they —not being mind-readers—can be expected to perform. As long ago as 1896, Lord Watson, one of the greatest of Law Lords, observed:

'"Intention of the Legislature" is a common but very slippery phrase, which, popularly understood, may signify anything from intention embodied in positive enactment to speculative opinion as to what the Legislature probably would have meant, although there has been an omission to enact it. In a Court of Law or Equity, what the Legislature intended to be done or not to be done can only be legitimately ascertained from that which it has chosen to enact, either in express words or by reasonable and necessary implication.'[1]

The same judicial protest has often been made in the United States. Mr. Justice O. W. Holmes once wrote: 'Only a day or two ago, when counsel talked of the intention of the legislature, I was indiscreet enough to say I don't care what their intention was. I only want to know what the words mean.'[2] It is here that we see a permanent, and apparently an insoluble, dilemma of written law: on the one hand no human language can be completely self-explanatory and all-embracing, and on the other hand the interpreters of the written word cannot and should not guess at undisclosed meanings which merely open

[1] *Salomon* v. *S.*, [1897] A.C. 22, 38.

[2] Quoted by Frankfurter J., 'Some Reflections on the Reading of Statutes', *Record of the Association of the Bar of the City of New York*, 1947, vol. 2, 228. Frankfurter J. adds: 'Legislation has an aim. . . . That aim, that policy, is not drawn, like nitrogen, out of the air; it is evinced in the language of the statute, as read in the light of other external manifestations of purpose. That is what the judge must seek and effectuate, and he ought not to be led off the trail by tests that have overtones of subjective design. We are not concerned with anything subjective. We do not delve into the minds of legislators or their draftsmen, or committee members.'

On the fallacy involved in the theory of 'intent', see Gény's theories discussed *apud* Stone, *The Province and Function of Law*, 152 ff.

the door to speculative ingenuity. It may be that no process of interpretation can entirely dispense with some element of what at its lowest is called 'guesswork' and at its highest 'insight', because all interpretation of statutory provisions suffers from the inevitable *generality* of their statement. A statute cannot, like most other forms of demonstration, provide illustrations of its meaning. As Lord Denning pointed out in *Escoigne Properties Ltd.* v. *I.R.C.*, [1958] A.C. 549, a clause of an Act, taken by itself, may be completely obscure unless one can find the clue to it in an illustration of the particular case at which it seems to be aimed. The 'mischief' which it seeks to prevent then becomes plain, or at least may be fairly deduced. This is particularly true of revenue Acts, which, more than any others, generally grow out of a 'wilderness of single instances', impossible to understand without penetration behind the veil of generality.

General estimate of statute and its interpretation

Nothing therefore could be farther from the truth than the notion that Parliament has only to express its will in appropriate words, and all legal and social consequences follow as the night the day. It is going too far to say that 'it is with the meaning declared by the Courts, and with no other meaning, that statutes are imposed on the community as Law';[1] for there are many parts of many statutes which have never been the subject of judicial interpretation at all, but which are unquestionably the law of the land. But a very great, and perhaps the most important, part of the operation of statute is indissolubly dependent on the function of the judge. To ignore this intermediate stage between the 'will' of the sovereign and the 'obedience' of the subject is to falsify completely the actual operation of statutory law in society. It is the unfortunate but inevitable consequence of this fact that interpretation sometimes results in the opposite of what the legislature seems to have intended.[2] For this anomaly the deficiencies of human

[1] Gray, *Nature and Sources of the Law*, 170.

[2] *Worthing Corpn.* v. *S. Ry.*, [1943] A.C. 593; *Field* v. *Gover*, [1944]

language and foresight are more responsible than the wisdom or unwisdom of the sovereign legislature.

VI. STATUTORY INTERPRETATION IN PRACTICE

We have now considered, though necessarily in outline only, some of the main orthodox principles which have been laid down for the interpretation of statutes during the course of ages and which are to be found, with full discussion and example, in the recognized textbooks on this difficult subject. We must now ask how these principles seem to work in practice, always remembering that in modern England, and probably in all modern States, the situation is very different from that which existed when lawyers first began to work out a body of doctrines for interpreting the written word. It must be confessed at the outset that we shall find much confusion and contradiction, and no very certain answer to some of the problems which are inseparable from this branch of legal technique.

Ratio legis and *ratio verborum*

The *ratio legis* and the *ratio verborum* have not shown themselves natural allies in our law—nor, perhaps, in any system of law. 'The question which I have to determine', observed Roxburgh J. in *In re Dark*, [1954] Ch. 291, 293, 'is interesting, if only as an example to show how dangerous it is to think that words in an Act of Parliament necessarily mean what they say.' Our reports abound in examples of the searchings of heart which judges have experienced in attempting to reconcile two uneasy yoke-fellows.[1] Perhaps there is no more striking

K.B. 200. 'This appeal', said Lord Evershed M.R. in *Walls* v. *Peake*, [1960] 2 Q.B. 413, 418, '. . . has left me with a most unhappy feeling that the parliamentary intention may, in the end, have been defeated. But it is the function of the court to construe the language of the Act. As I think Blackstone said, if Parliament plainly enacts that which is unreasonable, there is nothing that the judges can do to put it right.'

[1] See, for example, Wynn-Parry J. in *Minister of Health* v. *Fox*, [1950] Ch. 369. The main problem is neatly expressed by Frankfurter J. ('Some

illustration of the conflict than the much-litigated case of *River Wear Commissioners* v. *Adamson* (1877), 2 App. Cas. 743. In that case, the defendants' ship, while trying to make the port of Sunderland, was driven ashore in a gale. The crew were taken off, and the abandoned vessel was driven by the storm against a pier which was under the control of the plaintiffs as harbour authorities. The Harbours, Docks and Piers Clauses Act, 1847 (s. 74), provides that:

'The owner of every vessel . . . shall be answerable to the undertakers for any damage done by such vessel . . . or by any person employed about the same, to the harbour, dock or pier . . . and the master or person having the charge of such vessel . . . through whose wilful act or negligence any such damage is done, shall also be liable to make good the same.'

The plaintiffs claimed that, on this wording, the defendants were absolutely liable for the damage done, whether or not it had been occasioned by their fault or (as was the fact) by an Act of God. This contention prevailed at the trial at assizes before Quain J. and the plaintiffs were awarded heavy damages. The Queen's Bench, considering itself bound by *Dennis* v. *Tovell* (1872), L.R. 8 Q.B. 10 (a decision directly on the section, by a Court consisting of Cockburn C.J. and Blackburn and Quain JJ.), refused a rule, but Blackburn J. expressed a hope that the Court of Appeal would reverse this decision. The appeal ((1875), 1 Q.B.D. 546) then

Reflections on the Reading of Statutes', *loc. cit.*): 'What is below the surface of the words and yet fairly a part of them?' This essay contains much value and instruction for English students on the approach, which is in many respects different from orthodox English principles, to statutory interpretation in the Supreme Court of the United States. This experienced judge, however, does not profess to offer any key which will unlock all the mysteries. 'Though my business throughout most of my professional life has been with statutes, I come to you empty-handed. I bring no answers. I suspect the answers to the problems of an art are in its exercise.' Nor does the learned judge derive much comfort from canons of construction. 'Such canons give an air of abstract intellectual compulsion to what is in fact a delicate judgment, concluding a complicated process of balancing subtle and elusive elements. . . . The rules of construction are not in any true sense rules of law.'

came before a strong court, composed of Jessel M.R., Kelly C.B., Mellish L.J., Denman J., and Pollock B. Jessel M.R. said that the effect of the plaintiffs' contention was that 'if a vessel is driven by stress of weather, without the fault of any one, and is shipwrecked against the pier, the unfortunate owner of the vessel must not only lose his vessel by shipwreck, but have to pay for the damage done to the pier'. He added sardonically: 'It is something like the kind of hospitality which in the long past was shewn to vessels when they had the misfortune to be wrecked on this coast.' This conclusion was utterly repugnant to Sir George Jessel, whose liberal views on statutory interpretation we shall have occasion to remark later. He carried the court with him, though they were by no means unanimous in the reasons for their conclusions. Appeal was then made to the House of Lords and was argued before the Lord Chancellor (Lord Cairns) and Lords Hatherley, O'Hagan, Blackburn, and Gordon. Only Lord Gordon insisted on the strict literal interpretation of liability under the statute; but the other learned Lords arrived at their decision in favour of the defendants for such extraordinarily various reasons that inferior courts have had the utmost difficulty in ascertaining the *ratio decidendi* of a case which is of great importance to harbour authorities and to the owners of ships.[1] The reader of the report of this case in the House of Lords has the impression of treading water without ever touching bottom. Despite the most strenuous and ingenious efforts, the principles of the 'literal' and the 'liberal' are never reconciled. Perhaps the most interesting feature of the case is the extraordinary fluctuation of a legal mind as clear and erudite as that of Lord Blackburn. In *Dennis* v. *Tovell*, in a very short judgement, he had been a party to a decision in favour of the strict literal interpretation of the section. In the second stage of the *River Wear Case*, he repented of *Dennis* v. *Tovell* and hoped that it would be overruled. In the House of

[1] See *The Mostyn*, *ante*, p. 291.

Lords he again changed his mind and inclined to give a judgement in favour of the literal construction. Finally, he delivered judgement in the contrary sense. His speech is often quoted as a classical exposition of our principles of statutory interpretation, but it is no disrespect to one of the greatest Common Lawyers of the nineteenth century to say that it reads like the writhings of a soul in torment. When the mind of a Blackburn thus vacillates, it is not surprising if lesser lawyers suffer and struggle in the attempt to do justice according to statute law.[1]

The criticisms of our present rules of statutory interpretation have taken three principal forms.

Defects of literal interpretation

(1) It is objected that the whole doctrine of literal interpretation rests upon a fallacy. Words mean nothing by themselves; the very conception of interpretation connotes the introduction of elements which are necessarily extrinsic to the words themselves.

'The plain and unambiguous meaning of words', by which the courts so often believe themselves to be governed (frequently with inconvenient consequences), is really a delusion, since no words are so plain and unambiguous that they do not need interpretation in relation to a context of language or circumstances. Without this process, 'intention' is always undiscoverable.[2] There has, it is urged, been far too much tendency in our law to regard words as self-contained, self-sufficient 'things', whereas Continental jurisprudence is more ready to regard them as that which they should be—i.e. vehicles of meaning.[3] One of the most important contexts is that of the *whole* Act, and there is no more vicious method of argument than tearing words from a statute

[1] The meaning of s. 74 of the Harbours, Docks and Piers Clauses Act, 1847, is still controverted: see *Workington Harbour Board* v. *Towerfield (Owners)*, [1951] A.C. 112, and *Stonedale No. 1 (Owners)* v. *Manchester Ship Canal Co.*, [1956] A.C. 1.

[2] Cf. Max Radin, 'Statutory Interpretation', *H.L.R.* xliii. 863.

[3] Sir Maurice Amos, 'The Interpretation of Statutes', *Cambridge L.J.* v. 163. The Continental theories and methods are fully discussed in Gény's *Méthode d'interprétation* and *Science et technique*.

as some counsel do, without relating them to the whole purport of the enactment.[1]

Much of our case-law certainly suggests that the letter killeth more often than the spirit giveth life. We have a most elaborate code, slowly and painfully built up, for literal interpretation, and there is not a comma or a hyphen which has not its solemn precedent. No attempt has been made in these pages to enter into the details of this lore, for it is matter of pure technique which may be found in many books of reference. There is much reason for thinking that if the same amount of attention had been paid to the more difficult and elusive principles of *Heydon's Case*—if, in short, our statutory interpretation had not so weakly followed the line of least resistance—many existing anomalies in our law might have been avoided. The attractions of literal interpretation have not been enhanced by the characteristics of the English language, which does not, like Latin or French, readily lend itself to precise and lucid expression.

There are two other factors which tend to perpetuate the rigidity of literal interpretation in our law. The first is the effect of the doctrine of precedent, which exercises as important an influence here as in all other branches of judicial technique.

> 'Under our system', the Judicial Committee has said,[2] 'decided cases effectively construe the words of an Act of Parliament and establish principles and rules whereby its scope and effect may be interpreted. But there is always a danger that in the course of this process the terms of the statute may come to be unduly extended and attention may be diverted from what has been enacted to what has been judicially said about the enactment.'

What is true of 'undue extension' is also true of undue

[1] See Denning L.J., *Feyereisel* v. *Turnidge*, [1952] 2 Q.B. 29, 37.

[2] *Per* Lord Sankey L.C., *In re Aeronautics in Canada*, [1932] A.C. 54, 70, and see D. J. Llewellyn Davies, 'The Interpretation of Statutes in the Light of their Policy by English Courts', *Columbia L.R.* xxxv. 519, 525. See *Robinson* v. *London Brick Co.*, [1942] 2 K.B. 239 and [1943] A.C. 341.

restriction; a narrow literal interpretation, once established by precedent, may become fixed in perpetuity. Exactly at what point it becomes static is not easy to say. Sir George Jessel M.R., in *In re Bethlem Hospital* (1875), L.R. 19 Eq. 457, declared that he would not consider himself bound by a statutory interpretation of which he disapproved unless 'the authorities were numerous'. He went on to point out that when a certain interpretation has been thus established by a line of authorities, a judge, in approaching a statute, does not really 'interpret' it at all—that is, he is not free to exercise his own mind upon the meaning of the text before him. This combination, or conflict—whichever it may be considered—of the authority of precedent and the authority of statute cannot be described as happy.

The second petrifying factor is the real or supposed rule (now, however, questioned) that once a word or phrase has been given a certain judicial meaning, it is doomed to bear that meaning not only in all subsequent cases, but *in all subsequent statutes*.[1] This is an offshoot

[1] *Scilicet*, in the absence of a contrary intention; see *Barras* v. *Aberdeen Steam Trawling Co.*, [1933] A.C. 402. The classic statement of the rule is that of James L.J. in *Ex p. Campbell* (1870), L.R. 5 Ch. at p. 706: 'Where once certain words in an Act of Parliament have received a judicial construction in one of the Superior Courts, and the Legislature has repeated them without any alteration in a subsequent statute, I conceive that the Legislature must be taken to have used them according to the meaning which a Court of competent jurisdiction has given them.' I respectfully agree with Mr. W. H. D. Winder, 'The Interpretation of Statutes subject to Case Law', 58 *Juridical Review*, 93, that the rule, if it is to be accepted at all, is better and more moderately stated by the Judicial Committee in *Webb* v. *Outrim*, [1907] A.C. 81, 89, where the words of Griffith C.J. in the Australian case, *D'Emden* v. *Pedder* (1904), 1 C.L.R. 91, 110, are adopted: 'When a particular form of legislative enactment, which has received authoritative interpretation, *whether by judicial decision or by a long course of practice* [italics inserted], is adopted in the framing of a later statute, it is a sound rule of construction to hold that the words so adopted were intended by the Legislature to bear the meaning which has been so put upon them.' Even in this qualified form, however, the rule is not acknowledged without protest. It was briskly criticized by Lord Blanesburgh in *Barras* v. *Aberdeen Steam Trawling Co.*, *ubi sup.*, and was the occasion of a sharp division of opinion in the House of Lords in *Marshall* v. *Wilkinson*, [1943] 2 All E.R. 175 (whereon see Winder, *loc. cit.*). See also *Royal Court Derby Porcelain Co., Ltd.* v. *Russell*, [1949]

of the somewhat optimistic assumption that the legislature must be presumed to know the actual state of the law.[1] Consequently, if a word has once been given a particular meaning in any case of authority, however obscure, in connexion with any statute, however recondite, the draftsman who uses that word in a later enactment is, so to speak, 'affected with notice' of the judicial interpretation, however remote it may be from the matter in hand. It need hardly be said that in the huge mass of our case-law this assumption is a transparent fiction. Much labour on the part of draftsmen, and some elaborate devices,[2] are needed to guard against it.

These are grave defects, and give colour to the criticism that in English statutory interpretation a disproportionate emphasis has been laid on the body as opposed to the soul of statutes (to use Plowden's metaphor). But no system of law, so far as I am aware, has ever escaped the paradoxes of literal or grammatical interpretation or has ever found a completely satisfactory solution of them. Words are not telepathic communications, and daily experience teaches us that there is nothing more rare than the expression of a perfect *consensus ad idem*. Further, while it is true enough to say that words in themselves mean nothing, being mere 'verberations of the air', yet a statute is, of all human forms of expression, that which *ex hypothesi* purports to give to intention an explicit and comprehensive form of words. As we have seen (*ante*, p. 502), its very comprehensiveness is

2 K.B. 417, in which Denning L.J. said (at p. 429): 'I do not believe that whenever Parliament re-enacts a provision of a statute it thereby gives statutory authority to every erroneous interpretation which has been put upon it'. In *Paisner* v. *Goodrich*, [1955] 2 Q.B. 353, 358, Denning L.J. expanded his *dictum*, pointing out that a precedent of statutory interpretation applied to the situation *sub judice*, but did not necessarily apply to *all* situations. His dissenting judgement was upheld by the House of Lords ([1957] A.C. 65). On the whole, it may be said that the exigencies of modern legislation have compelled the courts to accept the rule, if they accept it at all, only with considerable qualifications which may in time render it obsolete.

[1] *Ante*, p. 457.

[2] e.g. the *Index to Statutory Definitions*, whereon see Amos, *op. cit.* 171.

often a snare rather than an illumination, for it does not and cannot help to understand the purpose which *lies behind* the general words.

Nor is it to be supposed that literal interpretation, however pedantic it may seem at times, is a mere disputation of Schoolmen. There is, no doubt, something slightly comic in the spectacle of a bench of judges anxiously dissecting a word or expression which the Plain Man *thinks*—though he is frequently mistaken—has a meaning too obvious for argument; and it is certainly depressing when the meaning which at last emerges is—whatever else it may be—manifestly *not* that which the legislator or testator or settlor had in mind. Or it may be that what the legislator did have in mind, and what he carefully defined (e.g. in his interpretation clause), is something deliberately different from the common acceptation of a particular word or phrase.[1] If rules of law are so framed that rights, liberties, and even lives may depend on vocables, then it is not mere intellectual exercise, but a positive duty—and one from which he would greatly prefer to be relieved—for the judge to give the most precise value to *minutiae*. Quibbles of the law may become mere perverse obstructions of justice, and it has been necessary at times to restrain them—e.g. the old niggling exceptions to indictments, the verbiage of statutes, and the tautologies of conveyances; but many refinements which appear to be judicial quibbles are in reality conscientious attempts to do justice within severely prescribed limits. It is even possible, in some circumstances, that the most ingenious literal interpretation of the law may be the most effective way of fulfilling its spirit. It was in such manner that Portia thwarted Shylock!

Background of statutes

(2) Much criticism has been directed against the rule which excludes extrinsic and explanatory matter from the interpretation of statutes, and which, in particular,

[1] See, e.g., *Deeble* v. *Robinson*, [1954] 1 Q.B. 77, on the difference between the 'common' and the 'statutory' meaning of the word 'shop'.

forbids the examination of the 'Parliamentary history' of a law as a means of arriving at the intention of the legislature.[1] The principle seems to be to divest the Act of all its clothing and leave only its naked, bony frame for clinical examination. Thus the official explanatory memorandum which usually accompanies the introduction of a Bill is not to be looked at—still less Departmental notes for guidance in administering the Act;[2] side-notes indicating the purport of clauses are taboo, being considered to be the product of the draftsman, not of Parliament;[3] and even the very title of an Act is of dubious relevance.[4] All these exclusionary inhibitions are certainly a heavy fetter on judicial analysis. It is urged, with much reason, that the real purport of a statute cannot be understood if these important surrounding circumstances are shut out, and that it is often impossible to discover 'mischief and remedy' from the mere phraseology of a statute. Anybody who has ever been concerned in drafting knows that a whole history of discussion, deliberation, or policy may lie behind a few words inserted or omitted in a formal instrument.[5]

We have seen[6] that the judicial approach to Parliamentary enactments has fluctuated greatly, at different periods, between elasticity and rigidity, and that 'strict' interpretation did not establish itself finally until the eighteenth century. This was not, as sometimes seems to be thought,[7] because the judges of the Augustan Age suddenly decided to place obstacles in the way of intelligent legislation, but because legislation had constantly grown both in quantity and in particularity, until it became quite impracticable, without confusing the

[1] *Ante*, pp. 493 ff.

[2] *L.C.C.* v. *Central Land Board*, [1958] 1 W.L.R. 1296.

[3] *Chandler* v. *D.P.P.*, [1962] 3 W.L.R. 694, 705.

[4] But it may have a bearing on a particular expression in an Act: see *Reg.* v. *Mackinnon*, [1959] 1 Q.B. 150.

[5] For a criticism of the English rule, and a contrast with the principles adopted in the United States, see Frankfurter, *op. cit.* 230 ff.

[6] *Ante*, pp. 492 ff.

[7] Sir Ivor Jennings, *opp. cit.*, *inf.*

functions of legislature and judiciary, to treat statutes with the flexibility which had been possible in the Middle Ages. The hardening process has gone on, until in our own day there is some reason for objecting that it has gone unnecessarily far. Hardness may be an admirable quality for many purposes, but it may also render a substance too intractable for use. Lord Blackburn, in the *River Wear Case*, placed statutes, for purposes of interpretation, on exactly the same basis as 'written instruments'. Written instruments in private relationships are governed by very strict rules of evidence in our law; and it may well be questioned whether instruments of government are not of too wide import to be bound with the same trammels as private transactions.

The severity, not to say pedantry, of the rule against 'Parliamentary history' was brought into relief by the case of *Ellerman Lines* v. *Murray*, [1931] A.C. 126, which has excited much comment.[1] In that case, a point of importance arose under the Merchant Shipping (International Labour Conventions) Act, 1925. This statute was passed in order to give effect in English law to an International Convention which was intended to ensure that a seaman should not lose his wages merely by reason of the wreck or loss of his ship. The text of the Convention was reproduced in a schedule to the Act. The House of Lords held that, as the words of the section in dispute were 'clear and unambiguous', it was not permissible to refer either to the preamble or the schedule of the Act in order to determine the intent of the section. The result was, in the words of Lord Blanesburgh, 'discordant with legislative precedent and . . . opposed to good sense and fairness'. There could hardly be a more startling example of treating words as 'things in themselves'.

[1] See, for example, H. C. Gutteridge, 'A Comparative View of the Interpretation of Statute Law', *Tulane Law Review*, viii. 1, and Sir W. Graham Harrison, 'Criticisms of the Statute Book', *Journal of the Society of Public Teachers of Law*, 1935, 9.

There are many reasons why our judges are extremely averse from considering the surrounding or extraneous circumstances of legislation.[1] A statute is the highest constitutional formulation of law, the means by which the supreme legislature, after the fullest deliberation, expresses its *final* will. The language of a statute 'can be regarded only as the language of the three Estates of the realm, and the meaning attached to it by its framers or by individual members of one of those Estates cannot control the construction of it'.[2] There is great reluctance to go behind this definitive formulation in search of possible motives, intentions, and influences. Our judges are in the habit of regarding all 'written instruments' in this austere manner; when once a man has committed his intentions to writing, he must be taken to mean what he writes, since the very act of writing implies the purpose of placing intention on permanent record; and if this is true of private documents, it is thought to apply *a fortiori* to writings produced after such exhaustive consideration, and with so much technical skill of expression, as statutes of the realm. Again, judges are accustomed to deciding *according to evidence*. They feel that Parliamentary debates, public speeches, statistical, economic, and technical material, and all the innumerable controversial elements which may surround the passing of a statute, are, as a body of evidence, extremely slippery and untrustworthy; and they also feel, rightly or wrongly, that once they embark on such speculations, their conclusions may be far more uncertain than interpretations within a strictly defined field, whatever their acknowledged limitations.[3] Besides, there is a practical question of time and convenience. Whatever may be customary in

[1] See Sir H. Lauterpacht, 'Preparatory Work in the Interpretation of Treaties', *H.L.R.* xlviii. 549.

[2] Maxwell (11th ed.), 26, citing *Dean of York's Case* (1841), 2 Q.B. 1.

[3] Well-known expositions of this attitude may be found in the judgements of Farwell L.J. in *R.* v. *West Riding of Yorkshire C.C.*, [1906] 2 K.B. 676 (reversed, [1907] A.C. 29) and Bramwell B. in *Att.-Gen.* v. *Sillem* (1863), 2 H. & C. at p. 537.

other countries, in English courts, if argument were once allowed to wander into all the surrounding circumstances and all the possible implications of statutes, it is difficult to see where it would stop. There is probably also in the minds of judges a feeling, not wholly unjustified, that strict interpretation is a stimulus to careful draftsmanship.

In most Continental countries recourse is had freely to *travaux préparatoires* in the interpretation of statutes, and not a few English and American critics cast longing eyes on this expedient.[1] In the United States the practice is not entirely settled, but the former strict rule against extraneous matter has been much relaxed, and references (though with caution) to the Congressional history of statutes, especially the reports of committees, are now fairly frequent, while in the interpretation of the constitution recourse has always been taken to the debates in Convention.[2] In France, the *travaux* commonly in use are tolerably well defined and not as extensive as is sometimes supposed. They consist of: '(1) textes des projets ou propositions de loi et exposés des motifs; (2) rapports déposés sur ces projets ou propositions; (3) discours des deux Chambres'.[3] All these are published in the *Journal Officiel*, together with certain *Impressions*, also published by authority. The extrinsic material in a French court is therefore of fairly limited scope, and it is not permissible to consult it at all except when 'la loi a statué, mais son sens est douteux'. When the sense gathered from the actual words is 'plain and unambiguous', the French rule, and indeed the rule of nearly all countries, is the same as the English: the words

[1] See Gutteridge, Lauterpacht, Amos, and Radin, *opp. cit.*

[2] Radin, Lauterpacht, *opp. cit.*

[3] Planiol, *Traité élémentaire de Droit Civil*, i. 86; cf. Aubry et Rau, *Cours de Droit Civil*, i, section 40. A *projet de loi* is what would be called in England a 'Government measure', while a *proposition de loi* is a 'private member's Bill'; for details of the constitutional and procedural difference see Esmein, *Éléments de Droit Constitutionnel*, ii. 438. On the *travaux préparatoires* of the Code Civil itself, see Josserand, *Cours de Droit Civil positif français*, i. 28.

must be loyally accepted and the law applied accordingly, however inconvenient the consequences.

English critics sometimes give the impression that the French system of *travaux préparatoires* is wholly enviable. It is probably true that French interpretation of statutes more nearly carries out legislative intention than our own, as it is certainly true that French statutes are better expressed than ours. But it is not to be supposed that French jurists are by any means satisfied with the system of interpretation in vogue. It is, for example, significant to find that so ardent a champion of liberal interpretation as François Gény was highly critical of the current use and interpretation of *travaux préparatoires* and actually desiderated the same kind of strict interpretation of laws as is applied to 'written instruments', such as wills.[1] The great treatise of Planiol is the Blackstone of France; yet we find this master of the law writing:[2] 'Les travaux préparatoires fournissent des armes à tous les partis et les diverses opinions en présence y trouvent des arguments qui s'annulent réciproquement. . . . Les procès-verbaux des séances sont souvent trop brefs pour qu'on puisse en tirer profit.' It may be that our judges are not wholly misled by their instinct when they distrust these uncharted waters.

The judicial approach

(3) Another kind of criticism relates to a general disposition of the judicial mind towards the work of Parliament rather than to any technical rules of interpretation.[3] Constructions are sometimes so restrictive that they excite the comment that judges resent the 'interference' of the legislature and delight in revealing

[1] *Méthode d'interprétation*, i. 287 ff.

[2] *Loc. cit.*

[3] Professor W. Friedmann, 'Statute Law and its Interpretation in the Modern State', *Law and Social Change*, ch. 2, distinguishes three kinds of judicial approach: (1) the 'pseudo-logical or text-book approach', (2) the 'social policy approach', and (3) the 'free intuition approach'. The first two correspond roughly with 'literal' and 'liberal' interpretation; the third, which is advocated by such Continental writers as Gény, has never had any following in England, nor could it do so without complete revolution in all accepted principles of statutory interpretation.

its imperfections. Let us hear the impressions of a Parliamentary draftsman who speaks from great experience:[1]

'We find that when an Act comes before a Court it is quite often held to mean something which we never intended, and we are told that this interpretation is inevitable, in view of well-established rules applicable to the construction of statutes; it seems to us, however, that these results are arrived at by subtleties and an excessive ingeniousness of argument which are out of place in construing legal documents prepared as Acts of Parliament necessarily are. More than that, we feel that the Courts are not altogether sympathetic to our objects and that they take rather a pleasure in showing how much cleverer they are than we are, and how ridiculous our statutes are.'

And again:

'I have certainly observed a tendency among some members of the legal profession to assume as the golden rule for the interpretation of Acts that they were not intended to mean what, to a plain man, they would appear to say.'

Stephen J., who had himself had large experience of draftsmanship, once referred[2] to Acts of Parliament as things which, 'although they may be easy to understand, people continually try to misunderstand', and observed that in draftsmanship 'it is necessary to attain if possible to a degree of precision which a person reading in bad faith cannot misunderstand'.

While it would be going too far to say that our courts read statutes 'in bad faith', it is difficult to resist the impression that some judges are always ready to think the worst of a statute and of its draftsman. Statutes are dreary reading, and perhaps the constant and enforced intimacy with them in all their jejune details—which forms so large a part of a judge's work nowadays—does not tend

[1] Sir W. Graham Harrison, *op. cit.* 16. Since the view of the draftsman is seldom heard, and his experience rarely made available, this article is of exceptional value to all students of modern legislation.

[2] *In re Castioni*, [1891] 1 Q.B. at p. 167.

to foster judicial patience! A deeper cause than this is the immemorial disharmony between the empirical tradition of the Common Law and the dictatorial method of legislation. And, whatever may be said in defence of the draftsman and in explanation of his many and formidable difficulties, the fact remains that a great many enactments upon our statute-book are *not* well drawn[1] and that they impose an exasperating task on the courts.

Again, part of the reluctance of judges to go questing beyond the literal meaning of words is due to their realization that guesses at the 'true intent' of the legislator cannot be more than guesses, and may often be completely mistaken. Sir William Graham Harrison himself cites a case[2] in which the draftsman was severely criticized for an omission which was supposed to be inadvertent, but which was in fact deliberate, and, indeed, unavoidable. To revert to the *River Wear Case*, who can say whether, under the general policy of the Act in question, the legislature did or did not intend the shipowner to be liable in the circumstances which happened? Nobody was to blame for the damage; it might well be argued that there was no more reason why the harbour authority should bear the loss than the shipowner. In the oft-cited case of *Reg.* v. *Hertford College* (1878), 3 Q.B.D. 693, there was clearly room for two equally reasonable opinions on the question whether the Universities Tests Act, 1871, was intended to apply only to Oxford colleges existing at the time of the enactment or to subsequent foundations as well. One result of the Law Reform (Miscellaneous Provisions) Act, 1934, is that the personal representatives of one who has been killed by negligence may recover damages for the 'expectation of life' which the deceased enjoyed almost in the article of death;[3] it is difficult to find two lawyers

[1] *Ante*, pp. 484 ff.

[2] *Sutcliffe* v. *Commissioners of Inland Revenue* (1928), 14 Tax Cases 1871.

[3] *Flint* v. *Lovell*, [1935] 1 K.B. 354; *Rose* v. *Ford*, [1937] A.C. 826; and other cases cited, *ante*, p. 329.

who agree whether this result was intended by the legislature or not.[1]

Incon-sistencies of doctrine

Whether or not, as some of these criticisms suggest, our whole doctrine of statutory interpretation rests upon false foundations, it is certain that this branch of our law exhibits inconsistencies which suggest radical weakness somewhere. This is evident in any of the standard treatises on the subject. There is scarcely a rule of statutory interpretation, however orthodox, which is not qualified by large exceptions, some of which so nearly approach flat contradictions that the rule itself seems to totter on its base. A few examples will illustrate inconsistencies which to the present writer seem fundamental.

The rule against 'Parliamentary history', as we have seen, is repeatedly asserted. It can go so far as to exclude an essential element from the decision of a case like *Ellerman Lines* v. *Murray* (*ubi sup.*); it prohibits a court, in the construction of income-tax provisions, from considering a Royal Commission Report on which those provisions were based.[2] It can exclude from the deliberations of the House of Lords valuable enlightenment of a term of art like 'reasonable cause' in interpreting a Regulation which vitally affects the liberty of the subject.[3] Unless the evidence can, by some feat of ingenuity, be gathered directly or indirectly from the language of the Act itself, 'it is wholly illegitimate to surmise or conjecture what those unrevealed motives, purposes or objects [of Parliament] may have been, and to construe and apply the statutes or resolutions as if they had been indicated'.[4]

[1] See also *ante*, p. 500, on *Edwards* v. *Porter*, [1925] A.C. 1. Cf. *Bynoe* v. *General Federation of Trade Unions Approved Society*, [1938] Ch. 164, where it is impossible to say that the apparently anomalous result was not intended by the Regulations in question.

[2] *Assam Railways and Trading Co.* v. *Commissioners of Inland Revenue*, [1935] A.C. 445.

[3] See *Liversidge* v. *Anderson*, [1942] A.C. 206, and contrast *Nakkuda Ali* v. *Jayaratne*, [1951] A.C. 66.

[4] *Per* Lord Atkinson, *Hollinshead* v. *Hazleton*, [1916] 1 A.C. at p. 438. Cf. *Edwards* v. *Att.-Gen. for Canada*, [1930] A.C. at p. 134.

Now it is manifest that if this rule is rigidly applied, it completely stultifies the doctrine of *Heydon's Case*. Except in its preamble (which has now been given up, and which, in any case, was never an operative part of the enactment),[1] a statute never declares its 'motives, purposes, or object'. It is couched in imperative form which does not admit of explanation of underlying causes. If, then, the statutory 'policy' is to be explored at all, it must either be deduced by pure inference from verbal indications (often very slender) in the text, or the court must look outside the statute for it. This, in fact, it constantly does. A casuistical distinction is drawn between 'all negotiation previous to the Act or the original form of the Bill' and 'the subject-matter with which the legislature was dealing, and the facts existing at the time with respect to which the legislature was legislating'.[2] On this ground, while in one case a Royal Commission Report is excluded as 'Parliamentary history', in another[3] it is admitted as a 'source of information'—i.e. as illuminating 'the subject-matter with which the legislature was dealing'. It is, perhaps, fortunate for our statutory interpretation that this conception of 'subject-matter' covers, I will not say a multitude of sins, but at all events a wide field. It enables a judge, in order to arrive at the true scope of a statute, to examine without apology 'the considerations that operated in the minds of those who presented to Parliament the Bill which when passed became the Act'.[4] It sanctions a method of analysis which is often highly valuable, and, indeed, indispensable—the consideration of a consistent course of legislation in order to determine the exact place of a particular enactment, or even of an expression therein, in a whole organic process. A very good example of

[1] But see *post*, p. 527, n. 3.

[2] *Per* Lord Halsbury L.C., *Herron* v. *Rathmines Improvement Commissioners*, [1892] A.C. at p. 502.

[3] *Eastman Photographic Materials Co.* v. *Comptroller-General of Patents*, [1898] A.C. 571.

[4] Greer L.J. in *Consett Iron Co.* v. *Clavering Trustees*, [1935] 2 K.B. 42, 56.

this historical method is the judgement of Scott L.J. in *Ledwith* v. *Roberts*, [1937] 1 K.B. 232, from which it appears that it is not really possible to extract from the statutes themselves, without recourse to a long social and Parliamentary history, the meaning of such expressions as 'suspected person', 'reputed thief', and 'idle or disorderly person' in modern enactments concerning vagrancy; and it is a matter of no small importance in criminal law that these terms should be precisely understood and defined.[1] The same method, with special reference to 'mischief', and even preamble, was adopted by Lord Parker C.J. in *R.* v. *Males*, [1962] 2 Q.B. 500. Sometimes judges discard fiction altogether and frankly ignore the rule against Parliamentary history. In *South Eastern Railway Co.* v. *The Railway Commissioners* (1880) 5 Q.B.D. 217, Cockburn C.J. said (at p. 236): 'Where the meaning of an Act is doubtful, we are, I think, at liberty to recur to the circumstances under which it passed into law.' The Chief Justice then described the legislative history of the Railway and Canal Traffic Act, 1854, in a manner which would probably have been forbidden to counsel in argument. There are many other examples of the same kind in our reports.[2] The lesson to be drawn from them all is that the principle of 'letting the statute speak for itself' frequently breaks down, and that once external circumstances have been admitted to explain it, it is difficult, without complete artificiality,

[1] See the historical considerations in the speech of Lord Maugham in *The Valverda*, [1938] A.C. at p. 199, and cf. the judgements in *Tumahole* v. *R.*, [1949] A.C. 253, and *R.* v. *Paddington Rent Tribunal*, [1949] 1 K.B. 666. An example of the analysis of a whole chain of legislation is the judgement of Lord Greene M.R. in *Shenton* v. *Tyler*, [1939] 1 All E.R. 827, and an interesting feature of this case is the use of the Report of a Royal Commission to throw light on the policy of a statute (see 55 *L.Q.R.* 488). *In re Orbit Trust*, [1943] Ch. 144 (Uthwatt J.), is another example of the historical approach to legislative policy; and cf. *Hutton* v. *Att.-Gen.*, [1927] 1 Ch. 427 (Tomlin J.), *Lawes* v. *Caulcutt*, [1952] 2 Q.B. 834 (Gorman J.), *R.* v. *Middlesex Confirming and Compensation Committee, Ex p. Frost*, [1956] 1 W.L.R. 995, and *Eton College* v. *Minister of Agriculture*, [1962] 3 W.L.R. 726.

[2] See Maxwell, *op. cit.* Cf. Lord Merriman P. in *Cooper* v. *C.*, [1953] P. 26, 31.

to confine the 'explanatory' to specific categories of evidence.

Again, it is an accepted maxim that a statute should not be reduced to absurdity if reasonable interpretation can avoid that result. But there seem to be two distinct judicial philosophies in this matter. Some judges take the view which was expressed by the Judicial Committee, *per* Lord Hobhouse, in *Salmon* v. *Duncombe* (1886), 11 App. Cas. at p. 634: 'It is a very serious matter to hold that when the main object of a statute is clear it should be reduced to a nullity, by the draftsman's unskilfulness or ignorance of law.' This is surely a reasonable application of the general legal maxim *ut res magis valeat quam pereat.*[1] Courts will therefore sometimes take great liberties with the language of a statute in order to fulfil its obscurely expressed intent,[2] or even to make sense of it when, grammatically, it makes nonsense.[3] A modern Lord Justice does not hesitate to say:

> 'When the purpose of an enactment is clear, it is often legitimate, because it is necessary, to put a strained interpretation upon some words which have been inadvertently used, and of which the plain meaning would defeat the obvious intention of the Legislature. It may even be necessary, and therefore legitimate, to substitute for an inept word or words that which such intention requires.'[4]

There is no doubt that some judges will 'read into' a statute, under the guise of the 'implied intention' of the legislator, what justice and convenience require. Thus it was a bold but necessary construction by which it was

[1] See Bowen L.J., *Curtis* v. *Stovin* (1889), 22 Q.B.D. at p. 517, and Lord Goddard C.J., *Gluchowska* v. *Tottenham B.C.*, [1954] 1 Q.B. at p. 445.

[2] See numerous examples in Maxwell, *op. cit.*

[3] See *R.* v. *Vasey*, [1905] 2 K.B. 748, a case remarkable, *e.g.*, because the statute in question was penal and the interpretation adopted operated against the accused.

[4] *Per* MacKinnon L.J., *Sutherland Publishing Co.* v. *Caxton Publishing Co.*, [1937] Ch. at p. 201. The Lord Justice cites the striking example of the Carriage of Goods by Sea Act, 1924, in which the word 'and' has been boldly substituted for 'or' by 'interpretation'. Cf. the observations of Denning L.J. in *Seaford Court Estates Ltd.* v. *Asher*, [1949] 2 K.B. 481, cited *ante*, p. 488.

held, in *Leicester* v. *Pearson*, [1952] 2 Q.B. 668, that negligence was a necessary element in the offence of running down a foot-passenger on a pedestrian crossing; and it was not without some clash of precedent that it was held, in *Frank* v. *F.*, [1951] P. 430, that when a statute spoke of a 'continuous' period of mental treatment, it could not have meant that continuity was broken by short periods of transfer from one mental hospital to another.[1]

All this, if it may be said with respect, is common sense; but obviously it is in flat contradiction of the principle that the 'plain language' of a statute is binding and that to correct it is to usurp the office of the legislator. Consequently, there is another school of judicial thought which holds that if a statute is absurd on its face, then absurd it must remain, whatever the consequences. This view is emphatically expressed by Lord Esher M.R. in *R. v. Judge of the City of London Court*, [1892] 1 Q.B. at p. 290: 'If the words of an Act are clear, you must follow them, even though they lead to a manifest absurdity. The Court has nothing to do with the question whether the legislature has committed an absurdity.'[2] It would be a mistake to regard this attitude as mere obscurantism; some judges feel that it is a positive duty to enforce, not to say accentuate, legislative absurdities, since that is the best way to call attention to them and to expedite their correction;[3] but it seems clear that there are two very different kinds of judicial approach to these cases of 'absurdity'.[4]

There is also, on the whole, a certain incompatibility between the Common Law and the equitable approach to the whole question of statutory interpretation. Mention has already been made (*ante*, p. 411, n. 1) of some of

[1] For further examples of the 'extension' of statutory provisions see Lord Goddard C.J., *Gluchowska* v. *Tottenham B.C.*, *ubi sup.*

[2] Cf. *Drakeley* v. *Manzoni*, [1938] 1 All E.R. 67.

[3] See du Parcq J. in *Newell* v. *Cross*, [1936] 2 K.B. 632, 638, 643.

[4] See Viscount Simon L.C., *Nokes* v. *Doncaster Collieries*, [1940] A.C. 1014, 1022.

the bold constructions which have been placed on certain statutes in the Chancery in order to mitigate the letter of the law by equitable remedies. Sir George Jessel was one of the great builders of modern Equity, and it is impossible to read his judgements without realizing that in his interpretation of statutes he allowed himself far more latitude than the ordinary Queen's Bench judge would think proper. This will be best realized by a study of the sharp difference of opinion which arose between this Master of the Rolls and a Common Law successor, Lord Esher, in that office, in *The Alina* (1880), 5 Ex.D. 227, and *Reg.* v. *Judge of the City of London Court* (*ubi sup.*), to which cases, without attempting a detailed discussion, I would refer the reader. *In re Bethlem Hospital*, to which I have already alluded, may be taken as the *credo* of Sir George Jessel with regard to statutory interpretation; 'there is', he said, 'such a thing as construing an Act according to its intent, though not according to its words'; and this principle he and many other Chancery judges have consistently followed to a degree which most Common Law judges, while they might envy it, would consider audacious.[1]

The greatest inconsistency of all is between 'broad' and 'narrow' interpretation. The antithesis is impossible of definition; all one can say is that sometimes a court will stretch interpretation to its farthest limit in order to effect the 'policy' of a statute,[2] and at other times it will prostrate itself before the 'foot of the letter' when, to

[1] In the *River Wear Case*, another great master of equity, Lord Cairns L.C., held that the true purpose of the statute was procedural, its intent being that, in case of damage, harbour authorities should have recourse against an ascertainable and probable solvent defendant, viz. the shipowner (who, in his turn, would have his remedy against the person or persons actually responsible for the damage). This was almost certainly the *provenance* of the statute; but it is to be noted that not a word of any such intention appears in the statute itself.

[2] See, e.g., *R.* v. *Vasey*, *ubi sup.*; *Norman* v. *N.*, [1950] W.N. 230; *Monk* v. *Warbey*, [1935] 1 K.B. 75, with which contrast *Daniels* v. *Vaux*, [1938] 2 K.B. 203; *In re Insole's Settled Estate*, [1938] Ch. 812, whereon see 55 *L.Q.R.* 2.

ordinary opinion, it would seem quite easy and reasonable to walk hand in hand with the spirit.[1] Is it, for example, necessary to rule out the heading of a section, on the ground that it is not an operative part of the statute, and to attach a meaning to words which, according to the heading, cannot possibly have been intended by the legislature?[2] Perhaps, in the last analysis, these disparities depend upon the moods and temperaments of individual judges; and yet even these are unpredictable from case to case. For example, it is surprising to find Lord Halsbury—a Lord Chancellor never given to heterodox interpretation—citing *Stradling* v. *Morgan* as a safe basis for statutory construction.[3] *Stradling* v. *Morgan*, as we have seen (*ante*, p. 455), belonged to a phase of theory which was (perhaps unfortunately) only a parenthesis in our law, and it is no disrespect to Lord Halsbury to say that if its full doctrine were applied today, a great deal of the law concerning statutory interpretation would have to be radically revised. Actually, it was only faintly relevant to the point in *Cox* v. *Hakes*.

The difference between the two kinds of judicial attitude has been forcibly illustrated in recent years. Lord Denning has repeatedly stood for the principle which (as Lord Justice) he expressed in simple terms in *Henry* v. *Taylor*, [1954] 1 Q.B. at p. 513: 'Where there is a fair choice between a literal interpretation and a reasonable interpretation, we should always choose the reasonable interpretation.' One might have supposed

[1] See, for example, *Mersey Docks* v. *Lucas* (1883), 8 App. Cas. 891, and Lord Dunedin's observations thereon in *Forth Conservancy Board* v. *Inland Revenue Commissioners*, [1931] A.C. at p. 549; and *Preston* v. *Norfolk C.C.*, [1947] K.B. 775.

[2] *R.* v. *Hare*, [1934] 1 K.B. 354. The effect of this decision may have been 'substantial justice', but the principle of interpretation seems to have been the extreme of literalism. 'While the marginal note to a section cannot control the language used in the section, it is at least permissible to approach a consideration of its general purpose and the mischief at which it is aimed with the note in mind': *per* Upjohn L.J., *Stephens* v. *Cuckfield R.D.C.*, [1960] 2 Q.B. 373, 383.

[3] In *Cox* v. *Hakes* (1890), 15 App. Cas. at p. 517.

this to be an elementary duty of the judicial office, but it has not appeared so to all our legal authorities. In *Magor and St. Mellons R.D.C.* v. *Newport Corpn.*, [1952] 2 All E.R. at p. 1236, the Lord Justice said this:

'This was so obviously the intention of the Minister's Order that I have no patience with an ultra-legalistic interpretation which would deprive them of their rights altogether. I repeat what I said in *Seaford Court Estates, Ltd.* v. *Asher*, [1949] 2 K.B. 481. We do not sit here to pull the language of Parliament and of Ministers to pieces and make nonsense of it. That is an easy thing to do, and it is a thing to which lawyers are too often prone. We sit here to find out the intention of Parliament and of Ministers and carry it out, and we do this better by filling in the gaps and making sense of the enactment than by opening it up to destructive analysis.'

This blasphemy was too much for the House of Lords (S.C., on appeal, [1952] A.C. 189). It was condemned by Lord Simonds in these words (at p. 191):

'The general proposition that it is the duty of the court to find out the intention of Parliament—and not only of Parliament but of Ministers also—cannot by any means be supported. The duty of the court is to interpret the words that the legislature has used; those words may be ambiguous, but, even if they are, the power and duty of the court to travel outside them on a voyage of discovery are strictly limited. . . . The second part of the passage that I have cited from the judgment of the learned Lord Justice is no doubt the logical sequel of the first. The court, having discovered the intention of Parliament and of Ministers too, must proceed to fill in the gaps. What the legislature has not written, the court must write. This proposition, which restates in a new form the view expressed by the Lord Justice in the earlier case of *Seaford Court Estates, Ltd.* v. *Asher* . . . cannot be supported. It appears to me to be a naked usurpation of the legislative function under the thin disguise of interpretation.'

Thus we have it on the authority of the House of Lords that it is not the business of the courts to try to discover what an Act of Parliament *means;* and that although, as we have seen, the courts have been stopping up holes in leaky statutes throughout the whole history of our law, this has been mere 'usurpation'. Here indeed is the triumph of Plowden's 'body' over the 'soul'. In this view *Heydon's Case* may be regarded as dead, though it is not as lifeless as the doctrine which this pronouncement of our highest tribunal lays down in such bleak terms.

Conclusions

On the whole, then, it cannot be pretended that the principles of statutory interpretation form the most stable, consistent, or logically satisfying part of our jurisprudence.[1] Some critics[2] have suggested that, in view of the erratic character of the judicial approach, we are driven to the conclusion that judges adopt rules of construction at their will 'as a device to achieve some desired result'. This is the so-called 'realist' view of the matter, but it does not explain why different judges should 'desire' different results. Unless we are to assume that they are governed entirely by their personal prepossessions—which would be to do the great majority of them a grave injustice—we must credit them with honestly trying to find the mode of interpretation which they believe to be consistent with their duty; and thus both they and we are still left asking what *is* the true doctrine applicable to the case. It would be comforting to be able to agree with the somewhat light-hearted assumption of the Committee on Ministers' Powers[3] that 'the principles of statute interpretation are clear and well-known', and that all that is needed is better drafting; but it is unfair and unconvincing to place the whole onus on the draftsman. Various means have been suggested for assisting the judiciary to arrive at the 'mischief and remedy' of statutes more easily than they seem

[1] Some judges themselves seem to be of this opinion; see 'The Impact of Statute on the Law of England', *Proceedings of the British Academy*, xlii. 247 (the Maccabaean Lecture, 1956), by Lord Evershed M.R., who pleads for a better science of statutory interpretation.

[2] See John Willis, 'Statutory Interpretation', 16 *Canadian Bar Review* (1938), 1. This is one of the most vivacious and challenging discussions of the subject and should be known to all students of it.

[3] *Report*, Cmd. 4060, 1923, p. 56.

to do at present. Nobody, so far as I know, has advocated that an unlimited and undefined mass of *travaux préparatoires* be cast upon the courts; but there are certain authoritative sources of information which it seems somewhat pedantic to withhold from the judicial purview. Many Bills in Parliament are accompanied by a memorandum, which is purely explanatory and scrupulously avoids any argumentative tone. Any Bill which imposes a charge on the public funds must, by the rules of the House of Commons, be accompanied by a memorandum of this kind, or by a White Paper in the case of a pure Money Bill. White Papers and Notes on Clauses are issued in connexion with certain highly technical measures. Sir William Graham Harrison asks, with much reason, whether the courts might not look at least for guidance to such carefully regulated aids, without any serious danger of becoming lost in a wilderness of loose speculations. He asks, again, whether the courts could not, with propriety, take cognizance of certain Parliamentary rules of procedure which in some cases would be conclusive evidence of the true scope of statutes or clauses.[1] Professor Laski[2] similarly advocated the explanatory memorandum and a return to the defining preamble[3]—not, however, suggesting that this

[1] *Op. cit.* 16, 37 ff. There are, however, difficulties in the drafting and amendment of an explanatory memorandum: see Sir Granville Ram, 'The Improvement of the Statute Book', *Journal of the Society of Public Teachers of Law*, 1951, 442, 455.

[2] *Report of the Committee on Ministers' Powers*, Annex V.

[3] It is a settled rule of interpretation that it is legitimate to consult preamble, headings, section-titles, &c., for guidance concerning intent, and it is submitted that a case like *R.* v. *Hare, ubi sup.*, is really a violation of this rule. There are, however, instances of errors in the placing or purport of sidenotes: see, e.g., the Married Women (Maintenance in Case of Desertion) Act, 1886, s. 1 (2). On the whole of this technique, see *Jenkins* v. *Shelley*, [1939] 2 K.B. 137, 145; *Dormer* v. *Newcastle upon Tyne Corpn.*, [1940] 2 K.B. 204; *Watkinson* v. *Hollington*, [1944] K.B. 16; *Butcher* v. *Poole Corpn.*, [1943] K.B. 48; *Re Carlton*, [1945] Ch. 280 and 372; *R.* v. *Surrey Assessment Committee*, [1948] 1 K.B. 28; and *Prince Ernest of Hanover* v. *Att.-Gen.*, [1957] A.C. 436. It was said in *Salmon* v. *Duncombe* (1886), 11 App. Cas. at p. 634: 'The title may be looked at for aid in finding out the object. The

material should be in any way binding on courts, but that judges should have authority to consult it for guidance if they so desire.

Again, it has been urged that statutes might be classified into categories to which different principles of interpretation should be applied—e.g. statutes which are constitutional, of 'social purpose', intended to effect specific reforms, or to implement international conventions, penal and taxation Acts, or those which are 'predominantly technical'.[1] It is to be feared, however, that any such attempted classification would merely add a series of ambiguous adjectives to the existing difficulties of interpretation. Categories of this kind, and others which might easily be suggested, could not possibly be precise and would overlap at many points. A whole new code of interpretation would be necessary to determine which description applied to which enactment. So far as these descriptive distinctions have existed already, they have not proved very secure. For example, the old rule that 'penal statutes must be construed strictly' was of full force and virtue in days when every technical device was employed to rescue offenders from the ferocities of the criminal law, but at present, when the strict conception of *mens rea* has been so much diluted by statutory provisions, this canon, though still not without value, has been greatly attenuated.

Whether or not new expedients would really assist

preamble is of great importance in finding out the object.' Cf. Co. Litt. 79a. Judges have sometimes regretted the disappearance of the preamble: see Lord Alverstone C.J., *London County Council* v. *Bermondsey Bioscope Co.* (1910), 80 L.J. (K.B.) 144, and *Powell* v. *Kempton Park Racecourse*, [1899] A.C. 143. Preambles are still used for short Acts with limited objective and for Private Acts; but the real difficulty is that many modern Acts are so wide in scope and so comprehensive in subject-matter that it is impossible to frame a preamble which is not either obscurely laconic or excessively verbose. The difficulty is as ancient as Plato: see *Laws*, iv. 718 ff. Already in the Tudor legislation to which Professor Laski refers some preambles had become intolerably cumbrous. The long title of an Act is some guide to its general scope, and it is a strict rule of Parliamentary procedure that nothing in the Act must go beyond the ambit of the long title.

[1] See Friedmann, *op. cit.*

interpretation would depend upon the spirit in which judges accepted them. If they were regarded as friends and guides in a process of interpretation which was liberal without being loose, they could render good service, and there seems to be no reason why they should not do so. If, on the other hand, they were regarded with suspicion (as some judges would certainly regard them) as being too vaguely 'extrinsic' or 'extra-legal', or even 'tendentious', or as 'usurpation', they would be either neglected or treated with hostility; and certainly, if they were regarded as additional specimens for the judicial microscope, they would merely add another stage to the rigours of literal interpretation.

Reviewing these many problems of interpretation, we are driven, in the end, to the unsatisfying conclusion that the whole matter ultimately turns on impalpable and indefinable elements of judicial spirit or attitude. Nothing could be more inimical to justice than that judges should exercise their functions upon subjective, political, or partisan considerations;[1] but while it would

[1] It goes beyond the scope of the present discussion to consider in detail a type of criticism to the effect that strict judicial interpretation is animated by a social or political bias which fetters the purposes of 'social legislation' (a question-begging term, since all legislation, properly considered, is 'social'); see Sir Ivor Jennings, 'Courts and Administrative Law', *H.L.R.* xlix. 426, and 'Local Government Law', 51 *L.Q.R.* 180, and cf. Laski, *Report of the Committee on Ministers' Powers, loc. cit.* I would only say that these charges of bias seem to me to be unsupported by any adequate evidence, and to be themselves notable examples of prepossession, since for the most part they merely mean that the results of interpretation are displeasing or inconvenient to the critics' own particular theories and aims. Sir Ivor Jennings charges 'individualistic' judges with an attachment to notions of private property which makes them hostile to 'collectivist' restrictions thereon. So long as private property is (rightly or wrongly) an important institution of our law, it is the duty of judges to enforce the proper legal safeguards both of private and public interest; but any judge who nowadays (or for many a long year past) attempted to govern his judicial policy by notions of *laisser-faire* or unrestricted private property could not perform his duties competently for twenty-four hours. 'Social legislation' is not a monopoly of the present age; and if judges are as obstructive as Sir Ivor Jennings suggests, they seem to have been singularly unsuccessful with the vast bulk of nineteenth-century 'social legislation', which in its day was even more bold, enterprising, and comprehensive than that of our own times.

be quite inaccurate to say that the English judicial approach to statutory law is invariably grudging and restrictive, there is no small reason for saying that on the whole, in modern times, it has leaned too readily towards the 'analytical' rather than the 'functional' (as Professor Laski expresses it), and has done so with too little consistency on one side or the other. If that be true, the real remedy lies, as it seems to me, not in any 'new found halliday' but in the existing law itself. There is ample warrant in settled rules of interpretation for a 'liberal' approach, and there are abundant and bewildering examples of judicial constructions which at one moment are treated as perfectly orthodox and at another as dangerously latitudinarian. What seems to be needed most of all is a more scientific consistency of principle.

VII

SUBORDINATE AND AUTONOMIC LEGISLATION

I. GROWTH OF THE PRINCIPLE OF DEVOLUTION

THE legislation which we have been considering so far is the only kind known to the strict theory of our constitution—that of sovereign Parliament. According to that theory, all government, properly so called, must proceed from the supreme representative body of the realm. To the school of English analytical jurisprudence this is the typical, indeed the only, direct exercise of sovereign power.

Throughout the civilized world, however, the theory and practice of legislative processes have been visibly changing for more than a century. There has been a widespread development of the principle known as *devolution*. The process has been forced on nations by the ever-growing complexity of social structure, which is the result of many factors beyond the scope of our present discussion.

Traditional doctrine of delegated powers

Nothing is more striking in the legal and social history of the nineteenth century in England than the development of subordinate legislation. Though its roots strike into early institutions, the rate of its extension during the last century could never have been guessed by our forefathers. It is now, beyond all doubt, an extremely large and important part of our social scheme and is bound to affect public and private law in every department. Every day it puts forth new shoots, and even within the memory of the present generation it has grown almost out of recognition—owing not only to the extraordinary conditions of war and the *sequelae* of war, but to its own inherent vitality. If we look at a work like

Sir Courtenay Ilbert's *Legislative Methods and Forms*,[1] written early in the present century, we shall be struck by the comparatively small and unimportant place which the author assigns to delegated legislation. If we refer to another well-known work, *Local Government in England* (Redlich and Hirst), written at about the same time (1903), we find the following general conclusions concerning the subordination of Departments to Parliamentary control:[2]

'In the earlier pages of this work it has been explained how the new central departments, created in the nineteenth century, have been fitted into parliamentary Government and brought under the sovereignty of Parliament. The task of the Legislature has been to extend and intensify the work of internal Government without reviving the ghost of the Star Chamber, to preserve the rule of law without stinting or starving administration. This task has been successfully accomplished. In spite of a vast expansion of governmental activity, England at the beginning of the twentieth century had no administrative law and no administrative courts in the continental sense. Every act of public authority, no matter by whom or against whom it is directed, is liable to be called in question before an ordinary tribunal, and there is no other means by which its legality can be questioned or established. And if the decision is unfavourable to the act in question, the proceeding complained of is immediately invalidated and nullified. There is no exception in England to the rule that every public proceeding, be it the issue of a warrant to arrest or a demand for rates, or a summons to pay money due to a public authority, or an order of Justices, is just as much a matter of ordinary law, and is liable to be questioned in the same way, as a private suit or action brought by one individual against another.'

A footnote adds:

'Some trifling relics of a *droit administratif* are still to be found, as in the Petition of Right . . . and in a few restrictions upon actions against constables and public authorities. More modern tendencies towards a continental system of administration appear in certain powers granted to the Local Government Board,

[1] Ch. iii. [2] ii. 364.

and described in a previous chapter, of adjudicating and finally deciding certain disputes arising out of modern laws of administration. After all that has been said in Part VI on the "quasi-judicial functions" of the Local Government Board it is enough here to repeat that they do not really encroach upon the unity and sovereignty of the law.'[1]

No longer accurate

These confident assertions, which will also be familiar to all readers of Dicey's *Law of the Constitution*,[2] can no longer be said to represent truly the system of government and judicature in England. Indeed, in some respects they express the exact reverse of the truth. Even in 1903 they were far from accurate. I would ask the reader to contrast with them some significant observations made in 1887 by a scholar who combined an incomparable learning with a quality of genius which can be described only as prophetic vision. Lecturing at Cambridge, Maitland made a forecast so striking that I make no apology for quoting it at some length:

Maitland's view

'The traditional lawyer's view of the constitution has become very untrue to fact and to law. By the traditional lawyer's view I mean that which was expressed by Blackstone in the middle of the eighteenth century, and which still maintains a certain orthodoxy. According to that view, while the legislative power is vested in King and Parliament, what is called the executive power is vested in the King alone, and consists of the royal prerogative. Now most people know that this is not altogether true to fact—they know that the powers attributed to the King are really exercised by the King's ministers, and that the King is expected to have ministers who command the confidence of the House of Commons. Still I think that they would say that this was a matter not of law, but of convention, or of constitutional morality—that *legally* the executive power is in the King, though

[1] *Scilicet*, the Local Government Board is now no more, its powers having been transferred, *mutatis mutandis*, first to the Ministry of Health and then to the Ministry of Housing and Local Government.

[2] In earlier editions. The first was published in 1885. By 1893, when the fourth edition was published, Dicey's Introduction showed that he had greatly modified his view, as was also shown by his article, 'The Development of Administrative Law', 31 *L.Q.R.* 148 (one of the last contributions from his vigorous pen).

constitutionally it must be exercised by ministers. But the point that I wish to make is that this old doctrine is not even true to law. To a very large extent indeed England is now ruled by means of statutory powers which are not in any sense, not even as strict matters of law, the powers of the King.[1] . . . The new wants of a new age have been met in a new manner—by giving statutory powers of all kinds, sometimes to the Queen in Council, sometimes to the Treasury, sometimes to a Secretary of State, sometimes to this Board, sometimes to the other. But of this vast change our institutional writers have hardly yet taken any account. They go on writing as though England were governed by the royal prerogatives, as if ministers had nothing else to do than to advise the King as to how his prerogatives should be exercised. In my view . . . we can no longer say that the executive power is vested in the King: the King has powers, this minister has powers, and that minister has powers. The requisite harmony is secured by the extra-legal organization of cabinet and ministry. The powers legally given to the King are certainly the most important, but I cannot consent to call them supreme.[2] . . . Year by year the subordinate Government of England is becoming more and more important. The new movement set in with the Reform Bill of 1832: it has gone far already and assuredly it will go farther. We are becoming a much governed nation, governed by all manner of councils and boards and officers, central and local, high and low, exercising the powers which have been committed to them by modern statutes.[3]

II. CHIEF SPHERES OF DELEGATED LEGISLATION

1. Powers directly delegated by Parliament

If this was true in 1887, it is infinitely more true today. The subject has now grown beyond the scope of summary treatment; but we can glance briefly at some of the outstanding features of the present situation.

As has been noted,[4] the great bulk of Parliamentary legislation nowadays is of the social and administrative rather than of the 'legal' kind. Parliament is obliged to delegate much of its legislative office, for two principal

[1] *Constitutional History of England*, 415.
[2] *Ibid.* 417.
[3] *Ibid.* 501.
[4] *Ante*, p. 311.

reasons: (1) it has not time to deal in detail with the multifarious matters which claim its attention; (2) many of these matters are so technical that there is a natural tendency to commit them to experts, while many others are of exclusively local importance.[1] Further, much of the time and interest of any Government in power is taken up with purely political exigencies, including foreign as well as domestic policy.

The result has been the rise of a number of organs of government which, though still subject in some measure to a general control of Parliament and of the courts, are rapidly acquiring a power nearly co-ordinate with that of the 'supreme' law-making and law-administering bodies. Let us consider a few of these new elements in our constitution.

(*a*) The Privy Council

The average citizen, it is to be supposed, thinks of the Privy Council only as a decorative and somewhat archaic body of little real moment in modern society. He would certainly never reckon it among the powers which govern him. Yet the field covered by Privy Council orders and regulations is immense; to set them out in detail would require many pages of print—indeed, a whole volume. They range from the minutest details of administration, e.g. the lighting and ventilation of cowsheds,[2] to legislation for dependencies, which latter it has been attempted to extend, though with doubtful legality, to the Channel Islands.[3]

Orders of the Privy Council are of two kinds. They may take the form of an original exercise of the prerogative, independent of the law-making power of Parliament. To this class, for example, belong legislative

[1] I believe these reasons, though doubtless substantially justified, are often exaggerated. The output of legislation, and its technical character, are no greater today than they have been at some periods in the past; see the present writer's *Law and Orders* (2nd ed.), 181, *et passim*.

[2] Contagious Diseases (Animals) Act, 1878, s. 34.

[3] *Re the States of Jersey* (1853), 9 Moo. P.C. 185; Anson, *Law and Custom of the Constitution* (4th ed.), ii, Pt. II, 58; Halsbury, *L. of E.* (3rd ed.), v, § 1393 and note.

Orders for the Crown Colonies, or regulations for trade and commerce in time of war. During the two world wars their number was immense and their effect far-reaching. An historic example was the celebrated Reprisals Order of 16 February 1917, which virtually imposed the economic blackade on Germany, inasmuch as it authorized the capture of vessels bound for neutral ports which afforded access to enemy territory. What is the legal force of Orders of this kind? The judgement of the Judicial Committee of the Privy Council in *The Zamora*, [1916] 2 A.C. 77, made it clear that an Order in Council, like every other act of the prerogative, is *sub lege*; it is subject to review by the courts, and cannot, of its own mere motion, override the ordinary law of the land. But with this reservation the courts must give the utmost weight to it.[1] Orders of this nature—again like every act of the prerogative—are in effect acts of the Cabinet; they may be concerned with questions either of the general policy of the realm, or of policy affecting only one particular Department of State.

A second, much larger, and constantly growing class of Orders in Council consists of those which are issued in accordance with powers expressly delegated to the Council by Acts of Parliament. The statute defines the strategy and leaves to the Council the control of tactics. This would seem to place a large power in the hands of a body little suited for the arrangement of details; in reality, it is a constitutional device for *legislation by the executive*, to which we shall have to refer again. The Council which nominally emits these Orders is as ill fitted as anybody could imagine to lay down minute rules for the ventilation of cowsheds and like matters. It consists of the Sovereign in person and a few Privy Councillors summoned by the Lord President, usually not less than six, and generally including one or two Cabinet Ministers. It meets at irregular times and places, its composition is variable, no member has an

[1] See also *The Canton*, [1917] A.C. 102; *The Oscar II*, [1920] A.C. 748.

enforceable right to be summoned to it, and the only constitutional convention—it is not more than that—which appears to govern it is that at least three Lords of the Council, and the Clerk of the Council, shall be present, besides the Sovereign.[1] Its procedure is in the highest degree formal, yet in the course of any year it issues many hundreds of Orders affecting a multiplicity of interests. All this means, as the reader will realize at a glance, that the Council merely lends formal sanction to legislation by Government Departments. It is they who are the true delegates of the legislature; the actual framing of the Orders is generally in their hands, and the sanction given by the Council is no more a real sanction than is the royal assent to Bills passed by the Houses of Parliament.[2]

(*b*) Rule-making authorities

Of more recent growth than the Privy Council are those 'rule-making' bodies which are now very numerous, and which possess important powers of many different kinds. A conspicuous example is the Rules Committee of the Supreme Court, first set up in 1875, and now, as the result of a long course of legislation, possessing an almost complete control over matters of procedure in the High Court. The rules must be laid before Parliament, and may be annulled on an address of either House,[3] but there does not seem to have been any occasion for the use of this power.[4] Let nobody suppose that this is a matter of merely professional import. It is true that we have progressed beyond the days when men could, by an artificial game of pleadings, reduce the law to the paradox *ubi remedium ibi ius*; but procedural law is still, and must always be, an indispensable adjunct to substantive law, and even today a good cause may easily

[1] Maitland, *op. cit.* 406.

[2] See *per* Lord Shaw, *R.* v. *Halliday*, [1917] A.C. 260, 287.

[3] Judicature (Consolidation) Act, 1925, s. 212.

[4] It would seem from *Birmingham Citizens' Building Society* v. *Caunt*, [1962] Ch. 883, that *Practice Directions* issued under these Rules are not absolutely binding. Rules which are repugnant to statute are *ultra vires* and void: *Hodge* v. *H.* [1963] 2 W.L.R. 297; *Bancroft* v. *B.*, [1963] 2 W.L.R. 309.

be thrown away by ignorance of procedural forms. Consequently, every practising lawyer has to know this body of adjective law as well as, if not better than, the juristic principles of substantive law. Here, then, is an example of pure court-made law. In its origin customary, this kind of law in modern conditions becomes subject to revision and formulation by specially constituted expert authority, such as the Rules Committee which we are considering. And this form of professional autonomy, ancient as it is, shows no signs of diminishing in present circumstances. It is noteworthy, on the contrary, that the example of the Rules Committee has been very widely imitated throughout the British Commonwealth. In England, this power is not confined to the Rules Committee, a fairly large and representative body of the profession; in comparatively new jurisdictions it may be entrusted to a more centralized authority. Thus, under the Matrimonial Causes Act, 1857, ss. 53 and 67, and the Judicature Act, 1875, s. 18, the President of the Probate, Divorce, and Admiralty Division has power to make rules for the procedure of his court. The power has been freely exercised in a jurisdiction where rules of practice are somewhat technical.[1] Of no less moment than the Rules of the Supreme Court are the County Court Rules for procedure and costs,[2] and among other important codes of Rules we may mention the Bankruptcy Rules, the Summary Jurisdiction Rules, and the Probate Rules.

In no true sense can these rules of procedure be described as the work of Parliament. They are essentially rules created by the profession for the profession, for the better conduct of litigation. They are, however, subject to regulations of publicity and revision which will be noted presently.

[1] See now the Matrimonial Causes Rules, 1950 (S.I. 1950, No. 1940), and Amendments (S.I. 1954, Nos. 138 and 1026), and the Matrimonial Causes Rules, 1957 (S.I. 1957, No. 619).

[2] County Courts Act, 1934, s. 99, and County Courts Act, 1955, ss. 10 and 11; Administration of Justice Act, 1956, s. 32.

(c) Local Authorities

Turning to local government, I should be going far beyond the scope of this chapter if I attempted, even in barest outline, to describe the present range and variety of this form of devolution. I must content myself with one example. By a series of enactments, notably the Public Health Acts, dating from 1875, local authorities —county, borough, rural and urban district councils —have powers to enact by-laws, binding upon the public generally, for public health and for 'good rule and government'. Offences against these by-laws are punishable on conviction by summary process by fines usually not exceeding £5. The range of subjects dealt with is immense; to take the commonest, we may note building, advertisements, care of the sick (hospitals, vaccination, infectious diseases), cleanliness of dwelling-houses, housing, town-planning schemes, protection against fire, offensive trades, public libraries, museums, nuisances, scavenging and cleansing, police, rating, education, traffic, highways, burials, and the conduct generally of persons in public places. All, however, as we shall see, are subject to a somewhat wider judicial scrutiny than most subordinate legislation. All these matters, and their many analogues in local government, count for no less in the daily lives of ordinary citizens than the enactments of Parliament. The far-off dignity of the House of Commons, though to the instructed it may symbolize the majesty of the constitution, to the plain law-abiding man is but a name compared with the immediate discipline of magistrates, policemen, and inspectors.

(d) Executive or Departmental legislation

Delegation to the executive, or departmental legislation, has already been mentioned, and we have seen that it often operates through Orders in Council. But the delegation is frequently more direct than this: a Minister, Board, or Committee is empowered to fill in, as it were, the interstices of a principal statute which Parliament has neither time nor inclination to fill in for itself. The extent to which this expedient has grown is one of the most remarkable features of our constitution at the present time. It has become almost the 'common form' of legislation. 'In mere bulk', writes Sir Cecil Carr,[1] who, as a former editor of the Statutory Rules and Orders, speaks with peculiar authority on this subject, 'the child now dwarfs the parent. Last year (1920), while 82 Acts of Parliament were placed on the statute-book, more than ten times as many Statutory Rules and Orders of a public character were officially registered under the Rules Publication Act. The annual volume of public general statutes for 1920 occupied less than 600 pages; the two volumes of the Statutory Rules and Orders for the same period occupy about five times as many. This excess in mere point of bulk of delegated legislation over direct legislation has been visible for nearly thirty years.'

The tendency has grown continuously since Sir Cecil Carr wrote, having been greatly augmented, as was inevitable, by the occurrence of another war.[2] The Emergency Powers (Defence) Acts of 1939 and 1940 were the parents of a vast number of Orders and Regulations, some of which are still in force, and a great deal of sub-legislation of the same 'emergency' character has been perpetuated in peace-time.[3] Perhaps the most remarkable example of Parliamentary delegation of very far-reaching and vague powers is provided by the Supplies and Services (Transitional Powers) Act, 1945, and the Supplies and Services (Extended Powers) Act, 1947. Under these Acts, Defence Regulations might be perpetuated for any of the following purposes:

(1) to secure a sufficiency of those [supplies and services]

[1] *Delegated Legislation*, 2, and the same writer's 'Administrative Law', 51 *L.Q.R.* 58. For the history of delegated legislation, see Sir William Graham Harrison, *Notes on Delegation by Parliament of Legislative Powers*, which, while most valuable and informative, seems to me to underestimate the growth of this method in the nineteenth and twentieth centuries. See, further, C. K. Allen, *Law and Orders* (2nd ed.), ch. 2.

[2] On the history of the whole process, see M. A. Sieghart, *Government by Decree*, 106 ff.

[3] See *Law and Orders* (2nd ed.), chs. 2 and 3.

essential to the well-being of the community, or their equitable distribution, or their availability at fair prices;

(2) to facilitate the demobilization and resettlement of persons and to secure the orderly disposal of surplus material;

(3) to facilitate the readjustment of industry and commerce to the requirements of the community in time of peace;

(4) to assist the relief of suffering and the restoration and distribution of essential supplies and services in any part of His Majesty's dominions or in foreign countries that are in grave distress as the result of war;

(5) for promoting the productivity of industry, commerce, and agriculture;

(6) for fostering and directing exports and reducing imports, or imports of any classes, from all or any countries and for redressing the balance of trade;

(7) generally for ensuring that the whole resources of the community are available for use, and are used, in a manner best calculated to serve the interests of the community.[1]

It is impossible to imagine a more sweeping code than this for regulating, by subordinate legislation, the entire economic life of the community; so wide, indeed, are the terms, especially of para. (7) above, that it would be almost impossible to challenge any Statutory Instrument made under them as being *ultra vires*;[2] and it is to be noted that these powers, which were originally sanctioned for five years only, lasted on in peace-time and were only very gradually reduced.[3] The last (23rd) edition (1957) shows that there are still 19 Defence (General) Regulations in force, applying to Ships and Aircraft, Essential Supplies and Work, and certain general and administrative provisions.

This is perhaps the high-water mark, up to the present time, of the delegation of legislative powers, but it is by no means uncharacteristic. The passing of any

[1] Further powers were conferred by the Emergency Laws (Transitional Provisions) Acts, 1946 and 1947, and the Supplies and Services (Defence Purposes) Act, 1951.

[2] See, however, the dissenting judgement of Denning L.J. in *Lewisham Borough* v. *Roberts*, [1949] 2 K.B. 608, 620.

[3] See *Law and Orders* (2nd ed.), 76 ff.

comprehensive new measure of social service, such as the National Health Service Act, 1946, involves, as a supplement, huge numbers, not only of Orders, but of whole codes of Orders, without which the Act could not operate. A glance at any annual volume of statutes will show that legislative functions are assigned to a great variety of authorities, such as the Privy Council, Ministers, Departments, Commissioners, Local Authorities, and a variety of separate functionaries, such as the Lord Chancellor, the Lord Chief Justice, the Master of the Rolls, the Senior Master of the Supreme Court, the Registrar-General, and many others. In short, the whole character of our legislation has fundamentally changed, and the average statute is merely a framework for details to be supplied by appointed authorities. The framework is entirely at the will of sovereign Parliament, the details are both devised and carried into effect by the executive, subject to certain constitutional controls the force of which, both *de jure* and *de facto*, we shall presently consider.

2. *Autonomic powers* (*a*) Corporations, Churches, &c.

Beside these distinct parts of our constitutional machinery, there are a large number of corporations, standing quite outside the governmental system, which are invested with the power of making by-laws for themselves and in many cases for the public at large. They are usually corporations of the so-called 'public utility' kind—authorities for transport, light, heat, water, and in general all essential public services corresponding to the commonest daily needs of the community. Though these by-laws are as binding on those whom they affect as Acts of Parliament themselves, they are, as we shall see, subject to a judicial scrutiny which is not applicable to statutes proper. Of that kind of corporation law which is most strictly called *autonomic*, inasmuch as it concerns directly only the members of a particular corporation, the most familiar example is the articles of association of a joint-stock company. Ecclesiastical bodies, again, have been conspicuous throughout history as autonomous societies-within-societies. The degree of autonomy has diminished in modern times, but it is still considerable. The Church of England, for example, though 'by law established'—i.e. by the general law of the land, and not by any peculiar authority or jurisdiction of ecclesiastical law—enjoys no small measure of self-government, now vested in the National Assembly by the so-called Enabling Act of 1919.[1] The Measures passed by this body affect the entirety of communicants, and in form and substance are statutes. Parliament controls them to the extent that they must be confirmed by a resolution of each House of Parliament, but with that reservation they are free to deal with 'any matter concerning the Church of England', *not excluding Acts of Parliament.* Thus in 1926 a Measure repealed eight whole Acts and twenty-one sections of other Acts.[2] Similarly the elaborate Clergy Pensions Measure, 1961, repealed ten whole Acts, dating from 1871. Not dissimilar to the autonomy of the Church is that of certain universities, especially Oxford and Cambridge and their colleges.

Effect of autonomic laws

Although it is a settled principle that subordinate laws of this kind, unlike by-laws issued by, say, a railway authority, are not directly binding on anybody outside the corporation which makes them,[3] that principle does not completely state their legislative effect. Negatively, they apply to everybody: that is to say, everybody is under a definite legal duty not to interfere with the rights which they confer. A Roman Catholic claims no rights under the Enabling Act, nor does he owe any positive duties of an ecclesiastical kind to the Anglican communion; but if he prevents a member of that communion

[1] Church of England Assembly (Powers) Act, 1919. A considerable number of Acts were amended by the Ecclesiastical Commissioners (Powers) Measure, 1938. For other examples of delegated powers co-ordinate with those of Parliament, see *Report of the Committee on Ministers' Powers*, 30 ff.

[2] First Fruits Measure, 1926.

[3] *London Assocn. of Shipowners, &c.* v. *London, &c., Joint Committee*, [1892] 3 Ch. 242, 255.

from exercising powers granted him by a Measure of the National Assembly, he commits a civil wrong no less than if he prevented a qualified voter from exercising his Parliamentary franchise. The same is true of anybody who interferes with a shareholder in the exercise of powers conferred by the article of association of a limited company, though the person interfering may have no rights or duties under the articles. All valid autonomic legislation, however restricted its positive scope, may be said to have this negative and by no means unimportant meaning for the whole body of citizens; and it therefore cannot be regarded as something altogether distinct and apart from the general rule of law.

(*b*) Industrial and professional organizations

In the foregoing examples autonomous rules originate in a specific antecedent legal sanction. The law does not formulate the articles of association of a joint-stock company, but it gives the company legal power to bind its members by articles upon which they agree among themselves. Neither does it formulate the Measures of the National Assembly, but it accords in advance binding force to such Measures, being *intra vires*, as the Assembly agrees to pass. There is another kind of autonomy, increasingly noticeable at the present time, which does not take its rise from any explicit statutory authorization, but grows up simply by the will and practice of a particular group which exists for a specific purpose —or what German jurists call a *Zweckverband*. The most conspicuous form of this species of autonomy in modern society is found in industrial organization; and this will serve as a good example to illustrate the difference between antecedently authorized autonomy and—if the tautology may be pardoned—purely autonomous autonomy.

For many and obvious reasons, fellow-workers in the same craft naturally tend to combine in guilds and unions. Trade guilds are of ancient origin in England; but for a long time our law refused, on grounds of supposed public policy, to recognize the kind of organization which came to be known as the Trade Union. As everybody knows, the industrial conditions of the nineteenth century made this policy of the law progressively inappropriate, and by a movement culminating in the Trade Unions Act, 1871, Trade Unions came to be recognized as legitimate associations with power to make autonomic rules for themselves.[1] This kind of industrial autonomy may therefore be said now to rest upon express legal recognition, and indeed it is governed by strict rules of law elaborated in a whole course of legislation.

But at the present time we are witnessing a totally different kind of trade autonomy which rests upon no such sanction. It proceeds in this case not from labour but from capital, and indeed may be said in some sort to be capital's answer to the very powerful autonomy now exercised by Trade Unions. Employers, producers, and distributors are now very commonly organized in associations which regulate output, supply, and prices, and regulate them with extreme strictness. Not only merchants and consumers, but lawyers also, are frequently reminded of this fact by cases of 'combination', 'coercion', 'conspiracy', or 'intimidation'—our law has not yet found even a satisfactory name for this new situation—in which the point of conflict is always the same, viz. that an individual in a particular industry refuses to submit to association rules and in consequence is virtually prevented from exercising his calling, the other members having agreed in advance that they will ostracize any recalcitrant trader. Rules of this kind are often said to be 'voluntary', and are cited as examples of 'autonomy by consent'; but in reality the voluntary element is largely fictitious. No man, it is true, is legally compellable to submit to the rules of a trade association, but the compulsion of bare existence is stronger than that of law. It does not completely meet the case to say that ultimately the courts exercise a control over the arrangements

[1] See Slesser and Baker, *Trade Union Law*, Pt. I.

of these voluntary associations, if they come into conflict with common right. We cannot disregard actual conditions as they affect ordinary social and industrial relationships. It is no satisfaction to a man who wishes to sell his goods at his own price, and who is prevented from doing so under pain of boycott and commercial annihilation, to know that Parliament has the power to declare price-maintenance associations illegal. This feature of modern industry has, in recent years, presented the courts with some of the most difficult problems which they have had to face, and it cannot be said that a wholly illuminating jurisprudence has yet emerged from their decisions.[1] Modern legislation,[2] by creating the Restrictive Practices Court, has established a control over these agreements, so far as they appear to be monopolistic or in restraint of trade, but this jurisdiction is concerned with 'the public interest'—the general effect on the economy of the country—and not with the rights and duties of the contracting parties *inter se*.

Like industrial organizations, most professions, such as the law, medicine, architecture, the Stock Exchange, impose upon their members certain rules of discipline and propriety. Some of these are of legal authority and effect, others purely voluntary. The difference is perhaps best illustrated on the one hand by the voluntary rules of the British Medical Association,[3] and on the other hand by the statutory powers vested in the General Medical Council and the elaborate machinery of discipline over doctors and dentists set up by regulations under the National Insurance Acts, the National Health Service Act, 1946, and the Medical Act, 1950. Contrast,

[1] The cases are too numerous to mention in full, but the most important in recent years are *Ware & de Freville* v. *Motor Trade Assocn.*, [1921] 2 K.B. 40; *Sorrell* v. *Smith*, [1925] A.C. 700; *Thorne* v. *Motor Trade Assocn.*, [1937] A.C. 797; *Crofter, &c., Harris Tweed Co.* v. *Veitch*, [1942] A.C. 435; and *Thomson* v. *Deakin*, [1952] Ch. 646.

[2] Monopolies and Restrictive Practices Acts, 1948 and 1953; Restrictive Trade Practices Act, 1956.

[3] See *Pratt* v. *British Medical Association*, [1919] 1 K.B. 244.

similarly, the rules of professional etiquette enforced by the Inns of Court and the General Council of the Bar and the powers of the Disciplinary Committee under the Solicitors Acts. These sub-laws, voluntary and compulsory, of professional bodies give rise to difficult legal problems,[1] and are the parent of many 'domestic tribunals',[2] which, however, lie beyond the scope of our present inquiry.

3. Forms of subordinate legislation

What has been said, though it touches only the fringe of this complex subject, will be enough to indicate the principal directions in which subordinate legislation has grown and is still growing.[3] It cannot be regarded as anything else than an integral part of the 'law of the land', if that term is to have any practical meaning. Since all men must at their peril know the law which governs them, or at least know how to obtain access to it, it is relevant to inquire into the forms in which this ever-expanding body of law is expressed. We have already seen that the 'statute-book' is not a book which he who runs may read. The sub-statute-book is an even more difficult, and a far more incomplete, text.[4] Its contents are now governed by the Statutory Instruments Act, 1946, which repealed the Rules Publication Act, 1893. The older Act, which was intended to ensure publicity for subordinate legislation, was highly defective and unsystematic, for reasons which have now fortunately

[1] See D. Lloyd, 'The Disciplinary Powers of Professional Bodies', 13 *M.L.R.* 281; Lord Morris, 'The Courts and Domestic Tribunals', 69 *L.Q.R.* 318; and J. D. B. Mitchell, 'Domestic Tribunals and the Courts', *British Journal of Administrative Law*, Jan. 1956, 80. See particularly *Abbot* v. *Sullivan*, [1952] 1 K.B. 189; *Lee* v. *Showmen's Guild*, [1952] 2 Q.B. 329; *Baker* v. *Jones*, [1954] 1 W.L.R. 1005; and *Byrne* v. *Kinematograph Renters Society, Ltd.*, [1958] 1 W.L.R. 762.

[2] See W. A. Robson, *Justice and Administrative Law* (3rd ed.), 317 ff.

[3] For further details, see W. A. Robson, *op. cit.*; F. J. Port, *Administrative Law*; G. E. Robinson, *Public Authorities and Legal Liability*; Sir Ivor Jennings, *Principles of Local Government Laws*, 30 ff., and *The Law and the Constitution*, ch. vi; M. A. Sieghart, *Government by Decree*; and the present writer's *Law and Orders*.

[4] On the whole subject, see evidence of Mr. C. T. (now Sir Cecil) Carr, *Committee on Ministers' Powers*, Minutes of Evidence, 204 ff.

become obsolete. The Act of 1946 repairs a number of erratic omissions in its predecessor and brings within the new and generic description 'statutory instruments' a large variety of subordinate legislation, including all orders, rules, and regulations made either by Order in Council or by a Minister under statutory authority. It also brings within the class of statutory instruments, after the passing of the Act, any statutory rules made by a 'rule-making authority' within the meaning of the Rules Publication Act, 1893; and power is given to add, by Order in Council, an important class of orders which that Act did not cover—namely, Ministerial orders confirming or approving, as required by numerous statutes, the sub-enactments of other subordinate authorities. All statutory instruments are to be numbered and sent to the King's Printer 'immediately after' their making and are to be printed and sold 'as soon as possible';[1] and lists are required to be printed showing the date of first issue. From this requirement, and from a number of others which need not be specified in detail, exceptions may be made by regulations issued by the Treasury, with the concurrence of the Lord Chancellor and the Speaker of the House of Commons; and any such regulations are subject to annulment by a resolution of either House of Parliament.

By this Act a reasonable degree of publicity is secured for a very large variety of sub-laws. There is, however, no *preliminary* publicity. Under the Rules Publication Act at least forty days' notice in the *London Gazette* was required for all orders which had to be laid before Parliament. This requirement, which was never very effectual, has been abandoned. Public information of statutory instruments therefore depends on the speed with which they are put forth in print, and it is thus easily possible

[1] The exact meaning of the terms 'immediately' and 'as soon as possible' has not, at the present date of writing, fallen to be interpreted. With regard to the effect of the similar expressions, 'as soon as possible' and 'as soon as may be', see *Law and Orders* (2nd ed.), 167 f., and 65 *L.Q.R.* 439 and 66 *ibid.* 299, though the reference there is not to publication but to laying before Parliament.

for anybody to contravene a recent order or regulation of which he had no knowledge and could hardly be expected to have any. This contingency, however, is provided for by s. 3 (2) of the Act; it is a defence to prove that the instrument under which a charge is brought had not been issued by the Stationery Office at the time of the alleged contravention. The absence of any provision for the publicity of a Ministerial Order displaces the maxim *ignorantia juris neminem excusat.*[1] There is, however, a proviso as vague as it is important: 'unless it is proved that at that date reasonable steps had been taken for the purpose of bringing the purport of the instrument to the notice of the public, or of persons likely to be affected by it, or of the person charged'. At the present date it is entirely obscure what is meant by 'reasonable steps' of publicity and who is empowered to take them. It is to be feared that the reference is principally to official announcements by broadcast—an expedient which became familiar during the war. This seems to be a highly unsatisfactory and uncertain method of making the law known, except, of course, in times of emergency.

Since the Statutory Instruments Act is silent on the point, it has been doubtful exactly when an Instrument takes effect,[2] but the better opinion seems to be that it comes into force as soon as it has been made and (if this is required by the parent Act) laid before Parliament,[3] unless, as often happens, a future date is assigned for its coming into operation.

The Statutory Instruments Act comprises far more sub-legislation than its predecessor, but it is not all-embracing; thus it does not include the orders of local authorities.[4] For reasons of sheer bulk, this is probably

[1] *Lim Chin Aik* v. *R.*, [1963] A.C. 160.

[2] In *Johnson* v. *Sargant*, [1918] 1 K.B. 101, Bailhache J. held that an order did not take effect until it 'became known', but the decision was unsupported by any other and has always been regarded as questionable.

[3] So held by Streatfeild J. in *R.* v. *Sheer Metalcraft, Ltd.*, [1954] 1 Q.B. 586.

[4] Except, *semble*, some Ministerial confirming orders, which are frequently required.

necessary; but it is an open and a difficult question whether either *sub-delegating* or *amending* orders come within the purview of the Act. S. 1 refers to the 'power to make, confirm or approve orders, rules, regulations or other subordinate legislation', and it is doubtful whether this expression, wide though it is, includes the very large number of amending orders (which, however, are in fact generally published) and the equally large number of instruments by which Ministers sub-delegate, e.g. to local authorities, the powers conferred on them by statute.[1] In *Blackpool Corpn.* v. *Locker*, [1948] 1 K.B. 349, Scott L.J. commented severely on the lack of publicity for sub-delegated legislative powers; but in *Lewisham Borough* v. *Roberts*, [1949] 2 K.B. 608, it was held, with express dissent from Scott L.J., that the powers there in question were not legislative but merely administrative, and that the Minister was entitled to delegate them as he did. Whichever decision is right, it is undoubtedly a great embarrassment in the whole sphere of administration that powers, whether they be technically described as executive, legislative, or judicial, are deputed by means which persons affected thereby cannot know or be expected to know, e.g. by 'confidential' circulars to local authorities and sometimes even by word of mouth (which may afterwards be repudiated).[2] In American administrative law the general rule, though with exceptions, is *delegatus non potest delegare*, but in our administrative law the question, so far as it relates to *legislative* delegation, is still at large and in a state of confusion which can be clarified only by some authoritative decision. It is remarkable that none has yet been given on so important a matter.[3] With regard to *administrative* powers, it is undoubted that a reasonable measure

[1] See S. A. de Smith, 'Sub-delegation and Circulars', 12 *M.L.R.* 37. See also *Erith Corpn.* v. *Holder*, [1949] 2 K.B. 46.

[2] See, e.g., *Falmouth Boat Construction Co., Ltd.* v. *Howell*, [1951] A.C. 16.

[3] See *Law and Orders* (2nd ed.), 204 ff., and *Report of the Committee on Ministers' Powers*, 50.

of sub-delegation is unexceptionable,[1] though its exact limits are difficult to define.

The power to sub-delegate may be expressly given by the parent statute, as was done by the Emergency Powers (Defence) Act, 1939, for Defence Regulations. The result is sometimes a whole descending series of delegations. In its Special Report for the Session 1945–6,[2] the Select Committee on Statutory Instruments, which will be mentioned later drew attention to what it called 'Five-tier legislation'. Referring to Defence Regulations, the Committee observed:

> 'Your Committee have sometimes had to take note of a pedigree of five generations: (*a*) the statute; (*b*) the Defence Regulations made under the statute; (*c*) the orders made under the Defence Regulations; (*d*) directions made under the orders; and (*e*) licences issued under the directions.'[3]

It is needless to observe that these successive devolutions cause great complexity in the law, and the Committee expressed the hope that more compendious methods might be adopted and that Departments would be 'content with the grandchildren of the statute and not bring its great-grandchildren or great-great-grandchildren upon the scene'. In a later Special Report (1947–8) the Committee expresssed doubts about the legality of some of these sub-delegations (which continue to appear), but up to the present time I am not aware that they have been tested in the courts.

A further complexity, and a frequent cause of complaint, is that the constant process of amendment and revision of Statutory Instruments leads to much 'legislation by reference', which makes it extremely difficult to discover the exact authority and effect of subordinate laws. As an example of the complexity which may result

[1] *Carltona Ltd.* v. *Commissioner of Works*, [1943] 2 All E.R. 560; *Lewisham Borough* v. *Roberts*, [1949] 2 K.B. 608, 621.

[2] H.M.S.O., 29 Oct. 1946.

[3] Licences, however, can hardly be regarded as 'legislation'.

from this process of sub-delegation, let me cite the preamble to one Order,[1] which reads thus:

'Whereas by the Aliens Order, 1920,[2] hereinafter referred to as the principal Order, made in pursuance of the Aliens Restrictions Acts, 1914–19, His Majesty was pleased, by and with the advice of His Privy Council, to impose certain restrictions on aliens, and to make provision in accordance with the said Acts for giving effect to the said Order:

'And whereas by the Expiring Laws Continuance Acts, 1920 and 1921, the Expiring Laws Act, 1922, and the Expiring Laws Continuance Acts, 1923 and 1924, s. 1 of the Aliens Restriction (Amendment) Act, 1919, was continued until 31st December 1925:

'And whereas His Majesty has power by Order in Council to revoke or add to any Order in Council made under the said Acts:

'And whereas the principal Order was amended by Orders in Council dated 3rd December 1920[3] and 12th March 1923:[4]

'And whereas it is expedient that provisions of the principal Order, as amended, should be further amended in the manner herein appearing:

'And whereas the provisions of s. 1 of the Rules Publication Act have been complied with:

'Now therefore His Majesty is pleased, &c.'

Even the draftsman of this Order must have had some difficulty in tracing its devious course to the fountain-head:[5] anybody less expert might well shrink from the mere attempt.[6]

[1] Restrictions on Aliens Order, S.R. & O., 1925, No. 760.

[2] S.R. & O., 1920, No. 448.

[3] S.R. & O., 1920, No. 2262.

[4] S.R. & O., 1923, No. 326.

[5] The draftsmanship of Statutory Instruments leaves much to be desired: see a severe criticism in *White* v. *Winterton Pottery, Ltd.*, [1932] 2 K.B. at p. 273. And see *Law and Orders* (2nd ed.), 244 ff.

[6] Of the 'classical example' of sub-sub-legislation provided by the Air Navigation Order (S.R. & O., 1923, No. 1508), Sir William Graham Harrison observes (*Committee on Ministers' Powers*, Minutes of Evidence, 50): 'There is a power to make this order regulating air navigation, but then instead of laying down exactly what is to be done in this, that and the other circumstances, it provides again and again that somebody else may say what is to be done. The Order does not say what is to be done; it says that somebody else may say what is to be done.'

Let us take another and quite characteristic example. An Instrument of 1946[1] is intended to provide that a launderer shall no longer be required to give notice to the Board of Trade if he intends to close down his business. This comparatively simple object is achieved by the following language:

'The Laundry (Control) Order, 1942, as amended by the Laundry (Control) (No. 2) Order, 1942, shall have effect as if subparagraph (3) of paragraph 2 were omitted, and the Laundry (Control) (No. 2) Order, 1942, is hereby revoked.'

The Select Committee on Statutory Instruments has repeatedly recommended the consolidation and redrafting of Orders so as to avoid this enigmatic form of expression, but the subject-matter is so diverse and extensive that the work proceeds very slowly, and it is often a labour of great intricacy to trace an Order through the maze back to its starting-point and to discover what the existing law really is. The task often defies the ingenuity even of trained lawyers and is certainly far beyond the capacity of the ordinary citizen, who is required to know the law at his peril. One regrettable result of this gratuitous obscurity is that it is sometimes wellnigh impossible for an individual to know what penalties he may incur by breach of an Order. For example, a person who is told that for certain offences in connexion with the keeping of poultry he will be liable to 'the penalties provided by the Diseases of Animals Acts, 1894 to 1937',[2] will have to make a diligent and exasperating search through a long course of legislation (chiefly concerned with horses) to learn that he is subject to penalties prescribed in s. 5 of the Diseases of Animals Act, 1927, and ss. 52 and 53 of the Diseases of Animals Act, 1894; and he must then, of course, refer to those Acts to

[1] S.R. & O., 1946, No. 890, cited in Special Report of the Select Committee on Statutory Rules and Orders, Session 1945–6, p. xxv.

[2] The Live Poultry (Regulation of Sales, Exhibitions and Movements) Order, S.R. & O., 1948, No. 333, discussed in *The Justice of the Peace*, 29 May 1948, p. 331.

discover exactly what the penalties are.[1] 'It is surely desirable', observed Lord Goddard C.J. in *Brierly* v. *Phillips*, [1947] K.B. 541, 543, 'that orders creating criminal offences should be stated in language which the persons who may commit the offences—in this case, quite humble people, like cottagers—can understand. It is a very serious thing to produce orders, whether under Defence Regulations or otherwise, which create serious offences, if they are couched in language which does not make clear whether a person is committing an offence or not.' It would be interesting to know what Bentham would have to say about the 'cognoscibility' of our modern statute-book. It has never been a completely 'open book', but it is in danger of becoming a sealed one. In any case, it is no longer a book—it is a bookstack.

III. RELATION BETWEEN SOVEREIGN AND SUBORDINATE LEGISLATION

1. *Constitutional checks*

Let us now ask what constitutional control is exercised over delegated legislation, considering first the theoretical powers possessed in this respect by legislative and judicial authorities, and second, the practical working of these checks at the present time.

Parliamentary control over delegated legislation is a complicated subject and involves technical questions of procedure which would be inappropriate for full discussion here. We cannot do more than give an outline of the present position.[2]

(*a*) Publicity and Parliamentary control

Parliament always has the general control that when a Bill is under consideration it may modify, amend, or refuse altogether the powers which the Bill proposes to confer on a Minister or other subordinate authority.

[1] For other examples of complex regulations, see *Langton* v. *Johnson*, [1956] 1 W.L.R. 1322; *Bryson* v. *Rogers*, [1956] 2 Q.B. 404.

[2] For details, see *Report of the Committee on Ministers' Powers*, *passim*; *Third Report from the Select Committee on Procedure*, H.M.S.O., 31 Oct. 1946; *Law and Orders* (2nd ed.), ch. 5; and Sieghart, *Government by Decree*, 123 ff.

This, however, does not often happen. A long Bill, if it is at all controversial, always presents a problem of time for debate, either in Committee or 'on the floor', or both; and of recent years a number of Acts have been passed through their stages only by the drastic method of the 'guillotine', which distributes a certain amount of time for debating different parts of the Bill. The available time is therefore concentrated on the principal subject-matter of 'skeleton' enactments, and the clauses which confer delegated powers tend to be 'taken as read' and are seldom debated at all. The result is that Members frequently acquiesce in delegating their legislative powers without realizing, or indeed inquiring into, the nature and effect of the powers which they grant.

Assuming that Parliament sanctions the powers proposed, they may be of two kinds. A large number are completely at the discretion of the specified authority, always provided that they are *intra vires*. Over these Parliament has no special supervision, except that complaint may be made about their mode of execution or any alleged abuse of them. This may be done either by questions addressed to a Minister, or, if the matter is important enough, by raising a debate on the adjournment, or, in extreme cases, by a motion of no confidence in a Minister, which takes the form of a vote on the estimates to reduce his salary.

The second class of subordinate enactments are those which are required by the parent statute to be laid before Parliament. Before we consider their different kinds, we should note that they are subject to a preliminary scrutiny.

In 1944 the Government agreed to a proposal which it had previously rejected, and set up a Select Committee on Statutory Rules and Orders (now known as Instruments), the function of which is to examine every Instrument laid or laid in draft before the House of Commons, with a view to determining whether the special attention of the House should be drawn to it on certain specified grounds. These are strictly defined and do not give the Committee any general censorship over the policy or effect of the Instrument, but rather over its form, extent, and publicity. The Committee has authority, however, to call attention to any 'unusual or unexpected' use of delegated powers—a phrase which has not yet been precisely defined and which has not been much prayed in aid by the Committee.[1] The task of the Committee, which had long before been suggested by the Committee on Ministers' Powers,[2] is extremely onerous. Since its inception it has examined many thousands of Statutory Instruments and has issued a continuous series of Sessional and Special Reports. It has power, which it has frequently exercised, to summon officials from Departments to explain delays or ambiguities; and in its Special Reports it has made a number of valuable observations on the general nature, form, and tendencies of delegated legislation, though it has no authority to suggest specific amendments. It has the advantage of the attendance and advice of Counsel to Mr. Speaker. It has effected steady and notable improvement in the form of Statutory Instruments,[3] and its mere existence is an incentive to care and restraint in the exercise of statutory powers. To that extent, though no farther, it is a valuable safeguard.

There are certain other preliminaries with regard to those orders which a statute requires to be laid before Parliament. The Statutory Instruments Act, 1946, s. 4, provides that a copy of the Instrument shall be so laid before it comes into operation. The ordinary reader would suppose this to mean that the Instrument does not take legal effect until it has been 'laid' as directed. It is not so, however. It seems to be beyond doubt that

[1] The other grounds on which the Committee is authorized to report are: (1) imposition of a money charge in consideration for a licence, services, &c.; (2) exemption from challenge in the courts; (3) unsanctioned retrospective effect; (4) unjustifiable delay in publication or 'laying'; (5) unjustifiable delay in notifying the Speaker of 'emergency' orders; (6) obscurity of form.

[2] *Report*, p. 63.

[3] See *Law and Orders*, 158 ff.

the provision is directory and not mandatory[1]—which means that failure by the responsible authority to 'lay' does not suspend the legal effect of the Instrument, but merely amounts to a breach of duty (presumably punishable as a Common Law misdemeanour) by the person responsible. There is an exception to this general provision. It sometimes happens that a Statutory Instrument is needed in a hurry to meet an emergency or an unexpected situation, and there may not be time to 'lay' it before it is needed. In that event the formality of 'laying' may be excused, but a notice and an explanation must be furnished 'forthwith' to the Lord Chancellor and the Speaker.[2]

We must now consider briefly the different kinds of delays or conditions applicable to those Statutory Instruments which are required to be laid before Parliament and which have passed the preliminaries. They may be summarized as follows:

(1) An Instrument may be 'quarantined' for a specified period after being laid, and at the end of the period it will automatically come into effect unless objection has been taken to it. This is not a very common method.

(2) It may be required to be laid in draft for a period of forty 'sitting days',[3] and will then automatically come into operation unless previously challenged.

(3) It may be required to lie before the House for forty sitting days, during which time it shall be subject to annulment (in rare cases annulment or modification) by resolution, or what is known as a 'prayer'. The Instrument

[1] See *Law and Orders*, 164 ff.; and on the West Indian case of *Springer* v. *Doorly*, see 65 *L.Q.R.* 439 and 66 *ibid.* 299, and C. B. Bourne in *Canadian Bar Review*, Aug.–Sept. 1950, 791.

[2] Statutory Instruments Act, 1946, s. 4 (1). The section merely says that this procedure may be adopted 'if it is essential', but does not state who is to decide that question or on what grounds. Under the Rules Publication Act, 1893, cases of urgency were met by Provisional Rules, which are now no longer known by that name.

[3] This period is made uniform by the Statutory Instruments Act, s. 6 (with certain exceptions specified in s. 9 (2)). Previously the period had varied erratically with different Orders.

takes effect at once, but lapses if a 'prayer' is successfully made against it. This is the method known as 'negative resolution' and is the one most commonly employed.

(4) Contrasted with this is the method known as 'affirmative resolution', by which the Instrument is laid before the House for a stated period, but does not come into operation until expressly approved by resolution. Variants of this form are that the Instrument may be laid in draft but not enacted unless the draft is approved within a specified time; or that the Instrument may come into operation at once, but will lapse after a stated period unless expressly approved.

(5) Finally, there are a considerable number of Statutory Instruments which are required to be laid before Parliament, but which are not subject to any form of affirmative or negative resolution, and are therefore not debatable, or, as the inelegant Parliamentary term has it, not 'prayable'.

Besides these kinds of Instruments there are certain types of orders to which a special procedure applies. Provisional Orders are preliminary to what is in effect Private Bill legislation for local or *ad hoc* requirements, and are given statutory form, after certain specified preliminaries, in periodical Provisional Order Confirmation Acts. The old procedure which applied to them has been considerably modified by the Statutory Orders (Special Procedure) Act, 1945—whether for better or for worse is matter of controversy. A variant of the Provisional Order is the Special Order, principally used in connexion with public utility undertakings and subject again to a procedure of its own. On the whole, there are for these special types of orders adequate though by no means perfect opportunities for Parliamentary examination and control, and they do not call for any detailed discussion here.[1]

[1] For further details, and some criticisms, see *Law and Orders*, 93 ff.; Sieghart, *op. cit.* 102 ff.; and John E. Kersell, 'Upper Chamber Scrutiny of Delegated Legislation', *Public Law*, Spring 1959, 46.

To sum up, there are, apart from the special types, four principal kinds of Statutory Instruments: (1) those which are subject to negative resolution; (2) those which are subject to affirmative resolution; (3) those which are required to be laid before Parliament, but are not 'prayable'; (4) those which do not require to be laid before Parliament at all. The two latter classes—those which are not open to any special Parliamentary supervision—comprise at least half of the total number of Statutory Instruments. These four types, as we have seen, have their variants, and the study of their different forms and effects is a highly technical matter. Various attempts[1] have been made to bring all Statutory Instruments under direct Parliamentary supervision, but they have not so far been successful. There is no uniform system upon which the responsible authorities choose one form rather than another for their orders and regulations. It is true in the main, though not invariably, that the method of 'affirmative resolution', either by a resolution of both Houses or of the House of Commons alone, is reserved for Orders which are considered to be of special importance or of an unusual character.[2] Otherwise the method adopted seems to be entirely at the option of the framers of the parent Act, and the practice varies considerably in different Departments, so that careful examination is necessary to determine in each case what kind of Instrument is in question.

It must be repeated that we have been dealing only with those Instruments which are required to be laid before Parliament, and are open to challenge, and a very large part of delegated legislation does not fall within this category. With regard, however, to those which do, what is the practical value of the safeguards which have

[1] See the Statutory Instruments (Parliamentary Control) Bill (*H.C. Deb.*, 21 Feb. 1951, col. 1299), introduced by Sir Herbert Williams, M.P., lost on a motion for rejection.

[2] e.g. (formerly) Rules made under the Government of India Act, 1936; and cf. Orders made by the Board of Trade under the Safeguarding of Industries Act, 1921.

been described? They do not in practice amount to any very effective check on sub-legislation. Parliament, as we have seen, grants the powers very freely and without much inquiry into their nature, and thereafter exercises little control; nor, it would seem, are many Members interested to do so. The preliminary screening of the Select Committee on Statutory Instruments is of considerable cautionary value; but the Committee has no mandate to control either the nature or the purpose of delegated legislation, and it may sometimes ask itself whether the limited results which it can achieve are proportionate to its heavy labours.

The opportunities for Members to take objection are extremely scanty and for the most part doomed to failure. Thus a 'prayer' is, under the Parliamentary procedure, 'exempted business', which in practice generally means that it can be taken only after 10 p.m., when the interest and attention of Members are not usually at their highest. For a good many years past many 'prayers' have been made against various Instruments which are subject to 'negative resolution'. They have generally come from Back Benchers who are concerned at the unrestrained growth of delegated legislation, and although they have been valuable in stimulating vigilance and in calling attention to anomalies, only an infinitesimal proportion of them have been successful. The reason is plain enough: most delegated powers are contained in Bills which are proposed by the Government of the day, and an attack on any of them is therefore in effect a criticism of Government policy and is almost certain to be defeated by the existing Parliamentary majority. Even when a 'prayer' is successful, the Instrument challenged and annulled is not necessarily disposed of; the Government, by ensuring a safe majority on a later occasion, can re-enact it; and this has happened in several instances.

Occasionally a 'prayer', or opposition to an 'affirmative resolution', may have the useful effect of extracting a concession or amendment from the responsible Minister;

but otherwise the process of negative or affirmative resolution provides no opportunity for amendment, unless this is specially sanctioned (as it is in very rare instances) by the parent Act. This is a grave defect in the whole system, for it means that if a Member feels objection to a part only of an Instrument, his sole recourse is to move for its entire rejection, which he may not wish to do. Many suggestions have been made that this rule should be changed, and this was proposed by the Liberties of the Subject Bill, 1950,[1] but there appears to be invincible Departmental objection to it and there is no doubt that it presents serious procedural difficulties.

Of all the methods of Parliamentary control, the most effective is the 'affirmative resolution', since this ensures that a proposed Instrument must at least have the attention of the House, and sometimes both Houses, before it can permanently become law, whereas in the 'negative resolution' procedure legal effect is automatic, after delay, unless some objector is sufficiently interested to demand the attention of the House. The Committee on Ministers' Powers was of opinion that the affirmative procedure might be more frequently employed; but here again there is strong Departmental resistance, which can be readily understood in many circumstances, for if it is desired to bring an Instrument into force quickly to meet a certain situation, it is obviously an embarrassment to the executive if the proposed measure is not only delayed but is uncertain of ultimate sanction.

Finally, the undoubted right of any Member, apart from any special forms or procedures of Instruments, to challenge what he believes to be an improper use of delegated powers is largely illusory; for in order to make himself heard, he must obtain time, which he is not likely to be given, for debate in a crowded legislative programme, or else contrive to raise a debate on the adjournment, or content himself with the inconclusive method of questions. In 1953, largely as the result

[1] See debate in the House of Lords, *H.L. Deb.*, Tuesday, 27 June 1950.

of anomalies which had been produced by reciprocal party manœuvres, the whole machinery of delegated legislation was examined by a Select Committee on Delegated Legislation, but its Report[1] is disappointingly barren of substantial proposals for reform. It cannot be discussed in detail here, but it is a document of first-class importance to the student of our complex legislative procedure. With one or two welcome exceptions, it has effected little change in the processes of sub-legislation.

Parliament, then, in theory is the legislative master, but in fact it surrenders a very substantial portion of its nominal sovereignty to its own servants. The issue is not whether there should or should not be delegated legislation. That question was answered centuries ago, for there has always been delegated legislation in our law and no responsible person doubts its necessity or usefulness. Nor is it a question of any rigid doctrine of separation of powers, for that, too, has been answered by our whole history, in which the separation of powers has never been an iron dogma. It is not our habit to make any constitutional principle a law of the Medes and Persians. The true issue is one of degree and proportion. We are here concerned with the sources of law, and we must recognize the fact that in our age one of the chief sources is a great mass of sub-enactments at the rate of between 2,000 and 3,000 Statutory Instruments per year. In strict theory, we can still call this legislation 'subordinate' and it is still true that in the last resort Parliament has sovereign authority over it; but in substance and in truth—and in fulfilment, to a degree which he can hardly have foreseen, of Maitland's prophecy (*ante*, p. 533)—the English lawgiver today is not one but legion, and the executive is the real origin of a vast amount of the law which it not only executes but creates. Whether or not this is an inevitable, or a desirable, feature of the

[1] H.M.S.O., 1953, No. 310. For a fuller account, see *Law and Orders*, 187 ff., *et passim*.

modern State, as many believe, is a question which lies beyond the scope of our discussion.

(*b*) Judicial control

Parliamentary control is direct, by way either of approval or of abrogation; the control of the courts is indirect; being an exercise of judicial interpretation, it cannot actually annul subordinate enactments, but can only declare them inapplicable in particular circumstances. The effect is practically the same in the two cases: the Rule or Order frowned upon by the courts, though not actually abrogated, becomes a dead letter, because in future no responsible authority will attempt to apply it, or, if it is applied, nobody will submit to it.

Doctrine of *ultra vires*

Judicial control operates, first, through the doctrine of *ultra vires*. As it is axiomatic that the enactments of Parliament can never be subject to judicial review, so it is axiomatic that all enactments made subordinately by virtue of specific statutory or Common Law authority are subject to the test whether or not they fall within the periphery of the power thus conferred. If they do not, they are of none effect. Even though a Rule or Order may have been made conditionally on ratification by Parliament, and may have received such sanction, it is still open to the courts to inquire whether it falls within the scope of the enactment from which it purports to derive its authority. The high constitutional importance of this function of the courts is well expresssed by Lord Shaw:

'The author of the power is Parliament: the wielder of it is the Government. Whether the Government has exceeded its statutory mandate is a question of ultra or intra vires. . . . In so far as the mandate has been exceeded, there lurk the elements of a transition to arbitrary government and therein of grave constitutional and public danger. The increasing crush of legislative efforts and the convenience to the Executive of a refuge to the device of Orders in Council would increase that danger tenfold were the judiciary to approach any such action of the Government in a spirit of compliance rather than of independent scrutiny.'[1]

[1] *R.* v. *Halliday, Ex p. Zadig*, [1917] A.C. 260, 287.

In short, this 'independent scrutiny' is one of the cardinal principles in a properly adjusted system of constitutional checks and balances. No general rule can be laid down for it. *Ex hypothesi* it is essentially a matter of interpretation turning upon particular considerations in each case. It is plain that much must depend on the terms, wide or narrow, in which the statutory power is expressed. The most remarkable example in our history of very extensive, indeed all-embracing, sub-legislation is the vast mass of defence and emergency regulations which have grown out of two world wars. The Defence of the Realm Act, 1914, at the beginning of the First World War, and in a lesser degree the Emergency Powers Act, 1920, at its conclusion, were the parents of sub-legislation of an extent and variety which had never before been dreamed of. Both during and after the war, however, a number of Regulations were challenged for *vires*, with varying success, in a series of decisions which are famous in our constitutional law.[1] This was possible because the general scope and purpose of the Regulations was the 'defence of the realm', and the number of 'competent authorities' who could apply the Regulations was comparatively limited. In the Second World War a far greater variety of purposes was assigned to Regulations made under the Emergency Powers (Defence) Acts of 1939 and 1940. The widest of them, besides the defence of the realm, were 'the efficient prosecution of any war in which His Majesty may be engaged' and 'maintaining supplies and services essential to the life of the community'. The purposes, indeed, are so diverse and far-reaching that they may be said to cover almost every aspect and activity of social life. As we have seen, some of these powers still survive, and others of them have now been made permanent, by the series of Supplies and Services Acts.

The result, at the present time, is that the doctrine of

[1] Especially *R.* v. *Halliday, ubi sup.*; *Att.-Gen.* v. *De Keyser's Royal Hotel, Ltd.*, [1920] A.C. 508; and *Chester* v. *Bateson*, [1920] 1 K.B. 829.

ultra vires is greatly attentuated and indeed, with regard to a large number of executive powers, it may be said to be completely paralysed. There are three main reasons for this: (1) The purposes assigned are so widely and vaguely expressed in the authorizing statutes that almost anything may be brought under them. What form or object of legislation, for example, could not be brought plausibly within the 'blanket' clause of the Supplies and Services (Extended Purposes) Act, 1947—'generally for ensuring that the whole resources of the community are available for use, and are used, in a manner best calculated to serve the interests of the community'? 'Best calculated' by whom, and by what kind of standard? To ask a court of law to interpret such phraseology is to invite it to embark on a number of economic and political considerations which are, or ought to be, quite outside its province. Vague language of this kind certainly serves its purpose—if such a purpose is intended—for it is a most effective deterrent to aggrieved persons. There may be—and, in the opinion of the present writer, there are—many Regulations under these and other Acts which are of questionable legality; but it is a brave litigant who will take the risk of disputing powers couched in such sweeping terms. In short, if the doctrine of *ultra vires* is to work at all, the powers which the courts are called on to interpret must be clearly defined and must be kept within ascertainable limits. The present tendency is to define them so loosely that interpretation becomes mere subjective guess-work, and therefore, in effect, is excluded altogether.

(2) It has become a common form of delegation, known in Whitehall as 'judge-proof', to empower a Minister to make (usually by the means of an Order in Council) such Regulations *as appear to him to be necessary or expedient* for a specified purpose. A series of decisions have held that when this form of words is used, the determination of necessity or expediency is entirely at the discretion of the delegated authority, and the courts

have no power to inquire into it; the only grounds on which the discretion can be challenged are that the Minister never properly directed his mind to the matter, or that he acted *mala fide*.[1] Both these grounds are illusory, since they are almost impossible to prove, even if there are any facts to substantiate them; and that is improbable, since Ministers of the Crown, advised as they are by conscientious officials, do not usually legislate without due consideration, and are, fortunately for England, seldom actuated by corruption or other palpable forms of *mala fides*. 'Bias', even if it can be proved, in favour of some predetermined policy, is not *mala fides*.[2] It was held in *Liversidge* v. *Anderson*, [1942] A.C. 306, that even the phrase 'if the Minister has reasonable cause to believe' was not subject to the doctrine of *ultra vires*, since the 'reasonable cause' was entirely 'subjective' in the mind of the Minister; but in view of the famous dissenting judgement of Lord Atkin, and of the subsequent decision and observations of the Judicial Committee in *Nakkuda Ali* v. *Jayaratne*, [1951] A.C. 66, there is ground for thinking that *Liversidge* v. *Anderson* was an *ad hoc* interpretation of an emergency measure and is not likely in future to be applied generally to Statutory Instruments governed by this form of delegation. Whether this be so or not, it is certain that when the law-making power is left to a Minister's judgement of 'necessity' or 'expediency', the courts disclaim any

[1] See *R.* v. *Comptroller-General of Patents, Ex p. Bayer Products, Ltd.*, [1941] 2 K.B. 306; *Progressive Supply Co.* v. *Dalton*, [1943] Ch. 54; *Franklin* v. *Minister of Town and Country Planning* (The Stevenage Case), [1948] A.C. 87; *Demetriades* v. *Glasgow Corporation*, [1951] 1 All E.R. 457; *Earl Fitzwilliam's Wentworth Estates Co.* v. *Minister of Town and Country Planning*, [1952] A.C. 362; *Allied Investors' Trusts, Ltd.* v. *Board of Trade*, [1956] Ch. 232.

[2] *Franklin* v. *Minister of Town and Country Planning, ubi sup.* Contrast the opinion of the Committee on Ministers' Powers (*Report*, p. 78): 'We think it is clear that bias from strong and sincere conviction as to public policy may operate as a more serious disqualification than pecuniary interest.' Of this fact the public had startling proof in the notorious Crichel Down affair, which does not fall for discussion here (see *Law and Orders*, 343 ff.).

right to consider the intrinsic reasonableness of his action.[1]

(3) The distinction between the administrative, the judicial, and the quasi-judicial is always difficult to draw with precision.[2] Powers delegated to executive authorities frequently partake of all three characteristics, which overlap and shade into each other. It is almost impossible to perform any important administrative act, which may affect liberty or property, without a preliminary weighing of evidence and a decision between alternatives, which is in essence a judicial or quasi-judicial exercise of the faculties. In the past, the leaning of the courts, when they found a judicial element in administrative action, has been to subject it to doctrines of natural justice by means of prerogative writs[3] (as they were formerly called), which will be described presently; at the present time, the marked tendency, which culminates in the case of *Franklin* v. *Minister of Town and Country Planning* (The Stevenage Case), [1948] A.C. 87, is to regard all discretionary executive action, authorized in wide terms by statute, as being purely administrative, and therefore exempt from any scrutiny by the courts.[4]

The combined result of these causes and tendencies is that at the present time, with regard to a very considerable area of delegated legislation, the doctrine of *ultra vires* is shut out on the threshold and of recent years very few attempts to invoke it have been successful.[5] It is

[1] *Point of Ayr Collieries, Ltd.* v. *Lloyd George*, [1943] 2 All E.R. 546; *Carltona, Ltd.* v. *Commissioners of Works*, [1943] 2 All E.R. 560.

[2] See *Report of the Committee on Ministers' Powers*, 71 ff.; D. M. Gordon, 'Administrative Tribunals and the Courts', 49 *L.Q.R.* 94, 419; W. A. Robson, *Justice and Administrative Law* (3rd ed.), ch. 1 *et passim*.

[3] See H. W. R. Wade, 'The Twilight of Natural Justice?', 47 *L.Q.R.* 103.

[4] See *Johnson & Co., Ltd.* v. *Minister of Health*, [1947] 2 All E.R. 395, especially the judgement of Lord Greene M.R., and *Nakkuda Ali* v. *Jayaratne*, *ubi sup*.

[5] When it has succeeded, it has generally been because certain statutory requirements have not been complied with—i.e. on purely procedural grounds; see *Commissioners of Customs and Excise* v. *Cure & Deeley, Ltd.*, [1962] 1 Q.B. 340, and *East Riding C.C.* v. *Park Estates (Bridlington), Ltd.*, [1957] A.C. 223. See also *Jones* v. *Farrell*, [1940] 3 All E.R. 608 (a decision of Bennett J.,

doubtful whether legislators, when conferring powers in the terms which are now commonly employed, realize the extent of the demission of their own theoretical authority. The doctrine of *ultra vires* has been for centuries a most salutary control, reasonably and intelligently exercised by our courts, over delegated powers. Today it is unquestionably in eclipse. There is a school of thought—to which, however, few lawyers belong—which regards it merely as 'judicial sabotage' of administrative policy. At present that kind of opinion seems to be having its way—whether for better or for worse the future must decide, presumably according to the democratic will of the people. If the will of the people desires government by decree—as it is, of course, entitled to do—the sure way to obtain it is by weakening, which means ultimately destroying, judicial safeguards against executive misuse of powers, which is not necessarily the result of any deliberate or improper usurpation but rather of genuine error or inadvertence, and oftener still of 'good intentions'.

By-laws

All by-laws made by subordinate authorities are subject to a system of checks. By statute, some require the approval of different Government Departments; thus by-laws made by local authorities for public health or 'good rule and government' are subject to supervision and alteration by the Minister of Housing and Local Government. Apart from this Ministerial scrutiny, by-laws have always been liable to review by the courts.[1] The judicial tests which they must satisfy are well established:[2] (1) They must be made, sanctioned, and published in the manner prescribed by the statute which

later disapproved by the Court of Appeal in *R.* v. *Comptroller-General of Patents, Ex p. Bayer Products, Ltd.*, [1941] 2 K.B. 306); *Fowler* v. *Duncan*, [1941] 2 All E.R. 577; *Harlow* v. *Minister of Transport*, [1951] 2 K.B. 98.

[1] The rule is very old. There are numerous cases in the Year Books concerning the by-laws of guilds and corporations: see Bacon or Rolle, *Abr. sub tit.* By-law. On the interpretation of by-laws generally, see Craies, *Statute Law* (3rd ed.), 267 ff., and Maxwell (11th ed.), 290 ff.

[2] Craies, *loc. cit.*

authorizes them; (2) they must not be repugnant to the laws of England;[1] (3) they must not be repugnant to the statute under which they are made; (4) they must not be vague or uncertain in their terms; (5) they must not be unreasonable. It is a settled rule of construction that the courts will interpret local by-laws benevolently and will not be astute to invalidate them on purely technical grounds.[2] Of the tests above-named, that of unreasonableness gives the courts the widest power of appraising the general expediency of a by-law; but the test is as variable and as difficult here as it is in all other branches of the law. In the leading case of *Kruse* v. *Johnson*, [1898] 2 Q.B. 91, it was held not unreasonable to give a policeman power to prevent street music of any kind within fifty yards of a dwelling-house, even without proof that the music was an annoyance to any person or persons. In *Da Prato* v. *Provost, &c., of Partick*, [1907] A.C. 153, it was held not unreasonable for a by-law to close all ice-cream shops at 10 p.m. In *Baird* v. *Corpn. of City of Glasgow*, [1936] A.C. 32, it was held not unreasonable for a Corporation, at its discretion, to exclude petrol stations from certain areas.[3] On the other hand, the following provisions in by-laws have been held unreasonable: not to keep swine within fifty feet of any dwelling-house;[4] to compel a person in charge of a vehicle selling a small quantity of coal to reweigh it at the request of the purchaser, or of anybody on behalf of the purchaser, or of an inspector of weights and measures, or of any constable;[5] to prohibit the sale in public places of newspapers, &c., devoted to tips and information about

[1] 'All [by-laws] which are contrary or repugnant to the laws or statutes of the realm are void and of no effect': *Chamberlain of London's Case* (1591), 5 Co. Rep. 63a. See *London, Midland & Scottish Ry.* v. *Greaver*, [1937] 1 K.B. 367; *Powell* v. *May*, [1946] K.B. 330.

[2] *Slattery* v. *Naylor* (1888), 13 App. Cas. 446, 543; *Kruse* v. *Johnson*, [1898] 2 Q.B. 91, 99; *Salt* v. *Scott Hall*, [1903] 2 K.B. 245, 248.

[3] See also *McQuade* v. *Barnes*, [1949] 1 All E.R. 154, *Reynolds* v. *John*, [1956] 1 Q.B. 650, and *Raymond* v. *Cook*, [1958] 1 W.L.R. 1098.

[4] *Heap* v. *Burnley Union* (1884), 12 Q.B.D. 617.

[5] *Alty* v. *Farrell*, [1896] 1 Q.B. 636.

horse-races.[1] It sometimes happens that a by-law which has been accepted as valid for a considerable period will eventually be declared unreasonable, and the same objection which is made to the irregular operation of case-law[2] becomes equally applicable to the operation of subordinate enactments. Thus in *Repton School Governors* v. *Repton R.D.C.*, [1918] 2 K.B. 133, the Court pronounced against a building by-law which had been long accepted without demur—viz. that every new building (including in that term *any addition to an existing building*) should have an open space of not less than 150 feet at the back.[3] The cases are not all easy to reconcile, but it is clear that the courts will uphold the regulations of local authorities so far as they can. It would appear that by-laws may be valid even when they interfere with, or take away, without compensation, existing rights of property;[4] and occasionally they are enforced in what seems to be a very high-handed manner.[5]

The doctrine of *ultra vires*, and the control of by-laws, are principles of wide and general application to delegated powers. In addition to these, and within a more technical sphere, the Court of Queen's Bench has certain specific procedures, known as prerogative orders, which will now be briefly described, for scrutinizing the conduct and the decrees of subordinate authorities. This is an ancient and a complex branch of the law—indeed, so complex that there is much to be said for reform in the nature of a more simple and uniform procedure. However, we must consider the law as it has grown historically, though in these pages it will not be possible to present more than a mere outline of the supervisory powers of the Queen's Bench. For a more exact and detailed description of them, the student should consult specialized works on the subject.[6]

[1] *Scott* v. *Pilliner*, [1904] 2 K.B. 855.

[2] *Ante*, p. 313.

[3] See also *Att.-Gen.* v. *Denby*, [1925] Ch. 596.

[4] *Slattery* v. *Naylor* (1888), 13 App. Cas. 446; *Att.-Gen.* v. *Hodgson*, [1922] 2 Ch. 429.

[5] See *L.C.C.* v. *Worley*, [1894] 2 Q.B. 826.

[6] Especially S. A. de Smith, *Judicial Review of Administrative Action*,

Mandamus

Mandamus is, in the words of Bowen L.J., 'a high prerogative writ,[1] invented for the purpose of supplying defects of justice. By Magna Charta the Crown is bound neither to deny justice to anybody, nor to delay anybody in obtaining justice. If, therefore, there is no other means of obtaining justice, the writ of mandamus is granted to enable justice to be done.'[2] When, therefore, any public authority or official is under an absolute (not discretionary) duty to perform a certain function, and, on demand duly made, refuses to perform it, any person who has a legitimate and sufficient interest in the performance of it may, provided that there is no other remedy equally convenient, beneficial, and effectual[3] open to him (e.g. by way of appeal), apply to the High Court for a mandamus to compel the performance of the duty. Disobedience amounts to contempt of court.[4] Before the establishment of local government as a national system in the nineteenth century, the writ was of very wide and miscellaneous range for compelling the performance of all manner of public duties,[5] but nowadays its scope has become more restricted and it is most commonly applied to inferior courts or tribunals, ordering them to 'hear and determine' a cause when they have refused to entertain it,[6] or to local and public utility authorities. It does not lie against the Crown, nor against any agent of the Crown acting as such, and this is a serious limitation on

which is the most authoritative work on the topic yet published. See also H. W. R. Wade, *Administrative Law*, and Griffith and Street, *Principles of Administrative Law*, 3rd ed., 1963.

[1] By the Administration of Justice Acts, 1933 and 1938, the writs now give place to Court Orders and the procedure is much simplified.

[2] *R.* v. *Commissioners of Inland Revenue, In re Nathan* (1884), 12 Q.B.D. 461, 478.

[3] *Per* Hill J., *In re Barlow* (1861), 30 L.J. (Q.B.) 271, approved *Reg.* v. *Leicester Guardians* [1899] 2 Q.B. 632, 639; *R.* v. *Dunsheath, Ex p. Meredith*, [1951] 1 K.B. 127.

[4] *R.* v. *Bristol and Exeter Ry. Co.* (1843), 4 Q.B. 162; *R.* v. *Income Tax Commissioners* (1888), 21 Q.B.D. 313. On the analogous remedy of *action for mandamus* in respect of so-called quasi-public duties, see G. E. Robinson, *op. cit.* 234 ff.

[5] See de Smith, *op. cit.* 264 ff., 430 ff.

[6] See, e.g., *R.* v. *Judge Dutton Briant*, [1957] 2 Q.B. 497.

its scope, which has not been altered by the Crown Proceedings Act, 1947. In exceptional circumstances it may lie against public authorities closely analogous to agents of the Crown.[1]

Certiorari

Certiorari is an order of the Court of Queen's Bench that a decision of an inferior jurisdiction, in which a defect is alleged, be transmitted to the Court for scrutiny. It is, like mandamus, of a prerogative character (formerly a writ), issued in the name of the sovereign on the motion of some interested or aggrieved party.[2] It is, in other words, an essentially disciplinary or supervisory process.

In the heyday of certiorari, as of mandamus, when this prerogative writ was employed to control the procedures of subordinate judicial and governmental authorities, little if any distinction was made between judicial and administrative functions;[3] but in modern times it is the accepted principle that this order is applicable only to *judicial* or *quasi-judicial* authorities. The distinctions between the judicial, the quasi-judicial, the legislative, and the administrative, have been the bugbear of our administrative law, and it is impossible to lay down any general test as to what is considered 'judicial' for the purposes of certiorari. It has been recently extended to inferior jurisdictions ranging from County Courts[4] to a Legal Aid Committee[5] and the Registrar of Building Societies.[6] On the other hand, it has been withheld from a Metropolitan Police Commissioner's withdrawal of a taxi-driver's licence[7] and from a Controller of Textiles'

[1] See, e.g., *R.* v. *Minister of Health, Ex p. Aldridge*, [1925] 2 K.B. 363; *Board of Education* v. *Rice*, [1911] A.C. 179.

[2] As to *locus standi* in the prerogative orders, see de Smith, *op. cit.* 305 ff.; *Law and Orders* (2nd ed.), 261 ff.

[3] See Wade, *op. cit.* 102 ff.; de Smith, *op. cit.* 281 ff.

[4] *R.* v. *Worthington-Evans, Ex p. Madan*, [1959] 2 Q.B. 145; *R.* v. *Hurst, Ex p. Smith*, [1960] 2 Q.B. 133.

[5] *R.* v. *Manchester Legal Aid Committee, Ex p. Brand*, [1952] 2 Q.B. 413.

[6] *R.* v. *Registrar of Building Societies, Ex p. a Building Society*, [1960] 1 W.L.R. 669.

[7] *R.* v. *Metropolitan Police Commissioner, Ex p. Parker*, [1953] 1 W.L.R. 1150.

cancellation of a trading licence.[1] It is indeed difficult to find here any consistent principle.

Another doctrine, of modern origin, which held the field for a number of years, was that certiorari was concerned solely with *jurisdiction*,[2] and was thus little more than a special procedure for *ultra vires*. This notion was based on a misunderstanding or misreading of old authorities, and was finally given its quietus in *R.* v. *Northumberland Compensation Appeal Tribunal*, *Ex p. Shaw*, [1951] 1 K.B. 711 and [1952] 1 K.B. 338,[3] which held that certiorari would also lie for *error on the face of the record*. The error must, of course, be one of law, not merely of fact.[4] What amounts to error of law, and what legitimately constitutes the record, have been the subject of more case-law than can be here discussed in detail.[5]

The decision in the *Northumberland Case* opened up new possibilities in certiorari when there was a 'speaking order'—i.e. a record of judgement or decision giving reasons which could, if necessary, be assailed for error of law. The absurdity resulted that if the inferior authority omitted, or did not choose, to place its reasons on record—which in most cases it was not obliged to do—

[1] *Nakkuda Ali* v. *Jayaratne*, [1951] A.C. 66.

[2] This limitation appears as late as 1924, in the oft-quoted definition of Atkin L.J. in *R.* v. *Electricity Commissioners*, [1924] 1 K.B. 171, 205 (prohibition).

[3] See *ante*, p. 245.

[4] *R.* v. *Minister of Fuel and Power, Ex p. Warwickshire C.C.*, [1957] 1 W.L.R. 861.

[5] For recent examples, the reader is referred to *R.* v. *Medical Appeal Tribunal, Ex p. Burpitt*, [1957] 2 Q.B. 584; *R.* v. *Medical Appeal Tribunal, Ex p. Gilmore*, [1957] 1 Q.B. 575; *Baldwin & Francis Ltd.* v. *Patent Appeal Tribunal*, [1959] A.C. 663; *R.* v. *Agricultural Land Tribunal, Ex p. Bracey*, [1960] 1 W.L.R. 911. As to the contents of the record, see *R.* v. *Medical Appeal Tribunal, Ex p. Gilmore, ubi sup.*; *R.* v. *Medical Appeal Tribunal, Ex p. Hubble*, [1959] 2 Q.B. 408; *R.* v. *Patent Appeal Tribunal, Ex p. Swift & Co., Ltd.*, [1962] 2 Q.B. 647. It has been held in *R.* v. *Chertsey JJ., Ex p. Franks*, [1961] 2 Q.B. 152, that the 'record 'may be the *oral* pronouncement of judgement in court, which would seem to be a novel kind of record without a 'face'; see 'R. E. M.', 77 *L. Q. R.* 157, and D. M. Gordon, *ibid.* 322.

—it did not lay itself open to certiorari. This situation was merely an historical survival. We shall see, however, that the anomaly was materially altered by the Tribunals and Inquiries Act, 1958.

The order, then, will go to a judicial or quasi-judicial authority on grounds of excess of jurisdiction (including failure to observe prescribed statutory requirements of procedure), of manifest error of law, and, we must add, of defect of natural justice.[1] But certiorari is essentially a discretionary remedy, and even when there is a technical ground for it, it may be refused if there is no adequate reason for it—as, e.g., that the complaint is trivial or that no injustice has been done.[2]

It is important to remember that certiorari is not an *appeal*. Where a form of appeal is provided by statute from a subordinate decision, certiorari is not applicable. If the complaint is made out, on any of the grounds already indicated, the Queen's Bench may quash the subordinate order, but it does not substitute a correct decision for an incorrect one, though it may combine its order with a mandamus to hear and determine afresh, or with a prohibition discontinuing the proceedings. This limitation on the effect of certiorari is one of several procedural disadvantages which make it, in many circumstances, an inconvenient remedy. The chief of these is that it must be brought within six months from the cause of complaint, and that it provides no opportunity for discovery of documents by means of interlocutory proceedings. The evidence before the Court is by affidavit, not usually susceptible of amplification or cross-examination, and the prerogative form of the order does not permit the plaintiff to include in his suit a demand for any alternative remedy, such as damages. The form of action, governed by the Rules of the Supreme Court,

[1] *R.* v. *Deputy Insurance Injuries Commissioner, Ex p. Jones,* [1962] 2 Q.B. 677.

[2] *R.* v. *Registrar of Building Societies, ubi sup.*; *Ex p. Fry,* [1954] 1 W.L.R. 730.

adds a stage to litigation and costs, since a preliminary application, with statement of reasons, must be made for leave to move. We shall see that for these and similar reasons there is a marked tendency at present for the declaratory judgement to displace certiorari.[1]

Several substantial improvements have been introduced by the Tribunals and Inquiries Act, 1958. First, the Act provides that on the demand of an interested party, the tribunal or other authority shall supply the reasons for its decision—in other words, shall furnish a 'speaking order'. This does much to modify the incongruity, mentioned above, which resulted from the *Northumberland Compensation Case*. Second, the Act provides for an appeal to the High Court from a number of tribunals (specified in a Schedule) which before the Act were not subject to appeal; and, as we have seen, where such an alternative remedy exists, certiorari is not usually applicable. Third, the Act puts an end to a form of legislation which previously was fairly common, namely, the specific exclusion of certiorari as a remedy for an aggrieved party. Apart from this definite prohibition of exclusionary clauses, it is now laid down[2] that the statutory form that the decision of a subordinate authority shall be 'final', or 'not subject to any legal proceedings whatever', does not exclude, in the absence of express provision, the supervisory operation of certiorari. To this general rule, however, there is at least one important exception. Under the Acquisition of Land (Authorization Procedure) Act, 1946, any challenge to a compulsory purchase order must be made within six weeks, and cannot be questioned after that comparatively brief period. The House of Lords held by a majority in *Smith* v. *East Elloe R.D.C.*, [1956] A.C. 736, that there was no escape from this exclusionary provision, not even on the ground of bad faith.[3]

[1] See *post*, pp. 579 ff.

[2] *R.* v. *Medical Appeal Tribunal, Ex p. Gilmore, ubi sup.* The decision emphasizes the essentially *disciplinary* nature of certiorari.

[3] The action was for a declaration, injunction, and damages, but doubtless

Prohibition

Prohibition is also a prerogative order, of ancient lineage, which differs from certiorari only in the fact that it can be brought at an earlier stage of the proceedings complained of: it is preventive rather than remedial. 'If the proceedings establish that the body complained of is exceeding its jurisdiction by entertaining matters which would result in its final decision being subject to being brought up and quashed on certiorari, . . . prohibition will lie to restrain it from so exceeding its jurisdiction.'[1] Though strictly the Order can issue only to an inferior 'court', 'as statutory bodies were brought into existence exercising legal jurisdiction, so the issue of the writ came to be extended to such bodies'. Thus it has gone to Tithe Commissioners, Commissioners of Woods and Forests, Commissioners of Taxes, the Comptroller-General of Patents, Light Railway Commissioners, the Board of Education, the London County Council, &c.[2] It may issue to Ministers,[3] but, like certiorari, it is not available if the applicant has another, prescribed form of appeal. Whether it lies for error on the face of the record is a disputed question, but in view of the anticipatory nature of the order, it is not likely to arise very often.[4] The Queen's Bench has always been tenacious of this writ as being in the nature of a salutary discipline exercised over inferior courts of limited jurisdiction. 'My view', said Brett L.J.,[5]

> 'of the power of probhibition at the present day is that the Court should not be chary of exercising it, and that wherever the Legislature entrusts to any body of persons other than to the superior Courts the power of imposing an obligation upon individuals, the Courts ought to exercise as widely as they can the power of controlling those bodies of persons, if those persons

the same principle would apply to certiorari. Cf. *Woollett* v. *Minister of Agriculture and Fisheries*, [1955] 1 Q.B. 103.

[1] *Per* Atkin L.J., *R.* v. *Electricity Commissioners*, [1924] 1 K.B. 171, 206.

[2] *R.* v. *Electricity Commissioners*, *ubi sup.*; and cases cited by Bankes L.J., *ibid.*, at p. 193.

[3] See *R.* v. *Minister of Health*, *Ex p. Villiers*, [1936] 2 K.B. 29.

[4] See de Smith, *op. cit.* 292.

[5] *R.* v. *Local Government Board* (1882), 10 Q.B.D. 309, 321.

admittedly attempt to exercise powers beyond the powers given to them by Act of Parliament.'

Even when the acts or regulations of a statutory body are subject to the approval of Parliament, the High Court may, even before Parliament has pronounced upon such acts or regulations, grant a writ of prohibition to restrain the doing of such things as it deems to be in excess of statutory authority.[1]

The essential difference between certiorari and prohibition is that the one is *ex post facto*—to undo what has been done—while the other is anticipatory, to prevent the doing of that which, once accomplished, may be difficult to revoke. The two remedies may be combined, so as to quash the *fait accompli* and prevent any futher action being taken on it.

Mandamus, certiorari, and prohibition are the special prerogative procedures which have been evolved in the course of our legal history for the supervision of subordinate jurisdiction. But they are not the only means of recourse to judicial protection. The general law of the land provides other safeguards for the citizen aggrieved by administrative action.

It is a fundamental principle of our constitutional law that, with few exceptions, an individual officer, if he commits a legal wrong in the course of his executive functions, cannot shelter behind the orders of his superiors. If, therefore, he commits a tort, he is liable to an action for damages for trespass, false imprisonment, negligence, fraud, or any other actionable wrong. Such actions for damages against individuals are not very common in administrative law, principally because the subordinate, unlike his superior, is not worth powder and shot. Sometimes, however, it may happen that while the superior is immune, the subordinate remains personally liable.[2]

[1] *R.* v. *Electricity Commissioners, ubi sup.*

[2] See *Smith* v. *East Elloe R.D.C.*, [1956] A.C. 736.

Injunction

Injunction[1] is an equitable remedy, available, since the Judicature Acts, in all superior courts, and enforceable on breach as a contempt of court. It may be, like prohibition, anticipatory—to nip in the bud a contemplated or threatened procedure—or retrospective—to put an end to an existing injurious or illegal state of things. It is in this sense usually negative in its effect, but more rarely it may be mandatory—to undo, even at expense, that which has been improperly done. The injunction may be either interim or perpetual. It is not as freely employed in England against administrative authorities as in some other countries, e.g. the United States, one powerful reason for this being that it is not, and never has been, available against the Crown. Some recent attempts to evade this rule by enjoining Ministers in their personal capacities have conspicuously failed.[2] Injunction is, however, important in the administrative sphere when it takes the form of a 'relator action', which involves an element of 'public interest'. In this process the nominal plaintiff is the Attorney-General, as representing a public, and not merely a private, interest, and he moves 'on the relation' of some aggrieved individual or corporation either to inhibit administrative action, or, in some cases, to assist it when other legal remedies are not available,[3] or are inadequate to meet a particular mischief.[4] The form of action commonly concerns local authorities, and is a not inconsiderable check on the legality of their procedures. The Attorney-General has discretion as to whether or not he will issue his fiat and lend his name to the action,[5] and conversely the court will not be overawed by the fact that the remedy is sought

[1] See de Smith, *op. cit.* 323 ff.

[2] *Harper* v. *Home Secretary*, [1955] Ch. 238; *Merricks* v. *Heathcoat-Amory*, [1955] Ch. 567. See *Law and Orders*, 168 ff.

[3] *Att.-Gen.* v. *Bastow*, [1957] 1 Q.B. 514; *Att.-Gen.* v. *Smith*, [1958] 2 Q.B. 173.

[4] *Att.-Gen.* v. *Harris*, [1961] 1 Q.B. 74.

[5] When a right, not of a charitable nature, is vested in a particular body of persons, e.g. the inhabitants of a parish, the Attorney-General may be a competent but is not a necessary party to a representative action: *Wyld* v. *Silver*, [1963] 1 Q.B. 169.

in the public interest by a Law Officer of the Crown—for injunction is always a discretionary remedy[1]—but it will be slow to disregard that aspect of the matter.[2]

Apart from relator actions, there is, of course, nothing to prevent the individual citizen from moving on his own account for an injunction against a subordinate authority to protect a *private* interest. The most frequent occasion of this form of action is when the individual claims that he has suffered special damage from a public nuisance created by a local authority; and the latter, in rare cases, may be joined as a defendant with others, not of a public character, who are alleged to have caused the nuisance.[3]

Declaration

The history of the *declaratory judgement*, or *declaration*, is somewhat obscure, but it is almost certainly of equitable origin. It was originally available in Chancery only when the plaintiff sought, in addition to the declaration, some consequential relief, but since 1883[4] this has been no longer necessary, though additional relief, e.g. injunction, can, and often does, accompany the declaration.

The action is peculiar in form, since it is not (unless accompanied by injunction) enforceable by execution, like most other judgements. It merely *declares* the rights and liabilities of the parties, sometimes in an existing state of facts, and sometimes (especially under Order 54a, r. 1) even *in futuro*. But the right claimed must not be purely hypothetical; it must have an actual basis in fact, though not necessarily a cause of action.[5] The fact that the judgement lacks, in many cases, compulsive

[1] See, e.g., *Att.-Gen.* v. *Colchester Corporation*, [1955] 2 Q.B. 207.

[2] *Att.-Gen.* v. *Harris, ubi sup.*

[3] *Pride of Derby etc. Angling Association, Ltd.* v. *British Celanese Ltd.*, [1953] Ch. 149.

[4] R.S.C. Order 25, r. 5. This was supplemented by Order 54a, r. 1, which gives power to any person interested in a 'deed, will or other instrument' (the meaning of 'other instrument' has been the subject of some doubt) to apply to the Court for a declaratory interpretation. A few statutory provisions, e.g. Administration of Justice (Miscellaneous Provisions) Act, 1933, s. 3, specially authorize the same recourse: see *In re Hodge's Policy*, [1958] Ch. 239 (liability for death duties).

[5] *Guaranty Trust Co.* v. *Hannay*, [1915] 2 K.B. 536.

force does not detract from its authority. It will be respected by all responsible parties, and even if it is not, any action brought in disregard of it will have short shrift as being vexatious. There does not seem to be any recorded instance of such defiance.

Declaration is of extremely wide scope and is surrounded by a vast and increasing amount of case-law. It has been particularly valuable in restraining *ultra vires* or prejudicial acts of local authorities, and in numerous other connexions. These are admirably set forth by Professor de Smith,[1] and here I cannot do better than follow, or attempt to summarize, his classification.

Where a *private* complaint is made (as we have seen, when a public interest is concerned, the proper procedure is a relator action), the action may be used to declare *ultra vires* a purported statutory order made by a local authority.[2] A party with sufficient *locus standi* may also take out an originating summons under the 'interpretative' Order 54a, r. 1A, to determine his rights under a subordinate decision.[3] A very large number of actions have been brought to challenge administrative acts, orders, or decisions. Many of them have been at the suit of ratepayers, or in defence of rights over land. Decisions of non-statutory[4] and even statutory[5] tribunals are subject to declaration, whether or not (*semble*) other remedies are available. A question of status, e.g. nationality,[6] may be established by declaration; and akin to status is the right of a party to remain in his employment when he has been wrongfully dismissed by a public

[1] *Op. cit.* 376 ff. The declaratory action has been used very freely in the United States, and is exhaustively examined by Professor E. Borchard's *Declaratory Judgments* (1934). A valuable and more recent study of the process in English jurisdiction is that of I. Zamir, *The Declaratory Judgement* (1962).

[2] *Brownsea Haven Properties* v. *Poole Corporation*, [1958] Ch. 574.

[3] *Taylor* v. *National Assistance Board*, [1958] A.C. 532.

[4] *Lee* v. *Showmen's Guild*, [1952] 2 Q.B. 329; *Davis* v. *Carew-Pole*, [1956] 1 W.L.R. 833.

[5] *Barnard* v. *National Dock Labour Board*, [1953] 2 Q.B. 18.

[6] *Att.-Gen.* v. *Prince Ernest Augustus of Hanover*, [1957] A.C. 436.

authority[1] or by the improper decision of a tribunal.[2] Similarly, traders who have been wrongfully refused permission or licences by public authorities to pursue their calling have been granted declarations to vindicate their rights.

Just as private individuals, and especially trustees, may take out originating summonses to ascertain their rights and duties, so may public authorities; and, as Professor de Smith observes, it is surprising that they do so comparatively seldom, instead of placing the onus on aggrieved citizens. When they do seek declaratory judgements, it is generally because they are at issue, in varying circumstances under our complicated legislation, with other local authorities.[3]

Finally, by statute,[4] declaration may be used as a means of testing the validity of membership of a local authority or of the House of Commons.

From this brief summary it may be seen that the declaratory judgement is of extremely wide range. Its advantages as a form of procedure over the prerogative orders, and especially certiorari, are many and striking. Thus certiorari must be brought within six months from the cause of complaint, and lies only to the Queen's Bench. A declaration, on the other hand, may be sought at any time within the ordinary six years of limitation of actions, and this is a particularly valuable characteristic when the plaintiff did not know, and could not have discovered, within the time limit of certiorari, the irregularity of which he complains.[5] The action for declaration allows discovery of documents and oral evidence about them, which, as we have seen, are not available in certiorari. The latter can relate only to statutory bodies,

[1] *Cooper* v. *Wilson* [1937] 2 K.B. 309.

[2] *Vine* v. *National Dock Labour Board*, [1957] A.C. 488.

[3] See de Smith, *op. cit.* 385.

[4] Local Government Act, 1933, and House of Commons Disqualification Act, 1957.

[5] *Barnard* v. *National Dock Labour Board*, [1953] 2 Q.B. 18. Cf. *Punton* v. *Ministry of Pensions and National Insurance*, [1963] 1 W.L.R. 186.

whereas declaration can apply also to non-statutory authorities, including domestic tribunals,[1] on many grounds, including defect of natural justice.[2] Certiorari, as we have seen, quashes a subordinate decision and puts nothing in its place; declaration is far more general in effect, and can be combined with other forms of relief, such as damages, injunction, or restoration of status. Though originating summonses for declaration under Order 54a, r. 1, are usually brought in the Chancery Division, actions for a declaration under Order 25, r. 5, may be initiated in any Division of the High Court, including Assizes.

Perhaps the most important advantages over the prerogative orders are (1) that declaration is available against both judicial and administrative acts, whereas certiorari, to its confusion, is limited to 'judicial' and 'quasi-judicial' decisions and to patent errors of law in their 'speaking' form; and (2) that under the Crown Proceedings Act, 1947, actions for declaration lie against the Crown, in the form either of an 'authorized' Government Department, or the Attorney-General, though in this case the judgement cannot grant a supplementary remedy, such as injunction, but is limited to a declaration of rights.

Questions have arisen about the availability of the declaration when another remedy, such as a prerogative order, might be thought more appropriate. The tendency of recent decisions is not to insist on this aspect but to encourage the declaratory action. In *Pyx Granite Co. Ltd.* v. *Ministry of Housing and Local Government*, [1960] A.C. 260, Lord Goddard said, apparently with the concurrence of his colleagues, that declaration and certiorari were not mutually exclusive.[3] Nor is a plaintiff

[1] *Lee* v. *Showmen's Guild*, [1952] 2 Q.B. 329; *Baker* v. *Jones*, [1954] 1 W.L.R. 1005.

[2] *Davis* v. *Carew-Pole*, [1956] 1 W.L.R. 833; *Hoggard* v. *Worsbrough U.D.C.*, [1962] 2 Q.B. 93; but see *Byrne* v. *Kinematograph Renters Society*, [1958] 1 W.L.R. 762.

[3] Cf. *Kanda* v. *Government of Malaya*, [1962] A.C. 322, 338.

excluded from a declaration because he has not availed himself (being out of time) of a statutory right of appeal.[1] Nor, again, is the Court debarred from making a declaration by a 'finality clause', to the effect that the decision of a Minister or similar authority 'shall be final'.[2] This, as in certiorari,[3] is somewhat ingeniously interpreted as meaning that the decision shall not be subject to any statutory form of *appeal*. The declaratory judgement is not an appeal, but a judicial pronouncement of rights. It seems, too, that even when certiorari might be thought to be the appropriate remedy, if counsel does not so argue but prefers a declaration, the Court will not be astute to insist on the point of procedure.[4] It will even encourage resort to declaration by an amendment of pleadings.[5]

Elastic and comprehensive though this remedy is, it remains always discretionary, both as to the plaintiff's cause of complaint and as to the nature of the relief granted. The Court may sometimes consider damages a sufficient remedy without a general declaration of status,[6] but on the other hand it may hold that a question of status (e.g. a right to continue in a certain employment) is the primary consideration.[7] Even when it does not consider it necessary to supplement its judgement with an injunction, it may grant 'liberty to apply' for it if that should prove necessary. And, as we have noted,

[1] *Francis* v. *Yiewsley and West Drayton U.D.C.*, [1958] 1 Q.B. 478.

[2] *Pyx Granite Case, ubi sup.* But where appeal is committed by statute to a specific jurisdiction, e.g. that of a Minister, declaration will not intervene; *Healey* v. *Minister of Health*, [1955] 1 Q.B. 221. In *Punton* v. *Ministry of Pensions and National Insurance*, [1963] 1 W.L.R. 186, where the decision of the Insurance Commissioner, as to eligibility for unemployment benefit, was expressed to be 'final', the Court allowed an amendment of pleadings to indicate that the Commissioner's findings of fact were not challenged, but that a declaration was sought, by originating summons, *solely as to his interpretation of a point of law.*

[3] *R.* v. *Medical Appeal Tribunal, Ex p. Gilmore, ante*, p. 575.

[4] *Hoggard* v. *Worsbrough U.D.C.*, [1962] 2 Q.B. 93 (an action before a single Judge at Assizes).

[5] *Punton's Case, ubi sup.*

[6] *Barber* v. *Manchester Regional Hospitals Board*, [1958] 1 W.L.R. 181.

[7] *Vine* v. *National Dock Labour Board*, [1957] A.C. 488, where the House of Lords differed from the Court of Appeal on this point.

declaration will not be granted on a mere *spes* or suppositious cause, nor on a trivial one, nor when no substantial injustice justifies it.

There is no doubt, however, that in recent years the courts have, in appropriate cases, leaned more and more towards the declaratory judgement for protection against judicial or administrative irregularities. Lord Denning, extra-judicially,[1] has compared the prerogative orders to the 'pick and shovel' of a bygone age, and declarations and injunctions to 'new and up-to-date machinery'. Recent tendencies seem to justify his suggestion, and it may well be that in future the prerogative orders will dwindle almost into insignificance—as they have done in the United States—under the shadow of this expanding and liberal form of action. Whether this will happen through the intervention of Parliament, or through the interpretative jurisdiction of the courts, it would be unsafe at present to predict.

2. Practical operation of these checks

Such are the principal constitutional and judicial checks upon the operation of delegated powers.[2] Parliament and the courts exercise a general control; but, as we have seen, Parliament shows an increasing readiness to surrender large portions of its control not only over the mandate itself but over the actual applications of the mandate. By a curious reversal of orthodox constitutional principles, Acts of Parliament are sometimes made to depend for their validity in whole or in part on the pleasure of subordinate authorities. To that extent, though they are the work of the sovereign assembly, yet they are provisional only, and therefore not really sovereign at all. It is of no great moment, perhaps, though it is often an inconvenience, that the operation of a Parliamentary enactment should be suspended, as it often is, until some subordinate Order, usually an Order in

Executive control over Parliamentary legislation

[1] *Freedom under the Law*, 126.

[2] For other (rare) judicial means of enforcing the liability of public authorities, such as *indictment* and *quo warranto*, see G. E. Robinson, *op. cit.*, ch. vi.

Council, calls it into being. A more innovating practice is that of giving subordinate authorities, again usually the Privy Council, the power of actually repealing existing statutes—the practice, in other words, of making statutes 'determinable upon condition subsequent'.[1] No less important is the delegated power of amending statutes, now becoming frequent. Here I cannot do better than quote some of the examples given by Sir Cecil Carr:[2]

'The Companies Act of 1908 (s. 118) contained certain tables and forms in schedules, but it allowed the Board of Trade to vary those tables and add to those forms. A schedule to the Metropolitan Police Act of 1839 contained a table of fees for taking out a summons or a warrant and so on. A later Act in 1897 provided that this table might be altered by the Home Office (60 & 61 Vict. c. 26, s. 2 (2)). An Act of 1799 specified the rates of brokerage to be charged by Dublin stockbrokers on dealings in Government securities. In 1918 Parliament allowed the Lord Lieutenant to approve rules fixed by the Dublin Stock Exchange in substitution for those in the 1799 Act.[3] The Weights and Measures Act of 1878 contained a table of metric equivalents. A later Act in 1897 sanctioned the varying of the table by Order in Council.[4] In 1882 it occurred to Parliament to protect ancient monuments such as Stonehenge and other similar relics of the past. For this purpose a number of Druid circles, earth-works, chapels, crosses, &c., were scheduled as "ancient monuments". Parliament at the same time permitted the Crown in Council to add other monuments to the original schedule.'[5]

These are amendments only in matters of detail; but a very much larger power, which is really a power of general legislation, of 'adapting' existing statutes to new

[1] e.g. Administration of Justice Act, 1920, ss. 2 (3) and 4 (2). See *Willcock* v. *Muckle*, [1951] 2 K.B. 844.

[2] *Op. cit.* 8.

[3] Stockbrokers (Ireland) Act, 1918, s. 1 (1).

[4] Weights and Measures (Metric System) Act, 1897, s. 2 (2).

[5] Ancient Monuments Protection Act, 1882, s. 10; Ancient Monuments Consolidation and Amendment Act, 1913, ss. 14 (4) and 24, and Sch. 2.

needs which have arisen or are likely to arise, is sometimes committed to the delegates of Parliament. Take, for example, the following provision:

'His Majesty may, by Order in Council, apply, with the necessary modifications and adaptations, in relation to the Air Council, and President of the Air Council, and the Air Force, and the officers and men thereof, and Air Force property and institutions, any of the enactments relating to the Army Council, the Secretary of State for the War Department, the Army, or the officers and soldiers thereof (including enactments conferring any powers, rights, exemptions or abatement from taxation or immunities or imposing any duties or disabilities on such officers or soldiers), or to military property or institutions, and every such Order in Council shall be laid before both Houses of Parliament.'[1]

Under this section,[2] His Majesty in Council (being here, as we have seen, the *alter ego* of the War Office) 'adapted' the Territorial and Reserve Forces Act, 1907, in such a way as to create and govern an Auxiliary Air Force, enacting for this purpose what is in all essentials no less a statute than the principal Act 'adapted'.[3]

Ousting the jurisdiction of the courts

We have already seen that the safeguard of *ultra vires* has been greatly abridged by certain forms, increasingly frequent, of delegated powers. The jurisdiction of the courts is also ousted by a not uncommon form of statutory provision that Instruments made under a particular Act 'shall have the same effect as if enacted in this Act'.[4] The House of Lords has held that the effect of this formula, provided that any specified formalities have been complied with, is to give the sub-legislation in

[1] Air Force (Constitution) Act, 1917, s. 13.

[2] As amended by the Territorial Army and Militia Act, 1921, s. 1.

[3] Auxiliary Air Force Order, 1924 (S.R. & O., 1924, No. 1212). Cf. the Air Force Reserve Order, 1924 (S.R. & O., 1924, No. 1213), and the Reserve Forces Act, 1882.

[4] e.g. National Insurance Act, 1911, s. 65; Restoration of Order in Ireland Act, 1920, s. 1 (4); Fertilizers and Feeding Stuffs Act, 1926, s. 23 (1); Sale of Food (Weights and Measures) Act, 1926, s. 9 (1). In some cases it is added that 'the validity of such order [Order in Council] shall not be questioned in any legal proceedings whatever': see, e.g., Extradition Act, 1870, s. 5. See *Report of the Committee on Ministers' Powers*, 40.

question the same force as legislation proper.[1] 'I have asked myself in vain', said Lord Herschell L.C.,[2]

'for any explanation of the meaning of those words[3] or any suggestion as to the effect to be given to them if, notwithstanding that provision, the rules are open to review and consideration by the Courts. The effect of an enactment is that it binds all subjects who are affected by it. They are bound to conform themselves to the provisions of the law so made. The effect of a statutory rule is precisely the same, that every person must conform himself to its provisions, and if in each case a penalty be imposed, any person who does not comply with the provisions whether of the enactment or of the rule becomes equally subject to the penalty.'

This interpretation was based on what appears to have been an historical misunderstanding,[4] but it was not until 1931 that a salutary limitation was placed upon the wide principle laid down in this case; the decision of the House of Lords in *Minister of Health* v. *R.*, *Ex p. Yaffé*, [1931] A.C. 494, is commonly interpreted[5] to mean that if an Order made by a Minister under an Act conflicts with the Act itself, it is void for repugnancy.[6]

[1] *Institute of Patent Agents* v. *Lockwood*, [1894] A.C. 347.

[2] *Ibid.*, at p. 359.

[3] 'Of the same effect as if they were contained in this Act': Patents, Designs, and Trade Marks Act, 1883, s. 101 (3).

[4] Sir William Graham Harrison, *Notes on Delegated Legislation*; and see *Law and Orders* (2nd ed.), 295 ff.

[5] e.g. by the Committee on Ministers' Powers: *Report*, 40.

[6] The position created by this case is an illustration of the curiously oblique manner in which our system of precedents sometimes works. There was acute difference of opinion in the various courts which considered the case. All three members of the Divisional Court arrived at the same conclusion for entirely different reasons. The Court of Appeal laid down the general principle that a Ministerial Order was invalid if inconsistent with the Act itself, and therefore, holding the Order in question not to be concerned with an 'improvement scheme' within the meaning of the Act, it decided against its validity. The House of Lords, on the other hand (Lord Russell of Killowen dissenting), while accepting the same general principle as the Court of Appeal, held the Order to be consistent with an improvement scheme, and therefore valid. The quaint result is that the doctrine which is usually ascribed to *Yaffé's Case* is to be found in a decision of the Court of Appeal which the House of Lords reversed! The position is by no means free from doubt, for in such a tangle of authority it is difficult to say what is *ratio decidendi* and what is *obiter dictum* (see *ante*, pp. 291 ff.). See further, *In re Bowman*, [1932] 2 K.B. 621, and *Miller* v. *Boothman*, [1944] K.B. 337.

Even so, it is difficult to agree with the conclusion of the Committee on Ministers' Powers that no ground is left for criticizing this form of clause, which is more than delegation, since it makes the executive not merely a deputy but a plenipotentiary. It has been used frequently in the past, and survives in a number of statutes, but it now seems, fortunately, to have fallen into disuse.[1] There can be little doubt that it showed a tendency not only to invest the executive with judicial powers, but to oust the control of the regular courts and to make the executive judge in its own cause.[2]

The tendency, however, goes farther than this. Modern statutes abound in examples of what the Committee on Ministers' Powers called[3] 'exceptional' types of delegated legislative powers. These the Committee classified as follows:

'(i) Instances of powers to legislate on matters of principle, and even to impose taxation;

(ii) Instances of powers to amend Acts of Parliament, either the Act by which the powers are delegated, or other Acts;

(iii) Instances of powers conferring so wide a discretion on a Minister, that it is almost impossible to know what limit Parliament did intend to impose;

(iv) Instances where Parliament, without formally abandoning its normal practice of limiting delegated powers, has in effect done so by forbidding control by the Courts.'

[1] Examples may be found in the Superannuation Acts, 1834 and 1859, which give the Treasury final decision of the amount of pension payable to a civil servant: see *Yorke* v. *R.*, [1915] 1 K.B. 852; Public Health Act, 1875, s. 268; Small Holdings Act, 1908, s. 39 (3); and particularly the Factories Act, 1937, and its predecessors (see *Law and Orders*, 456 ff.).

[2] See, on the whole subject, *Report of the Committee on Ministers' Powers*, Section III. One of the most remarkable examples of executive-judicial powers is the 'final and conclusive' disciplinary powers which the Minister of Health can exercise over doctors and dentists under the National Health Service Act, 1946, and its predecessors in National Insurance.

[3] *Report*, 31 ff., *q.v.* for the chief instances.

Some of the forms which these 'exceptional' types of sub-legislation have taken have been much criticized—in particular, the so-called 'Henry VIII Clause', which is found in eight modern Acts, and which gave the Minister power, during a specified period, to modify the provisions of the main Act 'so far as may appear to him necessary for the purpose of bringing the Act into operation'. This now seems, fortunately, to have been abandoned. Similar to it, and equally objectionable, is the power sometimes given to the Minister to 'remove difficulties' in bringing the Act into operation.[1] Perhaps the most arbitrary and unnecessary expedient of all is one which provides that the mere fact that a Minister has confirmed an Order shall be 'conclusive evidence' that he has complied with all the requirements of the Act.[2]

These anomalies result from allowing Departmental procedure, not subject to proper safeguards of appeal, to grow up independently of the ordinary legal procedure which has developed by ages of practice and experience. *Local Government Board* v. *Arlidge*, [1915] A.C. 120, is still the governing precedent for the principle that a statutory quasi-judicial authority is 'not bound to follow the procedure of a Court of Justice'. So far as mere *procedure* is concerned, the *dictum* is unobjectionable, for it would be both impracticable and undesirable to impose the Rules of the Supreme Court on all subordinate jurisdictions. The more substantial question, however, is whether such jurisdictions should not be bound by the *principles* of a Court of Justice (including natural justice).

Spirit of Crown litigation

It must also be added, regretfully but in candour, that an unfortunate spirit has often been shown in Crown litigation, and that in many of these matters, now so

[1] See strong observations hereon by Lord Hewart C.J. in *R.* v. *Minister of Health, Ex p. Wortley R.D.C.*, [1927] 2 K.B. 229, 236. A provision (cl. 120) of this kind in the Local Government Bill of 1929 was the occasion of a spirited debate in the House of Commons.

[2] Of this provision the Committee on Ministers' Powers said that 'we doubt whether it is ever justified'. See *Ex p. Ringer* (1909), 25 T.L.R. 718.

numerous through the extension of delegated powers, the representatives of the Government show a certain readiness to avail themselves of all technical, and sometimes unmeritorious, expedients in order to resist substantially just claims. In this matter we are much worse off than our French neighbours, who, in the remarkable jurisprudence of the Conseil d'État, possess not only a body of enlightened and consistent principles, but a stout defence against bureaucratic oppression. The position, however, has been much improved by the passing of the Crown Proceedings Act, 1947, which, besides removing many ancient anomalies in procedure, provides new remedies in tort against the Crown and in its general purport aims at placing litigation between subject and Crown on the same basis (with necessary exceptions) as between subject and subject. This was a reform advocated in all responsible quarters for many years, and long overdue. Many problems, however, still remain in the interpretation and functioning of this important Act.[1]

The Donoughmore Committee

In 1929, as the result of growing public uneasiness and criticism, a strong and representative Committee was appointed by the Lord Chancellor to inquire into the whole question of Ministers' Powers in relation to the constitution. The Committee reported in 1932. For the Committee's detailed recommendations, the reader is referred to its Report, to which frequent allusion has already been made in the foregoing pages, and which is a most valuable constitutional document. Here it need only be said that the Committee, while finding no cause for serious alarm, and while scouting the necessity for any special administrative jurisdiction, concurred in nearly all the criticisms which had been made of anomalies both in delegated legislative powers and in the quasi-judicial functions associated with them. The Committee made a number of substantive recommendations of a perfectly practicable nature—e.g. for the better

[1] See Glanville Williams, *Crown Proceedings*; and cf. R. M. Bell, *Crown Proceedings*.

defining and limitation of Departmental powers, for the abandonment, save in exceptional circumstances, of the more arbitrary forms of delegated powers, for a more effective scrutiny by Parliament through Committees, for simplification of the rules concerning publication of Orders and laying them before the House, for appeals to the courts from Ministerial decisions, for better procedure and form of such decisions, and many other matters. In several important respects the recommendations of the Committee bore fruit, though after long delay. Thus the Rules Publication Act, 1893, was supplanted by the Statutory Instruments Act, 1946; the Select Committee on Statutory Instruments was set up in 1944; costs in Crown proceedings were reformed by the Administration of Justice (Miscellaneous Provisions) Act, 1933; and the 'Henry VIII Clause' fell virtually into disuse. Otherwise the recommendations of the Committee bore little fruit. It has already been mentioned that the Select Committee on Delegated Legislation in 1953 recommended and effected very little substantial reform.

Growth of tribunals

The Donoughmore Committee in 1932 and the Select Committee in 1953 were concerned solely with delegated legislation and Ministers' powers. The judicial system in the administrative sphere was not within their terms of reference. It has now, however, assumed an importance which cannot be ignored in any consideration of the sources of law.

A vast change has come over our 'administration of justice'. It can no longer be considered as the monopoly of the courts of law. In 1932 there were comparatively few tribunals. Today, with the ever-increasing demands of the Welfare State, there are some 2,000[1] statutory tribunals under the supervision of the Council on Tribunals (to which further reference will be made), and

[1] This includes 706 under the National Health Service, 210 under National Insurance, 222 under National Insurance (Industrial Injuries), and 152 under National Assistance.

an unascertainable number of non-statutory tribunals in addition. I have elsewhere[1] reckoned that there must be some 18,000 persons who are liable to serve on tribunals, many, if not most, of them giving their services voluntarily.[2] The Government has created tribunals with a lavish hand. In the evidence given by Departments to the Franks Committee (see *post*, pp. 593 ff.) it appeared that there were at least 48, created by statute, which had never been called into being and whose existence was scarcely known in Whitehall itself. Even in the multitude which fall within the purview of the Council on Tribunals there seem to be 9 which have never yet been constituted.

Of course these are all subordinate jurisdictions and most of them, especially since the passing of the Tribunals and Inquiries Act, 1958, are subject to some form of appeal; while, as we have seen, even the determinations of non-statutory (e.g. domestic) tribunals are subject to control by the courts by declaratory judgement. But it is obvious that when we come to consider the 'administration of justice' in England, we are confronted with a system utterly different from that which prevailed a hundred or even fifty years ago. The courts of justice often have the last word, but the first word is usually of more importance to the citizen. The courts themselves, who spend most of their time interpreting modern statutes, have had to strengthen their numbers in response to social demands. For example, when the Donoughmore Committee reported, there were 20 Judges of the King's Bench. Today there are 34, all more than fully occupied.

Between 1949 and 1953 there occurred what has come to be known as the Crichel Down Affair. I have attempted to describe it elsewhere,[3] and need not retrace

[1] See *Courts and Judgments*, The Holdsworth Club, Birmingham, 1959.

[2] If we add, in the criminal sphere, the 16,000 or 17,000 unpaid Justices of the Peace, we have the remarkable figure of between 30,000 and 40,000 citizen judges of citizens, which I suspect must be unique in the world.

[3] *Law and Orders* (2nd ed.), 343 ff.

the ground. It did not reveal any illegality or corruption, nor did it at any stage impinge on the jurisdiction of tribunals, but it was a classic example of maladministration. In 1953 the Minister of Agriculture appointed a special Commissioner to inquire into the whole matter. His report, published in 1954, was a severe condemnation of the administrative methods which had been employed, and it resulted in the resignation of the Minister (who was personally blameless, but, according to Parliamentary convention, took the responsibility). The Report attracted lively public attention, and may be said to have been the climax of the dissatisfaction with administrative methods which had long been accumulating. In the following year the Lord Chancellor appointed a strong committee under the chairmanship of Sir Oliver Franks (as he then was) to report on Administrative Tribunals and Inquiries. Its Report (Cmd. 218) was published in 1957.

The Franks Committee

This was the first thoroughgoing investigation to be held for 25 years, during which the administrative situation, as we have seen, had greatly changed, and it is a constitutional document of capital importance. Its terms of reference were quite different from those of the Donoughmore Committee. It was not primarily concerned with the processes of delegated legislation, but with those of *statutory* tribunals and inquiries. Thus the Committee was precluded from examining many of the parliamentary and legal questions which its predecessor had been free to consider. The sprawling growth of tribunals and of inquiries, especially Public Local Inquiries held in connexion with the use of land, engaged its whole attention. It did not doubt the necessity and the usefulness, within reasonable limits, of tribunals, but its main purport was to recommend some general and systematic, yet reasonably elastic, principles in this judicial branch of our administrative law, in place of the haphazard disorder which had grown up piecemeal.

The Committee laid down at the outset three

extremely salutary principles: (1) that statutory tribunals are not mere appendages of the executive, but independent bodies; (2) that they are, or should be, essentially instruments of adjudication; and (3) that the indispensable characteristics of an adjudicating body are *openness*, *fairness*, and *impartiality*. These lighthouse-beams shine throughout all the Committee's recommendations.

Some discouragement is offered (para. 406) to the excessive proliferation of tribunals to which we have alluded (*ante*, p. 592). While they may be appropriate on grounds of cheapness, accessibility, expedition, and so forth, 'the administration should not use these methods of adjudication as convenient alternatives to the court of law'. The Committee stood in no fear of 'judicial sabotage'.

It was not recommended that all tribunals should be assimilated to courts of law,[1] but in accordance with the principles of openness, fairness, and impartiality some counterweights were offered to dangerous doctrines which have been derived from *Local Government Board* v. *Arlidge*, [1915] A.C. 120 (*ante*, p. 589), and which have sometimes been understood to mean that administrative adjudications are of wholly different substance from judicial determinations. Thus the Report urged that in all official procedures and inquiries the citizen should know the case which he has to meet, that reasons for decisions should be given not only by tribunals but by Ministers, and that reports of Inspectors intended to 'inform the mind' of a Minister after a public inquiry should be made available to all interested parties.

Procedure was recognized as of great importance in all adjudications, but the Committee did not favour a single uniform code similar to the American Administra-

[1] The difference between a court and a tribunal is often very difficult to determine. There is no satisfactory definition in our law, so far as I can discover, of either the one or the other. The question has arisen chiefly, but very uncertainly, in connexion with the privilege of witnesses; see *Courts and Judgments*, *ubi sup.*, and *post*, p. 599.

tive Procedure Act but proposed the consultative regulation of different tribunal procedures under the supervision, as will be mentioned, of the Council. Nor did it look kindly on the suggested establishment of a general Administrative Court of Appeal, but recommended a far more extensive and uniform system of appeals from tribunals than had previously existed.

The Committee evidently did not consider it within its terms of reference to examine the nature and operation of the prerogative orders of the Queen's Bench, or the other means of redress which have been discussed *ante*, pp. 563 ff. Its general recommendation, however, that tribunals should give reasons for their decisions—in other words, make 'speaking orders'—offset the anomaly which arose after *R.* v. *Northumberland Compensation Appeal Tribunal*, *Ex p. Shaw* (see *ante*, p. 573).[1]

Something has been said above (pp. 589 ff.) about the spirit of Crown litigation. On the general relationship between the executive and the public, the Committee had these pertinent observations to make (Report, para. 405):

> 'We wish to emphasise that . . . nothing can make up for a wrong approach to administrative activity by the administration's servants. We believe that less public resentment would be aroused against administrative action if all officials were trained in the principle that the individual has the right to enjoy his property without interference from the administration, unless the interference is unmistakably justified in the public interest. For example, the attitude of an owner or occupier may well turn on whether he receives reasonable and courteous notice of a proposal to inspect the land.'

The most imaginative recommendation of the Report, made largely at the instance of Professor H. W. R. Wade, was the establishment of a Council on Tribunals.

[1] The Committee recommended that reasons should be given in all cases, but the Tribunals and Inquiries Act provided that they should be given only if so required.

We shall see how this proposal was implemented by legislation.

The Franks Report enjoyed a far happier fate than its predecessor of 1932. It made altogether 95 recommendations, the great majority of which were accepted by the Government and were swiftly followed by the Tribunals and Inquiries Act, 1958.

The Council on Tribunals

Without going into excessive detail, the main provisions of the Act are as follows.

(1) A Council on Tribunals is appointed by the Lord Chancellor, of not less than ten nor more than fifteen members. (The Franks Committee had recommended two Councils, one for England and Wales and one for Scotland, but they are consolidated into one body by the Act, due regard being had to Scottish and Welsh representation.) The main function of the Council is to 'keep under review' the constitution and working of the large number of statutory tribunals which are designated in a Schedule to the Act; and this list may be augmented, as occasion demands, by statutory instrument.[1] It is the duty of the Council to 'consider and report on' such matters as may be referred to it concerning tribunals or statutory inquiries, and on its own initiative to report on any matter concerning inquiries which it may deem to be of special importance. References to the Council are to be made by the Lord Chancellor,[2] to whom the Council is to report, and an annual report on its work and conclusions is to be placed before Parliament.

The Chairmen of certain tribunals are to be appointed by the Lord Chancellor individually or from a nominated panel, and the Council is empowered to make recommendations to Ministers for appointments to certain other tribunals.

The Lord Chancellor is required to consult the Council

[1] Since the establishment of the Council, at least four new types of tribunals have been created by statute, perhaps the most important of which are the Mental Health Tribunals constituted under the Mental Health Act, 1959.

[2] Wherever this authority is mentioned, it should be read as including the Secretary of State for Scotland for all Scottish matters.

before making procedural rules for the scheduled tribunals or for statutory inquiries. Membership of most tribunals shall not be terminated without the consent of the Lord Chancellor.

There were a certain number of tribunals among those specified in the Schedule from which no appeal lay. For these an appeal to the High Court (Divisional Court of the Q.B.)[1] is provided, but only on a point of law. This provision may be extended by the Lord Chancellor, by statutory instrument, to other tribunals not within the Schedule. The supervisory powers of the High Court are also confirmed by the provision in s. 11 that the inclusion, in statutes passed before 1958, of clauses ousting the jurisdiction of the courts (see *ante*, pp. 586 ff.) shall not have effect so as to exclude the operation of certiorari and mandamus.

Finally, a partial but notable victory is won against the long and determined opposition of many civil servants by the provision of s. 12 that, *on demand* by an interested party, a tribunal or a Minister shall be bound to supply reasons for decisions. This, it is hoped, will put an end to the uncertainty of 'speaking orders' (*ante*, p. 573), since all orders will speak if so commanded. The requirement, however, may be denied on grounds of security (this, so far as we know, has not yet happened), or if, with the concurrence of the Lord Chancellor, it is deemed unnecessary or impracticable.[2]

The Act does not expressly adopt all the recommendations of the Franks Committee, nor attempt to cover all the ground which it surveyed, but not a few of the points which it urged have been adopted by administrative directions and instructions—e.g. legal qualifications of chairmen, publicity of proceedings, legal representation, and power to take evidence on oath. It certainly cannot be said that the Government was either

[1] By S.I. 1959, No. 450.
[2] As has happened in certain Income Tax matters: S.I. 1959, No. 452.

dilatory or reluctant in introducing much needed and overdue reforms.

The Council is a purely advisory and supervisory body. It has no executive powers, though its experience up to the present time is that its advice and queries have been sympathetically received. In its second Annual Report, the Council thus describes its own functions and limitations:

> 'It is our task to act as a watchdog for the ordinary citizen and to see that he gets fair play. We have no say in the issues to be decided, nor can we overrule the decisions that are made. Our duty is to supervise procedure, so as to ensure that tribunals and inquiries fulfil their purpose of always giving a fair hearing and do nothing which can offend the ordinary citizen's sense of justice. We can draw attention to any case where we think that these standards have not been observed, and we can comment on regulations intended to be made by Government Departments. Although our powers are purely advisory, there is thus much that we can do to make sure that mistakes are not repeated, that difficult questions receive study and that regulations conform to the principles of fair procedure laid down by the Franks Committee in 1957.'

A feeling has been evinced that the Council's statutory powers are unequal to its task,[1] principally because it has less control over inquiries, which inevitably trench on Ministerial policy and Parliamentary responsibility, than over the composition and procedure of tribunals. Even in its survey of tribunals, the Council is limited to those which are authorized by statute.[2] It cannot possibly take cognizance of the innumerable private, non-statutory adjudicating bodies which may be set up at pleasure by all manner of professional, trade, sporting, and similar organizations; but, as we have seen, the citizen is in large measure protected from any substantial

[1] See House of Lords debate on Wednesday, 12 July 1961, *H.L. Deb.* (Vol. 233, No. 108).

[2] Not even all statutory tribunals are subject to the supervision of the Council—e.g. the Patents Appeal Tribunal.

irregularity on the part of such 'tribunals' by the scope of the declaratory judgement.

Again, the Council is limited to *statutory* inquiries—i.e. those which a Minister or similar authority is *bound* by statute to hold before arriving at a decision. It has no control, for example, over *ad hoc* Departmental inquiries set up by a Minister. Nor has it, in general, supervision over matters of mere maladministration, though it may call attention to them. It is questionable whether, if it had then existed, it could have intervened at any stage in the Crichel Down imbroglio, which did not involve the functioning of any tribunal or statutory inquiry.

At the present date of writing, the Council has issued three annual reports to Parliament. The first was necessarily tentative, since in the first year of office the members were principally engaged in 'sizing up' the nature of their duties, in visiting typical tribunals, and in consultation with the Lord Chancellor and with Departments on many points of detail. On the whole, the Council has met with ready co-operation from Ministries when improvements have been suggested. Comments and advice have been tendered, and generally accepted, with regard to the considerable number of Statutory Instruments which have been made to govern the procedure of individual tribunals. Complaints from members of the public (which the Council has encouraged) have been carefully considered, and have been taken up with the appropriate authorities when (as has happened comparatively rarely) they have fallen within the Council's limited terms of reference and have seemed to disclose some substantial cause of complaint. Several questions of importance have been submitted for advice by the Lord Chancellor. Perhaps the most important of these is that of the privilege of witnesses before tribunals. On this point the carefully considered view of the Council was that, with certain exceptions, the existing law of qualified privilege is sufficient to protect witnesses. Again, the Council was of opinion, contrary to that of the Franks Committee, that tribunals should not have power to issue subpoenas, which were adequately available by the application of interested individuals. The difficult question of the costs of parties and witnesses before tribunals is, at this date, still under consideration.

The Council has always been conscious that with regard to statutory inquiries it stands on delicate ground. In its second report it said (para. 92): 'We have all along foreseen that this subject, since it touches directly on the decisions of both Government Departments and local authorities, was more likely to involve the Council in complicated and controversial issues than our other task of supervising administrative tribunals.' These prophetic words were soon to be fulfilled in what has come to be known as the *Chalk Pit Case*.

Briefly, the facts were that a firm of sand and gravel producers applied for permission to dig chalk on its land in Essex and was refused by the local authority. It appealed to the Minister, who, as required by the Town and Country Planning Act, 1959, caused a public local inquiry to be held. At this inquiry certain neighbouring landowners, of whom one was Major Buxton, were allowed to attend and to state strong objections to the proposed development, which they urged would injuriously affect their land by chalk-dust. It should be noted that they had no legal *locus standi*. The only parties who, by statute, have a *right* to attend an inquiry are the applicant and the local authority. It is the practice, however, by 'administrative concession', for the Inspector to allow the attendance, and to hear the objections, of any person who seems to have a reasonable interest in the inquiry, so that the 'person appointed' may be fully informed of all the local issues involved.

The Inspector reported against the appeal. The Minister, however, took advice from the Minister of Agriculture—who was himself advised by his experts—dissented from the Inspector's report, and allowed the appeal. Major Buxton and his friends then appealed against the Minister's decision, under s. 31 (1) of the Town and Country Planning Act, as 'persons aggrieved' by it.[1] Salmon J. held, with evident reluctance but on compelling authority, that only those whose *legal right* was, as they claimed, infringed were 'aggrieved persons'. The plaintiff had suffered no injury to any 'legal right'. Certiorari, which might possibly, but doubtfully, have been a means of recourse, was excluded by the Act.

The position then was that a person who was vitally interested in the project, who had been allowed to state his objections at the inquiry and had been upheld by the Inspector, had no further recourse against a Ministerial decision based on advice which he had never had the opportunity of examining or contesting. The Council on Tribunals, having the power to do so under its terms of reference, called the attention of the Lord Chancellor to this anomaly, which appeared to be contrary to the recommendations of the Franks Committee.

A storm ensued. There was intense public dissatisfaction with the situation which was disclosed. It was strenuously debated for over a year in Parliament, in the newspapers, in learned journals, and in correspondence between the Council and the Lord Chancellor. Much argument turned on the interpretation of 'new factual evidence' as it had been used in the Franks Report. What particularly offended Parliamentary and public opinion was that this decisive 'evidence' was not only anonymous, but came from persons who had never appeared at the inquiry and been subject to cross-examination. The Lord Chancellor defended his colleague's action as being perfectly within his statutory powers—as indeed it was—and of course the Minister defended his own action. But nobody was satisfied with an administrative act which seemed to be an arbitrary use of Departmental powers and a plain denial of justice. It is, however, unnecessary to follow this classic encounter, round

[1] *Buxton* v. *Minister of Housing and Local Government*, [1961] 1 Q.B. 279

by round,[1] for it ended, as usual, in a compromise. In July 1962 the Lord Chancellor issued his long-awaited rules of procedure for public local inquiries in connexion with planning appeals and the compulsory acquisition of land.[2]

Rule 10 provides that when the Minister is disposed to reject the Inspector's report, because he differs on a finding of fact or has received new evidence (including expert evidence) on a matter of fact, or taken into consideration some new issue of fact which was not raised at the inquiry, then before he reaches a decision he must notify the interested parties and give them the opportunity of making representations about the reasons for his dissent, or if necessary demanding the reopening of the inquiry, within twenty-one days.

An important exception is that if the Minister's reasons are based on 'a matter of Government policy', he is not bound to give this second opportunity to objectors. How 'Government policy' will be interpreted remains to be seen. Further, the position of 'third parties' is unchanged. Only the persons immediately concerned in the appeal have the rights conferred by Rule 10, though apparently other interested parties, without being 'aggrieved persons', will still be entitled, at the discretion of the Inspector, to make representations at the original inquiry. Major Buxton was such a 'third party' in the *Chalk Pit Case*, and under the new rules he would not have had the right to call for the reopening of the inquiry. To that extent the rules leave things as they were, but nevertheless the new opportunities made available to the parties to the appeal are a considerable and an overdue concession, and are to be regarded as conspicuously illustrating the usefulness and vigilance of the Council on Tribunals.

Whether the Council, within its limited terms of reference, can continue to be an efficient 'watchdog' is

[1] A summary of the stages in the controversy will be found in *Public Law*, Summer 1961, 121 ff.

[2] S.I. 1962, Nos. 1424 and 1425.

a matter for speculation. The task of supervising 2,000 tribunals (and probably more as time goes on), of extremely various kinds, many involving technical considerations, which render some 122,000 decisions a year, and of some 5,700 public local inquiries, may well be thought to be beyond the capacity of fourteen men sitting only at intervals and most of them busily engaged in other occupations. The Council itself has expressed concern at the growing volume of its work and seems to be somewhat anxious about its future. Apart from its prescribed duties, in its capacity of 'watchdog' it has encouraged, and indeed urged, members of the public to make representatations to it. A good many of these complaints have been laid, many of them (as was to be expected) without substance or beyond the jurisdiction of the Council, but not a few which have led to representations and remedy. This department of its work seems likely to grow and to make severe demands on time and labour. In short, the future of the Council cannot be regarded as secure. One can only regard it at present as experimental, but undoubtedly as an experiment in the right direction. More, perhaps, is too much to expect in the slow development of our administrative law.

Administrative Law in England today

As government, national and local, ever grows more complex in an overcrowded island, clashes between the citizen and the administrator are certain to increase. Very often they are not on matters of principle, which have to be left to the sovereign authority of Parliament, but on questions of *method* and attitude, which can hardly be covered by any legal rules. One has only to recall the Crichel Down affair, in which the subject had no recourse against maladministration short of Parliament itself, and to wonder in how many other instances the same causes of complaint may occur. For this reason, a proposal,[1] sponsored by 'Justice', the British Section

[1] *The Citizen and the Administration*, Director of Research, Sir John Whyatt; Stevens & Sons, Ltd., 1961.

of the International Commission of Jurists, has recently been made for the establishment of a Parliamentary Commissioner, roughly corresponding to the Ombudsman of the Scandinavian countries and of New Zealand, to act as a kind of 'grievance man'. The subject is too large for discussion here, and is certainly not free from difficulty. Suffice it that the suggestion, which has attracted much publicity, has now been somewhat brusquely rejected by the Government.[1] I venture to doubt, however, whether the last has been heard of it.

Government today operates through many different agencies, which tend constantly to multiply and to propagate their own species; for it is in the nature of administration to breed more administration. If Government, itself controlled (in theory at least) by popular will, loses control of the many agents which it employs, the result is that unhappy form of management which is known as bureaucracy, and which has proved the scourge of every country where it has been allowed to take control. The principal vices to which it is prone are inefficiency and corruption; for inefficiency invariably results from excessive complication of pretended efficiency, and corruption is certain to ensue when too much power is committed to too many hands.

In the modern State, therefore, a regulating influence is necessary to maintain a delicate three-sided relationship between the State and its agents on the one hand and between the State and the citizen on the other hand. That relationship is best maintained by an intelligent, explicit system of administrative law. It is unfortunate that this very term has for long had certain sinister connotations in England. This has been partly due to the obstinate conviction of many Englishmen that their own system of law is so far superior to all others that they have nothing to learn from foreign countries—the majestic Common Law being all-sufficient and all-embracing—and partly

[1] See *Public Law*, Winter 1962, 391.

to misrepresentations propagated (though later virtually renounced) by such popular expositors as A. V. Dicey. These misconceptions die hard, and there are still many Englishmen, laymen and lawyers alike, who imagine that a system like the French *droit administratif* is designed principally to afford officialdom some special privilege as against the ordinary citizen.[1] This is, to be frank, sheer nonsense. Whatever Napoleon Bonaparte's original intentions may have been in establishing the Conseil d'État, it has built up a remarkable jurisprudence, and on the whole is a more effective buffer between State and citizen than anything we possess, while, at the same time, far from acting as a clog on administration, it functions as an intelligent and expert adviser of the executive.[2] Yet sanctimonious delusions about it persisted for many years and are not yet quite dead.

Administrative law, then, has suffered a long gestation and a difficult birth in our legal system. It is still a delicate child, with an uncertain future, but it is beginning to take the shape of manhood. It has been forced upon us, against much blind prejudice, by irresistible circumstances. It is now taught in our law schools as a branch of law which is essential to an understanding of our whole legal system, though with all its growing complexities it is difficult to fit into a legal education. A copious literature begins to surround it, as it has done for many years past in the United States. The attempt which has been made in these pages to describe some of the stages of its growth is not more than a sketch of its adolescence. It will develop. So far, it has needed something like a periodical scandal to stimulate its overhaul. Let us hope that its future development, whatever it may be, may proceed without the aid of such galvanic shocks.

[1] This notion is implicit, for example, in a violent book like Lord Hewart's *New Despotism*, and even in the Donoughmore Report.

[2] There are not many satisfactory accounts in English of the *droit administratif*, but M. A. Sieghart's *Government by Decree* and Professor C. J. Hamson's *Executive Discretion and Judicial Control* will be found very helpful.

SUMMARY

In review of our conclusions concerning legislation as a source of law: Legislation is the characteristic law-making instrument of modern societies, expressing a relationship between the individual and the State. It is not, however, a relationship, taking the form of a command, merely between superior and subordinate. It represents a process of action and reaction between constitutionally organized initiative and spontaneous social forces. While it cannot be said of a great deal of modern legislation that it is in any real sense a direct product of 'popular consciousness' or 'the will of the people', and while it is true, in the phrase of Dicey, that 'laws foster law-making opinion', yet there is in society a prevailing current of opinion which necessarily and fundamentally influences the spirit of legislation. For the efficient working of the machinery of government, there should always be a harmony between legislative enactment and this dominant trend of public opinion. In contemporary societies, however, there are many different degrees and varieties of public opinion and of sections of it, and numerous influences, both of an expert and of a popular kind, enter into the consultative process which precedes a great deal of modern legislation of the 'social' type.

To understand the authority of statute, it is necessary to grasp the forms which it has taken in our law. In medieval England there was no conscious doctrine of the separation of powers: the legislative and administrative spheres had not yet become distinct. 'Legislation', not necessarily in imperative form, was primarily a rule emanating from the king; and it was not until the fourteenth century that there emerged something like a standard type of enactment of uniform authority and operation for the whole realm. Consequently, our early records of 'legislation' are highly imperfect. Until the activities of the Record Commission in the early nineteenth century, the only sources of information were private editions of statutes and the received tradition of the profession. From early times, many projects were mooted for the revision of the statute-book, which was in a state of the greatest disorder and obscurity, but it was not until the nineteenth century that the work of reform was thoroughly undertaken. Diversity of form often led to doubts concerning the authority of particular statutes. Though in the thirteenth and fourteenth centuries statutes, if proved to be executed in due form, had peculiar authority as emanating from the sovereign, and though they are not to be regarded as merely confirmatory of, or subsidiary to, a fundamental Common Law, it was probably not till the end of the fifteenth century that the absolute authority of statute, as understood today, settled itself in our law. It is now established beyond doubt: the modern doctrine is that Parliamentary enactment is absolutely unlimited in scope and authority.

Certain limits have sometimes been supposed to exist, viz. (1) Conformity to the law of God or to 'common right and reason' or to 'natural equity'. It is doubtful whether this supposed rule has ever been really applicable in our law; it amounts to little more than the principle that the courts will not, if they can avoid it, so interpret a statute as to produce injustice or absurdity; and in modern times it takes the form that, so far as possible, statutes are presumed to be in accordance with existing law, and especially existing Common Law. (2) Conformity to international law. This has never been a positive restriction, and it only means that as far as possible the courts will construe Acts of Parliament consistently with the comity of nations. But there are certain limitations more real than these: (1) Statute cannot prescribe that which is impossible of performace. (2) Penal statutes made *ex post facto*, and statutes directed against individuals, though theoretically still possible at the pleasure of the legislature, are so contrary to prevailing modern opinion that they may be said to be now unconstitutional for all practical purposes. There is, however, no embargo on retrospective legislation as such, though most Governments resort to it with caution, especially when its effect is detrimental to individuals; when its object is indemnification, there is no objection to it in proper circumstances. (3) No statute can immortalize itself by forbidding its own repeal in the future. (4) Public opinion is the real and actual, though not the legal, check upon legislation.

A statute, under the rule established after some fluctuations of theory, is of binding force for the whole realm as soon as it has received the royal assent. It may subsequently be repealed at any time either expressly or by implication. Express repeal explains itself, but has been complicated in the past by the unwieldy character of statutory records; implied repeal is governed by the principle *leges posteriores priores contrarias abrogant.* A statute in English law is never abrogated by mere disuse; but in practice a great many ancient statutes, being quite incongruous in modern surroundings, may be considered as dead letters even though they have never been formally repealed.

Statute has to be applied by the courts, and its purport and effect therefore become largely the product of judicial interpretation. The first task of the judge is to determine the literal or grammatical meaning of the words chosen by the legislator. Here the court is to a great extent in the hands of the draftsman, and the inevitable inadequacy of language which has to be strictly construed is, in any country, always a serious defect in legislation considered as a source of law. There can be no invariable rule for the interpretation of words and phrases in a statute; but words must always be considered in their context and subject to the *eiusdem generis* rule. And it is the 'golden rule' of the construction of all enactments that literal interpretation serves only as a means for the ascertainment and application of the general purport of the Act, or *ratio legis.* The expression of the legislator's will must invariably be considered not only by itself but with the natural consequences flowing from it. The judges should always endeavour to preserve the balance between the strict meaning of isolated expressions—which meaning they cannot disregard if it is plain and imperative—and a reasonable, just, and convenient interpretation of the statute as a whole. The general purpose as well as the literal terms of the enactment must be kept in view. Without considering extrinsic elements like the Parliamentary or social history of a course of legislation, or surrounding circumstances incidental to the enactment but not an integral part of it, a court must have regard to the general 'policy of the statute'. This embraces, according to the rules laid down in *Heydon's Case*, the existing Common Law at the time of the passing of the Act, the modification of the Common Law which the Act had in view, the nature of the remedy provided, and the reason for ordaining it.

The court also has to consider cases not expressly provided for in terms by the statute, but arising under it. Here judges are said to lay down the rule which the legislator would have laid down if he had considered the omitted case; but in reality it is often difficult to say what the will of the legislator would have been in the unforeseen circumstances, and the judge must then—and very frequently does—deal with the *casus omissus* according to his own discretion and the general principles of logic and social policy in which he has been trained. A very great part of the operation of statute-law therefore depends on the exercise of the judicial faculty, and all the rules of interpretation are subject to such marked variations that they do not form the most scientific or the best-settled part of our law. A judge, however, has no discretion where the phraseology of a statute is unambiguous; and since the language of statutes is often imperfect, and sometimes constrains the courts to results which do not seem to have been intended by the legislator, it is on the whole better that general principles of right and duty should be developed by the

Common Law than by the inelastic methods of Acts of Parliament.

There is a marked tendency at the present time for the legislative powers of Parliament to be delegated to a number of subordinate authorities. The traditional theory of the English constitution is that the legislative sovereignty of Parliament is unique and without competitor, and that the Rule of Law ensures a single and uniform administration of justice for all persons and all causes. This view cannot be said to accord wholly with present facts and tendencies.

Press of business and increase of purely technical problems have compelled Parliament to delegate extensively. The result has been the rise of a number of organs of government which gain increasing influence. Among these may be mentioned: (1) the Privy Council, which has wide powers to legislate by Order in Council, either as an exercise of the prerogative or, more commonly, under authority expressly conferred by statute, and which acts in reality as a sanctioning body for rules made by Government Departments; (2) various 'rule-making bodies' created by different Acts such as the Rules Committee of the Supreme Court, which controls matters of practice and procedure; (3) local authorities, which, with the great spread of local government during the nineteenth century, have acquired important powers of making by-laws of great variety and force in everyday affairs; (4) the executive, to which the power of making Statutory Instruments is entrusted by statute with growing frequency and widening scope. In addition to the authorities specially designated by legislation, a number of corporations within the State—such as public utility authorities, the Church, universities, &c.—have autonomous powers of providing for their own internal constitutions, and in many cases of making by-laws for the general public; while in industry there is a pronounced development of group or syndical government on the sides both of labour and of capital.

The actual form of subordinate legislation is largely governed by the Statutory Instruments Act, 1946, which aims at making sub-law as accessible to the public as the statutes of Parliament. The safeguard of publicity is supplemented by various constitutional means of control which are, in theory, exercised by Parliament and the courts. Some Statutory Instruments—variously named as Rules, Regulations, and Orders—become binding only after they have been approved by Parliament, or at least have not been disapproved, or have satisfied certain preliminary conditions laid down by particular enactments; but the actual exercise of Parliamentary veto is rare, though the possibility of its being imposed is a valuable check *in potentia*.

Judicial control operates chiefly through the doctrine of *ultra vires*, to which all subordinate legislation is *prima facie* subject. As to by-laws, certain judicial tests have become well established; but, on the whole, the courts lean towards a benevolent interpretation of them. A general disciplinary control is also exercised over public and quasi-public authorities by Court Orders of mandamus, certiorari, prohibition, and analogous processes such as injunction and declaratory judgement; by means of these, subordinate authorities may be compelled, on the one hand, to carry out their appointed duties, and, on the other hand, to keep within their proper powers.

Many of these checks tend to be weakened in present circumstances. It becomes more and more common to make the operation of Parliamentary legislation dependent for its commencement and validity on Orders made by the executive. There is a tendency to derogate from Parliamentary control by providing that Statutory Instruments when made shall have the same effect as an Act of Parliament. This expedient gives the executive original rather than delegated powers, and leads to confusion in the different spheres of government. Similarly, there is a tendency to oust the jurisdiction of the courts, and to remove a salutary judicial control, by making the

Department judge in its own cause both at first instance and on appeal. The functions of the executive are therefore constantly growing at the expense of the other powers in the State, the more so because Departments exercise a strong centralizing influence over local administration.

The tendency towards decentralization of government is irresistible and not in itself objectionable, but in order that decentralization shall not become mere disintegration a steady regulative power in the State is necessary. This, however, must be kept in due proportion to individual liberty and initiative, and a democratic constitution should aim at preserving a harmonious relationship between the State and its agents on the one hand, and the State and the citizen on the other hand. At the present time the English governmental system is not well adapted to this end. There is an uneven and confused working of constitutional machinery. The legislature exercises too little real control, both in the making and in the application of law, over its executive agents. The same is true of judicial control, which is ousted sometimes expressly and sometimes by the vague terms in which delegated legislation is couched; it has therefore lost much of its effectiveness in recent years, especially by the decline of the doctrine of *ultra vires*, and it stands in increasing danger from a school of thought which regards all judicial supervision as a mere impediment to administrative efficiency.

The only remedy for these growing ills is an acknowledged and stable system of administrative law, a branch of jurisprudence which has been only grudgingly accepted by many lawyers and executive officers, largely through the misconception that it confers special privilege and protection on the administration as against the individual. On the contrary, it can be, and is in other countries, the citizen's best shield against misuse of delegated powers, since it provides recourse to an impartial arbiter in case of dispute. There are, however, signs that administrative law is now beginning to take its proper place as an important, and indeed inescapable, branch of the English legal system, though its development is slow and spasmodic, and is acknowledged in many quarters with a certain scepticism and reluctance. Only by the systematic development of its principles shall we be able to ensure the just and proper functioning of social control and maintain equilibrium in the relations between the governors and the governed.

APPENDIX

REASONABLENESS OF CUSTOM

The number of cases, especially old cases (for the question seldom arises in modern conditions), concerned with the reasonableness of custom is large, and I cannot hope that my examination of them has been exhaustive. I have, however, endeavoured to scrutinize all those which are cited in the principal authorities, including the chief Abridgements, and I venture to hope that none of primary importance has escaped notice—though that is always possible in the mass of our case-law. Such decisions—and they are many—as deal only indirectly with the point have been purposely omitted from consideration here.

One preliminary observation must be made with regard to the older cases. The reports are often so scanty, or the decisions so much concerned with technical points of pleading, that it is difficult to know what evidence of the actual existence of the alleged custom was before the court. It is only when we come to later times and fuller reports that it is possible to gather any certain information on this point; and it is not always easy even in the more recent cases.

1. We may consider first a number of miscellaneous cases, not falling within any particular group, in which customs have been judicially declared unreasonable; and in all of them we shall find that proof of existence of the custom fails, or, at the least, is highly suspect.

Sara de Richford's Case (1330), Y.B. 3 Ed. 38 (Mich. pl. 12): In a writ of entry a custom was alleged that the inheritance was departible among male heirs. Stonore J.: 'In no place in England are tenements departible at common law, except in Kent, among male heirs; hence if any allege that tenements are departible among males anywhere else, this usage cannot be valid if is not actually observed, and you do not prove this in fact (*cest usage ne poit valer sil ne fuist use, et vous ne montres ceo en fait*).'

Sufficient evidence of actual user is clearly wanting here.

Anon. (1370), Y.B. 43 Ed. 3. 32 (Mich. pl. 30): A custom alleged in a vill that if a tenant was two years in arrears with his rent, the lord might enter and dispossess him until agreement was made for the arrears. 'And inasmuch as the usage was alleged solely in this one vill, and in no others in the neighbourhood, it was held by KNIVET and the whole Court, that it was a bad usage to oust a man of his inheritance, &c.'

The reason given seems to mean that the Court did not believe that the custom was really established as 'local law'. 'Inheritance' seems to be used loosely of a termor's possession.

Anon. (1469), Y.B. 8 Ed. 4. 18 (Mich. pl. 30): Trespass for digging in the plaintiff's close, which was four acres of land adjoining the sea in Kent. Defence, that 'all the men of Kent' had been used from time immemorial, when fishing in the sea, to dig in adjoining land in order to pitch stakes to hang out and dry their nets. *Nele:* 'He has said that the men have used, &c., and this is not a good prescription, for he ought to show *which men*, &c.'

This objection seems to have been the ground of decision. The custom is unreasonable because it is too vague and uncertain —i.e. on the facts and on the pleadings it is not shown to be appurtenant to any ascertained class of persons. There the case ends, so far as the *ratio decidendi* is concerned; but the rest of the discussion, on reasonableness generally, is interesting enough to be worth quoting:

CHOKE J.: 'This custom cannot be good, for it is against common right to prescribe to dig in my land, but there are other customs, which are used throughout the whole land, and such customs are legal: e.g. that of innkeepers who are chargeable for the goods of their guests, if the goods are stolen, &c. And also there is another custom that if my neighbour guard his fire negligently, so that through his negligence my house is burned, he will be liable to me: and such customs are good.'

LITTLETON J.: 'Custom which prevails throughout the whole land is common law, like the cases that you have cited, &c. And, Sir, a custom which can stand upon reason shall be allowed, e.g. the custom of primogeniture; but this custom is against reason, for if he can dig in one place, he can dig in another. And so if a man had a meadow adjoining the sea, they [the fishermen] by this custom could destroy the whole meadow, which would not be reasonable.'

DANBY J.: 'Those who are fishers in the sea can justify their going upon the land adjoining the sea, for such fishery is for the common wealth, and for the sustenance of all in the realm. This is common law.' *Quod fuit concessum. . . .*[1]

[1] This *dictum*, despite the *concessum*, appears to be a more than dubious statement of the law. It is in direct conflict with Hale, *De Portibus Maris*, 85 f., and is rejected by Holroyd J. in a very authoritative judgement in *Blundell* v. *Catterall* (1821), 5 B. & Ald. 268: see H. E. Salt, 'The Local

Fairfax: 'In the cases just mentioned of the innkeepers, &c., the customs are reasonable, for the innkeeper has a profit by his inn, and therefore a *quid pro quo*. And similarly my neighbour will have the same advantage against me if his house be burned by my negligence, as I shall have against him; but, Sir, this custom which goes to the destruction of my inheritance cannot be good, for though fishery may be for the common wealth, yet the common wealth cannot destroy my inheritance, for I shall not have advantage by such fishery, &c., and those who are fishers can be allowed parcel of [other?] land adjoining the sea for drying their nets.'

An interesting modern parallel with this case is *Mercer* v. *Denne*, [1905] 2 Ch. 538, where, however, there was no question of fishermen *digging* in land adjoining the sea, but merely of going upon it to dry and oil their nets. The custom was held to be good. The case is also instructive with regard to the kinds of documents which will be admitted in evidence in proof or disproof of the existence and reputation of a custom.

Barker *v.* Cocker (1621), Hob. 329: A claim for tithe-lambs. A custom was alleged that all the lambs in the parish were 'cast and reckoned together as if they were but one man's': the Vicar could then take his tithe where he chose, with the result, as the Court pointed out, that a man who owned one lamb might lose his all, whereas another who owned a great many might contribute nothing. The Court held that 'the pretended custom' was unreasonable and against law.

Small wonder that the custom was merely 'pretended'. It is highly improbable, though the report is silent on the point, that a custom so absurd and inequitable on the face of it can have been supported by any satisfactory evidence.

Owen *v.* Stainhow (1683), Tho. Jo. 199: An alleged custom to elect a canon to succeed in the next vacant place, there being no vacancy at the time. 'The Court thought that the custom was ridiculous, to chuse where no canonry was vacant.' An application for mandamus to hold the election was therefore refused.

Again absurd on the face of it, and unlikely to have any basis in fact.

Taylor *v.* Scott (1729), FitzG. 55: Alleged custom in a parish to

Ambit of a Custom', *Cambridge Legal Essays*, 288. In *Anon.*, Y.B. 8 Ed. 4. 23 (Mich. pl. 41) (a case also arising in Kent), Catesby argues at Bar that there is no right to enter and dig another's land even for defence against invasion, except by custom; but the contention appears to be unsound: see Salt, *loc. cit.* 286.

pay 10*d.* to the incumbent for churching every woman 'at the time of her being churched, or at the usual time when she should be churched'. *Held* (the sole ground of decision): too uncertain, there being no evidence as to what was 'the usual time', &c.

The uncertainty apparently existed in the pleadings rather than in the facts, for the custom does not seem unreasonable on the face of it.

Bastard *v.* Smith (1837), 2 Moo. & R. 129: The stanners of Devon claimed a right by custom to divert water from streams into their mines and dig trenches on the lands of third persons. The claim was founded on ancient charters, which appeared to confer this right in Cornwall; but it was disputed whether it extended to Devon, the Devon charter differing in material particulars from that of Cornwall. It was therefore contended that the custom in Devon, if it existed at all, had grown by mere usurpation.

Evidence was given of acts alleged to be done in pursuance of the custom, and of reputation.

It was contended (1) that the custom was unreasonable in itself even if established, (2) that it was not established by the evidence.

Tindal C.J.'s charge to the jury is so instructive an exposition of the relation between legal unreasonableness and evidence of actual user, that I venture to quote it at some length:

'As to the argument addressed to you, touching the unreasonableness of the custom, although you are not called on to say whether this be a reasonable custom or not (for that is matter of law, not submitted by the present pleadings to your decision), still you may properly thus far look to the nature of the custom, that, if you find it greatly affecting the rights of private property, you may fairly expect and require that it should be supported by evidence properly strong and convincing. . . . You cannot, indeed, reasonably expect to have it proved before you, that such a custom did in fact exist before the time of legal memory, i.e. before the first year of the reign of Richard I; for if you did, it would in effect destroy the validity of almost all customs: but you are to require proof, as far back as living memory goes, of a continuous, peaceable and uninterrupted user of the custom, and then you should enquire whether any document, or memorial, of more ancient times, is produced, tending to *disprove* the existence of the custom at that early period to which the law looks back.—If you think the custom is proved, either in the terms in which it is pleaded, or subject only to certain exceptions and qualifications, you will find your verdict for the defendants, telling me what those exceptions and qualifications are: if you think the custom is not proved at all, your verdict must be for the plaintiff.'

The issue is thus put to the jury as one purely of fact. They found for the plaintiff: which can only mean, on the Chief Justice's direction, that the custom was unreasonable because it was 'not proved at all'.

Rogers *v.* Brenton (1847), 10 Q.B. 26: This case concerned the interesting custom of 'bounding' in Cornwall. According to that custom, any person might enter on the waste land of another, and mark out, by four corner bounds, a definite area. A written description of the plot of land so marked out was recorded in the Stannary Court and proclaimed at three successive Courts; if no objection was made, the Court awarded a writ to the Bailiff of the Court to deliver possession of the said 'bounds or tin work' to the bounder, who thereupon had the exclusive right to take all tin and tin ore from the land bounded, paying a 'tin toll' to the owner of the soil.

Up to this point the custom was undisputed; but it was further claimed that the right, once established, might descend to executors and *might be preserved for an indefinite time, either by actually working or paying toll, or by annually renewing the four boundary marks on a day certain.*

It was with regard to the latter part of the custom that the dispute arose. The plaintiff, having 'bounded' an area of the defendant's waste, had ceased to work the minerals or to pay toll for eighteen years, and had merely renewed his boundary marks annually *pro forma.*

The custom was held unreasonable and void as to the latter part of it. Lord Denman C.J. (at p. 58) explains how the alleged right of maintaining a squatter's possession by a mere annual formality would defeat the whole purpose and utility of the custom, its reasonable basis being, in the common interest, that if the owner of the soil did not work the minerals, a bounder should be entitled to do so, on payment of a fair toll to the owner. This is certainly the view of the custom which commends itself to common sense and public policy.

Now it is true that in this case the jury had found the *whole* custom, including the disputed part of it, proved in fact. But on this finding of fact Lord Denman C.J. observes, at p. 59:

'When the evidence in this case is referred to, the variations and uncertainties in which those are involved who contend that the bound owner need not work strongly favour the conclusion in law at which we have arrived. The jury, indeed, have drawn a conclusion of fact from the whole, which, as such, we should not feel disposed to disturb; for it was their province to draw it from the statements submitted to them. But, on reading the report, and finding, among other things, that there is a conflict among the witnesses who from professional habits might have been supposed best able to speak to the point, whether even an annual renewal of the bounds be necessary to preserve the ownership in the bounds, and also that much reliance seems to have been placed on the fact, entirely inconclusive, that owners of land have in many instances not proceeded as for forfeiture of the bounds where the mines have not been worked, we see every reason to believe that the unqualified right now claimed is but an abuse of the original limits of the custom, inconsistent with its object, and not to be sustained on any principle.'

Although, therefore, the court was prepared to hold the custom unreasonable in any event, the actual observance of the custom claimed seems to have rested on a basis of fact which was slender, to say the least.

2. A group of decisions which may be called 'usurpation cases'. Something has been said already (*ante*, pp. 89 ff.) about customs which arise not so much from the *consensus utentium* as from imposition by a powerful upon a weaker class. This tendency is frequently to be found in cases concerning feudal customs. It was a natural temptation for feudal overlords, and others possessed of valuable customary rights against a servient class, gradually to extend or 'usurp' powers beyond the scope and *rationale* of the original custom. The courts constantly had to guard against these insidious encroachments, which were held to make the custom unreasonable. This principle is so important that in the highly authoritative *Case of Tanistry* it is stated as the *sole* ground of the unreasonableness of custom.

'And with regard to the various customs which have been adjudged void in our books, as being unreasonable, against common right or simply against law, if their nature and quality is considered, they will be found injurious to the multitude and prejudicial to the common wealth, and to have their commencement for the most part through oppression and extortion of lords and great men. [A number of examples are given.] . . . All these customs, while they are beneficial to lords in particular, still because they are prejudicial to the multitude of subjects, or to the common wealth in general, and commence by tort and usurpation and not by the voluntary consent of the people, are therefore adjudged unreasonable and void in law': *Tanistry Case* (1608), Dav. 28, 32b f.

These frequent usurpations have been steadfastly restrained by the courts (much more, of course, in past times than at present) on the principle that all excess is obnoxious to the Common Law. In Coke we read:

'It was also resolved that the reasonableness of the fine shall be judged by the Justices; and if it appears to them to be excessive, it is against law and shall not bind; for *excessus in re qualibet jure reprobatur communi*, an excessive distress is prohibited by the Common Law [and by Stat. Westm. I]. Excessive or outrageous Aid is against law. . . . An excessive fine at the will of the lord shall be said oppression of the people. And if tenant in dower has villeins or tenants at will who are rich, and she by excessive distress and fines makes them poor and beggars, it is by the law adjudged to be against law, and to be waste, as appears in, &c. . . . Such intolerable oppression of poor villeins and tenants at will is *ad exheredationem* of him in reversion, and against the Common Law of the land. . . . If fines and copyholders of a manor are incertain, the lord cannot demand or exact excessive and unreasonable fines; and the copyholder may deny to pay it, and the reasonableness of the fine shall be determined by the Justices': *Godfrey's Case* (1615), 11 Rep. 42a, 44a.

Usurpations of this kind may, indeed, be supported in some cases by fairly ancient practice, because 'the multitude' may not have had strength or opportunity, during a long period, to call them in question; in such circumstances the courts, looking at the original reasonable basis of the practice, will not hesitate, despite proved continuance of the usurpation, to repress it. But in the majority of cases we are left with a distinct impression that the attempted extension of a reasonable custom rests upon very questionable grounds of user and antiquity: that the lord is, in other words, 'trying it on', and when challenged, is unable to justify his usurpation by satisfactory proof of actual recognition of the usage. In that event, the court has still less hesitation in declaring the dubious custom 'unreasonable'.

The principal cases of this kind are as follows:

Robert-at-Mille *v.* Benet (1401), Y.B. 2 H. 4. 24 (Trim. pl. 20): A custom claimed in a manor that 'none shall put his cattle into his land before the lord'.—MARKHAM J.: 'This is a marvellous custom, &c.' 'And *tota Curia* said that the tenants cannot lose their profit, and that this cannot be a good custom.'

Markham's scepticism concerning the fact of user is undisguised. The result of the custom would be that before the tenants could put their cattle to graze, they would have to wait on the will and pleasure of the lord, and so 'lose their profit'. 'But if a day is limited it is otherways.' The custom seems to have been advanced somewhat half-heartedly, for '*Skrene* later waived the custom and avowed generally for damage feasant'.

Anon. (1431), Y.B. 9 H. 6. 44 (Mich. pl. 27): Custom alleged in a Court Leet that if the petty jury made any false presentment, and it was found false by the grand inquest, the petty jury should be fined. 'And all the Court held that this cannot be a custom: for it is against common right, and is extortion. But if it were used that if [the petty jurors] conceal anything which ought to be stated, they should then be amerced; this could be well founded in custom (*ceo peut gesir en custome*).'

The matter at issue was of more than local importance; for if the custom claimed had once crept into the many Courts Leet throughout the country, the already invidious task of the petty jurors might have become intolerable.

Anon. (1506), Y.B. 21 H. 7. 20 (Pasch. pl. 2): Custom claimed in a manor that every tenant who distrained for damage feasant should impound the offending cattle in the park of the lord, or else pay a fine.—KINGSMILL and FISHER JJ.: 'This prescription is invalid, because it is against common right and Common Law. Because whenever anybody finds cattle damage feasant on his land, by law and common reason he can distrain them there so found and impound them wherever he please on his land, and the lord is not thereby damnified, and has no loss; whence it follows that the distrainor ought not to be compelled to impound the cattle in the lord's pound. And if the tenants of a particular vill like to recognize as a legal rule that anybody who holds so much land shall pay annually to the church of that vill a certain sum, and shall pay 20*d*. fine to the lord for the said vill for every default: then although this constitution has been observed from time immemorial, nevertheless that custom is of no force, because by the default of payment to the Church the lord suffers no loss, since he has no gain by that payment. [*Aliter* if the penalty were payable to the guardian of the church.] . . . If any such custom as the present has been in use, the custom or prescription is of no validity.'

The last words seem to indicate some scepticism as to proof of the custom. The illustration has the air of being based on an actual case within the personal recollection of the judges.

Parton *v*. Mason (1561), Dyer 199b: The lord of a manor claimed the right by custom (1) to seize the best beast of any tenant of the manor dying within the manor, without saying 'for an heriot' or 'in the name of an heriot'; (2) if the best beast of such tenant were eloigned before seizure, to seize the best beast, levant and couchant, *of any other tenant of the manor*. In pursuance of the second part of the alleged custom, the plaintiff's ox was seized, and he sued in trespass.—*Held:* the plea stating the custom 'was not good for the matter of the prescription, nor for the form'.

There are no details of the evidence of the custom, which, on the face of it, certainly seems highly unreasonable, and was probably a somewhat barefaced attempt to extend unwarrantably a legitimate heriot custom. A similar custom, in much the same circumstances, was also held void and unreasonable in **Wilson *v.* Veise**, Dyer, *ibid.*

Here we may mention several cases, possibly hypothetical, possibly based on actual but unrecorded disputes, referred to by Littleton and Coke.

Litt. s. 209 (Co. Litt. 139b): Also if the lord of a manor will prescribe that there hath been a custom within his manor time out of mind of man, that every tenant within the same manor shall make fine *at the will of the lord* [these words, *a le volunte le d*[s], are found only in Letton and Machlinia's edition: see Wambaugh, *Littleton on Tenures, ad loc.*], and have made fine to the lord of the manor for the time being, this prescription is void. For none ought to make such fine but only villeins. For every free man may marry his daughter to whom it pleaseth him and his daughter. And for that this prescription is against reason, such prescription is void.

Coke adds an explanation of the distinction between this supposed custom and that of *merchetum.* Littleton then goes on to mention the valid customs of gavelkind and Borough English; and continues:

Litt. s. 212 (Co. Litt. 141a): But if a man will prescribe that if any cattle were upon the demesnes of the manor, there doing damage, that [*sic*] the Lord of the Manor for the time being hath used to distrain them, and the distress to retain till fine were made to him for the damages *at his will*, this prescription is void: because it is against reason that if wrong be done any man, that [*sic*] he thereof should be his own judge, for by such way, if he had damages but to the value of an halfpenny, he might assess and have therefor £100, which should be against reason. And no such prescription, or any other prescription used, if it be against reason, this ought not nor will not be allowed before Judges: *quia malus usus abolendus est.*

Apparently a hypothetical—and an extreme—case. Coke's chief illustration is the *Tanistry Case*, the reasons for suppressing which have been discussed above (*ante*, pp. 144 ff.).

Day *v.* Savadge (1615), Hob. 85, is chiefly famous for certain celebrated generalizations of Hobart C.J., but it also illustrates neatly how a custom may be pushed by its beneficiaries beyond all reasonable limits. The case presented a pretty tangle of customs, or alleged customs. The claim was for trespass to a bag of nutmegs, seized by way of distress at the wharf at Queenhithe, where the defendant was wharf-keeper in the employment of the Corporation of London. He alleged a custom of wharfage, which the plaintiff had refused to pay, on the goods. Plaintiff, being a freeman, alleged a custom that freemen of the City were exempt from the wharfage duty. This the defendant denied, and alleged a third custom (stated to have been confirmed, together with the other customs of London, by an Act of 7 Richard II) that proof of the Customs of London was furnished by a certificate of the Recorder, as representative of the Lord Mayor and Aldermen (see *ante*, p. 192, n. 4). The issue therefore narrowed itself down to the question whether the matter was to be tried by certificate or *per pais*. Hobart delivered the judgement of the Court, and held that it was unreasonable that the Corporation should be able to certify a custom in which it was itself an interested party. The case is one of the leading authorities in our law for the proposition that it is contrary to natural justice for a man to be judge in his own cause. It is not clear from the report whether the Court was satisfied that the custom was established in fact, or had been sanctioned by the Act of Richard II, but Hobart certainly seems to have been ready to reject it even though authorized by statute. This is extreme, but there would probably be every ground for saying, even according to modern interpretation, that no intention could be gathered from the statute that the custom should be used in defiance of natural justice. In short, the defendant's contention seems to have been an attempt on the part of the Corporation to apply a reasonable custom in a wholly unreasonable and unjustified manner.

We next come to two cases which raised substantially the same point:

Harbin *v.* Green (1617), Hob. 189: The Bishop of Sarum, as owner of certain mills in the city of Sarum, claimed a custom that all inhabitants of the city, being tenants of the Bishop, were bound to have all the grain *spent in their houses* ground at the Bishop's mills, and to pay for the grinding.—So much was allowed as a good custom; but the Bishop further claimed the same right as to all grain *brought into and sold in* the houses of his tenants. This part of the alleged custom was held unreasonable and void.

Coriton *v.* Lithby (1672), 1 Vent. 167, was a similar case and decision, but the judgement proceeded on points of pleading.

It was pointed out that the first part of the custom was perfectly reasonable, the 'considerations' being mutual: the Bishop maintained the mills and supplied machinery, servants, &c., while the inhabitants got their grain ground at a (presumably) reasonable price. But the second part of the custom looks like an attempt at extension unwarranted either in fact or reason; in effect, it would prevent the tenants from selling anything but ground grain. Its justification in actual usage may well be doubted.

Broadbent *v.* Wilkes (1742), Willes 360 (see *ante*, p. 139): The lord of a manor, and his grantees of mineral rights, claimed a right by custom to put earth, clay, stones, coal, timber, &c., anywhere on lands 'near' the mineral workings, at his and their will and pleasure. The plaintiff's close adjoined the mineral workings. The custom was held unreasonable. Apart from its vagueness, it 'tended to destroy his [the plaintiff's] estate, and defeat him of the whole profit of his land, and savours much of arbitrary power'.

The next case raised, in comparatively recent times, an important point concerning the liability of the grantees of mineral rights on certain estates for causing the subsidence of houses situate above the mineral workings.

Hilton *v.* Lord Granville (1845), 5 Q.B. 701: Action on the case for digging so as to withdraw support from the plaintiff's dwellings. Pleas: that the houses in question were situate in a royal manor, in which the defendant had licence to work mines. He claimed (1) a right *by prescription* to dig under houses, no more than was reasonably necessary for mining purposes, paying a reasonable compensation for any damage done; (2) the same right *by custom.—Held:* the prescription and custom claimed were oppressive and unreasonable. LORD DENMAN C.J.: 'A claim destructive of the subject-matter of the grant cannot be set up by any usage. *Even if the grant could be produced in specie, reserving a right in the lord to deprive his grantee of the enjoyment of the thing granted, such a clause must be rejected as repugnant and absurd.* That the prescription or custom here pleaded has this destructive effect, and is so repugnant and void, appears to us too clear from the simple statement to admit of illustration by argument.'

The case has been frequently attacked. The *dictum* of Lord Denman C.J. which I have italicized was disapproved in *Rowbotham* v. *Wilson* (1856), 6 E. & B. 593, 602 (affirmed 8 E. & B. 123 and 8 H.L. 348). In **Blackett *v.* Bradley** (1862), 1 B. & S. 940, Cockburn C.J. said of *Hilton* v. *Lord Granville:* 'It cannot be denied that the decision itself has not met with the universal approval of the profession.' Nevertheless, inasmuch as it had not been expressly overruled, it was followed in *Blackett* v. *Bradley*. It was accepted as good law in *Salisbury* v. *Gladstone* (1861), 9 H.L.C. 692. In *Wakefield* v. *Duke of Buccleuch* (*ubi inf.*), Malins V.C. was strongly pressed to regard *Hilton* v. *Lord Granville* as unauthoritative, but he refused to do so.

Wakefield *v.* Duke of Buccleuch (1867), L.R. 4 Eq. 613: The custom claimed was virtually the same as in *Hilton* v. *Lord Granville*. MALINS V.C. held that: (1) the law is settled that it is the duty of the grantee of mineral rights not to let down the surface to the prejudice of dwellings situate thereon; (2) against this settled rule of law, a custom is alleged. 'The evidence wholly fails to establish such a custom'; but even if it did, the custom, on the authority of *Hilton* v. *Lord Granville*, would be bad and void in law.

The evidence seems to have 'wholly failed' in both cases. Lord Denman's chief point, that the custom would involve a plainly paradoxical derogation by the lord from his own grant, raises a strong presumption against it, though his *dictum* is clearly too wide *quoad* a *royal* grant. *Hilton* v. *Lord Granville* was finally vindicated in *Wolstanton, Ltd.* v. *Newcastle-under-Lyme Corpn.*, [1940] A.C. 860, where Viscount Maugham said that the custom, if any, was 'probably founded in wrong and usurpation'.

It will be noticed in some of these cases that the words 'prescription' and 'custom' are used interchangeably. It need hardly be observed that this is mere looseness of language.

It will also be noticed that in several of the cases the unreasonableness turns largely on the fact that the lord, &c., is claiming something for nothing, whereas in the custom restrained to its proper limits he is reasonably claiming a *quid pro quo;* see, e.g., *Harbin* v. *Green* and the examples given by Littleton; see also the reasoning in *Anon.* (1466), Y.B. 8 Ed. 4. 18 (*ante*, p. 615), and *Anon.* (1506), Y.B. 21 H. 7. 20 (*ante*, pp. 621 f). This is what Comyns means by his principle that a custom is unreasonable 'if it be to the prejudice of any one, where there is not an equal prejudice or advantage to others in the same case' (*ante*, p. 142)

3. Another class of cases, not unlike the last, consists of those in which the 'usurpation' takes the form of attempting to extend a custom beyond its *local sphere of operation*. It is of the essence of custom that it is 'local law'. 'A custome, which is local, is alledged in no person, but layd within some mannor or other place': Co. Litt. 113b. 'All customs', said Lord Ellenborough in *R.* v. *Inhabitants of Ecclesfield* (1818), 1 B. & Ald. at p. 360, 'are purely local, and confined to particular places. There cannot be a custom in one place to do a thing in another.' 'Custom', said Willes J. in *Mayor, &c., of London* v. *Cox* (1866), L.R. 2 H.L.

239, 274, 'is the local law of and for inhabitants, and not for strangers casually in the place'; and the same principle is strongly insisted upon by Jessel M.R. in *Hammerton* v. *Honey* (1876), 2 W.R. 603.[1] But it not infrequently happens that by gradual encroachment the custom tends to be exported beyond its proper borders, or to be applied to persons who are not in any true sense 'inhabitants' naturally subject to it. It then loses the true characteristics of custom, and the unwarranted expansion of it, based not on long and continuous practice but on sporadic encroachments, is declared unreasonable. There can be no such thing as extra-territorial custom. Among the cases already discussed, *Bastard* v. *Smith*, in which a custom properly belonging to Cornwall was attempted to be extended to Devon, is a good illustration of this tendency. The other principal cases are:

Anon. (1579), 2 Dyer 363a: Claim by a copyholder in fee to a customary right to estovers in a strange manor, the custom being alleged in all tenants *ejusdem tenementi*. It cannot be good on this ground, though it might have been good if laid in all tenants *ejusdem manerii*.

The decision may have been on the pleadings solely: but it points to the distinction between claim by *estate* and by *locality*.

Gateward's Case (1607), 6 Rep. 59b: Trespass *quare clausum fregit* by depasturing beasts in the plaintiff's close in Horsington Holmes. Pleas, not guilty as to certain of the beasts: as to the rest, a common of pasture in the *locus in quo* for the inhabitants of the *neighbouring* vill of Stixwold from 1 August to the Feast of the Annunciation.

The custom was rejected. The right of common alleged is of no kind known to the law. The defendant has no estate in his house, but a mere habitation and dwelling; hence the custom is uncertain, 'for it will follow the person and for no certain time or estate, but during his inhabitancy'.[2] The remaining grounds of the judgement concern the dubious nature of the defendant's tenure and the vagueness of the persons ('inhabitants and residents') in whom the right of common is laid. Coke's note on the case states the general rule as to the locality of custom: 'The custom in the case at Bar was insufficient and repugnant in itself; for it was alledged, that the Custom of the Town of S. was, that every inhabitant thereof had use etc., to have Common within a place in the town of H. which was another town.'

[1] On the whole subject, see Salt, *op. cit.*

[2] Cf. *Ordeway* v. *Orme* (1613), 1 Bulstr. 183.

Topsall *v*. Ferrers (1618), Hob. 175: A custom was set up, applying generally to the City of London and particularly to the parish of St. Botolph's, that if any person died within the parish and was taken away to be buried elsewhere, a certain sum (not stated) was to be paid to the parson of the parish, as well as 'in the chancel' and to the churchwardens. The defendant's wife died within the parish and was buried elsewhere, and the customary sums were claimed; but she was not a parishioner, and it would appear (though it is not expressly stated) that she was merely passing through the parish, and was probably taken ill there. *Held*: that 'this custom is against reason, that he that is no parishioner, but may pass through the parish, or lie in an inn for a night, should be forced to be buried there, or to pay as if he were; and so upon the matter to pay twice for his burial'.

A clear case of attempting to extend 'local law', in the words of Willes J., to 'strangers casually in the place'.

We next come to a group of cases concerning tolls, all of which exhibit the same tendency to carry a local custom beyond due limits.

Haspurt *v*. Wills (1671), 1 Vent. 71: The City of Norwich claimed a custom that inasmuch as it maintained a common quay for the unloading of vessels, every vessel *passing through the river* should pay a toll, *whether it unloaded at the quay or not*. *Held:* unreasonable.

Prideaux *v*. Warne (1674), 2 Lev. 96: A similar claim was made, in respect of all ships *passing through* the river, by the Lord of the Manor of Padstow, on the ground of his maintaining, by custom, a quay at one point on the river. His riparian land was a very small portion of the whole river bank. He also claimed a right to distrain for tolls unpaid. *Held:* unreasonable.

These claims could have been dismissed on principles other than those of customary law. They are both cases of 'toll-thorough'—i.e. a toll claimed by a private individual in respect of the use of a *public* highway, stream, &c. Now it is settled law that a toll-thorough cannot be claimed by mere prescription, but 'must be supported by a good consideration performed in respect of the precise locality where the toll is claimed': *Smith* v. *Shephard* (1591), Cro. Eliz. 710; *Hill* v. *Smith* (1812), 4 Taunt. 520; *Brecon Markets Co.* v. *Neath and Brecon Ry. Co.* (1872), L.R. 7 C.P. 555. The toll-thorough therefore might well apply to those who used the quay, the 'good consideration' being that the corporation in the one case, and the lord in the other, maintained the quay; but it obviously could not be claimed from those who were merely *sailing past* the quay.

Somewhat similar is the ground of decision in the two following cases.

Geere *v.* Burkensham[1] (1683), 3 Lev. 85: A custom was alleged in the Manor of Miching that if any ship went ashore on the soil of the manor, the lord was entitled to take the best anchor and cable of the ship. *Held:* that the custom was void and 'without consideration'.

Simpson *v.* Bithwood (1702), 3 Lev. 307: A similar custom was set up in another manor, but, in contrast with the case last cited, it was stated as part of the custom that the lord should take care of the shipwrecked, bury the dead, &c.; and the anchor and cable were 'in consideration' of these services. The custom was therefore *held* good for 'although it be a charity, yet 'tis not unreasonable to have a recompence for a man's charity and charge'.

Simpson v. *Bithwood* enables us to understand the (at first sight) cryptic statement in *Geere* v. *Burkensham* that 'no custom of salvage was found': either the Lord of the Manor of Miching claimed a right without in fact observing any duty of 'salvage' towards the shipwrecked or, if any such duty existed in practice, it was not pleaded. In either case, the lord's claim, in the absence of any service rendered by him, becomes mere arbitrary extortion. It resembles the 'usurpation cases', but I have included it here, for convenience, among the cases concerned with shipping customs.

Fitch *v.* Rawling (1795), 2 H. Bl. 393: A custom for all the *inhabitants* of a parish to play cricket and other lawful games on certain land is good: but it does not extend to '*all persons* for the time being, being in the said parish'. In other words, it cannot be claimed, to use the expression of Willes J., by 'strangers casually in the place'.

A clear and simple case of a custom being imported into one locality from another is

Sowerby *v.* Coleman (1867), L.R. 2 Ex. 96: The inhabitants of the parish of Lilley claimed the right to enter upon the Manor of Lilley, at all seasonable times of the year, for the purpose of exercising and training horses thereon. The Manor of Lilley was not within the parish of Lilley. The same right was claimed for the inhabitants of the adjacent hundred of Hitchin and Pirton.

It is not clear what evidence was adduced of the antiquity and reputation of the custom; but in any case the Court held it void in law. Kelly C.B. doubted whether there was any recorded instance 'where the inhabitants of one parish have established a claim to the exercise of

[1] Burkenshaw? Levinz was careless in such matters.

such a right in another parish'. He pointed out the danger of allowing a custom of this kind to grow beyond its proper limits. 'The claim tends to widen its extent, and, if held valid in the smaller division, might spread in the course of time to the neighbouring hundred, or even to the neighbouring county': with the result that it might go very decidedly to the destruction of the lord's inheritance.—CHANNELL B.: 'I rest my judgment on the fact that the right . . . is claimed on behalf of a parish to be exercised in a place not within the parish.'[1]

Finally, there is a group of cases concerned with customs of the Lord Mayor's Court in the City of London. The most important of these deals with the custom of foreign attachment in that Court, and is another plain example of a custom extended beyond its proper sphere. The custom of foreign attachment (now fallen into disuse) is thus explained by Lord Selborne L.C. in *Mayor, &c., of London* v. *London Joint Stock Bank* (1881), 6 App. Cas. 393, 399: 'Foreign attachment is an incidental process against a Defendant to a suit, who has not appeared, having been summoned according to the course of the Court, to compel his appearance. The only thing which makes such a custom reasonable at all, and capable of being sustained in law, is, that the Court which has jurisdiction over the Defendant [the Lord Mayor's Court] is in substance, by this custom, acting against the Defendant alone, to compel his submission to that jurisdiction. For this purpose, it arrests or attaches his goods within the jurisdiction, or the debts owing to him within the jurisdiction (which are equivalent to his goods), by way of security to enforce his appearance, in whatever hands they may happen to be found. The stakeholder, the person in whose hands these goods of the Defendant may be, or from whom the debt is due to the Defendant, has no interest in the matter and does not suffer in any interest of his own, so long as he is properly indemnified; and the custom, if duly followed, indemnifies him.' The custom, in the case from which this quotation is taken, was

[1] *Mounsey* v. *Ismay* (1863), 1 H. & C. 719, seems to be contrary to the majority of these cases, and in *Sowerby* v. *Coleman* it was distinguished on the unsatisfactory ground that the custom in that case (for all freemen and citizens of Carlisle to hold horse-races on Ascension Day on the plaintiff's close, which was outside Carlisle) lasted only for a few days. There seems to be no objection to a custom for the inhabitants of a group of places to exercise rights in one place within the group, though Kekewich J. held otherwise in *Edwards* v. *Jenkins*, [1896] 1 Ch. 308. The decision has been questioned: see Salt, *op. cit.* 292.

declared by the House of Lords to be well established; but in the following case a growing abuse of it was restrained.

Mayor, &c., of London *v.* Cox (1866), L.R. 2 H.L. 239: *B.* sued *F.* in the Lord Mayor's Court for a debt of £86. *F.* having no attachable property in his own hands, the Court, by the custom of foreign attachment, made *C. & Co.* (Respondents) garnishees for an amount of £86, which they owed to *F.* Neither *B.*, *F.*, nor *C. & Co.* resided within the City, nor did the debt due from *F.* to *B.*, nor from *C. & Co.* to *F.*, arise within the City.—*Held*: that since neither the parties nor the property were within the jurisdiction, the custom of foreign attachment was not applicable; and, the Lord Mayor's Court being held to be an inferior Court, that the garnishee was entitled to a writ of prohibition to restrain the proceedings.

It should be added that, according to the later decision in *Mayor, &c., of London* v. *London Joint Stock Bank* (*ubi sup.*), *C. &. Co.*, being a corporation, would not have been liable in any case to foreign attachment. The rule laid down in *Mayor, &c., of London* v. *Cox* was followed in nearly similar circumstances in **Banque de Crédit Commercial *v.* de Gas** (1871), L.R. 6 C.P. 142, and in **Cooke *v.* Gill** (1873), L.R. 8 C.P. 107.

The following cases, though they turned on different considerations from those last discussed, may conveniently be mentioned here, since they also deal with customs of the Lord Mayor's Court. They are all in the nature of 'usurpations'.

Dean's Case (1600), Cro. Eliz. 689: Dean called Alderman Garret 'fool and knave' on the Royal Exchange, and was committed by the Mayor to Newgate, because he would not find sureties for good behaviour. He brought a *habeas corpus cum causa*, denying the right of the Mayor to commit for such an offence. The Mayor claimed the right by custom. *Held:* that no such custom existed, and that the statutes of 34 & 35 Ed. III under which it was claimed were 'principally for vagrant persons and such like, but were not intended for every private abuse'.

Lewis *v.* Masters (1697), 5 Mod. 75: *Held*: that the creditor of an intestate could not, by the custom of London, attach money in the hands of a debtor to the intestate before letters of administration were granted. The alleged custom was declared 'repugnant and unreasonable', and to 'overthrow the principles of law'.

Matthey *v.* Wiseman (1865), 18 C.B. N.S. 657: The custom of foreign attachment does not warrant proceedings against one who at the time of the commencement of the proceedings was dead. Hence a judgement and execution and payment by the garnishees in a suit so commenced in the Lord Mayor's Court cannot be set up by the garnishees as an answer to a claim against them by the personal representative of the deceased, for a debt due to him in his lifetime, notwithstanding that the letters of administration were granted before execution had, and that (as was suggested) by the custom of London the personal representative might have applied in the Lord Mayor's Court to dissolve the attachment.—PER CURIAM: 'We think that such a custom is unreasonable and void, if it is to be understood to mean that the non-appearance of the administratrix is to give life to a suit which was a nullity from its inception; and, if the custom does not mean this, we do not see how the fact that the plaintiff did not intervene can affect the position of the parties.'

4. Two cases must now be mentioned in which, on purely legal grounds, and apart from the considerations suggested above, the Court overruled as unreasonable a custom which seems to have been established by satisfactory evidence as of actual and ancient observation.

Rockey *v.* Huggins (1631), Cro. Car. 220: A copyholder for life set up a custom of cutting down and selling elm-trees on his tenement. The jury found the custom proved in fact. Nevertheless, it was held bad and unreasonable, though it would not have been so in the case of a copyholder *of inheritance*. 'And although it was urged at the Bar that it being found to be the custom, the Court shall not adjudge it ill and unreasonable, for it may have reasonable beginning . . . *held* that . . . it is against the nature of the estate of a copyholder that he should do acts in destruction of the estate; because customs which maintain them shall be allowable, but not *e converso*.'

This is a rare example of a copyholder 'usurping' against his lord.

Johnson *v.* Clark, [1908] 1 Ch. 303. This decision of Parker J. is discussed *ante*, p. 145. It was another of the rare cases in which a custom, though proved, was held to be contrary to a fundamental rule of law.

5. In conclusion, although, as I have already said, I have excluded from consideration many cases which bear only remotely on unreasonableness, I must make brief reference to two which have been commonly cited on the point, but which do not seem to me to be relevant. **Grimesby's Case** (1456), Y.B. 34 H. 6. 25 (Mich. pl. 33), though it is highly interesting with regard to the rights of pledgees according to the custom of London, turns not upon unreasonableness, but upon the question

whether time can run against the Crown. The Court did, however, hold that it was 'encounter reason' that a person having no title should be able validly to pledge the goods of another. It does not appear whether the Court considered that the custom had been proved in fact. Clayton *v.* Corby (1843), 5 Q.B. 415, was not a case of custom at all, but of prescription by an individual.

In Att.-Gen. *v.* Mathias (1858), 4 K. & J. 579, the defendants seem to have had so little ground for their claim to grant customary gales and licences to miners in the Forest of Dean, and to exact fees without accounting to the Crown, that the crushing logic of Byles J. in dismissing their wholly unfounded pretensions seems hardly worth reproducing. In Anon. (1561), Moo. 8, pl. 27, where a custom that a lessee for years should hold for half a year beyond his term is said to have been declared void; and in Lyne *v.* Bennet (1576), Ben. & D. 302, which concerned an alleged custom for the lord to take a heriot of the purchaser of lands within the manor, if the copyholder, the vendor, had no live beast, the reports are so meagre as to be valueless. The same remark applies to Fryer *v.* Johnson (1758), 2 Wils. 28.

INDEX

REPRINTED LITHOGRAPHICALLY IN GREAT BRITAIN
AT THE UNIVERSITY PRESS, OXFORD
BY VIVIAN RIDLER
PRINTER TO THE UNIVERSITY